O most-sweet Lord Jesus: how great is the gentleness of the pious soul admitted to your table, where the only food presented is yourself, her single beloved, the dearest object of all her heart's desires. Certainly, in the presence of you and your holy angels, my entire heart ought to be set ablaze and weep for joy; for you are truly present to me in this sacrament, although hidden beneath strange appearances. My eyes would not be able to bear seeing you in your own divine light; and the entire world would faint before the splendor of the glory of your majesty. It is thus out of care for my weakness that you hide yourself in the sacrament. I possess in a real way and adore the one adored by the angels in heaven; but I do not yet see except by faith, whereas they see him as he is, unveiled. In remembering these marvels, everything is heavily burdened, even spiritual consolations; for as long as I cannot see clearly my Lord in his glory, I count as nothing all that I see and all that I hear in this world. I sense that two things are supremely necessary here below, and that without them, this life of miseries would be unbearable to me. Enclosed in the prison of this body, I confess I need two things: food and light. Therefore you have given me, me in my weakness, your sacred flesh to be the food of my soul and my body, and *your word to enlighten as a lamp before my feet*. Without these two things, I would not be able to live; for the word of God is the light of the soul, and your sacrament the bread of life.

— Thomas à Kempis
The Imitation of Christ
(Book 4, chapter 11)

Since our light affliction of the present moment
produces for us, beyond all measure,
an eternal weight of glory,
our gazes never attach themselves to visible things,
but rather to invisible;
for visible things are only for a time,
while invisible things are eternal.

— 2 Corinthians 4:17-18

Visions of Amen

*The Early Life and Music of
Olivier Messiaen*

Stephen Schloesser

*William B. Eerdmans Publishing Company
Grand Rapids, Michigan*

© 2014 Stephen Schloesser
All rights reserved

Wm. B. Eerdmans Publishing Co.
4035 Park East Court SE, Grand Rapids, MI 49546

Hardcover edition 2014
Paperback edition 2022

Library of Congress Cataloging-in-Publication Data

Schloesser, Stephen, author.
Visions of amen: the early life and music of Olivier Messiaen /
Stephen Schloesser.
    pages   cm
Includes bibliographical references and index.
ISBN 978-0-8028-8262-2 (pbk.: alk. paper)
1. Messiaen, Olivier, 1908-1992.
2. Messiaen, Olivier, 1908-1992 — Childhood and youth.
3. Composers — France — Biography.
I. Title.

ML410.M595S44 2014
780.92 — dc23
[B]

2013050395

*For my parents,
childhood piano, and music lessons*

~ ~ ~

*and in memoriam
Garrett Stephen Schloesser
(1962-2011)*

Contents

Acknowledgments   ix

Introduction   xi

PART I
1883–1930
Pierre Messiaen and Cécile Sauvage

1. 1883–1914 ▪ Mixed Marriage, Literary Maternity, Postpartum Depression   3

2. 1914–1919 ▪ A Great War Childhood: Mourning and Melancholia   30

3. 1919–1930 ▪ Postwar Paris, National Conservatory, Death of Cécile   47

PART II
1927–1932
Budding Rhythmician, Surrealist Composer, Mystical Commentator

4. 1927–1931 ▪ First Works as Grief Works   79

5. 1927–1931 ▪ Decisive Coincidence: The Mystical Organ   130

6. 1931–1932 ▪ Synesthesia, Apparitions, the Gift of Fear   153

PART III
1932–1943
Theological Order, Glorified Bodies, Apocalyptic Epoch

7. 1932–1935 • From Apprentice to *Maître* — 197

8. 1935–1939 • Theological Turn, Young France, Baby Pascal — 228

9. 1940–1943 • Music for the End Times — 276

    1943: Résumé: *Visions of Amen*

        A Résumé of Three Decades: 1910s–1920s–1930s — 294

        Vision 1: Amen of Creation — 296

        Vision 2: Amen of the Stars, of the Planet with the Ring — 309

        Vision 3: Amen of the Agony of Jesus — 338

        Vision 4: Amen of Desire — 358

        Vision 5: Amen of the Angels, of Saints, of Birdsong — 373

        Vision 6: Amen of Judgment — 402

        Vision 7: Amen of Consummation — 433

PART IV
1943–1992
Legacy

10. 1943–1949 • Postwar *Liebestod* — 459

11. 1949–1959 • Cold War Ornithology — 488

12. 1960–1992 • *Et Exspecto Resurrectionem Mortuorum* — 507

    Appendix: Timing Indications for the Downloadable Recording of *Visions* by Hyesook Kim and Stéphane Lemelin — 533

    Abbreviations — 544

    Index of Names and Subjects — 545

    Index of Scripture References — 571

Acknowledgments

This book has been over a decade in the making. In September 2003, I joined pianists Hyesook Kim (Calvin College) and Stéphane Lemelin (University of Ottawa) in submitting a grant proposal to Professor James Bratt and the Calvin Center for Christian Scholarship. The project, entitled "Olivier Messiaen's Religious Perspective and Performance of *Visions de l'Amen*," received a generous grant from Calvin College in 2004.

During the academic year 2004-2005, the grant enabled Professors Kim and Lemelin and myself to present a lecture-concert at a number of sites in North America: University of Ottawa, Boston College, University of Notre Dame, Valparaiso University, University of St. Thomas (Minnesota), Baylor University, Santa Clara University, and Calvin College. At these events, after I had presented a brief lecture on Olivier Messiaen's life, works, and influences, Professors Kim and Lemelin would perform Messiaen's *Visions of Amen* (1943) for two pianos. Although Messiaen's music is frequently considered somewhat inaccessible to general listeners, audience reactions to these lecture-concerts of the *Visions* proved otherwise. Listeners expressed deep affinities with Messiaen's vast mental store of images: the creation of the universe; the frightening majesty of outer space; the intimate human suffering of Jesus Christ; the ecstasies and agonies of passionate love; the multicolored synesthetic vision of creation's consummation at the end of time; and, of course, Messiaen's trademark quotations of birdsong.

This experience led Professors Kim and Lemelin and myself to propose a publication to Eerdmans Publishing Company. In May 2005, the pianists had

Acknowledgments

recorded the *Visions of Amen* with a view to publication as a compact disc. We proposed that this disc would accompany a "document" that I would write; initially intended to be somewhat short, this work would reproduce in more systematic form the lectures that had originally accompanied the lecture-concert tour. In 2006, after editor in chief Jon Pott expressed both interest in and enthusiasm for the proposed publication, I began my research and writing.

However, I was not prepared for the bump in the road brought by the year 2007-2008 — ultimately a fortuitous and timely one, but a bump nonetheless. As the centennial year (2008) celebrating Messiaen's birth (1908) approached, a vast amount of new research was published and scholarly conferences introduced even more innovative discoveries. This flood of both information and interpretation — some of which substantiated and some of which undermined the narrative I had already composed — required a significant amount of time to absorb, sort out, and incorporate. Eventually, the proposed "document," originally intended to be somewhat short, grew rather significantly into a more substantial monograph.

Contemporaneously, the world of sound recording and online information storage underwent rapid change. (For example, the iTunes Music Store was launched by Apple in late April 2003.) Initial plans to insert a compact disc inside the published book increasingly appeared to be out of step with the move toward downloadable online music files. Consequently it was decided to make the recording of *Visions of Amen* by Professors Kim and Lemelin, to which my analysis is keyed by timing indications, available in downloadable format at the address below and in the appendix.

This book and recording are owed to the initial vision and generosity of the Calvin Center for Christian Scholarship in 2004. The completion of the monograph would not have been possible without a year's research sabbatical underwritten by the Office of the President at Loyola University Chicago during the academic year 2010-2011. The project's final fruition is owed to the assiduous attention of editor Tom Raabe and the unflagging patience of editor in chief Jon Pott.

STEPHEN SCHLOESSER
Loyola University Chicago
September 21, 2013

www.eerdmans.com/schloesser_audio

Introduction

During the course of writing this book, I have asked many people whether they have ever heard of the musician Olivier Messiaen. Most of them, caught off guard by the difficulty of the French ending ("-iaen" sounding something like a nasal "-aw"), have asked me to spell his name in case they had seen it in print. Even after this clarification, nearly all said no, they had not heard of him. The several people who had heard of him recalled three identifiers: he was the composer who used birdsong; he premiered his *Quartet for the End of Time* in a German prisoner of war camp; and he had synesthesia and "heard colors." Messiaen himself worked hard to mold and sustain his public image, and I think he would have been pleased that these aspects were remembered.

However, the actual Messiaen was a remarkably complex person with a sometimes tragic domestic life who lived in fascinating times. He was also a voracious reader with seemingly boundless interests. Fragments of this vast knowledge find their place in what is frequently a gumbo soup of his lyrics, commentaries, and analytic writings. The purpose of this book is to explore this enormous web of ideas and influences in the first part of Messiaen's long life.

The subject of Messiaen's life and work is vast. Two recent biographies cover the whole in detail. In 2005, anticipating the 2008 centennial celebration of Messiaen's birth, Peter Hill and Nigel Simeone published their sweeping, magisterial study entitled simply *Messiaen*. In 2007, Christopher Dingle published a more succinct volume, *The Life of Messiaen*. Although my own study is deeply indebted to both of these books, it is more narrowly focused on a

Introduction

very particular aspect of Messiaen's formation and identity: what might be called his "French Catholic avant-garde" music.¹ When I was asked by someone who had never heard of Messiaen what in particular stood out for me about him, I responded without hesitation: first, he had been ultra-Catholic in his religiosity; second, he had been avant-garde in his music. My questioner replied: "Ultra-Catholic and avant-garde — but those two things don't really go together, do they?" The immediate and unhesitating freshness of this response simplified things for me. True enough, we usually do not think of Catholicism and the avant-garde going together. But in Messiaen's case they did. This "charm of impossibilities" — a phrase of Messiaen's emanating from his immersion in the surrealists of the 1930s and 1940s — is perhaps one reason he continues to intrigue.²

Messiaen's paradoxical and seemingly unique ultra-Catholic avant-gardism is the primary lens through which this book approaches his early life and work. We now know that Messiaen self-consciously created his public persona by cultivating this apparent uniqueness. Not all of his autobiographical statements can be taken at face value. But the unusual juxtaposition of "Catholic" and "modern" must be seen not only within the personal details of his domestic life; it also emerges within the broader historical context of his times. The interactions between the Catholic Church and the French state throughout the first half of the twentieth century were shot through with tragedy, alternating at times in competition, conflict, and collaboration. Messiaen's ultra-Catholic avant-gardism intrigues and provokes thought even within narrow biographical confines; when situated within the broader historical context, his musical creations reverberate with much greater cultural, religious, and even political resonances. In reading Messiaen this way, I have located him as yet another character (along with the philosopher Jacques Maritain, the novelist Georges Bernanos, the artist Georges Rouault, and the musician Charles Tournemire) in the larger drama that I have written about in *Jazz Age Catholicism: Mystic Modernism in Postwar Paris, 1919-1933*.³ For readers unfamiliar with the history of France in general and of French

---

1. I owe this phrase to Jean-Marie Domenach and Robert de Montvalon, *The Catholic Avant-garde: French Catholicism since World War II* (New York: Holt, Rinehart and Winston, 1967).

2. Stephen Schloesser, "The Charm of Impossibilities: Mystic Surrealism as Contemplative Voluptuousness," in *Messiaen the Theologian,* ed. Andrew Shenton (Burlington, Vt.: Ashgate, 2010), 163-82.

3. Stephen Schloesser, *Jazz Age Catholicism: Mystic Modernism in Postwar Paris, 1919-1933* (Toronto: University of Toronto Press, 2005).

Introduction

Catholicism in particular, references to that work cited throughout this one will hopefully help in providing background.

Following this particular perspective has led to several emphases in this study:

1. *The religiosity of Messiaen's parents.* In later-life interviews conducted to establish his public persona, Messiaen asserted that his parents had been religious nonbelievers. As a corollary, he would then assert the surprising uniqueness and, as it were, spontaneous generation of his own religiosity by saying, "I was born a believer." This was one element among several that he used to fashion his self-image as a musician who was different and set apart from his peers. It also had the effect of erasing any lineage for his religiosity, one that rankled some critics. More particularly, it seemed to elevate his religiosity above the bitterly conflicted fray that was French Catholicism in the first half of the twentieth century. He could be abstractly "religious" without being aligned with any particular Catholic camp (each of which had political overtones).

In this book, I follow the lead of recent scholars who have uncovered the actual religious circumstances in Messiaen's childhood home. True enough, his mother had been an unbeliever. But his father, quite to the contrary, was not only a practicing Catholic; he was affiliated in numerous ways with Catholic Revivalism, a literary and cultural renaissance in overt competition with the dominant "laicist" (Americans would say "secular") culture and politics of France's Third Republic. Intriguingly, the years of his parents' courtship and marriage (from 1905 to 1907) overlap exactly with the high-water mark of Catholicism's bitter struggles with the state (the 1905 Act of Separation) and with its own internal critics (the 1907 condemnations of the "Roman Catholic modernists"). The memoirs of Pierre Messiaen, Olivier's father, are not entirely trustworthy as history. Still, his recurring allusions to his wife Cécile's unbelief suggest that religious tensions in the extremely cramped household were high and deeply felt by the young Olivier. One key to understanding his music is realizing that he inherited and interiorized elements of both his father's Catholicism and his mother's naturalism.

2. *A literary childhood.* Messiaen was frequently criticized for his writings, in terms of both the poetic lyrics he wrote for voice compositions, and the frequently lengthy commentaries on the music that he read out loud at performances and had printed with scores and recordings. Although this criticism most famously reached fever pitch in the "Messiaen Controversy" at the time of the liberation of Paris and the end of the German occupation in 1944, it was a constant both before and after. However, critics seem to have missed one

Introduction

of the most obvious of Messiaen's characteristics: he was a symbolist in the lineage of Richard Wagner, Claude Debussy, and the organist Charles Tournemire. Symbolism had long been out of fashion and made him somewhat anachronistic, but it was the world in which Messiaen lived and breathed. Literary texts were not optional for him; they were inextricably interwoven with musical texts.

Immersing oneself (as I do in this book's first chapter) in the writings and day-to-day lives of Messiaen's mother and father makes clear just how unusually saturated his childhood home was with words. Perhaps literature (and most especially poetry) was the one thing that the couple genuinely had in common. Both an editor and a translator, Pierre evolved into something of a literary historian and critic. Cécile not only wrote voluminously but read voraciously even as late as the last winter of her life when she was physically exhausted. They talked about literature constantly and, at least in the earlier days of their marriage, frequently commented on each other's work. When reading passages in Pierre's memoirs recalling discussions about poetic rhyme, it is impossible not to make immediate associations with Messiaen's elevation of "rhythm" as the most important element in music (he called himself a "rhythmician"). It is also impossible not to note the enormous number of pages in his vast multivolume *Treatise* that are devoted to rhythm, both literary and musical (and in Greek drama and poetry those two are the same), found in Greek, Roman, Hindu, Balinese, and other global sources.

Messiaen explicitly said that he did not consider himself a poet, and there is no need or suggestion here to conclude that he was. However, I have here followed the lead of one scholar who has suggested that, the more we look at Messiaen's parents, the more we would assume that he would become a literary figure, not a musician. I suggest that he did in fact become a literary figure to some degree — in his lyrics, in his commentaries, in his vast *Treatise*, and finally, in his operatic libretto for *Saint Francis of Assisi*. His somewhat anachronistic embrace of the symbolist vision was not merely a predilection stemming from personal preferences or temperament. It was also a consequence of having been raised in a family home saturated with literature.

As a corollary, Messiaen's form of Catholicism was of a particular kind. Certainly, there is a sense in which Catholicism's sacramental vision of reality is "symbolist" (in the broad sense) in every age. But in the nineteenth and twentieth centuries, especially in France, Catholic Revivalism became inextricably intertwined with the particularly fin-de-siècle symbolist movement: the works of Ernest Hello, Léon Bloy, Joris-Karl Huysmans, the Rosicrucians, and the organist Charles Tournemire serve as examples in this lineage. In true symbolist fashion, Messiaen privileged the invisible over the visible and believed (following Charles Baudelaire and Stéphane Mallarmé) that the truest realities could never be "seen" but only "suggested." Critics who attacked Messiaen's words simply did not understand his inseparable location in the literary.

3. *"Vulgarisation": consuming popular culture.* Messiaen was a voracious consumer of popular writings, what the French term *vulgarisation*. This is one important reason why scholars of his work soon find themselves in a dense forest of quotations from and citations of works that are initially difficult to identify. His embrace of Henri Bergson's philosophy of the "duration" is well known. But his primary introduction to that philosophy (and initial citations of it) came not from Bergson's writings directly but rather from a popular philosophy textbook. He loved reading about astronomy (a particularly important theme in *Visions*), but again, his sources were books of popular science. His fascination with synesthetic experiences of "hearing color" drew him to a popular study of mescaline-induced hallucinations. He was fascinated by books on dance and music in Africa, while his embrace of Hindu rhythms led him to study Hinduism. Many of these works, precisely because they are "popular" (and hence will never be translated), will be inaccessible to an Anglophone reader (even assuming that one had the time to procure them). Throughout this study, I have tried to present excerpts from these writings that are substantial enough to give the reader a sense of the richly varied imaginative world out of which the "literary Messiaen" produced his works.

4. *The emotion of "melancholy."* In the same later-life interviews used to fashion an enduring public persona, Messiaen liked to assert that, unlike most of his twentieth-century contemporaries, he was a "musician of joy." This was a key element in fashioning himself as an artist who didn't belong to his epoch. So much of the century's classical music gave emotional expression to the dismal, tragic, and horrific experiences of those decades: world wars, economic depression, totalitarian dictatorships, and genocide. By contrast, Messiaen fashioned himself a "musician of joy" whose eyes were firmly fixed on the glory of God and the world to come, blinding in their dazzlement. *Visions of Amen*, the centerpiece of this study, is the quintessential expression of this vision, both apocalyptic and eschatological.

In this book, however, I offer a different perspective, underscoring not the joy but rather the recurrent theme of melancholy in Messiaen's life, first in the experiences of his parents, and then in his own. In doing so, I have been inspired by recent scholars investigating the "history of emotions." Their work causes us to pause and think about how emotions are shared and talked about within communities and how they take on particular meanings in those set-

Introduction

tings. In Messiaen's case, a "music of joy" was clearly intended to set him apart from the mainstream of his twentieth-century peers, departing from a more common "music of despair," or at least "music of pain."

However, Messiaen is explicit about the object of his "joy": it is the religious promise of the world to come, the stability and eternity of which stand in sharp contrast to the fleeting ephemerality of our temporal terrestrial experience. Implicit in his vision is a melancholy about this world and this life, a melancholy that he seems to have first inherited from his mother. Her "melancholy" — which to a certain degree was also psychological depression — was already evident in the poetry she wrote while pregnant with Olivier, stemming from her naturalist worldview in which mortal beings were largely born to die. Later events only deepened these convictions and emotions. Such mournful melancholy also suffuses the memoirs of Messiaen's father, especially in his account of serving on the front lines in the Great War and of the many friends (and two brothers) killed in that war. Later experiences underscored life's ephemerality for Messiaen: his mother's untimely death when he was seventeen; his wife's multiple miscarriages; his capture and incarceration in a German prisoner of war camp; and, soon after his release, his wife's rapid mental degeneration to the point that she needed to be institutionalized until her death.

Throughout this book, then, the reader will recognize an underlying thread of a particular "history of emotions" in Messiaen: the explicit emotion he intends his music to convey is frequently the "joy" that will be experienced in the promised unchanging world of eternity to come. But the implicit emotion that drives this deep desire for stability is melancholy, a mournful awareness of the ephemerality of the present world and a deep sensitivity to accumulating losses: the passing away of vision, physical health, mental capacities, and eventually life itself.

5. *The emotions of "fear" and "awe."* As a corollary to this "history of emotions," I underscore the centrality of the emotion of fear throughout Messiaen's music. On one level this is simple enough: he was attracted to fearful and terrifying things, both in literature — in the works of Shakespeare, in the stories of Edgar Allan Poe, in the "abyss" (a central image in French literature from Blaise Pascal to Charles Baudelaire) — and in nature, especially the gorges of the Alps (his childhood) and the enormity of outer space.

On another level, however, his childhood affection for "fear" evolved into a sophisticated distinction between "fear" and "awe" (or "wonder" or "dread") — in French, between *la peur* and *la crainte*. This latter emotion is deeply rooted in both the Bible — "Fear of the Lord is the beginning of all wisdom" — and Catholic tradition (in which the last of the "seven gifts of the Holy Spirit" is "fear of the Lord"). But in modernity, this emotion had become an important marker of the most profound kind of "experience," whether "religious" or "aesthetic." While philosophers like Edmund Burke and Immanuel Kant had theorized about the "sublime," a complicated hybrid of both attraction and fear, Romantic poets, artists, and musicians created works intended to elicit an experience of the sublime in the reader, viewer, and listener. In Germany, Friedrich Schleiermacher applied this principle theologically: religion is piety and piety is the feeling of "absolute dependence." In France, Ernest Hello — a meditative writer whose impact on Messiaen cannot be overstated — distinguished between *la peur* and *la crainte*. The former, simple fear, ends up in cowering and retreating into smaller and narrower places of hiding. The latter, "fear of the Lord," has the potential to broaden our horizons indefinitely, open up a window onto "adoration" of what is utterly beyond us.

Rudolf Otto's *Idea of the Holy* (1917), a book that still influences theories of religion today, was published in the penultimate year of the horrifying Great War. Otto proposed that the distinguishing religious emotion was "awe," "dread," "wonder" — a response to encountering the "holy" (or "numinous") — a force "Wholly Other" than us, standing over against us, restoring us to a proper perspective of our place in the universe. In its simplest terms, this was Messiaen's own view of religion: God is wholly other than us. There is an unbridgeable distance between our temporal world and God's eternity. Nevertheless, God has in fact bridged those two worlds: historically, in the incarnation of Christ, and in our own day, in the Eucharist. For our part, we must keep our vision fixed on the wholly other world to come. Emotionally speaking, this entails *la crainte:* fear of the Lord.

6. *Rethinking time and eternity in light of emotions.* Messiaen's compositions and theoretical analyses focus on "rhythm": in fact, he considered any musician worthy of the name a "rhythmician." His fascination with Bergson's philosophy of the "duration" lay in the possibility of an alternative to "clock time" and the overcoming of the strictures of meter. He embraced Gregorian chant and Hindu ragas because they too offered alternatives to meter. His utilizations of the literary palindrome and the medieval isorhythm, and his own invention of the "non-retrogradable" rhythm, were all efforts at overcoming not merely meter but, indeed, time itself. Some of the most memorable moments in his music come when he employs all manner of musical tools to overcome time itself — paradoxically using an essentially temporal art form to give the reader an emotional experience of suspended time, of contemplative ecstasy, of "eternity" itself. Messiaen's identity as the "musician of time" has been much explored and established.

Introduction

However, this seemingly well worked terrain gains new interest and new significance when reconsidered in light of the "history of emotions." I suggest that Messiaen's attention to time emerged, whether consciously or not, from deep concerns over the human condition; in short, we are ephemeral beings who can imagine eternity, and this is a primary source of our melancholy and anxiety. Although they clearly differ from one another, both "melancholy" and "wonder" are emotional responses to the experience of time passing and things passing away — to the experience of being small and without control in the universe. For this reason, I have drawn connections throughout this work with a "modern" genealogy of thinkers associated with anxiety and the human condition: Blaise Pascal, Søren Kierkegaard, Edgar Allan Poe, Martin Heidegger, Paul Claudel, and John Updike. In both the micro- and macro-circumstances of his life, in world wars and domestic tragedy, Messiaen's was a life profoundly marked by ephemerality — wartime absence and separation, physical and mental illness, premature death, loss, grief, mourning, and melancholy. Messiaen's self-definition as a "musician of joy" takes on a possibly different meaning in this new context. Perhaps the "joy" he sought to represent came not from a lack of melancholy but rather from suffering it too much.

Considering Messiaen in this light allows us to reexamine his focus on time. Messiaen himself explicitly noted that the human experience of time is fundamentally emotional: it includes satisfaction with, regrets over, and unresolved melancholy about the past; both hope and fear of the distant future; and, in the flow of the "present moment" (which never really is but is only always-becoming), desiring, yearning for, straining after perceived possibilities in the more immediate future. From this perspective, *Visions of Amen* provides the ideal case study for considering Messiaen's attention to time in its emotional and experiential aspects — for he situated desire, in the form of the fourth movement ("Amen of Desire"), as the fulcrum upon which the other six movements are balanced.

Messiaen's desire, sometimes heartrending in its painful longing, is an awareness of ephemerality shot through with melancholy. It is (using his own words) a "terrible love," an insatiable longing symbolized by the wonders of creation, including the ancient and vast terrifying beauty of interstellar space, the gorges in the French Alps and the canyons in the American West plunging to great depths, and his beloved birds whose unchanging songs he traces back to prehistoric ancestors. At the same time, his desire is profoundly aware that time is ephemeral; it is always flowing, and all things must pass. In the end, then, Messiaen's desire — and vision — always aims at what is beyond this unceasing rhythm of coming into being and passing away. "For

Introduction

the things that are seen are temporal, but the things that are not seen are eternal" (2 Cor. 4:18).

*   *   *

The first part of this study is arranged chronologically and biographically. In the first section, three chapters are devoted largely to Messiaen's parents, Pierre Messiaen and Cécile Sauvage. Chapter 1 introduces them as young adults who are both passionate about literature: Pierre as a translator and editor, Cécile as a budding poet. Chapter 2 considers their respective encounters with tragedy and grief during the Great War of 1914-1918, a period suffused with mourning and melancholia. This was the period of Olivier Messiaen's childhood, aged six to ten. Chapter 3 follows the small family into Paris of the 1920s where Olivier spends the decade as a student at the National Conservatory. It ends with Cécile's untimely death from tuberculosis, a devastating blow for the late adolescent Olivier.

The second section is devoted to the first five years (1927-1932) of Messiaen's life as a composer and performer. Chapter 4 looks at his first works through the lens of his mother's death and interprets them as "grief works," attempts at "working through" mourning. Chapter 5 attempts to recover the surprising character of Messiaen's introduction to the organ, the fortunate obtaining of his prestigious position as organist of Trinité church in Paris, and the instrument's fortuitous advantages for a music of "time and eternity." Chapter 6 locates Messiaen's synesthesia within the larger historical context of nineteenth-century symbolism, early-twentieth-century investigations into synesthetic perception and "color-sound" machines, and almost a century of the association of multisensory perception with drug-induced visions. Messiaen's *Apparition of the Eternal Church* for organ is perhaps the most accessible work in which apparitions, color-sounds, and religious fear *(la crainte)* intersect.

The third section traces Messiaen's life and works through the 1930s, the "interwar" decade of the Great Depression that increasingly looked with dread toward another world war, and into the succeeding decade. In chapter 7, Messiaen and his wife Claire Delbos build a musical household. His great achievement during this period (1932-1935) is the composition of one of his most popular works, the *Ascension* suite, first for orchestra and then for organ. In chapter 8, as economic and political circumstances become more ominous, Messiaen shares the search for a "new order" characteristic of his contemporaries. One aspect of this desire for solidity is the study of explicitly

Introduction

"theological" ideas and their employment in compositions like the *Nativity* suite for organ. Chapter 9 considers the eschatological and even apocalyptic tenor of Messiaen's works as the 1930s pass into the Second World War. After the declaration of war, Messiaen is mobilized into the French army, captured by the Germans, and imprisoned. After he famously writes and premieres his *Quartet for the End of Time* in the prisoner of war camp, his release is secured and he is appointed to teach at the National Conservatory in Paris.

The fourth section interrupts this chronological narrative and embarks upon a close reading of Messiaen's *Visions of Amen* for two pianos. The work serves as a natural termination point for the first part of Messiaen's career: it is the last composition included in his *Technique of My Musical Language* (completed in the fall of 1942), Messiaen's own summation of his thought and work up to that point. Biographically, too, the work stands at a crossroads: Messiaen's wife, Claire Delbos, was succumbing to the mental illness that would eventually necessitate her institutionalization and lead to an early death. Meanwhile, he had begun teaching the brilliant young pianist Yvonne Loriod, for whose dexterity *Visions* was composed and who would eventually become his second wife. Both biographically and musically, *Visions* sums up the past and offers a preview of work to come.

Visions offers a kind of résumé of the vast reading and thinking Messiaen had done, from his childhood in 1910-1919, through the Conservatory years of the 1920s, and into his young adult years of the 1930s. Among the many topics treated in *Visions* are astronomy, dance, and rhythm (Vision 2); the overtly Christological "Agony of Jesus," one of the few "passion" works in Messiaen (Vision 3); complex human "desire," a surrealistic prefiguring of the Tristan works after the war (Vision 4); birdsong, the trait for which he is probably best known (Vision 5); and the eschatological consummation of time marked by color-sounds in the celestial city (Vision 7).

The fifth and final section returns to a chronological and biographical format as it surveys the next half century (1943-1992) of Messiaen's life and work. Necessarily brief and schematic, this survey attempts to revisit this much-better-known material by reconnecting it back to antecedents explored in the book's earlier sections. In chapter 10, the "Messiaen Controversy" is considered within the broader cultural crisis brought on by the end of the German occupation. At the same time, the "Tristan Trilogy" is seen against the tragic background of Claire's diminishment. Chapter 11 considers the 1950s — the decade of the monumental *Catalogue of Birds* — within both the decade's Cold War context and Messiaen's domestic heartbreaks. Finally, chapter 12 offers a thumbnail sketch of the large works composed between 1960 and Messiaen's

Introduction

death in 1992. Once again, an attempt is made to show continuity by referring these mature works of his later life back to themes already present in his youthful years.

*   *   *

I am aware that the interplay between biography and music is a contentious topic and that some scholars believe extramusical elements (like history and life stories) should not enter into discussions of compositions. However, many listeners find Messiaen inaccessible on first hearing (which often means he doesn't get a second hearing). I believe that knowing aspects of Messiaen's life opens his music up to listeners who might otherwise forgo it. By limiting the time span to Messiaen's earlier life and works, this study offers a glimpse into the formative years of the younger (and perhaps more approachable) Messiaen: a childhood marked by the Great War of 1914-1918; a late adolescence marked by grief, disillusionment, and eventual reconciliation with the untimely death of his mother; the attainment of a rare church position at the outset of the Great Depression; romantic love; marital and domestic bliss; the tragedy of the Second World War; and, of course, the "mystical" style for which he is known.

Similarly, in the "résumé" of Messiaen's youthful themes surveyed in *Visions of Amen,* I have again tried to keep the nonmusical reader in mind — even in the structural analysis that is offered in the appendix. The divisions in the work's seven movements are identified by timing indications corresponding to the downloadable online recording of the work, a performance of *Visions* by pianists Hyesook Kim and Stéphane Lemelin (available at the web address below). For readers preferring to follow the score published by Alphonse Leduc (Paris), measure numbers have also been included. For both musicians and nonmusicians alike, *Visions of Amen* summarizes Messiaen's vision — of things both visible and invisible.

www.eerdmans.com/schloesser_audio

PART I

1883–1930

Pierre Messiaen and Cécile Sauvage

CHAPTER 1

1883–1914

Mixed Marriage, Literary Maternity, Postpartum Depression

Until very recently, little had been known of Olivier Messiaen's parents beyond what he himself told interviewers. They were allegedly, in his account, both "unbelievers"; as a corollary, he himself had been "born a believer": *je suis né croyant*. This fabrication by Messiaen was just one element in his self-invention as a musician "set apart" from his contemporaries. In an unbelieving world, he seemed uniquely fated as a believing musician.

We now know this was untrue. His father had been thoroughly immersed in the deep piety of a northern French Roman Catholic family on the Belgian border. His mother, by contrast, came from a laicist family in the southern Alpine and Mediterranean region of France. As an adult, Messiaen combined aspects of both parents. From his father he inherited an extreme Catholicism and a "yearning for immortality"; from his mother came a deep and inconsolable melancholy about a world that is always passing away — a world in which the lives of human beings are as impermanent as "ephemeral mosquitoes." The roots of Messiaen's profoundly melancholic yearning for permanence preceded his birth.

Pierre Messiaen: Ultra-Catholic of the North

Pierre Messiaen was born in 1883 and raised on a large farm close to the Belgian border. A quick Wikipedia visit illustrates just how marginal the location was: the Messiaen farm was attached to what is today the village of Wervicq-

1883–1930: Pierre Messiaen and Cécile Sauvage

Sud (in Dutch: Zuid-Wervik), located at the northernmost tip of France. It is separated from Wervik, its Belgian sister town, by the Lys River. (The village had been divided between the Austrians and the French in 1713.)[1] Being raised in a border area in which both French and Flemish were spoken heightened Pierre's awareness of language and levels of "correctness" in French usage. In his memoirs, as both an author and a translator, Pierre makes observations both linguistic and nationalistic.

It is understandable that nationalist "patriotism" and religion were closely intertwined for Pierre and his ultra-Catholic childhood milieu. First, he had been born just a dozen years after France's humiliating defeat at the hands of the Germans in the Franco-Prussian War (i.e., in September 1870) and the loss of the Alsace-Lorraine region in the peace settlement. Second, the anticlerical Ferry Laws of 1879-1885, establishing the public school system and forbidding classroom teaching by unauthorized religious orders (including the Marists and the Jesuits, soon to be expelled from France), directly affected his childhood education. Third, his formative adolescent years were contemporaneous with the bitterly divisive Dreyfus affair, beginning in 1894 (when Pierre was eleven), culminating with Dreyfus's pardon in 1900 (when Pierre was seventeen), and concluding only with Dreyfus's exoneration in 1906 (the year before Pierre married). This parallelism between Pierre's youth and the rancorous fin-de-siècle church-state conflicts fills out the broader sociopolitical context of an ultra-Catholic upbringing and outlook.

"There were two things I heard repeated over and over again," writes Pierre in his memoirs.[2] The first was patriotic: that one day the "injustice

---

1. This account follows the authoritative biography established in Peter Hill and Nigel Simeone, *Messiaen* (New Haven: Yale University Press, 2005). See also Christopher Dingle, *The Life of Messiaen* (Cambridge and New York: Cambridge University Press, 2007). For Wervicq-Sud (France) and Wervik (Belgium), see http://en.wikipedia.org/wiki/Wervicq-Sud and http://en.wikipedia.org/wiki/Wervik.

2. Pierre Messiaen, *Images* (Paris: Desclée de Brouwer, 1944). The book's legal notice gives June 30, 1944, as the publication date in occupied Paris: "Achevé d'imprimer sur les presses de Curial-Archereau le 30 juin 1944. Autorisation No 19.411." Although Pierre's memoirs, published at age sixty-one, are an invaluable source for knowledge about Messiaen's parents, they are also somewhat problematic. First, the recent work of Béatrice Marchal radically recontextualizes Pierre's readings of Cécile Sauvage. Second, the publication date is important: the memoirs were put into final form during the German occupation, typeset in 1944, and printed just about a month and a half before liberation. Thus, the process of preparation occurred completely during wartime censorship. It is difficult to disentangle Pierre's political views (which seem to have been consonant with Vichy's "return to order" program) from what might have been perceived as politically exigent in 1942-1944. How-

1883–1914: Mixed Marriage, Literary Maternity, Postpartum Depression

against Alsace-Lorraine must be repaired." The second: that "the anti-religious politics of the [Third] Republic both divided and demoralized France." "One year it was the Jesuits evicted from their *collèges,* the following year the Brothers and the Sisters excluded from official schools. Under the cover of laicism we watched the French turned into a people with neither religious instruction nor moral discipline." All this, Pierre's father had told him, added to "the greatest pleasure" of Otto von Bismarck.[3]

Published in 1944, Pierre's memoirs vividly express, even at a distance of four decades, the memories and grievances of embattled Catholics at the turn of the century. Catholics had "let their [laicist] adversaries gradually seize all of the administration and directorships of the ministries or village schools.

---

ever, the memoirs are valuable to scholars insofar as they were written at exactly the time Messiaen was becoming well known: *Quartet for the End of Time* was written and first performed in January 1941 while Messiaen was imprisoned in a prisoner of war camp; *Visions of Amen* was composed in 1942-1943; in 1944, *The Technique of My Musical Language* appeared contemporaneously with Pierre's *Images.* Thus, Pierre certainly realized that the value of his memoirs depended significantly on the personality his son was in the process of becoming.

Their value also depended on the stature Pierre was achieving at this very moment with the publication of his life's work, a translation of the complete works of Shakespeare: William Shakespeare, *Œuvres. Nouvelle traduction française avec remarques et notes,* ed. Pierre Messiaen, 3 vols. (Paris: Desclée de Brouwer, 1939-1945). Note the exact dates of publication: vol. 1 *(Les Comédies):* March 15, 1939; vol. 2 *(Les Drames historiques et les poèmes lyriques):* August 31, 1944; vol. 3 *(Les Tragédies):* August 31, 1945; all published in Bruges, Belgium.

Of special note with regard to Pierre's Catholic connections is the third volume *(Tragédies),* which opens with Pierre's essay "Shakespeare et le catholicisme," 3:7-42. One critic observed: "The chief defect in this portion of the work seems to be his insistence upon Shakespeare's contact with the Catholic church. He believes that the dramatist was brought up as a Catholic and that, except for a period of depression when he wrote *Hamlet, Lear, Othello,* etc., he was largely inspired by a Catholic view of life.... His readers, however, will profit by his translation and need not concern themselves with his theological prejudice." H. Carrington Lancaster, "Reviewed Works: *William Shakespeare,* by Pierre Messiaen," *Shakespeare Quarterly* 3, no. 1 (January 1952): 60. Compare the critique by W. A. Gay in "*Walt Whitman: Choix de poèmes.* By Pierre Messiaen," *American Literature* 34, no. 2 (May 1952): 249-51, at 250: "The point of view seems to be that of a Catholic (he is the first to think that Whitman was much influenced by attending the Catholic cathedral in New Orleans)." Both reviews quoted in Yves Balmer, " 'Je suis né croyant...': Aux sources du catholicisme d'Olivier Messiaen," in *Musique, art et religion dans l'entre-deux guerres,* ed. Sylvain Caron and Michel Duchesneau (Lyon: Symétrie, 2009), 417-41, at 421 n. 25.

3. Pierre Messiaen, *Images,* 263. The "Iron Chancellor" Otto von Bismarck (1815-1898) had been the prime minister of Prussia during the Franco-Prussian War (1870-1871). He then oversaw the unification of Germany and served as the German Empire's first chancellor until 1890. He was also the architect of the *Kulturkampf* policy, an effort to break the power of the Catholic Church, especially in Bavaria.

Instead of clearly affirming their faith and their rights, they accepted being treated like pariahs and like conquered people." Then came the Dreyfus affair. "Everyone my age," writes Pierre, "knew that it wasn't at all about the lawsuit itself, but rather a campaign of some against the other, of officers and soldiers." A "normal regime" would have used the case to correct the abuses that had fossilized between "those who commanded and those who were commanded." Instead, it was "ir-religion that profited; the Church was robbed of its property and religious congregations lost the right to teach."[4] Everyone knew what the words "official neutrality" signified under the Third Republic:

> Antireligious propaganda had nothing standing in its way; it had the encouragement of the administration, whether declared outwardly or hidden underground. Catholicism, as timid, skimpy, and superficial as it was, occupied only a despised corner; schools without crucifixes, classes without prayers, religious instruction treated like an optional matter, an accessory, a bit less important than music and drawing. We let it happen; the priests themselves recommended discretion. It would have been more Christian and more effective to affirm that God is forever in charge of truth, salvation, life. (270-71)

In contrast to all this, Pierre underscores that it was "a grace to be born into a Catholic family. What light for the understanding and the will, what poetry for the imagination! Before the age of seven, we knew that God had ordered the heavens and the earth and that, thanks to the sacrifice of Our Savior, good thoughts and good actions, works, sufferings and joys would bring us to eternal life" (269). His mother practiced "a strict devotion" that "divided humanity into two categories": the "courageous folk, those who go to Mass, and the bad ones, those who never went." Each evening, immediately after dinner was finished, she "imposed on the whole family, including the domestic servants, a long prayer followed by the rosary and litanies." On Sundays, all were required to rise early in the morning, wash, change underwear, and be ready to leave for Mass "at least an hour in advance" (39). Pierre had an uncle who was a parish priest, a Franciscan aunt, two cousins who were Lazarists in China, and three more cousins who were Sisters of Saint Joseph in Algeria. Along with Pierre's mother, almost all the bourgeois and farm families of his childhood subscribed to the missionary periodical *Annals of the Propagation of the Faith* (12-13).

Even beyond the family circle, Pierre recalls that there was "nothing re-

---

4. Pierre Messiaen, *Images*, 264-65. The page numbers in the following text refer to this work.

publican" about the villages in which he was raised, and that his father had called the Third Republic a "band of gold-diggers who duped the electorate while fiercely engaging in the destruction of the country and of religion." In contrast, the villagers were "profoundly attached to the Catholic faith, rites, and clergy; they filled up their church at the Sunday Masses and Vespers; took their part all together in liturgical chants; honored and respected their priests as their spiritual fathers, consulted them about their projects and their concerns." Even in the wake of the Ferry Laws, the "official republican school [*école laïque*] had no more than 20 students whereas the independent Catholic school [*école libre*] had at least 500." At all the crossroads, "adorned with Calvaries and small chapels to the Virgin Mary," benches offered travelers the chance "to kneel and recite a prayer." Flowers and lighted candles celebrated the Marian month of May. The annual rural calendar was punctuated by feasts and celebrations; public processions featured marching contingents such as local societies, firemen, veterans of the Franco-Prussian War, and village bands. Perhaps the most important feast of the year was August 15, the Assumption of Mary. This festival celebrated the harvest, the purpose underlying all the other rhythms of agricultural life (21-23, 30).

Pierre's education only deepened his family and village formation. He was initially schooled by the Marist Brothers, who did not follow the official republican curriculum. (Their teaching was soon forbidden by the Ferry Laws.) The Marists taught orthography, sacred history, French history and geography, and arithmetic "according to the old methods and manuals established by the Brothers of Christian Schools" (51).

Pierre later had the good fortune to attend a boarding school designed to produce priests and missionaries "to serve the Church and France" (57). Although living so far away from home was difficult for both him and his family, the classical education he received was excellent. He was educated by Jesuits — who would also later be forbidden to teach and then expelled from France — whose Renaissance humanist curriculum Pierre criticized for being too secular in its Greek and Latin texts: "We read Homer, Xenophon, Plutarch, but never the New Testament in Greek. Texts of Cicero and Virgil were poured into us, but never those of Saint Augustine or Saint Jerome."

Returning closer to home in 1897, Pierre prepared for his *baccalauréat* exams at Sacré-Coeur (Sacred Heart) in Tourcoing, a city in the extreme north of France near the Belgian border.[5] His diocesan priest teachers introduced

---

5. The school is still in existence: http://fr.wikipedia.org/wiki/Institution_libre_du_Sacré-Cœur.

him to "modern" writers: Chateaubriand, Lamartine, Barbey d'Aurevilly, Verlaine, Mallarmé.[6] Once again, he recalls his clerical teachers with fondness: Abbé Lecomte, Canon Mainil, and Abbé Delbroucq, "the most passionate of the philosophy professors" and a fierce opponent of Kant and Nietzsche. Delbroucq in particular taught Pierre that one needed to follow the thought of Saint Thomas Aquinas and tackle head-on the problem of the origin of ideas.[7] Pierre's son Olivier would eventually become known for his embrace of and inspiration by Aquinas; he was following his father's lead.[8]

In 1900, Pierre became a student in letters and law at the Catholic University of Lille (Institut Catholique de Lille), a northern city close to Tourcoing. A Dominican priest gathered students to discuss theology and Christian socialism. Among the writers who "had the ears of the young around 1900" were Maurice Barrès and Charles Maurras (both closely associated with the far-right Action Française, founded in 1898), as well as prominent Catholic Revivalist writers like Francis Jammes, Paul Claudel, and the Comtesse Anna de Noailles. Pierre recalls the great interest taken by his cohort in the political turmoil of 1900-1905:

> A hot fever of ir-religion made our political leaders delirious. The newspapers recounted the violent stocktaking of the convents and churches, the expulsions of the religious and monks forced into exile. All this disgusted us. We were divided between two tendencies: on the one hand were those who believed that they could better the Republic, on the other, those who expected to take nothing good from it. The first, self-described Christian Democrats, believed that by participating in the fire and making concessions to the left, the house might still be saved; the second who were the ma-

---

6. Pierre Messiaen, *Images,* 73. François-René, vicomte de Chateaubriand (1768-1848); Alphonse de Lamartine (1790-1869); Jules-Amédée Barbey d'Aurevilly (1808-1889); Paul Verlaine (1844-1896); Stéphane Mallarmé (1842-1898).

7. Pierre Messiaen, *Images,* 80. For the 1879 restoration of the philosophy of Thomas Aquinas in worldwide Catholic educational institutions, see Stephen Schloesser, *Jazz Age Catholicism: Mystic Modernism in Postwar Paris, 1919-1933* (Toronto: University of Toronto Press, 2005), 33-35.

8. Messiaen later said he first read Aquinas at around age fifteen or sixteen, that is, in 1924-1925. See Brigitte Massin and Olivier Messiaen, *Olivier Messiaen: une poétique du merveilleux* (Aix-en-Provence: Alinéa, 1989), 31. "I read many theologians; I always return to Saint Thomas Aquinas, the most modern and richest of them all." Quoted in Vincent Benitez, "Messiaen and Aquinas," in *Messiaen the Theologian,* ed. Andrew Shenton (Burlington, Vt.: Ashgate, 2010), 101-23, at 101. See also Siglind Bruhn, "Traces of a Thomistic *De Musica* in the Compositions of Olivier Messiaen," *Logos* 11, no. 4 (Fall 2008): 16-56.

jority, read Barrès and Maurras, [Hippolyte] Taine and [Pierre-Guillaume-Frédéric] Le Play, and saw no national salvation except in a reversal of ideas, morals, and institutions.⁹

Several doctors and engineers founded a group called the Nationalist Youth (*Jeunesse Nationaliste*) and recruited followers from among the students. They published a small weekly periodical called the *Grand'Garde (Great Guard)* for which Pierre wrote literary critiques under a pen name.¹⁰

It was through this connection that the nineteen-year-old Pierre spent several hours one afternoon in 1902 with Barrès himself, who was "attentive to the efforts of a national and provincial renaissance." However, this encounter disillusioned the late adolescent, who realized that the nationalism of Barrès (like Maurras, a nonbeliever) did not extend deep into the roots: "how can you preach the tradition," asked Pierre, "when you don't first of all put it into practice?" He turned instead to writers of the Catholic Revival — Jammes, Paul Claudel, and Charles Péguy — who had "enlivened their rougher thought with eternity [*ont vivifié d'éternité leur pensée*] by supporting it with the permanent assistance of prayer and Mass." For Pierre, the positivist, agnostic, and even atheistic monarchism of Action Française was not enough: "France will no longer have heavenly protection, nor will it have a historical and supernatural *raison d'être*, if it does not remain the oldest daughter of the Church."¹¹ Pierre's reminiscences in this vein recur throughout his memoirs and reveal his religiously partisan milieu.

In short: Olivier Messiaen could hardly have had a father more fervently pious, politically opinionated, and ultra-Catholic than Pierre. Since Messiaen's claim in later life that he had been born of unbelieving parents was remarkably far from true, we can only speculate about his reasons for fabricating his religious origins. In any event, the breadth and depth of Olivier Messiaen's grounding in the classics, literature, and Catholicism have a clearly identifiable source: his father, Pierre Messiaen.

---

9. Pierre Messiaen, *Images,* 85.
10. Pierre Messiaen, *Images,* 87, 88.
11. Pierre Messiaen, *Images,* 88, 89. See Michael Sutton, *Nationalism, Positivism, and Catholicism: The Politics of Charles Maurras and French Catholics, 1890-1914* (Cambridge and New York: Cambridge University Press, 1982); Oscar L. Arnal, *Ambivalent Alliance: The Catholic Church and the Action Française, 1899-1939* (Pittsburgh: University of Pittsburgh Press, 1985). For Barrès see Ruth Harris, *Dreyfus: Politics, Emotion, and the Scandal of the Century* (New York: Metropolitan Books, 2010).

1883–1930: Pierre Messiaen and Cécile Sauvage

Cécile Sauvage: Agnostic Laicist of the South

Although Cécile Sauvage, Messiaen's mother, was born in the same year as Pierre (1883), her childhood milieu and upbringing could hardly have been more different. The contrast begins with geography: in contrast to Pierre's family in the far north, the Sauvage family lived in Provence, in the extreme southeast corner of France, and more specifically in the mountainous Alps region, bordering Italy. They lived in the commune of Digne-les-Bains (or more simply and historically, Digne), capital of the French department of Alpes-de-Haute-Provence.[12] "Cécile Sauvage was Provençal on account of her father and milieu," writes Pierre; "besides two or three excursions to Marseille and Avignon, she knew no other horizon except that of Digne."[13]

In sharp contrast to Pierre's upbringing — northern, rural, Catholic, and near-Flemish — Cécile was raised in a quasi-urban town setting, the daughter of a history teacher in the public lycée of Digne.[14] Several family details suggest that the family was firmly laicist in the fin-de-siècle sense. Teaching in a republican lycée gave Cécile's father a crucial role at the heart of the laicist project. More particularly, teaching history was even more so since the subject was used to undermine religious and monarchical traditions while at the same time legitimating the modern story of a liberal republican France.[15] "I never understood why he was ir-religious," Pierre writes of Cécile's father; "he had even done his studies at the minor seminary in Avignon. His thought, completely marked by Christian morality, never went beyond a conservative and resigned materialism."[16]

It is also significant that Cécile's brother, André Sauvage, was a medical student. The Republic used medical doctors and nurses to replace hospital sisters just as it used lay teachers *(instituteurs)* to replace priests, brothers, and sisters in the educational system.[17] One of the most famous and darkly

---

12. For Digne-les-Bains, see http://en.wikipedia.org/wiki/Digne-les-Bains.
13. Pierre Messiaen, *Images*, 127.
14. Pierre Messiaen, *Images*, 117.
15. The figure of the republican schoolteacher is beautifully illustrated in the film *My Father's Glory* (1990, directed by Yves Robert), based on the affectionate autobiographical novel by Marcel Pagnol (1957). Pagnol's anticlerical father was the archetype of this attitude. As a republican schoolteacher, he saw it as his job to inculcate in his students rational and scientific attitudes, as opposed to religious and other sentiments seen as primitive and superstitious.
16. Pierre Messiaen, *Images*, 192.
17. Jan Goldstein, *Console and Classify: The French Psychiatric Profession in the Nineteenth Century* (New York: Cambridge University Press, 1987); Jo Burr Margadant, *Madame le Professeur: Women Educators in the Third Republic* (Princeton: Princeton

1883–1914: Mixed Marriage, Literary Maternity, Postpartum Depression

amusing literary scenes in French literature occurs in Gustave Flaubert's *Madame Bovary* (1856). Emma Bovary has just died from suicide, having ingested poison to escape a miserable marriage and a failed affair. Hovering over Bovary's corpse, the priest Bournisien and the pharmacist Homais engage in their respective and opposed rituals of purification. "Monsieur Bournisien sprinkled the room with holy water and Homais threw a little chlorine on the floor."[18] In this archetypal scene, religion and science fought over the final word.

Since Pierre Messiaen paints an enormously affectionate portrait of the Sauvage family, it is difficult to know to what degree they might have been firmly laicist or anticlerical in their political leanings. However, in writing about their degree of religiosity, Pierre refers to Voltaire.[19] "Except for her mother who, around the age of 18, had considered becoming a nun," notes Pierre, "Cécile's grandparents and parents were respectable Voltaireans; they sent Cécile to Mass and catechism, but they painted a picture of religion for her as a commercial enterprise that traded [*spéculant:* 'speculated'] on the foolishness or ignorance of people."[20] Very likely the Sauvage family was laicist in a liberal bourgeois sense: embracing the separation of church and state, especially in education, hospitals, courtrooms, and marriage laws (including the legalization of divorce); and yet committed to republican law and order.

In practical terms, Pierre and Cécile seemed to have shared very little in common. What they did share, however, was a profound passion for literature. Their first encounter was in May 1905 when both were twenty-two. Pierre was a reader for a fairly obscure provincial literary review called *La Revue forézienne*. He received Cécile's first manuscript entitled "The Three Muses," a poem she had written three years earlier.[21] Pierre was smitten with Cécile's nature

---

University Press, 1990); Eugen Weber, "Lessons in Liberation: The Secular Vocation of Schoolteachers in the Third Republic," *Times Literary Supplement*, no. 4688 (February 5, 1993): 4, reviewing Jacques Ozouf and Mona Ozouf, *La République des instituteurs* (Paris: Seuil, 1992).

18. Gustave Flaubert, *Madame Bovary,* in Flaubert, *Œuvres,* ed. René Dumesnil and Albert Thibaudet, 2 vols. (Paris: Gallimard, 1951), 1:269-683, at 596; Flaubert, *Madame Bovary,* trans. and ed. Paul de Man (New York: Norton, 1965), 244.

19. Although the quintessential skeptic among the Enlightenment *philosophes,* Voltaire was nevertheless conservative in his attitude toward the role played by religion in maintaining social order. He allegedly quipped that those with possessions should not discuss the nonexistence of God and punishment for sin in the afterlife around domestic servants. Silverware might soon be discovered to have gone missing.

20. Pierre Messiaen, *Images,* 143.

21. Pierre Messiaen, *Images,* 117; for date see Cécile Sauvage, *Écrits d'amour,* edited, introduced, and annotated by Béatrice Marchal (Paris: Les Éditions du Cerf, 2009), 52. Of

poetry; marked by a descriptive "realism of minutiae" *(réalisme minutieux)*, it evoked for him his native Flemish sensibilities. And, indeed, he later happily discovered that Cécile was one of his "compatriots" since she descended from Flemish ancestors on her mother's side. Joseph Mounier and Jean Tenant, two of Pierre's young colleagues at the review, also shared his enthusiasm, and "The Three Muses" was published in the October 1905 issue of their provincial review.[22] In light of Olivier Messiaen's later preoccupations with immortality and eternity, it is worth noting that his mother's published poem was immediately followed by Pierre's fictional excerpt entitled "The Desire for Immortality."[23]

Wanting to know how old this "young girl" was, Pierre asked Cécile to send a photo of herself. When he went back home to the family farm during the summer for vacation and the harvest, his mother, a true matriarch, was intent on shaping his future. She asked whether he knew this poet whose "genuinely rustic" verses were the only ones she actually liked in his review. She also reminded him that the last possible deferment of his required military service would be in two years. "Think about creating a stable and durable situation for yourself," she told him; "about marrying, finding a woman who is a good Christian, who has good character and a good grasp of keeping house."[24]

---

all the new books he had received as a young reviewer, Pierre cites only four that he kept in his possession as late as 1942: two books by Maurice Barrès, one by Charles Maurras, and one by Francis Jammes, who, in 1905, had "converted" (i.e., returned) to the Catholicism of his childhood through the influence of Paul Claudel. This detail may have been consciously tailored to please a right-leaning audience in occupied France; it nevertheless demonstrates his lifelong association with conservative nationalism and Catholicism. See Messiaen, 119.

22. Cécile Sauvage, "Les Trois Muses," *Revue du Sud-Est*, no. 94 (October 1905): 243-62. (Starting in July 1905, the *Revue forézienne* became the *Revue de Lyon et du Sud-Est, bimensuelle illustrée.*) For annotated reprint of poem, see Cécile Sauvage and Béatrice Marchal-Vincent, *L'Œuvre poétique de Cécile Sauvage (1883-1927)*, 2 vols. (vol. 1: *Cécile Sauvage: Essai sur la Mélancolie dans l'écriture poétique*; vol. 2: *L'Œuvre poétique de Cécile Sauvage [1883-1927]*, edited and annotated by Marchal-Vincent), Ph.D. diss., Paris IV-Sorbonne, 1995 (Lille: Atelier National de Reproduction des Thèses, 1995): "Muse Antique" (2:218-19); "Muse Moderne" (2:219-22); and "Muse Revée" (2:222-30); critical notes (2:341).

23. Pierre Messiaen, "Le Désir de l'Immortalité," *Revue du Sud-Est*, no. 94 (October 1905): 263-73. A note at the bottom of the first page reads: "Chapter taken from a novel of M. Pierre Messian [sic] which will appear very soon, entitled: *At Age Twenty Years*, a sentimental and philosophical picture of contemporary French youth." This novel does not seem to have ever been published. This spelling of "Messian" also appears in the signature at the conclusion of the chapter (p. 273). See Béatrice Marchal, *Les Chants du silence. Olivier Messiaen, fils de Cécile Sauvage ou la musique face à l'impossible parole* (Sampzon: Éditions Delatour France, 2008), 27.

24. Pierre Messiaen, *Images*, 128.

1883–1914: Mixed Marriage, Literary Maternity, Postpartum Depression

Since Pierre's work moved him in November to Saint-Étienne, a southern city close to Lyon, the two were able to meet that fall. Cécile came to visit him accompanied by her brother André. (During this same month their father, Prosper Sauvage, underwent cataract surgery for his failing eyesight.) Pierre and Cécile were now able to carry on a courtship occasionally in person as well as by frequent correspondence. Cécile revealed to him that her poetry exacted a heavy toll on her, both emotional and physical: it "cost her great labor and great anxieties, frequent headaches, rough drafts and crossed-out passages" in her notebooks. Except for her father, who listened to her and encouraged her, Cécile said the rest of the family would have preferred to see her spend more time on housecleaning, small talk, and visiting.

Besides Cécile's lack of interest and skills in keeping house, the truly "great difference" Pierre noted between her and his mother "was religion." (This detail should be set within its wider ecclesiastical and political context: Pierre and Cécile first met in November 1905; the following month, the Act of Separation of Church and State [the "Law of 9 December 1905"] was passed, bringing the anticlerical campaign that had begun with the Dreyfus affair a decade earlier to its extremely bitter climax.) Whereas his mother "burned with Christian faith, beneficent charity!" it had been about a decade since Cécile had stepped inside a church, and from her period of catechism and first communion "she recalled only childishness."

Pierre recalls Cécile's vision of "human beings as nothing other than ephemeral mosquitoes who needed to be protected." After this observation, Pierre glosses the text with two lines from Cécile's poetry —

> To fly in the infinite without understanding the whirlwind [*la tourbe*]
> To buzz strangely between life and death.

The line evokes Blaise Pascal's vision of humanity as beings suspended between two infinities: being and nothingness. It also suggests the first lines of Paul Claudel's symbolist play *The City* (1893), in which Lambert declares his vision of "the city":

> Everything
> Matters. In a given area, not a single movement
> Is given over to chance, nor the human path.
>   I follow it with an eye as attentive as that of a scientist in a
>   whirlwind [*tourbillon*] studying the gyrations of wisps of straw.
>   *(He pauses, considering the City.)*

> Seeking to reunite, they cannot achieve it.
> The closer they become the faster they twirl.
> Such is the movement in cities.[25]

Cécile and Claudel were both closely attuned to the ephemerality of and apparent lack of directionality ("whirlwind") in human existence. However, where Claudel imagined a capacity to see purpose and pattern, Cécile saw only chance.

Pierre realized that his mother would never approve of his marrying "a woman without religion, with fragile health, having neither wealth nor the skills of maintaining a house." Even so, he had discovered this poet and literary fellow traveler: "why should I not try to bind her lot with mine?" Truth be told, it was probably Cécile's intriguing difference that attracted Pierre. He confesses in a touchingly transparent moment: "Discretion and meditation: she intimidated me; I spoke to her about everything except for that I wanted to say."

One topic about which they most certainly had frequent exchanges was poetry and Cécile's manuscripts, for Pierre went on to publish another seventeen of her poems in 1906 alone, three of them quite large with multiple sections.[26] In 1907 Cécile published a poem entitled "The Cow" in the *Mercure de France*. Founded in Paris in 1890 as a literary review associated with the symbolists and then expanded in 1894 to include a publishing house, the *Mercure de France* was one of the most prestigious cultural institutions at the turn of the century. The twenty-four-year-old Cécile, it seemed, had a bright future.

Throughout late autumn 1906 and the early winter months of 1907, "foggy, snowy, laced with a poignant melancholy," Cécile was "at the center of all my days! It was a dread. How had I arrived at living far from her?"[27] Then, in September 1907, they suddenly married one another without much preparation. In addition to its haste, the wedding was also somewhat irregular in that it preceded Pierre's military service; as a result, their first two years would be

---

25. Paul Claudel, *The City: A Play*, trans. John Strong Newberry (New Haven: Yale University Press, 1920), 5; Claudel, *La ville: édition critique*, ed. Jacques Petit (Paris: Mercure de France, 1967), 289-90. Translation altered. Claudel had originally published the drama in 1893; it was reproduced in the March 1901 issues of *Mercure de France*; its first and second versions would be published together as Claudel, *Théâtre: première série. 2, La Ville (première et seconde version)* (Paris: Mercure de France, 1911). This passage is from the second version.

26. For citations see Sauvage and Marchal-Vincent, *L'Œuvre poétique*, 2:342-44; cf. Sauvage, *Écrits d'amour*, 52-53.

27. Pierre Messiaen, *Images*, 129-30, 132.

1883-1914: Mixed Marriage, Literary Maternity, Postpartum Depression

largely spent separately. Although the Sauvage family was very happy with the marriage, the disapproval by Pierre's family, his employer, and "all [his] friends" was "complete." His mother "regretted not having the power to prevent me from committing a stupid mistake [*sottise*]; a wife who didn't go to Mass, this had never been seen in our family." Regardless, their marriage was celebrated at the little church at Sieyes (in Digne) on Monday, September 9, 1907.[28] Note again the broader context: on the day before the wedding (an important Marian feast), Pope Pius X had published his encyclical entitled *Pascendi Dominici Gregis*, a landmark event condemning Roman Catholic Modernism.[29] The turbulence in Catholicism continued at full tilt, caused by internal conflict as well as external opposition.

The newlyweds initially moved into Cécile's family home so that she could be close to her parents. During this first year of marriage, Pierre's military service meant that he was gone all day, often even on Sundays, and sometimes for several days on maneuvers. Cécile dealt with the loneliness by writing letters to Pierre as well as poetry. In mid-March 1908, Cécile became pregnant with Olivier. Three months later, her poem "Thyrsis and Gorgo" was published in the June 1 issue of *Le Feu*.[30] Pierre was appointed to teach at the Lycée Frédéric Mistral in Avignon, and the couple moved there.[31] In September, on their first wedding anniversary, Pierre discovered the first poems that Cécile had been writing during her pregnancy. These would become *The Budding Soul (L'Âme en bourgeon)*, the volume repeatedly referred to by Olivier Messiaen in later interviews.[32] Among many things Messiaen loved about these poems

28. For date see Marchal, *Chants du silence*, 32; and Hill and Simeone, *Messiaen*, 9. For contrasting dates see Pierre Messiaen, *Images*, 117 (Tuesday, September 10) and 134 (Sunday, September 8). Since a church wedding would have been added on to a civil marriage contracted at the local town hall, Pierre may have been thinking of two different ceremonies.

29. The feast of the Nativity of the Blessed Virgin Mary was celebrated on September 8: *Missel-Fr*, 1236-38; *Missel-En*, 1186-88. *Lamentabili Sane*, a syllabus of errors, had been issued earlier that summer on July 3. For the Roman Catholic Modernist crisis, see Schloesser, *Jazz Age Catholicism*, 54-56.

30. Cécile Sauvage, "Thyrsis et Gorgo," *Le Feu; revue occitane de l'humanisme méditerranéen* 4, no. 38 (June 1, 1908). Poem reprinted in Sauvage and Marchal-Vincent, *L'Œuvre poétique*, 2:250-51; notes 2:344; cf. Sauvage, *Écrits d'amour*, 53. *Le Feu* was published in Aix-en-Provence by the Imprimerie Mistral, named after Frédéric Mistral (1830-1914), Provençal writer and lexicographer of Occitan, a Romance language spoken in the "Occitania" region of France, Italy, Monaco, and Spain.

31. Hill and Simeone, *Messiaen*, 10.

32. For French-English bilingual version of the poem, see Cécile Sauvage, *L'Âme en bourgeon / The Budding Soul*, translation and afterword by Philip Weller, in *Olivier Messiaen: Music, Art, and Literature*, ed. Christopher Dingle and Nigel Simeone (Burlington, Vt.:

was his mother's prediction that she was pregnant with a son who would be a musician. His acute sense for symbolism delighted in this prenatal intuition.

However, Olivier Messiaen does not seem to have explicitly noted one of the most striking aspects of the poems — namely, their frequent tone of depression, sometimes to the point of despair. By contrast, his father Pierre underscored this melancholy in his memoirs. *The Budding Soul* was a "poem of maternal waiting, the parental pride of God spangling the heavens with planets and constellations; but also a despairing sadness insofar as love makes faces suddenly appear turned toward the sun, gives birth to skeletons who have no eyes and who return to dust. *Homo natus de muliere, brevi vivens tempore. The Budding Soul,* reuniting the crib and the tomb, without the spirit of super-terrestrial hope, can do nothing but scandalize a Christian."[33] Olivier Messiaen's music would later make this same connection between the crib and the tomb — although he would do it by a traditional medieval linkage between the star (of Bethlehem) and the cross (on Calvary).[34]

Pierre concludes:

> ... there is an immense sorrow in these poems. They depict both the lamb welcomed with a kiss when emerging from the maternal bosom as well as the poor mother who delivered and is now exhausted by loneliness and anxiety:
>
> *He is born, I have lost my young beloved,*
> *I held him so well in my enclosed soul. ...*[35]

Ashgate, 2007), 191-278. See also fully annotated version in Sauvage and Marchal-Vincent, *L'Œuvre poétique:* text 2:34-53; notes 2:308-23.

33. The interior Latin quotation is from Job 14:1 in the Vulgate. Translation: "Man born of a woman, living for a short time. ..." The passage continues: "... is filled with many miseries, who cometh forth like a flower, and is destroyed, and fleeth as a shadow, and never continueth in the same state." Cécile's vision of the "ephemerality" or "brevity" of human life likely found an echo in Lamartine's poem "Éternité de la Nature, Brièveté de l'Homme" ("Eternity of Nature, Brevity of Man"); see Alphonse de Lamartine, *Œuvres poétiques complètes de Lamartine,* ed. Marius-François Guyard (Paris: Éditions Gallimard, 1963), 465-67.

34. For the "star + cross" motif see discussion below of the *Twenty Gazes at the Infant Jesus* (1944).

35. Pierre Messiaen, *Images,* 135. This genre of internal dialogue marking Sauvage's *Budding Soul* may have been influenced by Lamartine, whose poetry, along with that of Marceline Desbordes-Valmore, "has been popular reading for generations of French children" and became "common sources for later nineteenth-century poets." One scholar discusses the "poetics of maternal echo" in Lamartine: "The poet, in fact, internalizes the dialogue

1883–1914: Mixed Marriage, Literary Maternity, Postpartum Depression

These lines written by Cécile and quoted by Pierre had accurately predicted what would be a severe case of postpartum depression.

Fifteen months after his parents' wedding, Olivier Messiaen was born on December 10, 1908, in Avignon. He was, fittingly enough, baptized two weeks later on Christmas Day at the church of Saint-Didier.[36] His grandfather Sauvage brought everyone at the dinner table to tears as he sang the ancient Noël: "Il est né, le divin Enfant . . ." (He is born, the divine Child . . .).[37]

1909–1912: *The Valley:* Companions in Poetry, Strangers in Worldview

In 1909, after Pierre had completed his military service, the couple finally began living together. Pierre received an assignment to teach in Ambert-en-Livradois, and the couple moved there with the four-month-old Olivier in April 1909.[38] This relocation into the Massif Central region of France, a harsh land of dormant volcanoes, entailed a difficult dislocation for Cécile — geographically, culturally, physically, and emotionally.[39] Pierre was used to harsh climates, having been raised in the extreme north of France and having traveled numerous times to the British Isles. But Cécile had spent her entire life in the sunny southern region of Provence, nestled in the Alps and not far from the Mediterranean Sea. Cécile's letters written in 1909 show how difficult it had been to leave her family for the first time. Additionally, her small family's financial situation, dependent entirely on a young teacher's salary, was dire.[40]

---

between self and other. Talking to himself is indeed the logical means of having a self-same interlocutor. In [Lamartine's] *Méditations* and *Harmonies,* the internalized dialogue remains embryonic, as the poet appeals to 'mon âme' [my soul] in 'Le Vallon' ['The Valley'] and in 'Pourquoi mon âme est-il triste' ['Why Is My Soul Sad?']. Embryonic dialogue reaches full maturity in 'La Vigne et la maison' ['The Vine and the House'] where the subject is split in two . . . 'moi' [me] and 'mon âme' [my soul]. But these two are one and the same. As Lamartine writes in *Nouvelles Confidences,* the poet is among those who have 'interrogé silencieusement leur âme et qui se sont répondus tout haut' [silently questioned their soul and who have answered themselves out loud]." Aimée Boutin, *Maternal Echoes: The Poetry of Marceline Desbordes-Valmore and Alphonse de Lamartine* (Newark: University of Delaware Press, 2001), 25, 79.

36. Marchal, *Chants du silence,* 41.
37. Pierre Messiaen, *Images,* 191.
38. Sauvage and Marchal-Vincent, *L'Œuvre poétique,* 1:96.
39. For Puy de Dôme, the large lava dome and dormant volcano in this region, see http://en.wikipedia.org/wiki/Puy_de_Dôme.
40. Marchal, *Chants du silence,* 46.

1883–1930: Pierre Messiaen and Cécile Sauvage

In multiple ways, then, Ambert came as a shock to Cécile's system: the change in climate; living full time with Pierre; caring for young Olivier; bidding farewell to her family and native region. The uncertainty of their situation appears in a letter written by Cécile to her parents: Pierre was dreaming of a teaching position in England, and they were thinking of moving the family across the Channel. (During the two years prior to their marriage [1905-1907], Pierre had become completely enamored of English literature and the English language, nourishing his hunger not only by studies in France, but also with several trips to London, Oxford, Cambridge, and Edinburgh.) The source of Cécile's extremely dark poetry written in Ambert is suggested by yet another comment made to her parents: the bleak autumn and winter "[force] us to look into ourselves."[41] Pierre would later wonder, reflecting in retrospect on Cécile's chronic poor health, whether the new climate had not simply been too severe for her.

Over the next three years (which Pierre curiously describes as the "best years" of Cécile's life with him),[42] she continued the "solitary, subdued, and meditative existence" of a poet followed previously in Digne and Avignon, writing each day between 9:00 and 11:30 A.M. It must have been sometime during that first year of 1909 that she initiated contact with Jean de Gourmont. Jean was the brother of the better-known Remy, cofounder of the *Mercure de France* (in which Cécile had published "The Cow" two years earlier). Born in 1877 (hence, six years older than Cécile and Pierre), Jean had a predilection for Romanticism and symbolism.[43] With his assistance and promotion, Cécile was arranging the publication of her first volume of poetry with Mercure de France (the publishing house associated with the literary review of the same name). (She wrote her parents: "Jean de Gourmont tells me that he will be as happy for my success as if it were his own. You see that he is kind.")[44] In mid-November, the Messiaens went to a professional photographer for Cécile to have her portrait taken. In spite of the financial imposition this meant for the impoverished family, Cécile needed to send a photograph to Jean for a forthcoming publication.

Earlier that month, in the November 1, 1909, issue of the *Mercure de France*, Jean had published a long article praising Cécile's work. It would be reprinted the next year in a volume entitled *Muses Today: An Essay*

---

41. Marchal, *Chants du silence*, 47.
42. Pierre Messiaen, *Images*, 139.
43. Marchal, *Chants du silence*, 60.
44. Cécile Sauvage to her parents, April 18, 1910, Archives Yvonne Loriod; in Marchal, *Chants du silence*, 61.

in Poetical Physiology (also published by the Mercure de France press).[45] This work considered eleven women poets, including the Comtesse Anna de Noailles, the somewhat notorious Lucie Delarue-Mardrus, and Cécile Sauvage. Jean's "poetical physiological" theory linked women poets with "beautiful animal sensuality," and his essay was imbued with his self-professed "immoralism" (following the leads of Nietzsche and of Gide's *Immoralist* [1902]).[46] Cécile was so embarrassed by the overtly sexual tone of the chapter dedicated to her that she begged her parents not to share it with anyone. Presumably Pierre read it, however, and one can only wonder how he reacted. In any event, Cécile was undoubtedly grateful for the wider recognition offered by the aristocratic Parisian critic with so prestigious a name.[47]

The volume being prepared for the Mercure de France, *While the Earth Turns,* included *The Budding Soul,* the collection of poems written during her pregnancy with Olivier. It was published in 1910 and positively received by Barrès, Jammes, Remy de Gourmont, and Frédéric Mistral (renowned publisher of a Provençal dictionary and winner of the 1904 Nobel Prize in literature).[48] It was not, however, a success in numerical terms: only 50 out of 500 copies were sold.[49] Refusing to be discouraged by the poor sales, Cécile immediately began work on a second volume entitled *The Valley* (or *The Dell = le vallon*), perhaps alluding to Alphonse de Lamartine's poem bearing the same title.[50] This collection's emotional tone would express Ambert's harsh

---

45. Jean de Gourmont, *Muses d'aujourd'hui: essai de physiologie poétique: comtesse de Noailles, Gérard d'Houville, Lucie Delarue-Mardrus, Marie Dauguet, Renée Vivien, Elsa Koeberlé, Hélène Picard, Jane Catulle-Mendès, Cécile Sauvage, Jeanne Perdriel-Vaissière, Laurent Évrard* (Paris: Mercure de France, 1910).

46. A "Voltairean aristocrat," skeptical, nonbelieving, and a proponent of "free morals," Jean de Gourmont would later publish *The Art of Loving* (1925) after returning from the war front, associating religion and sexuality. Marchal, *Chants du silence,* 60.

47. Marchal, *Chants du silence,* 48, 62.

48. Cécile Sauvage, *Tandis que la terre tourne. Poèmes* (Paris: Mercure de France, 1910). For annotated reprint, see Sauvage and Marchal-Vincent, *L'Œuvre poétique,* 2:1-53; notes 2:301-23.

49. As Pierre noted somewhat bitterly in his memoirs, *While the Earth Turns* would have to wait another eighteen years to be sold out and republished, that is, after the publication of a volume devoted to Cécile following her untimely death in 1928. See Pierre Messiaen, *Images,* 136.

50. Alphonse de Lamartine, "Le Vallon" ("The Valley"), in *Méditations poétiques* (1820), in Lamartine, *Œuvres poétiques,* 19-20. For English translation, see Lamartine, *Poetical Meditations / Méditations poétiques,* trans. Gervase Hittle (Lewiston, N.Y.: Edwin Mellen Press, 1993), 50-57.

new landscape in which Cécile now found herself. It would differ significantly from her earlier work written in her native Provence.

In these first years together, Cécile and Pierre were intellectual companions, steeped in literature, composition, and translation — literary passions that Olivier absorbed and later cultivated. Although the Anglophile Pierre still believed "that Racine [was] more perfect than Shakespeare, Corneille and Pascal more heroic, Molière more everyday and domestic," he found in English writers a "naive and confident freshness of the soul," a "Christian energy," a "smiling humor full of courage and practical reason in the face of difficulties, misfortunes, and idiocies."[51] These perceived characteristics would eventually drive him to the daunting task of translating and publishing the complete works of Shakespeare, an accomplishment eventually crowned with success.

In their long discussions over poetic style, Pierre shared his Anglophone passion with Cécile: "Keats, Shelley, and Wordsworth helped her become enamored of a more direct and concentrated sincerity, a more pure form, a more erudite and aerial music." Pierre's detailed description of his conversations about poetic meter uncannily evokes Olivier's intricate passages on the same subject published years later.[52] "[Cécile] attempted to express herself in varied meters," recalls Pierre, "alternating the stanzas [or verses = *strophes*] in alexandrines, octosyllables, heptasyllables, soothing the rhymes using means including assonance, *the tender melancholy* that inspired this countryside of Livradois."[53]

A touching account of an argument in March 1910 over a poem about the lark — the *alouette,* dear to both French and English writers and found throughout Pierre's memoirs — also brings Olivier to mind.[54] Olivier was particularly fond of the lark, and in his discussion of literary references to the bird, he specifically quoted his mother's verses over which his parents had argued decades earlier:

Listen to the lark lost at the bottom of the sky . . .

I saw the lark ascend,

---

51. Pierre Messiaen, *Images,* 118.
52. Olivier Messiaen's extensive analyses of Greek and Latin meters can be found in his *Traité de rythme, de couleur, et d'ornithologie (1949-1992) en sept tomes,* 8 vols. (Paris: Alphonse Leduc, 1994-2002). See especially 1:61-65, 69-243.
53. Pierre Messiaen, *Images,* 138, emphasis added.
54. Pierre Messiaen, *Images,* 140-41.

1883–1914: Mixed Marriage, Literary Maternity, Postpartum Depression

> Its voice constructing in the light air
> A landscape of brilliance [*clarté*]....[55]

"This poem was long," Pierre remarks; Cécile "had begun it twenty times without ever arriving at that which tugged the heart, the springtime voice of the lark that resurrects the sun and the buds." When Cécile showed Pierre the poem he told her, "It doesn't work, except for the first verse and the last ones." "You are always constricting me," she replied; "when a cathedral is needed a thatched cottage would be enough for you. It's silly of me to ask advice from others. *Voilà.*" And she threw her notebook to the ground.[56]

Two or three days later, while Pierre was dressing the fifteen-month Olivier for bed, Cécile conceded: "You're right about the lark, I'll only keep the first verse." "But there won't be any rhyme!" replied Pierre. "Too bad for the rhyme if it's lost its reason for being there." "But I also liked the final verses," he added." Cécile: "There will be another opportunity to put it somewhere else."[57] Olivier particularly loved these lines, especially the first verse, which his mother eventually preserved as a stand-alone poem. Undoubtedly he had heard the story of this argument, eventually committed to print by Pierre, retold multiple times.

In the poetry written between 1909 and August 1912, Cécile's melancholic juxtapositions of life and death — "the cradle and the skeleton" already seen in *The Budding Soul* — resurfaced and intensified. Cécile regarded human beings, writes Pierre, as living "in shadows, blind marionettes shooting up out of the abyss [*surgissant de l'abîme*], fulfilling in an eternal flight [or escape = *fuite*] their own unconscious gestures — birth, housework, weekly shopping,

---

55. Olivier Messiaen writes here (*Traité*, 5-1:254) that he is quoting his mother's poetic collection *Le Vallon* (1913). The first stand-alone line he quotes is indeed its own stanza in *Mélancolie*: see Sauvage and Marchal-Vincent, *L'Œuvre poétique*, 2:118 (LXXXV). However, the next three lines are not actually found in Cécile's *Le Vallon*. Where did Messiaen get these lines? He is partially quoting Pierre's account (in *Images*, 141) of Cécile's verse: "I saw the lark ascend, / Its voice constructing in the light air / A landscape of frosted trees [*d'arbres grêles*], / Leaning out over the streams." The modifier *grêle* comes from the verb meaning "to hail" (*grêler)*; the *arbres grêles* are trees that have become frosted or icy and thus sparkling. Since the words *l'arbre grêle* do occur in Sauvage's poem "Fuite," Pierre's quotation of *d'arbres grêles* would seem to be faithful to lines that Cécile had written. Olivier has taken Pierre's lines and modified his mother's sparkling "frosted trees" as simple "brilliance." See Sauvage and Marchal-Vincent, "Fuite," in *L'Œuvre poétique*, 2:75. I am grateful to Béatrice Marchal for her assistance here.

56. Pierre Messiaen, *Images*, 141.

57. Pierre Messiaen, *Images*, 141.

the [annual] harvest, engagements, marriages, funerals, sometimes a murder or a suicide — yet always haunted by the old Egyptian and Platonic myth of a Beauty which arranges the universe according to a rhythm of order and measure."[58] Pierre's lines suggest the influence of Pascal: human beings live unsteadily between two infinites, two "abysses" — infinite being and absolute nothingness. Anxiously aware of their inevitable return to dust, they nevertheless imagine the possibility of eternity even in their mortality and engage in various forms of escape *(fuites),* Pascal's "distractions" *(divertissements)* meant to temper or repress anxiety. Olivier absorbed his parents' metaphysical musings to a significantly large degree. His music evokes the paradoxical sense of the eternal — and eternally enervating — flux of becoming, coming into being, and passing out of existence.

However, mother and son differed in that Cécile does not seem to have believed in a transcendent eternity. Nor did she yearn for it as Pierre did — note his "Desire for Immortality" (1905) — or see it as the function of poetry as Claudel did.[59] Instead, she was resigned to the futility of life's unceasing ebb and flow. Commenting on this collection of poems written in Ambert (i.e., *The Valley*), Pierre offers this analysis: "Beauty for Cécile was not the Christian effort of finding the original paradise of intelligence and love in the mercy of

---

58. Pierre Messiaen, *Images,* 138.

59. Pierre Messiaen, "Le Désir de l'Immortalité." The scholar Wallace Fowlie summarizes Claudel's *Art poétique (Poetic Art),* published in 1907 (the year before Olivier's birth): "The poet sees every created thing in perpetual movement. We move by coming into contact with all the other things in the world. By this constant movement we waste ourselves and finally perish. 'Tout périt. L'Univers n'est qu'une manière totale de ne pas être ce qui est.' [Everything perishes. The universe is nothing but a total way of not being what is.] Existing within this movement, we unconsciously tend to deny that which is constant. This is our separation from God. . . .

"The human spirit alone is able to comprehend something of the bond which exists between the instability of the world and the stability of God. By naming an object, as the poet does, man rescues it from its fate of dissolution. In *Traité de la Connaissance* Claudel reaches a definition of man and of the poet as the one whose function is to *represent* (or reproduce) the creation of the Creator. 'Tout passe, et, rien n'étant présent, tout doit être *représenté.'* [Everything passes and, since nothing is present, everything must be *represented.*]. All the parts of the world find in man, in the incorruptible part of man, an intelligence which understands them and which is able to offer them to the One who created them in the beginning."

Wallace Fowlie, *Paul Claudel* (London: Bowes and Bowes, 1957), 31-32, emphasis in original, translations mine. See Claudel, *Art poétique: connaissance du temps, traité de la co-naissance au monde et de soi-même: développement de l'église* (Paris: Mercure de France, 1907); cf. Stephen Schloesser, "The Charm of Impossibilities: Mystic Surrealism as Contemplative Voluptuousness," in *Messiaen the Theologian,* 163-82, at 173.

Our Savior; it was rather, as in the eyes of the Greek philosophers and the Renaissance humanists, the eternal feminine of light and fertility accompanied by a child who plays among the flowers and is followed by death *which ceaselessly throws us back into nothingness [qui nous rejette sans cesse au néant].*"[60]

Indeed, as Cécile wrote:

Come, the earth itself hears and correctly perceives me
And calls me its human and sorrowful sister,
I who alone know, in my hollow bowels,
Every horror that death gives to living blood,
Death who watches me and who, upon my treasure of flesh,
Presses his bony and sepulchral hand,
And despoils the child of his native freshness,
And reveals the skeleton and reduces into dust
The skeleton itself and all of nature.[61]

Pierre would later wonder whether Cécile had not grown old before her time by reading nineteenth-century realist "novels of observation" (Balzac, Dickens, Tolstoy, and Dostoyevsky). Also on her night table were Villon, Lamartine, and Baudelaire; and she knew "thousands of verses" by Racine and Chénier, and almost all the fairy tales of La Fontaine — those so dear to Olivier's imagination throughout his life.[62] Pierre also speculated over whether *The Valley*'s pessimistic despair derived from "a latent physiological distress caused by the overly harsh and foggy climate" of Ambert; as well as from the births of Olivier and Alain whom she breast-fed (according to family custom)

---

60. Pierre Messiaen, *Images,* 139, emphasis added.

61. Pierre Messiaen, *Images,* 139. Analogous skeletal images are found in Charles Baudelaire's *Flowers of Evil (Les Fleurs du Mal)* and illustrations of his work by figures like Edvard Munch and Georges Rouault. See Stephen Schloesser, "From 'Spiritual Naturalism' to 'Psychical Naturalism': Catholic Decadence, Lutheran Munch, *Madone Mystérique,*" in *Edvard Munch: Psyche, Symbol, and Expression,* ed. Jeffrey Howe (Chestnut Hill, Mass.: McMullen Museum of Art, distributed by the University of Chicago Press, 2001), 71-110; and *Mystic Masque: Reality and Semblance in Georges Rouault, 1871-1958,* ed. Stephen Schloesser (Chestnut Hill, Mass.: McMullen Museum of Art, distributed by the University of Chicago Press, 2008).

62. For "realist" novelists, see Honoré de Balzac (1799-1850), Charles Dickens (1812-1870), Fyodor Dostoyevsky (1821-1881), and Leo Tolstoy (1828-1910). For poets, playwrights, and writers of fairy tales, see François Villon (ca. 1431-1463), Jean de La Fontaine (1621-1695), Jean Racine (1639-1699), André Chénier (1762-1794), Alphonse de Lamartine (1790-1869), and Charles Baudelaire (1821-1867).

for their first fifteen months. He was also sure that it must have come from "the complete absence of any Christian faith."[63]

However, Pierre, perhaps more than anyone (given his literary sensibilities), should have realized that the severe melancholy in *The Valley* was thoroughly compatible with Catholic belief and practice, as it seems probable that Cécile had taken the title from Lamartine's similarly dark poem, "The Valley." The first and final stanzas of Lamartine's work express religious belief, melancholic to the brink of despair.

> My heart, weary of all, even of hope
> Will no longer trouble fate with any prayers;
> Only lend me, valleys of my infancy,
> A day's asylum to wait for death....
> God, in order to conceive him, made intelligence;
> Through it nature finally discovers its author!
> A voice speaks to its spirit in the silence,
> Who has not heard this voice in his heart?[64]

Whatever the causes, Cécile's grim melancholy was shared by other members of her fin-de-siècle generation.[65] "We are in the universe as if in a cage," she frequently observed, "first at the breast of our mother, then in the crib, in our houses, in our destiny, and finally in our coffin. You can scream, cry, play or be bored, you never leave the cage. The fat calves who give the best meat [veal] are those you keep in the stable and force-feed with milk by imprisoning them in a mannequin's museum so they won't eat hay or straw."[66]

In addition to Cécile's generally bleak view of human nature (Voltairean

---

63. Pierre Messiaen, *Images*, 143.

64. Lamartine, "Le Vallon" ("The Valley"), trans. Hittle, 50, 56 (French), 51, 57 (English), translation altered. Cf. Lamartine, *Œuvres poétiques*, 19, 20. NB: the poem immediately following "The Valley" (in *Méditations poétiques*) is entitled "Le Désespoir" ("Despair").

65. See, for example, the 1901 mutual suicide pact made by Jacques Maritain (b. 1882) and Raissa Oumançoff (b. 1883, the same birth year as Cécile Sauvage); in Schloesser, *Jazz Age Catholicism*, 59-61. Jacques Barzun has summarized the fin-de-siècle's paradoxical "logic of progress": "All events had physical origins; physical origins were discoverable by science; and the method of science alone could, by revealing the nature of things, make the mechanical sequences of the universe beneficent to man. Fatalism and progress were as closely linked as the Heavenly Twins and like them invincible." Jacques Barzun, *Darwin, Marx, Wagner: Critique of a Heritage*, 2nd ed. (Chicago: University of Chicago Press, 1981; original 1941), 322.

66. Pierre Messiaen, *Images*, 144.

or Jansenist or both), she was also skeptical of education in particular. This seems especially ironic considering that she was both the daughter and the wife of schoolteachers: "Schools only serve to make people more inane, vain, unhappy, malicious, rebellious; they lose the slowly acquired harmony of their mores and customs, the poetry of their legends and their language."[67]

However, Pierre stresses in concluding that there was an enormous difference between Cécile's "everyday being" *(l'être quotidien)* and her "deep being" *(l'être profond)*. Outside of her "several hours each day, morning and evening, of silent meditation seated at her table of white wood," she "never spread any of her melancholy around her." Instead, in everyday interactions, she loved "to chat, to laugh, to joke." Everything "amused her and filled her with enthusiasm."[68]

Nevertheless, it is her "deep being," her view of life and of the purpose of poetry in the world, that most intrigues as a key to understanding her son's music. One day she passionately exclaimed to Pierre: "If you believe that it is the good God who invented poetry! It is rather human beings [who invented it] in order to give courage in misfortune [*du courage dans le malheur*]. Look at the greatest lyrics, the prophets of Israel; what is it that inspired them? Being conquered, captives, men who were hungry and who received blows; they consoled themselves in hoping that a savior would one day make them masters of the world. I have always been cold, I have always felt alone. My poetry is my hope of sunshine and friendship."[69]

Cécile's perceived sense of loneliness in the world led her to a self-imposed isolation that likely only exacerbated these feelings. Throughout these years in Ambert, from 1909 to 1913, Cécile maintained her distance from others. Afternoons were spent on walks in the countryside with Olivier and then, after his birth, Alain, while a housemaid took care of the home. Pierre doubted that, during those four years in Ambert, Cécile had gone into the city even ten times. Meanwhile, an increasingly exhausted Pierre shopped for food and made domestic purchases after work. Beginning in autumn 1909, he traveled once a month to Clermont to prepare his teaching license in English. In the evenings, having finished his course preparations for the next day, he would immerse himself in his own work as a graduate student, often falling asleep alongside Cécile as she reworked and polished her poetry.[70]

67. Pierre Messiaen, *Images*, 144.
68. Pierre Messiaen, *Images*, 146; cf. Sauvage and Marchal-Vincent, *L'Œuvre poétique*, 1:88.
69. Pierre Messiaen, *Images*, 146.
70. Pierre Messiaen, *Images*, 136; Marchal, *Chants du silence*, 48, 52.

1883–1930: Pierre Messiaen and Cécile Sauvage

Pierre was not aware, however, of Cécile's correspondence with Jean de Gourmont, which had been increasing in frequency since 1910 and which she kept locked away in a box. In August 1911 she published an extremely long poem extending over several pages in the *Mercure de France*. Entitled "Melancholy," it was enthusiastically received and promoted by Jean, who told Cécile she had finally found her voice. "I hope from now on to plunge into large and enduring works," she wrote her parents, "because I have found the austere and pure tone that suits me, this voice that Jean de Gourmont in one of his letters compares to the stylized song of a nightingale."[71] (Is it possible that Olivier heard this description as a boy and retrieved it for use in his adulthood: *the stylized song of a nightingale?*)[72] Jean later persuaded Cécile to include parts of "Melancholy" in her forthcoming volume, *The Valley*.[73] "Melancholy" would eventually be the last freestanding poem written by Cécile to be published during her lifetime.[74]

1912–1914: On the Eve of War

Around the end of November 1911, Cécile became pregnant a second time. The pregnancy was difficult, and during the Easter vacation in the second week of April 1912 she traveled south to spend most of the rest of the year with her parents in Grenoble. She was sorry to be separated from Pierre for so long and wrote him long letters.[75] She also worked hard on *The Valley* throughout this time and finished it before giving birth to Alain on August 30.[76] Pierre does not seem to have been very attentive. On October 12 she was still in the south and wrote him: "When are you coming to get us?" Cécile and the children returned to Ambert at the end of 1912.[77]

---

71. Cécile Sauvage to her parents, June 1911; in Marchal, *Chants du silence*, 62.

72. The nightingale has played a prominent role in French culture. In an interview, Igor Stravinsky responded to a question, saying: "For me, music is reality, as I have said before, and like Baudelaire, but unlike Messiaen, *'J'aime mieux une boîte à musique qu'un rossignol'* [I prefer a music-box to a nightingale]." Quoted in Daniel Albright, *Stravinsky: The Music Box and the Nightingale* (New York: Gordon and Breach, 1989), 23.

73. Marchal, *Chants du silence*, 63.

74. Cécile Sauvage, "Mélancolie" ("Melancholy"), written in 1909 with excerpts published in *Mercure de France* (August 1, 1911). The full poem was published as part of the collection *Le Vallon (The Valley)* (1913). See note for "Mélancolie" in Sauvage and Marchal-Vincent, *L'Œuvre poétique*, 2:344.

75. Marchal, *Chants du silence*, 55.

76. According to his father, Alain was a difficult child. Pierre Messiaen, *Images*, 219.

77. Marchal, *Chants du silence*, 56, 59.

1883–1914: Mixed Marriage, Literary Maternity, Postpartum Depression

The winter of 1912-1913 turned out to be long and horrible. In retrospect, it was perhaps a bad climate, both outside and within, in which to have *The Valley* appear.[78] Its January 1913 publication by the Mercure de France was initially an occasion of great joy for Cécile, who inscribed copies as gifts for her family members.[79] Pierre, however, recalled the reactions of those who had been her original supporters: "Mistral was scandalized by it; he no longer recognized his dear grasshopper from the Basses-Alpes. 'The wind blows where it will,' he wrote her. And Francis Jammes added: 'Go to Mass.'"[80] Jean de Gourmont was more enthusiastic than ever, however, and he paid a visit to the Messiaen home. Given the family's meager belongings, Cécile anxiously wrote her mother a request to send her precious tea set so that Jean might be received in a manner due an aristocrat.[81]

In the late spring of 1913, winter having been survived, Pierre successfully completed his diploma *(agrégation)* in English literature. He was immediately assigned by the state to teach at the lycée at Nantes in northwestern France, one of the nation's largest cities.[82] The Messiaens would be moving once again, although this time the distance was less and the climate similar. One might have thought that Cécile would find some relief in this large city with more literary connections than those available in small Ambert.

The academic year 1913-1914 passed quietly, and the city of Nantes was "cordial" and "generous" in its welcome. The Messiaen family lived in a neighborhood filled with houses of religious order priests, brothers, and nuns. "Since I took my children to Mass," writes Pierre, "greeted the priests and religious, and paid cash at the grocer and the butcher, we were taken to be decent folk." The time in Nantes seemed good; Alain grew into a boy, Olivier was "the best student in his class," and "the health of Cécile did not yet give me worry."

Significantly, Pierre's reflections on the lycée at Nantes underscore the extent to which the civil war between church and state, having reached its climax in the Act of Separation in 1905, continued to smolder during this final year before the world war. There was, he writes,

---

78. Cécile Sauvage, *Le Vallon* (Paris: Mercure de France, 1913). The volume contains four poems: "Fumées" ("Smoke"); "Fuites légères" ("Light Flights"); "Le Vallon" ("The Valley"); "Mélancolie" ("Melancholy"). For the annotated edition see Sauvage and Marchal-Vincent, *L'Œuvre poétique*, 2:54-125; notes 2:323-30.
79. Marchal, *Chants du silence*, 59.
80. Pierre Messiaen, *Images*, 139.
81. Marchal, *Chants du silence*, 60.
82. For Nantes, see http://en.wikipedia.org/wiki/Nantes.

a silent war [*une guerre sourde*] between the professors of a Catholic and French tradition and the *leftist* [*gauchards*] professors whose origins were Jewish or Protestant or the sons of *instituteurs,* keen on irreligious laicism. Among the former, I was scandalized by their resignation, perceptive but inert, with regards to the laws and programs revamping our bourgeoisie; among the latter, I was stupefied by their lack of culture which was compatible with a great deal of erudition and even knowledge, fiercely pursuing, under various names, the same suffocating enterprise, egalitarian and materialist.[83]

Pierre's description demonstrates his ongoing sympathy with the outlook of conservative Catholics who looked to writers like Barrès and Maurras for nourishment and inspiration.

In early 1914, the thirty-one-year-old Pierre foresaw for the future nothing but "years of calm, of fruitful and persevering work." Since Shakespeare was "poorly known in France; no one had ever done a proper job of translation; and our public was unaware of the exegesis that had stimulated his work in England and elsewhere," Pierre set himself the task of translating the complete works. The project would eventually take thirty years.[84]

Meanwhile, as Pierre occupied himself with his professional success, Cécile's epistolary relationship with Jean took a further step into physical involvement. As her biographer reasons, it is difficult to know exactly where and when this brief encounter took place: it seems impossible that it could have happened in tiny Ambert without neighbors noticing. But when would Cécile have been alone in Nantes? Or was it while Pierre was away on one of his trips to England? It seems unlikely that it would have occurred before the spring of 1914, but it may have been possible in early summer when Cécile took the children to Grenoble for the vacation period. She told her parents that the date of her arrival would be uncertain and that they ought not be worried or surprised if she didn't show up when expected. It is possible that she was preparing a detour to Paris, which would provide another possible opportunity for meeting Jean.[85] Whatever the timing, her writings recount a physical encounter expressed in the most passionate terms possible.

This was the state of the Messiaen household in late June 1914, the fi-

83. Pierre Messiaen, *Images,* 171-72, emphasis in original.

84. See note above: the complete works were published in three volumes between 1939 and 1945, that is, just before the outbreak of World War II and then immediately following the liberation.

85. Marchal, *Chants du silence,* 64-65.

1883–1914: Mixed Marriage, Literary Maternity, Postpartum Depression

nal peaceful hours of the Belle Époque. Pierre had been dreaming of "years of calm, of fruitful and persevering work" translating the complete works of Shakespeare. Cécile was inflamed with an escalating clandestine love affair. Olivier was six years old; Alain was about to turn two. Pierre was in Nantes; Jean was in Paris; Cécile was en route to or already in Grenoble for the summer months. The Archduke Franz Ferdinand of Austria was in Sarajevo, where he and his wife Sophie were assassinated on June 28. Concluding the monthlong July Crisis, France ordered mobilization on August 1. Among those called to the war front were Cécile's husband Pierre, her paramour Jean, and her brother André.

Popular sentiment held that the war would be over by Christmas. However, popular opinion was wrong. Years later, Pierre would rhetorically pose the question in his memoirs: "Why not get down to the job of this long-drawn-out task" of translating Shakespeare in 1914? He answers with understatement: "There were the four years of the Great War."[86]

---

86. Pierre Messiaen, *Images*, 172.

CHAPTER 2

1914–1919

A Great War Childhood: Mourning and Melancholia

The guns of August 1914 signaled the end of Pierre's brief one-year teaching stint in Nantes. Capitalizing on his proficiency in English, the military assigned him to the British army to act as a translator between French and English troops. By the time hostilities broke out, Cécile and the two boys had already arrived in Grenoble. Since her brother André had departed for the front to serve as a surgeon, Cécile and the children took over his apartment for the next four years.[1] Located in southeastern France and surrounded by mountains, including the Dauphiné Alps, Grenoble is called the "Capital of the Alps." Spending the formative years of six to ten in Grenoble, Olivier Messiaen would come to consider this majestic mountainous region of the Dauphiné his lifelong home.[2]

---

1. Pierre would later remark on André's "brilliant and productive surgical career" and explain how he "had saved the lives of so many wounded in his surgical ambulance, close to Verdun, and who, barely even going to Mass, was venerated as a god by the Sisters of the clinic at Eybens." Pierre Messiaen, *Images* (Paris: Desclée de Brouwer, 1944), 151.

2. See the small but lavishly illustrated volume by Claude Samuel, *Olivier Messiaen en Dauphiné*, with the collaboration of Nigel Simeone, Roger Muraro, Jean-Claude Roché, and Bernard Fort (Isère: Conservation du Patrimoine en Isère Musée Dauphinois, 2009).

1914-1919: A Great War Childhood: Mourning and Melancholia

In Flanders Fields: Pierre's Grief (1914-1918)

The war would impact Pierre in profound ways, as demonstrated in his memoirs. Although published toward the end of the German occupation of Paris in the Second World War, the memoirs are replete with references back to the catastrophic First World War three decades earlier.³ Pierre summarizes the war in terms reminiscent of many others who served at the Western Front: "muddy trenches, dugouts [*cagnas*] infested with lice and rats, bombardments of shells and bombs, bullets whistling by one after another, night work with pickaxes and shovels, horses frozen in the tangle of barbed wire."⁴ But the particular details of familial and personal loss convey the atmosphere of grief in whose aftermath Olivier would spend late childhood and adolescence.

The Messiaen family farm on the Belgian border had been prospering when war erupted in 1914. Pierre's brother Paul had put it back on firm footing after their father's death. However, as Paul left for the war front in Lorraine at the outbreak, half of the horses and cattle were taken by governmental requisition.⁵ "What desolation!" exclaims Pierre as he recalls seeing his native region later on, immortalized in the most popular English poem of the day, John McCrae's "In Flanders Fields" (1915).⁶ "Disemboweled and devastated villages, trees torn to shreds, fields cut up into trenches and bombed-out craters, a hellish horizon of mud, of ruins, of *chevaux de frise* [anticavalry obstacles], military emplacements, machine guns and cannons."⁷ Even the family's horse, requisitioned at the outset of the war in 1914, had not been spared. "Dear Minos! we learned later that he had returned to Verdun and perished after taking a bombshell in the stomach."⁸ A genuine "War Horse."⁹

---

3. One scholar notes how "disquieting" it is to read Pierre's wartime memories: "the vast majority of his portraits of friends and acquaintances of a similar age end with recording that they died during one or other battle of the war." Christopher Dingle, *The Life of Messiaen* (Cambridge and New York: Cambridge University Press, 2007), 9. For France's postwar decade as primarily a period of bereavement and mourning, see Stephen Schloesser, *Jazz Age Catholicism: Mystic Modernism in Postwar Paris, 1919-1933* (Toronto: University of Toronto Press, 2005), 8-11.

4. Pierre Messiaen, *Images*, 173.

5. Pierre Messiaen, *Images*, 106.

6. For analysis and criticism see Paul Fussell, *The Great War and Modern Memory* (New York: Oxford University Press, 2000), 248-50.

7. Pierre Messiaen, *Images*, 9.

8. Pierre Messiaen, *Images*, 33.

9. For a vivid portrayal of the role of horses in World War I, see the film *War Horse* (2011), produced by Steven Spielberg and Kathleen Kennedy; screenplay by Lee Hall and

1883–1930: Pierre Messiaen and Cécile Sauvage

Loss and grief pervade Pierre's story. Recalling the young men with whom he had associated when first working for the *Revue forézienne,* Pierre notes particularly Paul Forest, who "knew music, loved above all Mozart and Debussy, never spoke of Beethoven and Wagner except with a tone of contempt, played the piano with the lightness and tenderness of a woman; he was killed in Alsace at the beginning of the Great War." Pierre also cites Joseph Gourdon, who "only liked erudite and sibylline poetry; he wrote sonnets which were genuine conundrums; he too perished in Alsace (November 1914)."[10] Pierre remembers a father who "died before his son, killed at the Somme in 1917; then it was the turn of his inconsolable wife"; and "Chenevrier, the gardener of the chateau, a son who was also killed at the Somme in 1917."[11]

Other grieving mothers appear. Remembering yet another acquaintance from the *Revue forézienne* days, Pierre recalls how he heroically followed orders in a hopeless situation, took a rifle, led his men in the charge, and "disappeared in a cloud of bullets and smoke." His mother showed Pierre "his last letters. What a spirit of sacrifice! Such an acceptance of being offered as a holocaust so that France might be delivered!"[12] Decades later, when Pierre's infant son died soon after birth (in 1934), a friend of his mother wrote him about losing her own son in the war: "I remember how filled with despair I was after the death of my poor André. When I made my pilgrimage to the Monts de Champagne [cemetery], when I saw the ruins, these thousands of crosses, symbols of so many women, of mothers who wept like I did, I understood that in this mass of sorrows, my suffering was really a small thing. Even if I continued to suffer, I did not dare complain."[13]

Pierre notes that among all the sorrowful episodes he experienced, one in particular "brings tears to my eyes each time I think about it." On the eve of an attack, a New Zealander named Colonel King, a "great drinker of whiskey," told him stories of trips down under; and an Englishman named Colonel Smith, "the distant and reserved English type who only spoke in monosyllables," showed him pictures of his wife and their five children. "Undoubtedly,

---

Richard Curtis; directed by Steven Spielberg; based on Nick Stafford, *War Horse* (London: Faber and Faber, 2007), and Michael Morpurgo, *War Horse* (Tadworth: Kaye and Ward, 1982).

10. Pierre Messiaen, *Images,* 122.
11. Pierre Messiaen, *Images,* 99.
12. Pierre Messiaen, *Images,* 124. For Catholic discourse interpreting war losses as sacrificial holocausts in reparation for France's sins, see Schloesser, *Jazz Age Catholicism,* 87-96, 125-26.
13. Pierre Messiaen, *Images,* 252.

1914–1919: A Great War Childhood: Mourning and Melancholia

both had a presentiment that they would be killed the next day." The intuition was correct: at four o'clock the next day, Pierre received a frantic phone call telling him to translate: "Lengthen your range of fire, your shells are falling all around us." Less than five minutes later, the British post of Colonels King and Smith was "annihilated" by French friendly fire.[14]

Another memorable Englishman was Lieutenant Robert Eric Spinney, the son of an English consul to Morocco. Pierre recounts in detail his erudition: "He read the comedies of Shakespeare with a marvelous sense of the jokes, the poetry, and mimicry." After his left arm and shoulder were "horrifically torn to shreds by an aerial torpedo, he lived yet another ten hours and found the means by which, although no longer able to speak, to write down on a piece of paper that he was bequeathing me his beautiful illustrated ten-volume works of Shakespeare left behind with his mother in Morocco." Pierre went to visit Spinney's grave with Spinney's older sister, who said to him: "He is not there beneath the earth; his soul waits for me."[15]

The worst year for the Messiaen family was 1918, the war's last: his oldest sister died and his two brothers were killed. His older brother Paul (who had taken over the family farm) had "thought about marrying when in 1914 he was mobilized for the 237th infantry regiment; he fought in Lorraine, in Argonne, and Artois; his head was riddled with shrapnel during an attack at Craonne and he died in the hospital at Troyes, several months later, from meningitis, disfigured by a drilling [in his skull] and two or three other operations as cruel as they were useless." His brother Léon, eighteen months younger and a sculptor, was mobilized in the same division as Paul. He was wounded three times, at Lorraine, at Souchez, and at Verdun. "He was cleanly killed by a shell, with the entire telephone line post of his regiment, the day of the breaking of the Bulgarian front, 15 September 1918. We were able to bring his body back to France; he lies with his family, beneath a statue that he had designed as a monument in remembrance of the battles of Brienne-la-Rothière (1814). We understood too late why his last letters had been so melancholic."[16]

Finally, the eleventh day of the eleventh month.[17] Pierre recalls, however, that "no week of my existence was both more sorrowful and more exultant than that of the Armistice." On November 10, the final day of the war, he was in the Forest of Mormal near the Franco-Belgian border: "I had just learned

14. Pierre Messiaen, *Images*, 175.
15. Pierre Messiaen, *Images*, 188-89.
16. Pierre Messiaen, *Images*, 47.
17. Joseph E. Persico, *Eleventh Month, Eleventh Day, Eleventh Hour: Armistice Day, 1918, World War I and Its Violent Climax* (New York: Random House, 2004).

of the deaths of my two brothers." Since "the Germans held on to the very last minute," there was gunfire all around as comrades fell. "We were shivering; we were exhausted from no sleep; the minute we had an hour of relief we made huge fires with the piles of wood the enemy seemed to have prepared for us; refugees were sprouting out from everywhere, men, women, children, dragging along their packages, pushing wheelbarrows, begging us for drink and food, sleeping alongside us." On November 11, the morning of the cease-fire, they marched out led by the general on his horse, "saluting the cadavers in khaki or blue-grey stretched out on the sides of the road." Musicians played the "Marseillaise" and "God Save the King." The flood of refugees continued to renew itself without ceasing, and enormous craters frequently forced all to detour. For at least three days the Germans detonated their ammunition depots as they retreated, sending quivers as they exploded. "Not a single cow nor chicken remained in France."[18]

A Melancholic Homefront: Messiaen's Wartime Solitude

On August 30, 1914, Alain celebrated his second birthday. It must have been a somewhat cheerless observance. Pierre's account of Cécile's state of mind seems to have deliberately softened the truth of those years marked by her physical and mental decline as she "lost weight, sunk in melancholy."[19] "We only detected the decline of Cécile's health during the war," Pierre later recalled. "She no longer wanted to go out with the children; she locked herself in her room so as not to hear their games and their running across the apartment; she wrote me every day, but they were gloomy letters, distressing rather than comforting. Mistral had been correct in his perception: the dear grasshopper of the Basses-Alpes was no longer herself."[20]

Cécile did indeed lock herself in her dark room all day, along with her secret reasons, consumed with grief and desire for Jean de Gourmont, now at war. While she wrote vast amounts of passionate poetry — it was the only way to live out the relationship that the war had now severed — Olivier and Alain were in fact raised by their grandmother Sauvage.[21] Cécile's biographer imagines the effect this had on the six-year-old:

18. Pierre Messiaen, *Images*, 177-78.
19. Pierre Messiaen, *Images*, 172-73.
20. Pierre Messiaen, *Images*, 143.
21. Béatrice Marchal, *Les Chants du silence. Olivier Messiaen, fils de Cécile Sauvage ou la musique face à l'impossible parole* (Sampzon: Éditions Delatour France, 2008), 69.

1914–1919: A Great War Childhood: Mourning and Melancholia

Olivier [later] recalled, without ever having spoken about it to anyone, the anxiety that took hold of him many times, when he found his mother with her exhausted features, an air of depletion, sometimes in tears; he would press himself firmly into her arms, or stand still, his heart frozen over with deadly fear, powerless to comfort a sorrow whose seriousness he understood even if he did not know the cause. How could such a sensitive child so filled with love for his mother not have perceived it, when even the family circle attributed Cécile's state to her health? It is in fact starting at this moment that, according to general opinion, she began to decline and suffered the first attacks of tuberculosis.[22]

Six decades would transpire — September 1972, to be exact, when Messiaen was almost sixty-five years old — before he would discover the truth of what happened during that first year of the war. Following the death of his mother's sister, Germaine, Messiaen came into possession of and read the large volumes of mystical-erotic love poetry and prose that his mother had written in her dark isolation between August 1914 and August 1915.[23] They comprise three works: *The Mystical Embrace (L'Étreinte mystique)*, a reader in prose that was completed in August 1915; *Prayer (Prière)*, an extremely fragmentary reader in verse dating from 1914-1915; and *The Wing and the Rose (L'Aile et la rose)*, a short set of poems dating from the same period.[24]

Cécile used her intimate familiarity with Christian mystical literature in service of describing her passions. This appears immediately in the first paragraph of *The Mystical Embrace*, as she compares an erotic exchange to Christ's giving his flesh and blood in the Eucharist at Mass: "Side-by-side we ate together a food of love. The bread you touched, oh my lover, was your own flesh. The wine you poured out to me was the blood of your veins. The glass which I brought to my mouth was a chalice of love: I drank and faintness [*la défaillance*] reached down to my very depths with the penetrating drink."[25]

Similarly, in the second section, the lover's presence transfigures the beloved's vision of reality:

---

22. Marchal, *Chants du silence*, 70.
23. Yvonne Loriod-Messiaen did not read the manuscripts herself until October 1987, about five years before Messiaen's death in April 1992. Cécile Sauvage, *Écrits d'amour*, edited, introduced, and annotated by Béatrice Marchal (Paris: Les Éditions du Cerf, 2009), 24.
24. Sauvage, *Écrits d'amour*, 24.
25. *L'Étreinte mystique* (I): in Sauvage, *Écrits d'amour*, 61.

Your presence next to me was perhaps that of a God; because wherever you passed by a luminous trace remained. I went into the room where you lived and I fell to my knees: a real light of love spread itself throughout this room, on each object; the roses were no longer roses but rather a bouquet of trembling emotion, a bouquet that had served as the base of your dear head, — and, from the magnolia at the window with withered roses, to the bed, to the chairs, to the books, there extended a trellis, a long magnetism of love; and in reality, this room coalesced in a single kiss on my flesh and I remained there in faintness, pierced by the arrows of a sorrowful and ecstatic sensual [or sexual = *volupté*] pleasure.[26]

The final image directly evokes Bernini's Baroque sculpture *Ecstasy of Saint Teresa* in the Roman church of Santa Maria della Vittoria.

The third section also emphasizes the "visionary" aspect of mysticism, a motif that would become so important in Messiaen's works *(Apparition of the Eternal Church, Visions of Amen, Lightning Flashes of the Beyond . . .)*. Below the first two words ("visionary hours") Cécile had written and then deleted these words: "I am trying to relive these hours of sensual [or sexual = *volupté*] pleasure all the way down to their most mysterious sensations." "Visionary hours, in which we both were side-by-side in life, passing through life. The whole city was love, emerging from a religious dream [*d'un rêve religieux*], emerging from [*détaché*] ourselves: the houses, the avenues, the perspective of the river, the towers, the spires under a soft sky were all steeped in a spiritual sensibility, a luminous comprehension intimately linked to our path and our exchanges of wordless ardor."[27]

These brief excerpts provide a glimpse into numerous pages feverishly written by Cécile in her grief-stricken year of solitude. Although Olivier would not have read them in their written form until late in life, he seems to have absorbed such sentiments in some other way early on — for his own alliance (or at least juxtaposition) of mysticism and eroticism became a trademark feature in his own works.

Cécile seems to have begun to emerge from this emotional crisis in the summer of 1915. In July, for example, André, now a surgeon at the front, wrote his parents: "I am happy to know that Cécile is doing better: if morale didn't have a great influence on her physical being, she wouldn't be a Sauvage."[28]

---

26. *L'Étreinte mystique* (II): in Sauvage, *Écrits d'amour*, 61.

27. *L'Étreinte mystique* (III): in Sauvage, *Écrits d'amour*, 61-62.

28. Letter of André Sauvage (July 28, 1915), Archives Yvonne Loriod; in Marchal, *Chants du silence*, 71.

1914-1919: A Great War Childhood: Mourning and Melancholia

However, Prosper Sauvage, Cécile's father, died six months later, in December.[29] It must have been a very bitter additional blow for the fragile Cécile as well as the two grandsons.

"My children do not like to speak about the Great War and the years that followed," Pierre would later write. "They studied, amused themselves, skipped around, imagined spectacles and fantasies as one does between the ages 4 and 12. And 8 year old Olivier had the gift of music; he sight-read at the piano everything that fell beneath his hand, sang in his small young voice the entire scores of operas."[30] Indeed, much of Messiaen's childhood life was solitary. As he would later recall stoically, he had very few friends apart from a certain Jean Licou, "whom I liked very much, but he died when he was seven, so I was alone."[31] Literature and music — and opera, the hybridization of those two — became Olivier's enduring companions.

Cécile realized what an extraordinary child she had in Olivier, and she passed on to him her prodigious knowledge of literature and music. Both he and little Alain received many recountings of fairy tales, especially those of Madame d'Aulnoy, and they would not allow any variations from Cécile's standard versions. Two lines from Aulnoy's tales especially stand out for the budding musician-ornithologist who would later be famous for color-sounds and preoccupation with time:

Oiseau bleu, couleur du temps	Bluebird, color of time
Vole à moi promptement	Fly promptly to me.[32]

Cécile also told him that the deliciously terrifying stories she recounted were called "tragedies" and invented by a writer named Shakespeare. She also in-

---

29. Marchal, *Chants du silence*, 76.
30. Pierre Messiaen, *Images*, 153.
31. Dingle, *The Life of Messiaen*, 6.
32. Marchal, *Chants du silence*, 73, quoting "The Bluebird" ("L'Oiseau bleu") by Madame (or Countess) Marie-Catherine d'Aulnoy (1650/1651-1705), author of several volumes of "fairy tales" *(contes de fées)*. For background, see Sophie Heywood, *Catholicism and Children's Literature in France: The Comtesse de Ségur (1799-1874)* (Manchester, U.K., and New York: Manchester University Press, distributed in the U.S. exclusively by Palgrave Macmillan, 2011); Lewis C. Seifert and Domna C. Stanton, eds. and trans., *Enchanted Eloquence: Fairy Tales by Seventeenth-Century French Women Writers* (Toronto: Centre for Reformation and Renaissance Studies and Iter Inc., 2010); Ruth B. Bottigheimer, *Fairy Tales: A New History* (Albany: Excelsior Editions/State University of New York Press, 2009); Hilda Roderick Ellis Davidson and Anna Chaudhri, eds., *A Companion to the Fairy Tale* (Cambridge and Rochester, N.Y.: D. S. Brewer, 2003).

troduced him to operas — Mozart's *Magic Flute,* Berlioz's *Damnation of Faust,* Wagner's *Valkyries* and *Siegfried* — and piano music, including Debussy's *Estampes* and Ravel's *Gaspard de la nuit.*[33]

Messiaen himself dated his self-discovery as a musician to the age of seven and a half, that is, the summer of 1916. After learning music for a few months and precociously playing the piano, he went to Grenoble's largest music shop and purchased the score to Gluck's *Orphée.* He sat down in the large city park and opened the work to the first act's aria. As he read the notes, he experienced a revelation: he sensed that he was "hearing" the melody.[34] For Christmas 1916, he asked his mother for and received Gluck's *Alcestis* — to which she added Mozart's *Don Giovanni.*

In addition to the works of Shakespeare, Cécile introduced Olivier to the English Romantics, including Keats and Tennyson. Appropriately, his first piano composition, written in 1917 at the age of nine, was *The Lady of Shalott,* a response to Tennyson's poem of the same name.[35] The boy's choice seems uncanny when set in the context of his mother's hidden emotional life. The cursed Lady of Shalott must live in isolation in her tower and not look out directly into the world; the "bold Sir Lancelot" rides by and catches her eye; passion compels her to suspend weaving and look directly at him. The curse's punishment unfolds and the Lady dies an untimely death in her boat on the way to Camelot. Tennyson's Lancelot pronounces the final judgment: "She has a lovely face; / God in his mercy lend her grace, / The Lady of Shalott." Fifty years later Messiaen described it as "obviously a very childish piece, but neither quite silly nor completely devoid of sense. I still regard it with a certain tenderness."[36]

---

33. Marchal, *Chants du silence,* 75.

34. Peter Hill and Nigel Simeone, *Messiaen* (New Haven: Yale University Press, 2005), 12-13.

35. Marchal, *Chants du silence,* 73-75.

36. Olivier Messiaen and Claude Samuel, *Music and Color: Conversations with Claude Samuel,* trans. E. Thomas Glasow (Portland, Ore.: Amadeus Press, 1994), 258; originally Samuel, *Olivier Messiaen: Musique et couleur* (Paris: Éditions Belfond, 1986), quoted in Nigel Simeone, *Olivier Messiaen: A Bibliographical Catalogue of Messiaen's Works,* Musikbibliographische Arbeiten series, vol. 14 (Tutzing: Hans Schneider, 1998), 187; cf. Dingle, *The Life of Messiaen,* 7.

Messiaen's conversations with Claude Samuel played a major role in shaping and projecting his public image of himself from the late 1960s through the 1980s and then even after his death. As Christopher Dingle notes in his summary of this series of volumes, "Messiaen did not wish to appear as author of the conversations and, as a consequence, the author is given as Samuel." However, as Messiaen's corrections to the interview transcripts

1914–1919: A Great War Childhood: Mourning and Melancholia

One distinctive trait of Messiaen's temperament and music had its origins in Grenoble: his attraction to fearful things and, indeed, his pleasure in being frightened. Certainly, this attraction was partly temperamental. However, several factors in his wartime childhood would have developed this propensity. The first was the geographical fact of being surrounded by mountains. He would be marked throughout his life with a sensitivity to the sharp rises and plummeting depths of peaks and gorges. Like other compatriots immersed in the French imaginary from Pascal through Baudelaire, Messiaen was fascinated with the concept of the "abyss" and its corresponding "vertigo."[37] For the boy Messiaen living in the Dauphiné Alpine region, these literary and metaphysical spatial images were quite concrete. An indication of their impact appears sixty years later; in the large orchestral work entitled *From Canyons to Stars* (1974), the pivotal movement — entitled "Cedar Breaks and the Gift of Awe" — represents in sound-colors the deep gorge in Cedar Breaks, Utah.[38]

A second factor was intimately familial: the blindness of his grandfather Sauvage (who would die in December 1915). Tragically enough, especially for a schoolteacher, Messiaen's grandfather Prosper Sauvage had developed cataracts. After the November 1905 eye surgery (undergone just as Pierre and Cécile began their courtship) proved to be unsuccessful, Prosper eventually lost all of his sight. Pierre touchingly recalls that at Olivier's birth, grandfather Sauvage, "Short yellow man, bald, blind, walking with little steps, felt the face and the body of his grandson whom he had the sadness of not being able to

---

demonstrate, he shaped the final texts with a firm hand. Thus, unless otherwise indicated, references hereafter will be to "Messiaen and Samuel (1994)." For overview of the various editions, see Dingle, xii; for reproduction of Messiaen's corrections, see Claude Samuel, *Permanences d'Olivier Messiaen* (Arles: Actes Sud, 1999), 173; reprinted in Stephen Broad, "Recontextualising Messiaen's Early Career," 2 vols. (Ph.D. diss., University of Oxford, 2005), 1:81. For earlier editions see Olivier Messiaen and Claude Samuel, *Conversations with Olivier Messiaen,* trans. Felix Aprahamian (London: Stainer and Bell, 1976), 1; originally Samuel, *Entretiens avec Olivier Messiaen* (Paris: Pierre Belfond, 1967).

37. Suspended over the abyss, we are attracted to leap into it even as it repels us with terror. For a fuller account of this concept see below, pp. 280 n. 11, 424-27, 430.

38. The movement's epigraph quotes Ernest Hello: "The replacement of fear by awe [*de la peur par la crainte*] opens a window for adoration." Hello, *Paroles de Dieu. Réflexions sur quelques textes sacrés,* ed. François Angelier (Grenoble: Jérôme Millon, [1877] 1992), 176: "Ce magnifique remplacement de la peur par la crainte ouvre une fenêtre sur l'adoration." Used by Messiaen as the epigraph to *Des canyons aux étoiles* (1974), movement 5: "Cedar Breaks et le Don de crainte" ("Cedar Breaks and the Gift of Awe"). See Messiaen, titles and inscriptions to movements of *From Canyons to Stars,* in Olivier Messiaen, *Complete Edition,* 32 CDs (Germany: Deutsche Grammophon, 2008), 32-35, at 33.

see."³⁹ ("I would never wish on anyone," Pierre adds poignantly, "becoming blind in one's old age; an old man who can no longer see is imprisoned in his regrets and his anxieties.") However, Prosper's blindness had a lasting influence on the young Olivier, who enjoyed both frightening others as well as being frightened. "Alain and I played games with him, to frighten us. In the evening we would go into the room where he was, in darkness which didn't worry him at all, and we would say, 'Grandad, scare us!' which he did. Wasn't that an atmosphere quite close to Maeterlinck's [*Pelléas et Melisande*] in the old castle of Allemonde!"⁴⁰

A third factor in Messiaen's attraction to fear was literary. Even before Olivier's birth, when the newly-wed Messiaens were first living in Avignon, Pierre would read aloud his father-in-law's favorite novels, including those of Balzac, Dickens, and Tolstoy. "He preferred the tender and the gracious as opposed to that which was too real, too black," writes Pierre. "I remember the happiness he received from the love scenes and the rural work in *War and Peace*."⁴¹ Pierre also read Dostoyevsky to him; even as Prosper claimed not to like the dark Russian, he demonstrated an "insatiable" appetite for his work.⁴² When Pierre went off to war, Olivier, a precocious reader, followed his father's lead and read aloud for his grandfather until his death the following year.

In recognition of Olivier's interest (and perhaps Pierre's expertise), his uncle André gave him "an edition of Shakespeare's works which [he] loved very much, a romantic edition with woodcuts depicting all the characters in all possible attitudes — that made a deep impression on [him] as a child."⁴³ Messiaen created a toy theater for the staging of Shakespeare's works, experimenting with lighting and using model characters to block scenes. He would entertain Alain with performances in which he played all the parts. Later he recalled the importance of Shakespeare in his life:

> You know, all these things are contained in the plays of Shakespeare, not only the human passions, but also the magic, the witches, the sprites, the sylphs, the phantoms, and *apparitions of all kinds*. Shakespeare is an author who powerfully develops the imagination of his reader. I was inclined toward fairy tales, and Shakespeare is sometimes a super-fairy tale; it was this aspect of Shakespeare that impressed me. . . . I loved *Macbeth* most of

39. Pierre Messiaen, *Images*, 191.
40. Hill and Simeone, *Messiaen*, 12 n. 15.
41. Pierre Messiaen, *Images*, 192.
42. Pierre Messiaen, *Images*, 147.
43. Hill and Simeone, *Messiaen*, 14 n. 26.

1914–1919: A Great War Childhood: Mourning and Melancholia

all because of the witches and Banquo's ghost, also Puck [in *Midsummer Night's Dream*] and Ariel [in *The Tempest*] for the same reasons, and I felt very vividly the grandeur of the mad King Lear raging against the storm and lightning. As for the famous stage directions in the historical plays — "alarums, skirmishes, the enemy enters the city" — for me, they have always symbolized the idea of striking out for something new.[44]

At the age of ten, Messiaen said to his mother, "Mummy, you're a poet just like Shakespeare. Like him, you have suns, planets, ants, frightening skeletons. I prefer things which are frightening."[45] This connection between the supernatural and the dreadful or "awe-full" would last throughout his life.

Messiaen's wartime childhood was spent in the laicist environment of the Sauvage family from age five and a half until his tenth birthday in December 1918. Even at such a young age, he must have noticed the difference between that environment and the first five years of his life lived within Pierre's ultra-Catholic atmosphere. However, a letter from Cécile shows that this "Voltairean" milieu was supremely capable of accommodating religious sentiment when it had to. On November 28, 1918, seventeen days after the armistice and just about two weeks before Olivier's tenth birthday, Cécile wrote Pierre's sister Agnès a letter of condolence following the battlefield death of their brother Léon: "Give my best to your poor mother, for whose recovery I prayed when she was ill, and for whom I will pray now, that she will have the courage to bear this new tragedy. Tell her that I will *always* keep reverently the memory of her poor Léon. I have asked for a Mass to be said here which we will attend. . . . The children are well. They are at the Lycée, and Zivier [i.e., Olivier] has learnt the catechism. They join me in sending our warmest love, and both say that neither of them will forget their Uncle Léon."[46] Olivier would receive his first communion and confirmation half a year after this note was written.[47] The key Catholic doctrine of the Eucharist would prove to be central for the rest of his life (cf. *The Celestial Banquet*, 1928; *Book of*

---

44. Messiaen and Samuel (1994), 26, emphasis added.
45. Hill and Simeone, *Messiaen*, 12, 10-11.
46. Hill and Simeone, *Messiaen*, 9 n. 6.
47. Messiaen received these sacraments in Nantes on June 22, 1919, the Sunday following Corpus Christi; see Marchal, *Chants du silence*, 83. A decade earlier (by the decree *Quam Singulari* [August 15, 1910]), Pope Pius X had altered traditional sacramental practice, recommending that the first communion of children not be deferred too long after their seventh birthday, that is, the age of "discretion" or "reason." It seems likely that Messiaen's first communion was postponed from 1916 in anticipation of Pierre's return from war.

the Blessed Sacrament, 1984). Since he had been studying the catechism in preparation while in Grenoble, it is interesting to speculate how a precocious nine-year-old might have reconciled it all within a household whose adults did not attend religious services.

Reflecting on Cécile's progressively degenerating physical and psychological state, I can't help but think of Virginia Woolf, another writer whose emotional fragility would be similarly impacted by a world war. Given Cécile's attitudes toward "modern civilization," the catalyst provided by the First World War might also have been the way in which it verified her deepest convictions. The most important characteristic of the Great War as compared with previous conflicts — that is, its enormous scale — could initially be seen as the fruit of scientific progress. But then came the previously unimaginable casualties as well — the Somme, Ypres, Verdun — thanks to "progress" in technology like machine guns, mustard gas, submarines, and airplanes. In late 1916, one soldier wrote from the trenches: "Confronted by the spectacle of a scientific struggle in which Progress is used to return to Barbarism, and by the spectacle of a civilization turning against itself to destroy itself, reason cannot cope."[48] Mourning and melancholia permeated France, both during the war and in the postwar 1920s, and the small family of Pierre and Cécile did not escape it. By the time Pierre returned home as a war veteran and reunited with Cécile and the two boys, young Olivier had already been breathing this air for four years. There would be ten more.

Music Lessons in Nantes (January–June 1919): A Fortuitous Six Months

After his demobilization following the armistice in November 1918, Pierre was appointed to return to Nantes where he had taught for the year 1913-1914 following his completion of the English degree. It is difficult to imagine, even in geographical terms (let alone psychological ones), what a wrenching experience this was for him and his family. Pierre, of course, was relocating from the war front in Flanders where he had just managed to survive the past four years, to become a teacher once again of secondary-school English. Cécile and the children were moving from Provence in the extreme southeast back to the

---

48. Louis Mairet, letter of December 29, 1916; in Modris Eksteins, *Rites of Spring: The Great War and the Birth of the Modern Age* (Boston: Houghton Mifflin, 1989), 215-16; cf. Schloesser, *Jazz Age Catholicism,* 8-11.

1914–1919: A Great War Childhood: Mourning and Melancholia

Breton city of Nantes. Nevertheless, the move was fortuitous, for it was here that Olivier's musical gifts would be first honed.

In early 1919, as the family relocated from Grenoble to Nantes, Olivier's parents realized he needed specialized studies. According to Pierre, Olivier studied with two musical mentors: "the pianist Gontran Arcouët" (who taught at the École Nationale de Musique in Nantes) and "the organist Joseph de Gibon." The two of them took the ten-year-old into their "friendship and taught him the technical elements which he would develop later at the Conservatory of Paris."[49]

Pierre's recollection implies that Messiaen had been introduced to "the technical elements" of organ playing at the age of ten. This account diverges from that given by both Marcel Dupré and Messiaen himself. According to Dupré, it was not until autumn 1927 (i.e., eight years later) that the nineteen-year-old Messiaen first saw an organ: "he sat stupefied in front of my organ keyboards. He had never seen an organ console before. After an hour of explanations and demonstrations, I gave him the Bach C minor Fantasia to learn. He came back a week later and played it to me by heart, perfectly; an astonishing feat!"[50] However, Pierre's account, even with the misremembered first name, seems substantiated by the obituary Messiaen wrote years later on the occasion of Gibon's death: "I must also mention a beautiful *Pastorale* for organ, dedicated to me.... I have often played this *Pastorale* on my organ at the Trinité and will play it again regularly, along with his other works, *in memory of my old master*."[51] The master-apprentice relationship here would seem to have been that of studying the organ.

---

49. Pierre Messiaen, *Images*, 221. Pierre has the name wrong: it was Jean (sometimes Jehan) de Gibon. Hill and Simeone, *Messiaen*, 14.

50. Dupré letter dated December 27, 1967; in Hill and Simeone, *Messiaen*, 22. For the Tournemire-Dupré rivalry, see Schloesser, *Jazz Age Catholicism*, 297-99. In retrospect, this account would seem to be yet another street legend (not unlike the claim of having been raised by two unbelieving parents), devised to make Messiaen's artistry spontaneously generated. For a detailed study of Messiaen's self-inventions, see Broad, "Recontextualising Messiaen's Early Career." I am very grateful to Stephen Broad for his assistance.

51. Messiaen, 1952 obituary notice for Jean de Gibon; in Hill and Simeone, *Messiaen*, 15, emphasis added. Gibon seems to have been involved in the postwar revival of Gregorian chant in France. See his variations on the plainchant hymn for Easter, "O Sons and Daughters" ("O Filii et Filiae"): Jean de Gibon, *Variations sur "O filii": pour orgue ou harmonium (pédale non obligée)*, 2nd ed. (St. Laurent-sur-Sèvre: L. J. Biton, 1928). The piece is no. 26 in a series entitled "Collection of Selected Works for Organ or Harmonium in the Spirit of the *Motu Proprio* of His Holiness Pius X." For the 1903 *motu proprio* mandating the restoration of plainchant in Catholic worship, see Schloesser, *Jazz Age Catholicism*, 286.

1883–1930: Pierre Messiaen and Cécile Sauvage

Another significant aspect of this obituary is the description given of Gibon's work for piano dedicated to Arcouët, Messiaen's piano teacher. Entitled *Breton Cemetery* and written in 1919 — while Messiaen was a student of both dedicator and dedicatee, and just after his father had returned from the front — it immediately conjures images of grieving Brittany just after the armistice, a region (like all the rest of France) engaged in building monuments to its many lost youth.[52] It must have made a strong impression on the young boy since Messiaen remembered it with such clarity three decades later. Significantly, Messiaen's recollection of "the bell effects using superimposed fifths" suggests a source for his own *Visions of Amen,* in which allusions to bells (especially funeral bells and the wartime alarum) play a leading role. Finally, his description of the harmonic devices parallels exactly the liturgical musical style that Messiaen was about to discover most fully developed in Paris in the work of Charles Tournemire; Gibon's "imaginative harmonies, the use of the whole-tone scale and modes from plainchant must have sounded strangely 'modern' at the time."[53]

Since the linkage between the whole-tone scale and plainchant modes evokes the musicianship of Claude Debussy, it is fitting that Gibon is best remembered today for the gift he gave Messiaen in December 1919: the vocal score of Debussy's *Pelléas and Mélisande* (1902).[54] This symbolist opera, set to a libretto by Maurice Maeterlinck (which Messiaen had also received for Christ-

---

52. For the postwar surge in cemeteries and monuments, see Daniel J. Sherman, *The Construction of Memory in Interwar France* (Chicago: University of Chicago Press, 1999); cf. Schloesser, *Jazz Age Catholicism,* 330-31 n. 33.

53. Messiaen, 1952 obituary notice, in Hill and Simeone, *Messiaen,* 15. Gibon had very likely imitated this "modern" hybridization of the whole-tone scale and of plainchant modes as found in the music of Claude Debussy. In search of new modes that would contribute to a distinctively "modern" style, Debussy had engaged in *ressourcement* — a "return to the sources." Like other modernist-primitivists, including Pablo Picasso and Igor Stravinsky, he forged the future by mining the past. Ten years prior to the appearance of *Pelléas et Mélisande* (1902), Debussy had visited Solesmes in 1893. He also enjoyed going to concerts given by Charles Bordes' Chanteurs de Saint-Gervais, a Parisian group devoted to the plainchant revival. See letters of attestation in Julia d'Almendra, *Les modes Grégoriens dans l'œuvre de Claude Debussy,* rev. ed. (Paris: G. Énault, 1950), 183-87; cited in Katherine Bergeron, *Decadent Enchantments: The Revival of Gregorian Chant at Solesmes* (Berkeley and Los Angeles: University of California Press, 1998), 168 n. 54; in Schloesser, *Jazz Age Catholicism,* 285.

54. Judging from a letter written to his maternal grandmother and aunt and uncle Sauvage, Messiaen seems to have received the vocal score from Gibon in December 1919, either on his tenth birthday (December 10) or for Christmas two weeks later. Hill and Simeone, *Messiaen,* 15.

1914–1919: A Great War Childhood: Mourning and Melancholia

mas 1919),[55] tells the story of a doomed love and eventual *Liebestod*. Golaud discovers Mélisande by a stream in the woods. Her mysterious origins remain undisclosed throughout the opera. After they marry, Mélisande falls in love with Pelléas. Golaud kills Pelléas and wounds Mélisande, who eventually dies. Speculating about how young Olivier might have connected Mélisande with his mother, Cécile's biographer notes that Debussy's work could have provided

> an aesthetic and musical sublimation that offered him in a single opportunity a place to which he could escape, a refuge in which, if he could not forget, he could at least find support. Has anyone actually measured the impact that the story of Mélisande could have had on the sensibility of this ten-year-old boy, this Mélisande so beautiful, so mysterious and melancholic? How could the young Olivier not have unconsciously discovered the image of his mother in this young woman who sometimes enjoys herself but always repeats "I am not happy"? Could it not be said of her as of Mélisande, "that her soul was always cold"? In order to warm herself, Cécile sings in verses which yet again make her resemble Mélisande, "a bird from some foreign place."[56]

In the late 1940s, Messiaen would compose a trilogy of works inspired by the doomed love and love-death of Tristan and Isolde. But as Messiaen's interest in both "The Lady of Shalott" and *Pelléas and Mélisande* suggests, these magical stories shot through with star-crossed lovers had already left a deep

---

55. Hill and Simeone, *Messiaen*, 15.

56. Marchal, *Chants du silence*, 84-85. For these quotations see Maurice Maeterlinck and Claude Debussy, *Pelléas et Mélisande. Drame lyrique en 5 actes et 12 tableaux* (Paris: E. Front, 1904); reprinted as Maeterlinck and Debussy, *Pelléas & Mélisande in Full Score* (Mineola, N.Y.: Dover, 1985). Mélisande: "je ne suis pas heureuse ici" (act 2, scene 2), 107; "je ne suis pas heureuse..." (act 4, scene 2), 298. Arkel: "on dirait que son âme a froid pour toujours" (act 5, scene 1), 368. Pelléas: "Que fais-tu là à la fenêtre en chantant comme un oiseau qui n'est pas d'ici?" (What are you doing there at the window singing like a bird from some foreign place?) (act 3, scene 1), 155; cf. the Doctor: "Ce n'est pas de cette petite blessure qu'elle peut mourir; un oiseau n'en serait pas mort..." (It is not of this small wound that she might die; a bird would not die of it...) (act 5, scene 1), 367.

Other parallels would also have struck Messiaen, including allusions to Mélisande's fragile health and the specter of premature death. Mélisande: "Je suis malade ici..." (I am ill here); "C'est ici que je ne peux plus vivre... je sens que je ne vivrais plus longtemps" (I can no longer live here... I feel that I will not live much longer) (act 2, scene 2), 106, 111. cf. Arkel: "tu es trop jeune et trop belle pour vivre de déjà jour et nuit sous l'haleine de la mort..." (you are too young and too beautiful to be already living, day and night, breathing in death's air...) (act 4, scene 2), 267.

imprint on him during his wartime childhood. Given the postwar atmosphere between his veteran father and stricken mother, it is difficult not to imagine that the appeal was deeply personal as well as aesthetic and intellectual. In Messiaen's childhood world, passionate love is sparked by unseen forces and then doomed by fate to a resolution only in death. The words of King Arkel, sung as the tragedy of Golaud, Mélisande, and Pelléas moves inexorably to its destiny, might have echoed in the religious youth: "If I were God, I would have pity on the hearts of men."[57]

---

57. "Si j'étais Dieu, j'aurais pitié du coeur des hommes...." Marchal, *Chants du silence*, 86, quoting Maeterlinck and Debussy (act 4, scene 2), 298.

CHAPTER 3

1919–1930

Postwar Paris, National Conservatory, Death of Cécile

Six months after arriving in postwar Nantes, Olivier made his first communion and confirmation on June 22, 1919. The following month, the family moved to Paris where Pierre had been reassigned to teach at the Lycée Charlemagne, situated in the Marais district. This move from Brittany to the capital city, coming just over a year after the wrenching immediate postwar relocations from the fields of Flanders and the mountains of Provence, must have been simultaneously enervating and exhilarating: a dislocating expense of energy offering the promise of new beginnings. For the ten-and-a-half-year-old Olivier above all, the move was remarkably timely and fortuitous. He would now have at least the geographical possibility of attending the Paris National Conservatory of Music. Most immediately, he also suddenly found himself within walking distance of the ancient Sainte-Chapelle (whose stained glass would have a great effect on him), the Cathedral of Notre-Dame, and the church of Saint-Eustache, and just a short distance across the river Seine lay the Latin Quarter, including the church of Saint-Sulpice. How different his life might have been — and twentieth-century music, too — had his father not been reassigned from the provinces to the capital.

After an initial home on the quai de Bourbon on the Île Saint-Louis, the family settled into 67 rue Rambuteau, today located one block northwest of the Centre Pompidou in the Marais. Today's residential quarters sit above the street-level restaurant Le Marigny; back in 1919 this had been a *bar-tabac*, renowned for its oysters and snails, as well as its wines from Pouilly and Saumur. Pierre's memoirs recall this neighborhood with great picturesque detail:

across the street was another bar called the Martinique where, at 7 o'clock each morning, men dressed in rags who picked through the trash in the garbage cans would arrive, sacks on their backs, and order black coffee and a croissant. Pierre muses that if Christ himself had passed in front of the Martinique, "he would have repeated his *misereor super turbam*" ("I have compassion on the multitude" [Mark 8:2]). Indeed, Pierre's enthusiastically detailed description of the wider neighborhood of Les Halles suggests that he was fascinated by its extreme contrasts: "the most virginal devotion stood side-by-side with the most impudent prostitution, the wedding party in the luxury car narrowly missed the street person going through the streams of cabbage cores and half-rotted oranges; on the rue Saint-Denis, in front of the very door itself of the church of Saint-Leu, prostitutes took you by the arm and propositioned you."[1] From Pierre's perspective, Cécile seemed to have recovered from her wartime mental and physical illness. He observed that she had "rediscovered her appetite, her round cheeks, her vivacity, her good humor; she closely followed our children's studies, wrote inquisitive pages on her youth in Digne and about the Les Halles neighborhood in which we lived, which was too loud, but so picturesque in its ugliness and its vulgarity."[2]

However, the interior of the Messiaen apartment was a very different story, making family life "heavy and difficult."[3] In addition to being noisy, it was too cold because it faced north, and it was entirely too small: it had a dining room and only one bedroom, which was shared by Pierre, Cécile, Olivier, and Alain. A letter from Olivier to his uncle André described the difficult living situation.[4] The single bedroom resembled more closely a junk closet with the beds, the dressers, and everything else: "Mama, who is unable to find quiet in the dining room, is even less able to find it in the bedroom, where she does not have any elbow room. When she wants to sweep it, in order to remove the dust beneath the bed she needs to remove the table; to move the table she needs to remove the chairs; and so on." He also recalled that it was "a great heartbreak for her not to be able to receive those who invite us and who might even be useful for us, and to respond sadly: what do you want to do? We don't have a home." Understandably, Olivier grew to the point where he could no longer

1. Pierre Messiaen, *Images* (Paris: Desclée de Brouwer, 1944), 236-37.
2. Pierre Messiaen, *Images*, 154.
3. This and the following are from Béatrice Marchal, *Les Chants du silence. Olivier Messiaen, fils de Cécile Sauvage ou la musique face à l'impossible parole* (Sampzon: Éditions Delatour France, 2008), 88-89.
4. Olivier Messiaen to André Sauvage, May 8, 1925, Archives Yvonne Loriod; in Marchal, *Chants du silence*, 88-89.

stand sharing the same bed with his younger brother; but one wonders how his parents endured the lack of any adult privacy whatsoever.

As for work, it was difficult for all three. Olivier noted that when Alain was at school during the day, it was possible to work on his harmony lessons. But when Alain returned home, his play and roughhousing made work impossible for Olivier — and, implicitly, for his mother as well. As for Pierre, Olivier put it bluntly years later: "he was never there." He was at the lycée or perhaps at a library, presumably translating Shakespeare. Cécile's biographer observes that this chronic absence would have allowed Pierre to avoid his wife's company and to erase any sense of married life. Olivier had written this letter to his uncle to ask for money to obtain a larger and more workable apartment; apparently he had given up on his father's ability or desire to do anything about it. A measure of desperation set in when Olivier told his uncle that he would put some of the money he was sending for music lessons toward paying the rent. He was also beginning to make money as an accompanist and hoped to ask his teacher Jean Gallon to send some students his way for lessons in harmony and accompaniment. In short, the Messiaens' home life in Paris was sunk in penury; it was profoundly difficult for Olivier and his parents.

Not long after the family arrived in Paris in July 1919, Cécile paid a visit to the publishing house of the Mercure de France. Undoubtedly she went for professional reasons, hoping to renew a publishing relationship with the editorial house. But it would also seem likely that she went to see Jean de Gourmont for personal reasons; it had been almost five years since her relationship with Jean had abruptly ended in the summer of 1914 with the outbreak of war. Whatever the reason for her visit this summer, she discovered there that Jean was engaged to be married in a wedding set for the following February, 1920. The news came as a terrible shock, and during the remaining years of her life her despair presented itself as "a fierce determination to self-annihilation."[5] Pierre, who thought of her condition as nothing more than a self-evident form of madness, simply lamented that she was extremely "unreasonable" and begged her — to no avail — to eat and sleep sufficiently.[6]

As a matter of fact, whether she knew it or not, Cécile's life was being eaten away by tuberculosis. She refused to see any doctor — a tragic irony considering that her brother André was a prominent physician. Additionally, Cécile had a fear of germs, a "phobia" that prevented her from ever opening

---

5. Marchal, *Chants du silence,* 93.
6. Marchal, *Chants du silence,* 94.

a window.[7] Although such fear was undoubtedly personal, it was also a commonplace trait among those influenced by literary naturalism (as found, for example, in Zola), which magnified, as a matter of principle, nature's malevolence.[8] Cécile's biographer sums up the sad paradox:

> the strange life that she led in a room never aerated, never lighted, never swept, was exactly opposed to what her physical state [tuberculosis] would have recommended, the certain equivalent of a slow suicide. She had tried to fight, whatever one might say, but what could one do against the intimate wound on which neither tenderness nor understanding came to apply their balm? As she wrote in 1925, "A night's pause, and then take up again your life's collar, poor living creature, begin all over to shiver in a series of reactions against the cold, people, and the secret pain that towers over everything else."[9]

Apparently, Olivier too, perhaps as an empathic response to his mother's situation, also developed "phobias." In a letter written just three days after Cécile's death, Pierre estimated that Olivier's fretting over phobias made him waste "half of his time" in obsessions.[10]

---

7. Marchal, *Chants du silence*, 94.

8. Such "phobias" were also a cultural phenomenon upon whose imagery Cécile likely drew. Historian Michelle Perrot writes: "In the second half of the century, what Jean Borie has called 'mythologies of heredity' were developed by physicians and novelists (such as the Zola of *Fécondité* and *Docteur Pascal*), by fear of the great 'social scourges' — tuberculosis, alcoholism, and syphilis — and by terror of flaws transmitted by tainted blood." Michelle Perrot, "The Family Triumphant," in *A History of Private Life*, vol. 4, *From the Fires of Revolution to the Great War,* ed. Michelle Perrot, trans. Arthur Goldhammer (Cambridge: Harvard University Press, Belknap Press, 1990), 124. Tragically, Cécile's fear of tuberculosis was rooted in her own eventually fatal case of the disease.

See also Jean Borie, *Mythologies de l'hérédité au XIXe siècle* (Paris: Galilée, 1981); Kathleen Kete, "La Rage and the Bourgeoisie: The Cultural Context of Rabies in the French Nineteenth Century," *Representations* 22 (Spring 1988): 89-107; Ian Robert Dowbiggin, *Inheriting Madness: Professionalization and Psychiatric Knowledge in Nineteenth-Century France* (Berkeley: University of California Press, 1991); and a special issue of *Critical Quarterly* entitled "The Uses of Phobia by David Trotter: Essays on Literature and Film," 52/s1 (May 2010). See especially "Naturalism's Phobic Picturesque" (40-58) and "Feminist Phobia" (59-76).

9. Marchal, *Chants du silence*, 94; Cécile Sauvage, *Œuvres de Cécile Sauvage*, ed. Jean Tenant (Paris: Mercure de France, 1929), 341. Hereafter: Sauvage and Tenant, *Œuvres.*

10. Pierre Messiaen to Germaine Sauvage, August 29, 1927, Archives Yvonne Loriod; in Marchal, *Chants du silence,* 94.

1919–1930: Postwar Paris, National Conservatory, Death of Cécile

In spite of these domestic shadows, Olivier now had a vibrant life outside the home. Immediately after arriving in Paris, he was received by the Conservatory director, Gabriel Fauré, as an *auditeur* during the academic year 1919-1920. He would later frequently recall the experience that same year of seeing the ancient stained glass windows of Sainte-Chapelle for the first time. Thanks to his synesthesia (of which he was becoming more aware), he experienced the brilliant light as "dazzlement" *(éblouissement)*.[11]

In October of the following year (1920-1921), he was formally registered as a full-time student. In his second full year he won recognition for his piano performance and studies in harmony. That year he also composed *Two Ballads of Villon* (1921) for voice and piano, based on the texts of the rustic and bawdy late-medieval poet François Villon (1431-1463). Here, as elsewhere, Messiaen might have been following the lead of Claude Debussy, who had composed *Three Ballads of François Villon* (1910) just a decade earlier. Closer to home, Olivier's *Two Ballads* were composed contemporaneously with his mother's poem entitled "On Re-reading Villon."[12] The poem was the first she had written since arriving in Paris — and, perhaps more pointedly, the first she had written since learning of Jean de Gourmont's marital engagement.

Cécile's "On Re-reading" evokes Villon's lament over his long life in dire poverty, recorded in these lines from his *Testament:*

I myself have been poor since my childhood,
Born of poor and lowly origin;
... Poverty pursues us all and hunts us down.[13]

Cécile, who now found herself in a similar state of impoverishment in the great urban capital, creatively uses vocabulary imitating the medieval French to evoke Villon's Paris and compare it with her own five centuries later:

11. Sander van Maas, *The Reinvention of Religious Music: Olivier Messiaen's Breakthrough toward the Beyond* (New York: Fordham University Press, 2009), especially chapter 4: "The Gift of Dazzlement," 89-125.

12. Cécile Sauvage, "En Relisant Villon" (Paris, 1922); posthumously published in Sauvage and Tenant, *Œuvres,* 276-80; reprinted in François Villon and Pierre Messiaen, *Les Œuvres de François Villon commentées par Pierre Messiaen* (Paris: Desclée de Brouwer, 1946), 45-48; and in Cécile Sauvage and Béatrice Marchal-Vincent, *L'Œuvre poétique de Cécile Sauvage (1883-1927),* 2 vols. (Lille: Atelier National de Reproduction des Thèses, 1995), 2:267-69, 346-47.

13. François Villon, *Le Testament,* XXXV; in Villon and Pierre Messiaen, *Œuvres,* 79-146, at 87 (lines 273-74, 277); quoted in Sauvage and Marchal-Vincent, *L'Œuvre poétique,* 2:346 n. 2.

1883–1930: Pierre Messiaen and Cécile Sauvage

Poor Villon, I am your sister
Alone and stung in my dwelling.
The rumbling of the large city
Howls or sobs beneath my window;
My days pass with neither glory nor bird call
Nor without hope for a better time,
And if my song was once in a major mode
Paris now smothers it in my heart.

This Paris, Monsieur Villon,
Would make you open wide like a window,
Open your falcon-like eyes
To what appears in this epoch.
It is in automobiles that masters go
And in the sky, in a plane,
No longer with intoxicated heart in every being,
They launch themselves toward the rays.

Autobuses go to Saint-Jacques.
Trams go along Notre-Dame,
The Angelus, the Mass, Easter
All evaporate in the din.[14]

Throughout this poem, Cécile expresses the sentiments that Pierre had seen in their early marriage, namely, "a horror of modern progress, of everything that felt mechanical, the entire world fenced in by the same gestures and the same ideas." Whereas she enjoyed chatting with peasants, she detested the traveling salesmen who came to show a new kitchen stove model. Pierre recalls having had a quarrel with her the day he brought home an electric iron for pressing linen.[15] In this respect she again evokes her fellow poet Claudel, who always felt stifled in Paris and traveled far to escape it. In *The City*, the city as a product of modern civilization "emerges as a monstrous force, crushing and lacerating an individual, bringing him to stagnation."[16] And she prefigures her son, Olivier, who would later say: "I don't belong to

14. Sauvage and Marchal-Vincent, *L'Œuvre poétique*, 2:267, 268.
15. Pierre Messiaen, *Images*, 144, 145.
16. Or, as his friend André Gide remarked, for Claudel, "Modern civilization spelled ruination, waste." Bettina L. Knapp, *Paul Claudel* (New York: Ungar, 1982), 17, 27. For *La Ville*, see above, 13-14.

my era. I abhor skyscrapers, aeroplanes, I abhor everything which makes a din."[17]

Cécile's poem "On Re-reading Villon" concludes:

Sciences and the [steam] turbine
Will not change the ancient soul
And this is why the old world
Has the same [sun] flame in the morning;
You can change the garment but the pattern remains,
The same springtime, the same heartache,
The same love of a man for a woman,
So it goes with the human universe.
But this is what makes us what we are,
O my Villon, human brothers [*frères humains*],[18]
This sacred trembling of men
In the face of death and destiny. (Paris, 1922)[19]

Villon had been a familiar name in the Messiaen household; two decades later Pierre would coedit and publish not one but two editions of Villon's works.[20]

However, Olivier's *Two Ballads of Villon* seems to have been consciously influenced by his mother's "re-reading": relating her dislocating experience of

17. Messiaen, interview with Almut Rößler (April 23, 1979), in Rößler, *Contributions to the Spiritual World of Olivier Messiaen,* trans. Barbara Dagg and Nancy Poland (Duisberg: Gilles & Francke, 1986), 67-115, at 91. Compare Messiaen's comments on American cities: "[In] the States are also big cities, terribly big cities like New York, Chicago, and Los Angeles, where millions of people live, where frightening eighty-story skyscrapers tower above you. I'm not wildly fond of cities, and even less of that sort.... Mechanized civilization is overwhelming." Messiaen, in Olivier Messiaen and Claude Samuel, *Music and Color: Conversations with Claude Samuel,* trans. E. Thomas Glasow (Portland, Ore.: Amadeus Press, 1994), 155.

18. Cécile Sauvage here alludes to the first lines of Villon's "Ballad of the Hanged Men" ("Ballade des Pendus") — also known as "Villon's Epitaph" — generally believed to have been written during his imprisonment when he was awaiting execution: "Human brothers who live after us / Do not have hardened hearts against us" *(Frères humains qui après nous vivez / N'ayez les cuers contre nous endurcis).* See "L'Épitaphe Villon," in Villon and Pierre Messiaen, *Œuvres,* 166-67, at 166 (lines 1-2); quoted in Sauvage and Marchal-Vincent, *L'Œuvre poétique,* 2:347 n. 13.

19. Sauvage and Marchal-Vincent, *L'Œuvre poétique,* 2:269.

20. Villon and Pierre Messiaen, *Œuvres,* and Villon and Pierre Messiaen, *Œuvres complètes, présentées par Pierre Messiaen* (Lyon: Imprimerie Artistique en couleurs, 1948). The latter is from the series Les Chefs-d'oeuvre Français.

Paris to that of the medieval bard, criticizing the mechanization of the modern metropolis, and situating her own penury alongside that of her ancestral human brother's. It is not surprising that the next poetic fragments she wrote were *Souvenirs of Digne* (1924), verses recalling her life at age seventeen, gushing over with picturesque descriptions of birds, trees, butterflies, "a universe full of eggs, children, and insects, and flowers of every kind."[21] Self-confined in her small apartment, afflicted with phobias of contagion by germs, windows shutting out light and fresh air, struggling to breathe with weakened lungs, Cécile's imaginative memory transported her to kinder youthful days enjoyed in the Provençal mountains.

Even within this context of domestic pall, the fifteen-year-old Messiaen took second prize in harmony and in piano accompaniment during the 1923-1924 academic year. In 1924-1925, at age sixteen, he took first prize in piano accompaniment — a skill both artistic and pragmatic, capable of earning him money. One of the most lasting influences on Messiaen would be having Maurice Emmanuel as his music history teacher. Messiaen's musical education was marked by having entered the Conservatory in 1919; the 1914-1918 war had provoked a cultural "return to order" and a renewed emphasis on teaching history, intended to reestablish firm foundations. A prize in the course of the history of music *(cours d'histoire de la musique)* had been initiated by the French government during the war, and Messiaen's postwar generation "had the benefit of an uninterrupted, if conservative, education, in which the older prize system was again in force as a means to establish careers."[22]

Emmanuel, a close friend of Debussy (who died in March 1918), nourished Messiaen's budding interest in folk songs, ancient modes, and non-Western music.[23] Emmanuel had first come to prominence with his 1895 dissertation on the ancient Greek *orchestique* — the combination of what we might today call the dance and gymnastics used in the Greek theater. A scholar of Greco-Roman art, Greek and Hindu modes, and folk song, Emmanuel also published a study of Debussy's *Pelléas* in 1926.[24] As seen in his multivolume *Treatise*,

---

21. Cécile Sauvage, *Souvenirs de Digne* (1924); in Sauvage and Marchal-Vincent, *L'Œuvre poétique*, 2:270-71.

22. Jane F. Fulcher, "The Politics of Transcendence: Ideology in the Music of Messiaen in the 1930s," *Musical Quarterly* 86, no. 3 (Fall 2002): 449-71, at 463.

23. Peter Hill and Nigel Simeone, *Messiaen* (New Haven: Yale University Press, 2005), 19-20.

24. Maurice Emmanuel: *Essai sur l'orchestique grecque: étude de ses mouvements d'après les monuments figurés . . . : thèse presentée de la Faculté des lettres de Paris* (Paris: Hachette, 1895); published the next year as a monograph: Emmanuel, *La danse grecque antique d'après*

1919–1930: Postwar Paris, National Conservatory, Death of Cécile

Messiaen assimilated and synthesized Emmanuel's wide-ranging interests in meters, rhythm, dance, and modes, transforming it all into his highly idiosyncratic system.[25]

For Olivier, May 1925 seems to have signaled a critical moment in the ongoing decline of Cécile's mental and physical health. On May 8 he wrote the letter cited above to his uncle André, detailing the miserable living conditions of the family home and asking for four or five thousand francs to find a new apartment.[26] This was also the year in which he composed a piano piece entitled *The Sadness of a Great White Sky* — if he composed it in the spring semester of the 1924-1925 academic year, it would have been contemporaneous with his letter to André. Whether he composed it then or months later, the title suggests his mother's emotional state. One musicologist notes that the work's title "could well have fitted into the book of [*Eight Preludes*, 1928-1929] written four years later."[27] The observation is apt: the piano preludes were composed soon after Cécile's death two years later and may be viewed as a work of mourning.

The enigmatic title pointing to the "sadness" of the great white sky suggests that Messiaen had already seen a book published in this same year (1925) from which he derived imagery for *Eight Preludes* and many other works in future years. We know from the later work *Harawi* (1945) that Messiaen had

---

les monuments figurés (Paris: Hachette, 1896); and translated in 1916: Emmanuel, *The Antique Greek Dance, after Sculptured and Painted Figures,* trans. Harriet Jean Beauley (London: John Lane, [1916] 1927). Other scholarly works included *History of Musical Language* (1911; 1928); *Treatise on Modal Accompaniment of Psalms* (1913); the entry "Greece" and "Greco-Roman Art" in the Conservatory's encyclopedia and dictionary of music (1921); and a study of Debussy's *Pelléas et Mélisande* (1926). Composed works included a *Suite on Popular Greek Airs* for violin and piano (1907); *Thirty Songs* for soloist and piano based on popular folk songs collected from the Beaune region (1913); a *Sonatina No. 4* for piano based on Hindu modes (1920).

25. For Emmanuel's profound influence on Messiaen's self-conception as a "rhythmician," see Yves Balmer, "Édifier son œuvre: genèse, médiation, diffusion de l'œuvre d'Olivier Messiaen," 2 vols. (Ph.D. diss., l'Université Charles-de-Gaulle — Lille 3, 2008), 1:128-34. Balmer notes that rhythm's primacy was also central to the theory of Vincent d'Indy, founder of the Schola Cantorum; and that Greek rhythms also played a large part in Marcel Dupré's *Treatise on Organ Improvisation* (1925), published just two years prior to Messiaen's joining his organ class in the fall semester of 1927.

26. Olivier Messiaen to André Sauvage, 88-89.

27. Paul Griffiths, *Olivier Messiaen and the Music of Time* (Ithaca, N.Y.: Cornell University Press, 1985), 27; in Nigel Simeone, *Olivier Messiaen: A Bibliographical Catalogue of Messiaen's Works,* Musikbibliographische Arbeiten series, vol. 14 (Tutzing: Hans Schneider, 1998), 187.

1883–1930: Pierre Messiaen and Cécile Sauvage

been profoundly influenced by *The Music of the Incas and Its Vestiges* (Paris, 1925).[28] Given that Messiaen was at the Conservatory and studying music history (for which he won first prizes) under Emmanuel at this time, it seems likely that he had been introduced to this seminal work when it first appeared. Note, for example, this lament in the Incan tradition:

> My mother gave birth to me
> In the midst of a rain cloud,
> Inasmuch as I weep like a downpour,
> Inasmuch as I wander like the cloud.[29]

The Sadness of a Great White Sky seems inspired by Incan poetry; both composition and monograph date from 1925.[30]

Pierre, too, identified May 1925 as the moment he first felt "a weight of sorrow and the presentiment that [Cécile] would soon be leaving us." He specifically recalls one evening when she read these verses to him, taken from a poem composed that same year entitled "Destiny."

> When I shall indeed have suffered from my voiceless soul,
> Which restrains both rhythm and human rays,
> Men [*des hommes*] will nail it, to secret boards,
> Without having ever seen it, ironic destiny!
>
> For what I have sung is still only silence,
> And my heart, my eyes and my constrained elan,
> Will perish without a word, forever unknown,
> Across the torpor of immeasurable matter.[31]

---

28. Raoul d'Harcourt and M. d'Harcourt, *La Musique des Incas et ses survivances,* 2 vols. (Paris: Librairie Orientaliste Paul Geuthner, 1925).

29. D'Harcourt and d'Harcourt, *La Musique des Incas,* 1:192.

30. For more on the d'Harcourts, see pp. 92-95 below.

31. Cécile, quoted in Pierre Messiaen, *Images,* 154; poem is "Destin" ("Destiny") (1925), in Sauvage and Marchal-Vincent, *L'Œuvre poétique,* 2:272. Here again, Cécile's use of the word "soul" evokes its repeated usage in the poetry of Lamartine. In connection with Cécile's fear of dying in obscurity, note that Lamartine's poem "Pourquoi mon âme est-elle triste?" ("Why Is My Soul Sad?") is preceded by "Le Génie dans l'Obscurité" ("The Genius in Obscurity") in Alphonse de Lamartine, *Harmonies poétiques et religieuses* (Paris: C. Gosselin, 1830), in *Œuvres poétiques complètes de Lamartine,* ed. Marius-François Guyard (Paris: Éditions Gallimard, 1963), 422-23 and 424-30.

The "nailing" of Cécile's feminine soul *(âme)* by men (the word *hommes* here specifically implies males) alludes to the nailing of Christ's body to the cross. However, whereas Christ's instrument of death was all too public, the "secret boards" of Cécile's cross ensure that she will forever remain unknown.

Pierre seems to have been unaware that Cécile's anxieties about dying as an unknown poet were very real. Cécile paid at least one visit to Marie Dormoy in the publishing offices of the Mercure de France to ask about her two earlier books of poetry. Dormoy recalled that telling Cécile that her books rarely sold seemed "to sadden her a bit, because it seems to her, as she says, that people have put her under a bushel [*sous le boisseau*]."[32] (Once again a Gospel allusion: "No one lights a lamp and puts it in a cellar or even under the measure [bushel].")[33] It seems that Cécile had at this time despaired of her poems selling and considered another form of writing. In the May 8, 1925, letter to his uncle André cited above, Olivier reported his mother's ambitions: "It's necessary for you to know," he wrote André, "that mama's work is very important, because she wants to try her hand at journalism like papa, under the pen name of a man." A woman poet was somewhat acceptable, perhaps; but being a female journalist was a different story.[34]

Pierre recalled that this same presentiment — that Cécile was not long for this world — came back to him several times over when she would read her favorite passage from the Gospels (perhaps Matthew 25?) and then say: "Jesus Christ died for everyone, yet there are the elected and the condemned! I just cannot understand this."[35] If these episodes were as frequent as Pierre said, it suggests that religion had moved into the foreground as a serious site of conflict in the Messiaen home. Pierre's ultra-Catholicism had been exacerbated by the laicist milieu in which he taught at the Lycée Charlemagne in Paris.

---

32. Marie Dormoy, *Souvenirs et portraits d'amis* (Paris: Mercure de France, 1963); in Marchal, *Chants du silence*, 90.

33. Luke 11:33 (Douay-CCD). "Personne n'allume une lampe pour la mettre dans un lieu caché, ou sous le boisseau" (Fillion).

34. For women's journalism see Mary Louise Roberts, *Disruptive Acts: The New Woman in Fin-de-Siècle France* (Chicago: University of Chicago Press, 2002), and Lenard R. Berlanstein, "Selling Modern Femininity: *Femina,* a Forgotten Feminist Publishing Success in Belle Epoque France," *French Historical Studies* 30, no. 4 (Fall 2007): 623-49.

35. Pierre Messiaen, *Images,* 154. Anticipating *Visions of Amen:* when reading Messiaen's commentary for the "Amen of Judgment" (Vision 6) — "In truth, I say to you, Amen. 'Condemned, away from me!' (Gospel according to Saint Matthew). The damned are fixed in their state." — one wonders what he had thought when he heard his mother's anguish. See Messiaen, "Note de l'Auteur," *Visions de l'Amen* (Paris: Durand, 1943), n.p.

1883–1930: Pierre Messiaen and Cécile Sauvage

For refuge, he frequented both the church of Saint-Séverin and the Centre Catholique des Intellectuels in the Latin Quarter.[36]

But perhaps more generally, Pierre may have shared the rage, suppressed or expressed, of many war veterans throughout the postwar decade of the 1920s who had returned to a France they blamed for their generation's massacre. Probably the most notorious of these was Georges Bernanos (1888-1948), wounded several times, a survivor of the horrific slaughters at the Somme and Verdun, and now an ultra-Catholic monarchist associated with the Action Française. His first novel, *Under the Sun of Satan* (1926), was a work fueled by tremendous anger at the laicist state; it was published in April 1926 by Jacques Maritain, a leading spokesman of postwar Catholic Revivalism with whom Pierre was acquainted. Maritain had been prolific in the publication of his own sharply polemical works, including *Antimodern* (1922) and *Three Reformers* (1925).[37] This was the charged air that Pierre would have breathed in his engagement with postwar Catholic intellectuals.

Whatever the nature and content of Cécile's and Pierre's arguments over religion and the disturbing implications of both salvation and damnation, Cécile pondered such theological problems during the two years preceding her death in a large lyrical drama entitled *To Love after Death* (written 1925-1926).[38] This dialogue poem imitated the philosophical allegories that Cécile studied in her readings of Pedro Calderón de la Barca (1600-1681), a Catholic priest and dramatist of the Spanish Golden Age best known for his play *Life Is a Dream* ("Life is a dream from which only death awakens us"). *To Love after Death* is based on the Morisco Revolt in Spain (1568-1571), an insurrection of Moriscos (Muslims who had converted to Christianity) in Granada against the kingdom of Castile. The episode was particularly brutal: after the city of Galera was defeated, its survivors were sold into slavery, the city was leveled, and salt was plowed into its soil. In Cécile's play, Maléha, a Muslim who has converted to Christianity, is nevertheless killed by a Spanish soldier during the

---

36. Brigitte Massin and Olivier Messiaen, *Olivier Messiaen: une poétique du merveilleux* (Aix-en-Provence: Alinéa, 1989), 134; in Siglind Bruhn, *Messiaen's Contemplations of Covenant and Incarnation: Musical Symbols of Faith in the Two Great Piano Cycles of the 1940s* (Hillsdale, N.Y.: Pendragon Press, 2007), 30.

37. Stephen Schloesser, *Jazz Age Catholicism: Mystic Modernism in Postwar Paris, 1919-1933* (Toronto: University of Toronto Press, 2005), 245-81.

38. Cécile Sauvage, *Aimer après la mort,* in Sauvage and Marchal-Vincent, *L'Œuvre poétique,* 2:164-216. The French title plays on words: "To love after death" *(Aimer après la mort)* and "To love after love" *(Aimer après l'amour)* are near homonyms. For Pierre's account of the composition, see Pierre Messiaen, *Images,* 153-54.

sacking of Galera. Her fiancé, Touzani, is also a Morisco — and yet he swears to take revenge for the killing. Maléha's soul appears to him among a choir of angels and reminds him of the divine precept to forgive sins. Cécile noted in her preface: "The title of this piece is taken from Calderon. The basic idea came from chapters twenty-two and following of the *History of the Civil Wars of Granada* by the archpriest Ginés Pérez de Hita. I transformed the subject giving to it a mystical atmosphere [*une atmosphère mystique*] and making its heroes those Christians who had been born into the Muslim religion and had so recently converted to Christianity."[39]

What might have been a conventional morality tale about forgiveness, however, turned out to be a reflection on the insignificance of human beings and the vastness of the universe — perhaps the central theme in her son Olivier's musical compositions in adulthood. For example, the Angel of Death sings:

> May our hymn carry its harmony toward God,
> May it raise up in its flight both space and life.
> Worlds, suns, minds and hearts
> Enter in movement in its vast rumblings.
> Amplitude shuddered in its serene heights
> And the soul pours itself out into distant [sound] waves
> Where thought flies in a supreme soaring
> Beyond life, beyond death [*Au-delà de la vie, au-delà de la mort*],
> Into the infinite lightning flash [*l'éclair infini*], into the eternal idea
> That raises up the created immensity of love.[40]

For the reader familiar with *Éclairs sur l'au-delà . . . (Lightning Flashes of the Beyond . . .)* (1991) — Olivier Messiaen's final completed work, premiered posthumously — Cécile's words, written just a year before her death sixty-four years earlier, carry an additional weight of poignance.

Another angel adds its voice, conjoining the weight of temporality with the infinite lightness of eternity:

> Human beings, remember that we have sung
> About this world, joining to its corporeal heaviness
> The imponderable concord of eternal hymns.[41]

---

39. Sauvage, preface to *Aimer après la mort*, 2:165.
40. Sauvage, *Aimer après la mort*, 2:215.
41. Sauvage, *Aimer après la mort*, 2:216.

Finally, the Angelic Chorus concludes the drama with words Cécile borrowed from the Catholic service for Ash Wednesday. As the priest makes a sign of the cross on the forehead with ashes, he recites the formula "Souviens-toi, ô homme, que tu es poussière, et que tu retourneras en poussière" (Remember, man, that thou art dust and unto dust thou shalt return).[42] Cécile's usage contrasts human forgetting and recommends remembrance:

> Human beings, *remember* that our songs have dandled
> Our eternal summer on your wandering globe
> So that the planet, *having forgotten its origins in dust* [*oubliant sa poussière*],
> Might have the sparkling of a star in the bosom of its atmosphere,
> In the elan of ardor that spreads out across it:
> Thus sparkles the love that increases itself in loving.

The imagery here (most notably interstellar "dust") strikingly resembles Messiaen's notes on "Amen of the Stars, of the Planet with the Ring" in *Visions of Amen* some twenty years later.

Cécile's monumental work concludes with stage directions:

> *(Maléha and Touzani reach out to one another; the angels and the young human beings also lean towards one another in the same way, thus forming the figure of a mystical union between earth and heaven.)*[43]

Thus ends Cécile's allegorical drama: a mystical union between the ephemeral and the eternal.

The sheer volume of this work indicates that Cécile had once again begun writing intensely and consequently needed more solitude in the tiny apartment. Pierre records that he began taking his sons out more frequently, to visit both friends' houses and churches, because the boys "demonstrated a genuine passion for religious ceremonies and music."[44] We can only imagine what it was like for young Olivier to walk to close-by churches and listen to the organists of his day: Louis Vierne (1870-1937) at the Cathedral of Notre-Dame; Joseph Bonnet (1884-1944) at Saint-Eustache; Charles-Marie Widor

---

42. *Missel-Fr*, 304; *Missal-En*, 217; translations of the Latin liturgical formula accompanying the imposition of ashes: "Meménto, homo, quia pulvis es, et in púlverem revertéris." The formula builds on the Latin Vulgate translation of Gen. 3:19.

43. Sauvage, *Aimer après la mort*, 2:216.

44. Pierre Messiaen, *Images*, 153.

1919–1930: Postwar Paris, National Conservatory, Death of Cécile

(1844-1937) at Saint-Sulpice; and Charles Tournemire (1870-1939), the great improvisor at the Basilica of Sainte-Clotilde.

Cécile also frequently asked Pierre to take the two boys out for dinner at restaurants in the evenings, saying that "they were too loud and demanding, that she would prefer a few hours of calm and a bowl of café au lait." When people would ask, "Is your wife ill?" Pierre would respond, "A bit tired." He didn't want to disclose that "Cécile, struck by a kind of melancholic loneliness, refused all recreation."[45] When her brother André, her sister Germaine, and her mother pressed her to return to the mountains of Dauphiné for vacation, she refused, saying that the train trip exhausted her. Similarly, she stopped visiting the cathedral at Chartres, even though she was enamored of it and they had found an affordable nearby *pension* in which the whole family could stay. Rather, she "complained over and over again that in Beauce [the farm surroundings of Chartres] the roads were hard on the feet and the fields had no trees or shade."[46]

In conclusion, although Cécile claimed that "I write little, I haven't done anything worthy of being known," both her writing and her reading were in fact voluminous.[47] Having completed *To Love after Death*, Cécile spent the winter of 1926-1927 rereading all of Euripides, Homer's *Odyssey,* and all of Racine, Shakespeare, and the medieval devotional classic *Imitation of Christ.* Pierre later judged that, although there were some worthwhile passages in Cécile's large final work, her "personality was no longer there, this luminous freshness of realism, this immaterial music of landscapes and of the soul."[48]

The Death of Cécile Sauvage

In the spring of 1927, Cécile's condition declined precipitously as she lost a great deal of weight, coughed frequently, and looked chronically exhausted. In June one of her legs became inflamed, a condition Pierre thought to be "a small crisis." Although he professed to be seriously anxious about this, he relied on the diagnosis of one of his aunts, who attributed it to Cécile's undergoing her "change of life."[49] As for Olivier, he too seemed sickly, and, in a June 1927 letter

---

45. Pierre Messiaen, *Images*, 153, 155.
46. Pierre Messiaen, *Images,* 153-55.
47. Jean Tenant, *Sous le balcon de Prudent-Modérat* (Paris: le Rouge et le Noir, 1930), 68.
48. Pierre Messiaen, *Images,* 153-54.
49. Letter of Pierre Messiaen to Germaine Tatin-Sauvage, August 26, 1927, Archives Yvonne Loriod; quoted by Marchal, *Chants du silence,* 95.

to Cécile's sister Germaine, Pierre wrote: "He is very anemic."[50] No one was yet aware that Olivier's anemia was a symptom of his own case of tuberculosis.

In July, Cécile asked Pierre to take Alain to Chartres in order to give her some solitude and quiet. The fourteen-year-old Alain "irritated her by running from one room to another looking for a saw, a knife, a hammer, nails, pieces of wood and fabric in order to make theater props." It wasn't necessary to take the eighteen-year-old Olivier since he did not fatigue Cécile, being "a dear, unobtrusive and obedient." She asked for just one month of rest in which she would have no other worry except what clothes to wear for eating out at a small restaurant on the boulevard Saint-Germain and walking in the Luxembourg Gardens. In September, she promised, they would all travel north for a vacation at grandmother Messiaen's farm on the Belgian border, staying there until the new school year began. Pierre later said that he agreed to Cécile's request because her health was not discernibly worse than normal.[51] He and Alain left for Chartres on July 16.[52]

And, in fact, Cécile seemed to be doing better — at least judging from her long letters arriving at Chartres every two or three days. She and Olivier went for "excellent meals" at the Auberge de la Reine Blanche, a quaint old restaurant still going strong today on the Île Saint-Louis. "We have just signed, Olivier and I, a new lease on good health," she wrote Pierre. "Enthusiasm for work has come back to me."[53] But on Monday, August 22, Cécile must have had some difficulty breathing since she and Olivier went to a small hotel in Montlhéry, about sixteen miles from Paris, to get some cleaner air. By Wednesday the twenty-fourth, Cécile could not get out of bed and Olivier rushed her to the Hôtel-Dieu hospital (next to the Cathedral of Notre-Dame of Paris).[54] She died two days later, on Friday, August 26, 1927. Four days later, Alain would celebrate his fifteenth birthday.

Pierre received a telegram saying that Cécile "was dying, had been taken

---

50. Pierre Messiaen to Tatin-Sauvage, June 24, 1927, Archives Yvonne Loriod; in Marchal, *Chants du silence*, 95.

51. Pierre Messiaen, *Images*, 155.

52. Marchal, *Chants du silence*, 14.

53. Pierre Messiaen, *Images*, 155. However, it is difficult to know whether or not this line is authentically Cécile's since it is immediately followed by a reference to *Primevère*, that is, the book of poetry invented by Pierre after her death: "This fall, I am going to get back to work on *Primevère* [*Primrose*]. I need to rediscover this poetry of super-terrestrial borders [or 'boundaries' = *confins*] which is my very reason for being, somewhat bright blue and bright red like the windows of Chartres." Even if forged by Pierre, this reference to stained glass accurately evokes the influence of the teenaged Olivier on his mother.

54. Marchal, *Chants du silence*, 14.

to the Hôtel-Dieu, one of these pulmonary congestions which are merciless."
Significantly, the telegram came from the family doctor, not from Olivier. It
would seem that Olivier was respecting his mother's stated wishes throughout
this entire episode since he had not alerted his father to the urgent attempt to
find fresh air in Montlhéry the preceding Monday.[55] After Pierre hurried back
from Chartres with Alain, he was able to see Cécile only twice, and even then
only for barely a half hour in a public area where others had also come to see
their sick loved ones. The first time, "she apologized for not having alerted
me earlier, she did not believe she was that seriously ill, she didn't want to
worry me." The second time, "she wasn't able to articulate anything except
the name of her husband and children." Pierre recalls that the hospital staff
"pressed us to go by pointing to the pendulum" — a curiously haunting detail
given Olivier's later attention to the image of clock time, Edgar Allan Poe's
"The Pit and the Pendulum," and Baudelaire's associations with the funeral
bell. Pierre's brief account of the episode ends: "God preserve me from dying
in a hospital!"[56]

The small sad trio accompanied Cécile's body back south to Grenoble
for burial. Pierre recalled that in January 1907, while traveling back to Lyon
after visiting Cécile in Digne, "under a dreary night sky of frost and snow,"
he had first contemplated his "declaration of love" to her. Now, "[T]wenty
years later, in August 1927, under the clearest and warmest summer night sky,
traveling from Paris to Grenoble, the carriage attached to our car carried, in
a small crate, what had once been Cécile Sauvage." He then concludes with
these observations:

> I often reproach myself for not having tried more insistently to bring Cécile
> Sauvage back to the Christian faith. Her poetry would have increased in
> joy, perhaps also in fullness and love. Perhaps she would have gathered the
> courage to rise above this melancholy which played a part in her premature
> death, to conquer this lonely and silent despair of which my children have
> kept a memory so heavy that they rarely speak to me of their mother. For
> myself, I ceaselessly see her as I did in the first years of our marriage, with
> her brown eyes gilded with a bit of mist, her ivory face, her mischievous
> mouth and voice, opening our shutters in early morning to hear the twit-
> tering of the swallows. . . .
>
> Each human being must carry their cross, suffer a great sorrow. My

---

55. Marchal, *Chants du silence*, 13.
56. Pierre Messiaen, *Images*, 156.

great sorrow is that some inescapable destiny I do not fathom crushed the being I most loved and admired, just as it crushed John Keats.[57]

We have no comparable autobiographical reflections from Olivier about that final month spent alone with his mother as she lay dying, surely a catastrophic emotional event for an eighteen-year-old. He would soon become enamored of the surrealist poet Paul Éluard, a Great War veteran whose *Capital of Pain*, published the previous year in 1926, became a sensation.[58] Perhaps it is at just this time that Olivier encountered Éluard's work, suffused with loss, grief, and rage, giving expressive form to the inchoate feelings of a "sacrificed generation."[59] For example:

Unknown, she was the form I preferred,
The one who freed me from the weight of being a man,
And I see her and I lose her and I bear
The pain like a little sunlight in cold water.[60]

And another:

The lamp lit up at the mischief of the storm
In the fine days of August without fail,
With one of her caresses she kissed the air,
    her companion's cheeks,

---

57. Pierre Messiaen, *Images*, 156-57. Like Cécile, the English Romantic poet John Keats (1795-1821) died prematurely from tuberculosis. For Pierre's translation of Keats, see Pierre Messiaen, *Les romantiques anglais: textes anglais et français* (Paris: Desclée de Brouwer, 1955), 795-897.

58. Paul Éluard, *Capitale de la douleur* (Paris: Éditions Gallimard, 1926). Twenty years later, Messiaen would write Éluard: "Dear Monsieur, I have received the copy of *Dignes de vivre* which you have so kindly sent me with a beautiful dedicatory inscription. *Merci beaucoup!* But I already have it! just as I already have *Capitale de la douleur, l'Amour la Poésie, Donner à voir,* and your admirable *Choix de Poèmes* and others as well. . . . Perhaps one day we might collaborate? I would be happy and proud to do so!" Olivier Messiaen to Paul Éluard, March 13, 1945, Carlton Lake Collection of French Manuscripts, Harry Ransom Center, The University of Texas at Austin, 66.1. I am grateful to the Harry Ransom Center for kind permission to consult these documents.

59. Schloesser, *Jazz Age Catholicism*, 88.

60. Paul Éluard, "Les petits justes" ("Just and Small"), X, in *Capital of Pain*, trans. Mary Ann Caws, Patricia Terry, and Nancy Kline (Boston: Black Widow Press, 2006), 146, trans. 147.

1919–1930: Postwar Paris, National Conservatory, Death of Cécile

Closed her eyes
And like leaves in the evening
Faded out on the horizon.[61]

Rewriting Cécile Sauvage: A Martyr to Maternity?

In September 1927, while Pierre was going through his deceased wife's letters and notebooks, he first discovered with certainty what he might well have suspected earlier: Cécile's secret relationship with Jean de Gourmont.[62] At the very end of the manuscript *Mystical Embrace (Etreinte mystique)*, Cécile had written:

> Let it be said: Jean and Cécile loved one another. Their life of love was divine and a trembling of ecstasy like an open flower bathing in the rain from heaven. The book of their love is a fainting of tenderness, the pages in it are mornings moistened from tears or sun, days of gray life and of gray homes but also of delicious days in the countryside where the bindweed has been woven into a spider's web with the dew, *everything there is prayer and adoration*. Their mouths were joined like those of doves, their bodies were without sin like the rose that opens the divine secret of its thousand folds to the day.
> They were so thoroughly intertwined and loved that they formed only a single heart in the breast of tenderness and love.
> They were so thoroughly intertwined that their love will shine in the marvelous history of love.[63]

In a strange twist, Jean de Gourmont also died prematurely — on February 19, 1928, six months after Cécile.

One can only imagine what it was like for Pierre to discover these writings in the month following Cécile's death. He faced a conundrum: on the one hand, he wanted to produce a volume that would establish Cécile's place — finally, if posthumously — in French literature; on the other hand, preserving his own respectability demanded eliminating any possible trace of evidence of

---

61. Éluard, "L'impatient" ("The Impatient One"), in *Capital of Pain*, 48, trans. 49.
62. Marchal, *Chants du silence*, 105.
63. Sauvage manuscript *L'Étreinte mystique* (XXIII), in Sauvage, *Écrits d'amour*, 87-88, emphasis added; cf. Marchal, *Chants du silence*, 102.

1883–1930: Pierre Messiaen and Cécile Sauvage

this affair. Pierre applied himself to this task almost immediately and tapped connections he had made during his first job as a reviewer at the *Revue forézienne* twenty years earlier. Pierre had first encountered Cécile when he received the manuscript of poems she sent to the review back in 1905; he specifically noted that both "Joseph Mounier and Jean Tenant shared" his enthusiasm for the manuscript.[64] It was now to Tenant, a literary figure associated with the postwar extreme political right, that Pierre turned for assistance.[65]

Thanks largely to Tenant's efforts, four works appeared in the three years following Cécile's death that at least established a beachhead for her legacy in French literature. The first was a special issue of the literary review *Les Amitiés,* edited by Tenant and published in Saint-Étienne, where Pierre and Tenant had first worked two decades earlier. Entitled *Cécile Sauvage, 20 July 1883–26 August 1927: Studies and Remembrances,* the issue was published in September 1928 as a one-year anniversary volume commemorating Cécile's death.[66] Two more volumes appeared in 1929 published by Mercure de France. (This must have been a bitter bargain Pierre made with himself given Jean de Gourmont's linkage. And yet, Jean himself was now deceased.) One of these volumes was the *Works of Cécile Sauvage,* also edited by Tenant; it would remain the definitive edition for many years.[67] A second was the forty-ninth edition of a regularly appearing French anthology entitled *Poets Today: Selected Works with Biographical Notices and Bibliographical Essays* (1929).[68] This edition included

64. Pierre Messiaen, *Images,* 126.

65. Pierre described Tenant before the Great War as always being "pink like a lady apple, with large round blue eyes." He regularly read Barbey d'Aurevilly and Léon Bloy, both extremist writers in the Catholic Revivalist movement heavily influenced by the Decadents; and "in literature as in politics," he approved of Charles Maurras, founder of the extreme-right Action Française. Editing his memoirs in 1942-1943 for their 1944 publication in occupied (and heavily censored) France, Pierre noted that Tenant "is today at the head of a daily newspaper," that is, the *Mémorial de la Loire.* See Pierre Messiaen, *Images,* 123. Tenant had been associated with Action Française, especially with Léon Daudet, cofounder (with Maurras in 1907) and editor of the *Action Française* newspaper, from the first decade of the century up to and including the 1940-1944 German occupation and Vichy regime. For Tenant's praise of Daudet in July 1939, that is, on the very eve of the Second World War, see Paul Renard, *L'Action française et la vie littéraire (1931-1944)* (Lille: Presses universitaires du septentrion, 2003), 162.

66. *Cécile Sauvage, 20 juillet 1883–26 août 1927: études et souvenirs,* ed. Jean Tenant (Saint-Étienne: Édition des Amitiés, 1928).

67. Sauvage and Tenant, *Œuvres.*

68. *Poètes d'aujourd'hui: morceaux choisis accompagnés de notices biographiques et d'un essai de bibliographie,* ed. Adolphe van Bever and Paul Léautaud, 49th ed. (Paris: Mercure de France, 1929). Although Cécile Sauvage appeared only (posthumously) in this 1929 edi-

1919–1930: Postwar Paris, National Conservatory, Death of Cécile

a short biographical entry on Sauvage and selections of her poems; the reason she was included in the forty-ninth edition after so many years of obscurity would have been the preceding publication of Tenant's edition of her works. Finally, in 1930 Tenant brought together a collection of his own essays entitled *Under the Balcony of Prudent-Moderate*. This included a reprint of his introductory essay for *Cécile Sauvage, 20 July 1883–26 August 1927*.[69]

Cécile Sauvage, the 1928 homage edited by Tenant, was an uneven assortment of sixteen "testimonials" by writers, some well known and others somewhat obscure, who for the most part had never met Cécile or even previously known of her work. Describing this collection, Tenant enthused that it was "a miracle" that such a diverse group could have been assembled, "all voicing their regret at not having known her whose voice sang with such perfect pitch." In fact, he seemed overly self-conscious about the somewhat bizarre collection — "And yet, how much they differ!" — and emphasized the common "agreement of their praise and friendship."[70] Fortunately, authoritative approbation was conferred by the Comtesse Anna de Noailles, a writer at that time synonymous with "feminine poetry" — in effect, "the official muse of the Republic"[71] — whose salon was attended by writers particularly associated with the cultural, religious, and nationalist right: Jammes, Mistral, Alphonse Daudet (father of Léon), and Barrès, a close friend of de Noailles. "No poet," de Noailles wrote of Sauvage, "has ever amassed and brought together with so much ease her prodigious collection. A dazzling intervention."[72]

Indeed, even if not dazzling, the collection intrigued. It included both Émile Baumann and Bernanos, eminent figures in the Catholic literary revival.[73] Morever, after the recent publication of *Under Satan's Sun* (1926),

---

tion, both Lucie Delarue-Mardrus and Anna de Noailles had been regularly included during the previous two decades. For example, both appeared in the 1927 (45th) and 1913 (23rd) editions.

69. Jean Tenant, "Avant-propos" (October 1927–January 1928), in *Cécile Sauvage*, ed. Tenant, 9-29; reprinted (with a two-page introduction) as Tenant, "La brève journée et le chant d'amour de Cécile Sauvage," in Tenant, *Sous le balcon*, 57-87.

70. Tenant, "La brève journée," *Sous le balcon*, 58.

71. See Tama Lea Engelking, "Anna de Noailles (1876-1933)," in *French Women Writers*, ed. Eva Martin Sartori and Dorothy Wynne Zimmerman (Lincoln: University of Nebraska Press, [1991] 1994), 335-45, at 335 and 342.

72. [Anna], Comtesse de Noailles, "Le lyrisme de Cécile Sauvage" (August 20, 1928), in *Cécile Sauvage*, ed. Tenant, 5-7, at 6; quoted by Tenant in Sauvage and Tenant, *Œuvres*, xv.

73. Georges Bernanos, "Cécile Sauvage ou le Miracle de la vie intérieure," and Émile Baumann, "Les deux rythmes de Cécile Sauvage," both in *Cécile Sauvage* (1928), ed. Tenant, 43-44, 45-47, respectively.

Bernanos was the preeminent novelist associated with the Action Française, outspoken in his contempt for the Third Republic, Jews, and homosexuals.[74] He was a strange bedfellow with another writer in the collection, the prolific journalist, poet, and novelist Lucie Delarue-Mardrus. Known for her lesbian affairs and extensive writings on lesbian love, Delarue-Mardrus was about to publish *The Angel and the Perverts* (1930), detailing her involvement with her lover, Natalie Clifford Barney.[75] Far from being inconceivable, such paradoxical juxtapositions characterize the postwar "crazy years" *(les Années Folles)*.

In fact, Delarue-Mardrus fit in perfectly with Tenant's aggressively antifeminist agenda. A nonconformist and a notorious contrarian, she did not see her lesbianism at odds with overt antifeminism (including a facile dismissal of women's suffrage).[76] Delarue-Mardrus thought she saw in the late Sauvage a fellow traveler: "At a time when womanhood is howling so much for equality of the sexes, it is good to keep in mind the lines of this simple young woman who, thanks to her being a poet, responded in advance to all of its errant ways."[77] When Tenant quoted this line a year later in his introduction to Sauvage's *Works* (1929), he softened it by attributing it to "Mrs. Lucie Delarue-Mardrus," who had been "struck by [Sauvage's] realism and high spirituality."[78] But this realist-mystical hybrid did not reflect Delarue-Mardrus's outlook (she did not use Tenant's words); it came rather from the postwar dialectical realism of Léon Daudet, *Action Française,* and Tenant himself, who asked rhetor-

74. "[Jean] Cocteau, the conversion of Cocteau and his little 'fairies' from Le Bœuf sur le Toit; come now, is this what they call the Catholic Revival?" Georges Bernanos, quoted in Henri Massis, *Maurras et notre temps,* 2 vols. (Paris and Geneva: La Palatine, 1951), 1:212; in Bernard Doering, *Jacques Maritain and the French Catholic Intellectuals* (Notre Dame, Ind.: University of Notre Dame Press, 1983), 47; in Schloesser, *Jazz Age Catholicism,* 186.

75. Lucie Delarue-Mardrus, *The Angel and the Perverts,* trans. Anna Livia, Cutting Edge Lesbian Life and Literature (New York: New York University Press, 1995); originally Delarue-Mardrus, *L'ange et les pervers, roman* (Paris: J. Ferenczi et fils, 1930). See introduction to "Lucie Delarue-Mardrus (1874-1945)," in *French Women Poets of Nine Centuries: The Distaff and the Pen,* ed. and trans. Norman R. Shapiro (Baltimore: Johns Hopkins University Press, 2008), 800-819, at 801.

76. Shapiro, *French Women Poets,* 800.

77. Lucie Delarue-Mardrus, "La fierté d'être femme" (Paris, April 1, 1928), in *Cécile Sauvage,* ed. Tenant (1928), 33-37, at 37; quoted by Tenant, in Sauvage and Tenant, *Œuvres,* xv; and in translation in Shapiro, *French Women Poets,* 945. Sauvage's poetry appears on 944-55.

78. Sauvage and Tenant, *Œuvres,* xv. By the time of Tenant's publication, "Mrs." Delarue-Mardrus's fifteen-year marriage to the translator J. C. Mardrus had already been over for fourteen years. She was divorced from Mardrus in 1915 and never remarried.

ically: "Are there many examples, in contemporary poetry, of such an accord between realism and spirituality?"[79]

Above all else, Cécile Sauvage had been a mother: this was the central image, created by Tenant with Pierre's assistance, that smoothed over all the smaller dissonances found within this strange volume. It is important to set this maternal image within the context of the postwar 1920s. "Maternity" was a loaded term in this era of the "new woman" who rejected childbearing, fought for suffrage, dressed like a man, and was associated with lesbianism.[80] Issues of sexuality and gender were thoroughly politicized as conservative nationalist forces promoted a natalist campaign against feminist reproductive concerns. Political forces on the right (including the Catholic Church) argued that national security was at stake: after the decimation of the male population in the Great War, they argued, France needed to reproduce a new generation as quickly as possible. In his article launching the 1928 homage to Cécile, Léon Daudet played his part in fashioning the overall message as he wrote in *Action Française*: "Unique poetess, diamond of flesh, she grasped reconciliations and brought them into center focus: the woman and the tree, understanding and maternity."[81]

Tenant traced Cécile's declining health and withdrawal into isolation back to Alain's birth in late August 1912: "Her health had not been so good since the birth of a second son. The first son had already stolen her youth." (Alain and Olivier can hardly have been pleased with this reading of their mother's life!) Tenant then pushed the chronology back even further, placing Cécile's decline squarely on Olivier's shoulders. The "subtle shadow" that Cécile had written about in her poem entitled "Melancholy" was "not merely that of the Ambert valley" volcanoes; nor was the mourning simply over the loss of "the southern light" of Provence. Rather, argued Tenant, Cécile's degeneration resulted from having given birth: "Chronologically, 'Melancholy' came after *The Budding Soul*, that is, after the birth of her first son, Olivier. The break is very apparent."[82]

And yet, Tenant continued, this was precisely what made Cécile a model, for she now appeared as

---

79. Tenant, preface to Sauvage, *Œuvres* (1929), x. For this dialectical aesthetic of realism and spiritualism, see Léon Daudet's literary "launch" of Georges Bernanos's *Under Satan's Sun* (1926) in the pages of *L'Action Française*: "Révélation d'un Grand Romancier: *Sous le soleil de Satan*" (April 7, 1926); "À propos de Georges Bernanos. Le succès littéraire" (April 26, 1926); in Schloesser, *Jazz Age Catholicism*, 250-56.

80. Mary Louise Roberts, *Civilization without Sexes: Reconstructing Gender in Postwar France, 1917-1927* (Chicago: University of Chicago Press, 1994).

81. Léon Daudet, quoted by Tenant in Sauvage and Tenant, *Œuvres*, xvi.

82. Tenant, preface to Sauvage and Tenant, *Œuvres*, xii, xiii.

a sorrowful mother, sacrificed to maternity [*sacrifiée à la maternité*]. She gave everything to her sons, even before having brought them into the world: her strength, her joy, and the flower of her life. As she waited for her first son to arrive, we saw her already submitted to her destiny [*soumise à son destin*]. These tender conversations, these caressing words are, without her knowing it, the sign of this total donation [or self-sacrifice: *don total d'elle-même*] of her very self which was accomplished in the depths of her flesh.[83]

However, one page later, Tenant fudged a bit on the chronology again, now refocusing the blame on Alain: "A second son, Alain, was born to her in 1912. This same year she finished 'The Valley.' She never published anything again."[84] Tenant then immediately added a gloss on the allegorical piece that Cécile had been working on at her death: "*To Love after Death,* a lyrical drama of Christian inspiration that bears witness to her intimate being's ascension toward the elevated truths of the Faith. This work, like her religious evolution, remained incomplete."[85] Presumably at Pierre's pushing, Tenant also reinvented Cécile as having been en route back to her childhood Catholicism.

Tenant's most explicit politicization of Cécile came in his appeal to the authority of Maurras himself. In *Feminine Romanticism* (1903), Maurras had written: "Yes, to be truly *feminine* is to hide eternally. The woman who confesses and rends the voluptuous drapery sacrifices to her art something of her sex. The sphinx is disfigured the instant it reveals itself."[86] In 1903, Maurras's attack had been on Anna de Noailles; Tenant's retrieval of it almost three decades later in this collection (in which de Noailles was a preeminent contributor) was crass. Nevertheless, Tenant proceeded:

> In praising Cécile Sauvage one wouldn't even know how to leave what distinguishes her from her Romantic predecessors, — these "feminine heads full of thoughtful revolt and feverish meditation," against whom Charles Maurras [in *Feminine Romanticism*] directed the blistering lines of his criti-

---

83. Tenant, preface to Sauvage and Tenant, *Œuvres*, xiii.
84. Tenant, preface to Sauvage and Tenant, *Œuvres*, xiv.
85. Tenant, preface to Sauvage and Tenant, *Œuvres*, xiv.
86. Charles Maurras, *Le romantisme féminin* (1903); quoted in Catherine Perry, *Persephone Unbound: Dionysian Aesthetics in the Works of Anna De Noailles* (Lewisburg, Pa.: Bucknell University Press, 2003), 150. For further context, see Elaine Marks's entry "1929 'Odor di Femina' [sic]," on Jean Larnac's 1929 *Histoire de la littérature féminine en France*, in *A New History of French Literature*, ed. Denis Hollier (Cambridge: Harvard University Press, 1989), 888-91.

cism. She whom [Eugène] Marsan wants to call "The Shepherdess" did not feel any less deeply than others, but she knew that "overworked sensitivity can only burn out" [again, quoting *Feminine Romanticism*], and with all her soul she strove for simplicity. What distinguishes her from the "little souls, quivering slaves of sensation" [quoting Barrès] is above all this entire donation of herself, without return, without taking back and without demand; next, this noble submission to the duties of love and of maternity; finally, this progressive self-effacement we saw doggedly applied. But let there be no mistake. Tempered and mastered, the fervor was real. A large part of her work testifies to this: the poems of *The Budding Soul*.[87]

By means of these antifeminist somersaults, Tenant could explain why Cécile's self-imposed isolation and self-effacement were not the result of emotional depression but rather, in fact, intentionally deployed tools of "feminine romanticism." One would never suspect that Cécile, knowingly trapped in this patriarchal literary world, had secretly hoped to become a journalist by adopting a masculine pseudonym.

As if he were not yet clear enough, Tenant concluded his essay by underscoring his point:

> Only those who knew [Cécile] are able to imagine the surprise that she would have felt in hearing herself praised this way. She was so little a woman of letters! A mother before everything else, she was more proud of her children than of her poems. Secondly, she was a woman, and not at all feminist [*et point féministe*]. . . .
>
> This book will make her known as she was: simple and cheerful, subdued and melancholic, loving wife and admirable mother. This was the woman. As to the poet, she is one of those, "in small number" — as Georges Bernanos says — "who watch over the threshold of our homes."[88]

Tenant's essay, first appearing in the 1928 homage volume, reappeared with slight alterations as the preface to the 1929 *Works*. Olivier Messiaen never liked this edition and tried (without success) to have a new one published

---

87. Tenant, preface to Sauvage and Tenant, *Œuvres,* ix-x; alluding to Eugène Marsan's essay, "Cécile Sauvage la Bergère [the Shepherdess]," in *Cécile Sauvage,* ed. Tenant, 66-74; reprinted from *Comœdia* (November 15, 1927). Marsan (1882-1936) wrote literary criticism for *L'Action Française* under the pen name Orion.

88. Tenant, preface to Sauvage and Tenant, *Œuvres,* xvi, xvii; quoting the final line of Bernanos, "Cécile Sauvage ou le Miracle de la vie intérieure," in *Cécile Sauvage,* ed. Tenant, 47.

during his lifetime.[89] In addition to the *Works* not actually being "complete," the 1929 volume produced by Pierre and Tenant extolled Cécile as the ideal 1920s woman of the natalist right, devoted so completely to the ideal of maternity that she had "sacrificed" herself on its altar. This same agenda can be seen in the unpublished fragments from notebooks and letters Pierre selected for publication in the section following the poems. Most of them are from Cécile's life before moving to Paris in 1919, and a large portion of them focus on motherhood and nature. Certain passages, especially from Digne just before her marriage in 1907, also contributed to imagining Cécile as a Catholic believer who might one day return to the faith.

However, Messiaen likely also detested this volume because he realized that it omitted something substantial. Although he did not yet know what final form they had taken, he knew of his mother's feverish wartime writings in her secluded room in Grenoble while he was a boy. For a long time he thought that these had constituted a "lost" manuscript entitled *Book of Love (Livre d'amour)* that his father said had been a casualty of the Germans' pillaging of the family home in the Second World War. When Messiaen asked his father where this volume was, he received such an angry response that he suspected Pierre had destroyed the work. And in fact, Messiaen did not find it when he searched Pierre's belongings after his death.[90] It would not be until 1972 that Messiaen learned of his mother's actual manuscripts: *The Mystical Embrace* (completed August 1915); *Prayer* (fragments from 1914-1915); and *The Wing and the Rose* (also 1914-1915).[91]

Only recently have scholars been able to determine the complicated steps undertaken by Pierre Messiaen to preserve both his wife's literary heritage and his own sense of marital respectability in the 1929 edition.[92] First, Pierre fabricated a single document he entitled *Primrose:* this French word *(Primevère)* is easily created by adding three letters *(mev)* to the word *Prière (Prayer),* the actual title of Cécile's 1914-1915 reader. Pierre then predated this document by saying that it had been begun in 1911 — this invented chronology meant that it would have been written contemporaneously with *The Valley,* completed at the latest by Alain's birth in August 1912, and published the next year by Mercure de France. This chronology is confirmed in Pierre's memoirs: "It is

---

89. Unfortunately, the most widely available current edition is basically a reprint of Tenant's 1929 edition: Cécile Sauvage, *Œuvres complètes* (Paris: Table ronde, 2002).

90. Marchal, *Chants du silence,* 107; Hill and Simeone, *Messiaen,* 223.

91. Sauvage, *Écrits d'amour,* 24.

92. Béatrice Marchal, introduction to Sauvage, *Écrits d'amour,* 9-56; see 18-32; cf. Marchal, *Chants du silence,* 105-13.

during the 1911 summer vacation... that Cécile Sauvage, commemorating our engagement and our marriage, began to write a third volume: *Primrose*."[93] This dating not only made sure that the actual period of composition (i.e., 1914-1915, during which Pierre was away at the war front) was erased; it also meant that the intimate sentiments were tied to married love in general and to the first, happier years of their marriage in particular. Finally, having invented a single work, given it a fabricated title, and predated it to Cécile's healthier years, Pierre cut and pasted (and occasionally altered) material from the three actual documents — *The Mystical Embrace, Prayer,* and *The Wing and the Rose* — and used them to create this new work, *Primrose,* which appeared in the *Works* edited by Tenant.[94]

Finally, even the 1929 dedications of the previously published poems were altered to make them seem more maternal and familial. *The Budding Soul* had not had an explicit dedication in the 1910 edition; it was now addressed "For Olivier Messiaen." *The Valley* (1913) had originally been dedicated to Jean de Gourmont; however, the 1929 volume replaced this seemingly collegial dedication — only Pierre knew of its amorous nature — with a maternal one: "For Alain Messiaen," who had been born just after its composition. *Primrose,* the fragmentary collection invented by Pierre, dated "1913" and attributed to Cécile, was dedicated "To my dear Pierrot, in memory of our engagement and of our marriage. C.S." In a very strange twist, the only nonfamilial dedication was the one assigned to *Wisps of Smoke (Fumées)* (1910). Whereas it had previously borne no dedication, it now read: "For Jean Tenant and Henri Pourrat"![95]

93. Pierre Messiaen, *Images,* 151; quoted in Sauvage and Marchal-Vincent, *L'Œuvre poétique,* 1:151.

94. See "Primevère" (1913 [*sic*]), attributed to Cécile Sauvage; in Sauvage and Tenant, *Œuvres,* 211-62. At the bottom of the first page is a note: "Death did not allow Cécile Sauvage to complete this collection of poetry and prose."

95. See Sauvage and Tenant, *Œuvres,* 33, 177, 211, 147. Dedications analyzed by Philip Weller, afterword to translation of *The Budding Soul,* in *Olivier Messiaen: Music, Art, and Literature,* ed. Christopher Dingle and Nigel Simeone (Burlington, Vt.: Ashgate, 2007), 252-278, at 271.

Henri Pourrat wrote a long essay of remembrances for the 1928 volume in memoriam: see Pourrat, "Souvenirs," in *Cécile Sauvage,* ed. Tenant, 84-107. Like Tenant, Pourrat (1887-1959) came to be associated with the far right. He spent most of his life in his native Ambert (where Cécile wrote *Fumées* and the rest of *Le Vallon*). A French anthropologist and writer (winner of the Grand Prix du Roman of the Académie Française [1931] and the Prix Goncourt during the occupation [1941]), he collected oral folklore, supported the Vichy regime's "back to the earth" program, and wrote for the extreme right-wing newspapers *Croix-de-feu* and *Le Flambeau.* Christian Faure, "*Vent de Mars* d'Henri Pourrat, Prix Goncourt 1941, ou la consécration d'une œuvre littéraire par le Régime de Vichy," *Bulletin du Centre d'Histoire*

Tenant recycled his preface yet a third time (again with only slight alterations) as a chapter in his 1930 collection of essays, *Under the Balcony of Prudent-Moderate*.[96] Since this chapter was only slightly modified, of greater interest are the collection's overall content, tone, and intended audience in which Cécile was now situated. Tenant's volume, appearing at the beginning of the Great Depression and its increasingly polarized political world, was intended as an attack on "moderates" and a defense of "extremists" on the right. The allegorical figure of "Prudent Moderation" (Prudent-Moderate in the title), explained in Tenant's own dedication, was a straw man, a representative of those middle-class "moderates" offended by Action Française.

As a consequence of being placed within this broad political agenda at the outset of the ominous 1930s, Cécile Sauvage was now memorialized as one of "Four Great Deceased" writers, including the extremely acerbic and polemical Catholic pamphleteer Léon Bloy (d. 1917), with whom she would have shared nothing in common. This section of the book paralleled another: "Four Great Living" writers, all of them highly visible members of Action Française: the cofounders Maurras and Léon Daudet; the novelist Bernanos; and René Benjamin, a recipient of the Prix Goncourt (1938), a prolific pamphleteer who attacked democracy and liberalism, and the biographer of Barrès and Maurras.

Thus, Cécile Sauvage had been rewritten, indeed, reinvented between 1928 and 1930, for a public that had not actually known her — as an antifeminist devotee of the natalist cause, a martyr who had willingly sacrificed her promising literary career on the altar of childbearing and child rearing. More specifically, Sauvage's name was now associated with the writers of the Action Française: Barrès, Bernanos, Maurras, Tenant. In the years 1928-1930 this association was an extremely volatile one for Catholics following the papal condemnation of Action Française in 1926.[97] On the one side were those like Jacques Maritain who

---

économique et sociale de la région lyonnaise 1 (1982): 5-25; Faure, *La mystique vichyssoise du retour à la terre selon l'œuvre d'Henri Pourrat* (Gonfaron: Association Française d'Archéologie Métropolitaine, 1988); Faure, *Le Projet culturel de Vichy. Folklore et Révolution nationale 1940-1944* (Lyon and Paris: Coédition Presses Universitaires de Lyon and Éditions du CNRS, 1989), 118-19. For the newspapers see Samuel Kalman, *The Extreme Right in Interwar France: The Faisceau and the Croix de Feu* (Burlington, Vt.: Ashgate, 2008).

96. Tenant, "La brève journée et le chant d'amour de Cécile Sauvage."

97. In late December 1926, Pope Pius XI had issued his condemnation of the Action Française, prohibiting Catholics from belonging to the movement and placing a number of Maurras's writings on the Index of Forbidden Books. The condemnation was traumatic for Catholics (especially for numerous French clergy), and Action Française became a hotly contested site, forcing integralist Catholics to choose between Maurras and Rome. See Schloesser, *Jazz Age Catholicism*, 189-90.

had followed the pope's lead. On the other were those like Bernanos; leaving the church rather than abandon Maurras, Bernanos attacked Maritain in 1928 for siding with the "enthusiastic cries of a small number of esthetes and epileptic Jews." This is the same Bernanos with whom Tenant closed his essay, in this very same year, on Cécile Sauvage: he referred to her as guardian "of the threshhold of our homes."[98] Pierre Messiaen does not seem to have followed Bernanos out the door of the church, and it is difficult to know what precisely he thought of Tenant's work. However, regardless of Pierre's intentions, Tenant's essay conveyed right-wing sensibilities both political and ecclesiastical.

In the domestic sphere, Pierre moved on quite quickly, marrying Marguerite Élie, a longtime friend from Orange. Although Pierre avoids giving a precise date in his memoirs, his first son with Marguerite, Charles-Marie (Messiaen's first half brother), was born in 1930, about twenty-two years after Messiaen himself.[99] Pierre and Marguerite (hereafter designated in Messiaen's diaries as "The Pio's") must have married sometime in 1929, in the second year after Cécile's death. The 1929 edition of Cécile's works can be seen from Pierre's point of view as a means of putting closure on his earlier life.

In Messiaen's adult accounts of his upbringing, Pierre was largely erased; when he was mentioned at all, he was rewritten as an "unbeliever" — which, it seems fair to say, would have been a grave insult in Pierre's eyes. Although we can only speculate why Messiaen framed his life in this way, the story of his parents' lives is strongly suggestive regarding the source of the composer's signature mixture of Catholicism set within an aggressively modernist aesthetic. Throughout Messiaen's life, the influence of Catholic doctrine, practice, and iconography played a prominent role. Certainly, the extremely religious household of Pierre had its influence.[100]

Even so, Messiaen's primary devotion was to his mother, both during her

---

98. Georges Bernanos to Jacques Maritain, April 21, 1928, in *Combat pour la vérité, correspondance inéditée, 1904-34,* ed. Albert Béguin and Jean Murray (Paris: Plon, 1971), 321ff.; in Doering, *Jacques Maritain,* 52-53; in Schloesser, *Jazz Age Catholicism,* 189. Tenant, quoting the final line of Bernanos, "Cécile Sauvage ou le Miracle de la vie intérieure," in *Cécile Sauvage,* ed. Tenant, 47.

99. Pierre Messiaen, *Images,* 237-39; cf. Christopher Dingle, *The Life of Messiaen* (Cambridge and New York: Cambridge University Press, 2007), 48. For the tragic birth and death four years later of Messiaen's second half brother, twelve-day-old Jacques, see Dingle, 53.

100. On the problem of raising religious sons in the Third Republic, see Paul Seeley, "O Sainte Mère: Liberalism and the Socialization of Catholic Men in Nineteenth-Century France," *Journal of Modern History* 70 (December 1998): 862-91. Messiaen's situation reverses the usual paradigm of a religiously practicing mother and a nonpracticing father. My thanks to Suzanne Kaufman for this reference.

life and after her death. It must have been difficult for an adolescent to make sense of such a volatile mixture of ultra-Catholic religiosity and an equally extreme naturalist nihilism — much of it wrapped in "mystical" language — sharing the same impossibly small household in the impoverished Parisian quarter. This is perhaps what makes Messiaen's religiosity so unique: the traditional iconography is there throughout, and in the hands of a more conventional Catholicism it might have been largely inconsequential or smugly suffocating. But in Messiaen's hands, the transcendent always has an eye firmly fixed on the tragically ephemeral passing of a seemingly insignificant human existence. Primordial canyons and gorges, light-years of stars, nebulae, galaxies, eternity itself — against such enormity, the psalmist's cry comes to mind: "What is man, that thou art mindful of him or the son of man that thou art concerned about him?"[101]

---

101. Ps. 8:4 (Douay-CCD).

PART II

1927–1932

Budding Rhythmician, Surrealist Composer, Mystical Commentator

1927–1932: Budding Rhythmician, Surrealist Composer, Mystical Commentator

1. 1928 summer (Fuligny)   *Le Banquet céleste (The Celestial Banquet)* — organ
2. 1928 summer (Fuligny)   *Préludes (Preludes)* — piano, begun
   1929 summer (Fuligny)   *Préludes (Preludes)* — piano, completed
3. 1929-1930 (Paris)   *Diptyque (Diptych)* — organ
4. 1930 (Paris)   *Trois Mélodies (Three Melodies)* — voice and piano
5. 1930 summer (Fuligny)   *Les Offrandes oubliées (The Forgotten Offerings)* — orchestra
6. 1930-1931 (Paris)   *La Mort du nombre (The Death of Number)* — piano, voice, violin
7. 1931 summer (Fuligny)   *Le Tombeau resplendissant (The Resplendent Tomb)* — orchestra

Before considering *The Celestial Banquet,* Messiaen's self-designated "first work" composed in the summer of 1928, it is worth contemplating an autobiographical fragment that emerged almost as an aside in a 1989 interview. He noted that "during the first year he studied the organ" — the academic year 1927-1928 that opened one month following his mother's death in late August — he was sick in bed "for several weeks."[4]

We now know that Messiaen had been confined because an X-ray examination revealed that what Pierre had called "anemia" in the spring of 1927 was in fact a symptom of his son's own case of tuberculosis. The illness worsened to the point that Messiaen had to be brought to his aunts' family farm, where the open air and a solid diet restored his health.[5] During this period of bed rest, Pierre gave him a book to read by Jacques Maritain — philosopher, leading figure of postwar French Catholic Revivalism, an acquaintance and contemporary of his father (they had been born just a year apart). Messiaen did not specify which work it was, saying only that he found it "difficult" reading.[6]

---

4. Messiaen, in Brigitte Massin and Olivier Messiaen, *Olivier Messiaen: une poétique du merveilleux* (Aix-en-Provence: Alinéa, 1989), 178.

5. Béatrice Marchal, *Les Chants du silence. Olivier Messiaen, fils de Cécile Sauvage ou la musique face à l'impossible parole* (Sampzon: Éditions Delatour France, 2008), 95.

6. "I never met [Maritain]. My father knew him. I only read one of his books, at age eighteen [i.e., in 1927], during my first year of the organ. I was sick for several weeks, I used the time to read Maritain, a book of high philosophy which seemed very difficult to me." Messiaen, in Massin and Messiaen, *Olivier Messiaen,* 178. See also Douglas Shadle, "Messiaen's Relationship to Jacques Maritain's Musical Circle and Neo-Thomism," in *Messiaen the Theologian,* ed. Andrew Shenton (Burlington, Vt.: Ashgate, 2010), 83-99.

CHAPTER 4

1927–1931

First Works as Grief Works

Messiaen would not have found Pierre's rewriting of Cécile Sauvage via Jean Tenant an accurate monument of bereavement.[1] By contrast, Messiaen's first musical compositions dating from the summer of 1928 through the summer of 1931 — from *The Celestial Banquet* through *The Resplendent Tomb* — might profitably be read as his own working through grief. At the very least, they challenge the evaluation, made after Messiaen's own death six decades later, that his music is marked by "a refusal to mourn."[2]

Trauerarbeit (Grief Work): 1927–1931

During the four years immediately following his mother's death, Messiaen spent summer vacations at the farm of his paternal aunts in the north of France at Fuligny, Aube. Here he composed works out of personal inspiration; during the academic months in Paris he composed works intended for Conservatory assignments. Later on, he established his own official catalogue, laying out his seven earliest published works in the following order:[3]

[1]. From now on "Messiaen" refers to Olivier Messiaen; his father continues to be referred to as "Pierre."

[2]. Bernard Holland, "Remembering Messiaen with Works of His Own," *New York Times,* November 10, 1992, C15.

[3]. Nigel Simeone, *Olivier Messiaen: A Bibliographical Catalogue of Messiaen's Works,* Musikbibliographische Arbeiten series, vol. 14 (Tutzing: Hans Schneider, 1998), xvii.

1927–1931: First Works as Grief Works

Most likely it was Maritain's greatly revised and enlarged second edition of *Art and Scholasticism*, which had recently been published on May 25, 1927.[7] Messiaen's suggestion that the work had little effect on him due to its difficulty rings untrue. By that time he had been reading writings of Saint Thomas Aquinas for two or three years;[8] reading Maritain's modern usage of the Thomistic texts should hardly have been a problem. Moreover, *Art and Scholasticism* was read by a broad general audience, and its endnotes were filled with contemporary references. Messiaen's ultramodern deployment of traditional Catholic and Thomistic tropes is the musical epitome of Maritain's theory (although there were reasons both in 1927 and in the composer's 1989 interview to downplay the impact of reading the philosopher).[9]

Maritain's extended argument in *Art and Scholasticism* made two principal points: first, religion and the avant-garde are eminently compatible as they meet in the artistic and aesthetic arena; second, there is no particularly "religious" form of art. As opposed to the Ultramontanist vision that had governed Catholic arts and literature for nearly a century by the 1920s, Maritain's

---

7. Jacques Maritain, *Art et scolastique,* rev. ed. (Paris: Louis Rouart et Fils, [1920] 1927); English: *Art and Scholasticism: With Other Essays,* trans. J. F. Scanlan (New York: Charles Scribner's Sons, 1930). See bibliographical notice in Jacques Maritain and Raïssa Maritain, *Œuvres complètes / Jacques et Raïssa Maritain,* ed. Jean-Marie Allion et al., 17 vols. (Fribourg, Switzerland: Éditions universitaires; Paris: Éditions Saint-Paul, 1982-2008), 17:28-31, at 29. The 1927 edition differed from the original 1920 text most significantly in its greatly expanded endnotes. It was also augmented with an essay, "Frontiers of Poetry," as well as four annexes: "Discourse on Art," "Several Reflections on Religious Art," "The Triumph of Saint Thomas in the Theatre," and "Georges Rouault" (the painter). See Stephen Schloesser, *Jazz Age Catholicism: Mystic Modernism in Postwar Paris, 1919-1933* (Toronto: University of Toronto Press, 2005), 190-98.

8. Massin and Messiaen, *Olivier Messiaen,* 31.

9. In 1927, Messiaen would likely have reacted badly to Maritain's strong emulation of Jean Cocteau and his postwar neoclassicism — most notably, Cocteau's assault on Claude Debussy as the representative of what his own movement aimed at eradicating. In 1989, sixteen years after his death in 1973, Maritain had fallen into obscurity, having been regarded as an extreme reactionary voice after the Second Vatican Council (1962-1965) and the publication of *Le Paysan de la Garonne, un vieux laïc s'interroge à propos du temps présent* (Paris: Desclée de Brouwer, 1966); translated as *The Peasant of the Garonne: An Old Layman Questions Himself about the Present Time* (New York: Holt, Rinehart and Winston, 1968). For Maritain, Cocteau, and Debussy, see Stephen Schloesser, "Maritain on Music: His Debt to Cocteau," in *Beauty, Art, and the Polis,* ed. Alice Ramos (Washington, D.C.: American Maritain Association, distributed by Catholic University of America Press, 2000), 176-89, and Schloesser, *Jazz Age Catholicism,* 142-48, 190-98. See also Stephen Broad, "Messiaen and Cocteau," in *Olivier Messiaen: Music, Art, and Literature,* ed. Christopher Dingle and Nigel Simeone (Burlington, Vt.: Ashgate, 2007), 1-12.

neoscholastic aesthetic located the religiosity of a work in its interior formal principle and not in any outward imitation of some prototype.[10]

Messiaen himself embraced Maritain's vision; in fact, a decade later he explained his own music in nearly identical terms (without, notably, giving Maritain any attribution). In an apologia for *Songs of Earth and Sky* (1938), Messiaen wrote in 1939:

> First of all, I wanted to write a religious, Catholic work [*une oeuvre religieuse catholique*]. I wrote recently in *Art sacré:* "Religious art, if it is 'one' is also essentially 'many.' Why? Because it expresses the search for a single thing, which is God, but a single thing that is everywhere, that may be found in everything, above and below everything." All subjects may be religious when they are in the eye of a believer. Why should "Bail avec Mi (pour ma femme)" be any less religious than "Antienne du silence (pour le jour des Anges gardiens)"?[11]

Or, quoting the title of a chapter by Ernest Hello: "Diversity of Words and the Unity of God."[12]

Messiaen's rhetoric in another article appearing at the same time again echoes Maritain:

> Is this to say that this music must necessarily be circumspect, limited to certain subjects, of a style and language more or less out of date? No, a thousand times no! The religious subject encompasses all subjects: it is God and all of his creation.... As for language, it is only clear when it is "true." It must always be contemporary and original to an epoch and personality.... Let us be innovative, join the chain, without attaching ourselves to such and such a chain-link of the past. The fake Bach partisans [*les partisans du faux Bach*] can never write a lasting and "true" work.[13]

---

10. Schloesser, *Jazz Age Catholicism*, 148-51, 194-98, 203-6.

11. Olivier Messiaen, "Autour d'une Parution" ("Around a Publication"), *Le Monde musical*, April 30, 1939, 35, in *Olivier Messiaen: Journalism, 1935-1939*, ed. Stephen Broad (Surrey, U.K., and Burlington, Vt.: Ashgate, 2012), Fr 57-59, at 58; Eng 119-21, at 119. Messiaen quotes from his own article: "Autour d'une Œuvre d'orgue" ("Around an Organ Work"), *L'Art Sacré*, April 1939, 123; in *Olivier Messiaen: Journalism,* Fr 73-74; Eng 134-35, at 134.

12. Hello, "La diversité des paroles et l'unité de Dieu," in *Du néant à dieu*, ed. Jules-Philippe Heuzey, 2 vols. (Paris: Perrin et Cie, [1921] 1930), 1:46-47.

13. Messiaen, "De la Musique sacrée" ("On Sacred Music"), *Carrefour*, June-July 1939, double issue, 75; in *Olivier Messiaen: Journalism,* Fr 74-76, at 75; Eng 135-37, at 136.

1927–1931: First Works as Grief Works

Compare Maritain's *Art and Scholasticism* (1927): "There is no style *peculiar to religious art*, there is no *religious technique*. . . . [Religious art follows] the example of God Himself who speaks the language of men [and can] assume . . . every means and every form of technical vitality, so to speak, placed at its disposal by the contemporary generation."[14] Indeed, even Messiaen's final quip imitated Maritain's own impish advice a decade earlier: those who wanted to practice sacred art should "begin by doing still-life studies, accustom themselves to discovering a religious significance in the inevitable apples, jam-jar, pipe and mandolin."[15] Even more suggestively, given Messiaen's line about "fake Bach partisans," it seems he might also have run across Maritain's lines in *Antimoderne* about the neo-Gothic: "We love the art of the cathedrals, of Giotto and [Fra] Angelico. But we detest the neo-Gothic and the pre-Raphaelism. We know that the course of time is irreversible; as much as we admire the century of Saint Louis, we do not want *to return to the Middle Ages* on that account, along an absurd path which certain penetrating critics generously accuse us of."[16]

The novelty of Messiaen's *Celestial Banquet*, then, should be seen within this context: it was written shortly after he had read Maritain during a bedridden Christmas vacation of December 1927–January 1928. Maritain gave a Catholic artist license to jettison received external forms and set out on an avant-garde path. One thing alone mattered: the eternal formal principle that radiated clarity *(clarté)* from within and gave unity and meaning to the organic whole.[17]

---

14. Maritain, *Art et scolastique*, 215; *Art and Scholasticism*, 143.

15. Maritain, *Art et scolastique*, 215-16; *Art and Scholasticism*, 143-44.

16. Maritain, *Antimoderne* (Paris: Éditions de la Revue des jeunes, 1922); in Schloesser, *Jazz Age Catholicism*, 163.

17. "A certain splendour is indeed according to all the Ancients the essential character of beauty, — *claritas est de ratione pulchritudinis, lux pulchrificat, quia sine luce omnia sunt turpia,* — but it is a splendour of intelligibility: . . . *splendor formae,* said St. Thomas with a metaphysician's precision of language: for *form* . . . is above all the peculiar principle of intelligibility, the peculiar *clarity* of every thing. . . . So, to say with the Schoolmen that beauty is the *splendour of form shining on the proportioned parts of matter* is to say that it is a lightning of mind on a matter intelligently arranged." Maritain, *Art et scolastique*, 37-39; cf. 45-47; *Art and Scholasticism*, 24-25; cf. 28-30.

1927–1932: Budding Rhythmician, Surrealist Composer, Mystical Commentator

1928: *Le Banquet Céleste (The Celestial Banquet)*

Messiaen composed *The Celestial Banquet* at his aunts' farm in Fuligny during the summer of 1928.[18] At first glance, the meaning of this relatively small piece for organ seems conventional enough: the "celestial banquet" refers both to the Eucharist here on earth and to the "eschatological banquet" (or wedding feast) at the end of time. (In the words of the hymn "Ave Verum Corpus" composed by Saint Thomas Aquinas, the Eucharist is a "foretaste" [*praegustatum*] of the eschatological banquet.) Thus, the "celestial banquet" is an intersection of temporality and eternity — one of those "unions of opposites" that marks Messiaen's vision of the world, a vision both sacramental (mystic-realist) and surrealist. The composer's preoccupation with temporality and eternity is expressed in the scriptural quotation he employs as the work's epigraph, which, in the first edition, appeared on the front cover just beneath the title: "Celui qui mange ma chair et boit mon sang demeure en moi et moi en lui" (Whoever eats my flesh and drinks my blood abides in me and I in him).[19] In terms of temporality and duration, the keyword is "abide" *(demeurer)*; to the Anglophone reader, it recalls a venerable Anglican hymn: "Abide with me. Fast falls the eventide." Time passes quickly; we are in search of one who will remain steady, who will endure, abide.

Liturgically, this line occurs in the Gospel reading for the summer feast of Corpus Christi (Body of Christ); falling on the Thursday after Trinity Sunday (itself following Pentecost Sunday and hence ending the springtime Easter cycle), the feast was traditionally celebrated by outdoor processions with the Blessed Sacrament in many cultures and especially in rural areas.[20] In 1928 it was celebrated on Thursday, June 7.[21] Since Messiaen wrote the work at his

---

18. The 1960 revised edition gives a dating of 1926 — that is, before Messiaen began to study the organ and before his mother's death. For its actual 1928 dating, see Simeone, *Bibliographical Catalogue*, 2-5, and Peter Hill and Nigel Simeone, *Messiaen* (New Haven: Yale University Press, 2005), 23.

19. For reproduction of covers for both the first edition (1934) and "new edition" (1960), see Simeone, *Bibliographical Catalogue*, 2, 5. The scriptural quotation does not appear on the 1960 cover.

20. For thirteenth-century origins, see Barbara R. Walters, Vincent J. Corrigan, and Peter T. Ricketts, eds., *The Feast of Corpus Christi* (University Park: Pennsylvania State University Press, 2006).

21. In 1928, Easter Sunday was celebrated on April 8; Corpus Christi on Thursday, June 7. For calculating feast days dependent on Easter, note the number of days following Easter Sunday: Ascension Thursday = 39; Pentecost Sunday = 49; Trinity Sunday = 56; Corpus Christi (Thursday) = 60.

aunts' home in Fuligny that summer, it is possible that he had been struck by the day's Mass and procession. As Pierre notes in his memoirs, such processions were common fare in his rural origins.

Whatever the initial catalyzing spark, the Eucharist preoccupied Messiaen that summer. *The Celestial Banquet* was originally just one part of a larger work (written for orchestra) entitled *The Eucharistic Banquet* that he set apart and reworked for organ. "I was only nineteen years old when I composed *The Eucharistic Banquet*," he said later; "it was a very long work, neither very well scored, nor very well constructed. But I never hesitated about the title. It always seemed obvious to me."[22]

On a general level this is all straightforward: the Eucharist was at the center of Catholic identity and remained at the center of Messiaen's own faith throughout his life. Nearly sixty years later (and not long before he died), he would write his massive organ cycle, *Book of the Blessed Sacrament* (1984), the last of his organ works, bringing his life's work back full circle to its beginning. He described the 1984 work as "a great act of faith in the Real Presence of Jesus Christ in the Blessed Sacrament."[23] In addition to its appeal for personal piety, the doctrine of transubstantiation had profound appeal for Messiaen on a more metaphysical level: it affirmed the penetration of the Eternal into the temporal, the capacity of the temporal to become the Eternal.[24]

But on a more personal level, the matter was less straightforward: for *The Celestial Banquet* was scored for organ during the latter part of the sum-

---

22. Messiaen, in Massin and Messiaen, *Olivier Messiaen*, 45; and in Simeone, *Bibliographical Catalogue*, 188.

23. Olivier Messiaen and Claude Samuel, *Music and Color: Conversations with Claude Samuel*, trans. E. Thomas Glasow (Portland, Ore.: Amadeus Press, 1994), 258; hereafter "Messiaen and Samuel (1994)"; in Simeone, *Bibliographical Catalogue*, 168. Translation altered.

24. In Catholic theology, this ontological capacity for human divinization is known by its scholastic name as *potentia oboedientia*: "Nature, as created, should always be seen as accompanied by a supernatural existential and as a *potentia oboedientia* ('obediential potency') for grace as God's communication of himself. Its created state can, moreover, be characterized not as a state of *natura pura*, but rather as a precondition for God's free action of self-communication becoming 'exterior.' . . . God's creation is an aspect of his power to give himself freely in grace and in the incarnation to the other aspect of himself." Karl Rahner, *Encyclopedia of Theology: The Concise Sacramentum Mundi* (New Delhi: Continuum, [1975] 2004), 326. One theologian puts Rahner's abstract formulation more simply: "For Rahner, human nature is nothing less than the ability to be God in the world!" Harvey D. Egan, "Theology and Spirituality," in *The Cambridge Companion to Karl Rahner*, ed. Declan Marmion and Mary E. Hines (Cambridge and New York: Cambridge University Press, 2005), 13-28, at 17.

mer of 1928 — that is, contemporaneous with the first anniversary of Cécile's death (August 26). As a work of mourning, Messiaen must have been inwardly conflicted about it. For although the scriptural quotation on the work's front cover boldly recalls Christ's assurance of an abiding beyond death, its wider textual source links that endurance with the physical act of consuming the Eucharist — something that Cécile had neither believed in nor practiced for many years. And in fact, a Catholic's sensibilities would immediately link this Gospel passage with funerals and memorials since it was the text appointed to be read at daily masses commemorating the dead: "Then Jesus said to them, Amen, amen, I say unto you, Except you eat the flesh of the Son of man, and drink His blood, you shall not have life in you. He that eateth My flesh, and drinketh My blood, hath everlasting life: and I will raise him up in the last day" (John 6:51-55).[25] Not insignificantly, Messiaen's epigraph quotes only from the verse that follows two lines after the passage appointed for the Mass, thereby excluding the negative ("you shall not have life in you") and stating only the positive: "He who eats my flesh and drinks my blood, abides in me and I in him" (John 6:57).[26]

Messiaen has left no indications of how, at age nineteen, he worked through these conflicts in his own mind; while he shared his father's deeply fervent Catholicism (and its insistence on the need for sacraments), his mother had passed away without receiving the last rites, let alone any sacramental practice for many years. In short: the Eucharist, a marker of Messiaen's own identity and inclusion within a religious communion that offered solace (at least in principle) during a period of bereavement and grief, simultaneously excluded his mother from that same communion. One might speculate that it was precisely this exclusion that would push Messiaen later

---

25. See "Masses and Burial Services for the Dead: The Common or Daily Mass for the Dead [Missa Quotidiana]," *Missal-En,* 1501-9, at 1505-6; cf. "Messes des Défunts. Messe Quotidienne pour les Défunts," *Missel-Fr,* 978-82, at 980. Perhaps even less consoling for Messiaen vis-à-vis his mother's unbelief would have been the Gospel passages appointed for use at the funeral mass on the day of burial (John 11:21-27) and for the mass offered on the anniversary of death (John 6:37-40); cf. *Missal-En,* 1520-21, 1533; and *Missel-Fr,* 990 *("Messe des Funérailles"),* 987; *("Messe pour le Jour Anniversaire des Défunts").*

26. A recent study argues that French belief in and devotion to the Catholic doctrine of purgatory (and, by extension, masses for the dead) waned during the 1920s. Faced with the fact of millions of youth killed in the First World War, the bereaved were reluctant to imagine those who had died glorious deaths *(morts glorieux)* for the fatherland spending time suffering in the flames of purgatory prior to entering celestial glory. See Guillaume Cuchet, *Le crépuscule du purgatoire* (Paris: Armand Colin, 2005).

on to broader and more inclusive notions of Catholicity in particular and religion in general.[27]

In any event, Messiaen explicitly designated *The Celestial Banquet* as his first opus. Primarily it conveys an experience of eternity and duration — abiding, remaining, perduring, and enduring — and the conviction that we can be rescued from the ravages of time. The piece's remarkably slow tempo would become a trademark of Messiaen's work, an attempt to represent imaginatively (insofar as this is possible) the timeless "duration" of eternity within time.[28] This is a singular advantage of the organ that Messiaen fully exploited in his life. A wind instrument, the sound flows steadily and without interruption as long as the key is depressed and air is supplied to the pipes. Igor Stravinsky regarded this as the organ's liability: "the monster never breathes."[29] But Messiaen took this potential vice and turned it into virtue, utilizing the organ's unending and invariant flow of sound to represent the intersection of temporality and eternity, the union of the creature with the Creator, a union whose foretaste *(praegustatum)* is experienced in consuming the Eucharist, the eschatological banquet already manifest here and now in time.

One might finally consider Messiaen's *Celestial Banquet* as a tone poem, a musical song without words, evoking his mother's last written lines — "What celestial life" *(Quelle céleste vie)* — from her unfinished "Saint Mary the Egyptian":

> Here my pure soul imitates the desert.
> Against this vast horizon that escapes towards the infinite
> I mold my thought and am beneath the blue sky
> A single expanse of both dream and fire;
> With an immense kiss I embrace all the azure

---

27. As noted above, Cécile would say: "Jesus Christ died for everyone, yet there are the elected and the condemned! I just cannot understand this." Pierre Messiaen, *Images* (Paris: Desclée de Brouwer, 1944), 154.

28. See Jan Christiaens, "Sounding Silence, Moving Stillness: Olivier Messiaen's *Le banquet céleste*," in *Silence, Music, Silent Music*, ed. Nicky Losseff and Jenny Doctor (Burlington, Vt.: Ashgate, 2007), 53-68; cf. Diane Luchese, "Olivier Messiaen's Slow Music: Glimpses of Eternity in Time" (Ph.D. diss., Northwestern University, 1998).

29. Stravinsky commented while speaking about his *Symphony of Psalms* (1930): "My first sound-image was of an all-male chorus and *orchestre d'harmonie*. I thought, for a moment, of the organ, but I dislike the organ's *legato sostenuto* and its blur of octaves, as well as the fact that the monster never breathes. The breathing of wind instruments is one of their primary attractions for me." Igor Stravinsky and Robert Craft, *Dialogues* (Berkeley: University of California Press, 1982), 46.

1927–1932: Budding Rhythmician, Surrealist Composer, Mystical Commentator

> Resting on me. Oh! what pure happiness
> I have enjoyed in these places! What celestial life [*Quelle céleste vie*]
> Has consoled my days!
>
> (Paris, 1927)[30]

It is unknown when Messiaen first performed *The Celestial Banquet*. A decade later, however, he would complain "that the label of 'mystic' — which was so kindly pinned to my back at the first performance of my *Banquet céleste* — does not correspond to the truth."[31] But this was the assessment of Messiaen with ten years of hindsight. Around 1929, far from minding the label "mystic," he seemed to encourage it.

1928–1929: *Préludes (Preludes for Piano)*

Messiaen's eight preludes for solo piano were composed either entirely in the summer of 1929 or else (more likely) during the summers of 1928 and 1929.[32] Both the music and the titles of the movements are impressionistic, imitating those of Debussy, whose own *Preludes* (1909-1913) include these evocative images:

> *The Wind in the Plain:* Lively
> *What the West Wind Has Seen*
> *"Sounds and Fragrances Swirl through the Evening Air":* Moderate
> *The Submerged Cathedral:* Profoundly calm
> *Dead Leaves:* Slow and melancholic
> *Egyptian Canopic Jar:* Very calm and sweetly sad[33]

Messiaen follows Debussy's impressionistic and symbolist lead even though he ventures into the 1920s' surrealism of Éluard:

---

30. Cécile Sauvage, "Sainte Marie l'Egyptienne" (1927), in Cécile Sauvage and Béatrice Marchal-Vincent, *L'Œuvre poétique de Cécile Sauvage (1883-1927)*, 2 vols. (Lille: Atelier National de Reproduction des Thèses, 1995), 2:272-74, at 274.
31. Messiaen, "Autour d'une Œuvre d'orgue," Fr 73-74, at 73; Eng 134-35.
32. Simeone, *Bibliographical Catalogue*, 6-7.
33. François Lesure and Roy Howat, "Debussy, Claude," in *Grove Music Online. Oxford Music Online,* http://www.oxfordmusiconline.com.proxy.bc.edu/subscriber/article/grove/music/07353. "Sounds and fragrances swirl through the evening air" is a line from Charles Baudelaire's poem "Evening Harmony" ("Harmonie du Soir"). A canopic jar was used by ancient Egyptians to inter the deceased's internal organs.

1. The Dove
2. Song of Ecstasy in a Sad Landscape
3. The Light Number [*Le nombre léger*]
4. Deceased Instants [*Instants défunts*]
5. The Impalpable Sounds of Dreaming
6. Bells of Anguish and Tears of Farewell
   [*Cloches d'angoisse et larmes d'adieu*]
7. Quiet Lament
8. A Reflection in the Wind[34]

The titles tell us much about Messiaen's intellectual formation at age twenty. The association of bells with "anguish" and "farewell tears" evokes Baudelaire and the traditional "funeral bell" *(cloche funèbre)*, tolled to let the village know that someone was in the process of dying. The organist at Notre-Dame of Paris, Louis Vierne, had just written his *Poems of Funeral Bells* (*Poème des cloches funèbres,* op. 39) in 1916.[35] In addition to the general association of the "Quiet Lament" with mourning, the *plainte* (lament) is more specifically a Russian folk song genre that attracted Messiaen.[36]

Most striking is Messiaen's embrace of surrealism, the most distinctive movement of the postwar 1920s. The crux of surrealist thought is the association of paradoxical images that normally can only be imagined together in the dream state. Pierre Reverdy had proclaimed in 1918, as the Great War was ending:

> The image is a pure creation of the mind.
>   It cannot be born from a comparison but from a juxtaposition of two more or less distant realities.
>   The more the relationship between the two juxtaposed realities is distant and true, the stronger the image will be — the greater its emotional power and poetic reality.[37]

---

34. Simeone, *Bibliographical Catalogue,* 7.

35. Louis Vierne dated the completion of "Le Glas" (i.e., "The Toll" of a funeral bell), the second of two *Poems of Funeral Bells,* as December 28, 1916. The manuscript for the other poem ("Bells and the Nightmare") was lost. Opus 39 now consists of just "The Toll." See Rollin Smith, *Louis Vierne: Organist of Notre-Dame Cathedral* (Hillsdale, N.Y.: Pendragon Press, 1999), 659; and Louis Vierne, "Le Glas," op. 39, in Vierne, *Complete Piano Works,* vol. 3 (Kassel: Bärenreiter, 2008).

36. Mily Alexeïewitch Balakirew, ed., *Recueil de chants populaires russes, notés et harmonisés par M. Balakirew,* trans. J. Sergennois (Leipzig: M. P. Bélaïeff, 1898).

37. Pierre Reverdy's remarks in his journal *Nord-Sud* (March 1918), quoted by André

1927–1932: Budding Rhythmician, Surrealist Composer, Mystical Commentator

Messiaen's titles juxtapose sadness and ecstasy, sound and touch, image and no image. The "sad landscape" is one where another has been lost; yet it is simultaneously a place of ecstasy, the union with another that is so absolute that one is literally taken out of oneself *(ek-stasis)*.[38]

In "The Impalpable Sounds of Dreaming," to be "impalpable" is to be "intangible," not perceptible to the touch; more generally, it means the incapacity of being perceived or grasped by the mind. In this piece, the intangible or imperceptible is "sound" — and even more, sound produced by "dreaming," an implicit reference to Breton's surrealism: "I believe in the future resolution of these two states, dream and reality, which are seemingly so contradictory, into a kind of absolute reality, a *surreality,* if one may so speak."[39] It is in dreaming, Breton theorized, following Freud, that we can express wishes that can be neither acknowledged nor fulfilled in our conscious waking state. As for the (invisible?) "Reflection in the Wind": like sound, wind is also impalpable in

---

Breton in his (first) *Manifesto of Surrealism* (1924), in Breton, *Manifestoes of Surrealism,* trans. Richard Seaver and Helen R. Lane (Ann Arbor: University of Michigan Press, [1969] 1972), 20; cf. Schloesser, *Jazz Age Catholicism,* 111. One wonders whether Pierre Messiaen didn't have an influence in Olivier's turn to surrealism. At the end of the Second World War, Pierre published a study of Gérard de Nerval, a writer André Breton in particular acknowledged as a strong influence on the surrealist movement. See Pierre Messiaen, *Christianisme et occultisme: Gérard de Nerval* (Paris: Morainville, 1945).

Compare Henri Bergson: "In this regard, the philosopher's sole aim should be to start up a certain effort which the utilitarian habits of mind of everyday life tend, in most men, to discourage. Now the image has at least the advantage of keeping us in the concrete. No image will replace the intuition of duration, but many different images, taken from quite different orders of things, will be able, through the convergence of their action, to direct the consciousness to the precise point where there is a certain intuition to seize on. *By choosing images as dissimilar as possible,* any one of them will be prevented from usurping the place of the intuition it is instructed to call forth, since it would then be driven out immediately by its rivals. By seeing that in spite of their differences in aspect they all demand of our mind the same kind of attention and, as it were, the same degree of tension, one will gradually accustom the consciousness to a particular and definitely determined disposition, precisely the one it will have to adopt in order to appear unveiled to itself." Bergson, "Introduction to Metaphysics" ("Introduction à la métaphysique") (1903), in *The Creative Mind,* trans. Mabelle L. Andison (New York: Philosophical Library, 1946), 187-237, at 195, emphasis added.

38. Perhaps he was prepared for surrealism by his childhood immersion in Shakespeare. For example: "THESEUS: Merry and tragical? tedious and brief? / That is hot ice, and wondrous strange snow! / How shall we find the concord of this discord?" William Shakespeare, *A Midsummer Night's Dream,* act 5, scene 1, lines 58-60; in *The Arden Shakespeare Complete Works,* ed. Richard Proudfoot, Ann Thompson, and David Scott Kastan, rev. ed. (London: Arden Shakespeare, 2011), 908.

39. Breton, *Manifestoes of Surrealism,* 14.

itself, insubstantial, invisible, incapable of reflection. Undoubtedly, Cécile had read young Messiaen poems from Christina Rossetti's book of nursery rhymes:

Who has seen the wind? / Neither I nor you.
But when the leaves hang trembling, / The wind is passing through.
Who has seen the wind? / Neither you nor I.
But when the trees bow down their heads, / The wind is passing by.[40]

It seems fitting that Messiaen should conclude his preludes with this juxtaposition of what could, in theory, be an enduring thing — a visual reflection — with what is essentially temporal and always in the process of coming into and passing out of existence — the wind — perceived only indirectly by inference (i.e., seeing its effects on trembling leaves and bowing branches).

The series begins and ends with air: the dove and the wind. The French love their doves, and Cécile Sauvage was no exception. In 1908, while pregnant with Olivier, she wrote in Avignon: "I have a golden-throated dove. It holds wisps of straw in its beak to carry back to its nest. As it rises, its flight makes the sound of a wheel [*un bruit de roue*] that flaps and whooshes. It has elongated eyes. Its male has a beautiful shimmering throat that moves like water."[41] A year later, writing the long poem "Melancholy" in Ambert-en-Livradois, Cécile used the dove to convey a darkly different tone:

Melancholy, O my dove
With tender eye, with grey feather,
You who are with me as daylight ends
At the pond made iridescent by the moon.[42]

When listening to Messiaen's "The Dove," one of the pieces most imitative of Debussy's impressionistic style, we can hear both sets of his mother's associations: the shimmering gold throat, the flapping and whooshing of wings; and the grey-feathered melancholy, tender companion alongside shimmering water beneath moonlight.

40. "Who Has Seen the Wind?" in Christina G. Rossetti, *Sing-Song: A Nursery Rhyme Book* (London and New York: Macmillan, 1893), 98.
41. From a fragment dated "Avignon, 1908," in Cécile Sauvage, *Œuvres de Cécile Sauvage,* ed. Jean Tenant (Paris: Mercure de France, 1929), 328; hereafter: Sauvage and Tenant, *Œuvres.* The *"bruit de roue"* may be a play on words: *roucouler* = to coo.
42. *Mélancolie,* in Sauvage and Tenant, *Œuvres,* 124; in Sauvage and Marchal-Vincent, *L'Œuvre poétique,* 2:113 (LXVI).

1927–1932: Budding Rhythmician, Surrealist Composer, Mystical Commentator

However, there is another likely source for the dove image: *The Music of the Incas* (1925) by Marguerite and Raoul d'Harcourt, introduced above in discussing Messiaen's *Sadness of a Great White Sky*.[43] The d'Harcourts' work was published in two volumes: the first volume was textual, devoted to a wide-ranging descriptive overview of instruments, feasts and dances, folklore, and numerous examples of folk songs (both poetical verse and musical melodies). The second volume was pictorial: a marvelous compilation of illustrations. The work identifies seven indigenous musical genres:

1. religious songs
2. funerary lamentations *(les lamentations funéraires)*
3. songs of love *(chants d'amour)*, most especially the *harawi*
4. songs of patriots and travelers
5. dances — both sung and instrumental
6. songs of farewell *(les chants d'adieux)*
7. pastorals marked by melancholy[44]

Messiaen's preludes, especially the "tears of farewell" *(larmes d'adieu)* and "quiet lament," suggest direct parallels.

---

43. Raoul d'Harcourt and M. d'Harcourt, *La Musique des Incas et ses survivances*, 2 vols. (Paris: Librairie Orientaliste Paul Geuthner, 1925). Marguerite Béclard d'Harcourt (1884-1964) studied composition at the Schola Cantorum. Her teachers included both Vincent d'Indy and Maurice Emmanuel; she received "an education that revealed the enormous resources of modality and which gave her an extensive knowledge of Gregorian chant, of ancient Greece and of folksong. After her marriage to the ethnologist Raoul d'Harcourt, she accompanied him on voyages to South America" — the result was this 1925 volume on the music of the Incas. See Anne Girardot's entry for d'Harcourt in *The Norton/Grove Dictionary of Women Composers*, ed. Julie Anne Sadie and Rhian Samuel (New York: Norton, 1995), 54.

Marguerite's musical publications included *Pasña pitači: Maiden's Dance Place; Peruvian Inca Melody for Flute and Piano* (New York: G. Ricordi, 1923) and *Mélodies populaires indiennes (Équateur, Pérou, Bolivie). Recueil de 55 mélodies harmonisées* (Milan: Ricordi et Cie, 1923). Scholarly writings include "La musique Indienne chez les anciens civilisés d'Amérique: Le folklore musical de la région andine: Équateur, Pérou, Bolivie," in *Encyclopédie de la musique et dictionnaire du Conservatoire*, ed. A. Lavignac and L. de La Laurencie, 11 vols. (Paris: C. Delagrave, 1913-1931): I/v (1922): 3353-71; and an article dedicated to Emmanuel three years before his death, "L'œuvre musical de Maurice Emmanuel," *Revue musicale* 152, no. 6 (1935): 22-33. See Barbara L. Kelly, "Béclard d'Harcourt, Marguerite," in *Grove Music Online. Oxford Music Online*, http://www.oxfordmusiconline.com.proxy.bc.edu/subscriber/article/grove/music/02494 (accessed January 24, 2011).

44. D'Harcourt and d'Harcourt, *La Musique des Incas*, 1:567. References to this work have been placed in the following text.

However, the most curious and peculiarly "Incan" of these genres is the *harawi*, a type of love song to which Messiaen would notably return later (*Harawi* [1945]). The oldest and most distinctive Peruvian type, the *harawi* is primarily dominated by its atmospheric sadness (1:172-75). In their deeply anthropological and historical study, the d'Harcourts explained the sadness that runs throughout the Peruvian genres (lament, farewell, melancholy) by observing that, even after the Spanish conquest and forced conversions to Christianity, "the pantheistic spirit remained intact among these beings in constant contact with the forces of nature, particularly brutal and violent in the high elevations of the Andean valleys. Certain manifestations of solar religion [sun worship] would seem to survive even to this day" (1:192).

For the natives, then, "man is not free; he directs [or is in control of = *dirige*] very little of his life!" This consciousness "weighs heavily on his destiny in its entirety." His determinism, write the d'Harcourts, "subsists in love. If one loves, or if one no longer loves, the responsibility lies not with a person's will but rather with an event, act, or coincidence." Even in the 1920s, "Love potions and practices of sorcery still maintain, of course, all their power today: 'Why, my dove, was I made to drink from the vase of the water of forgetting!' [love song no. 50]." Attributing ruptures of love relationships and departures of loved ones to nonhuman causes means that a lover can content oneself "with projecting responsibility for changes in feelings" back onto plants and other such objects. Conversely, "this resigned fatalism" is also found when the lover has run away and is now found in the arms of another, "not because jealousy isn't torturing his heart, but rather, more logically than in many Europeans, the Indian realizes that to eliminate the happy successor will not restore him any of his lost happiness" (1:192-93).

The *harawi* genre of the love song has this element of sadness and melancholy because it specifically sings about love that has ended, either through a relationship's rupture or, more grievously, through death. In the *harawi*, the dove appears frequently as a symbol of the departed beloved. For example:

My dove has left / For its native land,
Ah! my dove, I don't know, I don't know ...
My dove has flown away, / I myself, miserable, I remain weeping.
Ah! my dove, I don't know, I don't know ... (song no. 32, 1:278-82, at 281)

In another example, the dove is not the one that has flown away but the one left behind. The words begin with "onomatopoeia imitating the soft cooing of the dove, then, through five couplets, the poet questions the bird about the causes of its eternal sadness, indifferent to the changing spectacle of nature."

1927–1932: Budding Rhythmician, Surrealist Composer, Mystical Commentator

> Toungou, toungou, toungou, / Toungou, soft dove,
> Toungou, what do you have? / Toungou, do you suffer greatly?
> Tell me about your grief.

The final verses of this song make one wonder whether Messiaen thought about his mother's seemingly "lost" book of love poems:

> Why when everything / Is resting
> In your nest, do you, / With weeping eyes,
> Softly sing?
> Is it the beautiful tenderness / Of a mother with loving heart,
> Or is it rather the prolonged moans, / Of a forgotten lover,
> That your lament sadly [*ta plainte tristement*] expresses?
> (song no. 39, 1:292-93)

In other songs the subject is "the loss of a beloved dove and the sorrow of the one who searches for it": "I raised up a dove, / With all my heart I loved it" (song no. 47, 1:303-4); "I lost my dove, / How far can it have gone?" (song no. 49, 1:306-7); "I lost my pet dove / All of a sudden" (song no. 63, 1:323-26).

Yet another example laments experiences that cannot now be unlearned:

> Why, dove, / Did you instruct me?
> Did you make me drink / From the vase of the water of forgetting?
> Did you make me sleep / In your arms? (song no. 50, 1:307-8)

In a song that is meant to be "sung by a young man," the dove is creatively transformed into the singer himself:

> I would like to have new love, / But I do not have it, from fear of
>   suffering,
> I am a young dove learning to fly, / When night comes, I put myself
>   to sleep crying!   (song no. 52, 1:310-11)

The most piercing song for Messiaen might have been one that is not merely about abandonment but about its irreversible finality.

> Two doves in love / Are in pain, are sad, sighing, weeping,
> They are covered in snow / At the foot of a hollow tree trunk.

1927–1931: First Works as Grief Works

One of them, abandoned, / Laments sorrowfully.
For the first time, / It feels alone in the world.

Believing its dove dead, / It laments bitterly,
Expressing its sadness / In this plaintive song. (song no. 64, 1:326-28)

We cannot know whether Messiaen had already encountered this volume of Incan music by 1925 *(Sadness of a Great White Sky)*, or whether he read it three years later. The positioning of "The Dove" as the first of his eight *Preludes*, likely written in the summer of 1928 (along with *The Celestial Banquet*), is highly suggestive. He seems already to have been aware of the dove's privileged position: the symbol of lost love in a fatalistic universe.

Finally, depending on when they were composed, two pieces of *Preludes* ("The Light Number" and "Deceased Instants") indicate that Messiaen had also been introduced to Henri Bergson's metaphysical thought by the summer of 1928 or 1929. He had most likely discovered Bergson in Armand Cuvillier's philosophy manual (first edition 1927), a textbook cited by Messiaen and intended for use in lycées as students prepared to enter the *grandes Écoles*.[45]

---

45. Armand Cuvillier, *Manuel de philosophie, Tome II: Logique, Morale, Philosophie générale* (Paris: Librairie Armand Colin, 1927). The second revised and corrected edition appeared in 1928. In 1931, volume 1 appeared: *Introduction générale: Psychologie*. In 1938, a third volume was published: *Appendices Psychologie expérimentale. Science du langage. Esthétique Logique formelle*. Each volume went through numerous editions over the years until the final printing in 1951. Cuvillier's specialty was philosophical psychology, and he was deeply informed by Bergson's thought. His massive first volume *(Psychologie)* of the *Manuel de philosophie* can be seen in nascent form in Cuvillier, *ABC de psychologie* (Paris: Librairie Delagrave, 1923).

Cuvillier's imposing work was a response to the government's "Instructions Relative to the Programs of Secondary Education in the Lycées and Collèges" (September 2, 1925). They included the directive that philosophical problems should appear to students "not as the artificial product of the tradition particular to the world of philosophers, not as the result of the collision of certain 'categories' or of certain prejudices decorated with some name of a system, *but as issues of reality itself,* moral or physical, and of the obscurities they present to someone wanting to make them intelligible." Cuvillier accordingly counseled his young readers to read in light of their own experience: "this is why you will find, in the present work, at the beginning of each chapter, observations and appeals to experience." Cuvillier, *Manuel de philosophie. Tome I: Introduction générale. Psychologie.* (Paris: Librairie Armand Colin, 1931), vii. This postwar approach to philosophy reflected the influence of the majority of historians of philosophy, including Henri Bergson, Étienne Gilson, and the late Victor Delbos, for whom "past philosophical texts were still relevant to the modern reader, even if they had been written centuries earlier; in this respect, they were different from

1927–1932: Budding Rhythmician, Surrealist Composer, Mystical Commentator

Although Messiaen might have encountered Cuvillier's volume in his Conservatory curriculum, a more likely source would have been his father, Pierre, a teacher at the Lycée Charlemagne. Just as Pierre had introduced Messiaen to Maritain's *Art and Scholasticism* in the winter of 1927-1928, he might also have given him Cuvillier for a broad overview of philosophy in the 1920s.[46]

In a chapter devoted to "space and time," under the rubric "The New Realism," Cuvillier provides a remarkably succinct introduction to Bergson's philosophy of duration.[47] The first and most fundamental distinction made is between the "duration" — the "concrete duration," the "lived duration" *(la durée concrète, la durée vécue)* — and "abstract and uniform time" *(le temps abstrait et uniforme),* that is, time measured by a clock.[48] Having laid out these two terms, Cuvillier immediately quotes a line from Bergson's *Essay on the Immediate Data of Consciousness* (1889), one Messiaen himself will quote later in his own *Treatise*.[49] "Pure duration might well be nothing but a succession of qualitative changes, which melt into and permeate one another, without precise outlines, without any tendency to externalize themselves in relation to one another, *without any affiliation with number:* it would be pure heterogeneity."[50] Bergson's distinction between "number" (or clock or "mathematical time") and "duration" is what struck the young Messiaen — it appears in the piece "The Light Number" in *Preludes* and is about to be used more explicitly in *The Death of Number*. For Bergson, the concrete lived "duration" cannot be quantified or measured. It is the internal experience of a succession of quali-

---

scientific texts, which were superseded by more recent ones." Delbos had been a member and then president of the Société d'Études pour les Questions d'Enseignement Secondaire (Society of Studies for Questions of Secondary Education). Christina Chimisso, *Writing the History of the Mind: Philosophy and Sciences in France, 1900 to 1960s* (Burlington, Vt.: Ashgate, 2008), 5, 13.

46. Massin and Messiaen, *Olivier Messiaen*, 178.

47. Cuvillier, *Manuel de philosophie, Tome II* (1927), 557-65; for preceding discussion of Bergsonian intuitionism, see 539-44; cf. 22, 44, 188, 507, 510, 532, 577, 585-86, 592-94, 596, 618-620, 653. For historical background, see Pierre A. Buser, *Le temps, instant et durée: de la philosophie aux neurosciences* (Paris: Odile Jacob, 2011), especially 57-88.

48. Cuvillier, *Manuel de philosophie, Tome II* (1927), 557.

49. Henri Bergson, *Essai sur les données immédiates de la conscience* [1889], 36th ed. (Paris: Félix Alcan, 1938); Bergson, *Time and Free Will: An Essay on the Immediate Data of Consciousness*, trans. F. L. Pogson (New York: Macmillan, [1910] 1959).

50. Bergson, *Essai sur les données immédiates*, 79; Bergson, *Time and Free Will*, 104; quoted in Cuvillier, *Manuel de philosophie, Tome II* (1927), 557; quoted and slightly altered in Messiaen, "Philosophie de la durée: Durée vécue, temps structuré," in *Traité de rythme, de couleur, et d'ornithologie (1949-1992) en sept tomes*, 8 vols. (Paris: Alphonse Leduc, 1994-2002), 1:9-10. Emphasis added. Compare Salvador Dali's surrealist "melting" clocks.

tative changes that cannot be interrupted until the integral organic event has achieved its completion. Think of a melody: it has no existence if it is dissected into parts. Similarly, although a duration takes "time" to unfold, it cannot be cut up and still remain a melodic whole.

By contrast, as Cuvillier observes, space is mathematical. Consider a Cartesian coordinate system: it allows for the abstract measurement by numbers of any concrete motion whatsoever. Similarly, measured time is "clock time": it is not based on internal subjective experience of a succession of qualitatively distinct (heterogenous) states but rather on the steady uniform (homogenous) swing of the pendulum.[51] Each second measured out by the pendulum's swing is like every other second; every minute like every other; every hour like every hour; every year like every year. Although this may be true of clock time or mathematical time, Bergson maintained, it is not true of the concrete lived duration experienced by a human being. Some hours fly by while others drag on. One year is felt as glorious while another as an *annus horribilis*. Thanks in part to the image of the pendulum, Bergson calls clock time "spatialized" time: we lay time out and visualize it in space (as when we look at a day calendar divided up into fifteen-minute segments) so that we can measure it with numbers. But this practicality should not mislead us; for although spatializing time might be necessary pragmatically to arrange our everyday lives, it is not how we actually experience time.

Cuvillier's Bergsonian account of measured time as duration's "death" *(la durée morte)* and its dissection into homogenous "instants" *(morcelée en instants)* must have impacted Messiaen, not only as a deeply philosophical musician but more particularly as a recently bereaved twenty-year-old.

It is precisely because [space] is a principle of dividing up [*morcellement*], of division in the simultaneity, that space makes measurement possible: *space is the principle of number,* and not the inverse; space is the fundamental concept of mathematics. For, in order to count, it is necessary to "retain the successive images" and to "juxtapose them with each of the new units" that one has an idea of. Thus, "every clear idea of number [*toute idée claire du nombre*] implies a vision in space." The very idea of the number two is already "that of two different positions in space." — It follows that homogenous and measured time, *mathematical time, is nothing other than*

---

51. Compare the distinction between clock time (time *measurement*) and "existential time" in Joan Stambaugh, "Existential Time in Kierkegaard and Heidegger," in *Religion and Time,* ed. Anindita Niyogi Balslev and J. N. Mohanty (New York: Brill, 1993), 46-60.

1927–1932: Budding Rhythmician, Surrealist Composer, Mystical Commentator

the deceased duration [*la durée morte*], laid out in space and parceled out into instants [*morcelée en instants*], juxtaposed with one another on the model of space.[52]

Bergson (via Cuvillier) offered Messiaen a way of reimagining time and existence. The "light number" or even the "death of number" — the death of clock time or measured time — is not to be mourned. For what remains is the duration. Put otherwise: what remains is the internal life of the spirit, not subject to mathematical time, measurement, or number. Cuvillier summarizes the philosophy of duration: "Thus we are in the presence of a fundamental opposition between pure duration and space. *The duration is what is given to intuition: succession without exteriority, it is essentially qualitative, and it characterizes the world of spiritual life* [*le monde de la vie spirituelle*]. *Space is a construction of the intelligence: exteriority without succession, it is the underpinning of quantity and measurement; it belongs to the world of matter* [*au monde de la matière*]."[53] These few pages in Cuvillier seem to have affected Messiaen as he thought through time and rhythm in the midst of grieving his mother's passing. His prelude entitled "Deceased Instants" ("Instants défunts") plays on Cuvillier's *la durée morte . . . morcelées en instants* ("deceased duration parceled out into instants"). At the same time, Messiaen smiles sadly; *instants défunts* is a close homonym for *infante défunte*, evoking Maurice Ravel's *Pavane pour une infante défunte* (1899/1910), to which the composer referred as his "Pavane for a Dead Princess."

1930: *Diptyque (Diptych) for Organ: An Essay on Terrestrial Life and Blessed Eternity*

In the spring of 1930, Messiaen triumphantly completed his formal studies at the Conservatory by winning the first prize in composition.[54] His success was doubled by having secured the May publication of his *Diptych for Organ: An Essay on Terrestrial Life and Blessed Eternity*. It was his earliest work in print (quickly followed by the appearance of *Preludes* in June and *Three Melodies* in October).[55]

---

52. Cuvillier, *Manuel de philosophie, Tome II* (1927), 558, quoting phrases from Bergson, *Essai sur les données immédiates*, 59-68, emphasis added.
53. Cuvillier, *Manuel de philosophie, Tome II* (1927), 558, emphasis in original.
54. Hill and Simeone, *Messiaen*, 17.
55. Simeone, *Bibliographical Catalogue*, 8-9; Jon Gillock, *Performing Messiaen's Organ*

1927–1931: First Works as Grief Works

Forty years ago, a scholar called *Diptych* "the black sheep of the organ works in that it is the only [one] which does not bear the imprint of Messiaen's distinctive personality." Judging it "a strange retreat into academicism" whose "tonal scheme," "academic application of augmentation," and "quasi-canonic entries" only made matters worse, he judged it "a pity" that Messiaen wrote it for and dedicated it to his "dear Masters Paul Dukas and Marcel Dupré."[56]

Four decades later, *Diptych* can be revisited with fresh eyes, most particularly through the lens of Messiaen's late-adolescent interest in time and eternity, especially within the optic of mourning. True to its title, the composition forms a "diptych" by being divided into two panels. The first is a fast-moving toccata that imitates Dupré's style, manifest especially in his *Three Preludes and Fugues* (1920), a virtuosity extending that of his own teacher, Charles-Marie Widor. In Messiaen's first panel ("Terrestrial Life"), rapid dissonant chords provide a kind of perpetual motion machine while a simple legato line played in either the left hand or the pedals sings out a mournful modal melody. The diptych's second panel ("Blessed Eternity") can seem initially deceiving. Since it provides an absolute contrast to the first in terms of tempo — it is so slow as to seem that nothing happens — it can sound completely unrelated to the first. And yet, closer listening reveals that the melodies are identical: the mournful melody in the first movement, somewhat disguised because of the Dupré-like velocity, is stated and then developed in the extremely slow melody in the second movement — slow to the point of near stasis. More to the Bergsonian point: this is near timelessness; the death of number; pure "duration."

As in *The Celestial Banquet,* then, the relationship between terrestrial temporality and celestial eternity is the issue at stake. In terms of measured clock time, the contrast between the frenetic anxiety of "terrestrial life" and the peaceful stasis of "blessed eternity" could not be more explicit. And yet, since the near-static melody in the second "celestial" movement restates the anxious melody of the first "terrestrial" movement in a radically altered context, Messiaen plays with these notions and with his listeners. The two movements are not, in his hands, as opposed to one another as it might seem. Messiaen's notes for the first performance in February 1930 make his intention explicit: "The first part of this work expresses *the anguish and useless torment of life.* It is a prelude in C minor containing four statements of the same theme, separated

---

Music: 66 Masterclasses (Bloomington: Indiana University Press, 2010), 22-31; Olivier Latry and Loïc Mallié, *L'œuvre d'orgue d'Olivier Messiaen. Œuvres d'avant-guerre* (Stuttgart: Carus, 2008), 77-87.

56. Stuart Waumsley, *The Organ Music of Olivier Messiaen* (Paris: Alphonse Leduc, 1968), 25. For dedication see Simeone, *Bibliographical Catalogue,* 8-9.

by short developments. The second part takes up the theme of the first and transforms it. An Adagio in C major, based on a single ascending phrase, it expresses the peace and charity of Christian paradise."[57] *Diptych* is yet another in service of the work of mourning — an attempt to make peace with "the anguish and useless torment of life" as well as the problem of time and eternity.

It is also yet another experiment with Bergsonian thought as channeled through Cuvillier. A corollary of the emphasis on the concrete lived duration's "heterogenous" and "qualitative" character (as opposed to clock time's "homogenous" and hence "quantitative" aspects) is that duration is experienced in emotionally diverse ways. Cuvillier observes that duration is simply "the flow, sometimes slow, sometimes rapid, of our internal states of consciousness" *(l'écoulement, tantôt lent, tantôt rapide, de nos états de conscience en nous).*[58] When Cuvillier greatly expanded his analysis of "The Psychical Life according to M. Bergson" in the next volume of his philosophy manual (1931), he devoted considerable attention to this key element of the "duration" — namely, that differences in *intensity* experienced in internal states lead to differences in *quality,* not quantity. In other words, time as measured by a clock is different quantitatively; but inwardly experienced duration differs qualitatively and is thus always relative: we pass from disgust to dread, from dread to sympathy, from sympathy to humility. Intensity is felt as a certain quality, nuance, or "color."[59]

Twenty years later, in his completely revised textbook for lycée students, Cuvillier formulated a principle summarizing this awareness of qualitative relativity in experiences.[60] Messiaen quoted it at the very beginning of his multivolume theoretical *Treatise.* These two laws, writes Messiaen, "perfectly summarize lived duration":

57. Messiaen, in Hill and Simeone, *Messiaen,* 26, emphasis added.
58. Cuvillier, *Manuel de philosophie, Tome II* (1927), 557.
59. Cuvillier, "La vie psychique d'après M. Bergson," in *Manuel de philosophie, Tome I* (1931), 40-48, at 46.
60. The last edition of *Manuel de philosophie* (1951) was succeeded by Cuvillier's new textbook, *Précis de philosophie,* 2 vols. (Paris: Armand Colin, 1953). Like its predecessor, the work's first volume was dedicated to psychology: *Psychologie, psychologie sociale et esthétique.* The second volume was given to *Logique et philosophie des sciences, morale, philosophie générale.* This work also went through several editions until its final printing in 1962. After the new national norms governing education were published in 1960 *(l'arrêté du 18 juillet 1960),* Cuvillier published yet a third textbook conforming to the new regulations entitled *Nouveau précis de philosophie,* 2 vols. (Paris: Armand Colin, 1963). The first volume was now entitled simply *La Connaissance (Knowledge)* and the second *L'Action (Action).* The fifth and final edition was published in 1968, the year that student revolts led to educational reforms.

a) *Feeling of the present duration.* Law: in the present, the more that time is filled with events, the more it will appear short — the more that it is empty of events, the more it will appear long.
b) *Retrospective appreciation of time passed.* Inverse law of the preceding: in the past, the more that time was filled with events, the more it will appear long now — the more it was empty of events, the more it will now appear short.[61]

Put simply, time is relative. One experiencing events interiorly senses them differently than one observing or measuring the "same" events against an external standard from the outside. In the first case, while we are "in the present" and experiencing joy, work, or anything else that occupies us and captures our attention, we feel an increase in tempo — "Time flies when you're having fun." Conversely, the experience of waiting and inaction — *Waiting for Godot* — opens up a void that slows down the tempo.

In the second case, looking back at a duration that is now past, the opposite holds true. The remembrance of an event that no longer has any interest for us now, even if it took place over a long "time" measured in clock hours, will seem short to us in retrospect — short because in hindsight it was insignificant. Conversely, writes Messiaen, a period of life that was filled with "events of all orders (physiological and psychological work, affective shocks, esthetic shocks, actions that were accomplished or avoided)" will seem in retrospect "long and even very long if the events were very numerous, and its tempo expands or contracts in proportion to the number of remembrances it has left in us."[62]

The score of *Diptych* offers a visual analogue to Messiaen's observed laws. When considered from the perspective of the "first law" (the experienced feeling of the present duration), the first movement, filled with events, seems to pass quickly — the time is "short." Conversely, the second movement, "empty of events," passes slowly — the time is "long." However, when considered from the perspective of the "second law" (retrospective appreciation of time passed, that is, from a vantage point "external" to the experience and in terms of "objective" measurement), the first movement seems to be "long" in appearance: the activity requires 7⅔ pages (120 measures) of printed score for its notation. By comparison, the second, slow movement is remarkably "short"

---

61. Messiaen, *Traité*, 1:10, 23; summarizing Cuvillier, *Nouveau précis de philosophie. Tome I: La connaissance* (1963), 224-26.
62. Messiaen, *Traité*, 1:10.

1927–1932: Budding Rhythmician, Surrealist Composer, Mystical Commentator

in appearance, requiring a mere 1⅓ pages of score (33 measures) — it is only one-eighth as "long" as the first.[63]

Diptych is also Messiaen's first musical application of André Breton's surrealist theory, not merely in the texts of titles (as in *Preludes* above), but also in juxtapositions of musical elements such as rhythm, tempo, and dynamics. Breton intended the juxtaposition of seemingly contradictory images to produce an imaginative explosion (as in a dream), transcending the limitations of the waking state over which the law of noncontradiction rules. In *Manifesto of Surrealism* (1924), Breton complains: "We are still living under the reign of logic." Regarding the waking state: "I have no choice but to consider it a phenomenon of interference."[64]

Five years later, in *Second Manifesto of Surrealism* (published in 1930, the same year as Messiaen's *Diptych*), Breton clarifies his aims.[65] The opening lines declare: "Everything tends to make us believe that there exists a certain point of the mind at which life and death, the real and the imagined, past and future, the communicable and the incommunicable, high and low, cease to be perceived as contradictions. Now, search as one may one will never find any other motivating force in the activities of the Surrealists than the hope of finding and fixing this point."[66] *Diptych* performs Breton's theory: to "find and fix" that "certain point of the mind" at which opposites were no longer perceived to be contradictions. *Diptych* gives the listener an experience of overcoming the oppositions between terrestrial and celestial, neck-breaking speed juxtaposed with glacial stasis, anxiety with absolute peace. Its two panels represent the same theme considered differently from "a certain point of the mind."

Rather than being a "black sheep" in Messiaen's musical progeny, *Diptych* — his first published work — seems instead to introduce his audience to the juxtaposition of apparent opposites, one of his lifelong signatures. As his student Pierre Boulez once said, Messiaen "does not compose; he juxta-

---

63. In June 1956, Messiaen recorded himself playing his own complete organ works. In his recording of *Diptych,* the first section clocks in at about 5:15 minutes; the second at about 9:15 minutes. In Olivier Latry's recent performance, the first section clocks in at about 5:10, approximately the same duration as Messiaen's. However, it seems that Messiaen's performance is unbearably slow for Latry: he plays the second section in about 6:00, that is, in two-thirds the time of Messiaen's recording. See Messiaen, *Oeuvres complètes pour orgue: interprétées par l'auteur* ([London]: Ducretet-Thomson, 1957); digitized and reprinted as *Messiaen par lui-même: œuvres pour orgue* ([France]: EMI France, 1992); and Messiaen and Latry, *Complete Organ Works* (Hamburg: Deutsche Grammophon, 2002).

64. Breton, *Manifestoes of Surrealism,* 12.

65. André Breton, *Second manifeste du surréalisme* (Paris: Éditions Kra, 1930).

66. Breton, *Manifestoes of Surrealism,* 123-24.

poses."[67] This trademark can be frustrating for a newcomer to Messiaen's music: one moment the listener is luxuriating in the middle of a beautiful adagio and then, suddenly without preparation, transition, or warning, a frenetic and crashing barrage erupts, assaults, and terrifies. A little while later, absolute serenity returns. If we are used to musical works being self-enclosed — a fast movement that is loud; a slow movement that is soft — Messiaen's method of constantly juxtaposing the two side by side can be initially unnerving and perhaps irritating. Enjoying Messiaen demands an appreciation for extreme contrasts. They are two aspects of reality perceived from Breton's surrealist "certain point of the mind." In *Diptych,* terrestrial and celestial are no longer perceived as contradictions.

1930: *Trois Mélodies (Three Melodies)*

Three Melodies was written in Paris in 1930 and published in October that year, following closely on the eight *Preludes* for piano (issued in June) and *Diptych* for organ (appearing in May), all three from the publisher Durand & Cie.[68] (Although written earlier than these pieces, *The Celestial Banquet* was not published until late 1934.) It made a superb launch for the twenty-one-year-old as the variety demonstrated his versatile fluency in writing for voice, piano, and organ.

Like *Preludes* and *Diptych, Three Melodies* is a work of grief; indeed, among the three 1930 publications, it provides the clearest reference to Messiaen's mother. *Three Melodies* consists of three songs:

1. "Why?"
2. "The Smile"
3. "The Lost Fiancée"

The words to the first and third were written by Messiaen himself while the middle was set to a brief poem by his mother. The distinction is made subtly in Messiaen's indications heading up each song: in the first and third, the reference reads, "Words and Music by Olivier Messiaen." For the second, "Poem by Cécile Sauvage" is at the top left while "Music by Olivier Messiaen" is at

---

67. Pierre Boulez, *Notes on Apprenticeship,* trans. Herbert Weinstock (New York: Knopf, 1968), 64; originally *Relevés d'apprenti* (Paris: Éditions du Seuil, 1966).
68. Simeone, *Bibliographical Catalogue,* 10-11. Lyrics following in Olivier Messiaen, *Complete Edition,* 32 CDs (Germany: Deutsche Grammophon, 2008), 302-3.

the top right. The work, a triptych, can be heard as a dialogue between Cécile and Olivier.

The first movement elaborates a simple plaint: "Why?" Why do the birds of the air, the reflections in the water, the clouds in the sky, the leaves of autumn, the roses of summer, and the songs of spring "no longer have any charm for me"? This is nature poetry of the sort his mother wrote in her youth; it is about terrestrial time as it names the seasons. The singer is melancholic as the world has been drained of all appeal. The piece ends with six insistent cries: "Why? Why, Ah! Why? Why? Why? Why?"

In response comes "The Smile,"[69] a short, extremely slow piece in which the soprano sings the words of Cécile Sauvage with chant-like simplicity and tender expression:

> A certain word murmured / By you is a kiss
> Intimate and prolonged / Like a kiss on the soul.
> My mouth wants to smile / And my smile trembles.

"The Lost Fiancée," the third and final song, identifies "The Smile" as the words of a fiancée who has gone away. The song is itself a diptych juxtaposing two opposed moods. In the first section, a quick and lively movement evoking Debussy's impressionism, the bereft equates the lost fiancée with all the joys that had lost their charm in the song "Why?": the gentle fiancée, the angel of goodness, a sunny afternoon, the wind rushing through flowers, a smile as pure as a child's heart, a large lily white like a wing, very high in a golden cup!

This collage makes little sense as it imitates surrealist verse. All these images are prefixed by the simple "It is" *(C'est);* they are contrasts and opposites swirling together in a single montage, a fluid dream state. The "smile" refers back to "The Smile," here no longer erotic but rather childlike in its "purity"; the purity is immediately linked to the "large lily," the standard symbol in Renaissance depictions of the annunciation (in which the angel Gabriel announces to Mary — the fiancée of Joseph — that she, even in her virginity, will conceive a child, and not by means of the man to whom she is betrothed); the pure lily is then glossed as being "white like a wing" (ambiguously the wing of an angel or perhaps a dove), elevated "very high up" in a golden cup like the Holy Grail of medieval legend.

---

69. Much later in life Messiaen will compose *Un Sourire (A Smile)* (1989) for orchestra to celebrate the bicentenary of Mozart's death. It was published posthumously in 1994. Simeone, *Bibliographical Catalogue,* 176-77.

1927–1931: First Works as Grief Works

Here the frantically paced first panel of the diptych suddenly stops and passes over immediately into the second, a slow quiet prayer. We now see that the lover is not merely bereft; he is also bereaved. The fiancée is not lost but rather deceased.

> O Jesus, / bless her! Her!
> Grant her your powerful grace!
> That she might know neither suffering nor tears!
> Grant her rest, Jesus [*donnez-lui le repos*].

In this newly revealed context, the final image of the diptych's first wing — the pure white and gold — evokes the elevation of the host and chalice at Mass, the representation of Christ's sacrifice that, in Catholic theology, atones for sin and releases souls from their sufferings in purgatory. This resets the scene as a Requiem Mass in which the final lines of the *Dies Irae* sequence read:

> Mournful day that day of tears,
> When from dust shall man arise
> Stained with guilt his judgment know
> Mercy, Lord, in mercy spare him.
>
> Sweet Lord Jesus,
> grant them rest. Amen.

This last couplet occupies a special place in French Romantic music as Gabriel Fauré separated it out and concluded his *Requiem* (1890) with what has become perhaps its most beloved movement: *Pie Jesu Domine, / dona eis requiem. Amen.*[70]

Messiaen's final verses are a close paraphrase of *Pie Jesu;* they also include a softer version of *Dies Irae*'s final day of "tears" *(lacrimosa dies illa)* and being "spared" ("that she might not know": *qu'elle ignore*). Although *Dies Irae* is both bleak and terrifying, there are moments of tenderness, and one in particular might have touched Messiaen: the first line of the thirteenth stanza reads *Qui Mariam absolvisti* — "You who absolved Mary [Magdalene]," that is, she whom tradition had identified with the nameless woman caught in adultery

---

70. *Dies Irae,* in *Missal-En,* 1505, translation altered. Gabriel Fauré was director of the Paris Conservatory when Messiaen first arrived in 1919; deafness forced him to retire in 1920. Fauré's *Requiem* was played at his own state funeral in the Église de la Madeleine in November 1924. Did the almost sixteen-year-old Messiaen attend?

1927-1932: Budding Rhythmician, Surrealist Composer, Mystical Commentator

and about to be stoned before Jesus' intervening rescue. Thanks in part to the legendary church named after her (the Madeleine — where, incidentally, Fauré was organist until his death in 1924), Mary Magdalene has a firm place in the Parisian imaginary.

Three Melodies expresses an important aspect of Messiaen's piety and theology: the priority of grace and overriding importance of predestination. A traditionally "Protestant" emphasis on "grace" and a corollary de-emphasis (or negation altogether) of the importance of "works" are perhaps not entirely foreign to French Catholicism, given the importance of Jansenism in France. In fact, the popular spiritual writer Dom Marmion also emphasized predestination. But Messiaen's embrace of the overriding priority of grace is perhaps more deeply rooted in his mother's death. If Catholic "works" (including an active sacramental life) are necessary for salvation, Cécile Sauvage is lost. Hence Messiaen's heart-wrenching appeal: "Grant her your powerful grace! [*Donnez-lui votre Grâce puissante!*]." His faith and trust must be placed in the ability of God's grace to cancel any debt incurred by human will.

Three Melodies can seem both simplistic and even nonsensical at first glance. However, it is a carefully considered work and in some sense functions as a small requiem prayer. In this sense it both looks back to *The Celestial Banquet* and looks ahead to *The Forgotten Offerings*.

1930: *Les Offrandes oubliées (The Forgotten Offerings)*

Having successfully shepherded his first three works through publication, Messiaen spent the summer of 1930 composing at his father's sisters' farm in Fuligny. In a letter to Charles Tournemire of August 30, Messiaen wrote that he had "just finished the music for a symphonic poem."[71] This was *The Forgotten Offerings*, subtitled a "Symphonic Meditation for Orchestra." Premiered at the Théâtre des Champs-Élysées the following February, it would be Messiaen's first publicly performed and reviewed orchestral work.[72]

---

71. Messiaen to Tournemire, August 30, 1930, in Brigitte de Leersnyder, ed., *Charles Tournemire (1870-1939), Cahiers et Mémoires de l'Orgue* 41 (Paris: Les Amis de l'Orgue, 1989), 80; cf. Stephen Schloesser, "The Charm of Impossibilities: Mystic Surrealism as Contemplative Voluptuousness," in *Messiaen the Theologian*, 167. Tournemire eventually wrote a review of the second performance (December 6, 1931) of *The Forgotten Offerings*, published in *Le Courrier musical* 32, no. 20 (December 15, 1931): 594; reprinted in Simeone, *Bibliographical Catalogue*, 208.

72. Simeone, *Bibliographical Catalogue*, 12-15.

The Forgotten Offerings is a triptych, a form conducive to Messiaen's juxtapositions of extreme contrasts. The first movement is slow and meditative; the second movement, both frantic and violent, opens with an unprepared-for terrifying crash; the third returns to the initial meditative ambience, now much slower, approaching the stasis of eternity. Messiaen's preface poetically explains the significance of each:

I. Cross
Arms extended, sad unto death,
on the tree of the Cross you poured out your blood.
You love us, sweet Jesus, we had forgotten that.

II. Sin
Driven by madness and the serpent's tongue,
in a panting, frantic, relentless race,
we descended into sin as if into a tomb.

III. Eucharist
Behold the pure table, the fountain of charity,
the banquet of the poor, behold adorable Mercy offering
the bread of Life and of Love.
You love us, sweet Jesus, we had forgotten that.[73]

The influence of Cécile's final work (*To Love after Death* [1925]) seems to reappear here five years later. The angelic chorus counsels: "Human beings, remember... The planet, having forgotten...."[74]

Messiaen's cryptic title reverses expectations. The forgotten offerings are not those made by human beings; rather, they are the "offerings" extended by God as signs of love — it is God's self-offering that has been forgotten by human beings. The sign of this love is the Eucharist — quite literally, it is the memorial *(anamnesis)* created to prevent forgetting *(amnesia)* — again, a devotion much in Messiaen's purview these first years of composition. However, again keeping in mind the conundrum posed by his nonpracticing mother, Messiaen does not view the Eucharist as a sign of exclusion or a requirement

---

73. Simeone, *Bibliographical Catalogue*, 15; English translation in Christopher Dingle, *The Life of Messiaen* (Cambridge and New York: Cambridge University Press, 2007), 25-26.

74. Sauvage, *Aimer après la mort,* in Sauvage and Marchal-Vincent, *L'Œuvre poétique,* 2:216.

1927–1932: Budding Rhythmician, Surrealist Composer, Mystical Commentator

of redemption (through "works"). Rather, as in *Three Melodies*, the priority of grace and the extension of "adorable Mercy" are Messiaen's chief concerns. Indeed, perhaps this work is in reparation for what he himself had forgotten. His eye is redirected back to what is important: not to humanity but rather to God's grace, not to temporality but to eternity.

Since time and eternity are a central concern, the idiosyncratic nomenclature that Messiaen invented for this work is intriguing. In the score's first section ("Cross"), marked "Very slow, sorrowful, profoundly sad," Messiaen places symbols above the string quartet that "sings" the melody against the harmonic backdrop of flutes and woodwinds. A *nota bene* at the bottom of the first page says that these symbols are meant for the conductor: | = ½ time; ⊓ = 1 time in binary; ∧ = 1 time in ternary.[75] The phrasing of the melody follows this system as notes are grouped as singles, doubles, or triples. In other words, there is no predictable meter because there is no recurrent "strong" beat. Rather, a single beat is strong; the first beat of a double is strong; and the first beat of a triple is strong — and these combinations are mixed and matched throughout this first section. In the absence of any established meter: the first measure has 10 beats; the second measure has 11; the third has 9; the fourth 7; the fifth 9 again; and so on. The first five measures look like this:

Measure 1 (marked 10/8 time)	⊓∧|⊓⊓	1+1 1+2+3 1 1+2 1+2
Measure 2 (marked 11/8 time)	⊓∧⊓⊓⊓	1+2 1+2+3 1+2 1+2 1+2
Measure 3 (marked 9/8 time)	|⊓⊓⊓⊓	1 1+2 1+2 1+2 1+2
Measure 4 (marked 7/8 time)	⊓⊓∧	1+2 1+2 1+2+3
Measure 5 (marked 9/8 time)	⊓∧⊓⊓	1+2 1+2+3 1+2 1+2

Without doubt, Messiaen's attempt to bring about the "death of number" here is owed to Bergsonian theory. However, the letters exchanged between Messiaen and Tournemire during the summer of composition point to yet another source of inspiration: the theorization of Gregorian chant as a "free" musical form by the monks of Solesmes Abbey, especially in the writings of Dom André Mocquereau.[76] Solesmes's musicological research divided chant

---

75. The work is also available in study score form. See Olivier Messiaen, *Les offrandes oubliées* (Paris: Éditions Durands, 1931). The sign system is introduced at the bottom of the first page.

76. For Mocquereau, see Messiaen, "Dom Mocquereau et *le Nombre musical Grégorien*," in *Traité*, 4:43-51; cf. Messiaen, "Théorie simplifiée de la rythmique grégorienne," in *Traité*, 4:52-65. While Mocquereau's first volume had been published in 1908, the second was not published until 1927 — that is, the year Tournemire began his preparation for *L'Orgue Mys-*

into groups of twos and threes. However, unlike in metered music, each note in a grouping received equal time; this meant that the notes in a group of three, for example, did not become a "triplet," shrinking their time values to fit the same temporal space as two notes. And yet, the groupings into doubles and triples meant that the first strong beat was entirely unpredictable "free" music. It was the "end of meter" — a first step on the journey to the "death of number" and the "end of time."

By employing this notation, Messiaen was engaging in modernist primitivism, pointing ahead to his future by aligning himself with a certain faction of the past. The idea of plainchant being a music of "freedom" or "liberty" went all the way back to Canon Gontier's revolutionary *Rational Method of Plainchant* (1859): "plainsong is an inflected recitation in which the notes have an unfixed value, whose essentially free rhythm is that of ordinary speech."[77] Plainsong was performed in the seventeenth and eighteenth centuries by giving each note its own accent; it was sung in what sounds to us an unbearably slow and heavy tempo.[78] By contrast, the Romantic method invented by nineteenth-

---

tique by engaging with the monks at Solesmes; the year Messiaen's mother died; and the year he began studying the organ with Dupré. See Mocquereau, *Le Nombre musical grégorien, ou Rhythmique grégorienne, théorie et pratique*, 2 vols. (Rome, Tournay, and Paris: Société de Saint Jean l'Évangeliste, Desclée & Cie, 1908-27); Mocquereau, *"Le Nombre Musical Grégorien": A Study of Gregorian Musical Rhythm*, trans. Aileen Tone (Rome, Tournay, and Paris: Société de Saint Jean l'Évangeliste, Desclée & Cie, 1932). For Tournemire and Solesmes, see Schloesser, *Jazz Age Catholicism*, 299-305; cf. 283-85, 287.

77. Canon Augustin-Mathurin Gontier, *Méthode raisonée de plain-chant. Le plain-chant dans son rythme, sa tonalité et ses modes* (Paris: V. Palmé, 1859); in Benjamin Van Wye, "The Influence of the Plainsong Restoration on the Growth and Development of the Modern French Liturgical Organ School" (Ph.D. diss., University of Illinois at Urbana-Champaign, 1971), 75; in John Rayburn, *Gregorian Chant: A History of the Controversy concerning Its Rhythm* (Westport, Conn.: Greenwood Press, [1964] 1981), 10. For the genesis of Gontier's book see Dom Pierre Combe, *The Restoration of Gregorian Chant: Solesmes and the Vatican Edition*, trans. Theodore N. Marier and William Skinner (Washington, D.C.: Catholic University Press of America, 2003), 26-30; originally Combe, *Histoire de la restauration du chant Grégorien* (Sablé-sur-Sarthe: Abbaye de Solesmes: Ed. Vaticane, 1969). See also Katherine Bergeron, *Decadent Enchantments: The Revival of Gregorian Chant at Solesmes* (Berkeley and Los Angeles: University of California Press, 1998).

78. For a performance of plainchant as sung before the nineteenth century "restoration," see François Couperin, *Messe solennelle à l'usage des paroisses*, performed by Olivier Vernet, Jean-Yves Hameline, and Ensemble Jacques Moderne (Vichy, France: Ligia Digital, 2000). Viollet-le-Duc provided a pointed definition of "restoration" in his *Dictionnaire raisonné de l'architecture française du XIe au XVIe siècle* (1854): "RESTORATION, s.f. Both the word and the thing are modern. To restore an edifice means neither to maintain it, nor to repair it, nor to rebuild it; it means to reestablish it in a finished state, *which may in fact never*

century Solesmes directed the notes "to be sung quickly and lightly," grouped either according to principles of ordinary speech or in unpredictable groups of two and three.[79]

In Paris, this theory (or ideology) of plainchant as being the truly "free" musical art was taken over and institutionalized by Charles Bordes and Vincent d'Indy at the Schola Cantorum, an independent school of music founded in 1894.[80] In the wake of the Dreyfus affair (ca. 1894-1900), French music became politicized and polarized, and the Schola took on a new meaning as the "counteridentity" of the National Conservatory in Paris.[81] If the Conservatory was Republican, laicist, and pro-Dreyfusard, the Schola opposed it by being nativist, religious, and anti-Dreyfusard.[82] The Schola "took pride in inculcating in its students a sense of the majestic sweep of a unified, contiguous and elegantly unfolding music history, resplendent with musical masterpieces reflecting summits of achievement."[83] Bordes and d'Indy viewed the Conservatory, rooted in the Enlightenment both historically and ideologically, as endorsing an ideology of "scientific" and "natural" tonal harmony.

At the Schola, they inverted these values: now tonal harmony was "artificial" and "utopian" while plainchant, in sharp contrast, was a "free discourse" both "natural" and "logical." "Free" was the keyword: plainchant was a "free recitative" in a "free music"; a "free-flowing chant with infinite variation"; "freedom" in the "musical phrase"; a "cult of nature" and — in a phrase reminiscent of Johann Gottfried Herder's *Voices of the Folk (Stimmen der Völker)*

---

have actually existed at any given time." Eugène-Emmanuel Viollet-le-Duc, *The Foundations of Architecture: Selections from the* Dictionnaire raisonné, trans. Kenneth D. Whitehead (New York: George Braziller, 1990), 195, emphasis added.

79. Van Wye, "The Influence of the Plainsong Restoration," 75.

80. Schloesser, *Jazz Age Catholicism*, 30-32, 283-87. See also Philip Michael Dowd, "Charles Bordes and the Schola Cantorum of Paris: Their Influence on the Liturgical Music of the Late 19th and Early 20th Centuries" (Ph.D. diss., Catholic University of America, 1969).

81. Jane Fulcher, *French Cultural Politics and Music: From the Dreyfus Affair to the First World War* (New York: Oxford University Press, 1999), 15-63. See also "La Schola et le Conservatoire," *Mercure de France* 16 (September-October 1909): 234-43; Vincent d'Indy, ed., *La Schola Cantorum: Son histoire depuis sa fondation jusqu'en 1925* (Paris: Librairie Bloud et Gay, 1927).

82. See Fulcher, *French Cultural Politics,* 31-35; Fulcher, "In Preparation for Vichy: Anti-Semitism in French Musical Culture between the Two World Wars," *Musical Quarterly* 79, no. 3 (Autumn 1995): 458-75; and Fulcher, "Vincent d'Indy's 'Drame Anti-Juif' and Its Meaning in Paris, 1920," *Cambridge Opera Journal* 2, no. 3 (November, 1990): 295-319.

83. Stephen Broad, "Recontextualising Messiaen's Early Career," 2 vols. (Ph.D. diss., University of Oxford, 2005), 1:38.

(1807) — "music of the people." Bordes in particular took these complex musical works produced in medieval monasteries and reconfigured them as something natural, rooted in simplicity, and erupting spontaneously from the heart. Recalling that he had once heard a Basque countryside shepherd sing the song "Balatsa," Bordes remarked, "In hearing this theme sung so freely, I sensed the admirable art which is true plain chant. . . . It was the unexpected confirmation of the logical and natural precepts of Gregorian plain chant, the *basic condemnation of all utopias of measured music.*"[84] Bordes is echoed in Messiaen's condemnations of "measured" or "military" music as unfree and antinatural: the marching " 'without cadence' of soldiers, frighteningly antinatural! Free walking — the true walking — is never composed of two groups of footsteps with absolutely identical durations."[85] Messiaen's avant-garde insistence on "rhythm" was paradoxically rooted in a somewhat reactionary movement, the study and propagation of plainchant at both Solesmes and the Schola Cantorum.

Why did Messiaen use this occasion, his first performed and published orchestral work, to employ these rhythmic signs that were so embedded in a very specific meaning context? The most likely answer is Charles Tournemire, the organist at the basilica of Sainte-Clotilde with whom Messiaen corresponded in the summer of 1930.[86] The crux of being a "mystical" composer for Tournemire was the art of improvisation based on plainchant.[87] Messiaen derived a great deal of his self-understanding from Tournemire, and the use of such markings in *The Forgotten Offerings* may have been an experiment in bringing this emerging self-understanding to his compositions for the concert hall.

But this leads to an intriguing question: Might Messiaen's thinking in the summer of 1930 also have been influenced by his future wife, the violinist Claire Delbos, a student at the Schola? Where and when Messiaen met Delbos is shrouded in mystery; "he kept their courtship and engagement a secret until shortly before the invitations to the wedding [in June 1932] were

---

84. Bordes, cited by André Coeuroy, *La Musique et le peuple en France* (Paris: Stock [Delamain et Boutelleau], 1941), 95; in Dowd, "Charles Bordes ," 50; in Schloesser, *Jazz Age Catholicism,* 284-85. Emphasis added.

85. Messiaen, *Traité,* 1:58.

86. See Schloesser, *Jazz Age Catholicism,* 282-322.

87. In 1886, at age sixteen, Tournemire had left the provinces for Paris and studied composition with d'Indy at the Schola Cantorum. However, Tournemire, a firm republican and Conservatory professor, had little esteem for the Schola, which he dubbed the "Schola 'cancro'-rum," that is, "School of Dunces" (*cancre* = dunce). Schloesser, *Jazz Age Catholicism,* 287-88.

sent out."[88] But the autumn 1930 composition of *The Death of Number,* in which the violin plays a signature role — just months (or perhaps weeks) after finishing *The Forgotten Offerings* earlier that summer — suggests that Delbos might have influenced the composition.

Whatever the source of Messiaen's decision to invent a rhythmic symbol system derived from plainchant, *The Forgotten Offerings* takes another important step forward in Messiaen's exploration of the relationship between time and eternity. The first section ("Cross") is profoundly sorrowful and slow. The overwhelming grief, suffused with an aimlessly wandering melancholy, is made possible by the chant-like melody frustrating any desire to locate a steady beat or meter.

The second section ("Sin") is marked "Quick, ferocious, desperate, breathless," and it too uses Messiaen's rhythmic symbols in several places as part of an overall strategy to overcome any unified meter. As one scholar observes, "Sin" recalls both *The Rite of Spring* (1913) by Stravinsky and *The Sorcerer's Apprentice* (1897) by Paul Dukas (Messiaen's composition teacher) — "notwithstanding the latter's darker side having since been neutered by Mickey Mouse in the Walt Disney film *Fantasia*"![89]

But resistance to meter in these two first sections is nothing compared to the third — "Eucharist" — which extends to even greater extremes Messiaen's preceding experiments in near stasis *(The Celestial Banquet* and the second half of *Diptych).* If the second section calls to mind Stravinsky and Dukas, the third evokes Richard Wagner's *Parsifal* "in its quest to evoke a mystical experience" by destroying "the traditional Western notion of time."[90] (The symbolist parallelism between Wagner's "Grail" and Messiaen's "Eucharist" further deepens the linkage.) Marked "Extremely slow (with great mercy and great love)," the "Eucharist" movement is a study in stasis with no discernible melody and no need for rhythmic groupings. Messiaen has repeated here the experiment of *Diptych,* that is, representing the Bergsonian contrast between duration as inwardly experienced and time as externally analyzed in retrospect. As printed, the first section is 3 pages long; the second, filled to the brim with "events," is 28½ pages long; the third a trifling 1½ pages. In performance time, however, the first two sections are nearly equal in length (3:30 and 3:00 minutes, respectively) while the third section is twice as long (6:00 minutes).[91]

88. Hill and Simeone, *Messiaen,* 41.
89. Dingle, *The Life of Messiaen,* 25.
90. Jane F. Fulcher, "The Politics of Transcendence: Ideology in the Music of Messiaen in the 1930s," *Musical Quarterly* 86, no. 3 (Fall 2002): 449-71, at 465.
91. Timings based on Olivier Messiaen, *Concert à quatre. Les Offrandes oubliées. Le*

1927–1931: First Works as Grief Works

1930: *La Mort du Nombre (The Death of Number)*

Messiaen composed *The Death of Number* in the autumn of 1930 after returning to Paris from summer vacation. In contrast to his later self-described "theological" works emphasizing doctrines of the body (transfigured and resurrected), this early "theosophical" text concerns two "souls": the First Soul (presumably departed), a soprano; the Second Soul (left behind on earth), a tenor — accompanied by piano and a violin.[92] The introduction of the violin, playing a significant soloist's role, again suggests that Messiaen had met Claire Delbos by this time and that this work is, in the end, about her new role in his life. Born on November 2, 1906, Delbos was two years older than Messiaen. She had studied at the Schola Cantorum as well as the Paris Conservatory and was both a violinist and an accomplished composer.[93]

The opening melodic line in *The Death of Number* seems to be derived from one of the laments in Balakirew's *Collection of Russian Folk Songs*, a book Messiaen used for material elsewhere (for example, in *Visions of Amen*). But the text too seems to have inspired Messiaen. The Russian song opens with words of grief: "Oh! what a heart, what a sad heart, is mine! Stop, my heart, doing me so much harm, and wearing me out with grief!" The folksinger then notes how all the beauties of nature have lost their charm. (The theme repeats that of "Why?" from Messiaen's *Three Melodies* composed earlier in 1930 and published in autumn.) Then, finally, the "beautiful soul of a girl" *(la belle âme de fille)* appears in the prairie beyond the river; she has come to harvest the wheat. However, perspiration of this "beautiful soul" is so heavy that it makes her clothes stick to her body. A "brave young man" appears from out of the woods: "May God come to your aid," he prays. The young man has not come with empty hands but with

---

Tombeau resplendissent. Un Sourire, performed by Orchestre de l'opéra Bastille; conducted by Myung-Whun Chung (Deutsche Grammophon 445 947-2, 1995); also available as disc 24 in Messiaen, *Complete Edition.*

92. Commenting on *The Death of Number*, Michael R. Bundy observes: "Clearly influenced by Tournemire, not just in its theosophical content — it is a dialogue between two souls, the words being written by Messiaen himself — both stylistically and harmonically." Bundy, *Prophets without Honour: The Forgotten* Mélodies *of Widor, Vierne, and Tournemire* (Leicester, U.K.: Matador, 2011), 316.

93. Nigel Simeone, "Delbos, Claire," in *Grove Music Online. Oxford Music Online*, http://www.oxfordmusiconline.com/subscriber/article/grove/music/51575 (accessed June 18, 2009); cf. Dingle, *The Life of Messiaen*, 48.

1927–1932: Budding Rhythmician, Surrealist Composer, Mystical Commentator

> A small gift — a half flask of brandy [*eau-de-vie:* literally, "water-of-life"],
> And to eat afterwards — bread spiced with honey.[94]

In Messiaen's transforming imagination, this exchange between the brave young man and the "beautiful soul of a girl" becomes a conversation between a "First Soul" (soprano) and a "Second Soul" (tenor) in *The Death of Number*.

The work opens with a solo by the violin, to be played "muffled" *(sourdine)* as it sounds its plaintive lament (derived from the Russian folk melody) very slowly *(Très lent)*. Then the Second Soul (tenor) sings with chant-like simplicity and minimal piano accompaniment. The tenor's text reveals something of Messiaen's imaginative transformations. In the original Russian folk song, the singer straightforwardly laments:

> Toward the light my eyes no longer see anything joyful,
> During the day, they do not see the sunbeams [*rayons du soleil*]
>   in the sky.[95]

Messiaen takes this thoroughly naturalist and realist rural imagery and spins it into surrealistic verse.

> There was a sunbeam [*un rayon de soleil*] that slept in your hand.
> You lifted your small fingers very high.
> It began to shine with such brilliance [*d'un tel éclat*] that I could
>   see nothing other than it.[96]

Now the sunbeam is not in the sky but sleeping in the hand of the First Soul. She lifts it "very high" — compare again *Three Melodies,* in which the lily (white as a wing) is lifted "very high" in the golden cup. And whereas the singer could "no longer see anything joyful" in the original because of grief, here too the Second Soul is blinded — not by grief, but by the dazzling bright sunbeam. Throughout the rest of his life, Messiaen will use this image of a light so bright that it blinds us — that is, dazzlement *(éblouissement)*, the blindness experienced when overwhelmed by the radiant brilliance of truth.[97] And yet, here it is already in nascent form at age twenty-one.

---

94. "Complainte" (#23), in Balakirew, *Recueil de chants populaires russes,* 35.
95. "Complainte" (#23), 35.
96. Olivier Messiaen, *La Mort du nombre* (Paris: Durand et Die, 1931), 1.
97. Sander van Maas, "The Gift of Dazzlement," chapter 4 in *The Reinvention of Religious Music: Olivier Messiaen's Breakthrough toward the Beyond* (New York: Fordham University

1927–1931: First Works as Grief Works

Messiaen continues the fantastical imagery as the sunbeam unwinds itself, stretches to the four corners of the earth, and in its ascension back to the skies carries the Second Soul (tenor) upward to the soprano's "untroubled soul" *(ton âme sereine)*. The violin enters once again and repeats its opening solo lament, "very slow" and "still muffled." In what can now be seen as Messiaen's emerging trademark surrealism, this extreme quiet and slowness are immediately juxtaposed with agitated frenzy. The Second Soul had left off before, being carried upward to the serene First Soul; but his mood has shifted once again:

I am still very far away from you.
Who can push me even further away?
Why this goodbye [*Pourquoi l'adieu?* — cf. "Why?" in *Three Melodies*]?
Nothing can destroy the dream [*détruire le rêve*]![98]

Immediately and again in contrasting juxtaposition, the First Soul serenely sings a single slow line recalling the myth of Narcissus:

Press, 2009), 89-125; Siglind Bruhn, *Messiaen's Interpretations of Holiness and Trinity: Echoes of Medieval Theology in the Oratorio, Organ Meditations, and Opera* (Hillsdale, N.Y.: Pendragon Press, 2008), 33-35. For example, see Messiaen's opera *Saint Francis of Assisi* (1983), completed at age seventy-five: "God dazzles us through excess of Truth. Music carries us to God through default of Truth. . . . Hear this music, which suspends life from the ladders of heaven, *hear the music of the invisible.*" Olivier Messiaen, *Saint François d'Assise*, act 2, tableau 5: The Angel Musician; libretto translation in Bruhn, 207-18, at 213; cf. Bruhn, "Traces of a Thomistic *De musica* in the Compositions of Olivier Messiaen," *Logos* 11, no. 4 (Fall 2008): 16-56, especially 48-51.

Perhaps Saint John of the Cross laid out the image most clearly: "The sun so obscures all other lights that they do not seem to be lights at all when it is shining, and instead of affording vision to the eyes, it overwhelms, blinds, and deprives them of vision since its light is excessive and unproportioned to the visual faculty. Similarly, the light of faith in its abundance suppresses and overwhelms that of the intellect." John of the Cross, *The Ascent of Mount Carmel*, chapter 3, quoted in Matthew Hill, "Faith, Silence and Darkness Entwined in Messiaen's 'Regard du silence,'" in *Silence, Music, Silent Music*, 37-52, at 52.

For Messiaen's own explanation, see Messiaen and Samuel (1994), 233. Benitez summarizes: "Music carries us to God 'by an absence of truth,' until the day when He Himself will dazzle us 'by an excess of truth.' [Messiaen] believes that music, despite its lack of truth, has the capacity to bring a person closer to God, who one day will reveal a superabundance of truth." Vincent Perez Benitez, *Olivier Messiaen: A Research and Information Guide* (New York: Routledge, 2008), 59; cf. Benitez, "Messiaen and Aquinas," in *Messiaen the Theologian*, 101-23, at 122.

98. Messiaen, *La Mort du nombre*, 2-3.

1927–1932: Budding Rhythmician, Surrealist Composer, Mystical Commentator

Motionless water does not flee the flower,
the flower that looks at it.

The Second Soul responds again in agitation: he wants to come closer and yet he is held back by an invisible force as he tries to climb "this staircase that doesn't end." (This image will return years later in *Harawi* as "The Stairs Repeat," referring perhaps to the staircase in Dukas's version of the Bluebeard story.)[99] The First Soul responds quietly. The two souls personify the two characteristics of *Diptych:* "Terrestrial Life" and "Blessed Eternity."

The Second Soul responds frenetically with key motifs in Messiaen's imaginary. We have already seen the association of bells and death in the "Bells of Anguish and Tears of Farewell" (in *Preludes*). Here they sound as "Bells

---

99. Messiaen loved the operatic setting of Maurice Maeterlinck's libretto (after the fairy tale by Charles Perrault) by his Conservatory teacher, Paul Dukas: *Ariadne and Bluebeard (Ariane et Barbe-bleue)*, first performed in Paris at the Opéra Comique in March 1907. (In fact, Messiaen recalled being at a performance of *Bluebeard* with Dukas in the hall of the old Paris Conservatory; cf. Messiaen and Samuel [1994], 143.) In Dukas's version (as distinguished from Bartok's *Bluebeard's Castle* [premiered 1918]), the rooms are filled with multicolored gems. Messiaen later recalled: "I was a pupil of Paul Dukas, whose masterpiece, the opera *Ariane et Barbe-bleue,* contains in the first act the amazing scene of the gemstones. Ariane successively opens seven doors, and out of each door rushes a stream of gems.... Thus Dukas was able to link orchestration and tonality to the color of the stones, and this correspondence struck me when I was eighteen." Messiaen and Samuel (1994), 143, 167.

In the second act of *Bluebeard,* as Ariadne leads the other five wives out of their dark entombment: "We have lived in this darkness [*dans cette obscurité*] a long time. Come here, it is clearer [*il y fait bien plus clair . . .*]. Yes, lead us into the brilliance [*menon-la dans la clarté*]. Is there a brilliance in the very deepest darkness? [*Il y a donc une clarté dans les plus profondes ténèbres?*] Yes, there is!" They finally reach the top of the staircase and emerge into the noonday light, "the blinding sea of brilliance [*l'aveuglante nappe de clarté*] that forces them to lower their heads." In the end, however, the tale is a psychological tragedy: the five wives cannot choose the light and instead return to the darkness. "Adieu," concludes Ariadne, "be happy..." See Paul Dukas and Maurice Maeterlinck, *Ariane et barbe-bleue = Ariadne and Blue-Beard: conte en trois actes. Partition pour chant et piano réduite par l'Auteur* (Paris: Durand, [1906] 1950), 120, 136, 245-46. The emotional struggle of the Second Soul in Messiaen's *Death of Number* echoes that in Dukas's masterpiece. (Also worth noting: the "repeating" aspect of the staircase may be owed to Rembrandt's *Philosopher in Meditation* [1632], which Messiaen would have seen at the Louvre.)

It seems worth noting the parallel of the wives in *Ariadne* with Cécile Sauvage's condition (the inability to leave the darkness). For gender parallels between Debussy's *Pelléas et Mélisande* and the story of Bluebeard's castle, see Elliott Antokoletz and Juana Canabal Antokoletz, *Musical Symbolism in the Operas of Debussy and Bartok: Trauma, Gender, and the Unfolding Unconscious* (New York and Oxford: Oxford University Press, 2004).

of horror!" *(Cloches d'horreur!)*. And we have already seen the d'Harcourts' discussion of the enduring belief in love potions among the Peruvians. Here again: "dreadful potion!" *(breuvage affreux!)*. Finally, Messiaen (like Debussy) loved Edgar Allan Poe's stories, most especially "The Pit and the Pendulum," in which moving walls close in on a prisoner of the Spanish Inquisition, threatening to crush him to death. The image appears here: "wall that crushes me!" *(mur qui m'écrase!)*.[100] These references to horror, dread, and terror all show Messiaen's literary consolidation of a childhood fondness for fear into a maturing interest in dread.

So too the apocalypse — as the Second Soul transforms a somewhat conventional expression of lament over lost love into a lament for the end of time and space:

> Time and space are dying!
> So far off, joy! So far off, light!
> Bells of horror! dreadful potion! wall that crushes me!
> The earth opens up, the stars fall, the world is swallowed up!
> The end, the end, who can tell it? [*La fin, la fin, qui la dira?*]
> I suffer! I suffer!

The First Soul responds with serene simplicity: "Wait! hope!"

Now, a sea change in character as the violin enters "without muffling" *(sans sourdine),* assuming a soloist's role and boldly soaring in a song without words, accompanied by a lavish piano reminiscent of both Debussy and Chopin. (One can imagine Messiaen accompanying Delbos.) Messiaen takes the minor sixth forming the Russian folk song's arc and extends it to a major sixth while the sonority moves from D minor to E major.

---

100. Nearly twenty years later, Messiaen will have this same image in mind as he composes *Turangalîla Symphony:* "the double terror of the pendulum blade slowly getting nearer the heart of the prisoner while the wall of red-hot iron closes in on him . . . in Edgar Allan Poe's celebrated story *The Pit and the Pendulum.*" Messiaen, analysis of movement 7, "Turangalîla 2," *Turangalîla-Symphonie,* in Messiaen, *Complete Edition,* 281. By means of Charles Baudelaire's translations, Poe's *fantastical* works had an important influence on Catholic Revivalist authors like Ernest Hello and Villiers de l'Isle Adam. See Schloesser, *Jazz Age Catholicism,* 35-37; and Schloesser, "Charm of Impossibilities," 176-77. For a useful study underscoring Poe's short story as a *fantastical* work, see David R. Saliba, *A Psychology of Fear: The Nightmare Formula of Edgar Allan Poe* (Washington, D.C.: University Press of America, 1980), especially 190-205. Saliba notes: "And what the narrator takes to be his salvation by the General is nothing more than his final awakening — caused probably by the noise of his own screams" (205).

1927–1932: Budding Rhythmician, Surrealist Composer, Mystical Commentator

The violin eventually ascends to the heavens in a chromatic scale and falls away imperceptibly as the First Soul returns in this new emotional universe of hope and joy:

> Lighter than feathered birds,
> lighter than empty space [*le vide*],
> lighter than what is not,
>   we will glide [*planer* = like birds] above a dream.
> The weight of number will be dead.
> The weight of number will be dead.
> It will be dead! dead![101]

The meaning of the work's opaque title, an extension of the "Deceased Instants" *(Instants défunts)* of *Preludes,* is now revealed. In a tradition stretching back to Greek antiquity and most especially Plotinus, "number" — that is, multiplicity in matter, the fragmentation of the original One into many — produces weight.[102] As the voices unite into a single entity, number is destroyed and the souls become weightless: *The Death of Number.*[103] Messiaen's birds,

---

101. Messiaen, *La Mort du nombre*, 9-11.

102. Messiaen's use of the "Soul" in *The Death of Number* would seem to be at least partly owed to its frequent recurrence in his mother's poetry and dramatic scripts, in turn influenced by its usage in Lamartine's poetry (among others): see Aimée Boutin, *Maternal Echoes: The Poetry of Marceline Desbordes-Valmore and Alphonse de Lamartine* (Newark: University of Delaware Press, 2001). But "the death of number" also suggests that Messiaen's personification of the "Soul" might have been influenced by the thought of Plotinus (especially *Enneads* 3 and 4), perhaps via his study of Henri Bergson. Curtis L. Hancock, "The Influence of Plotinus on Bergson's Critique of Empirical Science," in *Neoplatonism and Contemporary Thought,* ed. R. Baine Harris, 2 vols. (Albany: State University of New York Press, 2002), 1:139-64, at 139; cf. Louis Delaunay, *M. Bergson et Plotin* (Angers: J. Siraudeau, 1919). Evelyn Underhill had published the essay "The Mysticism of Plotinus" (1919); reprinted the following year in Underhill, *The Essentials of Mysticism and Other Essays* (London: J. M. Dent, 1920), 116-40. Interest in Plotinus was also part of the postwar "mystical" vogue; cf. Abbé René Arnou, *Le désir de Dieu dans la philosophie de Plotin* (Paris: Alcan, 1921); Franz Cumont, *Le culte égyptien et le mysticisme de Plotin* (Paris: E. Leroux, 1921-1922); Édouard Krakowski, *Une famille spirituelle de penseurs: Plotin, Pascal, Maine de Biran, Bergson* (Paris: Union Interalliée, 1930). Messiaen quotes Plotinus (*Enneads* 6.3) on colors in *Traité,* 7:14-15.

103. Note the opening line of Bergson's second chapter: "Number may be defined in general as a collection of units, or, speaking more exactly, as the synthesis of the one and the many" (On définit généralement le nombre une collection d'unités ou, pour parler avec plus de précision, la synthèse de l'un et du multiple). Throughout this chapter, Bergson opposes any possibility of measuring the experience of lived duration by "number": num-

which will later become his trademark, are here only implicit; souls can glide like birds, figures of freedom, release, and transcendence.

The work's conclusion seems to be a personal one deliberately encoded. Immediately following the repeated jubilant exclamation "It will be dead! dead!" the violin enters and joins with the First Soul in a duet (accompanied by piano) lasting nearly to the end of the piece. The soprano ambiguously sings: "Listen to the song of our single soul [*de notre âme unique*]!" Since the Second Soul (Messiaen's bereaved alter ego?) no longer sings, it might be that "our single soul" refers to the Second Soul's absorption by the First. However, more suggestively, since this line is sung in duet with the violin, "our single soul" might instead be the union of the First Soul and the violin — namely, Cécile and Claire, recently departed mother and newly arrived wife-to-be. The play on words immediately following this line would support this reading: "Clear smile [*Claire sourire*], pure look, trembling ecstasy."[104] The first two French words are a punning juxtaposition of "clear" — that is, Claire's name — and "smile" — that is, the title of Cécile's poem in *Three Melodies* and the description of "The Lost Fiancée": "She is a smile as pure as a child's heart . . ."

The final text adds yet more Messiaen motifs: the song of "this single soul" rises higher and "leaps toward new brilliances [*clartés nouvelles*], / In an eternal springtime!" The word for "brilliances" — *clartés,* etymologically linked with *claire* — is a complicated one in Messiaen, evoking complex connotations.[105]

---

ber is homogenous whereas duration is heterogenous. See, for example: "a continuous or qualitative multiplicity *with no resemblance to number*"; "Withdraw, on the other hand, the pendulum and its oscillations; there will no longer be anything but the heterogeneous duration of the ego, without moments external to one another, *without relation to number*"; "duration properly so called has no moments which are identical or external to one another, being essentially heterogeneous, continuous, *and with no analogy to number*"; "What is duration within us? A qualitative multiplicity, *with no likeness to number*." Bergson, *Time and Free Will,* 75, 105, 108, 120, 226; and Bergson, *Essai sur les données immédiates,* 57, 80, 82, 91, 174. Emphasis added.

104. Messiaen, *La Mort du nombre,* 13-15.

105. Jacques Maritain notes that *clarté* — "clarity" or "brightness" (Lat. *claritas*) — along with "integrity" *(integritas)* and "proportion" *(proportion),* is also one of the three formal aspects of beauty in Aquinas following the tradition of Abbot Suger and Hugh of St. Victor. In *Art et scolastique,* the newly published book that Messiaen likely read during recovery from tuberculosis in the winter of 1927-1928, Maritain underscores *clarté* as "the essential character of beauty." See Maritain, *Art et scolastique,* rev. ed., 37-38, 44-45; *Art and Scholasticism,* 24-25, 28-29; quoting Aquinas, *Summa Theologiae,* Ia, Q. 39, 1. 8; Aquinas, *Commentary on the Book of Divine Names,* 6. See also: John Roger Dodds, "*Claritas:* A Central Concept in the Aesthetics of Joyce and Aquinas" (Ph.D. diss., University of Chicago, 2010); Umberto Eco and Hugh Bredin, *The Aesthetics of Thomas Aquinas* (Cambridge:

1927–1932: Budding Rhythmician, Surrealist Composer, Mystical Commentator

Most specifically, *clarté* is one of the four properties of resurrected ("glorified") bodies in the theology of Thomas Aquinas. Clarity (Lat. *claritas*), also translated as "lightedness," denotes the diaphanous transparency characterizing glorified bodies raised from the dead. Messiaen's use here recalls his introduction to Aquinas around age fifteen or sixteen (about five or six years earlier); so too his introduction to Maritain's *Art and Scholasticism* (in which *claritas* figures prominently) in the winter of 1927-1928. However, this association of *clarté* with disembodied "souls" is an initial youthful understanding. Aquinas's theology underscores, rather, that the property of "lightedness" belongs to bodies — a doctrine that Messiaen will explore at the other end of the decade (in *Glorified Bodies* [1939]).

Finally, the First Soul's text ends with eternity: "In an eternal springtime [*un éternel printemps*]!"[106] If (as the Second Soul cried) both "space and time" have "died," this "death of number" — that is, the death of Bergson's "spatialized" time (the "end of time") — inaugurates a new life, an "eternal springtime," unified, indivisible, and immeasurable. The work concludes with the violin singing solo for a final thirteen measures, rapturously accompanied by the piano. If this biographical reading of the work accurately represents Messiaen's intentions, then the beginning of "an eternal springtime" means: Claire Delbos has entered the void left by Cécile Sauvage. *The Death of Number* — the death of multiplicity — ends with Claire's violin accompanied by Olivier's piano, the two becoming one.

1931: *Le Tombeau Resplendissant (The Resplendent Tomb)*

The last of the seven works to be considered a work of mourning is *The Resplendent Tomb*, the tomb that is brilliant, radiant, shining brightly.[107] Scored

---

Harvard University Press, 1988), especially 102-21; Otto Georg von Simson, *The Gothic Cathedral: Origins of Gothic Architecture and the Medieval Concept of Order* (New York: Harper Torchbooks, [1956; 2nd rev. ed. 1962] 1964), 50.

106. Messiaen, *La Mort du nombre*, 17-18.

107. The titles of four poems by Lamartine in the *Third Book* of his *Harmonie poétiques et religieuses* (Paris: C. Gosselin, 1830) are suggestive with regard to *The Resplendent Tomb:* "Le Cri de l'Âme" ("The Cry of the Soul"), "Le Tombeau d'une Mère" ("The Tomb of a Mother"), "Le Génie dans l'Obscurité" ("The Genius in Obscurity"), and "Pourquoi mon âme est-elle triste?" ("Why Is My Soul Sad?"). The last three of these follow one another in sequence. The "resplendence" in Messiaen's work provides an exact counterpart to Lamartine's "obscurity" (or "darkness"). See table of contents in Alphonse de Lamartine, *Œuvres poétiques complètes de Lamartine,* ed. Marius-François Guyard (Paris: Éditions Gallimard, 1963).

1927–1931: First Works as Grief Works

for a symphony orchestra, the piece was composed at Fuligny in the summer of 1931. It is a work filled with both rage and beatitude. The rage is extremely understandable given Messiaen's situation: his father Pierre had married Marguerite Élie sometime in 1929, about two years after Cécile's death. Their first son, Charles-Marie (Messiaen's half brother), was born in 1930, about twenty-two years after Messiaen himself.[108] Although Pierre and Marguerite made their home at 44 quai Henri IV (with Alain, who lived in rooms at the top of the house), an interview conducted with Messiaen in October 1931 suggests that at this time the family was still living in the cramped quarters of 67 rue Rambuteau.

In the October interview, which took place in Messiaen's home, José Bruyr wrote that the dining room "was filled with a feminine presence." He then drew on imagery borrowed from Tenant's collection of essays in memoriam (which either Olivier or Pierre had passed on to him): "[Georges] Bernanos described Cécile Sauvage as one of those poets who watch over the threshold of our homes. Above all, she watches over the threshold of this room where her son shakes my hand."[109] Messiaen was quoted as saying: "It often seems to me now that it is my mother, after her death, who guides my hand or my spirit."[110]

Thus, in 1931, when he composed *The Resplendent Tomb,* Messiaen was living with his father, stepmother, brother Alain (now twenty years old), and half brother Charles-Marie — apparently in the same quarters that had already been unbearably close for Messiaen as an adolescent. The two boys had now grown into late adolescence; it is difficult to imagine how they now managed with an additional toddler as well. However, this domestic context was about to change in June when Messiaen would marry Claire Delbos, leave the apartment in which he had lived for the past dozen years, and move to the newlyweds' home at 77 rue des Plantes in the Fourteenth Arrondissement.[111] Perhaps this imminent change accounts in part for *The Resplendent Tomb*'s abrupt shift from blind rage to serene beatitude.

The work is divided into four main sections corresponding to four stanzas in a handwritten preface. (The preface was printed in facsimile for the rental

---

108. Dingle, *The Life of Messiaen,* 48.
109. José Bruyr, "Olivier Messiaen," in *L'Écran des musiciens, seconde série* (Paris: José Corti, 1933), in Hill and Simeone, *Messiaen,* 38; quoting the final line of Bernanos, "Cécile Sauvage ou le Miracle de la vie intérieure," in *Cécile Sauvage, 20 juillet 1883–26 août 1927: études et souvenirs,* ed. Jean Tenant (Saint-Étienne: Édition des Amitiés, 1928), 47.
110. Messiaen to Bruyr; in Hill and Simeone, *Messiaen,* 38.
111. Dingle, *The Life of Messiaen,* 48.

1927–1932: Budding Rhythmician, Surrealist Composer, Mystical Commentator

score published for string parts in 1932. The other orchestral parts were left unpublished in manuscript.)[112]

> [Section 1] My youth is dead: it is I who killed it. Anger that soars, anger that overflows! anger like a spurt of blood, anger like a hammer blow! Hands around the throat, Encircling the throat, rage-filled hands, cold hatred on the face! Despair and tears![113]

This section, marked "Fast" *(Vif)* and lasting about four minutes (pages 1-45; sections 1-22 in the score), is driving, violent, and "savage." Compare Messiaen's language with that of Éluard in a poem about "your life without me":

> I shattered myself on the rocks of my body
> with a child I was strangling.[114]

Another parallelism:

> Messiaen: "Encircling the throat."
> Éluard: "let's seize them by the throat."[115]

Though not resplendent, a tomb also appears in Éluard's "Like an Image":

> a tomb decorated by three pretty trinkets
> a veil of silk over the slowness of lust
> to an end
> an axe in the back with a single blow.[116]

Compare Messiaen: "anger like a hammer blow!"

---

112. Messiaen's text is in Dingle, *The Life of Messiaen*, 35. A facsimile of the autograph preface is in Simeone, *Bibliographical Catalogue*, 25.

113. Messiaen, *Resplendent Tomb*; in Dingle, *The Life of Messiaen*, 35.

114. Paul Éluard, "Défense de savoir" ("Knowledge Forbidden"), II:III, in *Love, Poetry*, trans. Stuart Kendall (Boston: Black Widow Press, 2007), 188, trans. 189. Originally *L'amour la poésie* (Paris: Éditions Gallimard, 1929).

115. Éluard, "Le diamant qu'il ne t'a pas donné" ("The Diamond He Didn't Give You"), in *Capital of Pain*, trans. Mary Ann Caws, Patricia Terry, and Nancy Kline (Boston: Black Widow Press, 2006), 188, trans. 189.

116. Éluard, "Comme une image" ("Like an Image"), IV, in *Love, Poetry*, 136-41, at 138, trans. 139.

1927-1931: First Works as Grief Works

The breathless pace of section 1 is achieved not only by the tempo but, more importantly, by the rhythm. Although Messiaen has left behind the previous year's experiment (in *The Forgotten Offerings*) with invented symbols denoting unitary, binary, and ternary groupings derived from Gregorian chant, it is still the unpredictable mixing and matching of those groupings that contribute to the irregular — and in this movement, "savage" — quality of the theme.

The main reason that the earlier experiment will no longer work is because the primary grouping is now 5 (3+2), a number (following both Stravinsky and Bartók) that resists traditional meters based on 2 or 3. The outstanding driving theme in this section might be represented thus:

⌈1+2+3+4+5⌉ (rest) ⌈1+2⌉ ⌈1⌉ ⌈1+2+3+4+5⌉

This rhythm is something of an experimental halfway house. It retains elements of *The Forgotten Offerings* in that the 1+2 1 grouping would have been represented ⌈⌉|; additionally, if there had been another invented symbol (perhaps a pentagon), the groupings of five would have been an evolution of the ∧⌈ (i.e., 1+2+3 1+2) combination (although there would be no strong accent following the initial ternary group). But this is precisely why the old system no longer works: Messiaen is moving on from 1s, 2s, and 3s to the 5s (and soon 7s) that cannot be reduced to meters based on 2s and 3s.

Messiaen's new rhythmic experiments engaged in the summer of 1931 suggest that he was trying to apply insights gained during recent visits to that year's International Colonial Exposition. Held in Paris from May through October 1931, the exposition was a mammoth undertaking highlighting peoples and cultures from France's overseas colonies.[117] (Josephine Baker was selected as "Queen of the Colonies" and photographed with her troupe at the Togo-

---

117. Didier Gransart, *Paris 1931: revoir l'Exposition Coloniale* (Paris: FVW Éd., 2010); Laure Blévis et al., *1931, les étrangers au temps de l'exposition coloniale* (Paris: Cité nationale de l'histoire de l'immigration, 2008); Barbara L. Kelly, *French Music, Culture, and National Identity, 1870-1939* (Rochester, N.Y.: University of Rochester Press, 2008); Elizabeth Ezra, *The Colonial Unconscious: Race and Culture in Interwar France* (Ithaca, N.Y.: Cornell University Press, 2000); Patricia A. Morton, *Hybrid Modernities: Architecture and Representation at the 1931 Colonial Exposition, Paris* (Cambridge: MIT Press, 2000); Herman Lebovics, *True France: The Wars over Culture Identity, 1900-1945* (Ithaca, N.Y.: Cornell University Press, 1992); Catherine Hodeir and Michel Pierre, *1931, l'exposition coloniale* (Brussels: Éditions Complexe, 1991). For the surrealists' antiexhibition, La Vérité sur les Colonies (The Truth about the Colonies), held from September 1931 to February 1932, see Jody Blake, *Le Tumulte Noir: Modernist Art and Popular Entertainment in Jazz-Age Paris, 1900-1930* (University Park: Pennsylvania State University Press, 1999), 133-35; and Blake, "The Truth about the

1927–1932: Budding Rhythmician, Surrealist Composer, Mystical Commentator

Cameroun Pavilion.)[118] Messiaen recalled being deeply affected by the "sublime male and female dancers of Bali (one of the Sunda Islands, celebrated for its dances and its music)." Noting especially the "visual and sonic rhythms" of Anak Agung Gede Mandera and his Balinese gamelan orchestra as well as "the marvelous dances of the eyes, the neck and the hands," Messiaen said he was "marked, permeated and transformed" for his entire life. "I pause here to salute my sisters and brothers of Bali, who love rhythm as I do."[119]

At the other end of the spectrum from such unpredictability, Messiaen's rhythmic experiments offer a first inkling of what will become one of his signature tools: the rhythmic palindrome, symbolic stasis, what he will call the "non-retrogradable rhythm." In his later work, the motif here,

⌈1+2+3+4+5⌉ (rest) ⌈1+2⌉⌈1⌉ ⌈1+2+3+4+5⌉,

will instead become

⌈1+2+3+4+5⌉ ⌈1+2+3⌉ ⌈1+2+3+4+5⌉,

a rhythmic motif (5+3+5) that reads the same both forward and backward. However, it will play exactly the opposite function that the similar motif does here. In this work, the motif's jagged irregularity is used to effect a sense of frantic breathlessness, a rhythm that inexorably pushes us forward. In later work, the "non-retrogradable" palindrome will be used for exactly the opposite purpose: stasis representing simultaneity (i.e., eternity). If time can be read both forward and backward in the same way, it is, quite literally, the "end of time."

These reflections get us ahead of the present work. But they also show that *The Resplendent Tomb* is a threshold or turning point both musically and emotionally.

> [Section 2] My youth lived within a music of flowers. An enchanted staircase offered itself to my eyes. It was lit up [*l'éclairait*] by the plumage of the

---

Colonies, 1931: Art Indigène in the Service of the Revolution," *Oxford Art Journal* 25, no. 1 (2002): 35-58.

118. Baker was used to inaugurate the new Musée de l'Homme at the Palais de Chaillot. Bennetta Jules-Rosette, *Josephine Baker in Art and Life: The Icon and the Image* (Urbana and Chicago: University of Illinois Press, 2007), 140.

119. Messiaen, *Traité*, 1:88-89. For the gamelan see Michael Tenzer, *Gamelan Gong Kebyar: The Art of Twentieth-Century Balinese Music* (Chicago: University of Chicago Press, 2000).

bluebird of illusions. Joyously melancholic [*joyeusement mélancolique*], the melody of the atmosphere rose up.[120]

This section is alternately marked "Moderate" and "Almost slow" and lasts about five minutes (pages 1-45; sections 23-30 in the score). It is enchanted and atmospheric, achieving precisely the contradictory — indeed, surrealist — effect of being simultaneously joyful in its jagged rhythms and melancholic in its modalities. The rhythms are effected largely by frequently alternating time signatures, especially those in odd numbers (5/8 and 7/8) alternating with duple or triple meters (10/8 and 9/8) and resisting any reduction to them.

Its imagery, too, is fantastical and surrealist: the "staircase" appears here again — in *The Death of Number* it was an "endless" staircase, ascending to the beloved who kept receding out of reach, likely alluding to Dukas's and Maeterlinck's *Bluebeard*. Now it is simply "enchanted," luminous as it is lit up by the "bluebird of illusions," referring to the key symbol of the "Bluebird of Happiness" (aided by the good fairy Bérylune) in Maeterlinck's *The Bluebird* (1909).[121] (Perhaps Madame d'Aulnoy's *"oiseau bleu"* is also remembered?) Birds and light, associated with fairy tales, enchantment, and childhood more generally — all of which transcend what commonly passes for "realism" — are now perceived as disenchanted illusions.

> [Section 3] My youth is dead: it is I who killed it. Rage [or craze = *fureur*], where are you leading me? Trees, why do you sparkle [or burn = *brillez*] through the night? Advance, retreat, hold out your arms! Waves in my ears! it cracks, spins, dances, shouts, screams: the void enters into me![122]

This section, lasting about three minutes (pages 55-89; sections 31-47 in the score), is largely a reprise of the first section with a few alterations. This is accomplished textually by repeating the first line of the first section. As such, the work thus far can loosely be thought of as written in sonata form: exposition, development, recapitulation. As the sonata form implies, the exposition returns with a difference. The difference here is that, having reflected on the enchanted illusions of youth, the rage has become even worse, threatening to fall over the edge into crazed insanity.

---

120. Messiaen, *Resplendent Tomb*; in Dingle, *The Life of Messiaen*, 35.
121. Maurice Maeterlinck, *L'oiseau bleu, féerie en six actes et douze tableux* (Paris: Fasquelle, 1909).
122. Messiaen, *Resplendent Tomb*; in Dingle, *The Life of Messiaen*, 35.

1927–1932: Budding Rhythmician, Surrealist Composer, Mystical Commentator

Again, the imagery, dominated by the metaphor of light, transforms naturalist and realist artifacts. Trees suggest dry land while waves evoke the sea: such juxtaposed topographies call to mind not only surrealists but also Rimbaud's cross-fading of contradictory spaces:

> The silver and copper chariots —
> the steel and silver prows —
> churn up the foam, —
> raise up the bramble stumps.[123]

Messiaen's rage burns like luminous trees, evoking fires found abundantly in Éluard:

> Eyes burning with wood.... / Only pain catches fire.[124]

> in nocturnal plains the fire looked for the dawn.[125]

> chest like an isolated fire beaten / this fire no longer knows its equal who sleeps.[126]

> this gush of water that fevers / crowned by fire of tears.[127]

> silent eyes / open and offer themselves to flames.[128]

And perhaps most directly:

> The heart of the forests the sleep
> of a burning flare
> the nocturnal horizon
> that crowns me.[129]

---

123. Arthur Rimbaud, "Seascape" [Marine]; in *A Season in Hell and Other Works = Une saison en enfer et œuvres diverses,* trans. Stanley Appelbaum (Mineola, N.Y.: Dover Publications, 2003), 79.
124. Éluard, "Seconde nature" ("Second Nature"), IX, in *Love, Poetry,* 98, trans. 99.
125. Éluard, "Seconde nature," 106, trans. 107.
126. Éluard, "Seconde nature," 108, trans. 109.
127. Éluard, "Seconde nature," 124, trans. 125.
128. Éluard, "Défense de savoir," 186, trans. 187, translation altered.
129. Éluard, "Comme une image," 130, trans. 131.

Éluard's complaint works equally for *Resplendent Tomb*:

> I am unable to lose you
> this is the flower of the secret
> a fire to discover.[130]

In *The Death of Number,* the lightness of "the void" had been a blessing; but now it is the emptiness of nothingness.

Messiaen: "the void enters into me!"

Éluard: "In the periphery of hope / in pure loss / *calm creates a void.*"[131]

> There is no longer anything around me
> if I stray there is nothing on either side
> nothing and me.[132]

While the second section is indebted to fin-de-siècle symbolism, sections 1 and 3 derive largely from postwar surrealism. Just as surrealism expressed the disillusionment of the postwar era, so too it would become even more politicized and apocalyptic in the 1930s' era of the Great Depression. In *The Resplendent Tomb,* it provided a vocabulary for expressing the rage of betrayed youth.

However, the work does not end here. After thunderous crashes of full orchestra with drums, twelve seconds of absolute silence follow. Then begins this fourth section, marked "Slow" and lasting about three minutes (pages 90-92; sections 48-49 in the score). Strongly reminiscent of Mahler, it echoes the representation of "eternity" concluding *The Forgotten Offerings*.

> [Section 4] What is this resplendent tomb? It is the tomb of my youth, it is my heart. The flame burning without end, the blinding clarity [*l'aveuglante clarté*] of an inner voice illuminates it:
> "Come unto me, all ye that labour and are heavy laden, and I will give you rest. Blessed are the meek, for they shall inherit the earth. Blessed are

---

130. Éluard, "Défense de savoir," 194-99, at 194, trans. 195.
131. Éluard, "Comme une image," 136-41, at 140, trans. 141, emphasis added.
132. Éluard, "Défense de savoir," 192, trans. 193.

they that mourn, for they shall be comforted. Blessed are the pure in heart, for they shall see God."[133]

Once again the metaphor of light dominates the imagery, and the word *clarté* appears as it had in *The Death of Number* — although now the "brilliance" more closely follows the thought of Aquinas, one so bright that it blinds the viewer (dazzlement = *éblouissement*) to the divine presence.

However, it is also a surrealist image employed by Éluard:

What a beautiful spectacle indeed a beautiful spectacle
to banish. Its perfect visibility
blinds me [*me rendrait aveugle*].[134]

This is the mystical vision in the "dark night of the soul": the overwhelming presence "appears" as its contrary — absence.

The final lines of the text spoken by the illuminating "inner voice" are a quotation from Christ's beatitudes in the Sermon on the Mount. The surrealist passes seamlessly into the scriptural: the beatitudes themselves are surrealistic in their unions — the meek inherit and the mournful are comforted. The ultimate promise for Messiaen is that the pure of heart shall *see*. Messiaen's fondness for visual metaphors is supported by the Scriptures: the hoped-for result of all this earthly turmoil will be *vision* — although perhaps not until after death.

During an interview conducted just weeks after completing this work, Messiaen said he had "wanted to write a kind of Beatitude for those who discover in their faith something more than illusions of a distant youth."[135] This sense of deepening belief accords with his statement much later in life that his Catholic faith was primarily dominated by aspects of the "marvelous" of Shakespeare, fairy tales, and surrealism. However, "it was no longer a matter of theatrical fiction but of something true."[136] The maturation and internaliza-

---

133. Messiaen, *Resplendent Tomb*; in Dingle, *The Life of Messiaen*, 35.
134. Éluard, "Défense de savoir," 178, trans. 179.
135. Bruyr, "Olivier Messiaen," 124-31; Nigel Simeone, "Offrandes oubliées 2: Messiaen, Boulanger and José Bruyr," *Musical Times* 142 (Spring 2001): 17-22, at 21-22; in Dingle, *The Life of Messiaen*, 35. Bruyr (1889-1980) was a prolific Belgian music critic.
136. "It is certain that in the truths of the Catholic faith, I found this attraction of the marvelous multiplied a hundredfold, a thousandfold, and it was no longer a matter of theatrical fiction but of something true. *I chose what was true.*" Messiaen and Samuel (1994), 26; cf. Dingle, *The Life of Messiaen*, 36. Note that "the marvelous" was a key concept in

tion of his faith had certainly been catalyzed by the death of Cécile Sauvage; but they were also very likely aided by his having met Claire Delbos. Her presence facilitated the transformation of blinding rage into dazzlement: the breakthrough vision of *clarté*.

Intriguingly, Messiaen never submitted *The Resplendent Tomb* for publication as a whole during his lifetime. The first edition appeared only in 1997, five years after his death, under the supervision of his second wife, Yvonne Loriod.[137] He seems to have been almost immediately uncomfortable with such a public outburst of profoundly personal emotion. Moreover, by the time of its completion, Messiaen had become a more public figure, having obtained the titular organist post at La Trinité contemporaneously with composing *The Resplendent Tomb* that summer. Messiaen's ambivalence about the work mirrors its liminal location: it was composed in the last summer Messiaen would spend with his aunts at Fuligny; the last summer as an unmarried man; and the last before assuming the organist's post at La Trinité in September. As the poetic preface notes, crossing the threshold from youth into adulthood is the work's overt subject: the tomb containing the remains of Messiaen's self-killed youth now shone with resplendence.

---

surrealism, as Breton declared: "Let us not mince words: the marvelous is always beautiful, anything marvelous is beautiful, in fact only the marvelous is beautiful." Breton, *Manifestoes of Surrealism*, 14. cf. Pierre Mabille, *Mirror of the Marvelous: The Classic Surrealist Work on Myth*, trans. Jody Gladding (Rochester, Vt.: Inner Traditions, 1998); originally Mabille, *Le miroir du merveilleux* (Paris: Sagittaire, 1940).

137. Simeone, *Bibliographical Catalogue*, 22-25; Hill and Simeone, *Messiaen*, 45.

CHAPTER 5

1927–1931

Decisive Coincidence: The Mystical Organ

The pipe organ as an instrument must have been linked in Messiaen's mind with the memory of his mother. According to some accounts, he began studying it in Dupré's class during the fall semester of 1927, just weeks after Cécile's death. In broader terms, Messiaen's turn to the organ decisively influenced his career and music in at least two respects: in terms of his developing interest in time ("duration") and the musical representation of "eternity"; and in the way he imagined what he was doing as a "mystical" composer and improviser. Becoming an organist and having to serve the requirements of the liturgical year imposed a concretely practical channel for Messiaen's energies. The organ would function as a means by which he could represent the kinds of metaphysical questions and struggles life posed — those for which he would become known as a "mystical" composer.

1927: A Decisive Coincidence

Because we are so accustomed to the settled fact of Messiaen's life — that he became the titular organist at La Trinité in autumn 1931 and held this post until his death sixty-one years later — it is easy to overlook just what a turn of fortune this was. As one scholar observes: "Extraordinary as it may seem now, the [organ] played no part in his original career plans.... From his childhood, Messiaen's vocation, as he told various interviewers, was to be a composer. Although a committed Roman Catholic, it was not Messiaen's faith that led him

1927–1931: Decisive Coincidence: The Mystical Organ

to take up the organ. Rather his skill as an improviser prompted Jean Gallon, his harmony teacher, to recommend Messiaen to Marcel Dupré."[1] To see his turn to the organ as unexpected, it helps to examine where his interests had lain until the year 1927.

A review of the prizes he won at the Conservatory suggests alternative paths.[2] Messiaen's prizes in harmony and fugue composition (won in 1922, 1924, and 1926) pointed toward possible success as an orchestral composer. Prizes in piano performance and accompaniment (which also involved other keyboard skills like score reading and improvisation)[3] — won each year from 1922 to 1925 — pointed ahead to the song cycles he would compose for voice and piano as well as writings for accompanied violin (after meeting Claire Delbos). Nothing in his Conservatory career through the spring of 1927 suggested a future career as a church organist.

However, the previous autumn semester of 1926 had been marked by two significant events. First, Messiaen's composition teacher that fall was Charles-Marie Widor, the eighty-two-year-old titular organist at Saint-Sulpice in the Latin Quarter for the preceding fifty-six years. Second, thanks largely to Widor's active lobbying, his forty-year-old student, Marcel Dupré,

---

1. Christopher Dingle, "Forgotten Offerings: Messiaen's First Orchestral Works," *Tempo* 62, no. 241 (2007): 2-21, at 4.

2. Peter Hill and Nigel Simeone, *Messiaen* (New Haven: Yale University Press, 2005), 16-17.

1919 (Age 10)	Fall: Messiaen enters the Conservatory as an *auditeur*	
1920 (Age 11)	October: Messiaen first appears as a formally registered student	
1922 (Age 13)	2nd Medal	Piano
	2nd Certificate of Merit	Harmony
1923 (Age 14)	1st Medal	Piano
1924 (Age 15)	2nd Prize	Harmony (Maurice Duruflé won 1st)
	2nd Prize	Piano accompaniment
1925 (Age 16)	1st Prize	Piano accompaniment
1926 (Age 17)	1st Prize	Fugue (counterpoint)
1927 (Age 18)	*No prizes*	*(Cécile Sauvage's death in August)*
1928 (Age 19)	2nd Prize	History of Music
	1st Certificate of Merit	Organ and improvisation
	2nd Certificate of Merit	Composition
1929 (Age 20)	1st Prize	History of Music
	1st Prize	Organ and improvisation
	2nd Prize	Composition
1930 (Age 21)	1st Prize	Composition

3. Hill and Simeone, *Messiaen,* 19.

1927–1932: Budding Rhythmician, Surrealist Composer, Mystical Commentator

assumed the professorship of organ performance and improvisation at the Conservatory.

Widor had succeeded to the post of organ professor at the Conservatory in 1890 (following the death of César Franck). As his student Louis Vierne (organist of Notre-Dame de Paris, 1900-1937) later recalled, Widor instituted a change in direction with his opening remarks: "In France we too greatly favor improvisation over execution. This is more than a mistake. It is nonsense."[4] Widor's class became known as a composition factory — "along the lines of M. Citroën rather than *père* Franck!" quipped Messiaen's mentor, Paul Dukas[5] — producing annual winners of the Grand Prix de Rome. (Dupré won the Prix de Rome in 1914 for his cantata *Psyché*.) Studying composition with Widor and listening to his performances at Saint-Sulpice would have exposed Messiaen to the organ's overwhelming power to dazzle the listener, especially due to the formidable technique and brilliant toccatas for which both Widor and Dupré were famous.

As early as 1922, Widor had been urging Dupré to aim at succession to the Conservatory's organ chair. Once belonging to Franck, the chair had been occupied since 1911 by the aging Eugène Gigout (born in 1844, the same year as Widor), organist at the Parisian church of Saint-Augustin. Gigout's death on December 9, 1925, left the chair vacant. Dupré's astonishing technique reflected Widor's own preference for virtuosity in execution over improvisation as well as strictness in rhythm, phrasing, and legato.[6] (Indeed, Dupré's *Three Preludes and Fugues,* composed by 1911 but not published until 1920, were initially deemed unplayable.)[7] In a series of recitals during 1921-1922, Dupré had dazzled Parisian audiences by performing the complete organ works of J. S. Bach from memory. He had also traveled abroad extensively as a concert performer. Thus, when Gigout died, the charismatic and photogenic Dupré

---

4. Louis Vierne, "Mes Souvenirs," quoted in Michael Murray, *French Masters of the Organ* (New Haven: Yale University Press, 1998), 114.

5. Dukas did not intend this as a compliment and stated his aim as Widor's successor: "I shall very gently try to deindustrialize music. For the moment I think that's the most urgent job before me." Letter of Paul Dukas to Guy Ropartz, November 13, 1927, quoted in Roger Nichols, *The Harlequin Years: Music in Paris, 1917-1929* (Berkeley and Los Angeles: University of California Press, 2002), 184; in Hill and Simeone, *Messiaen,* 20.

6. Murray, *French Masters,* 83, 114-18, 160, 169.

7. Gerard Brooks, "French and Belgian Organ Music after 1800," in *The Cambridge Companion to the Organ,* ed. Nicholas Thistlethwaite and Geoffrey Webber (Cambridge: Cambridge University Press, 1998), 263-78, at 276, and Graham Steed, *The Organ Works of Marcel Dupré* (Hillsdale, N.Y.: Pendragon Press, 1999), 2.

became a celebrity with a cult following. Widor's campaign promoting Dupré's candidacy eventually succeeded.[8]

However, for the young Messiaen, the plot was thicker and the web stickier. Dupré's victory meant the defeat of Messiaen's early mentor, Tournemire. Tournemire had been a twenty-year-old student at the Conservatory when Widor took over the organ class after Franck's death in 1890. Tournemire had idolized Franck; conversely, he came to despise Widor and was convinced that Widor developed "a profound and absurdly enduring hatred with regard to me."[9] Since 1919, when Tournemire became the Conservatory professor of the instrumental ensemble class, he had taken for granted that he would eventually ascend to the organ chair of Franck and Gigout. The expectation was not unreasonable: Tournemire's own practice followed Gigout's teaching, emphasizing improvisation and plainsong accompaniment over virtuosity in performance. Tournemire's own freedom with respect to rhythm, phrasing, and legato would have continued this approach.

Thus, when Tournemire came in second place to Dupré in the competition for succeeding Gigout, he reacted with bitter rage, blaming "the hateful support of Widor" as well as both Dupré and his wife for their instigation "of this disgraceful act." (This was not entirely paranoia on Tournemire's part; Dupré was perfectly capable of conniving against a mentor, as an episode with Vierne demonstrated in 1920-1924.)[10] This tangled web of 1926 sets the stage for Messiaen's organ studies beginning the following year.

In 1927, just after Easter (April 17) — that is, about four months before his mother's unanticipated death (August 26) — Messiaen was sent by Jean Gallon (who had been impressed by the youth's improvisational ability) to attend Dupré's organ class as an *auditeur*.[11] Six months later (a month after his mother's death), Messiaen entered Dupré's fall semester class as a registered student. (Not insignificantly, this is the same fall semester in which Messiaen also entered the composition class of Paul Dukas, newly appointed

---

8. Murray, *French Masters,* 160.

9. Later in life, Tournemire wrote that Widor's arrival had been "catastrophic." For this and following, see Stephen Schloesser, *Jazz Age Catholicism: Mystic Modernism in Postwar Paris, 1919-1933* (Toronto: University of Toronto Press, 2005), 297-99.

10. Later recalling Dupré's instruction to let Vierne come to Sainte-Clotilde and "play like a pig," organist Jean Langlais (Messiaen's classmate and close friend) later confided: "Dupré's meanness was like that." Rollin Smith, *Louis Vierne: Organist of Notre-Dame Cathedral* (Hillsdale, N.Y.: Pendragon Press, 1999), 331-43; Langlais at 343.

11. Christopher Dingle, *The Life of Messiaen* (Cambridge and New York: Cambridge University Press, 2007), 13.

successor to Widor.) Years later (as noted above), Dupré would describe his initial encounter with Messiaen in quasi-mythical terms: "He joined my class in October 1927. When he came out to Meudon [the Parisian suburb in which Dupré lived] for the first time (he was nineteen), he sat stupefied in front of my organ keyboards. He had never seen an organ console before. After an hour of explanations and demonstrations, I gave him the Bach C minor Fantasia to learn. He came back a week later and played it to me by heart, perfectly; an astonishing feat! In class he didn't fidget, but seemed to me to be rather distracted."[12] It seems safe to assume that major contributions to Messiaen's "distraction" were not only the death of his mother just over a month earlier but also his own struggle with tuberculosis that semester.

In yet another account given forty years later, Dupré recounted: "In my preparatory course for the organ class, you played to me, by heart and impeccably, the Fantasia in C minor by Bach. You had been playing the organ for... eight days!"[13] These recollections, regardless of their accuracy, served both Dupré and Messiaen: Dupré because he became so closely identified with his iconic student; Messiaen because his destiny as an organ performer and composer, like his religious faith, seemed to have been fated and to have come out of nowhere. But can Dupré's reports of Messiaen's complete stupefaction and ignorance of the organ — "He had never seen an organ console before" — be believed?

The accuracy of these accounts seems unlikely. First, the nine-year-old Messiaen had studied with the organist Jean (sometimes Jehan) de Gibon in Nantes.[14] Messiaen himself spoke of de Gibon only as his first teacher of "harmony"; but Pierre Messiaen's description of him having "taught [Olivier] the technical elements" suggests the possibility that Messiaen had already been introduced to organ playing in 1919 in the church at Nantes; or, at the very least, he had seen an organ console![15] Second, as Pierre took the boys out for walks in churches because they "demonstrated a genuine passion for religious ceremonies and music"[16] — especially from May 1925 onward (as Cécile's condition worsened) — it seems difficult to believe that the young Conservatory student would neither have asked to see nor gained admittance to the great

12. Marcel Dupré, quoted in Hill and Simeone, *Messiaen*, 22.
13. Marcel Dupré, quoted in Hill and Simeone, *Messiaen*, 22.
14. Pierre Messiaen, *Images* (Paris: Desclée de Brouwer, 1944), 221; cf. Hill and Simeone, *Messiaen*, 14.
15. Messiaen's account appeared in January 1952 in an obituary notice for de Gibon; in Hill and Simeone, *Messiaen*, 14-15.
16. Pierre Messiaen, *Images*, 153.

1927–1931: Decisive Coincidence: The Mystical Organ

organs of his day, including that of Saint-Sulpice, instrument for both Widor and his assistant Dupré.[17]

Third and most importantly was Jean-Yves Daniel-Lesur. He had been born on November 19, 1908, just weeks before Messiaen.[18] His mother, Alice Lesur (née Thiboust), was an accomplished and published composer whom Tournemire considered his "brilliant" and "best" student and friend.[19] Alice sent her young son to study with Tournemire, who took a particular interest in him. As a teenager, Daniel-Lesur was Messiaen's classmate at the Conservatory, and the two became lifelong friends. From 1927 to 1937, Daniel-Lesur served as Tournemire's deputy organist at Sainte-Clotilde; eventually Messiaen also served Tournemire as deputy until assuming his own post in 1931. Given the close bond Daniel-Lesur had with his fatherly mentor Tournemire, it seems extremely unlikely that he had not taken Messiaen with him into Sainte-Clotilde's organ tribunal — Franck's legendary instrument — and introduced him to Tournemire before October 1927. Indeed, given the chronology, Messiaen's decision to study the organ after Easter 1927 would more likely have been catalyzed at Sainte-Clotilde where Daniel-Lesur had begun serving as deputy.[20]

Given the bitter context of Tournemire's and Dupré's competition for the vacated Conservatory organ chair in late 1925 and early 1926, the fact that such a relationship between Tournemire and the adolescent Messiaen would have been suppressed is easily explained. The poisonous relations between Widor, Dupré, and Tournemire would have made difficult terrain for the teenaged Messiaen to negotiate. Especially in a guild in which employment and career opportunities depended largely on a patronage system, the task of not offending anyone would have required a great deal of finesse. For all these reasons, it seems highly unlikely that Messiaen had not thought of studying the organ before April 1927; it is even less plausible that Dupré's account of Messiaen's first contact is reliable.

---

17. Marcel Dupré had been assistant organist at Saint-Sulpice since the age of twenty (1906).

18. Nigel Simeone, "Daniel-Lesur. In Memoriam," *Musical Times* 143, no. 1881 (Winter 2002): 6-8. See also Andrew Thomson, "Daniel-Lesur: The Athenian of Paris," *Musical Times* 132, no. 1781 (July 1991): 333-36; Alexia Tye, "The 'Jeune France' Group in the 1930s — Daniel-Lesur and the Charles Tournemire Lineage," *Organ* 89, no. 353 (Autumn 2010): 42-44.

19. Cécile Auzolle, "Daniel-Lesur et Charles Tournemire: une filiation," in *Musique, art et religion dans l'entre-deux guerres,* ed. Sylvain Caron and Michel Duchesneau (Lyon: Symétrie, 2009), 155-79.

20. Dingle, *The Life of Messiaen,* 13.

Nevertheless, it remains true that, until 1927, Messiaen's studies at the Conservatory did not suggest he would eventually become so closely identified with the organ. According to his own established list, Messiaen's earliest known composition for organ (unpublished) was entitled *Modal Sketch (Esquisse Modale)* and written in 1927, presumably late that fall.[21] The title suggests the influence of Tournemire, who had made the superiority and versatility of "modal" music the key to his mammoth organ work.[22] (Not incidentally, this is the same autumn in which Tournemire began to compose *L'Orgue Mystique,* dating the first completed composition — Easter — November 11, the anniversary of the Armistice.)[23] In the organ class exams for the following May, 1928, Messiaen composed a set of variations *(Scottish Variations)* on the given theme of the Scottish folk song "Comin' through the Rye," for which he received a "First certificate of merit in organ."[24]

Later that summer of 1928 Messiaen composed *The Celestial Banquet* at Fuligny for the December examination of the composition class.[25] *Scottish Variations,* composed for the earlier May exams, undoubtedly demonstrated the influence on him of both Dupré and Dukas — we cannot know for sure, since Messiaen's variations have been lost (or were purposely destroyed). But the character of *The Celestial Banquet* — specifically designated by Messiaen as his first opus — is instead owed to the influence of Tournemire and *L'Orgue Mystique,* the first scores of which had been finished and were going to press that summer.[26]

Messiaen's self-understanding as a liturgical organist came from Tournemire — namely, as a symbolist who contemplates and "comments on" or

---

21. Nigel Simeone, *Olivier Messiaen: A Bibliographical Catalogue of Messiaen's Works,* Musikbibliographische Arbeiten series, vol. 14 (Tutzing: Hans Schneider, 1998), 187.

22. Schloesser, *Jazz Age Catholicism,* 304-5, 308. Marie-Louise Langlais, "'L'École de Sainte-Clotilde' à Paris, son rôle dans le développement d'une musique française pour orgue inspirée par le chant grégorien et sa modalité dans les années 1930," in *Musique, art et religion dans l'entre-deux guerres,* 181-99.

23. Schloesser, *Jazz Age Catholicism,* 309.

24. Hill and Simeone, *Messiaen,* 23, 17; cf. Simeone, *Bibliographical Catalogue,* 188.

25. Simeone, *Bibliographical Catalogue,* 2-5; Jon Gillock, *Performing Messiaen's Organ Music: 66 Masterclasses* (Bloomington: Indiana University Press, 2010), 12-21; Olivier Latry and Loïc Mallié, *L'œuvre d'orgue d'Olivier Messiaen. Œuvres d'avant-guerre* (Stuttgart: Carus, 2008), 62-65.

26. Hill and Simeone, *Messiaen,* 25. For Tournemire's chronology in composing *L'Orgue Mystique,* see Robert Sutherland Lord, "Liturgy and Gregorian Chant in L'Orgue Mystique of Charles Tournemire," *Organ Yearbook* 15 (1984): 60-97; cf. Schloesser, *Jazz Age Catholicism,* 309-11.

1927–1931: Decisive Coincidence: The Mystical Organ

"paraphrases" appointed texts. Messiaen would later use this very word *(commenter)* to describe his work: "Insofar as I was an organist, I had the duty of commenting on the texts proper to the office of the day."[27] *The Celestial Banquet,* for example, "comments on" or "paraphrases" the appointed text from Saint John's Gospel: *demeure* ("abide" or "remain").

Tournemire's influence is evident in Messiaen's unusual registration for the pedal. As one scholar has noted, while *The Celestial Banquet* created "an exciting new effect" by emancipating the pedal "from its traditional role," Messiaen was in fact following Tournemire's lead. The third *L'Orgue Mystique* composition (for Pentecost [no. 25]) — finished on January 9, 1928 — employed similar scoring in the pedal.[28] This was the January during which Messiaen was presumably confined to bed for tuberculosis at his aunts' place in Fuligny; when he read Maritain on the modernity of religious art; and about six months before he composed *The Celestial Banquet.* Given Messiaen's association with Daniel-Lesur, familiarity with Tournemire's recently finished score seems eminently certain.

27. "En tant qu'organiste, j'ai eu le devoir de commenter les textes propres à l'office du jour." Messiaen, in Antoine Goléa, *Rencontres avec Olivier Messiaen* (Paris: Editions Slatkine, 1984), 38, emphasis added. Messiaen said that his epigraphs (taken from biblical, theological, meditative texts) were "of the greatest significance" for the artist to study, inseparable from the origins of his music. See Almut Rößler, *Contributions to the Spiritual World of Olivier Messiaen,* trans. Barbara Dagg and Nancy Poland (Duisberg: Gilles & Francke, 1986), 27-37, at 28. Compare Messiaen's 1938 review of Tournemire: "The *'terminale* piece' is the triumph of Tournemire's art. It is always very long, and it provides a resume of the important religious ideas of each feast by paraphrasing the texts [*en paraphrasant les textes*] of the sequences, hymns, or alleluias proper to the day." Olivier Messiaen, "*L'Orgue Mystique* de Tournemire," *La Syrinx: revue musicale indépendante* (May 1938): 26-27, at 27. It seems likely that Messiaen took Béranger de Miramon Fitz-James's assessment of Tournemire's weekly "feverish inspirations" (in July 1929) as a model for himself: namely, a "liturgical metaphysician, and illustrator, and a musical preacher." For this and more on Tournemire's symbolist method of "paraphrasing" and "commenting on" given liturgical texts, see Schloesser, *Jazz Age Catholicism,* 303, 304, 306, 308, 311, 312.

28. Stuart Waumsley, *The Organ Music of Olivier Messiaen* (Paris: Alphonse Leduc, 1968), 24, referring to the third movement (accompanying the elevation of the eucharistic host) of Charles Tournemire, *L'Orgue Mystique,* "In Festo Pentecostes (Pentecôte)," No. 25 (Paris: Heugel, 1928), 7. Tournemire puts the Gregorian melody into the pedal, which is coupled to the Récit playing a Flûte 4 and Nazard $2\ ^{2/3}$. Messiaen's *Banquet céleste* (1934 edition) similarly has the pedal coupled to the Positif playing a Prestant 4 and Piccolo 1. Waumsley's work was published by Alphonse Leduc (Messiaen's own publisher) and thus functioned as a quasi-authoritative directory to his organ music. Since this specific reference to Tournemire is extremely obscure, it seems probable that Messiaen gave it to Waumsley. For date of Tournemire composition see Lord, "Liturgy and Gregorian Chant," 73.

1927–1932: Budding Rhythmician, Surrealist Composer, Mystical Commentator

The chronological intersection of Tournemire's commencement of *L'Orgue Mystique* and Messiaen's initial studies of the organ following his mother's death was extremely fortuitous. Tournemire gave Messiaen a mode of expressing his literary symbolism, initially prefigured in his ten-year-old encounter with Debussy's *Pelléas and Mélisande*. Anyone looking at Pierre and Cécile Messiaen would have predicted a literary career for their son, not a musical one.[29] Thanks in some part to Tournemire, Messiaen did in fact live out a quasi-literary career: he quoted or wrote textual epigraphs for a great many of his works (placing him squarely in the symbolist lineage); he wrote most of the texts for his own scores (including the libretto for *Saint Francis of Assisi*); and he wrote out detailed explanations or commentaries on his own work. In a sense, then, he did pursue a "literary" career — a fact that would lead to severe criticism in the mid-1940s (during the so-called Messiaen Controversy).[30]

As a corollary, the organ's nature served as the ideal physical instrument for Messiaen's fascination with Bergsonian "duration" and representations of "eternity." The organ's ability to provide sound that endures as long as the key is depressed and air continues to be supplied to the pipes allowed him to indulge one aspect of his signature interest in rhythm — in this case, the near absence of it, approaching the point of stasis.

Messiaen's self-understanding as a church organist, derived from Tournemire, was at one with the Catholic Revivalist project of *la mystique* — the mystical.[31] It aimed not so much at conveying *information* — the job of the historical and the practical; the task of the theologian — as at leading the listener

---

29. Dingle, *The Life of Messiaen*, 1.

30. Discussed below; cf. Hill and Simeone, *Messiaen*, 142-67. See also Radosveta Bruzaud, "Entre verbe et musique: l'épigraphe dans les œuvres d'Olivier Messiaen des années 1930," in *Musique, art et religion dans l'entre-deux guerres*, 405-16.

31. As early as 1999, Julian Tölle suggested that Messiaen's work should be situated within the broader cultural context of the *renouveau catholique*. More recently, Siglind Bruhn has also connected Messiaen to this movement by pointing to his father's associations. The research of Yves Balmer offers the most substantial evidence of both Pierre's and Messiaen's acquaintance with this milieu. See Julian Christoph Tölle, *Olivier Messiaen, Eclairs sur l'au-delà-: die christlich-eschatologische Dimension des Opus ultimum* (New York: Peter Lang, 1999), 223-24; Siglind Bruhn, *Messiaen's Contemplations of Covenant and Incarnation: Musical Symbols of Faith in the Two Great Piano Cycles of the 1940s* (Hillsdale, N.Y.: Pendragon Press, 2007), 19-30; Balmer, "'Je suis né croyant...': Aux sources du catholicisme d'Olivier Messiaen," in *Musique, art et religion dans l'entre-deux guerres*, 417-41; and Balmer, "Religious Literature in Messiaen's Personal Library," in *Messiaen the Theologian*, ed. Andrew Shenton (Burlington, Vt.: Ashgate, 2010), 15-25. See also Robert Fallon, "La spiritualité gothique de Messiaen et le renouveau catholique," trans. Martine Rhéaume, in *Musique, art et religion dans l'entre-deux guerres*, 387-403.

into an *experience*. It sought to act as the midwife of a *presence:* not so much an increase in knowledge as an increase in *emotion*.[32]

1927–1930: Calls of the Orient — a Mystic Vogue

In addition to the literary influence of his parents and the symbolist influence coming from Debussy and Tournemire, Messiaen was fascinated by music history, both European and beyond, thanks in large part to Maurice Emmanuel. Messiaen's multivolume *Treatise on Rhythm, Color, and Ornithology (1949-1992)* is brimming with references to historical works.[33] As already seen in the 1927-1930 works, Messiaen included elements of plainchant, Russian folk songs, and music of the Incas, along with the current vogue of surrealist poetry and imagery.

There was also the turn to "the Orient": Emmanuel's *Sonatina IV: On Hindu Modes (Sonatine IV: sur des modes hindous)* had already been composed in 1920 and published in 1923 — the same year as Albert Roussel's opera-ballet *Padmâvatî*.[34] This eastward musical turn, most especially to Hinduism and Islam, paralleled contemporaneous postwar works in "mystical" studies: for example, R. A. Nicholson, *Studies in Islamic Mysticism* (1921); Louis Massignon, *The Passion of al Hallâj, Mystical Martyr of Islam* (1922); Louis Renou, *The Value of Perfection in Vedic Hymns* (1925); works by René Guénon (who took the name Abd al-Wahid Yahya), including *General Introduction to the Study of Hindu Doctrines* (1921), *East and West* (1924), *Man and His Becoming according to the Vedânta* (1925); and numerous works in translation by Rabindranath Tagore, to name just a few. In the middle of the postwar decade, a massive compendium of thought on the "Orient" by French intellectuals, writers, and

---

32. See Jan Plamper, "The History of Emotions: An Interview with William Reddy, Barbara Rosenwein, and Peter Stearns," *History and Theory* 49, no. 2 (May 2010): 237-65; Barbara H. Rosenwein, *Emotional Communities in the Early Middle Ages* (Ithaca, N.Y.: Cornell University Press, 2006); Penelope Gouke and Helen Hills, eds., *Representing Emotions: New Connections in the Histories of Art, Music, and Medicine* (Burlington, Vt.: Ashgate, 2005); Rosenwein, "Worrying about Emotions in History," *American Historical Review* 107, no. 3 (June 2002): 821-45; and William M. Reddy, *The Navigation of Feeling: A Framework for the History of Emotions* (New York: Cambridge University Press, 2001). See also Jerome Neu, *A Tear Is an Intellectual Thing: The Meanings of Emotion* (New York: Oxford University Press, 2000).

33. Messiaen, *Traité de rythme, de couleur, et d'ornithologie (1949-1992) en sept tomes*, 8 vols. (Paris: Alphonse Leduc, 1994-2002).

34. Hill and Simeone, *Messiaen*, 19-20.

artists was published as *Appeals of the Orient* (or Calls = *appels* [1925]). Two years later, the right-wing writer Henri Massis felt compelled to publish his *Defense of the West*. By the end of the 1920s, Jacques Maritain's "Thomistic Study Circle" — founded to deepen understanding of Thomas Aquinas — was sponsoring lectures on the Vedanta Sara and Bhagavad Gita.[35] Interest in the "mystical" East, especially Hinduism, pervaded the Parisian scene in the 1920s and 1930s. Messiaen breathed this air.

Finally, not unlike Maurice Emmanuel, Tournemire was himself a pioneer in promoting a renaissance of "ancient" (i.e., pre-Baroque) music and especially "modalism."[36] In a letter to Dom Gajard, the Benedictine musicologist and plainchant expert at Solesmes, Tournemire expounded his strongly held vision of music history: "The grand masters of modality" had been "Frescobaldi in Italy, Buxtehude in Germany, Titelouze and Grigny in France," all of them "pioneers of ancient modality."[37]

The prizes that Messiaen won at the end of the academic years 1927-1928 and 1928-1929 — those in organ, composition, and music history — reflected the future direction his life would take. The years 1926-1927 proved to be the exception rather than the rule: he received no honors at the end of that academic year (following the Easter at which he decided to study the organ). It seems that something interiorly at age eighteen (during the year preceding his mother's death) was shifting directions. One factor may have been the

---

35. Reynold Alleyne Nicholson, *Studies in Islamic Mysticism* (Cambridge: University Press, 1921); Louis Massignon, *Al-Hallâj: martyr mystique de l'Islam*, 4 vols. (Paris: P. Geuthner, 1922); Louis Renou, *La valeur du parfait dans les hymnes védiques* (Paris: E. Champion, 1925); René Guénon, *Introduction générale à l'étude des doctrines Hindoues* (Paris: M. Rivière, 1921); Guénon, *Orient et Occident* (Paris: Payot, 1924); Guénon, *L'homme et son devenir selon de Vêdânta* (Paris: Bossard, 1925); Rabindranath Tagore, *Art et anatomie hindous* (Paris: Éditions Bossard, 1921); Tagore and André Gide, *L'offrande lyrique*, 18th ed. (Paris: Éditions de la Nouvelle revue française, 1921); Tagore, *La religion du poète*, trans. A. Tougard de Boismilon (Paris: Payot, 1924); *Les Appels de l'Orient, Les Cahiers du Mois* 9/10 (Paris: Émile-Paul, Frères, 1925); and Henri Massis, *Défense de l'Occident* (Paris: Plon, 1927). For Maritain see Schloesser, *Jazz Age Catholicism*, 204-5.

36. Dietrich Buxtehude, *Passacaile, chacones, préludes et fugues, toccatas, canzonette: pour orgue*, ed. Charles Tournemire (Paris: Éditions Salabert, 1923); Louis-Claude d'Aquin, Nicolas Antoine Lebègue, and Jean François Dandrieu, *Douze noëls anciens pour orgue*, ed. Charles Tournemire (Brussels and Paris: Schott frères, 1938). Between 1903 and 1907, Tournemire's intellectual formation had been steeped in and profoundly shaped by Eastern thought and religions. See Schloesser, *Jazz Age Catholicism*, 291.

37. Charles Tournemire to Dom Gajard, date unknown, in Schloesser, *Jazz Age Catholicism*, 305; cf. Tournemire, "La Musique modale à l'orgue," *La Tribune de Saint-Gervais* 26, no. 12 (November 1929): 165-67.

1927–1931: Decisive Coincidence: The Mystical Organ

family's dire financial situation and the increasing pressure he felt to provide more income, something that organ substitution would provide. Whatever the causes, a more specific new direction seems evident in 1927-1928, the year following Cécile's death:

1927-28	Age 19:	Composition — Second certificate of merit
		Organ — First certificate of merit
		History of Music — Second prize
1928-29	Age 20:	Composition — Second prize
		Organ — First prize
		History of Music — First prize
1930	Age 21:	Composition — First prize

In 1929 he was "also presented with the coveted *Diplôme d'études musicales supérieures,* an award from the governing body of the Conservatoire in recognition of consistently high achievement by a student." Finally, in 1930 (at age twenty-one) he won first prize in composition.[38]

This trifecta of superior performance in organ, composition, and history reflected the strong influence of Messiaen's Conservatory teachers — Dupré, Dukas, and Emmanuel — as well as Tournemire.

1930–1931: Titular Organist and Mystic Composer

The spring of 1930 was not the best of times to graduate from school. The New York stock market crash in October 1929 had triggered the worldwide Great Depression. Although its arrival would be somewhat delayed in Europe, crisis was in the air. The *années folles* (crazy years) of the postwar 1920s were ending as the "menacing years," "hollow years," and "dark valley" of the interwar 1930s arrived.[39] Messiaen, impoverished before the Great Depression, now needed to engage activity that would provide income. He was enormously

---

38. Hill and Simeone, *Messiaen,* 17.

39. Suzanne Pacé, *Années 30 en Europe: le temps menaçant 1929-1939: exposition du 20 février au 25 mai 1997, Musée d'art moderne de la ville de Paris* (Paris: Paris musées; Flammarion, 1997); Eugen Weber, *The Hollow Years: France in the 1930s* (New York: Norton, 1994); Piers Brendon, *The Dark Valley: A Panorama of the 1930s* (New York: Knopf, distributed by Random House, 2000); Serge Berstein, *La France des années 30,* 2nd ed. (Paris: Armand Colin, 1995); Philippe Bernard and Henri Dubief, *The Decline of the Third Republic, 1914-1938,* trans. Anthony Forster (New York: Cambridge University Press, 1985).

fortunate in having published three works in 1930: *Diptych, Preludes,* and *Three Melodies.*

Messiaen was also extremely lucky to have *The Forgotten Offerings* receive its premiere in February 1931 at the Théâtre des Champs-Elysées; this was the first public performance of one of his orchestral works.[40] In a review of this performance, Messiaen was first publicly described as a "mystic" composer. A listener would need to have completely missed Messiaen's point, wrote the reviewer, not "to recognize a musician, an artist, a nature 'in depths'; and what pleases me best of all, a mystic [*un mystique*]." Although he did observe that Messiaen seemed largely incapable of representing sin in the second part ("Sin"), the triptych's framing slow movements ("Cross" and "Eucharist") demonstrated that he was "infinitely more capable of representing tenderness, sorrow, and the humanly perceptible part of the ineffability of music and his mysticism [*sa mystique*]."[41]

This public designation of Messiaen as "a mystic" undoubtedly assisted him when, one year after graduating from the Conservatory and five months after this review, fortune opened up a very rare, prestigious post. Messiaen had been the regular organ deputy for the ailing Charles Quef, titular organist at the Parisian church of La Trinité since 1929. When Quef died on July 2, 1931, Messiaen sought assistance in obtaining his vacated post, turning to both Dupré and Widor. He also sought out Tournemire, for whom he also deputized occasionally at Sainte-Clotilde and with whom he corresponded while in Fuligny for the summer break.[42]

Messiaen's choice of Tournemire as a mentor and advocate, in addition to his Conservatory teachers, suggests the self-conscious persona he was adopting as a "mystical" musician. In April 1930, Tournemire's interview with the music critic José Bruyr had appeared in *Guide du Concert.* Bruyr quoted Tournemire: "Nourished by mysticism, I aspire to nothing other than to make music participate with all possible piety in the mysteries of Sacrifice."[43] Tournemire actively promoted this self-identity: his 78-rpm recording of his master

40. Hill and Simeone, *Messiaen,* 29-31.

41. Review by A. Febvre-Longeray of performance (February 19, 1931); in *Le Courrier musical* 33, no. 6 (March 15, 1931): 186; in Simeone, *Bibliographical Catalogue,* 208.

42. See letters of Olivier Messiaen to Charles Tournemire dated August 4 and 10, 1931, and September 17, 1931; in Joël-Marie Fauquet, "Correspondance inédite. Lettres d'Olivier Messiaen à Charles Tournemire," in *Charles Tournemire (1870-1939),* ed. Brigitte de Leersnyder, *Cahiers et Mémoires de l'Orgue* 41 (Paris: Les Amis de l'Orgue, 1989), 80-85. See also Schloesser, *Jazz Age Catholicism,* 308.

43. Charles Tournemire, interview with José Bruyr, "Un entretien avec . . . Charles

1927–1931: Decisive Coincidence: The Mystical Organ

César Franck's *Chorale in A Minor* for organ won the 1931 Prix Candide for best recording on a solo instrument. (For a Jazz Age comparison, the prize in the category of "light music" [*musique legère*] went to "Mlle. Joséphine Baker" for her Columbia Records recording of "Suppose.") This recording appeared at the same time as Tournemire's small study entitled *César Franck* (1931), rewriting his master as a "mystical" composer.[44] Tournemire's version of Franck, which had very little to do with the actual late-nineteenth-century bourgeois music professor, was rivaled by one created by Dupré.[45]

Later that year, in July and August 1931, along with Widor and Dupré, Tournemire lobbied vigorously for the candidacy of his "protégé," Messiaen.[46] On July 15, he wrote to the curate at La Trinité:

> The musical value and the future of this Christian organist are of the highest order: a transcendent improviser, an astonishing performer, and a biblical composer, my protégé is growing very clearly into someone well above the majority of artists about whom too much is said, in my opinion.
>
> With Messiaen, all is prayer.

A week later, Tournemire wrote another letter asking for an intermediary's support: "I am particularly concerned about the young and magnificent Chris-

---

Tournemire," *Guide du Concert*, April 18, 1930, 791-93, at 793; quoted in Schloesser, *Jazz Age Catholicism*, 310. Capitalization of "Sacrifice" in original.

44. Charles Tournemire, *César Franck* (Paris: Delagrave, 1931). See Schloesser, *Jazz Age Catholicism*, 300, 319.

45. As Andrew Thomson notes, Tournemire's small book presented Franck as the incarnation of "the spirit of the 13th century, summit of Catholic civilization, that which had produced the Gothic cathedrals, Saint Thomas Aquinas and Dante." In actuality, however, Franck "remained to the end of his life a bourgeois professor of music, of limited general culture, typical of his epoch, and in no way responsible for this image." Tournemire's version was instead an example of the kind of psychological projection of "acolytes intoxicated by Wagner and by the neo-medieval writings of Huysmans and Péladan." Thomson, "Les enregistrements de Charles Tournemire," trans. Jacqueline Englert-Marchal, in *Charles Tournemire (1870-1939)*, 47-59, at 57. Cf. Thomson, "The Mystic Organist: Charles Tournemire (1870-1939)," *Organists' Review* 3-5 (March-May 1989).

Three years after Tournemire's 1930 recording session at Sainte-Clotilde, Dupré recorded all three of Franck's *Chorales* at Saint Mark's Church, London. Lawrence Archbold, "'We Have No Idea of the Liberty with Which Franck Played His Own Pieces': Early French Recordings of César Franck's A-Minor Chorale and the Question of Authenticity," in *The Organist as Scholar: Essays in Memory of Russell Saunders* (Festschrift Series), ed. Kerala J. Snyder (Hillsdale, N.Y.: Pendragon Press, 1994), 83-116, at 90.

46. Hill and Simeone, *Messiaen*, 34-36; cf. Schloesser, *Jazz Age Catholicism*, 308.

tian artist, and a pure Christian *whose mysticism is well-balanced:* Olivier Messiaen.... His future is splendid — and what is better, much better, he prays and he conceives his musical works to the glory of Xrist."[47] The campaign was successful. Messiaen was named organist at La Trinité in the fall of 1931. Fortune had smiled on him, providing at least some means of steady income as the Great Depression settled in. He would maintain the post until his death sixty-one years later.

Messiaen's reputation as a "mystical" composer grew. After a second performance of *The Forgotten Offerings* at the Conservatory in December 1931 (three months after he had taken over the post at La Trinité), a brief but important review written by Tournemire declared: "The very young composer Olivier Messiaen pursues a very pure ideal; *he belongs to the lineage of mystics* [*des mystiques*]."[48] Five years later the appellation had become standard: reviewing yet another performance of *The Forgotten Offerings,* a critic wrote that the work made manifest in Messiaen "a mysticity [*une mysticité*] that is passionate, elevated, reflective, and expressed in a subtle language in its purity."[49] A year later the image appeared across the English Channel in the *Times:* "A Mystic Composer" (December 11, 1937).[50]

Messiaen himself encouraged the "mystical" appellation. Shortly after his appointment at La Trinité, he sat down with José Bruyr (who had interviewed Tournemire a year earlier). When Bruyr asked what the almost twenty-three-year-old thought of the state of music in 1931, Messiaen replied in terms echoing Tournemire and perhaps repaying his patronage: "I think that today the most important thing is not to destroy tonality but to enrich it. In this regard we have terribly neglected Gregorian chant: a source which is still living.... I think it's above all in the mystic sense that this source can give life to our art."

At the interview's end, Messiaen was more precise: "we must return to Charles Tournemire, whose *L'Orgue mystique,* washed clean of any sentimentality, also relies on the art of Gregorian chant.... The only admissible way

---

47. Letters of Charles Tournemire; quoted in Nigel Simeone, "'Chez Messiaen, tout est prière': Messiaen's Appointment at the Trinité," *Musical Times* 145, no. 1889 (Winter 2004): 36-53, at 40. Emphasis added.

48. Charles Tournemire, review of the second performance of Messiaen's *Forgotten Offerings* (December 6, 1931); in *Le Courrier musical* 33, no. 20 (December 15, 1931): 594; in Simeone, *Bibliographical Catalogue,* 208. Emphasis added.

49. Roger Vinteuil, review of the first concert of La Jeune France (June 3, 1936); in *Le Ménestrel* 98, no. 24 (June 12, 1936): 192; in Simeone, *Bibliographical Catalogue,* 209.

50. "E. E." [Edwin Evans], "A Mystic Composer," *Times* (London), December 11, 1937; cited in Dingle, *The Life of Messiaen,* 66 n. 54.

[of relying on chant] is . . . to rediscover the depths of the soul — the mystical soul — and faith." Bruyr quipped: "Olivier Messiaen seems to want to claim a kingdom for which there is little competition: that of the mystical composer."[51]

Since Bruyr's review did not appear in print until 1933, it was able to solidify the already-growing impression of Messiaen's "mystical" character as his works were performed more and more in public. In March-April 1933, Messiaen's ten-minute orchestral work entitled *Hymn to the Blessed Sacrament* (1932), described by the composer as "a song of praise to Jesus present in the Host," received its first performance and reviews.[52] In 1932-1934 Messiaen composed his four-movement *Ascension* suite for orchestra, self-consciously "mystical" in its enormously slow (to the point of being nearly static) representations of "eternity" in the inner life of the divinity. Premiered in early 1935 (in both its orchestral and organ transcription versions), it represented the summit of Messiaen's self-representation as a "mystical composer."

Symbolist Commentator

Messiaen's new vocation as organist obliged him to improvise — that is, "comment on" or "paraphrase" — the assigned musical and linguistic "texts" given in the Catholic office books. This in turn amplified his self-understanding as a "mystical" musician: "during the office, I participate in the mystery that unfolds, that inscribed in the consecration of bread and of wine, that of the transubstantiation. There the Blessed Sacrament is present while I improvise, and I know that it is under these conditions that what I produce is better [than in concerts]."[53]

Messiaen's contract specified that he would be present each Sunday for the 9 A.M., 11 A.M., and noon Masses, and for the vespers service at 5 P.M. At the sung "High Masses" of 9 and 11 he was constrained to accompany the

---

51. Olivier Messiaen, interview with José Bruyr; Bruyr, "Olivier Messiaen," in *L'Écran des musiciens, seconde série* (Paris: José Corti, 1933), 124-31; quoted in Hill and Simeone, *Messiaen*, 37-39. On April 25, 1932, Messiaen assisted Tournemire by playing pieces from *L'Orgue Mystique* the following spring (along with Daniel-Lesur and several other young star organists) at a grand concert at Sainte-Clotilde, an evening aimed at making the massive work familiar to a wider audience. Tournemire's handwritten program is reproduced in Leersnyder, *Charles Tournemire (1870-1939)*, 28-29. See Schloesser, *Jazz Age Catholicism*, 320.

52. Quoted by "F.D." in review of the first performance (March 23, 1933); *Le Courrier musical* 35, no. 8 (April 15, 1933): 196; in Simeone, *Bibliographical Catalogue*, 215-16, at 215.

53. Brigitte Massin and Olivier Messiaen, *Olivier Messiaen: une poétique du merveilleux* (Aix-en-Provence: Alinéa, 1989), 66.

choirs as they sang both the ordinary and proper works for the liturgy. But the noon Mass gave him greater latitude for improvisation.[54] (He nicknamed this service "The Mass of the crazies" [*La Messe des fous*] since "the congregation expressed themselves with violence against a presence at the organ.")[55] Even before attaining the titular post, as Quef's deputy Messiaen knew the congregation's negative attitudes toward his performances. In a letter responding to Messiaen's application for the position, the parish curate felt obliged to report earlier reactions to the young substitute's improvisations: "Finally, the deputizing you have done at the Trinité during M. Quef's illness has not won over the general congregation. You are one of the leading representatives of a young school which likes dissonances and which some consider to be too noisy. Note that in saying this I am not passing judgment on one style or another, but giving you the spontaneous reactions of those who like music and who, without knowing who is playing the instrument, have been in a state of revolt. This is something that needs to be faced."[56]

Because the noon Mass was a "Low Mass" (i.e., not sung by a choir), Messiaen had no obligations other than "to play at the given moments my choice, or to improvise." At first, fresh out of the Conservatory, he played mostly Bach. But later he began improvising, and it was because of this experience that he acquired "the desire to fix certain moments, to organize them, and in the end, to compose."[57] The Parisian writer Julien Green recalled hearing a Messiaen improvisation: "It is of monstrous beauty, opening up immense caverns where rivers flow, where piles of precious stones glitter. We do not know where we are — in India perhaps. The composer was playing on the organ of the Trinité. Never have the vaults of this hideous edifice heard more

---

54. Olivier Messiaen and Claude Samuel, *Music and Color: Conversations with Claude Samuel*, trans. E. Thomas Glasow (Portland, Ore.: Amadeus Press, 1994), 25, hereafter "Messiaen and Samuel (1994)."

55. Massin and Messiaen, *Olivier Messiaen*, 65.

56. Letter of Curé Hemmer to Olivier Messiaen, early August 1931. Messiaen responded: "Dissonant music. When I was deputizing at the Trinité, I know that I sometimes exhibited tendencies which were a little too modern, and I regret that now. I was only twenty years old when I deputized for the first time; I am now twenty-two-and-a-half, and at this time of life one evolves very quickly. My current view is that . . . [f]or the organ, especially the organ in church, what matters above all is the liturgy. The environment and the instrument are not well suited to modern music and it is important not to disturb the piety of the faithful by using chords which are too anarchic." Messiaen to Hemmer, August 8, 1931, from Fuligny. Both letters quoted in Simeone, " 'Chez Messiaen, tout est prière': Messiaen's Appointment at the Trinité," 41, 42.

57. Massin and Messiaen, *Olivier Messiaen*, 65.

disturbing sounds. Occasionally I had the impression that hell was opening, suddenly gaping wide. There were cataracts of strange noises *dazzling* the ear."[58] Aaron Copland offered a more reserved account: "Visited Messiaen in the organ loft at the Trinité. Heard him improvise at noon. Everything from the 'devil' in the bass, to Radio City Music Hall harmonies in the treble. Why the Church allows it during service is a mystery."[59] John Cage, too, went up to the organ loft to hear Messiaen improvise: "Glorious and shocking sounds," he recalled; "such a sweet person too."[60]

The religious "office" Messiaen most enjoyed playing was not any of the three Masses but rather the Sunday vespers at 5:00 P.M. "There I was able to improvise, and it is without doubt the moment when I was able most to unite myself to the texts [*m'unir aux textes*], because they were sung in plainchant. Thus I improvised on the psalms and the Antiphonal texts."[61] Following Tournemire's style — one Messiaen termed "half-Gothic, half-ultra-modern" (*mi-gothique, mi-ultra moderne*) — a line of Gregorian chant would be taken from the vespers proper to the day and freely improvised on in sonorities that could be ultramodern precisely because they were medieval, that is, modal.[62]

It is easy to forget that the "line" in the vespers service was both a linguistic text of words (usually taken from the Scriptures) and an accompanying melody to be sung. In preparation for *L'Orgue Mystique*, Tournemire wrote out the liturgical (linguistic) texts on which he was to musically "comment" (*commenter*). The composition was thus intended not only as musical variations on the melodic line but also as a "paraphrase" of or a "commentary" on the linguistic texts. Messiaen's earliest example of this was *The Celestial Banquet*, intended as a "commentary" on words from the Gospel of John: "He who eats my flesh and drinks my blood abides in me and I in him." As Tournemire wrote in his letter of endorsement for the Trinité post, Messiaen was "a Biblical composer."[63]

---

58. Julien Green, quoted in Hill and Simeone, *Messiaen*, 185.

59. Aaron Copland, quoted in Alex Ross, *The Rest Is Noise: Listening to the Twentieth Century* (New York: Farrar, Straus and Giroux, 2007), 446.

60. John Cage, quoted in Kenneth Silverman, *Begin Again: A Biography of John Cage* (New York: Knopf, 2010), 82.

61. Massin and Messiaen, *Olivier Messiaen*, 65.

62. Messiaen, "*L'Orgue Mystique* de Tournemire" (May 1938), 27; quoted in Schloesser, *Jazz Age Catholicism*, 311. At least as far back as Claude Debussy (who visited Solesmes in 1893), composers found in modalism an extension of melodic vocabulary allowing them to go beyond tonalism's strictures. See Schloesser, 284-85.

63. Tournemire to Hemmer, July 15, 1931, quoted in Simeone, " 'Chez Messiaen, tout est prière': Messiaen's Appointment at the Trinité," 40.

Fifteen years later, during the so-called Messiaen Controversy at the end of the German occupation, critics would attack Messiaen viciously, accusing him of using too many words and providing too much commentary (which they considered distracting and irrelevant) on the "pure music." Yet this was the way he understood his task as a musician; one interiorized by the weekly obligation of improvisation. Although not so fundamental to American church services, this understanding of the organist's task endures to this day in France — exemplified by Jean Guillou at Saint-Eustache; Olivier Latry, Jean-Pierre Leguay, and Philippe Lefebvre at Notre-Dame; Daniel Roth at Saint-Sulpice; Thierry Escaich at Saint-Etienne-du-Mont; and Jean-Baptiste Robin at the Royal Chapel in the Palace of Versailles, to name but a few. It is easy for an American reader to miss how deeply associated music and text are in this practice of improvisation, especially when the linguistic text is not explicitly articulated. In the organ Messiaen found sustenance on both a religious level (meditating on religious texts) and a literary level (inherited from Pierre and Cécile). This need and gift for textual meditation would be strengthened in his introduction to the writings of Dom Columba Marmion.

Lectio Divina: Dom Columba Marmion and Art of Contemplation

Shortly after Messiaen took the Trinité post, his spiritual confessor said to him, "you have become an organist, you must now understand the liturgical cycle as it is inscribed over the course of a year. You should read *Christ in His Mysteries* by Dom Columba Marmion, you will find there everything you need in order to reflect on the liturgical cycle. Your position [as organist] effectively obligates you from now on to a liturgical work concerning what you do not yet understand."[64]

Who was Dom Marmion and what kind of book is *Christ in His Mysteries*? Marmion (b. 1858) was made abbot of Maredsous Abbey in 1909 and remained so until his death in 1923. Situated in the Ardennes Forest near the city of Namur in southern Belgium, the abbey was founded in 1872 by Henri and Jules Desclée, the two brothers who established Desclée de Brouwer, the publishing house renowned for Roman Catholic literature. The abbey was intended to

---

64. Massin and Messiaen, *Olivier Messiaen*, 68. For the French edition used in the present study, see Dom Columba Marmion, *Le Christ dans ses mystères. Conférences spirituelles* (Namur, Belgium: Abbaye de Maredsous; Paris and Bruges: Desclée de Brouwer et Cie, [1919] 1928); for English translation see Columba Marmion, *Christ in His Mysteries*, trans. Alan Bancroft (Bethesda, Md.: Zaccheus Press, 2008).

serve as a refuge for Benedictine monks expelled from Germany during the *Kulturkampf*, and, inspired by its German motherhouse, it developed a school of applied arts and crafts. Marmion's own curious background contributed a curious accent to this jumble of cultures: although born in Ireland and natively Anglophone, he would eventually write his works in French; they would then need to be retranslated into English to be published in Anglophone countries.

It is difficult to overstate the popularity of Marmion's *Christ in His Mysteries* in the postwar epoch. First published in 1919 just after the Armistice, the work sold 45,000 copies by 1930 (the latest edition as Messiaen took over his new post). Over the next three years — during which the work was translated into at least Flemish, English, German, Polish, Spanish, and Italian — another 25,000 copies were sold.[65] As the work's subtitle ("spiritual conferences") suggests, its chapters consist of the kinds of edifying retreat lectures *(conférences)* delivered to fellow monks as preparation for their personal meditation.[66] One indication of this originally clerical audience is that the scriptural passages saturating Marmion's text — both as the starting point for commentaries and as glosses on those meditations — are always quoted from the Vulgate edition of the Bible without translation, which presumes that the readers (and original listeners) could read Latin. It should be added, however, that lay readers who had attended Catholic schools (and even many who had attended state schools) would have been able to read Latin in the 1920s and 1930s.

The genre is that of devotional literature, and Marmion excludes any hint of historical exegesis or theological criticism. As such, his work directly descends from that of his Benedictine ancestor, Dom Guéranger, whose multi-volume *Liturgical Year* had been given to Tournemire and inspired *L'Orgue Mystique*.[67] Guéranger's work carefully distinguished between three genres of textual commentary: the historical, the mystical, and the practical *(l'his-*

---

65. Massin and Messiaen, *Olivier Messiaen*, 70. See successive editions following the initial 1919 printing: 1921, 1922, 1923, 1925, 1926, 1928, 1929, 1930, 1932, etc. "A survey was made among Belgian Catholics during the [First World] War which asked, 'Do you read religious books? Which titles and authors?' The name most frequently mentioned was that of Marmion." J. Cardolle, *Aux Jeunes. Et toi, connais-tu le Christ, vie de ton âme? D'après l'œuvre de Dom Marmion* (Paris and Bruges: Desclée de Brouwer, 1949), n.p.; quoted in Balmer, "Religious Literature," 20.

66. *Christ in His Mysteries* is the middle work in a trilogy, the first and last books of which are *Christ, the Life of the Soul* (1914) and *Christ, the Ideal of the Monk* (1923): Columba Marmion, *Le Christ, vie de l'âme: conférences spirituelles* (Maredsous, Belgium: Abbaye de Maredsous, 1914); Marmion, *Le Christ: idéal du moine: conférences spirituelles sur la vie monastique et religieuse* (Maredsous and Namur, Belgium: Abbaye de Maredsous, 1923).

67. Schloesser, *Jazz Age Catholicism*, 299-303.

1927–1932: Budding Rhythmician, Surrealist Composer, Mystical Commentator

torique, la mystique, la pratique). Although the historical indulged in historical exegesis and theological criticism, Guéranger considered this merely preparatory to the most important value of the *Liturgical Year*, the mystical. In this genre, as Guéranger wrote, "we purposely avoid everything which would savor of critical discussion."[68] The point was not to add any more to the demystification of the faith being produced by nineteenth-century historical and theological studies. Rather, the mystical aimed at precisely the opposite: rekindling the inner fervor of believers whose souls had been cooled by approaches too rational. The mystical was this interior sanctification and even divinization that came by participating in the mysteries.

So too for Marmion's much shorter and accessible (and thereby more popular) work. He makes the mystical purpose of this volume explicit in the foreword to the original edition: "And so the mysteries of the God-man are not only models that we ought to ponder; they also contain within themselves treasures of merit and of grace. By His almighty power Christ Jesus, ever living, *produces the interior and supernatural perfection of His states in those who are moved by a sincere desire to imitate Him,* and who put themselves in contact with Him through faith and love."[69] Here Marmion echoes Guéranger, for whom Christ's coming into the soul in a present-day appropriation is "mysterious and full of love." Even the form of his presentation imitates Guéranger, who had written, "These longings for a Messiah ... are *not a mere commemoration* of the ancient Jewish people; they have *a reality and efficacy* of their own. ... In vain would the Son of God have come, nineteen hundred years ago, to visit and save mankind, *unless He came again for each one of us and at every moment of our lives.*"[70]

For Marmion, the key word is not "events" or "circumstances" but rather "mysteries" as laid out in the first chapter's title: "The Mysteries of Christ Are Our Mysteries."[71] The tradition, writes Marmion, should not be "buried,

---

68. Stephen Schloesser, "The Charm of Impossibilities: Mystic Surrealism as Contemplative Voluptuousness," in *Messiaen the Theologian*, 168-70; Guéranger at 169.

69. Marmion, "Foreword to the Original Edition [March 25, 1919]," in *Christ in His Mysteries*, xiii-xv, at xiii, emphasis added.

70. Guéranger, quoted in Schloesser, "Charm of Impossibilities," 169. Compare Marmion: "Our Lord did not come solely for those inhabitants of Palestine who were living in His time, but for all men throughout all ages: 'Christ died for all.' The gaze of Jesus, being a divine gaze, was cast upon every soul; His love extended to each one of us." Marmion, chapter 1 in *Christ in His Mysteries*, 3-22, at 21.

71. Marmion, chapter 1 in *Christ in His Mysteries*, 3-22; on the word "mysteries" see translator's note, 12 n. 48.

like a dead letter, in the depths of the Holy Scriptures." Rather, we ought to "contemplate" the "mystery of Christ." This should not be through a "purely intellectual study," for "such a study is often dry and sterile." Rather, we ought "to contemplate Him so as to conform our own lives . . . so that our thirst may be fully quenched"; for this knowledge is "a fountain of water, springing up into life everlasting." (Compare Messiaen's words in *The Technique of My Musical Language:* "to give our century the spring water for which it thirsts.") "It is true that in their historical, material duration the mysteries of Christ's life on earth are now past; but *their power remains,*" and we can have a share in them. The mode is clear: it is "through the choice of quotations from the sacred books and from holy authors," and through the church's "symbolism" and "rites," that our interiors are disposed for "a full and generous assimilation of the spiritual fruit of each mystery."[72]

Messiaen would certainly have appreciated the way Marmion's text echoes the nineteenth-century symbolist project of clothing the invisible with the visible. It is "a psychological law of our nature — our nature being matter and spirit — that we go from the visible to the invisible." The "exterior elements of the celebration of the mysteries are to serve for our souls like the rungs of a ladder"; by means of them we can contemplate and love "realities that are heavenly and supernatural." These exterior elements are therefore useful, but they are only the "fringe of Christ's garment." We ought not to stop there but go beyond: "The glory, the splendor, the power of the mysteries of Jesus are chiefly *interior,* and are what we should be seeking above all." To repeat, when we contemplate these mysteries, it is not for a historical project — "not only for the purpose of recalling to our minds the events accomplished for our salvation." Rather, the point is so that "our souls may participate in a special set of circumstances of the sacred humanity" of Christ.[73]

For Messiaen, Marmion's method would have been a logical and seamless extension of the symbolist vision undergirding both Debussy and Tournemire. The meaning of improvisation as "commenting on" or "paraphrasing" a sacred text can easily be seen as a musical mode of doing what Marmion does: the devotional "reader" (literary or musical) takes texts and meditates on them in such a way that they lead auditors to prayer and then, ideally, to a transformation of the self. Marmion's method is thoroughly Benedictine and a recovery

---

72. Marmion, chapter 1 ("The Mysteries of Christ Are Our Mysteries") and chapter 2 ("How We Assimilate the Fruit of the Mysteries of Jesus"), in *Christ in His Mysteries,* 3-22 and 23-38, at 9, 20, 26; cf. "spring" water, 11.

73. Marmion, chapter 2 in *Christ in His Mysteries,* 23-38, at 28, 30.

of the ancient monastic practice of *lectio divina* in which words on the page are gradually transformed into mystical union with God.[74] After reading the text *(lectio)*, one meditated on the words *(meditatio)*, an action that in turn led to prayer *(oratio)*. From here, if so moved, divine action brought one into contemplative union with itself *(contemplatio)*. Marmion's work is a modern recovery of this ancient *lectio divina*. A recent writer put his words poetically:

We read	(Lectio)
under the eye of God	(Meditatio)
until the heart is touched	(Oratio)
and leaps to flame.	(Contemplatio)[75]

From Cécile and Pierre, Messiaen inherited a profound appreciation of literature. From Tournemire (following Guéranger), he apprenticed a "mystical" improviser's identity as being a "commentator" on liturgical texts. Reading Marmion, descended from Guéranger's Benedictine tradition, Messiaen deepened these earlier paths. His improvisations and compositions were a musical application of *lectio divina*. One of the first and most enduring of these would be his *Apparition of the Eternal Church* (1931-1932).

---

74. For the classic study see Dom Jean Leclercq, *L'Amour des lettres et le désir de Dieu: initiation aux auteurs monastiques du Moyen-Age* (Paris: les Éditions du Cerf, 1957); translated as Leclercq, *The Love of Learning and the Desire for God: A Study of Monastic Culture* (New York: Fordham University Press, 1961). Recent studies both scholarly and popular include Duncan Robertson, *Lectio Divina: The Medieval Experience of Reading* (Trappist, Ky.: Cistercian Publications; Collegeville, Minn.: Liturgical Press, 2011); Raymond Studzinski, *Reading to Live: The Evolving Practice of Lectio Divina* (Trappist, Ky.: Cistercian Publications; Collegeville, Minn.: Liturgical Press, 2009); Christine Valters Paintner and Lucy Wynkoop, O.S.B., *Lectio Divina: Contemplative Awakening and Awareness* (New York: Paulist, 2008); M. Basil Pennington, *Lectio Divina: Renewing the Ancient Practice of Praying the Scriptures* (New York: Crossroad, 1998); Mario Masini, *Lectio Divina: An Ancient Prayer That Is Ever New,* trans. Edmund C. Lane (New York: Alba House, 1998); Mariano Magrassi, *Praying the Bible: An Introduction to Lectio Divina* (Collegeville, Minn.: Liturgical Press, 1998); Michael Casey, *Sacred Reading: The Ancient Art of Lectio Divina* (Liguori, Mo.: Triumph Books, 1996).

75. Thelma Hall, *Too Deep for Words: Rediscovering Lectio Divina* (New York: Paulist, 1988), 44. No citation given for Marmion quotation.

CHAPTER 6

1931–1932

Synesthesia, Apparitions, the Gift of Fear

Apparition of the Eternal Church (1931-1932) for organ, like *The Resplendent Tomb* (1931) for orchestra, stands pivoted on the threshold between two epochs in Messiaen's life. On the one hand, insofar as its subject matter is the suffering in terrestrial life as a preparation for eternal life, it looks back to the death of his mother. On the other hand, being the first organ work composed for his newly obtained position as organist of La Trinité, and utilizing intensive research he had been doing on synesthesia and "colored-hearing," it points ahead. Although the exact date of composition is not known, it can be established within two key events in Messiaen's life: after his September 1931 assuming of the Trinité post and prior to his marriage to Claire Delbos on June 22, 1932.

However, since the text on which it "comments" is taken from autumnal celebrations of the Dedication of a Church, it likely dates from November 1931, perhaps in improvisations Messiaen performed at vespers services. The feast day of the Dedication of Saint John Lateran, November 9, fell on the month's second Monday in 1931. The first vespers of the feast would have been held the evening before, that is, on Sunday the eighth — Messiaen's preferred service.

Synesthesia: A Literary, Scientific, and Cultural Genealogy

Beginning in 1931-1932 and continuing throughout the 1930s and 1940s, Messiaen employed words like "apparition," "vision," "looks" *(regards)*, "lightning flashes" *(éclairs)*: *Apparition of the Eternal Church; Seven Brief Visions of the Resurrected Life* (1939); *Visions of Amen* (1943); *Twenty Gazes at the Infant Jesus* (1944). He finally returned to the image in the last work he finished before his death, *Lightning Flashes of the Beyond . . .* (1991). The year 1931 marks a turning point: whereas the *Diptych* for organ (1930) was subtitled an "essay" and *The Forgotten Offerings* (1930) a "meditation," the "apparition" of the eternal church comes in 1931-1932.

The word "apparition" suggests that Messiaen incorporated synesthetic research into this first organ work at La Trinité. The unity of opposites sought in surrealism was also the dream of synesthesia, and in this regard symbolism, surrealism, and synesthesia cluster around this romantic dream.[1] For Baudelaire, "So scent and sound and color correspond. / As cool as babies' flesh are some perfumes, / Sweet as an oboe, verdant as a lawn." The surrealist Éluard follows Baudelaire's symbolist lead: "To the great floods of sunlight / that discolor perfumes."[2] One scholar clarifies Messiaen's synesthetic experience by observing that colors were produced by "the *interaction of notes* and *not the individual notes themselves.*" In Messiaen's own words: "It is childish to assign a color to each note. It is not isolated tones which produce colors, but chords, or better, complexes of tones. Each complex of tones has a well-defined color."[3]

Whatever the physiological components of synesthesia, its cultural significance goes back to late-eighteenth-century Romantics protesting divisions resulting from both the mind-body dualism of Cartesianism and the mecha-

---

1. Given how fertile the years 1926-1927 were in Messiaen's imaginative development, note that Debussy's "Apparition" for voice and piano, set to a poem by symbolist Stéphane Mallarmé, was published posthumously in 1926. See Debussy, "Apparition," in *Quatre mélodies,* Supplément musical du numéro spécial de mai 1926 (Paris: La Revue musicale, 1926), 18-23.

2. Victor Segalen, *Les Synesthésies et l'école symboliste* (n.p.: Éditions Fata Morgana, 1981); reprint in *Œuvres complètes,* ed. Henry Bouillier, 2 vols. (Paris: R. Laffont, 1995), 1:61-81; Charles Baudelaire, "Correspondances" ("Correspondences"), in *The Flowers of Evil and Other Poems of Charles Baudelaire,* trans. Francis Duke (Charlottesville: University Press of Virginia, 1961), Fr 18; Eng 19; Éluard, "Seconde nature" ("Second Nature"), XI, in *Love, Poetry,* trans. Stuart Kendall (Boston: Black Widow Press, 2007), 102-5, at Fr 102, Eng 103.

3. Vincent Perez Benitez, *Olivier Messiaen: A Research and Information Guide* (New York: Routledge, 2008), 128; Olivier Messiaen, *Conférence de Notre-Dame* (1977), trans. Timothy J. Tikker (English) and Almut Rößler (German) (Paris: Alphonse Leduc, 2001), 11; in Benitez, 128. Messiaen reputedly saw colors when he read music as well as when he heard it, complicating the matter even further. See Kevin T. Dann, *Bright Colors Falsely Seen: Synaesthesia and the Search for Transcendental Knowledge* (New Haven: Yale University Press, 1998), 193 n. 8; citing Jonathan W. Bernard, "Messiaen's Synaesthesia: The Correspondence between Color and Sound Structure in His Music," *Music Perception* 4 (1986): 41-68.

nistic strain of Newtonianism.[4] Romantics, fascinated with "invisibles" and "seeing the unseen," embraced Wordsworth's "correspondent breeze" as the mediator "between outer motion and inner emotion."[5] In our ability to "see" the wind only by its effects (including not only seeing it move other things but also feeling it with the sense of touch), its invisibility overthrew "the tyranny of the eye and the obsession with material substance." (Compare Messiaen's "Reflection in the Wind" [1928-1929].) When Coleridge spoke of "A light in sound, a sound-like power in light," or when Shelley linked light and music in his metaphors, "they were not, as seven decades of literary criticism has assumed, experiencing synaesthesia but were reaching beyond the bounds of the five senses for language to express the ineffable." In *Art and Revolution* (1849), Richard Wagner first proposed his theory of the ideal *Gesamtkunstwerk*, a "total art work" that would unify performing arts, visual arts, and literature. Eight years later, Baudelaire's theory of "correspondences" (a translation of Swedenborgian doctrine) imagined synesthesia as the dedicated seeker's capacity to experience "the deep unity of the cosmos."[6]

The French symbolist movement coincided with others, including studies of psychological disorders or altered physiological states (hysteria, nervousness [*nevrosité*], and degeneration). The synesthetic visionary — whose physiological gift perhaps manifested a psychological alteration — can "lift the painted veil" (Shelley) and gain privileged access to the underlying "reality" that remains invisible to the masses. In 1883, Arthur Rimbaud published his "Voyelles": the work began "Vowels / *A* black, *E* white, *U* green, *O* blue"; it concluded with " — *O*, the Omega, violet beam from His Eyes!" This "chromaesthetic assertion" was accompanied by Paul Verlaine's testimonial that Rimbaud was a genuine *voyant* (seer).[7] In *On the Spiritual in Art* (first German edition 1911), Wassily Kandinsky laid out his revolutionary doctrine of synesthetic creation: "Color is the keyboard. The eye is the hammer. The soul is the piano, with its many strings. The artist is the hand that purposefully sets the soul vibrating by means of this or that key. Thus it is clear that the harmony of colors can only be based upon the principle of purposefully touching the human soul."[8]

4. For this and following see Dann, *Bright Colors Falsely Seen*, 14.

5. David Sandner, *The Fantastic Sublime: Romanticism and Transcendence in Nineteenth-Century Children's Fantasy Literature* (Westport, Conn.: Greenwood Press, 1996), 43; citing M. H. Abrams, "The Correspondent Breeze: A Romantic Metaphor," *Kenyon Review* 19, no. 1 (Winter 1957): 113-30; commenting on Wordsworth, *Prelude*, I, 35.

6. Dann, *Bright Colors Falsely Seen*, 13, 42.

7. Dann, *Bright Colors Falsely Seen*, 42, 43, 22.

8. Kandinsky, *On the Spiritual in Art* (1911); in Judith Zilczer, "Music for the Eyes:

1927–1932: Budding Rhythmician, Surrealist Composer, Mystical Commentator

In the fin-de-siècle, scientific investigations into "synesthesia" continued the Romantic dream by offering "a new and expanded form of wholeness" that seemed to affirm the "inherent unity" of reality — not merely metaphorically, but scientifically, offering counterevidence against Descartes and Newton in their own terms. Scientific interest "focused on the peculiar phenomenon of *audition colorée*, or 'color[ed] hearing' (*Farbenhören* in German), the rare condition in which certain individuals always see within their visual field distinct, vivid patches of color in conjunction with particular sounds."[9] In 1893, the French psychologist Alfred Binet published an article entitled "The Problem of Color Hearing" in which he observed: "A question of much interest in these days is that of color hearing. It has been repeatedly discussed in the daily press and literary and scientific reviews; it has been the subject of medical theses... it has figured in poetry, in romance and even in the theater."[10]

During the first half of the twentieth century, a number of inventors created "color organs," instruments capable of displaying abstract light shows: Australian Alexander Hector, in 1912; American architect Claude Bragdon, in 1915; Englishman Leonard Taylor, in 1920; Italian Achille Riccairdo, between 1920 and 1925; members of the Bauhaus, in 1922; Hungarian Alexander László, whose instrument was called the Sonochromatoscope, first shown in 1925; Austrian Count Vietinghoff-Scheel, whose Chromatophon was played at the second Hamburg Congress for Color-Music Research in 1930; and numerous others. The most famous color-music practitioner was the American Thomas Wilfred, who built his first Clavilux in 1921.[11]

Between 1927 and 1936, four international congresses devoted to color-sound research (Farbe-Ton-Forschungen Kongress) were held at the University of Hamburg.[12] The first, organized by Dr. Georg Anschütz, an expert on synesthesia, foregrounded research on color-light music and synesthesia. However, as the new technology of cinema promised the unification of ab-

---

Abstract Painting and Light Art," in *Visual Music: Synaesthesia in Art and Music since 1900*, ed. Kerry Brougher and Olivia Mattis (London: Thames and Hudson; Washington, D.C.: Hirshhorn Museum; Los Angeles: Museum of Contemporary Art, 2005), 25-86, at 31.

9. Dann, *Bright Colors Falsely Seen*, 11-12.

10. Alfred Binet, "The Problem of Color Hearing" (January 1893); in Zilczer, "Music for the Eyes," 26.

11. Clark Farmer, "'Every Beautiful Sound Also Creates an Equally Beautiful Picture': Color Music and Walt Disney's *Fantasia*," in *Lowering the Boom: Critical Studies in Film Sound*, ed. Jay Beck and Tony Grajeda (Urbana: University of Illinois Press, 2008), 183-97, at 186.

12. See Lauren Hebert and Heather McGuire, "Chronology," in *Visual Music*, 235-47.

1931–1932: Synesthesia, Apparitions, the Gift of Fear

stract painting, color-hearing composition, and color-organ performance, the congresses turned in this direction. Between 1928 and 1932, the German Oskar Fischinger made fourteen short films in which he animated particular pieces of music, a number of which were screened at the second and third congresses in 1930 and 1933.[13] His eighth, completed in 1931, was a filmstrip meant to accompany *The Sorcerer's Apprentice* by Messiaen's composition teacher and mentor, Paul Dukas.[14] Fischinger contacted Leopold Stokowski, conductor of the Philadelphia Orchestra, about the possibility of a film based on Bach's *Toccata and Fugue;* Stokowski then suggested the project to Walt Disney. Although it was not initially successful at the box office, the most famous example of visual music ferment would eventually be Disney's *Fantasia,* released in 1940 (and known to Messiaen).[15] Disney had seen a color organ demonstration in 1928, and Stokowski (who arranged and conducted the music for *Fantasia*) had used the Clavilux color organ to perform Rimsky-Korsakov's *Scheherazade* and Scriabin's *Prometheus.*[16] Disney's vision was thoroughly indebted to these European currents.[17]

In addition to scientific explorations of physiology and technological inventions, experiments with altered states of consciousness by use of drugs also became popular. Hashish and opium had possessed a double attraction for the public: they were not merely drugs; they were from "the Orient," enhancing their exotic aura.[18] Between 1838 and 1846, the French poet Théophile

13. Jörg Jewanski, "Die neue Synthese des Geistes. Zur Synästhesie-Euphorie der Jahre 1925-1933," in Hans Adler and Ulrike Zeuch, *Synästhesie: Interferenz — Transfer — Synthese* (Würzburg: Königshausen & Neumann, 2002), 239-48, at 245-46; cf. Jörg Jewanski, "Eine neue Kunstform — Die Farblichtmusik Alexander Lászlós," in *Farbe — Licht — Musik: Synästhesie und Farblichtmusik,* ed. Jörg Jewanski and Natalia Sidler (New York: Peter Lang, 2006), 211-65, at 251-53.

14. Esther Leslie, *Hollywood Flatlands: Animation, Critical Theory, and the Avant-garde* (London and New York: Verso, 2002), 188.

15. For Messiaen on Disney's use of Stravinsky's *Rite of Spring,* see Olivier Messiaen and Claude Samuel, *Music and Color: Conversations with Claude Samuel,* trans. E. Thomas Glasow (Portland, Ore.: Amadeus Press, 1994), 162, hereafter "Messiaen and Samuel (1994)." Messiaen, *Traité de rythme, de couleur, et d'ornithologie (1949-1992) en sept tomes,* 8 vols. (Paris: Alphonse Leduc, 1994-2002), 2:118.

16. Leslie, *Hollywood Flatlands,* 187.

17. "Disney's *Fantasia* is simply the best-known example of a process that was already well underway by its release, one that blurred the line between the avant-garde and mass culture." Kerry Brougher, "Visual-Music Culture," in *Visual Music,* 88-178, at 96; for Fischinger and *Fantasia,* see 89-96.

18. Martin Booth, *Cannabis: A History* (London and New York: Doubleday, 2003), 85. Cf. Baudelaire: "Hashish, of course, comes to us from the Orient; the stimulating char-

Gautier, knowing how to attract a wide readership, published *The Opium Pipe* (1838), *Hashish* (1843), and *The Hashish-Eaters Club* (1846). This literary vogue engaged in dialogue with scientific research: in 1843, a neuropathologist first published his book *Hashish,* arguing that hashish "can give a sort of prophetic intimation of what the future might hold."[19] That same year, the medical journal *Annales médico-psychologiques (Medical-Psychological Annals)* reproduced some of Gautier's text about the experience of hashish; it appeared again in *On Hashish and Mental Alienation* (1845) by the French proto-psychologist Joseph Moreau ("who liked to style himself 'Moreau de Tours' ").[20]

Synesthesia played a crucial role: "My hearing was inordinately developed," related Gautier. "I heard the sound of colors. Green, red, blue, yellow sounds came to me perfectly distinctly."[21] In 1857, a Union College undergraduate named FitzHugh Ludlow quoted Gautier in his own account of drug-induced visions: "Thus the hasheesh-eater knows what it is . . . to *smell* colors, to *see* sounds, and much more frequently, to *see* feelings."[22] In 1851, Baudelaire treated the subject of drug addiction in *On Wine and Hashish.* He continued this interest with the publication of *Artificial Paradises* (1860), the first chapter of which is entitled "A Taste for the Infinite." The volume included significant portions of Thomas De Quincey's *Confessions of an English Opium-Eater* (1821), translated by Baudelaire, as well as his own major essay, *The Poem of Hashish.* Once again, artificially induced synesthesia plays a significant role: "At this stage of the intoxication, the drug sharpens the senses and the powers of perception, of taste, sight, smell, hearing — all participate equally in the progression. *The eyes pierce the infinite.* The ear hears sounds that are almost imperceptible amid even the most tumultuous din. Then the hallucinations begin. By gradations, external objects assume unique appearances in the endless combining and *transfiguring of forms.* Ideas are distorted;

---

acteristics of hemp were well known in ancient Egypt and its use, under various names, was widespread in India, Algeria, and Arabia Felix. . . . It is more or less valued, depending on its various regional origins; the hashish of Bengal is the most prized by enthusiasts; yet the hashish of Egypt, Constantinople, Persia, and Algeria is pleasing in the same fashion, although to a lesser degree." Baudelaire, *Artificial Paradises,* trans. and ed. Stacy Diamond (Secaucus, N.J.: Carol Publishing Group, 1996), 35, 36.

19. Booth, *Cannabis,* 85; cf. Harry Cockerham, "Gautier: From Hallucination to Supernatural Vision," *Yale French Studies,* no. 50 (1974): 41-53; the issue was entitled "Intoxication and Literature."

20. Brian M. Stableford, *Glorious Perversity: The Decline and Fall of Literary Decadence* (San Bernardino, Calif.: Borgo Press, 1998), 59.

21. Théophile Gautier, in Dann, *Bright Colors Falsely Seen,* 15.

22. FitzHugh Ludlow, in Dann, *Bright Colors Falsely Seen,* 15.

1931–1932: Synesthesia, Apparitions, the Gift of Fear

perceptions are confused. *Sounds are clothed in colors and colors in music.*"[23] Baudelaire's account is a hymn to the ultimate unity of the universe: all the senses "join equally"; eyes see the invisible and ears perceive the "almost inaudible." Finally, sound and color merge into *l'audition colorée:* colored hearing, visual music.

Charles Blanc-Gatti: *Sounds and Colors*

This cultural historical overview of synesthesia as a drive toward unity allows us to situate Messiaen's encounter with the Swiss painter Charles Blanc-Gatti. Having become aware of seeing flashes of color when he heard sounds, Messiaen avidly researched synesthetic phenomena, guided in part by the painter. "Without suffering from physiological synesthesia (as did my friend Blanc-Gatti, the painter, who had a disorder of the optic and aural nerves that allowed him actually to see colors and shapes when he heard music), when I hear a score or read it, hearing it in my mind, I visualize corresponding colors which turn, shift, and combine, just as the sounds turn, shift, and combine, simultaneously."[24]

---

23. Baudelaire, *Artificial Paradises,* 50, emphasis added. Cf. Jörg Fachner, "Drugs, Altered States, and Musical Consciousness: Reframing Time and Space," and Benny Shanon, "Music and Ayahusca," both in *Music and Consciousness: Philosophical, Psychological, and Cultural Perspectives,* ed. David Clarke and Eric F. Clarke (Oxford and New York: Oxford University Press, 2011), 263-80 (quoting Baudelaire at 263) and 281-94.

24. Messiaen and Samuel (1994), 37. Vincent Benitez compares the musician and painter: "When comparing Blanc-Gatti's synesthesia with that of his own in a conversation with Claude Samuel in 1967, Messiaen employed the term 'synopsia' ('synopsie') to describe their respective synesthetic conditions. He probably derived the term, moreover, from Blanc-Gatti himself ('that strange disease which Blanc-Gatti . . . called "synopsia"'). In its general definition, synesthesia is a blending of the senses in which one experiences a sense-perception other than the sense actually being stimulated. For example, one might perceive a scent when a particular pitch is sounded. With colored-hearing synesthesia, one sees colored effects or phenomena when listening to sound. Messiaen characterized Blanc-Gatti's colored-hearing synesthesia as physiological and his own as more inward. In Messiaen's view, Blanc-Gatti possessed 'a synaesthesia in its most commonly occurring form: a spontaneous association of the senses of seeing and hearing.' In other words, the painter actually saw colors and shapes when he heard music. (In the later conversations with Claude Samuel in 1986, 'physiological synesthesia' ['synesthésie physiologique'], not synopsia, is used to describe Blanc-Gatti's colored hearing.) Conversely, Messiaen described his hearing of color as not involving what he saw in the physical world but what he saw inwardly: when reading or hearing a score, he visualized corresponding phenomena of color." Vin-

1927–1932: Budding Rhythmician, Surrealist Composer, Mystical Commentator

Since Messiaen would later recall having met the painter at age twenty (i.e., ca. 1929), he might well have seen Blanc-Gatti's work entitled *Organs* at the 1930 Salon des Indépendants in Paris (January 17–March 2).[25] *Organs* is reproduced in his book *Sounds and Colors (Sons et couleurs)* — a work Messiaen refers to in his *Traité* — along with this fragment of a critical review: "A colorist, rich in nuances, used to creating chromatic harmonies or oppositions. His compositions, after Liszt, Bach, Beethoven, Wagner, Rimsky-Korsakov, Debussy, are interesting symphonies of colors. Moreover, we have not forgotten that at the last Salon des Indépendants, he displayed, with the title *Organs,* an important transposition of chromatic images from the field of musical sensations."[26] Given Messiaen's fascination with the soundscape of bells that once pervaded rural life, it is worth noting that Blanc-Gatti reproduced another work on the same page as *Organs;* the

---

cent P. Benitez, "Simultaneous Contrast and Additive Designs in Olivier Messiaen's Opera, *Saint François d'Assise,*" *Music Theory Online* 8, no. 2 (August 2002): note 3. http://mto.societymusictheory.org/issues/mto.02.8.2/mto.02.8.2.benitez_frames.html. For references, see Messiaen and Samuel (1994), 40; and Almut Rößler, *Contributions to the Spiritual World of Olivier Messiaen,* trans. Barbara Dagg and Nancy Poland (Duisberg: Gilles & Francke, 1986), 43. Cf. Jonathan W. Bernard, "Messiaen's Synaesthesia: The Correspondence between Color and Sound Structure in His Music," *Music Perception* 4 (1986): 41-68; Bernard, "Colour," in *The Messiaen Companion,* ed. Peter Hill (London: Faber and Faber, 1995), 203-19.

25. In a filmed interview, Messiaen said: "When I was 20 years old I met a Swiss painter who became a good friend by the name of Charles Blanc-Gatti, he was synaesthesiac which is a disturbance of the optic and auditory nerves so when one hears sounds one also sees corresponding colors in the eye." See the documentary video directed by Michel Fano and Denise Tual, *Olivier Messiaen et les oiseaux* (1973), produced by SOFRACIMA, Denise Tual et Fondation Royaumont; 80 min.; this segment excerpted in Olivier Mille, Paul Barge, ARTE France, Artline Films, et al., *La liturgie de cristal = The Crystal Liturgy: Olivier Messiaen* (London: Medici Arts, [2002] 2008) (Juxtapositions DVD9DS44). I am grateful to Malcolm Ball for providing this reference, which is also found on his page dedicated to Messiaen: http://www.oliviermessiaen.org/messbiog.html However, Messiaen says elsewhere he met Blanc-Gatti "just after the death of Paul Dukas," that is, in May 1935. Brigitte Massin and Olivier Messiaen, *Olivier Messiaen: une poétique du merveilleux* (Aix-en-Provence: Alinéa, 1989), 43.

If not this identical painting, Messiaen owned one like it: "At home, I have a Blanc-Gatti painting depicting an organ with a stained-glass window, in which colored circles surround the organ pipes and the stained glass." Messiaen and Samuel (1994), 167. For a reproduction of this work, see Charles Blanc-Gatti, *Les Orgues,* in *Sons et couleurs,* 2nd ed. (Paris and Neuchâtel: Attinger, [1934] 1958), hors-texte p. XVI.

26. A. Tabrant, *L'Œuvre, Paris,* on the Exposition Bernheim-Jeune, Paris, 1931; in Blanc-Gatti, *Sons et couleurs,* xvi. Messiaen's seventh volume of the *Traité* is devoted to "sound-color." For Blanc-Gatti see *Traité,* 7:6-9.

1931–1932: Synesthesia, Apparitions, the Gift of Fear

image of a large crucifix juxtaposed next to a bell tower, it is entitled *Church of Mase (Valais)* and carries this epigraph: "When the evening Angelus calls to prayer."

In 1931, it is difficult to imagine Messiaen missing Blanc-Gatti's show entitled *The Painter of Sounds* at the Galeries Bernheim-Jeune (October 19-30).[27] The exhibition's date seems especially important: it immediately preceded the feast of the Dedication on November 9, the text upon which *Apparition of the Eternal Church* "comments."

In December 1932, Blanc-Gatti's paintings were praised at the first Artistes Musicalistes show (an exhibition of "musical painters") in Paris. At the third Farbe-Ton-Forschungen Kongress in 1933, he performed his "chromophonic orchestra," an instrument that projected light synchronized with music. Here he also viewed nine of Fischinger's works and was inspired to turn to producing his own abstract films, the most well known of which would be *Chromophonie* (1939). If he is remembered today, it is perhaps largely with respect to Walt Disney's *Fantasia* (1940). When Disney visited Paris in 1935, Blanc-Gatti approached him about making a synesthetic film, only to be turned down. After hearing that Disney was making *Fantasia*, Blanc-Gatti wrote Disney in 1939 and told him about his film *Chromophonie*, which premiered on November 24 (four months into the Second World War) in Switzerland that year. Disney never replied; *Fantasia* was released the following year. Following the war, when *Fantasia* was released in Europe in 1946, critics pointed out that Disney had largely plagiarized the work of the Artistes Musicalistes in general and Blanc-Gatti in particular.[28]

While Blanc-Gatti's *Sounds and Colors* (1934) covers a wide range of subjects regarding color and sound, two would have interested Messiaen. The first, closely linked to surrealism's method of juxtaposing (or "connecting") opposites and contradictories, is the juxtapositions of colors and their effects on emotions.

There are colors that "excite and stimulate physical and psychic forces," writes Blanc-Gatti, and others that have a "calming, serene, pacifying action." Sounds in the lower registers evoke the tragic; they are associated with the male human voice, the growling of a tiger, and the color red. Serenity, on the other hand, is associated with the female voice, the song of the nightingale,

27. Charles Blanc-Gatti and Galerie Bernheim Jeune, *Exposition Blanc-Gatti: le peintre des sons* (Paris: Bernheim Jeune, 1931).

28. Blanc-Gatti recalls the affair in *Sons et couleurs*, 174-79; cf. Leslie, *Hollywood Flatlands*, 187; and Robin Allan, *Walt Disney and Europe: European Influences on the Animated Feature Films of Walt Disney* (Bloomington: Indiana University Press, 1999), 110.

1927–1932: Budding Rhythmician, Surrealist Composer, Mystical Commentator

and the softness of blue.²⁹ Of great significance, especially for *Visions of Amen*, Blanc-Gatti makes this contrast specific by using the example of two kinds of bells: the tocsin (alarm bell) and the Angelus bell.

> In all bell towers and campaniles, the bell that sounds the tocsin is always the largest, the one having the greatest surface, sounding the lowest note, the sound that is most low-pitched [*grave*].
>
> By contrast, the bell announcing the morning Angelus is the most crystalline, the purest, the lightest, the smallest, sounding the highest note, the most high-pitched sound [*aigu*].³⁰

Fascinated by the "parallelism established between the 'musical spectrum' of the scale and the spectrum of colors," Blanc-Gatti draws on Alexandre Dénéréaz's *Course in Harmony*, in which the classic theory of complementary colors by Chevreul is applied to "modern complementary harmony."³¹ As with Messiaen, colors are not associated with single notes but rather with chords: the dominant (I) symbolizes red, the hottest color and associated with tragedy; the subdominant (IV) corresponds to the cold color purple, passive and ecclesiastical, spiritual and transcendent; the diminished chord (VII) corresponds to indigo, less straightforward than the others; the minor degrees (III and VI) correspond to blue and green, last of the cold colors; the "spiritual dynamic center" of the tonal system (II) corresponds to yellow, "color of the sun's rays," the "archetypal vital center"; finally, the major degrees (dominant and tonic, I and V) correspond to the hottest colors, red and orange.³² Blanc-Gatti then applies these associations to topics as varied as rose windows in cathedrals, color therapy *(chromotherapie)* for emotional disturbances, clothing and the lighting of interiors, and even human productivity (e.g., the automaker Ford experienced a rise of 10-20 percent in productivity after equipping its factories with "judiciously selected colors").³³

---

29. Blanc-Gatti, *Sons et couleurs*, 16.
30. Blanc-Gatti, *Sons et couleurs*, 16.
31. For influence of Michel Eugène Chevreul on Messiaen via Robert Delaunay, see Benitez, "Simultaneous Contrast and Additive Designs in Olivier Messiaen's Opera, *Saint François d'Assise*." Compare parallel in Georges Rouault: Tara Ward, "French Resistance: Rouault's Partisan History of the Modern," in *Mystic Masque: Reality and Semblance in Georges Rouault, 1871-1958*, ed. Stephen Schloesser (Chestnut Hill, Mass.: McMullen Museum of Art, distributed by the University of Chicago Press, 2008), 357-64.
32. Blanc-Gatti, *Sons et couleurs*, 18.
33. Blanc-Gatti, *Sons et couleurs*, 42.

1931–1932: Synesthesia, Apparitions, the Gift of Fear

If we read Blanc-Gatti in light of Messiaen's preoccupation with creating experiences of feelings — especially sharply contrasted emotions — we can see the appeal and influence of his thought. As in the paintings of Robert Delaunay, Messiaen's favorite artist (who was strongly influenced by Chevreul), it is the simultaneous juxtaposition of contrasts that provokes strong effects. Musicologist Andrew Shenton explains:

> A concept Messiaen did draw from painting is that of "simultaneous contrast" — a phenomenon whereby, as a result of staring hard at a color next to a white area, its complementary color can be seen, evoked by the mind's eye. Painters also use the concept when describing the interaction of two colors and how our perception of one color is shaded by the other. For Messiaen, natural resonance (the overtone series) was the aural equivalent of simultaneous contrast, and he believed that his musical colors were perceived differently depending on what surrounded them.[34]

The linkage is with the surrealist project of finding that "point of the mind" *(point de l'esprit)* in which contradictory concepts or images can be grasped as simultaneously valid and ultimately one. For example, blue and orange (as Blanc-Gatti notes) are complementary colors that, when joined together, "reconstitute the white light" from which they were originally refracted (as through a prism).[35] In 1929, Éluard began one of his poems with the lines: "The earth is blue like an orange / faultless words don't lie";[36] a decade later, in his preface to *Quartet for the End of Time,* Messiaen wrote: "[I]n my dreams . . . I submit in an ecstasy to a wheeling, gyrating interpenetration of superhuman colors. These swords of fire, these blue and orange lava flows, these sudden stars: here is the jumble, here the rainbows!"[37] It is not merely that blue and orange are complementary opposites of cold and hot; it is that, when connected, they bring us back to ("reconstitute" = *reconstituent*) the original source: white light. The synesthetic dream is thus about both uniting the senses of sight and sound in some primal unseen unity and simultaneously juxtaposing contrasting color-sounds that bring us back to the original source.

A second topic among the many Blanc-Gatti covers gives a particularly physical undergirding to the dream of unity: the fact that both color and

---

34. Andrew Shenton, *Olivier Messiaen's System of Signs: Notes towards Understanding His Music* (Aldershot, U.K., and Burlington, Vt.: Ashgate, 2008), 51.
35. Blanc-Gatti, *Sons et couleurs,* 136.
36. Éluard, "Premièrement" ("Firstly"), VII, in *Love, Poetry,* 34-35.
37. Messiaen, preface to *Quatour pour la fin du temps* (Paris: Éditions Durand, 1942), i.

sound are composed of waves. Although the mention of "ether" dates Blanc-Gatti's remarks, the fundamental point remains: like sound, "*light* is also a *vibration* of ether." Similarly, as with sound, "it is possible to measure the length of the wave and the frequency of vibrations of light in each of the different colors of the spectrum." Blanc-Gatti's highly specific numerical references resemble those that Messiaen would also find in the astronomical texts that fascinated him: "If we take the numbers, red rays begin at 483 trillion vibrations per second and arrive at 700 trillion vibrations per second with violet. . . . Red begins at 7,000 angstroms and violet ends at 4,000 angstroms." This leads to a first rule: "Low sounds correspond to hot shades, reds and oranges, then going higher, the chromatic scale passes by successive interpolations to yellows and greens, corresponding to mid-range sounds, and finish up with the highest sounds, in the cold shades of blues and violets. Dogs and wolves, among others, can hear sounds that humans cannot."[38] Blanc-Gatti ends with a final parallelism: *"Luminous intensity will correspond to sonorous intensity."*[39]

Why is it so important that these fundamental sense-data of sound and color be, at base, expressions of waves? The answer for Blanc-Gatti (and Messiaen too) can be expressed in one word: rhythm.

> The great lesson of nature demonstrates that nothing has been let up to the chance of fantasy and that everything is the result of a divine *order!*
>
> This immutable rhythm that is our whole life, beginning with our walking, our respiration, our pulse, is a rhythm in double time.
>
> Rhythm of the solstices and equinoxes, the flux of the oceans, the spectacle of universal gravitation in sidereal space. . . .
>
> Everywhere the mark of a magnificent order from the smallest to the greatest, from the structures revealed to us by the microscope up to the solar systems which we know by telescope. . . .
>
> Then, synthesizing light, the three fundamental colors, and their three complementaries; the three states of matter, the three dimensions, the three angles of the triangle: ternary rhythm.
>
> Binary rhythms, ternary rhythms, always rhythms.
>
> It is thus normal that all the arts would be permeated with this immutable law of rhythm, architecture, painting, sculpture, music, dance, poetry, and even prose.

---

38. Blanc-Gatti, *Sons et couleurs*, 136-37.
39. Blanc-Gatti, *Sons et couleurs*, 142, emphasis in original.

1931–1932: Synesthesia, Apparitions, the Gift of Fear

How rightly Hans von Bülow sensed when he wrote: "In the beginning was rhythm."[40]

Blanc-Gatti's imagery and language resemble Messiaen's so closely that it is difficult to know which was the source of the other's thinking on a given topic. However, since Blanc-Gatti was almost two decades older than Messiaen, he undoubtedly provided the young composer with the invaluable collection of resources on synesthesia, *audition colorée,* and "the aesthetic of sounds and colors" that may be found in *Sounds and Colors.*[41]

Peyote: The Plant That Makes Eyes Open with Wonder

Blanc-Gatti was the most probable source for Messiaen's introduction to two books he cites.[42] The first was published the same year as his mother's death: *Peyote: The Plant That Makes Eyes Open with Wonder* (1927).[43] *Peyote* is filled with descriptions of mescaline-induced "visions" and "apparitions" that cause the eyes "to fill with wonder" — or, imitating the French, to become "enmarvelled."[44] The second, published in 1930, bears an elaborate title whose topics suggest why it would have been of such interest for Messiaen: *Studies*

---

40. Blanc-Gatti, *Sons et couleurs,* 143, 145.
41. Blanc-Gatti, *Sons et couleurs,* 146-55, 160-79.
42. See Messiaen quotations of Blanc-Gatti, Rouhier, and Quercy in *Traité,* 1:67.
43. Alexandre Rouhier, *La plante qui fait les yeux émerveillés: le peyotl* (Paris: Gaston Doin et Cie, 1927). "Peyote" appears in Blanc-Gatti, *Sons et couleurs,* 155: "It has been called 'the plant that makes eyes open with wonder.'" Messiaen discusses both Blanc-Gatti and Rouhier's *Peyotl* and makes the connection explicit: "Mescalin visions have a sibling resemblance to those of Synopsia.... A parallel between sound and light vibrations seems to me full of information." Messiaen, *Traité,* 1:67-68, at 68. He also puts the connection negatively: "Whenever I hear music, I see corresponding colours. Whenever I read music (hearing it in my mind), I see corresponding colours. This is not a matter of visual perception, after a manner of the dangerous and monstrous hallucinations which can be induced by, say, mescalin. Neither is it a case of that strange disease which Blanc-Gatti (the painter of sounds) called 'synopsia.'" Messiaen, in Rößler, *Contributions,* 43.
44. The verb *émerveiller* does not translate into English; it means that the eyes are altered or filled with "marvel" in the same way that they might be filled with brightness or light ("brightened" or "enlightened," hence, "emarvelled"). Note the same root in *émerveiller* and *le merveilleux* ("the marvelous") — the key concept for the surrealists (see Pierre Mabille, *Mirror of the Marvelous: The Classic Surrealist Work on Myth,* trans. Jody Gladding [Rochester, Vt.: Inner Traditions, 1998]; originally Mabille, *Le miroir du merveilleux* [Paris: Sagittaire, 1940]) and for Messiaen himself. "The Marvelous is my natural climate, at the

1927–1932: Budding Rhythmician, Surrealist Composer, Mystical Commentator

on Hallucination. 1, The Philosophers: Theory of Perception, Image, and Hallucination in Spinoza, Leibniz, Bergson; The Mystics: Saint Teresa, Her Miseries, Her Perception of God, Her Visions.[45]

Blanc-Gatti's own book notes that the alkaloid extract of peyotline has "the property of *transforming auditory sensations into visually-colored sensations.*"[46] "It is undeniable," he argues later, "that a close connection exists between natural synesthesias and those experienced under the influence of the alkaloid taken from peyote. There is in fact a strange similitude between the observations gathered from individuals gifted with *audition colorée* and those experiencing peyotline-induced synesthesia."[47]

Peyote is exactly the kind of book that Messiaen loved. First, it is thoroughly literary, filled with pithy epigraphs from a variety of times, places, and genres: the Bible, Juvenal, Lucien, the *Song of Roland*, Shakespeare, Flaubert, Baudelaire, Rabindranath Tagore, and the *Dictionary of Orientalism*, to name but a few. The chapter "Prohibitions of Peyote and Its Use" includes epigraphs from Victor Hugo's *Man Who Laughs* ("It is not a god in these herbs but rather a demon, I have verified it") and Genesis ("You shall not eat of the tree of the knowledge of good and evil").[48] Second, in addition to being a work of popular science (beginning with an initial "botanical and geographical" overview of the plant), it is a work of anthropology. The chapter "The Cult of Peyote in Mexico and the United States" contains illustrations of statuary and woven votive shields, and photographs of native Huichols with painted faces ("Great Father of Fire"; "Goddess of Eastern Rains"; "Mother of Maize"; "The Sun Father") and wearing ceremonial costumes. And, like the book published one year earlier on the music of the Peruvians (see above discussion on the *harawi* genre), there are Huichol songs in musical notation, including those for "The Dance of Peyote." A schematic diagram accompanies the text outlining the ritual of the Great Feast of Peyote and the Dance of Fire. ("You will never find a single ancient mystery," says the epigraph from Lucien, "where there is no dancing.") Given the centrality of the Eucharist in his thought and art, Messiaen would undoubtedly have been intrigued by these remarks on syncretism:

---

breast of which I feel good. I have experienced the need to live a Marvelous, but a Marvelous that might be true!" Messiaen, in Massin and Messiaen, *Olivier Messiaen*, 27.

45. Pierre Quercy, *Études sur l'hallucination. 1, Les Philosophes: Théorie de la perception, de l'image et de l'hallucination chez Spinoza, Leibniz, Bergson; Les Mystiques: Sainte Thérèse, ses misères, sa perception de Dieu, ses visions* (Paris: F. Alcan, 1930).

46. Blanc-Gatti, *Sons et couleurs*, 155, emphasis in original.

47. Blanc-Gatti, *Sons et couleurs*, 156.

48. Rouhier, *La plante qui fait les yeux émerveillés*, 170, 171.

1931–1932: Synesthesia, Apparitions, the Gift of Fear

The ancient ethnic atavisms, wakened from their torpor and reappearing with the mysterious and mystical call of the divine Cactus, are going to . . . incite the Red Man to reconcile his intimate ancestral beliefs with those newly acquired in contact with Whites. Blending together the indigenous cult and the eastern cult with the greatest possible faith, [the call of the Cactus] obtains a third cult which represents for [the native] an even greater perfection, but which makes Protestant or Catholic ministers quiver with a holy indignation: [in 1923] the Indians of Oklahoma and of South Dakota founded the "Peyote Church of Christ" which substitutes Peyote for the wheat of the Sacred Species and, during communion, replaces the white eucharistic host with the brown disc of a "mescaline button."[49]

The attached footnote reads: "This strangely recalls the ancient Aztec belief in which Peyote was qualified as *teonanacall:* 'divine flesh.'"

The most intriguing aspect of the book, however, is the minutely detailed recording of numerous experiences of "peyote intoxication." These "observations" include measurements of the prepared drug, the exact date and time of ingestion, the exact times of observations (e.g., 3:30, 4:20, 4:35, 5:20, 5:25 P.M.), and accounts of the subject's physical states and spoken experiences and visions. This last detail is what is most striking in light of Messiaen's music: the repeated recurrence, many times over, of the words "visions" and "apparitions." The first observation is a self-observation:[50]

> The product employed for this experience is a fluid extract of P.E. from "mescaline buttons," prepared with alcohol at 70c and a proof of 2 gr., 50% alkaloids in total.
>
> Age of subject: 33 years. Height: 1 m. 77. Weight: 78 kg. Robust health even with a delicate stomach and frequently subject to migraines originating in the stomach.
>
> Sunday 8 February 1914 — I finished the mid-day meal at 2:00 p.m.

Notations are made at fifteen- or thirty-minute intervals, in which the pulse and amount of liquid ingested are noted. At 7:30 P.M. he reports that he is "able to stand up and walk with ease. However, this upright position is made

---

49. Rouhier, *La plante qui fait les yeux émerveillés*, 167. The cited source for this information is the September 20, 1924, issue of the weekly Jesuit publication *America, a Catholic Review*.

50. Rouhier, *La plante qui fait les yeux émerveillés*, 233-40.

painful by a vertiginous state provoking unpleasant desires to vomit.... I feel the effects, slightly heightened, of a certain feeling of unreality [*d'irréalité*] or light intoxication. The room and its objects appear more clear than usual." He lies down and closes his eyes, upon which he places a thick headband "in order to keep the light out of them."

Then, at 8:30, "The visions begin to occur, the eyes being closed." At first they are geometrical designs; then they begin to move; then come a series in the form of an hourglass. The "visions come one after another with a progressively building intensity until 9:00 p.m. at which vomiting occurs, then they decrease, ceasing completely at 9:30." In reflections afterward, light plays an important part: "The majority of forms perceived during this intoxication were of a weak luminosity, as if badly lit and seen in semi-darkness, but certain details were, by contrast, of an intensely luminous coloration, of a vivacity in shade, of an incomparable purity of color scale, and as small as they might be, they seem to have been illuminated interiorly with a clarity [*clarté*] so *lively* [*vivante*] that they gave the sensation of never having been perceived in such a manner and were a genuine motif of enchantment." He underscores that "all the visions were described in the real time of their production to a friend who took notes. Nothing whatsoever was perceived by open eyes." Then follows the section entitled "Enumeration of the Visions." The list of images, extremely detailed, reads exactly like an account of someone's dream: dark masses; a human figure; the descent of a stairway; "a great quantity of masks of all forms and colors"; a candelabra in an archaic style; the human figure seen at the beginning "reappears at my left, very close to me and watches me [*me regarde*]"; the corner in an unknown apartment, "reduced to a chimney viewed laterally"; a public hall with a wall decorated with colored masks. After intense vomiting at 9:00 P.M., he lies down horizontally and visions continue: "Vision of irregular fragments"; "Vision of vague engravings"; "Vision of a tunnel"; "A final vision hazy and confused." "9:30 p.m. — All the visions are finished." In his concluding notes, "Regarding the subject of these diverse visions," he emphasizes precise points, including:

> All the visions were able to be clearly localized in diverse sectors of the visual field;
> The vivid shades (blue, red, green, purple, yellow) possessed a luminosity, vivacity, purity and sweetness that is inexpressible;
> The visions were never perceived by open eyes;
> The apparition, the procession and the nature of the visions was never, in any degree, subject to the influence of the will.

1931–1932: Synesthesia, Apparitions, the Gift of Fear

Over the next twenty-five pages of similar, minutely detailed recordings of experienced images, the words "vision," "apparition," and "appear" recur over and over: "Vision of a virgin forest"; "Vision of a painting dominated by green shades, then mauve"; "She announces a blue vision"; "Vision of green grass"; "Vision of a Russian peasant"; "Apparition of a cross, lively red"; "Their apparition is so unexpected that it provokes each time a quivering of surprise"; "A sister completely white appears"; "With closed eyes, the following [images] appear"; "Apparition of a thin jagged garland of Asparagus."

In the analysis provided in the chapter "Peyote Intoxication," the conversation turns to those effects of the drug called *"peyote-induced synesthesias* of which one of the most remarkable and most frequent is that of *audition colorée.*" In fact, one could say that "Peyote tends to realize that 'dark and deep unity' of the senses of which Baudelaire spoke, by means of which 'perfumes, colors and sounds respond' and to provoke the apparition of a general synesthetic state." Baudelaire had affirmed that "all sounds contain a color" and, before, Hoffmann had felt "these mysterious correspondences." Rouhier cites a 1926 journal article in which Hoffmann was quoted: "In the state of delirium which precedes sleep, there is produced in me a *confusion between colors, sounds and odors.* It is as if one and the others were mysteriously born all together in a single ray of light and then united in order to form a marvelous concert."[51]

Rouhier then recalled the mescaline experience of "M.T.," which was "filled with manifestations of *audition colorée.*" Upon hearing strikes on a "bronze mortar that vibrated like a bell," M.T. explained that "the sonorous vibrations provoke luminous waves [*des ondes lumineuses*] formed out of small points of color ..., which created circles that expanded and spread out in the same direction as the sounds." A note tapped on the piano "changed the shade of the vision in course," and "each sonority made colors appear, amplifying those which had already been seen or provoking apparitions which moved, modified themselves, and changed with the following vibration." The lowest notes of the piano almost always appeared as purple to M.T., while the high notes were of a pinkish-red mixed with white.[52]

Several pages later, in figure 44, Rouhier reproduced an artwork by Elmiro Celli entitled *Sounds of a Bell.* The image is accompanied by this commentary: "The same vibratory wave will give two different manifestations, one

---

51. Rouhier, *La plante qui fait les yeux émerveillés,* 308ff.

52. Rouhier, *La plante qui fait les yeux émerveillés,* 310-11. For a more complete account of M.T.'s visions, Rouhier directs the reader to *Revue métapsychique* 3 (May-June 1925).

1927–1932: Budding Rhythmician, Surrealist Composer, Mystical Commentator

sonorous and the other visual, according to the nature of that upon which it exerts itself: a tightened rope or a plate sprinkled with fine sand [i.e., Celli's work reproduced in the photograph]. Why should a Celli not have translated into forms on a vibrant plate that which the bell expresses in sound? Forms are the luminous expression of things, because each thing exists in light, just as everything exists in music."[53]

Two final observations from *Peyote* seem worth mentioning. The first has to do with the concept of the "mystic": "The numerous visions having a religious character perceived by Mme. de S., agnostic and detached from every formal cultic practice, revealed to both herself and those surrounding her, very real mystical tendencies that were recognized following a sustained introspection and a meticulous psychological analysis."[54] The second has to do with the felt duration of time: mescaline intoxication frequently entails a "loss of the *notion of time*," although perhaps not more than "many other poisons of the intelligence." The diminishment of attention and "error of the brain" lead to the experience of being "surprised by an abundance of images when one is not used to perceiving so many in the same period of time [*laps de temps*]." The brain's "creatively imaginative activity prodigiously heightens the error, just as it is mistaken in a hashish intoxication or in normal dreaming."[55]

Evidently, much in *Peyote* would have fascinated Messiaen; yet it should be seen as continuous with his earlier life. Visions and apparitions had fascinated him since childhood, and one of his favorite plays had been Shakespeare's *Midsummer Night's Dream*. When the fairy Queen Titania finally wakes from the spell cast on her — "This hateful imperfection of her eyes" — she exclaims: "My Oberon! what visions have I seen! / Methought I was enamour'd of an ass." Soon after, Bottom too awakens from his dream state and meditates on its irreducible mystery using synesthetic language that confuses the five senses: "I have had a most rare vision. I have had a dream, past the wit of man to say what dream it was. Man is but an ass, if he go about to expound this dream.... Man is but a patched fool if he will offer to say what methought I had. The eye of man hath not heard, the ear of man hath not seen, man's hand is not able to taste, his tongue to conceive, nor his heart to report, what my dream was."[56] In Messiaen's "visions," there is continuity from Shakespeare to peyote.

53. Rouhier, *La plante qui fait les yeux émerveillés*, 315.
54. Rouhier, *La plante qui fait les yeux émerveillés*, 314.
55. Rouhier, *La plante qui fait les yeux émerveillés*, 325-26.
56. Shakespeare, *A Midsummer Night's Dream*, act 4, scene 1, lines 203-12; in *The Arden Shakespeare Complete Works*, ed. Richard Proudfoot, Ann Thompson, and David Scott Kastan, rev. ed. (London: Arden Shakespeare, 2011), 907.

1931–1932: Synesthesia, Apparitions, the Gift of Fear

November Apparition: Chiseled Souls and the Gift of Fear

Messiaen wrote an introductory poem for *Apparition:*

Made of living stones,
Made of stones of heaven,
It appears [*apparaît*] in heaven:
It is the Spouse of the Lamb!
It is the Church of heaven
Made of the stones of heaven
That are the souls of the elect.
They are in God and God in them
For the eternity of heaven![57]

Keeping in mind Blanc-Gatti, synesthesia, and "sound-color," note that these living stones in the book of the Apocalypse and poetically paraphrased by Messiaen are luminous gems of twelve colors: jasper, sapphire, chalcedony, emerald, sardonyx, carnelian, chrysolite, beryl, topaz, chrysoprase, hyacinth, and amethyst.[58] Colors imply sounds as well along the full wave spectrum, hot, cold, and in between. Messiaen described *Apparition* as the "alternation of bright colors of the 2nd, 3rd and 7th 'Modes of Limited Transposition,' their opposition with empty fifths, hard and cold," and few other pieces imitate so closely this sensation of endless rotating colors.[59] He described his much later

---

57. Nigel Simeone, *Olivier Messiaen: A Bibliographical Catalogue of Messiaen's Works,* Musikbibliographische Arbeiten series, vol. 14 (Tutzing: Hans Schneider, 1998), 26-27; Jon Gillock, *Performing Messiaen's Organ Music: 66 Masterclasses* (Bloomington: Indiana University Press, 2010), 32-36; Olivier Latry and Loïc Mallié, *L'œuvre d'orgue d'Olivier Messiaen. Œuvres d'avant-guerre* (Stuttgart: Carus, 2008), 88-94. For the medieval practice of celebrating dedications, see Lee Bowen, "The Tropology of Mediaeval Dedication Rites," *Speculum* 16, no. 4 (October 1941): 469-79.

58. Rev. 21:19-20. For information on the precious stones, see Gregory K. Beale, *The Book of Revelation: A Commentary on the Greek Text* (Grand Rapids: Eerdmans, 1998), 1080-90.

59. Olivier Messiaen, jacket notes for *Apparition;* in his set of eight vinyl LP discs recorded and released in 1957: *Olivier Messiaen. Œuvres complètes pour orgue. Interprétées par l'Auteur au Grand Orgue de l'Église de la Trinité à Paris* (Paris: Ducretet-Thomson, 1957), catalog numbers 260 C 074–260 C 081. Messiaen's notes for these Ducretet-Thomson recordings have been compiled and translated in Jon Gillock, "Messiaen's Organ Works: The Composer's Aesthetic and Analytical Notes," *Music: The AGO-RCCO Magazine* 12, no. 12 (December 1978): 42-54, at 43.

Messiaen's form of "synopsia" did not consist of a one-to-one correspondence between pitches and colors; rather, the addition of even one note changed the chord's color; hence, the kaleidoscope is turned by changing juxtapositions of chords. Vincent Benitez quotes Messiaen — "It is childish to assign a color to each note. It is not isolated tones which produce colors, but

1927–1932: Budding Rhythmician, Surrealist Composer, Mystical Commentator

Colors of the Celestial City (1963) in similarly kaleidoscopic terms: "The work does not end, having never really begun: it turns on itself, interlacing its temporal blocks, like the rose window of a cathedral with its vivid invisible colors."[60]

Messiaen bases his poem on the ancient Latin plainchant hymn entitled "Caelestis urbs Jerusalem" ("Celestial City of Jerusalem"). The hymn is designated to be sung at the first vespers service for liturgies associated with the Dedication of a Church.[61] Messiaen would have encountered this particular office quite soon after his appointment in September 1931: first, on November 9, for the feast of the Dedication of Saint John Lateran (in older calendars, feast of the Dedication of the Arch-Basilica of Our Savior); and again on November 18, at the memorial of the Dedication of the Basilicas of Saints Peter and Paul.[62] The textual imagery of these feasts, replete with shining living stones, seems to have had a deep effect on Messiaen. He would return to the same subject thirty years later in *Verset for the Feast of the Dedication* (1961), his first organ work after nearly a decade's absence (since *Mass of Pentecost* [1950]), and in the just mentioned work for orchestra, *Colors of the Celestial City*.

These two feasts of church dedications are situated within Catholicism's larger tradition of November, the last month of the liturgical year, devoted to remembering and praying for the deceased as well as an emphasis on eschatological topics. (In December the new church year begins with Advent, the four-week period preceding Christmas at the winter solstice.) This monthlong remembrance of deceased loved ones begins on November 1 with the feast of All Saints (Halloween being the "eve" of "All Hallows"). This is immediately followed on November 2 by the strongly contrasting sober commemoration of All Souls. The feast of All Saints (a holy day of obligatory Mass attendance), definitively concluding the annual harvest season, remembers those human

---

chords, or better, complexes of tones. Each complex of tones has a well-defined color" — and then comments: "Thus it is the *interaction of notes* and *not the individual notes themselves* that produce colors in Messiaen's synesthesia." Benitez, *Olivier Messiaen*, 128, emphasis in original; quoting Messiaen, *Conférence de Notre-Dame* (1977), 11. Cf. Benitez, "Simultaneous Contrast and Additive Designs in Olivier Messiaen's Opera, *Saint François d'Assise*."

60. Quoted in Paul Griffiths, *Olivier Messiaen and the Music of Time* (London: Faber and Faber, 1985), 201; in Jeremy S. Begbie, *Resounding Truth: Christian Wisdom in the World of Music* (Grand Rapids: Baker Academic, 2007), 170.

61. See the office of First Vespers for the "Common of the Dedication of a Church" ("Commune Dedicationis Ecclesiae. In I. Vesperis"), in *Vesperale Romanum* (Tournai, Belgium: Desclée & Cie, [1924] 1936), second part (following p. 544), 72-76, at 74-75.

62. The feast of the Lateran Dedication was appointed for the Sunday following the octave of All Saints. In 1931, November 1 fell on a Sunday, as did its octave (November 8); thus it seems that the dedication would have been celebrated on November 15 that year.

beings successfully "harvested" into eternal glory — the "church triumphant." On the following day, the "church suffering" is remembered; it is comprised of loved ones still in purgatory undergoing the purgation of imperfections that lie in the way of their becoming stones in the celestial city.[63]

The subsequent celebrations of the dedication of churches are intimately linked to these commemorations of All Saints and All Souls; as Thomas Aquinas summarized this ancient allegorical understanding, "the faithful become the Temple of God."[64] Thus the month of November is woven together by linking these important memorials at octave or novena intervals: November 1 (All Saints), November 2 (All Souls), Sunday after the Octave of All Saints (Arch-Basilica), and November 18 (Basilica of Saints Peter and Paul).

The first stanza of the vespers hymn "Caelestis urbs Jerusalem" celebrates the celestial city:

Jerusalem, heavenly city, blessed vision of peace![65]
Built of living stones, thou risest to the very stars;
and like a bride art circled round with thousand, thousand angels.[66]

---

63. This image of the church is one of eternity intersecting time, peace transmuting suffering. In terms of time, the church is the past (the temple of Solomon in ancient Jerusalem), the present church on earth, and the future (the heavenly Jerusalem at the end of time). In Catholic medieval tradition, it is the threefold church: the church militant here on earth; the church suffering in purgatory; and the church triumphant (saints and angels). "It may signify the whole body of the faithful, including not merely the members of the Church who are alive on earth but those, too, whether in heaven or in purgatory, who form part of the one communion of saints. Considered thus, the Church is divided into the Church Militant, the Church Suffering, and the Church Triumphant." George Joyce, "The Church," in *The Catholic Encyclopedia*, vol. 3 (New York: Robert Appleton Co., 1908); http://www.newadvent.org/cathen/03744a.htm.

64. See Frederick Christian Bauerschmidt, "'That the Faithful Become the Temple of God': The Church Militant in Aquinas's *Commentary on John*," in *Reading John with St. Thomas Aquinas: Theological Exegesis and Speculative*, ed. Michael Dauphinais and Matthew Levering (Washington, D.C.: Catholic University of America Press, 2005), 293-311.

65. Note that Messiaen has taken the peaceful "vision" *(pacis visio)* and transformed it into a hallucinatory "apparition." In addition to *Peyote* and Blanc-Gatti, one wonders whether Messiaen had been influenced by Claude Debussy's posthumously published "Apparition," which had appeared just five years earlier. Debussy's text would certainly have appealed to Messiaen, who loved fairy tales: "When with the sun in your hair, in the street and in the evening, / You appeared to me laughing, / Appeared [*Apparue*] / And I believe I saw the fairy [*Et j'ai cru voir la fée*] / With the hat of brilliance [*Au chapeau de clarté*]." Debussy, "Apparition," in *Quatre Mélodies de Claude Debussy* (Paris: La Revue musicale, 1926). The work was published in the musical supplement in a special May 1926 issue of the *Revue musicale:* "The Youth of Debussy."

66. "Caelestis urbs Jerusalem," hymn for the dedication of churches, in *Vesperale Ro-*

1927–1932: Budding Rhythmician, Surrealist Composer, Mystical Commentator

The second stanza is devoted to the image of the "heavenly jeweled city" as the bride of Christ, a bride "blessed with happiest fortunes" and given "the Father's glory" for her dowry. The fourth stanza is the source for Messiaen's words about the stones being human souls — "Made of the stones of heaven / That are the souls of the elect. / They are in God and God in them":

> After the strokes of the salutary chisel [*Scalpri salubris ictibus*],
> and many a blow [*Et tunsione plurima*],
> the stones, polished by the workman's hammer [*Fabri polita malleo*]
> raise up this stately pile [*Hanc saxa molem construunt*],
> and being well fitted together [*Aptisque juncta nexibus*]
> are placed in the highest summit [*Locantur in fastigio*].

However, Messiaen textually understates the terror that his music captures viscerally. For the dreadful point of the third stanza is the problem of suffering, persecution, and even martyrdom as the necessary preconditions on which the foundation of the church is built. The saints are able to endure such torments — *"Tormenta quisquis sustinet"* — only because they are propelled by the love of Christ — *"Amore Christi percitus."* For the human "stones" to be capable of fitting into spaces in the city's foundation appointed by the divine Architect, they must be gradually and painstakingly cut down to size with "strokes of the salutary chisel" (or "strokes of the healthful chisel" = *scalpri salubris ictibus*) and repeated hammering with the mallet *(Et tunsione plurima / Fabri polita malleo)*. Brilliantly shining living stones — human souls — are shaped and polished by such instruments of pain, torture, and even death.[67]

---

manum, 74-75. Translation here and following from Dom Prosper Guéranger, O.S.B., *The Liturgical Year*, trans. Benedictines of Stanbrook, 15 vols. (Westminster, Md.: Newman Press, 1949), 15:217. For other translations and commentaries, see Joseph Connelly, *Hymns of the Roman Liturgy* (New York: Longmans, Green and Co., 1957), 158-61; Cornelius Canon Mulcahy, *The Hymns of the Roman Breviary and Missal* (Dublin: Browne and Nolan, 1938), 246-47; Matthew Britt, O.S.B., *The Hymns of the Breviary and Missal* (New York: Benziger Brothers, 1924), 343-46.

67. Compare the English Jesuit George Tyrrell's meditation on this hymn:

> While, therefore, the members of the visible Church are upon earth, those of the invisible are both in Heaven and on earth — on earth, a handful; in Heaven, as the sands on the sea-shore. That portion which is in Heaven is formed and perfected — has passed into its changeless condition; while the portion on earth is in process of formation, not yet accepted, shaped, or perfected. Here the stones of Solomon's temple are hewn and fashioned with many a rough

1931–1932: Synesthesia, Apparitions, the Gift of Fear

Messiaen might have understood all this from reading Dom Guéranger's text (via Charles Tournemire) on which *Apparition of the Eternal Church* may be considered a "commentary":

At the same time, Christ is the Corner-stone on which other living stones, all the predestined [*l'assemblée des prédestinés*], are built up by the apostolic architects into the holy temple of the Lord. Thus the Church is the bride, and by and with Christ she is the house of God. She is such already in this world of miseries [*dès ce misérable monde*], where in labor and suffering the elect stones [*des pierres élues*] are chiseled, and are laid successively in the places assigned them by the divine plan [*prévu par le plan divin*]. She is such in the happiness of heaven, where the eternal temple [*le temple éternel*] is being constructed of every soul that ascends from earth [*de toute âme en-volée d'ici-bas*]; until, when completed by the acquisition of our immortal bodies [*nos corps immortels*], it will be consecrated by the great High-Priest on the day of the incomparable dedication which will close time [*au jour de l'incomparable dédicace qui clora les temps*].[68]

As Messiaen's October 1931 interview with José Bruyr shows, his mind was clearly preoccupied with his departed mother when the feasts of All Saints, All Souls, and the two dedications came around between November 1 and 19 in 1931. As a pious Catholic believer in that epoch, he must have wondered: In spite of her conscious rejection of Christianity, since she had

---

blow and sharp incision; there they are noiselessly laid each in its peculiar and predestined place in the living structure.

... In Heaven the invisible Church consists of the spirits of the just made perfect in love, purged seven-fold in the fire of suffering and great tribulation, developed into full correspondence with that Divine plan and pattern thought out and loved by God from all eternity, and then by Him infused slowly and laboriously into the often reluctant mind and conscience, into the heart and affections of each saint; a light that haunted the soul when it would cower in the darkness; a fire that leaped up after every futile quenching; a tormenting thought that would not rest unlistened-to and unloved.

George Tyrrell, *Hard Sayings: A Selection of Meditations and Studies* (London and New York: Longmans, Green, [1898] 1904), 417-19.

68. Dom Guéranger's commentary in *The Liturgical Year*, 15:212-13; original, *L'Année liturgique. Le temps après la Pentecôte. Tome 6: Propre des saints du Ier au XXX novembre, la Toussaint, les morts, la dédicace,* 12th ed. (Tours: Maison Alfred Mame et Fils, 1930), 260, translation altered. A close reading of this short text reveals how much influence it would soon have on both the *Ascension* (1932-1934; cf. the "soul") and *Nativity* (1935; cf. predestination of the elect and the eternal divine plan) suites via Dom Marmion.

1927–1932: Budding Rhythmician, Surrealist Composer, Mystical Commentator

suffered greatly in both body and spirit, was it possible that she had been polished and fitted as a foundation stone in the celestial city by means of her own hammering and chiseling? He would have found more consolation for this interpretation in another hymn for the feast, "Urbs Jerusalem beata," a more primitive version of "Caelestis urbs Jerusalem," which Guéranger reproduces in the office for second vespers. Those who have suffered for the name of Christ gain entry to the heavenly city by their merits; other images also stand out, including the "brilliant" pearls out of which the celestial city's doors are made; and the city being "nothing but praise, nothing but melody":

> The doors are made of brilliant pearls [*Les portes en sont
>   de perles brillantes*].[69]
> They are always open:
> whoever suffers in this world [*quiconque souffre en ce monde*]
> for the name of Jesus Christ
> Will find entrance there by right of merit [*par le droit du mérite*].
>
> The hammer of suffering [*Le marteau des souffrances*] polishes the stones;
> and thus equipped by the worker, they are placed [*elles sont
>   posées*],[70] fixed
> in their respective places in the holy edifice.
>
> This entire beloved city, consecrated to God,
> is nothing but praise, but melodies [*n'est que louange, que mélodies*]:
> songs of joy [*chants d'allégresse*] whose fervent love
> pays homage to one God in three persons.[71]

Although Messiaen leaves out the suffering in his poetic paraphrase, his description written for his own recording of the work in the mid-1950s explicitly made the connection: "Like the hymn for the 'Dedication of Churches' says: chisel, hammer, some suffering and some tests, tailoring and polishing the elected persons, living stones of the spiritual edifice (ex-

---

69. Compare Messiaen, "Resurrection," in *Songs of Earth and Sky* (1938): "Perfume, portal, pearl [*Parfum, porte, perle*]."

70. Again compare Messiaen, "Resurrection": "An angel [*Un ange*] / Posed atop the rock [*Sur la pierre il s'est posé*]."

71. In Guéranger, *The Liturgical Year*, 15:230-31, translation from French altered. Cf. *L'Année liturgique*, 284ff.

1931–1932: Synesthesia, Apparitions, the Gift of Fear

pressed by the unceasing pulsations of the bass). The vision is very simple, almost brutal at its climax. Established slowly, it will take a long time to disappear."[72]

It is difficult to miss the terror in Messiaen's *Apparition*. In this respect, two Catholic Revivalist works seem likely to have influenced Messiaen. The first is Ernest Hello's *Words of God* (1877), which would later inspire *Visions of Amen*.[73] Although Messiaen later said he had received his copy of this nineteenth-century classic from his brother Alain around 1933 or 1934, one of Hello's lines in particular suggests that Messiaen might have had it already in 1931.[74] It is a line he will quote three decades later as an epigraph in *From Canyons to Stars* (1974): "This magnificent replacement of fear by awe [*de la peur par la crainte*] opens a window for adoration."[75] (In 1927, Hello's thought was implicitly rephrased by Daniel-Rops in *Our Anxiety*: "For, in place of material fear [*la peur matérielle*], human beings quickly substitute metaphysical fear [*la crainte métaphysique*].")[76] Hello explicitly delineates two meanings of the word "fear" that are distinguished in French: simple "fear" *(la peur)* and the "dread," "awe," or "wonder" *(la crainte)* theologically known as "fear of the Lord." For Hello, simple fear is an emotion that makes us all too aware of our smallness; it cripples us and makes us cower. By contrast, the emotion of "dread" or "wonder" opens up the possibility of self-transcendence.[77]

Messiaen's *Apparition* is terrifying; indeed, it seems to be a written-down version of the kind of organ improvisation on which Julien Green reported:

72. Messiaen, jacket notes for recording of *Apparition* (Ducretet-Thomson, 1957); in Gillock, "Messiaen's Organ Works," 43, translation altered.

73. Ernest Hello, *Paroles de Dieu. Réflexions sur quelques textes sacrés,* ed. François Angelier (Grenoble: Jérôme Millon, [1877] 1992). It seems likely that Messiaen was also acquainted with a two-volume collection of unpublished fragments by Hello entitled *From Nothing to God*. Originally published in 1921, the two-volume edition was reprinted in 1930, just prior to Messiaen's succession to the Trinité position. See Hello, *Du néant à dieu,* ed. Jules-Philippe Heuzey, 2 vols. (Paris: Perrin et Cie, [1921] 1930). Messiaen would most likely have learned of it from Tournemire, who was intimately familiar with the work. Hello's themes permeate Tournemire's "préface-poème" for his massive trilogy entitled *Faust — Don Quixote — Saint Francis of Assisi* composed between 1921 and 1929. For Tournemire's text see Joël-Marie Fauquet, *Catalogue de l'œuvre de Charles Tournemire* (Geneva: Éditions Minkoff, 1979), 90-93.

74. Messiaen, in Massin and Messiaen, *Olivier Messiaen,* 155.

75. Hello, *Paroles de Dieu* (1992), 176: "Ce magnifique remplacement de la peur par la crainte ouvre une fenêtre sur l'adoration."

76. Henri Daniel-Rops, *Notre inquiétude, essais* (Paris: Perrin et Cie, 1927), 23.

77. Hello, *Paroles de Dieu* (1992), 225-29.

1927–1932: Budding Rhythmician, Surrealist Composer, Mystical Commentator

"It is of monstrous beauty, opening up immense caverns where rivers flow, where piles of precious stones glitter. . . . Occasionally I had the impression that hell was opening, suddenly gaping wide. There were cataracts of strange noises *dazzling* the ear."[78] But the fear experienced is not meant to be *la peur;* it is, rather, an exercise in *la crainte* — Hello's window opened on to adoration.

The second Catholic Revivalist text that likely influenced Messiaen's *Apparition* is one we encountered with respect to *lectio divina: Christ in His Mysteries* (1919), by the Benedictine abbot Dom Columba Marmion.[79] Messiaen's spiritual director had instructed him shortly after obtaining the Trinité post to get this book; his job was now to comment on or paraphrase the texts of the liturgical year, and he did not yet understand them. Did Messiaen have *Christ in His Mysteries* in hand by the feast of All Saints on November 1, 1931? We cannot know for sure.

However, if he did have the book, he would immediately have noticed one of its most curious features: it concludes its mammoth consideration of the "mysteries of Christ" celebrated throughout the liturgical year not, as one might expect, with Pentecost, Trinity Sunday, or Corpus Christi in early summer. Rather, Dom Marmion ends with the November feast of All Saints, which he considered the logical (and theological) end point of Christ. Marmion reasoned: insofar as the church is the mystical body of Christ, as the saints constitute those who have finally become stones in that living temple, and as the goal of every human being is to become a saint by contemplating and interiorizing the "mysteries of Christ," the feast of All Saints is the ultimate terminus of the liturgical year, the life of the Christian, and the life of Christ.

At the end of what is an extremely long book, Marmion's final chapter in *Christ in His Mysteries,* "Christ, Crown of All the Saints," begins with the introductory remark: "Christ is inseparable from His mystical body," which is the church.[80] Marmion underscores the point of celebrating "the glory of the kingdom of Jesus in one solemn feast, All Saints [November 1]" at the end of the annual liturgical cycle:

---

78. Julien Green, quoted in Peter Hill and Nigel Simeone, *Messiaen* (New Haven: Yale University Press, 2005), 185.

79. Massin and Messiaen, *Olivier Messiaen,* 68; citing Marmion, *Le Christ dans ses mystères. Conférences spirituelles* (Namur, Belgium: Abbaye de Maredsous; Paris and Bruges: Desclée de Brouwer et Cie, [1919] 1928).

80. Columba Marmion, chapter 20 ("Christ, Crown of All the Saints [Feast of All Saints]") in *Christ in His Mysteries,* trans. Alan Bancroft (Bethesda, Md.: Zaccheus Press, 2008), 441-66, at 441.

1931–1932: Synesthesia, Apparitions, the Gift of Fear

It joins together as the object of its praise the whole multitudinous company of the elect, in order to extol their triumph and their joy and at the same time urge us to follow their example, so that we may share their felicity.

For that society is one, as Christ is one. Time will be followed by eternity; souls here below are formed to perfection, but the end of the journey is found only in that glorious society.... In this "great multitude which no man could number" [Apoc. 7:9], each saint will shine with a distinctive splendor; and God will take delight for ever in the efforts, the struggles, the victories, of that saint (which are like so many trophies at the feet of God, to honor His infinite perfections and recognize His rights).[81]

Blood dominates Marmion's imagery; he associates the church's life-source with sacrificial blood.

Look at this indeed: what song is sung by the elect whom St. John shows in his Apocalypse casting themselves down before the [sacrificial] Lamb? "You were slain, and have redeemed us for God with your blood.... To you blessing and honor and glory and dominion, forever and ever" [see Apoc. 5:9, 13]. The saints acknowledge that they are trophies of the blood of the Lamb — trophies that are more glorious the higher their holiness is.

Let us, then, seek with all the ardor of our souls to purify ourselves more and more in the blood of Jesus, seek to produce those fruits of life and holiness that Christ Jesus merited for us by His Passion and death. If we become saints, our souls will, for all eternity, thrill at the joy we shall give Christ by singing the triumphs of His divine blood and the almighty power of His grace.[82]

Blood dominates even in the celestial Jerusalem: "all the glory of the saints ... all the splendor of their triumph is fed by that one and only source; it is because they are tinctured with the blood of the Lamb that the robes of those chosen are so resplendent." In a genuinely medieval fashion, Marmion's method consistently points to and underscores the paradoxes that run throughout Christian imagery. "In heaven," he says, we shall arrive at that mental vantage point (very surrealist!) "from which we shall understand that all the mercies of God have Calvary as their starting-point; that the price of the unending happiness in which we shall then rejoice for ever was the blood of Jesus. Let us not forget this: In the heavenly Jerusalem we shall be inebriated with divine bliss; but

---

81. Marmion, *Christ in His Mysteries*, 442, 443.
82. Marmion, *Christ in His Mysteries*, 445.

this bliss — all of it, every instant — will have been paid for by the merits of the blood of Jesus Christ. 'The stream of the river' that, eternally, 'makes the city of God joyful' [Ps. 45 (46):4]."[83] The celestial city is joyful, indeed — but it is the "joy of the blood of the stars."[84]

Whether or not Marmion was thinking explicitly of the hymn for the Dedication of a Church, he follows this ancient liturgical tradition of interpreting human suffering as purgatorial:

> God has a powerful hand and His purifying activity reaches depths that only the saints know. By the temptations He permits, by the adversities He sends, by the feelings of being deserted and the frightful loneliness He sometimes produces in the soul, He tries that soul in order to detach it from what is merely created. He digs deep into it, in order to empty it of itself; He "pursues" it, He "persecutes it, in order to possess it" [words of Dom Pie de Hemptinne]; He delves to its very marrows; He "breaks its bones," as Bossuet says somewhere, "in order to reign in it alone."
>
> Blessed the soul that abandons itself into the hands of this Divine Worker! Through His Spirit — that Spirit, all fire and love, who is "the Finger of God's right hand" [hymn "Veni, Creator Spiritus"], God the Eternal Artist will engrave on it the features of Christ, so as to make it resemble His Beloved Son according to the ineffable design of His wisdom and mercy.[85]

Reading Marmion's lines, Messiaen might well have remembered lines from Dostoyevsky he would have heard read out loud by his father in childhood:

> I took the book out of his hand and opened it at another place: the Epistle to the Hebrews, Chapter X, Verse 31. I handed it to him.
> "It is a fearful thing to fall into the hands of the living God," he read and flung the book violently away. I saw that he was trembling.
> "A frightening verse.... Well, you certainly know how to pick them!"[86]

---

83. Marmion, *Christ in His Mysteries*, 464.

84. "Joy of the Blood of the Stars" ("Joie du Sang des Étoiles") is the fifth movement of Messiaen's *Turangalîla Symphony*. Marmion's passage is yet another example of the "star + cross motif," that is, the intersection of the "star" of Bethlehem and the "cross" of Galilee, invented by Messiaen for *Twenty Gazes at the Infant Jesus* (comp. 1944). See also note 22 on p. 468 below, on T. S. Eliot's *Murder in the Cathedral* (1935).

85. Marmion, *Christ in His Mysteries*, 461-62.

86. Fyodor Dostoyevsky, *The Brothers Karamazov*, trans. Andrew R. MacAndrew (New York: Bantam Dell, [1970] 2003), 413-14.

1931–1932: Synesthesia, Apparitions, the Gift of Fear

For Messiaen, such a message would certainly have made a strong impact, for its logical conclusion is that those moments in which "the soul is plunged into sorrow and suffering, into aridity and dryness" are paradoxically "moments that are rich in graces."[87] And Marmion's emphasis on always keeping one's eyes on the prize — "The whole mystery of Christ, the Incarnate Word, leads to this final goal"[88] — would have propelled Messiaen's quest even further, looking beyond this ephemeral world to what is lasting and eternal.

Several decades later, Messiaen explained his single-minded attention to eternity in a published conversation:

> You said that I express only joy and glory in my music.... On the one hand there are people whose view of the next world is obstructed by the suffering on earth; there is Job, who is driven by suffering to reproach God. On the other hand, there are those who, despite suffering, constantly assert afresh their hope of everlasting life.... Do you think it's easy to constantly convince oneself of the latter?... When the apostle Peter saw Christ walking on the water, he asked Him to give him His hand, so that he could walk on the water along with Him. Christ gave him His hand. Peter looked at Him and was able to walk on water in the same way. Suddenly he became aware of this, began to stumble, and was in danger of drowning. He had doubted Christ, who then said to Peter: "Oh, man of little faith!" That's how it is for all of us every day. We must constantly strive afresh not to doubt and not to drown. *We must direct our gaze towards the life hereafter and try to forget about this life.*[89]

We cannot know whether Messiaen had already read Dom Marmion by All Saints' Day in November 1931. But if he had, Marmion's gloss on words of Saint Paul would have mirrored the direction that Messiaen's own internal path had already been heading. "All the sufferings He permits or sends are so

---

87. Marmion, *Christ in His Mysteries*, 463.
88. Marmion, *Christ in His Mysteries*, 465.
89. Messiaen, in Rößler, *Contributions*, 52-53, emphasis added. I am grateful to Hyesook Kim for alerting me to this passage. Compare Daniel-Rops quoting Fr. Sanson (discussed on pp. 209-10): "For the Christian, terrestrial life has no other meaning than that of a waiting for eternal life: '*And far from being troubled by the reproach addressed to Christianity for orienting ourselves in our entirety toward the beyond [de nous orienter tout entier vers l'au-delà], I say that it is by this, and by this alone, that [Christianity] reveals itself to us as being the truth of life [la vérité de la vie].*'" Daniel-Rops, *Notre inquiétude*, 285. Quotations from Sanson are in italics; emphasis in original.

many titles to glory and heavenly beatitude. St. Paul declares himself powerless to describe the splendor of the glory, and the depths of happiness, which will crown the slightest of our sorrows that are endured through divine grace: 'The sufferings of the present time are not worthy to be compared with the glory to come that will be revealed in us'; 'For our present light affliction, which is for the moment, prepares for us an eternal weight of glory that is beyond all measure.'"[90]

Messiaen recorded this "apparition" of the "eternal church" just as he was about to leave his mother's home and create his own home with his newly-wed. He recorded it in minute detail, just as accounts of mescaline-induced apparitions and visions are recorded with exactitude in *Peyote*. Messiaen's is a vision of eternal joy, certainly; but inextricably embedded in that joy is a tremendous amount of blood, suffering, and sorrow. It is an easy paradox to overlook in Messiaen: yes, he self-consciously insisted that he was a "musician of joy." But at the same time — from "the joy of the blood of the stars" in *Turangalîla Symphony* to the "perfect joy" motif in the *Saint Francis of Assisi* opera — joy is saturated with blood, suffering, and sorrow, whether named or left unspoken.[91] From the standpoint of surrealism or of mystic-realism, joy and blood are actually one.

The Eternal Church: Time, Duration, Nonretrogradability

Doctrines of the Eucharist and the church share a common trait that would have appealed to Messiaen the "rhythmician": they represent a reality that is simultaneously temporal and eternal.[92] Or perhaps better: one in which eter-

---

90. Marmion, *Christ in His Mysteries,* 462, quoting Rom. 8:18 and 2 Cor. 4:17.

91. "Perfect joy" in the *Little Flowers of Saint Francis of Assisi (Fioretti di San Francesco d' Assisi)* is the cheerful suffering and self-abnegation explained in the eighth chapter, "How St. Francis, Walking One Day with Brother Leo, Explained to Him What Things Are Perfect Joy." Messiaen's libretto for the opera *Saint Francis* puts it this way: "For, above all the favors and gifts of the Holy Spirit that Christ grants his friends, there is the power of vanquishing oneself and bearing voluntarily, for the love of Christ, sorrows, injuries, opprobrium, and discomfort." Libretto translated in Siglind Bruhn, *Messiaen's Contemplations of Covenant and Incarnation: Musical Symbols of Faith in the Two Great Piano Cycles of the 1940s* (Hillsdale, N.Y.: Pendragon Press, 2007), 207-18, at 208; for "theme of joy" leitmotif see p. 178. Messiaen's self-description as a "musician of joy" needs to be interpreted within the context of his works, including the "star + cross" motif *(Twenty Gazes),* the "Joy of the Blood of the Stars" *(Turangalîla),* and the "theme of joy" *(Saint Francis).*

92. For time intersecting eternity, see n. 63 above.

1931–1932: Synesthesia, Apparitions, the Gift of Fear

nity intersects time. In comparison with Messiaen's innovative experiments with unpredictable meters in immediately preceding compositions, *Apparition* does not seem to indicate innovation. However, it is precisely the hypnotic sameness of the piece's rhythm that suggests further reflections on Bergsonism, time, and duration.

Messiaen wrote notes for his own recorded performance of this piece in 1957. They can be summarized in bullet points:

- Rhythm: "An iamb and a double long."
- Harmony: "The alternation of bright colors of the 2nd, 3rd and 7th 'Modes of Limited Transposition,' their opposition with empty fifths, cold and hard."
- Dynamics: "An immense crescendo gathering together little by little all the forces of the organ's fortissimo — a diminuendo also progressive."
- Summary: "That is all the rhythmic, harmonic, and dynamic material of this piece."[93]

One scholar expands on Messiaen's words, describing *Apparition of the Eternal Church* as "an immense, hypnotic crescendo calling upon the characteristic piling of tier upon tier of sound rising from the symphonic organ — indissociable from Messiaen both as organist and improviser — followed by a long decrescendo in mirror image. One perpetual and unchanging rhythm, linking an iambus to two long notes, sustain the entire structure of the work."[94]

The simple, unchanging, and perpetually recurrent rhythmic element is at the heart of the "hypnotic" experience: it is a paradoxical hybridization of time — time that is eternal in its repetitiveness. Is it possible that Messiaen, so acquainted with English writers (thanks to his father Pierre), and who explicitly points to ocean tides (especially Debussy's) in his listed examples of "natural" rhythms,[95] had in mind Matthew Arnold's "Dover Beach"?

Listen! you hear the grating roar
Of pebbles which the waves draw back, and fling,

---

93. Messiaen, jacket notes for recording of *Apparition* (Ducretet-Thomson, 1957); in Gillock, "Messiaen's Organ Works," 43. Translation altered.

94. Michel Roubinet, liner notes, *Olivier Messiaen. Œuvres pour orgue*, performed by Olivier Messiaen, trans. Denis Ogan (Paris: EMI France, [1957] 1992), 13. This set of four compact discs is a reedition of Messiaen's eight vinyl LP discs cited above (Ducretet-Thomson, 1957).

95. Messiaen, *Traité*, 1:42, 53.

1927–1932: Budding Rhythmician, Surrealist Composer, Mystical Commentator

> At their return, up the high strand,
> Begin, and cease, and then again begin,
> With tremulous cadence slow, and bring
> The eternal note of sadness in.[96]

Arnold develops the image as he reflects on Sophocles, who, hearing this eternally repetitive rhythm on the Aegean Sea, had been reminded of

> the turbid ebb and flow
> Of human misery.[97]

Although viewed through a different lens, this is not far from the subject matter of *Apparition*.

The unending forward impulsion of *Apparition*'s rhythm is implicit in its basic element: it is an iambus (a weak-strong pairing of syllables) followed by a "double-long" — in medieval notation, a *longa*, equal to four *breves*. Concretely, the piece's fundamental rhythmic unit is:

⌈1⌉⌈1+2⌉⌈1+2+3+4⌉.

Use of the iambic combination — an initial weak beat (⌈1⌉) followed by a strong beat of twice the duration (⌈1+2⌉) — makes the fundamental beat unstable; it wants immediately to move to something sturdier. Pictorially, we might imagine the listener always impelled to leap off an ice floe that is drifting away and on to more stable footing. This sense of incessant impulsion and the need to leap is amplified by the lowest range of the pedals playing the same rhythmic pulse — yet juxtaposed so as to produce syncopation with the rhythm above:

Manuals: ⌈1⌉⌈1+2⌉⌈1+2+3+4⌉
Pedal: ⌈1⌉⌈1+2⌉⌈1⌉⌈1+2⌉⌈1⌉

In other words, although the "melody" in the hands sustains the steady chord for four beats (⌈1+2+3+4⌉), the pedals continue the eternal ebb and flow: weak-strong-weak (⌈1⌉⌈1+2⌉⌈1⌉). The "hypnotic" element is intensified by a recurrent second motif in the pedals of three recurrent beats of equal strength:

---

96. Matthew Arnold, "Dover Beach," in *Poems by Matthew Arnold*, ed. G. C. Macaulay (London and New York: Macmillan, 1896), 65-66, at 65.
97. Arnold, "Dover Beach," 66.

1931–1932: Synesthesia, Apparitions, the Gift of Fear

⌈1⌉⌈1⌉⌈1+2⌉ ⌈1⌉⌈1⌉⌈1+2⌉ ⌈1⌉⌈1⌉⌈1+2⌉. This triple repetition, the inexorable hammer of the mallet, presumably represents the three aspects of the "eternal church": the church militant (human beings on earth), the church suffering (souls in purgatory), and the church triumphant (saints and angels in the Celestial City). Like the Eucharist (or "celestial banquet"), the church is a paradoxical intersection of time and eternity. In Bergsonian terms, it has just one indivisible "duration," unified and bounded by its initial onset and its final end.

The "sound-colors" that Messiaen notes — the warm and hot "lively" colors of his own modal system contrasted with the "hard and cold open fifths" — are integrated with the rhythm so as to amplify this forward impulsion. The iambs are hot-warm: the chord on the weak beat is almost unbearably "hot" in its dissonance; it is impelled to leap onto the strong beat that opens up the clustered chord and conveys somewhat less dissonant heat. The double-long beat is fully resolved in the harsh cold of open fourths and fifths. This an example of the "simultaneous contrast" central to Messiaen's "sound-colors."[98]

In addition to the hot-cold contrast, the open fourths and fifths evoke the medieval sonority of the *organum*, that is, voices moving in parallel motion with the melody at an interval of a fourth or fifth. Similarly, the extreme dissonance produced by chord clusters formed by multiple tightly formed intervals of seconds strikes the listener as "ultramodern." Taken together, *Apparition*'s open fifths and clenching seconds are thus — once again recalling Messiaen's laudatory description of Tournemire's *L'Orgue Mystique* as "half-Gothic, half-ultra-modern" — yet another paradoxical intersection

---

98. Compare Vincent Benitez: "Rather, sound-color relationships in Messiaen's music should be viewed from the perspective of simultaneous contrast. . . . Messiaen compared the way he structures his music to the way a painter structures colors on a canvas. . . . Both of their approaches to color involve the mutual enhancement of their materials through simultaneous contrast; the distinctive characteristics associated with a particular musical entity or color are secondary considerations. In other words, a painter juxtaposes two complementary colors on a canvas because they intensify one another to an appreciable degree, not because they lie directly opposite one another on a color wheel. Similarly, Messiaen combines, for example, two chords in his music because they enhance one another from sound-color perspectives, not because both chords define larger harmonic areas or happen to be literal pitch-class complements that form an aggregate. Aggregates and larger harmonic areas should be viewed as by-products of Messiaen's more fundamental use of simultaneous contrast and not as fundamental constructs that determine harmonic activity on the musical surface." Benitez, "Simultaneous Contrast and Additive Designs in Olivier Messiaen's Opera, *Saint François d'Assise*"; cf. Messiaen, in Rößler, *Contributions*, 76-80, 87-88, 115; and Messiaen and Samuel (1994), 61-62.

characteristic of Charles Baudelaire: "all *modernism* is worthy of becoming antiquity someday."[99]

Messiaen employs an overall "mirror" construction. The piece seemingly arises out of some far-off distance, thanks to the mechanics of closed organ boxes muffling the enormous sound. (Messiaen's interest in the "far-off" seems to extend back to lines from *Pelléas et Mélisande*.)[100] It builds steadily as the ranks of pipes are drawn systematically (as an improviser would) until reaching the instrument's full capacity. At this point, emphasizing the threefold character of the church, three chords are played for long durations: an A-flat minor chord whose inverted sixth makes it unstable (church militant); a stepwise motion to B-flat minor that is stable in its root position but nevertheless minor in mode (church suffering); and a final stepwise motion to C major with doubled pedals and full chords in both hands stretching the entire spectrum of the organ from lowest to highest pitches (church triumphant). This threefold movement is repeated two more times, the second of which is "false" as it initiates the reverse (mirror) process by which the piece will now gradually return, by means of gradual subtraction of ranks, to its original muffled far-off distance.

---

99. Messiaen and Baudelaire, quoted in Stephen Schloesser, *Jazz Age Catholicism: Mystic Modernism in Postwar Paris, 1919-1933* (Toronto: University of Toronto Press, 2005), 311, 331 n. 36. "Baudelaire's solution of the problem of 'modernity' famously defined beauty as being 'always and inevitably of a double composition . . . made up of *an eternal, invariable element*, whose quantity it is excessively difficult to determine, and of *a relative, circumstantial element*, which will be, if you like, whether severally or all at once, the age, its fashions, its morals, its emotions.' Baudelaire amplified the terms: 'By "modernity," I mean the ephemeral, the fugitive, the contingent, the half of art whose other half is the eternal and the immutable. . . . This transitory, fugitive element, whose metamorphoses are so rapid, must on no account be dispensed with. By neglecting it, you cannot fail to tumble into the abyss of an abstract and indeterminate beauty. . . .'" Schloesser, 166.

100. Messiaen's interest in the "far-off" has already been seen in *The Death of Number* — "I am still very far away from you. / Who can push me even further away?" — and extends back to Debussy's *Pelléas et Mélisande*. In video footage from his Conservatory class, Messiaen draws the students' attention to Golaud's first encounter with Mélisande: "Mélisande says, 'I'm not from here. I was born far from here.' 'Far.' She repeats it over and over, drifting further away as if she doesn't even belong to our planet, as if she's from another world, another plane. . . . Golaud asks, 'Where are you from, where were you born?' . . . She replies, 'Far from here. Far . . . Far . . .' [*loin d'ici. Loin. Loin . . .*]." See the documentary video *Olivier Messiaen et les oiseaux*. Excerpts available on YouTube ("Messiaen on Debussy and Colour").

For his published version of this analysis, see Messiaen, *Traité*, 6:59-60. The passage under consideration is in *Pelléas*, act 1, scene 1, "A Forest," section 12-13; E. Fromont edition (1904); reprinted as Debussy, *Pelléas et Mélisande in Full Score* (Mineola, N.Y.: Dover Publications, [1985] 2010), 12.

1931–1932: Synesthesia, Apparitions, the Gift of Fear

Messiaen applied the symmetry of palindromes (for example, "Able was I ere I saw Elba") to rhythm. Reading the same both "forward" and "backward" (retrograde), palindromic rhythms can represent the stasis of eternity. He was particularly inspired by Guillaume de Machaut, and especially his lyrical work "My End Is My Beginning."[101]

Ma fin est mon commencement	My end is my beginning
Et mon commencement ma fin	And my beginning my end
Et teneure vraiement	And the tenor [is sung] in the normal way
Ma fin est mon commencement.	My end is my beginning
Mes tiers chans trois fois seulements	My third voice three times only
Se retrograde et einsi fin.	Turns back on itself and thus ends.
Ma fin est mon commencement	My end is my beginning
Et mon commencement ma fin.	And my beginning my end.[102]

Messiaen later claimed that he was unaware of Machaut's work as late as 1941. And yet, the correspondences between the two seem remarkably coincidental, especially in Messiaen's own threefold repetition at the fulcrum of *Apparition*, that is, just before the work "turns back on itself" and proceeds to its end (which mirrors its beginning).[103] For Messiaen, these palindromes could symbolize eternity because they are not linear or unidirectional like space-time.

101. Messiaen quotes Machaut's *Ma fin* twice in the *Traité:* see 1:45 ("the retrograde movement, forgotten since Guillaume de Machaut [see the Rondo 'Ma fin est mon commencement, Et mon commencement ma fin']"); and 3:180 ("Ma fin est mon commencement — Et mon commencement ma fin"); cf. 4:28 on Machaut's "isorhythms" and 5.1:16. Gareth Healey identifies nonretrogradable rhythms in movements 2, 5, and 6 of *Visions of Amen* (1943); and movements 6, 13, 16, 18, and 19 of *Vingt Regards* (1944). See Healey, "Form: Messiaen's 'Downfall'?" *Twentieth-Century Music* 4, no. 2 (September 2007): 163-87, at 173 (table 2). He does not discuss the *Apparition*.

102. For an accessible overview of Machaut's musically, textually, and visually complex puzzle, see Anne Stone, "Music Writing and Poetic Voice in Machaut: Some Remarks on B12 and R14," in *Machaut's Music: New Interpretations,* ed. Elizabeth Eva Leach (Rochester, N.Y.: Boydell Press, 2003), 125-38. This translation of *Ma fin* is by Virginia Newes, "Writing, Reading and Memorizing: The Transmission and Resolution of Retrograde Canons from the 14th and Early 15th Centuries," *Early Music* 18 (1990): 218-34 (225-28); in Stone, 137. (I have added the arrows.) Newes notes that copyists after Machaut's death who did not understand his puzzle miscopied the work in a way that was unintelligible. This would partly explain its being "unknown."

103. Messiaen claimed that he had not yet encountered Machaut's work as late as the writing of *Quartet for the End of Time* (1940) — see Messiaen in Antoine Goléa, *Rencontres*

1927–1932: Budding Rhythmician, Surrealist Composer, Mystical Commentator

The true endgame or meaningful center of a palindrome is not (as in a linear construction) the end point. Rather, it is the center fulcrum that holds together both the forward motion and its reversal mirror image. *Apparition* both begins and ends in some far-off distance: its nonlinearity symbolizes the church's character as "eternal." A much more self-conscious and rigorously applied theory of "nonretrogradability" will appear in Messiaen's treatment of "The Gaze of the Church of Love," the culminating movement in *Twenty Gazes* (1944).[104]

In this deceptively simple rhythmic scheme, Messiaen continues experimentation with representing atemporality using a medium that is irreducibly temporal. In *The Forgotten Offerings* he had usurped meter by using alternations of binary and ternary groupings inspired by plainchant. In *The Resplendent Tomb* he had introduced irregular rhythmic patterns not reducible to more basic numbers. And in both of these as well as in *Diptych*, he had experimented with reducing the tempi to near stasis. *Apparition* represents yet another phase in Messiaen's experiments with representing "eternity": in addition to the extreme slowness of the tempo and the syncopated pulses, the entire movement can be seen as one large palindrome — a duration complete in itself with both image and mirror.

Finally, an observation that initially runs against common sense: *Apparition* shares much in common with the "perpetual motion machine" character of the French symphonic organ toccata. One has only to think of well-known toccatas by Gigout, Boellmann, Dupré — and most famously, that from the fifth organ symphony by Messiaen's first Conservatory composition teacher,

---

avec Olivier Messiaen (Paris: René Julliard, [1960] 1961), 66; quoted in Robert Sherlaw Johnson, *Messiaen* (Berkeley: University of California Press, 1975), 62.

However, this claim seems unlikely, not only because of the parallels in *Apparition* (1931-1932) a decade earlier, but also because the scholarly edition of Machaut's works published between 1926 and 1929 — during his Conservatory years in Maurice Emmanuel's history class — was a significant event in ancient music research. See Guillaume de Machaut, *Musikalische Werke*, ed. Ludwig von Friedrich, 3 vols. (Leipzig: Breitkopf & Härtel, 1926-1929). The first volume, published in 1926, contained Machaut's ballades, rondos (including *Ma fin*), and virelais. As one musicologist notes, Machaut scholarship had to wait until 1904 to begin in earnest since "Even late in the nineteenth century, in spite of impressive knowledge of medieval art, architecture and literature, medieval music was still considered to exhibit a primitive state." See Lawrence Earp, *Guillaume de Machaut: A Guide to Research* (New York: Garland, 1995), 279; cf. 277-83, 339-41; and Margaret Bent, "What Is Isorhythm?" in *Quomodo Cantabimus Canticum? Studies in Honor of Edward H. Roesner*, ed. Cannata et al. (Middleton, Wis.: American Institute of Musicology, 2008), 121-43.

104. Jean Marie Wu, "Mystical Symbols of Faith: Olivier Messiaen's Charm of Impossibilities," in *Messiaen's Language of Mystical Love*, ed. Siglind Bruhn (New York and London: Garland, 1998), 85-120, especially 98-104.

1931–1932: Synesthesia, Apparitions, the Gift of Fear

Charles-Marie Widor. They are marked by a seemingly limitless amount of energy produced by an internal spontaneous combustion engine that continues to produce a steady source of breathless velocity. This toccata tradition exploited technological innovations pioneered by Aristide Cavaillé-Coll, later enhanced by the electrification of wind sources. But its imagery was also thoroughly nineteenth century; the ancient dream of a perpetual motion machine had been quashed by the midcentury formulation of the second law of thermodynamics. As the fin-de-siècle seemed a harbinger of the end times, there was much popular talk about the inevitable heat death of the universe (since finite sources of energy such as the sun would eventually burn themselves out). In addition to being entertaining and thrilling, French organ toccatas that could seemingly go on forever came into vogue alongside this morbidly popular fascination with heat death and impossible perpetual motion.[105]

Although it is at the opposite end of the tempo spectrum from Widor's toccata, Messiaen's *Apparition* is its own hypnotic perpetual motion machine. It goes on and on and on and on — like the unbounded "free energy" of a self-combustion engine. Or the primordial Aegean Sea.

Seventy Years Later: Postmodern *Apparition*

Although well known to organists, Messiaen's *Apparition* has not been a piece familiar to broader audiences. However, that may change as it has recently been given a fresh lease by a documentary film: Paul Festa's *Apparition of the Eternal Church* (2008), reviewed by one critic as "perhaps the finest film ever made on how people experience music."[106]

Festa puts headphones on thirty-one persons and plays Messiaen's *Apparition* for them without telling them what they are hearing. He then films them as

---

105. Arthur W. J. G. Ord-Hume, *Perpetual Motion: The History of an Obsession* (New York: St. Martin's Press, [1977] 1980); Stephen G. Brush, *The Temperature of History: Phases of Science and Culture in the Nineteenth Century* (New York: B. Franklin, 1977); Brush, "Nietzsche's Recurrence Revisited: The French Connection," *Journal of the History of Philosophy* 19, no. 2 (April 1981): 235-38; Greg Myers, "Nineteenth-Century Popularizations of Thermodynamics and the Rhetoric of Social Prophecy," in Patrick Brantlinger, ed., *Energy and Entropy: Science and Culture in Victorian Britain* (Bloomington: Indiana University Press, 1989); Helge Kragh, *Entropic Creation: Religious Contexts of Thermodynamics and Cosmology* (Burlington, Vt.: Ashgate, 2008).

106. Andrew Patner, "A Great Movie about Music," review of Paul Festa's *Apparition of the Eternal Church, Chicago Sun-Times,* October 6, 2008. For the film's Web site see http://www.apparitionfilm.com/.

they are listening to the work and speaking (sometimes shouting) about what they are feeling and what images come to mind. From the standpoint of visual imagery, the reactions are extremely varied. However, from the perspective of felt emotion, the responses are surprisingly singular. They are about fear, or at least a sense of the uncanny. For example:

> It's church, or zombies, or it's, or mutant creatures that have gone wild, right? Frankenstein, so —
> It sounds a little bit like some sort of horror film as well as if something *bad* was going to happen to somebody, although, you know, generally that sort of thing's just in the *movies,* people are *acting.* Bad things happen in real life and this sort of music isn't playing at all!

> It evokes, on the one hand, something very earthy, and earthly, yet even as deep as it is, it also in a strange way evokes something celestial. The earthly part of it then seems to me very interior. Underneath the crust. Magma, miasma — All of those kinds of things that have to do with the formation of the earth, and of a world.

> Cosmic! Like *2001 Space Odyssey.*

> It's kind of space age, kind of Gothic . . .

> It's all very . . . scary! *Oh my god!*

> I almost feel like it's Yom Kippur.

> Day of Judgment — if you've taken Ecstasy.

> I see a huge stairway, you can't see the top of it — literally an infinite staircase.
> It's like an acoustic Escher staircase!

> A feeling of fear, anxiety, and stress but it always kind of resolves itself.

> Unresolved, it's not going to resolve.

> The music is nondirectional, really — that is, yeah, there is an overall . . . but it just floats!

1931–1932: Synesthesia, Apparitions, the Gift of Fear

This has a kind of . . . victorious sound to it.

It's triumphant here, even though it's quieter.

The drama is over, you know? The — it's gotten a little sad.[107]

Remarkably, many of the images actually reflect Messiaen's own personal catalogue: images of monsters, zombies, horror, ghostly apparitions; images from both geology and astronomy that have to do with unimaginable quantities of space and time approaching infinity; images of the end of time and judgment; an "infinite staircase"; the feeling of unending suspended duration made possible through prolonged nonresolution; a final triumph that is, at the same time, a melancholic one.

Underlying the variety of images in Festa's documentary is a striking unity in the experience of some kind of fear — or at least representative images triggered by what sounds like a fear-inducing encounter. And rightly so, for Messiaen's *Apparition* is in fact meant to conjure up and provoke an experience of fear — just as Messiaen enjoyed doing with his brother and blind grandfather as a child. Probably the reaction to his composition Messiaen would most have enjoyed is that of a six-year-old boy named Aiden. Festa writes that when the music began and a broad smile spread across Aiden's face, Festa checked his iPod to make sure it was playing the right track. "Do you like it, Aiden?" asked Festa. "I love it," replied the six-year-old. "Why do you love it?" "Because it's scary."[108]

One of Festa's most invaluable inclusions in the film (although he received criticism for it) is "Squeaky Blonde," a New York club personality dressed up in Goth costume (perhaps as a mummy), drinking beer and smoking from a bong as she speaks: "But then! When they start lowering your friend's body into the uh — tomb they've dug — (unintelligible). Is that all there is? Is that all there is? I don't think it is. But — some people will beg to differ."[109] Although one of Festa's critics attacked Squeaky as an "anti-Christ" figure, one suspects that Messiaen would have considered this criticism nonsense. Indeed, because he grew up in the Jazz Age shock-erotic atmosphere of surrealism and was fascinated by experiments in synesthetic and mescaline-induced apparitions,

---

107. All quotations in Paul Festa, *OH MY GOD: Messiaen in the Ear of the Unbeliever* (San Francisco: Bar Nothing Books, 2008), 34-36, 42-43, 45, 48-49, 52-53, 55, 64, 72, 78-79, 84-85, 90-91.

108. Six-year-old Aiden, quoted in Festa, *OH MY GOD*, 71.

109. "Squeaky Blonde," quoted in Festa, *OH MY GOD*, 91-93.

it seems more likely that "Squeaky Blonde" would have been one of Messiaen's favorite moments — a twenty-first-century expression of a long trajectory associating drugs and visions.[110]

And yet, at least for this audience, *la peur* never translates into *la crainte*. The passage from emotion to referent seems impossible. The one auditor who tries to articulate Messiaen's own image in theological terms, the late Juilliard professor Albert Fuller, seems promising at the beginning — "The image that Messiaen had about what church means" — but then runs off track as imagery stalls in pietism and pathos: "Jesus as the son of God, who was *crucified* — which ain't fun! Not when they drive nails through your hands, and your feet, and you choke to death because you can't take a breath."[111]

Festa's experiment is highly suggestive. On the one hand, it demonstrates that Messiaen was a master at producing music evoking feelings of fear, dread, and terror (or perhaps simply pain) in its listeners — an emotional experience he had delighted in since childhood. On the other hand, the emotion interpreted as *la peur* does not translate easily into *la crainte:* "fear of the Lord." Listeners interpreted the "experience" in terms largely shaped by their common experience of horror films; this is not entirely inaccurate, since the "Gothic" was one popular place to which the "sacred" migrated in the late eighteenth century.[112]

These observations point to the importance of recent work on the "history of emotions."[113] Interpreting one's experience as a certain emotion (e.g., *la crainte*, a wonder-response to the numinous) and not another (e.g., *la peur*, fear of cinematic zombies and serial killers) depends on being a member of a specific "emotional community" from which one's images are derived. The

---

110. For associations between the *fantastique, hallucinatoire,* and drug use in nineteenth-century decadence and Catholic Revivalism, see Schloesser, *Jazz Age Catholicism*, 36.

111. Albert Fuller, quoted in Festa, *OH MY GOD*, 100.

112. Peter Brookes, *The Melodramatic Imagination: Balzac, Henry James, Melodrama, and the Mode of Excess*, with a new preface (New Haven: Yale University Press, 1995; original 1976).

113. Jan Plamper, "The History of Emotions: An Interview with William Reddy, Barbara Rosenwein, and Peter Stearns," *History and Theory* 49, no. 2 (May 2010): 237–65; Barbara H. Rosenwein, *Emotional Communities in the Early Middle Ages* (Ithaca, N.Y.: Cornell University Press, 2006); Penelope Gouke and Helen Hills, eds., *Representing Emotions: New Connections in the Histories of Art, Music, and Medicine* (Burlington, Vt.: Ashgate, 2005); Rosenwein, "Worrying about Emotions in History," *American Historical Review* 107, no. 3 (June 2002): 821–45; and William M. Reddy, *The Navigation of Feeling: A Framework for the History of Emotions* (New York: Cambridge University Press, 2001). See also Jerome Neu, *A Tear Is an Intellectual Thing: The Meanings of Emotion* (New York: Oxford University Press, 2000).

community's shared vision allows its members to interpret an emotional event as being one type and not another.

What does this mean for postmodern listeners as they encounter Messiaen's musical representations meant to signal *la crainte de Dieu* — fear of the Lord? This question is provoked by both *Apparition* itself and Festa's documentary. But whatever the future of Messiaen's "fear" factor, he reveals his intentions about it in a kind of coda to a discussion of Blanc-Gatti's *Sounds and Colors* and the influence of "nonmusical rhythms" on musical rhythm:

> Before leaving the painting-music and sound-color relationships, allow me to share a small secret. Due to a peculiar tendency of my mind, I have always loved monsters (all those of the Cretaceous period: Brontosaurus, Diplodocus, Stegosaurus, Tyrannosaurus), and the painters of monsters: Hieronymus Bosch, Goya's *Los Caprichos* [cf. "The Sleep of Reason Produces Monsters"] and *Los Disparates,* Picasso, Max Ernst, Dali, [Félix] Labisse. In turn, I tried to produce monsters in music: but I never succeeded in doing so. Music is able to depict terror, fright, the supernatural [*la terreur, l'effroi, le surnaturel*] (witness the Wolf's Glen of cursed bullets in [Weber's] *Freischütz*, the "Commander scene" in [Mozart's] *Don Giovanni,* the scene between Alberich and Hagen in [Wagner's] *Twilight of the Gods* and its dark prelude, the "hallucination scene" in [Mussorgsky's] *Boris Godunov,* the "underground rooms" of the castle vault in [Debussy's] *Pelléas,* the "murder of Marie" in [Berg's] *Wozzeck*). However, in the art of sounds and rhythms there is an intellectual voluptuousness [*une volupté intellectuelle*] absolutely unsuitable for monstrosity and vileness — just as in laughter and the comical — indeed, [unsuitable for] all things excluded by an anthropomorphic criterion very distant from musical abstraction.[114]

Apparition of the Eternal Church may not depict the "monstrous," and perhaps it would be musically impossible to do so. But it certainly succeeds in representing terror, fright, and the supernatural — and Messiaen's personal list of favorite precedents (in Weber, Mozart, Wagner, Mussorgsky, Debussy, and Berg) clarifies his intentions in composing *Apparition*.

---

114. Messiaen, discussion of visual arts *(arts plastiques)* in the chapter on rhythm; in *Traité*, 1:65-68, at 68.

PART III

1932–1943

Theological Order, Glorified Bodies, Apocalyptic Epoch

CHAPTER 7

1932–1935

From Apprentice to *Maître*

The entry of Louise ("Claire") Delbos into Messiaen's life has been noted: in *The Death of Number,* the violin mediates between the First Soul and the Second Soul. First performed on March 25, 1931 — about a year before their marriage in June 1932 — the work suggests that the couple had met at least by the time of its composition in fall 1930.[1] It also indicates Delbos's role in Messiaen's passage through the grieving of his mother's death.

Claire Delbos, baptized Louise Justine, was born on All Souls' Day, November 2, 1906, almost exactly two years before Messiaen. As indicated on a program for a violin recital given on February 5, 1932 (on which her name appeared as "Louise Delbos"), the name Claire (i.e., "clear" or "bright") was adopted a few months before marrying Messiaen.[2] Throughout the 1930s, Claire retained her maiden name (Delbos) for professional engagements such as recitals and published compositions.

Given this practice, her signature on a letter in October 1939, written on behalf of Messiaen, who had been mobilized into the military, stands out: "Cl. Olivier Messiaen (Claire Victor-Delbos)."[3] The use of this French hyphenation

---

1. The first performance took place under the auspices of the Société Musicale Indépendante at the École Normale de Musique with Messiaen at the piano. Nigel Simeone, *Olivier Messiaen: A Bibliographical Catalogue of Messiaen's Works,* Musikbibliographische Arbeiten series, vol. 14 (Tutzing: Hans Schneider, 1998), 21.

2. Peter Hill and Nigel Simeone, *Messiaen* (New Haven: Yale University Press, 2005), 42.

3. Claire Delbos-Messiaen (from Neussargues) to unidentified recipient, Saturday,

convention (Victor-Delbos) signals that, even after several years of marriage, Claire linked herself with her father, the philosopher Victor Delbos, who had by that time been deceased for twenty-three years. This linkage in turn suggests the extent to which Messiaen was marrying not merely a fellow practicing Catholic, but one whose father had once been at the very center of the prewar Catholic Revivalist ferment.

Victor Delbos: Philosopher of Authentic *"Clarté"*

From 1909 to 1913, Victor Delbos was professor of philosophy and psychology at the Sorbonne. In 1913 he was appointed to a new chair that had been created for him: philosophy and history of philosophy.[4] Known as both a prominent Spinoza scholar and a sympathetic interpreter of Kant, Delbos was one of several "proficient linguists whose interpretations and translations of major Kantian texts transformed the character of French philosophy after 1890."[5] Among Delbos's closest friends was Maurice Blondel, the philosopher of "action" associated circa 1905 with the Roman Catholic Modernists; Delbos's

---

October 23, 1939, Carlton Lake Collection of French Manuscripts, Harry Ransom Center, The University of Texas at Austin, 186.1. I am grateful to the Harry Ransom Center for kind permission to consult these documents.

4. Christina Chimisso, *Writing the History of the Mind: Philosophy and Sciences in France, 1900 to 1960s* (Burlington, Vt.: Ashgate, 2008), 24. After Delbos's death, the chair was suppressed and not re-created until 1933. Delbos's works published during his lifetime include the following: *Le Problème moral dans la philosophie de Spinoza et dans l'histoire du Spinozisme* (Paris: Félix Alcan, 1893); *La Philosophie pratique de Kant* (Paris: Félix Alcan, 1905), awarded by the Académie Française; translator and editor of Immanuel Kant, *Les Fondements de la métaphysique des mœurs de Kant*, 7th ed. (Paris: Ch. Delagrave, 1934); *Le Spinozisme* (Paris: La Société française d'Imprimerie et de Librairie, 1916). For intellectual biography, see Abbé Joannès Wehrlé, *Victor Delbos: membre de l'Institut, professeur de philosophie à la Sorbonne* (Paris: Bloud et Gay, 1932); from the series Les Maîtres d'une Génération. In 2002, the Academy of Moral and Political Sciences established the Prix Victor Delbos, a biennial prize awarding works making known "spiritual life and religious philosophy." See http://www.asmp.fr/prix_fondations/fiches_prix/victor_delbos.html.

5. For Spinoza, see Alan D. Schrift, "The Effects of the *Agrégation de Philosophie* on Twentieth-Century French Philosophy," *Journal of the History of Philosophy* 46, no. 3 (July 2008): 449–73, at 461. For Kant, see Martha Hanna, *The Mobilization of Intellect: French Scholars and Writers during the Great War* (Cambridge: Harvard University Press, 1996), 36; cf. 121. See Victor Delbos, *La Philosophie pratique de Kant* (Paris: PUF, 1969); cited by Michel de Certeau, *The Practice of Everyday Life*, vol. 1 (Berkeley: University of California Press, [1984] 2002), 216 n. 19.

students included Étienne Gilson, who would become (along with Jacques Maritain) one of the two main voices in postwar Catholic philosophy. In fact, while Gilson served in the trenches during the Great War, Delbos mailed philosophy books to him at the front.[6]

An indication of Delbos's centrality in prewar Catholic Revivalism can be glimpsed in a 1912 *New York Times* article: "French Catholic Revival: Marked Reaction toward the Church Has Set In."

> PARIS, June 14 — Among the most important of many changes which are now passing over the spirit of the French nation is the reaction toward Catholicism which is being remarked on all sides. The view is often expressed that the contempt for religion which was so universal a few years ago has now quite gone out of fashion, and that the most brilliant and talented thinkers and writers of the younger generation are now turning toward the Church as their guide in life.
>
> An influential critic of contemporary France, who adopts the pseudonym "Agathon," writing *l'Opinion* on the Catholic movement points out that the strongest tendencies among the youth of France are cult of character and personality, a taste for the heroic, and not a preference for abstract ideas and systems. It is this, he says, which is leading the young people more and more toward the deepest source of all activity, namely, moral and religious life. The intellectual youth who twenty years ago seemed to be won over by anti-clerical doctrines is now turning toward Catholicism, a fact the importance of which cannot be exaggerated. . . . *At the Sorbonne the students in philosophy have chosen for professor a Catholic, Victor Delbos.*[7]

The article's conservative Catholic provenance tells us a great deal about Delbos's milieu. The "writer" referred to under the pseudonym "Agathon" was in fact two men, Henri Massis and Alfred de Tarde, strongly influential youthful members of the Action Française. In 1912, Massis and de Tarde had conducted a newspaper survey for the Parisian daily *l'Opinion* — the prompt for this *New York Times* article.[8] In 1913 they published their results as a book with a title that outlined their thesis: *The Young People of Today: The Taste for*

---

6. Alan D. Schrift, *Twentieth-Century French Philosophy: Key Themes and Thinkers* (Malden, Mass.: Blackwell, 2006), 131; Hanna, *The Mobilization of Intellect*, 58.

7. "French Catholic Revival: Marked Reaction toward the Church Has Set In," *New York Times*, June 23, 1912, emphasis added.

8. For following see Stephen Schloesser, *Jazz Age Catholicism: Mystic Modernism in Postwar Paris, 1919-1933* (Toronto: University of Toronto Press, 2005), 77-78.

Action; Patriotic Faith; A Catholic Renaissance; Political Realism. The work, an apologia for proto-fascist ideals, redefined both youth and modernity by constructing an activist younger generation in opposition to "the generation of 1885" they defamed. Amplifying their earlier work attacking the dominant intellectual trends in the university — *The Spirit of the New Sorbonne: The Crisis of Classical Culture; The Crisis of French* (1911) — Massis and de Tarde accused the "1885 generation" of having perverted the Sorbonne by forming its fundamental orientation out of imported German historicism and idealism. They accused that older generation of having been "pessimistic, self-doubting, morally flabby, overly intellectual and introspective, relativistic, incapable of energetic action, lacking faith, obsessed with decadence, and ready to accept the defeat and eclipse of their country."

By contrast, the "young people of 1912" were turning their backs on these Sorbonne professors and putting away all such decadent self-doubt. They were patriots, prepared "and even eager to give up" their lives — especially if that sacrifice would lead to throwing off the "German yoke" and the regeneration of France. (Although they could not have known it, the outbreak of world war one year later would provide this opportunity for self-sacrifice en masse.) Tired of relativism, they hankered after moral "absolutes" and joined in a Catholic renaissance *(renaissance catholique)* that offered *order*: a basis for both discipline and coherent action. In sum, whereas the 1885 generation had created "disorder and ruins" in "all matters," the new generation of 1912 was creating "order and hierarchy."

Massis's identification of Victor Delbos tells us, at the very least, that he was seen as the professorial mentor of these extreme-right-leaning youth — youth like Pierre Messiaen himself — both ultra-Catholic and ultranationalist. Delbos stood out as an anomaly: simultaneously both a Sorbonne professor and a fervent Catholic, he was a rare bridge in the civil war between church and state, Catholicism and positivism. He continued this *engagement* on behalf of the Third Republic when the Great War broke out, undertaking a lecture survey of "French thought" *(la Pensée française)* at the Sorbonne in 1915-1916.[9] (Blondel christened Delbos's series a wartime "sacred union of our philosophers.")[10] And in fact, Delbos's bold ambition was to be both patriotic and

---

9. Hanna, *The Mobilization of Intellect,* 158.

10. Maurice Blondel, "Avertissement," in Victor Delbos, *La Philosophie française* (Paris: Plon-Nourrit et Cie, 1919), i-iv, at iii. For France's wartime *l'union sacrée* between right and left, see Schloesser, *Jazz Age Catholicism,* 84; cf. 81-82, 86, 97, 100, 106, 123-24, 143-45, 199, 357 n. 3.

1932–1935: From Apprentice to Maître

religious, as demonstrated in a letter written in May 1916 (during the bloodiest phase of the war):

> As an ensemble, French souls have shown themselves to be simple, courageous, noble. They have revealed or created incomparable moral forces (or strengths = *forces*).... May this dreadful war purify in making the energies of our country triumph! As a human conclusion, let us summon all of our vows [*nos voeux*] to the coming of new national and international orders [*d'un ordre national et d'un ordre international nouveaux*]; and as the most elevated thought, the single notion of sacrifice may give some meaning to everything that is taking place.... Our excellent, our admirable young people [*jeunes gens*]! they are the ones who are giving to the present hour the greatest subjects of joy and of hope. How much they merit to obtain later on the moral direction of our country! and how good this will be![11]

We can see what attracted "Agathon" and his generation, who were repelled by the sterility of "abstract ideas and systems." For although Delbos gave Descartes and his cult of "clear and distinct ideas" their due pride of place in the history of French thought, he argued (in terms related to Blondel's *Action* [1893]) that clearness *(la clarté)* could extend beyond ideas into the tangible world of "reality" and "action." Patriotically acknowledging the "penchant for clearness" *(ce penchant à la clarté)* characteristic of the "French spirit" *(l'esprit français),* Delbos cautioned that many came too quickly to the conclusion that "the clearness being sought is a purely logical or mathematical clearness" *(la clarté qu'il recherche est une clarté purement logique ou mathématique).*[12] He encouraged an alternative vision, one with deep appeal to the wartime "realist generation" *(génération réaliste):* "Indeed clearness [*la clarté*] can be brought to bear on the things of observation, and on their concrete relations as well as on abstract concepts and their concatenation; it can be united with a most

---

11. Excerpt of a letter written just a few days before his death (June 16, 1916) by Victor Delbos to Abbé J. Werhlé; quoted in Blondel, "Avertissement," iii-iv. Delbos's rhetoric of the need to establish a new national order so as to make sense of the enormous sacrifice of France's youth again echoes Catholic Revivalist discourse. See especially the book by Henri Massis (the prewar "Agathon"), *Le Sacrifice 1914-1916* (Paris: Plon, 1917); cf. Schloesser, *Jazz Age Catholicism,* 87-96.

12. These remarks are from Delbos's introductory lecture to his wartime series on French philosophy, posthumously reproduced from his notes and published as "Caractères Généraux de la Philosophie Française," in *Revue de Métaphysique et de Morale* (January 1917): 4-5; and republished as the first chapter in Delbos, *La Philosophie française,* 1-15, at 4.

subtle perception of the real [*une perception plus subtile du réel*] as well as to a most finished systematization of ideas; it can mean nicety of vision as well as rigor of reasoning [*aussi bien la vision nette que le raisonnement rigoureux*]."[13] In light of this passage, Louise Delbos's adopted "Claire" — a word prominent in Messiaen's attachment to the central role of *clarté* (as "brightness" or "brilliance") in medieval aesthetics, especially in Aquinas (and as explicated by Maritain) — might have also paid homage to her father. Delbos straddled two worlds by advocating for an intellectual *clarté* (clearness) that was traditionally French while at the same time not inevitably positivist, that is, not necessarily incompatible with Catholicism.[14]

As noted by Harvard philosopher Ralph Perry immediately after the war, Delbos's wartime survey of French clarity was "tragically interrupted by the lecturer's death."[15] He died quite suddenly at age fifty-three on June 16, 1916. As his bereaved daughter Louise (Claire) was just nine and a half, Messiaen and Claire shared the experience of losing a mother prematurely. Two decades later, the first years of the Second World War coincided with a serious decline in mental health for which Claire would eventually need to be committed institutionally and from which she would later die. Both world wars would be traumatic for her on an immediate, personal level.

Delbos's death would have been traumatic in another way for young members of the Catholic Revivalist movement who were, at that moment, experiencing the most horrific year of the Great War. The battle at Verdun had been raging since February; the battle of the Somme would begin two weeks later. These were terrible days. Delbos's importance to this generation — dubbed by Massis as the "sacrificed generation"[16] — endured throughout

---

13. Delbos, "Caractères Généraux," 4; Delbos, *La Philosophie française*, 4; translated in Ralph Barton Perry, *The Present Conflict of Ideals: A Study of the Philosophical Background of the World War* (New York: Longmans, Green and Co., 1922), 455. Perry was a philosophy professor at Harvard University. Note that Delbos's method is eminently representative of postwar Catholic Revivalism, a dialectical hybridization of the "real" and the "ideal," "concrete" and "abstract." See Schloesser, "Mystic Realism: A Faith That Faced the Facts," in *Jazz Age Catholicism*, 107-37.

14. Note the numerous occurrences throughout Delbos's introductory chapter, which serves as his manifesto. In addition to the passage already cited, the following are found on just one page: "clear ideas" *(les idées claires)* (twice); "clear relationships" *(des rapports clairs);* "light up the mind" *(éclairer l'esprit);* "French thought's taste for clarity" *(le goût qu'a la pensée française pour la clarté);* "a series of ideas clearly linked together" *(une suite d'idées clairement liées)*. Delbos, "Caractères Généraux," 4; Delbos, *La Philosophie française*, 3-4.

15. Perry, *Present Conflict of Ideals*, 455.

16. Schloesser, *Jazz Age Catholicism*, 87-90, 107-10.

the 1920s. Thanks largely to the efforts of Blondel, Delbos's wartime lectures were edited and published immediately after the war as *French Philosophy* (1919).[17] Several other works of Delbos were published posthumously as others assumed the effort to keep his ideas and influence alive.[18] As late as the first two years of Claire's marriage, there was an effort at establishing Delbos's legacy for further research. First, in 1932, Abbé Joannès Wehrlé (identified on the title page as a member "of the Clergy of Paris"), "faithful friend and fel-

---

17. Delbos, *La Philosophie française*. See also Blondel's profoundly personal preface that underscores Delbos's aims at renewing French thought both for the war and after the war. Blondel quotes a letter of Delbos to his friend Abbé J. Wehrlé, written just a few days before his death, heralding "the coming of a new national order and a new international order" after the war.

18. Victor Delbos, *Étude de la philosophie de Malebranche* (Paris: Bloud et Gay, 1924); Delbos and Maurice Blondel, *Maine de Biran et son œuvre philosophique* (Paris: J. Vrin, 1931). For Delbos's posthumous publications in the *Revue de métaphysique et de morale* (on method in the history of philosophy, Kant, and post-Kantianism), see Chimisso, *Writing the History of the Mind*, 39 n. 21, 48 n. 66. Note the citation of Delbos's study of Malebranche in Armand Cuvillier, *Manuel de philosophie. Tome I: Introduction générale. Psychologie* (Paris: Librairie Armand Colin, 1931), xxvii.

Yet another indicator of Delbos's involvement in Catholic circles is his association with the staunchly Catholic publishing firm Bloud et Gay. In addition to being the publishers of Delbos's 1924 study on the philosophy of Malebranche, they also published two booklets of his during the war: *L'Esprit philosophique de l'Allemagne et la Pensée française (The Philosophical Spirit of Germany and French Thought)* (1915, 43 pages), and *Une Théorie allemande de la culture: W. Ostwald (A German Theory of Culture: Wilhelm Ostwald)* (1915?, 34 pages). The firm's origins (as Bloud et Barral) had been in the fin-de-siècle's virulent anticlerical years; beginning in 1897, a collection entitled "Science et Religion" attempted to build bridges with subjects like "Social Christianity," "Art and Religion," and "Faith and Reason." In February 1915, just six months after the outbreak of the Great War, Edmond Bloud, the firm's majority partner now in association with Francisque Gay, assisted Monsignor (later, Cardinal Archbishop) Alfred Baudrillart in founding the Comité Catholique de Propagande Française à l'Étranger (Catholic Committee of French Propaganda Abroad). By means of Bloud et Gay, the Comité waged a war of words in Catholic countries (especially Spain) against the German propaganda campaign designed to convince those abroad that France was anticlerical and that they should choose the Germans as allies. The publishing house effectively became the center of the committee's activities, producing collections including "Bibliothéque de la Guerre" ("War Library") and "Guerre et Religion" ("War and Religion"). See Anne-Lise Péreon, "La Librairie Bloud et Gay entre 1911 et 1939," Mémoire de D.E.A. d'Histoire contemporaine (Université de Paris IV–Sorbonne, July 1992), 7, 10, 18-20; and Schloesser, *Jazz Age Catholicism*, 96-100, 118-19; cf. Barbara de Courson, "The French Clergy and the War," *American Catholic Quarterly Review* 42, no. 168 (October 1917): 529-45, especially 542-44. I am deeply grateful to Messieurs Denis and Antoine Bloud for generous assistance in researching their grandfather's works.

low student at the École Normale," published an intellectual biography with Bloud et Gay. It shared the Victor Delbos prize of the Academy of Moral Sciences that year with another book.[19] (The book's imprimatur was granted on June 25, 1932, just three days after Claire's marriage.) Entitled *Victor Delbos: Member of the Institute, Professor of Philosophy at the Sorbonne*, the biography appeared in the series commemorating "The Masters of a Generation."[20] Second, in 1933, an extensive bibliography of Delbos's publications was compiled and published in Danish, then translated into German and French, aiming at "rendering a service to researchers who will be studying the personality or work of Delbos."[21]

Claire Delbos

Claire Delbos would be "the great female inspiration of Messiaen's life" after his mother's death.[22] Undoubtedly, their mutual attraction was owed in great measure to music, as Claire was both a violinist and a composer. Given the family background, it is unsurprising that Claire would have done her musical studies at the Schola Cantorum. In addition to the school's overall project dedicated to plainchant and ancient music, she would have been attracted to d'Indy's teachings on composition, summarized in his *Course of Musical Composition* (1902).[23] However, assuming that Claire's mother had raised her daughters in an intellectual milieu much like the one characteristic of Victor

---

19. André Lalande, "Philosophy in France, 1933-34," *Philosophical Review* 44, no. 1 (January 1935): 1-23, at 13, 23. The description of Werhlé is Lalande's. Werhlé shared the Delbos prize with (Pastor) Victor Monod, *Dieu dans l'univers: essai sur l'action exercée sur la pensée chrétienne par les grands systémes cosmologiques depuis Aristote jusqu'à nos jours* (Paris: Fischbacher, 1933).

20. Joannès Wehrlé, *Victor Delbos*. See note above on Bloud et Gay. Other such "masters" included abbés and bishops Batiffol, Duchesne, Julien, Lemire, Mignot, and Naudet; as well as Pierre Duhem (a scientist firmly immersed in Catholic Revivalism): R. N. D. Martin, *Pierre Duhem: Philosophy and History in the Work of a Believing Physicist* (La Salle, Ill.: Open Court, 1991); Stanley L. Jaki, *Uneasy Genius: The Life and Work of Pierre Duhem* (The Hague and Boston: Nijhoff, distributed by Kluwer Academic Publishers, 1984).

21. Berthe Verhaeghe, "Bibliographie de Victor Delbos (1862-1916)," *Revue néoscholastique de philosophie* 35, no. 40 (1933): 555-64.

22. Christopher Dingle, *The Life of Messiaen* (Cambridge and New York: Cambridge University Press, 2007), 48.

23. Stephen Broad, "Recontextualising Messiaen's Early Career," 2 vols. (Ph.D. diss., University of Oxford, 2005), 1:28; cf. Hill and Simeone, *Messiaen*, 41.

1932–1935: From Apprentice to Maître

Delbos, Messiaen must also have found in Claire a soul mate sharing similar passions in religion and philosophy as well as music. The fortuitousness of such an encounter, especially in Paris circa 1930, and even more so in the midst of mourning, cannot have escaped Messiaen.

Messiaen's relationship with Claire came as a surprise to his friends: they knew nothing about her or the couple's courtship until his last-minute announcement of the marriage.[24] After their wedding on June 22, 1932, Messiaen moved out of the Marais into a home significantly more distant from the center of Paris, at 77 rue des Plantes in the city's southern Fourteenth Arrondissement. On November 22 Claire played the violin and Messiaen played the piano in the premiere of his *Theme and Variations* for violin and piano, a wedding present.[25] The work was dedicated to "Mi," Messiaen's pet name for Claire. ("Mi" is the third syllable of the solfège scale [C-D-E = Do-Re-Mi] and the highest note reached by a violin.) In a letter sent to his fellow student and organist Jean Langlais, Messiaen said Langlais would be "very kind" if he were to "make a lot of noise and call for an encore of this work which is one of my best."[26]

In 1932 Messiaen also composed the *Ascension* suite, subtitled "Four Symphonic Meditations for Orchestra." The work was quickly completed: it was begun in May; Messiaen's wedding was in June; and the composition was concluded in July.[27] The May date suggests a Tournemire connection: on April 25, Messiaen had played the organ at Sainte-Clotilde along with Daniel-Lesur and several other young virtuoso organists at a grand concert of pieces selected from Tournemire's *L'Orgue Mystique*.[28] The aim of the event (by invitation only) was to make the mammoth work better known as its composition drew to a close. (However, its publication was another story: now in its fourth year, it would eventually have four more long years before completion.) Was the deeply "mystical" *Ascension* prompted by having just worked up Tournemire's pieces?

However, a quick composition did not mean a speedy publication. The fact that Messiaen could not find time to orchestrate *Ascension* for another year (in May-July 1933 in Monaco) conveys a sense of just how much his employment commitments (including La Trinité and also much teaching) consumed his

24. Hill and Simeone, *Messiaen*, 40-41.
25. Simeone, *Bibliographical Catalogue*, 33.
26. Marie-Louise Jaquet-Langlais, *Jean Langlais, 1907-1991: ombre et lumière* (Paris: Éditions Combre, 1995), 71; in Simeone, *Bibliographical Catalogue*, 33. For "Mi," see p. 246 n. 48.
27. Simeone, *Bibliographical Catalogue*, 38-39.
28. Schloesser, *Jazz Age Catholicism*, 320.

time. Yet another year (summer 1934) would be required to complete the organ transcription of movements I, II, and IV as well as to compose an entirely new third movement for this solo version (eventually published in 1934).[29]

The time constraints might have been fortuitous; since Messiaen was unable to compose any new work between the *Ascension* (1932-1934) and the *Nativity* organ suite (summer 1935), a three-year pause provided time for Messiaen's thought to develop. The *Ascension* suite would be the last work in his youthful "mystical" period. Changing circumstances in 1932-1935 would lead him to embrace a sense of new order and a more rigorous self-understanding as a "theological" musician, leaving behind the "mystical" appellation.

Forty-five years later he would famously say: "Personally, I deeply distrust this word [mysticism]. It doesn't suit me at all, and I'd like to say why not. As soon as one starts talking about mysticism, people think of a diseased state, of a neurotic who has vague sentiments and ecstasies. I don't like that; I'm a devout man and I love the sound, solid gifts of Faith."[30] The opposition between what is "vague" and what is "solid" resonates with the cultural mood circa 1933. As Henri Daniel-Rops had already noted of the younger generation in 1927: "Finally, even more recently, a group of mystics [*un groupe de mystiques*] has appeared whose tendencies seem to want to assert themselves with a precise vigor, in the sense of an abandonment of human values, i.e., in the sense of a fusion with the absolute."[31] As the world turned upside down, Messiaen was among many in search of more distinct order.

1933: Henri Daniel-Rops and New Order

After Messiaen's premiere of *The Resplendent Tomb* (1931) on February 12, 1933, a richly nuanced review appeared in the March 1933 issue of *Le Courrier musical*. Before examining this complex text, recall the ominous historical context:

---

29. Simeone, *Bibliographical Catalogue,* 40-41; Jon Gillock, *Performing Messiaen's Organ Music: 66 Masterclasses* (Bloomington: Indiana University Press, 2010), 37-48; Olivier Latry and Loïc Mallié, *L'œuvre d'orgue d'Olivier Messiaen. Œuvres d'avant-guerre* (Stuttgart: Carus, 2008), 95-118.

30. Messiaen, April 23, 1979; in Almut Rößler, *Contributions to the Spiritual World of Olivier Messiaen,* trans. Barbara Dagg and Nancy Poland (Duisberg: Gilles & Francke, 1986), 89; cf. Stephen Schloesser, "The Charm of Impossibilities: Mystic Surrealism as Contemplative Voluptuousness," in *Messiaen the Theologian,* ed. Andrew Shenton (Burlington, Vt.: Ashgate, 2010), 168 n. 26.

31. Henri Daniel-Rops, *Notre inquiétude, essais* (Paris: Perrin et Cie, 1927), 73.

1932–1935: From Apprentice to Maître

the beginning of the "menacing years," the "hollow years," and the "dark valley" of the interwar 1930s.[32]

Following the stock market crash of October 1929, the Great Depression slowly began to settle over Europe (as well as the United States). American banks called in the loans they had made to German banks; these loans had been the foundation of the postwar German economy. As German banks failed, unemployment rose from 1.6 million in October 1929 to 6.12 million in February 1932; the unemployment rate was 33 percent. (For comparison, America's unemployment rate in 1932 was 23.6 percent.) In November 1932, Americans turned leftward for a solution and elected Franklin Delano Roosevelt as president. By contrast, many Europeans turned rightward and pinned their hopes on fascism.

On January 30, 1933, Adolf Hitler was appointed chancellor of Germany. On February 27 a fire broke out at the Reichstag (the German parliament), giving the Nazis a chance to establish emergency powers so as to defend the nation from the alleged communist instigators. They rounded up political opponents and imprisoned them mostly in Dachau, the first of the concentration camps. (In the United States, Roosevelt was inaugurated into office the following week, on March 4.) On March 23 the Nazis achieved a two-thirds majority in the parliament. That same day they passed the Enabling Act, giving Hitler dictatorial powers. In November, Benito Mussolini's essay "The Doctrine of Fascism" was published in English translation in the British journal *Living Age*.[33] Meanwhile, France's Third Republic, never known for stability, had become a caricature of parliamentary democracy's failings.[34] In short: March

---

32. See Suzanne Pacé, *Années 30 en Europe: le temps menaçant 1929-1939: exposition du 20 février au 25 mai 1997, Musée d'art moderne de la ville de Paris* (Paris: Paris musées; Flammarion, 1997); Eugen Weber, *The Hollow Years: France in the 1930s* (New York: Norton, 1994); Piers Brendon, *The Dark Valley: A Panorama of the 1930s* (New York: Knopf, distributed by Random House, 2000); Serge Berstein, *La France des années 30*, 2nd ed. (Paris: Armand Colin, 1995); Philippe Bernard and Henri Dubief, *The Decline of the Third Republic, 1914-1938*, trans. Anthony Forster (New York: Cambridge University Press, 1985).

33. Benito Mussolini, "The Doctrine of Fascism," trans. Jane Soames, *Living Age* (November 1933): 235-44; originally published in *Political Quarterly*. The issue also included articles entitled "Life in a Nazi Camp" (authored by "A Prisoner") and "Jazz in Japan."

34. Even a brief slice of the time line shows how short were the durations and how frequent the changes of prime ministers: Pierre Laval (January 27, 1931–February 20, 1932); André Tardieu (February 20, 1932–June 3, 1932); Édouard Herriot (June 3, 1932–December 18, 1932); Joseph Paul-Boncour (December 18, 1932–January 31, 1933); Édouard Daladier (January 31, 1933–October 26, 1933); Albert Sarraut (October 26, 1933–November 26, 1933); Camille Chautemps (November 26, 1933–January 30, 1934); Édouard Daladier again (January 30, 1934–February 9, 1934); and so on.

1932–1943: Theological Order, Glorified Bodies, Apocalyptic Epoch

1933 marked the edge of a precipice, the moment in which Europe, wittingly or not, began to hurtle toward 1939.

This is the historical context in which to read the March 1933 review of Messiaen's *The Resplendent Tomb*.[35] The reviewer ("F.D.")[36] began simply enough: "This new work, essentially romantic, testifies to the mystical aspirations of the author." But F.D. then took a literary turn, comparing Messiaen's "mystical" vision to that of Henri Daniel-Rops, a brilliant young history professor seven years older than Messiaen. Daniel-Rops had begun his literary career with a book of essays published in 1927 entitled *Our Anxiety: In Praise of Anxiety; On a New Generation; Positions in the Face of Anxiety*.[37] The work was a response to a cultural conversation about whether the postwar generation had been "born under the sign of anxiety" (Daniel-Rops) and was suffering a new *mal du siècle* (malady of the century).[38] Daniel-Rops wanted to distinguish between anxieties that he considered superficial and historically contingent (e.g., a result of wartime trauma) and "metaphysical" anxiety, the profound

---

35. Review by "F.D." of the first performance of *The Resplendent Tomb* (February 12, 1933); in *Le Courrier musical* 35, no. 5 (March 1, 1933): 113; reprinted in Simeone, *Bibliographical Catalogue*, 213-14.

36. "F.D." might be Fernand Drogoul, a pupil of Vincent d'Indy who was already writing for the *Courrier musical* before the war. He was a great inspiration to the Catholic poet Pierre-Jean Jouve, who later dedicated his book on Mozart's *Don Juan* to him (a book that Messiaen was to use); and his wife was Thérèse Aubray, a poet who was close to Éluard and other surrealists, and who corresponded with the Catholic critic Charles du Bos. My thanks to Toby Garfitt for assistance.

37. Daniel-Rops, *Notre inquiétude* (1927). Note that in 1927 Martin Heidegger published his landmark book in which anxiety *(Angst)* plays a defining role in human existence: Heidegger, *Sein und Zeit* (Halle: Niemeyer, 1927); cf. Ethan Kleinberg, *Generation Existential: Heidegger's Philosophy in France, 1927-1961* (Ithaca, N.Y.: Cornell University Press, 2005). For this generation's self-understanding, see Schloesser, *Jazz Age Catholicism*, 108-10.

38. The topic of *inquiétude* — which can also be translated as agitation, concern, or simply inquietude — had been launched in the postwar era by Benjamin Crémieux's "Le Bilan d'une enquête," *Nouvelle revue française* 21, no. 120 (1923): 287-94. Crémieux, a Great War veteran who had been wounded three times, proposed that his generation was afflicted by a "new malady of the century" *(nouveau mal du siècle)*, just as François-René de Chateaubriand's postrevolutionary Romantic generation had been in the early nineteenth century. In 1924, Marcel Arland took up the theme and described postwar literature: "It is possible that one day such torments will appear naïve and that people will be surprised by that taste for moral suffering, for this masochism, for this 'inquietude' which leads us to rather peculiar attempts." See Arland, "Sur un nouveau mal du siècle," *Nouvelle revue française* (February 1924): 156; in Frédéric J. Grover, *Drieu La Rochelle and the Fiction of Testimony* (Berkeley: University of California Press, 1958), 101; cf. Jean Grenier, "Les Directions présentes de la littérature," *La Vie des lettres et des arts* 12 (1924): 75-79; 13:63-69. My thanks to Toby Garfitt for assistance.

1932–1935: From Apprentice to Maître

type of instability or "inconstancy" (following the thought of Blaise Pascal) from which the human condition cannot escape.

Whereas literary critics were arguing about the emotional instability manifesting itself in postwar literature, Daniel-Rops wanted to emphasize that the search for stability, although perhaps inevitable, was (again following Pascal) illusory. "For if it is true that in searching to create a new order [*à créer un ordre nouveau*] the mind admits disorder, and if it pleases, that it would be vain to affirm that once this order is attained, it would be able to rest content with it."[39] Daniel-Rops praised metaphysical anxiety as the only one worth considering: "The foundations of the soul are only reached by means of anxiety. It alone indicates the meaning of great problems. . . . Anxiety appears to us formally as the only creator of art." By contrast, he criticized the postwar modernist cult of machines and mechanism: "how mediocre does this humanity appear to us: while it knows only how to build machines, the notion of the absolute completely escapes it!"[40]

Daniel-Rops, who had left behind his childhood faith in the 1920s for agnosticism, nevertheless quoted at length the afternoon Sunday sermons preached at the Cathedral of Notre-Dame in Paris during the Lenten season of 1925 entitled "Human Anxiety [*L'Inquiétude humaine*]: The Message of Jesus Christ."[41] With respect to Messiaen, one quotation stands out:

39. Compare Pascal: "Let us, therefore, not seek certainty and stability. Our reason is always deceived by inconstant appearances; nothing can affix the finite between the two infinites [of being and nothingness] that both enclose and escape it." Pascal, *Pensées* (Pléiade), 185; (Lafuma) 199; (Sellier) 230; for Pléiade, see Pascal, *Œuvres complètes*, 2 vols. (Paris: Éditions Gallimard, 2000), vol. 2; for Lafuma, see Pascal, *Pensées,* trans. A. J. Krailsheimer, rev. ed. (New York: Penguin, 1995); for Sellier, see Pascal, *Pensées,* ed. and trans. Roger Ariew (Indianapolis: Hackett, 2005); cf. Schloesser, "Notes on the *Miserere* Plates Exhibited in *Mystic Masque*," in *Mystic Masque: Reality and Semblance in Georges Rouault, 1871-1958,* ed. Stephen Schloesser (Chestnut Hill, Mass.: McMullen Museum of Art, distributed by the University of Chicago Press, 2008), at 176, and Schloesser, "1871-1901: Realism, Symbolism, Mystic Modernism," in *Mystic Masque,* 23-43, at 37.

40. Daniel-Rops, *Notre inquiétude,* 20-22, 31, 18, 27, 31.

41. "Even though we do not share the Catholic faith of Fr. Sanson," wrote Daniel-Rops, "we would like to render him this homage. In a striking way, he has summarized, in one of his lecture series (published under the title *Human Anxiety*), the facts of this problem." In another passage, he judged that "the Rev. Fr. Sanson, Oratorian priest, was correct in affirming the universality of the fact of human anxiety [*l'inquiétude humaine*]." Daniel-Rops, *Notre inquiétude,* 34 n. 1; 29. The 1925 Lenten conferences given by the Rev. Pierre Sanson at the Cathedral of Notre-Dame of Paris were entitled, and later published as, *L'Inquiétude humaine: le message de Jésus-Christ (Conférences de Notre-Dame de Paris)* (Paris: Éd. Spes, 1925). The volume's cover quoted a famous phrase from Saint Augustine's *Confessions* (1.1)

1932–1943: Theological Order, Glorified Bodies, Apocalyptic Epoch

For the Christian, terrestrial life has no other meaning than that of a waiting for eternal life: "*And far from being troubled by the reproach addressed to Christianity for orienting ourselves in our entirety toward the beyond [de nous orienter tout entier vers l'au-delà], I say that it is by this, and by this alone, that [Christianity] reveals itself to us as being the truth of life [la vérité de la vie]."*

"Orient humanity in its entirety toward the beyond [*vers l'au delà*]." Words profound in both meaning and influence, words which adolescent souls cannot hear without emotion. It is true that at the moment in which the intransigence of youth speaks alone in the heart of humanity, religion is willingly turned into this superhuman idea: a passionate waiting for the beyond [*une attente passionnée de l'au-delà*], a constant desire for God, a renunciation of the earth in favor of heaven [*à la terre en faveur du ciel*]. The love of God appears alongside the first passion of the adolescent. However, very quickly, what we call reason takes up residence in the aging soul.[42]

Reading this passage, it is difficult not to think of both the passionate late-adolescent Messiaen who was about to compose *The Resplendent Tomb* and the composer in old age who, just before dying, finished his last fully completed work, *Lightning Flashes of the Beyond . . . (Éclairs sur l'au-delà . . .)* (1991).

Beginning in 1931, Daniel-Rops's writing, increasingly on Catholic topics, was advised by the philosopher Gabriel Marcel, newly converted to Catholicism in 1929.[43] (Daniel-Rops himself returned to practicing Catholicism in the early 1930s.) Both were members of L'Ordre Nouveau, an intellectual movement later dubbed the "Non-Conformists of the 1930s" *(les non-conformistes des années trente),* and both signed the first manifesto for a "New Order" in March 1931.[44] Catalyzed by the apparent catastrophic failure of republicanism and capitalism, these nonconformists sought a "third way" that would avoid

---

in both Latin and French: "inquietum est cor nostrum . . ."; "Notre cœur est inquiet . . ." (Our hearts are restless . . .).

42. Daniel-Rops, *Notre inquiétude*, 285. Quotations from Sanson are in italics; emphasis in original.

43. H. Stuart Hughes, *Between Commitment and Disillusion: The Obstructed Path and the Sea Change, 1930-1965* (reprint, with a new introduction, Middletown, Conn.: Wesleyan University Press; Scranton, Pa.: Harper and Row, 1987), 65-67.

44. See Jane F. Fulcher, *The Composer as Intellectual: Music and Ideology in France, 1914-1940* (New York: Oxford University Press, 2005), 285-87; John Hellman, *The Communitarian Third Way: Alexandre Marc's Ordre Nouveau, 1930-2000* (Montreal: McGill-Queen's University Press, 2000), especially 30-33; cf. Jean-Louis Loubet Del Bayle, *Les non-conformistes des années 30: Une tentative de renouvellement de la pensée politique française* (Paris: Seuil,

the extremes of dualistic oppositions between individualism and collectivism, capitalism and communism, nationalism and internationalism. L'Ordre Nouveau aimed at nothing less than the "spiritual rebirth" of Europe.[45]

In March 1932, Daniel-Rops published *The World without Soul*, a scathing critique of the cult of "machinism" and of mechanized industrial society, especially as represented in America, Henry Ford, and Taylorism.[46] This attack was set within a broader analysis of modern culture as one in which the cult of logical reason had "hypertrophied" and other nonrational (but not necessarily "irrational") mental functions — like "instinct" and "intuition" — had "atrophied." (In this respect, Daniel-Rops and the surrealists were of one accord in their attack on the cult of reason alone.) In the book's first chapter, "Adieu à une Inquiétude" ("Farewell to an Anxiety"), Daniel-Rops followed the argument he had made in *Notre inquiétude* (1927): postwar discourse over anxiety had grown tiresome. It was time to bid farewell to all the forms of anxiety except the eternal metaphysical one. Ironically, however, modernity had itself long ago bid farewell to this only true form of anxiety:

> True anxiety, the only one which is valuable in itself, is metaphysical anxiety [*l'inquiétude métaphysique*]. . . . Every anxiety is vain which does not seek to transform itself into order, which, without hope, does not aspire to rest [from inconstancy]. . . .
>
> Without doubt, we have become blind and deaf with respect to an immense number of phenomena with which our ancestors were able to establish some communication. To take an example from the material do-

---

[1969] 2001). In May 1933, two months after the review by "F.D.," the first issue of *Ordre Nouveau* appeared.

45. Historian Julian Jackson observes: "The most striking phenomenon of the 1930s is that all these various themes of republican renewal no longer exerted any claim on the imagination of the younger generations." The two most significant strands of the "spirit of the 1930s" *(esprit des années 30)* were, "first, an assertion of the 'primacy of the spiritual' (Mounier's *Esprit*, Aron and Dandieu's *Ordre Nouveau*) . . . ; secondly, a technocratic disillusion with the ineffectiveness and squalidness of republican government (X Crise, Coutrot)." Jackson, "The Long Road to Vichy" (review article), *French History* 12, no. 2 (1998): 213-24, at 221.

46. Daniel-Rops, *Le monde sans âme* (Paris: Plon, 1932). The book was at least partly written in response to Crémieux, *Inquiétude et reconstruction; essai sur la littérature d'après guerre* (Paris: Éditions R.-A. Corrêa, 1931). For the ongoing *inquiétude* debates, see François Hertel, "Essai sur l'inquiétude des jeunes," *L'Action Nationale* (Quebec) 6, no. 12 (December 1935): 219-37; and Hertel, "Essai sur l'inquiétude des jeunes . . . II," no. 1 (January 1936): 6-37; cf. André Laurendeau, "Lettre de Paris. Le chrétien et le monde moderne (entretien avec Daniel-Rops)," *L'Action Nationale* 8, no. 2 (October 1936): 111-17.

main, the diminution in quality of our instincts is a significant fact. . . . For almost three centuries, every action of humanity has replaced instincts and intuitions by rational volitions.[47]

Given Messiaen's attraction to surrealism, synesthesia, sound-colors, apparitions and visions, Bergsonian intuition and duration, and the fantastical in literature (Hamlet's ghost, Poe's pit and pendulum) — not to mention Roman Catholic ritual, imagery, and doctrine — connections with Daniel-Rops's diagnosis of the "hypertrophy" of reason and the "atrophy" of nonreason are readily apparent.

Exactly one year after the appearance of *The World without Soul*, "F.D." quoted it in his review of Messiaen's *Resplendent Tomb:*

> [Messiaen] seems to feel with M. Daniel-Rops that "metaphysical" anxiety [*inquiétude*] is "the only kind that is worthy in itself and which tends to transform itself into order." [Messiaen] seems to regret, with the same philosopher (who joins Bergson, Massis, Mauriac and Ch. Gillouin), "the atrophy of certain instincts of ours" and to think that in recognizing the primacy of reason "we are rendered blind and deaf with respect to a great number of phenomena with which our ancestors knew how to establish valuable communications."[48]

By situating Messiaen not only alongside Daniel-Rops but also in the genealogical line of Henri Bergson (who had just published *The Two Sources of Morality and Religion* [1932]), Henri Massis (of the now-condemned Action Française), the Catholic Revivalist novelist François Mauriac, and Charles Gillouin (who had just published his *Diary of a Christian Philosopher, 1915-1921* [1932]), the reviewer created the composer as a bold new "nonconformist."[49] For although these figures were in one sense political opponents — Bergson and Mauriac

---

47. Daniel-Rops, *Le Monde sans âme*, 12, 13, 195. By 1935, Daniel-Rops was arguing that "the French had not completely succumbed to 'materialist productivism' because their peasants were the repository of *'ancestral'* values. A romantic Péguyist notion that peasants were not materialistic but *instinctive* communitarians was common among Catholics in this period." See Hellman, *The Communitarian Third Way*, 115, emphasis added.

48. "F.D." (March 1, 1933), 213-14. Daniel-Rops's *Le Monde sans âme* had been published on March 18, 1932.

49. Henri Bergson, *Les deux sources de la morale et de la religion* (Paris: F. Alcan, 1932); Charles Gillouin, *Journal d'un chrétien philosophe: 1915-1921* (Paris: Nouv. Libr. française, 1932).

1932–1935: From Apprentice to Maître

on the left; Massis and Gillouin on the right — all shared an opposition to the "primacy of reason," a trait that French republicans valued as their distinguishing mark, the heritage of Descartes's "clear and distinct ideas." Victor Delbos's words bear repeating: "Indeed clearness can be brought to bear on... concrete relations as well as on abstract concepts and their concatenation."[50]

"F.D." concluded that the "excesses" *(outrances)* of Messiaen's *Resplendent Tomb,* "justified by the subject," might well have come as a surprise, explaining why "part of the audience applauded while another part booed." However, he insisted that Messiaen's work signaled a new generation's turn toward concerns more profound than those of their predecessors:

> Whatever one might think, it is necessary to recognize a sign of the evolution of the mind [or spiritual evolution: *l'évolution de l'esprit*] among certain young people, of which M. Daniel-Rops, cited above, is the torch. Judging, it seems, with the author of *A World without Soul,* that revolutionary existence will consist in recovering a presently-lost knowledge of the nature of the world and its laws, the sense of being, M. Messiaen has desired, against all the practices in honor since the manifestations of the impressionist school, to reintegrate the human being in music and to make him express his passions, this interior impulsion of which Huysmans spoke, the "silent voice that the tumult of noisy machines cannot suppress in us," "the hope that does not define itself."[51]

By recalling the figure of Joris-Karl Huysmans, a primordial figure of nineteenth-century Catholic Revivalism, F.D. planted the young Messiaen in a long and venerable Catholic genealogy.[52]

Just a month and a half after this review, the same F.D. published a review of the first performance of *Hymn to the Blessed Sacrament* (1932), a ten-minute work for orchestra described by Messiaen as "a song of praise to Jesus present in the Host."[53] In this April 1933 review, F.D. referred back to his own earlier, March review:

50. Delbos, "Caractères Généraux," at 4-5; in Perry, *Present Conflict of Ideals,* 455.

51. "F.D." (March 1, 1933), 214. The reviewer misquotes the title as *Un Monde sans âme (A World without Soul).*

52. See Schloesser, *Jazz Age Catholicism,* especially 39-45.

53. Review by F.D. of the first performance of *Hymne au Saint-Sacrement* (March 23, 1933), in *Le Courrier musical* 35, no. 8 (April 15, 1933): 196; in Simeone, *Bibliographical Catalogue,* 215-16, at 215. Composed in 1932, the work was lost during the war around 1944 and had to be reconstituted from memory. See Simeone, 28-31.

1932–1943: Theological Order, Glorified Bodies, Apocalyptic Epoch

As we said just a while ago, the spiritual tendencies of this young composer full of gifts and rich in talent excuse us for defining the climate of his thought. Even more than *The Resplendent Tomb,* this *Hymn* demonstrates that the desire for eternal beatitude has been given to him from above and that he aspires to come out from the prison of the body in order to contemplate the divine light, just as it is said in *The Imitation* [*of Christ* by Thomas à Kempis]. Messiaen means for his music not only to speak to the soul but moreover to edify it. He leads the concert audience into "the sounds of truth and of life," along the flowery paths of poetry he learned to frequent from his infancy. The blood of the author of *The Budding Soul* and *To Love After Death* [i.e., Cécile Sauvage] flows in his veins.[54]

These were very personal and even obscure references that Messiaen must have provided F.D.: references to his mother's writings; and the *Imitation of Christ,* a copy of which "traveled everywhere" with Messiaen and that had likewise been one of his mother's favorite books (reread the winter before her death).[55]

F.D. assisted Messiaen by exegeting the symbols embedded in the *Hymn to the Blessed Sacrament,* which likely would not have been at all apparent to the listener. These details must have come from Messiaen himself: for example, the description of the communicant who has just received the Blessed Sacrament and finds himself "plunged into rapture"; and Messiaen's affinity with fairy tales: the listener hears the sound of "small bells coming from distant places" and is "transported into the very middle of fairyland [*est transporté en pleine féerie*]."[56] F.D. juxtaposes the Eucharist with fairy tales a second time: after quoting Messiaen's final poetic lines in the piece — "The living bread that gives life, / eternal life!" — the reviewer adds that not only is this ending a bit too short, but it also will not be replacing Dukas's ballet *The Peri* anytime soon.[57]

---

54. "F.D." (April 15, 1933), 215-16.

55. Hill and Simeone, *Messiaen,* 374. Cf. Pierre Messiaen, *Images* (Paris: Desclée de Brouwer, 1944), 153-54; Brigitte Massin and Olivier Messiaen, *Olivier Messiaen: une poétique du merveilleux* (Aix-en-Provence: Alinéa, 1989), 52, 147; Gillock, *Performing Messiaen's Organ Music,* 22, 327.

56. Messiaen himself self-consciously connected Catholicism and fairy tales in a discussion of the "Marvelous": "I very much believe that it is because of fairy tales that I became a believer.... You could say that I passed over without thinking from the sur-real of fairy-tales to the supernatural of faith." Massin and Messiaen, *Olivier Messiaen,* 27-28; cf. discussion above of the "marvelous" as a key concept in surrealism.

57. *The Peri,* or *The Flower of Immortality (La Péri)* (1912) is a ballet by Paul Dukas, Messiaen's composition teacher. In it, a young man's search for immortality involves interactions with a Peri, that is, the descendant of a fallen angel in Persian mythology. (Compare

1932–1935: From Apprentice to Maître

Even this apparent aside likely came from knowing Messiaen's devotion to his Conservatory master (who would pass away two years later).

These obscure details suggest that F.D. was in conversation with Messiaen about his works. At least to some extent, then, F.D. functioned as the budding composer's own frame for reception. If so, then Messiaen, in this crucial year of 1933, seems to have self-consciously associated himself with this wider cultural stage of the "new order," a spiritual revolution against the "primacy of reason" symbolized by Bergson, Maritain, Mauriac, Daniel-Rops, and, in the beginning, Huysmans.

1934–1935: Heated Politics and Maternal Sorrows

Events continued to unfold on both global and domestic fronts. On February 6, 1934, the "Stavisky Riots," fomented by right-wing mobs, catalyzed the increasing polarization of France. To those on the left, the riots seemed ominous in their suggestion that fascist forces would soon take over France as they already had in Germany and Italy, and were attempting to in Spain. The panic triggered alliances between left-wing groups that would soon result in the victory of a French socialist government in 1936. In the meantime, divisions in France deepened.

On the home front, sadness and loss reigned over the bearing of children. On July 21, 1934, after less than two weeks of life, Jacques Messiaen (the second son of Pierre and Marguerite and Messiaen's half brother) underwent a painful death, recounted with heart-wrenching detail in Pierre's memoirs.[58] This tragedy likely prompted a composition by Claire that would be published the following year: *Two Pieces for Organ*.[59] The first of the two pieces bore the biblical title *Man, Born of a Woman, Living for a Short Time (Book of Job)*. The line, from the book of Job, underscores the ephemerality and instability of human existence:

Man that is born of a woman is of few days, and full of trouble.
He comes forth like a flower, and withers;
   he flees like a shadow, and continues not.[60]

---

the subtitle of *Iolanthe* [1882], Gilbert and Sullivan's "fairy opera": *Or the Peer and the Peri*.) For *La Péri*'s influence on Messiaen's compositional technique, see Stuart Waumsley, *The Organ Music of Olivier Messiaen* (Paris: Alphonse Leduc, 1968), 16, 18.

58. Pierre Messiaen, *Images,* 241-52.
59. Claire Delbos, *Deux pièces pour orgue* (Paris: Hérelle et Cie, 1935).
60. Job 14:1-2. As seen above, Pierre Messiaen quoted this passage from the Latin

1932–1943: Theological Order, Glorified Bodies, Apocalyptic Epoch

Vividly evocative of the shortness of human life, the verse is even more poignant when set within the context of the death of a child. This particular chapter of lament concludes:

> But the mountain falls and crumbles away,
>   and the rock is removed from its place;
> the waters wear away the stones;
>   the torrents wash away the soil of the earth;
>   so thou destroyest the hope of man.
> Thou prevailest for ever against him, and he passes;
>   thou changest his countenance, and sendest him away.
> His sons come to honor, and he does not know it;
>   they are brought low, and he perceives it not.
> He feels only the pain of his own body,
>   and he mourns only for himself.[61]

Claire's second organ piece provided a stark contrast: *The Virgin Rocks the Child*. The title evokes the serenity of the nativity scene and the infant Christ; but next to the meditation on Job, it might also recall the *Pièta*. As a diptych, *Two Pieces* appears to memorialize the death of the newly born Jacques.

Meanwhile, Claire experienced her own loss and grief while suffering several miscarriages from 1932 to 1936. This very private domestic fact is known because of notes made by Hilda Jolivet, the wife of composer André.[62] In 1934, Claire confided her condition to Hilda, whose recorded private reaction was acerbic: "We had heard about the white wedding of these two ethereal beings, so I was astonished when my hostess started to confide in me about her difficulties with pregnancy, and her regret at not having children. The conversation between our two husbands must have been more enthralling, because it went on, and on. . . ."[63]

Claire's surprising bluntness about the miscarriages might be explained in a way that Madame Jolivet would not have guessed. Given the Messiaens'

Vulgate with reference to Cécile's vision of life: *Homo natus de muliere, brevi vivens tempore.* Pierre Messiaen, *Images*, 135.

61. Job 14:18-22.

62. The Jolivets happened to be neighbors of the Messiaens; Messiaen would soon be deeply influenced by Jolivet's immersion in Balinese music and other Eastern influences; conversely, Jolivet's music would receive a new direction after hearing Messiaen's *Nativity* (1935).

63. Hill and Simeone, *Messiaen*, 57.

fervent Catholicism, it is likely that Claire wanted to make clear that the couple was not practicing birth control. Four years earlier, in the summer of 1930, the Anglican Communion's Lambeth Conference had reversed its position reached in 1920 and voted to allow contraception in some circumstances. The decision was immediately responded to by a papal encyclical promulgated by Pope Pius XI on December 31, 1930. Entitled *Casti Connubii (Chaste Wedlock)*, the encyclical stressed the sanctity of marriage and restated the traditional prohibition of using any form of artificial birth control by Roman Catholics.

The issue was especially volatile in France; birthrates had been low for nearly two centuries, from even before the French Revolution. During the nineteenth century, after the church had narrowly avoided extinction during the Napoleonic empire, French confessors adopted a "don't ask, don't tell" policy out of fear that Catholics would reject religious practice entirely. After World War I, birth control, abortion, and other feminist issues became front-burner issues, especially in the wake of France's "depopulation" crisis provoked by the decimation of an entire generation of males. The 1920s in particular were marked by bitter opposition between left and right (including Catholic natalist) factions over legislation designed to roll back liberalizing measures achieved in the prewar period.[64]

Following the publication of the encyclical — which arrived as the Great Depression was about to settle in with full force — priests were inundated throughout the 1930s with inquiries from lay Catholics trying to reconcile the newly-explicit condemnation of contraception with their marital practices.[65]

64. For prerevolutionary France, see Roger Chartier, *The Cultural Origins of the French Revolution* (Durham, N.C.: Duke University Press, 1991), 97-100; for the nineteenth century, see Claude Langlois, *Le crime d'Onan: le discours catholique sur la limitation des naissances, 1816-1930* (Paris: Belles lettres, 2005); for postwar France, see Mary Louise Roberts, *Civilization without Sexes: Reconstructing Gender in Postwar France, 1917-1927* (Chicago: University of Chicago Press, 1994). Articles published in *New Blackfriars*, the periodical review published by Dominican friars in Great Britain, suggest the flavor of the time: Vincent McNabb, O.P., "The Crime of Birth Control," 2, no. 16 (July 1921): 213-20; Denis Gwynn, "France and Birth Control," 4, no. 38 (May 1923): 806-16; M. A. Standish, "William Cobbett on Birth Control," 7, no. 80 (November 1926): 700-709; Reginald Ginns, O.P., "Financial Control and Birth Control," 11, no. 123 (June 1930): 366-75; Vincent McNabb, O.P., "The Ethics and Psychology of Neomalthusian Birth-Control," 11, no. 126 (September 1930): 549-57.

65. Martine Sevegrand, "Limiter les naissances. Le cas de conscience des catholiques français (1880-1939)," *Vingtième siècle. Revue d'histoire* 30 (April-June 1991): 40-54; Sevegrand, *Les enfants du bon Dieu: les catholiques français et la procréation au XXe siècle* (Paris: Albin Michel, 1995); Sevegrand and Jean Viollet, *L'amour en toutes lettres: questions à l'abbé Viollet sur la sexualité, 1924-1943* (Paris: Albin Michel, 1996). For parallels in the United States, see Leslie Woodcock Tentler, *Catholics and Contraception: An American History*

1932–1943: Theological Order, Glorified Bodies, Apocalyptic Epoch

In this context, the Messiaens, fervent Catholics just married in June 1932 and thus in the immediate wake of the papal promulgation, might have wanted to make Claire's miscarriages publicly known. The message was implicit: their marriage was not childless for want of trying.

At about the same time as *Two Pieces for Organ,* Claire composed *Primrose* (1935), a set of five aphoristic songs for voice and piano. The lyrics were poems from Pierre's 1928 forged collation of Cécile's three texts of love poems. In retrospect, Claire's desire to evoke Messiaen's mother (whom she had never met) — or for that matter, any aspect of motherhood at all — seems deeply painful. *Primrose* was published by Alphonse Leduc (Messiaen's publisher) and prominently featured the two women's names on the cover: "On poems of Cécile SAUVAGE. Music by Claire DELBOS."[66] Only Pierre would have known the text's actual provenance.

As 1934 passed into 1935, the *Ascension* suite that had been begun so long before finally began to emerge. The organ version, a transcription of the orchestral score (with a completely new third movement), was published in November 1934. Messiaen himself premiered it on January 29, 1935, at Saint-Antoine-des-Quinze-Vingts in Paris. When he performed it for the second time, at Sainte-Clotilde on April 4 (at Tournemire's invitation), only seventy persons were in the audience! Meanwhile, the orchestral version was premiered on February 9, a week after the organ version's premiere.

On May 28 at La Trinité, Messiaen played the *Ascension* suite a third time, at an evening concert brimming with symbolism.[67] First, it was the Tuesday preceding Ascension Thursday, the fortieth day of Easter and the liturgical feast on which the *Ascension* suite "comments." Second, it was the concert inaugurating the organ that had undergone a yearlong restoration and enlargement beginning in 1934.[68] Third, the concert featured both Messiaen and his Conservatory teacher, Dupré. Master and student divided the program into five sections:

(Ithaca, N.Y.: Cornell University Press, 2004); John T. McGreevy, *Catholicism and American Freedom: A History* (New York: Norton, 2003), 216-49.

66. Claire Delbos and Cécile Sauvage, *Primevère: cinq mélodies avec accompagnement de piano* (Paris: A. Leduc, 1935).

67. Olivier Latry and Loïc Mallié, *L'œuvre d'orgue d'Olivier Messiaen. Œuvres d'avant-guerre* (Stuttgart: Carus, 2008), 95-118, at 95; facsimile of program brochure for inaugural concert (May 28, 1935) at 99-101; cf. Simeone, *Bibliographical Catalogue,* 41.

68. On organ restoration, see Gillock, *Performing Messiaen's Organ Music,* 353-59; also includes facsimile of program brochure for inaugural concert (May 28, 1935). For *L'Ascension,* see 37-48.

1932–1935: From Apprentice to Maître

1. Dupré played the Choral and Fugue from the Sonata for Organ no. 5 in C Minor (op. 80, 1894) by his own teacher, Félix-Alexandre Guilmant, organist of La Trinité from 1871 to 1900. (He also played J. S. Bach.)
2. Messiaen played his *Ascension* suite as well as two movements from Dupré's *Way of the Cross* (op. 29, 1931).
3. Dupré played Messiaen's *Celestial Banquet* and excerpts from Charles-Marie Widor's *Gothic Symphony* (op. 70, 1895). (In 1934, Dupré had just assumed the post of titular organist at Saint-Sulpice, succeeding Widor, who retired at age ninety.)
4. The church's choir sang four hymns in honor of the "Very Blessed Sacrament" (of the Eucharist).
5. Dupré played his own Final in G Minor from the *Seven Pieces* (op. 27, 1931).

In addition to what must have been a spectacular sonic and musical experience, the program displayed a tapestry of generations, interweaving teachers and students, and traced the organ's evolution from Romanticism to the ultramodern.

The *Ascension* Suite: Titles and Epigraphs

Messiaen's literary texts for the *Ascension* suite offer clues to his growing sophistication in religious texts. The organ transcription of movements I and IV of the orchestral version was likely made in the summer of 1933 (following the May-July completion of the orchestration); the transcription of movement II and the new composition of III were likely made in the summer of 1934 in preparation for publication that November.[69] The titles for movements I, II, and IV of the orchestral and organ versions are identical:

> I. MAJESTY OF CHRIST PRAYING THAT
> HIS FATHER SHOULD GLORIFY HIM
> Father, the hour is come: glorify Thy Son,
>   that Thy Son also may glorify Thee.
>   *(Prayer from Christ, the Gospel*
>   *according to St. John)*

---

69. For varying dates see Simeone, *Bibliographical Catalogue*, 41.

1932–1943: Theological Order, Glorified Bodies, Apocalyptic Epoch

II. Serene Alleluias from a Soul [d'une âme]
Longing for Heaven
We beseech Thee, Almighty God, that we
may in mind [*en esprit*] dwell in Heaven.
(Mass on Ascension Day)

IV. Prayer from Christ Ascending towards His Father
And now, O Father, I have manifested Thy name unto men ... and now, I am
no more in the world, but these are in the world and I come to Thee.
*(Prayer from Christ, the Gospel
according to St. John)*[70]

The sources of Messiaen's epigraphs inserted beneath the titles — the texts upon which the music "comments" — are easily located in his reading of Dom Marmion's chapter on the Ascension in *Christ in His Mysteries*.[71] The epigraph for the first movement comes from Marmion's quotation of John's Gospel read at the Mass of the Vigil of the Ascension: "Father, the hour has come! Glorify thy Son, that thy Son may glorify thee."[72] The epigraph for the second comes from Marmion's quotation of the priest's opening prayer (Collect) for the Mass of the Ascension.[73] The prayer's emphasis on already "dwelling in heaven" here and now "in mind" (or "spirit") is also Marmion's; the prayer, he says, "points to the grace for our souls that is attached to this mystery."[74] It is underscored by

---

70. These titles and epigraphs appear on the second and third pages of the organ score: first in French, then in English translation. Messiaen, *L'Ascension. Quatre Méditations Symphoniques pour Orgue = Ascension Day. Four Symphonic Meditations for Organ* (Paris: Alphonse Leduc, 1934).

71. Columba Marmion, chapter 16 ("'And Now, Father, Glorify Your Son' [The Ascension]"), in *Christ in His Mysteries,* trans. Alan Bancroft (Bethesda, Md.: Zaccheus Press, 2008), 347-70.

72. John 17:1 (Douay-CCD); quoted in Marmion, *Christ in His Mysteries,* 353; cf. *Missel-Fr,* 680; *Missal-En,* 582.

73. "Let us therefore say a few words on this glorification; on what the grounds of it are for Jesus, on the special grace it brings us. The Church sums up these points in a prayer for the Mass of the Ascension: 'Grant, we beseech thee, Almighty God, that we who believe thy only-begotten Son, our Redeemer, to have this day ascended into heaven, may ourselves live there in spirit [*en esprit*].'" Note that *esprit* can be translated as either "mind" or "spirit." Marmion, *Christ in His Mysteries,* 348; quoting the Collect for the Mass of the Ascension in the Roman Missal: *Missel-Fr,* 682-83; *Missal-En,* 585.

74. Marmion, *Christ in His Mysteries,* 348.

Messiaen putting this in the mouth of "a soul who desires [*qui désire*] heaven." The epigraph for the fourth is the Gospel assigned for the Mass of the Vigil, a passage from which Messiaen takes fragments connected by ellipses.[75] Messiaen labels this the "Priestly prayer of Christ" *(Prière sacerdotale du Christ)*, again closely following Marmion's text: "High Priest who is always heard, He repeats, for us, His priestly prayer at the Last Supper."[76]

The epigraph for the third movement — which was, remember, composed a year later especially for the organ — is initially puzzling:

III. OUTBURST OF JOY FROM A SOUL [TRANSPORTS DE JOIE D'UNE ÂME] BEFORE THE GLORY OF CHRIST WHICH IS ITS OWN GLORY
Giving thanks unto The Father which hath made us meet to be partakers of the inheritance of the Saints in light . . . has raised us up together and made us sit together in heavenly places in Christ Jesus.
(The Epistles of Paul the Apostle to the Colossians and to the Ephesians)

The epigraph's second half, as one might expect, again follows Marmion: "raised us up with Him, and together seated us with Him in heaven."[77] However, the first half, taken from Colossians 1:12, is not found in Marmion's chapter on the Ascension; it occurs in his chapter on the Epiphany, the preeminent festival of light: "Let us offer God a ceaseless thanksgiving for having made us capable of 'having a share in the inheritance of the saints in light.'"[78] It might seem at first glance that Messiaen has picked this passage somewhat arbitrarily, given his love for the metaphor of light.

However, another look demonstrates how closely Messiaen was reading Marmion. This particular Epiphany conference focuses on light — entitled "The Manifestation to the Magi Signifies the Calling of the Pagan Nations to the Light of the Gospel" — and concludes with an appeal to the "Father of Lights" from John's Gospel: *"Father, glorify your Son, that your Son may glorify*

---

75. John 17:1-11 (Douay-CCD); cf. *Missel-Fr,* 680-81; *Missal-En,* 582-83.
76. Marmion, *Christ in His Mysteries,* 367. The passage comes from Conference 16.5: "Why an unshakeable confidence should likewise animate us on this solemnity of the Ascension: Christ enters the Holy of holies as Supreme High Priest and remains there as our one and only Mediator." Marmion, 362-68.
77. Marmion, *Christ in His Mysteries,* 357; quoting Eph. 2:4-7.
78. Marmion, chapter 8 ("The Epiphany"), in *Christ in His Mysteries,* 154-74, at 162; quoting Col. 1:12.

you."⁷⁹ This same text recurs as the title of the entire later chapter of conferences devoted to the Ascension: "And Now, Father, Glorify Your Son."⁸⁰ This intertextual linkage of the two feasts already indicates Messiaen's deepening appropriation of Marmion's liturgical theology.

More particularly, the linkage is also a play on words. Since Marmion normally quotes his scriptural texts in the Latin Vulgate, this section's conclusion ends with a rhetorical flourish: "Pater, clarifica Filium tuum ut Filius tuus clarificet te!"⁸¹ Because of the Vulgate's interchangeable use of *clar-* cognates (like *claritas* and *clarifica*) for both "light" and "glory," the imperative might also read: "Father, illuminate (or brighten or 'clarify') your Son so that your Son may illuminate (or brighten or 'clarify') you!"⁸² Later on, Messiaen's *Glorified Bodies* (composed in 1939) will also entail "illuminated" bodies, brilliant with the trait of *claritas (clarté)* — "clearness" or "clarity." The pun does not transfer into either the French or the English translations.

Most significantly, what began as a wordplay and misunderstanding based on translation — *clarifica* as both "glorify" and "brighten" — ended up being a founding principle of Messiaen's theological aesthetics. In an interview four decades later, Messiaen drew the equivalence between glory and light: "Glory, Grace, Light: it's all linked up together. For that reason, my music is cheerful, it contains glory and light. Of course suffering exists for me, too, but I've written very few poignant pieces. I'm not made for that. I love Light, Joy, and Glory in the divine sense."⁸³

One final textual puzzle remains: the source of Messiaen's title for the newly composed third movement of *Ascension*'s organ version. In 1933, the title for the orchestral version had been "Alleluia on the Trumpet, Alleluia on the Cymbal." The origin of this orchestral title is not mysterious: the Alleluia verse and response preceding the Gospel reading for the Mass on Ascension Day quote Psalm 46:6: "Dieu est monté dans l'allégresse; le Seigneur, au son de la trompette, alleluia" (God has ascended amid rejoicing, the Lord with the sound of the trumpet). The same verse is repeated as the Offertory chant; it

---

79. Marmion, *Christ in His Mysteries*, 163; quoting John 17:1.

80. Marmion, chapter 16 ("'And Now, Father, Glorify Your Son' [The Ascension]"), in *Christ in His Mysteries*, 347-70; again quoting John 17:1.

81. Marmion, chapter 8 ("L'Épiphanie"), in *Le Christ dans ses mystères. Conférences spirituelles* (Namur, Belgium: Abbaye de Maredsous; Paris and Bruges: Desclée de Brouwer et Cie, [1919] 1928), 147-66, at 155; quoting John 17:1 (Vulgate).

82. This Latin usage is discussed more fully below: see Messiaen's quotation of *"De clarté en clarté"* for Vision 7, *Visions of Amen*.

83. Messiaen, interview with Rößler, April 23, 1979, in Rößler, *Contributions*, 92.

1932–1935: From Apprentice to Maître

occurs three more times as it opens the first vespers for the feast, serves as the verse for the hour of Terce, and concludes the hymn at second vespers.[84] Few liturgical texts carry such weight; here Messiaen's choice is immediately clear.

However, the source of the title for the newly composed organ version in 1934 — "Outburst of Joy from a Soul [*Transports de joie d'une âme*] before the Glory of Christ Which Is Its Own Glory" — is more obscure. Messiaen most likely derived the title's French phrase *Transports de joie* from the word *transportée* found in the prophet Zechariah:

> *Sois transportée d'allégresse, fille de Sion!* — Rejoice greatly, O daughter of Sion!
> *Pousse des cris de joie, fille de Jérusalem!* — Shout for joy, O daughter of Jerusalem![85]

The words *sois transportée* do not follow the traditional Catholic translation: *Tressaille d'une grande joie, fille de Sion!* (Crampon).

Rather, they follow Abbé Louis-Claude Fillion, a professor of Scripture and Hebrew at the Institut Catholique of Paris and also a member of the Pontifical Biblical Commission. The eight volumes of his Bible translation had originally been published individually between 1888 and 1904; they were later published as a collection in 1927-1931, just prior to Messiaen's composition of *Ascension*.[86] Intended for use in seminaries and by clergy, Fillion's was a bilingual Bible with the Latin Vulgate and French translation printed in parallel columns. If Messiaen had not yet been acquainted with this version prior to assuming his post at Trinité, he was probably introduced to it soon afterward along with Marmion's work. Fillion's Latin-French parallel format would have facilitated reading Marmion's quotations from the Vulgate.

But why, in the summer of 1934, did Messiaen turn to the prophet Zechariah for this title in the newly composed third movement of the *Ascension* organ version? It seems to have no connection with the other material from the

---

84. Ps. 46:6 (47:5) "Ascéndit Deus in jubilatióne, et Dóminus in voce tubæ." See *The Liber Usualis with Introduction and Rubrics in English,* ed. Benedictines of Solesmes (Tournai, Belgium: Desclée & Co., [1939] 1949), 844, 846, 848, 849, 853; cf. *Missel-Fr,* 684, 685; *Missal-En,* 586, 587. English here: Douay-CCD; contrast Fillion: "Dieu est monté au milieu des cris de joie, et le Seigneur au son de la trompette."

85. Zech. 9:9, trans. Fillion, Douay-CCD.

86. Fillion had originally published the eight volumes individually between 1888 and 1904: vol. 1 (1888); vol. 2 (1889); vol. 3 (1891); vol. 4 (1892); vol. 5 (1894); vol. 6 (1896); vol. 7 (1901); vol. 8 (1904). For full citation see list of abbreviations.

liturgical texts, John's Gospel, or Marmion. Perhaps he was already thinking ahead to the following year in which he would write the *Nativity* suite; there he would use this verse as the epigraph for the *Nativity*'s first movement, quoting Fillion's translation directly.[87] The connection there is clear since the passage occurs prominently as the Communion refrain: *Exsulta, filia Sion, lauda filia Jerusalem* [*Tressaille de joie, fille de Sion! Chante, fille de Jerusalem!*].[88] But with the *Ascension*, no immediate connection seems to exist.

A more intriguing source is posited, however, in Henri Rossier, a Swiss Protestant medical doctor who produced a vast amount of popular writing on biblical books, persons, and themes. Rossier's death in 1928, the same year as Messiaen's mother, very likely provided a new impetus to revisit his works. In 1905 he had published biblical reflections in the form of three letters on the glory of the Father and of the Son.[89] Although it is impossible to know whether Messiaen was aware of Rossier's work — it is not cited in his *Traité* or elsewhere — the connection intrigues. Rossier's reflections on "glory" open almost immediately with his quotation of Zechariah 9:9; moreover, he uses a Swiss Protestant biblical translation in which the word *transports* appears directly: "Réjouis-toi avec transports, fille de Sion; pousse des cris de joie, fille de Jérusalem!"[90] The figures of Rossier and Fillion suggest an image of Messiaen in 1934 — this moment in which he is self-consciously adopting the public persona as a "theological" musician (as opposed to a "mystical" one) — immersed in various biblical translations, nourishing his literary appetite for words richly layered with multiple meanings.

87. "Sois transportée d'allégresse, fille de Sion!": Messiaen's epigraph to movement 1 ("La Vierge et l'enfant") of the *Nativité* (1935) suite; quoting Zech. 9:9 (Fillion). Compare the epigraph to movement 9 ("Dieu parmi nous"): "Mon âme glorifie le Seigneur, mon esprit a tressailli d'allégresse en Dieu mon Sauveur" (Luke 1:46-47 [Fillion]). At least in 1934-1935, Messiaen seems to have preferred using the literary *l'allégresse* to name "joy": contrast Crampon: "mon esprit tressaille de joie"; and Segond: "mon esprit se réjouit." As noted below, *l'allégresse* has nineteenth-century precedents in both Chateaubriand and Léon Bloy.

88. Communion antiphon for Christmas Mass (Second Mass) at Dawn, quoting Zech. 9:9; see *Missel-Fr*, 224; *Missal-En*, 143; cf. Dom Prosper Guéranger, O.S.B., *The Liturgical Year*, trans. Benedictines of Stanbrook, 15 vols. (Westminster, Md.: Newman Press, 1949), 2:194.

89. Henri Rossier, "La gloire du Père et du Fils. Trois lettres à un frère" (1905); reprinted in Rossier, *Vie et ministère de personnages bibliques. Considérations sur quelques thèmes* (Chailly-Montreux, Switzerland: Éditions Bibles et Littérature Chrétienne, 2006), 253-71. This is the seventeenth volume (out of eighteen) of Rossier's collected works.

90. Rossier, "La gloire du Père et du Fils," 256; quoting Zech. 9:9 from the biblical translation of Jean-Frédéric Ostervald (1724) or John Nelson Darby (1885). Both the Ostervald and Darby Bibles were produced for Francophone Swiss readers.

1932–1935: From Apprentice to Maître

Whatever the exact source of the word *transports,* the source for the rest of the title is immediately clear. Marmion dedicates his fourth conference on the Ascension to "Feelings of deep joy to which this glorification of Jesus gives rise in us."[91] Messiaen's third movement follows Marmion closely here, and here again Messiaen's recurrent trope as the "musician of joy" — looking beyond the travails of temporal life and fixing our gaze on eternal glory — would have found profound affirmation:

> The ascension of Jesus gives rise to multifarious feelings in the faithful soul that contemplates it with devotion. Even though Christ no longer merits now, His Ascension nevertheless has the power of producing efficaciously the graces it signifies or symbolizes.... Raising our souls towards heavenly realities, it brings alive in them *detachment from things that are passing....* It gives us *patience with the adversities of here below.* For as St. Paul says, if we have shared the sufferings of Christ, we shall be associated also with His glory: "sharing His sufferings so as to share His glory."...
>
> Yes, let us rejoice! Those who love Jesus *experience a deep and intense joy in contemplating Him* in the mystery of His ascension, in thanking the Father for having given such glory to His Son, and in felicitating Jesus at His being the object of it.
>
> Let us rejoice, as well, that *this triumph and glorification of Jesus is ours also....*
>
> *Let our hearts be given up wholly to this joy,* this intimate and altogether spiritual joy. Nothing dilates our souls so much as this feeling, nothing makes us go more generously forward along the running-track of obedience to the Lord's precepts: "I have run the way of your commandments, when you enlarged my heart." During these holy days of Ascensiontide, let us repeat often to Christ Jesus the ardent aspirations of the hymn of the Feast: "Be our joy, O you who will one day be our reward; and may all our glory dwell in you, for ever and ever":
>
> Oh, be our joy — thou who will be
> Our prize throughout eternity:
> Our future glory now in store
> In thee, O Christ, for evermore![92]

---

91. Marmion, *Christ in His Mysteries,* 359-62.
92. Marmion, *Christ in His Mysteries,* 359, 361-62, emphasis added.

1932–1943: Theological Order, Glorified Bodies, Apocalyptic Epoch

Messiaen translated this remarkable appeal to joy into music. His third movement for the organ, newly composed in 1934, opens with a brilliant outburst of joy: a statement answered by a thunderous motif in the pedal evoking the dynamic clanging of a carillon transports the listener. Undoubtedly, Messiaen knew Chateaubriand's classic passage (in *Genius of Christianity* [1802]) recalling public bells before their silencing during the Revolution: "The carillons and clamorous voices of bells, in the midst of our festivals, seemed to augment public joy [*semblaient augmenter l'allégresse publique*]; it was joy expressed at the level of great sound."[93]

Somewhat mysteriously, Messiaen almost immediately distanced himself from the *Ascension* suite after the two versions were completed in 1934-1935. In his *Technique of My Musical Language*, when Messiaen rated his own works composed up until 1942 — one star for "characteristic of my musical language"; two stars for "very characteristic" — *Ascension* received no star; he judged it not at all characteristic.[94] Remarkably enough, the orchestral score would not be published until June 1948 — only after the world war had been survived and as Messiaen was introduced to an American audience.[95] It was only near the

---

93. "Les carillons et les voix bruyantes des cloches, au milieu de nos fêtes, semblaient augmenter l'allégresse publique; c'était la joie exprimée sur une échelle de sons immenses. . . ." François-René de Chateaubriand, "Des Cloches," *Génie du christianisme, ou beautés de la religion chrétienne* (1802), in *Essai sur les révolutions. Génie du christianisme,* ed. Maurice Regard (Paris: Éditions Gallimard, 1978), 894, using variants *e* and *f,* 1832; cf. Chateaubriand, "Of Bells," in *Genius of Christianity; or, The Spirit and Beauty of the Christian Religion,* trans. Charles I. White, 13th rev. ed. (Baltimore: John Murphy and Co., [1856] 1880), 479-81, at 480. This standard English translation is based on a variant omitting the words underlined above. Translation altered.

In yet another use, Léon Bloy concluded his (published) journal entry for April 16, 1894: "Cris de joie, transports d'allégresse dans ma maison! Carillon des cœurs! Qu'on mette la table du joyeux festin de la Misère!" (Cries of joy, transports of joy in my house! Carillon of hearts! Let the joyous banquet table of poverty be set!). Bloy, *Le Mendiant ingrat* (1892-1895), in *Journal de Léon Bloy,* ed. Joseph Bollery, 2 vols. (Paris: Mercure de France, [1956] 1963), 1:99.

94. Simeone, *Bibliographical Catalogue,* 75-76. Neither the organ nor the orchestral version of the *Ascension* receives a star in the French (1944), English (1956), German (1966), or trilingual (1979) editions of the *Technique.* See Messiaen, *Technique de mon langage musical,* 2 vols. (Paris: Alphonse Leduc, 1944), 1:64-67, at 66 (organ) and 67 (orchestral); and Messiaen, *The Technique of My Musical Language,* trans. John Satterfield (Paris: Alphonse Leduc, 1956), 1:71-74, at 73 (organ) and 74 (orchestral).

95. Messiaen, *Technique de mon langage musical,* 107-9, at 109. The orchestral score of *Ascension* was published in June 1948; a year later it was conducted by Serge Koussevitsky in the final concert of the Berkshire Festival (August 14, 1949), concluding the Tanglewood

1932–1935: From Apprentice to Maître

end of his life, when Messiaen revised his *Technique* in order to incorporate the original two volumes into a single book interposing the text with musical examples, that Messiaen changed the designation. (Perhaps he was persuaded by Mstislav Rostropovich's four performances of *Ascension* in Washington, D.C., in November 1978 — two years after the American bicentennial, for which Messiaen composed *From Canyons to Stars* [1974]. During this visit Messiaen, Loriod, and Rostropovich were received by President Jimmy Carter and First Lady Rosalynn at the White House.)[96] Published in 1999, the posthumous edition of the *Technique* awarded two stars to both the organ and the orchestral version of *Ascension*. They were now to be considered "very characteristic" of his musical language.

After such an enormous investment of time from beginning to completion (1932-1934), why did Messiaen leave *Ascension* behind? The reason lies in 1935: it is the year in which he composed *Nativity,* a work he considered a definitive break with not only his past but also the "Franckist" past of the French tradition since César Franck. And it is the year he and Claire collaborated in forming La Spirale, the group preceding La Jeune France, a self-conscious association of the new generation of "under-thirty" musicians. The year 1935 marks Messiaen's transition: at age twenty-six, his apprenticeship was finished. He could now be called *maître*.

---

season at which Messiaen had taught. Simeone, *Bibliographical Catalogue,* 39; Hill and Simeone, *Messiaen,* 188.

96. Hill and Simeone, *Messiaen,* 320-21. My thanks to Elizabeth McLain.

CHAPTER 8

1935-1939

Theological Turn, Young France, Baby Pascal

The three years that passed between beginning the composition of *Ascension* (1932) and that of *Nativity* (1935) were contemporaneous with a changing world at large. The historical importance of 1935-1936 can hardly be overestimated. Situated midway between the February 1934 right-wing Stavisky Riots and the June 1936 left-wing victory of the Socialist Popular Front, the summer of 1935 was a period of enormous instability, one fraught with both peril and possibility.[1] This was the summer in which Messiaen attempted a musical revolution while writing *Nativity*, a work based on "theological doctrine." He would soon help form La Jeune France, a musical alliance calling for a generational revolution and new "nonconformism" in French musical aesthetics. The fertile outburst of activity in this period exhibits Messiaen's evolving sense that a "new order" was being called for. Messiaen seems to have wanted to make the transition from the "mystical" — whose symbolist vagaries, shrouded in incense, may or may not be true — to more sure-footed "theological" compositions, possessing doctrinal certitude. In this sense as elsewhere, Messiaen echoed Marmion: "These, you will say to me, are very elevated truths; this state is a very sublime one. That is true; and yet have I

---

1. Eugen Weber, *The Hollow Years: France in the 1930s* (New York: Norton, 1994), 134-36; Philippe Bernard and Henri Dubief, "6 February: Day of Crisis," in *The Decline of the Third Republic, 1914-1938,* trans. Anthony Forster (New York: Cambridge University Press, 1985), 219-28; Serge Berstein, *Le 6 février 1934* (Paris: Gallimard, 1975); Wilfrid Knapp, *France — Partial Eclipse: From the Stavisky Riots to the Nazi Conquest* (New York: American Heritage Press, 1972).

done anything other than to repeat to you what the Word Himself has revealed to us, what St. John and St. Paul have restated to us after Jesus? No, these are not dreams, but realities — divine realities."[2]

1935: Predestination: Reading Dom Marmion on "Divine Adoption"

There is an appropriateness to the late-May 1935 performance at La Trinité of *Ascension* bringing the school year to a close. During the upcoming summer vacation in Grenoble, Messiaen took his first step as a "theological" musician, composing the large organ cycle dedicated to Christmas themes, *The Nativity of the Lord*.[3] Its adventurous employment of registrations and distributions of labor between manuals and pedals reflect additions Messiaen had made to the Trinité organ in the 1934-1935 renovation. These included especially a 2⅔ Nazard (on both Positif and Récit manuals), a 1⅗ Tierce (Positif), and the III Cymbale (Récit) — the latter would play a crucial syncopated rhythmic role (coupled to the pedals) in the ninth movement, "God among Us." Messiaen had obtained new sonic possibilities; now it was time to compose in a new style. Messiaen would later say that *The Nativity*, especially in its use of Hindu rhythms, "produced the proof, at least I believe I did, that it was possible to write for organ other than in a post-Franckist aesthetic" — an appellation, we can be sure, that would have appalled Tournemire.[4]

It is difficult to imagine that these nine meditations on Christ's birth did not evolve out of reflections on the difficulties and even dangers of bearing and rearing children. If we recall Claire's *The Virgin Rocks the Child* from *Two Pieces for Organ* (1935), composed after her several miscarriages as well as the death of the two-week-old Jacques Messiaen, the decision to devote a very large composition to the subject of the nativity suggests even a votive offering.

2. Columba Marmion, chapter 3 ("*'In Sinu Patris'* — in the Heart's-Embrace of the Father"), in *Christ in His Mysteries,* trans. Alan Bancroft (Bethesda, Md.: Zaccheus Press, 2008), 41-65, at 63.

3. Nigel Simeone, *Olivier Messiaen: A Bibliographical Catalogue of Messiaen's Works,* Musikbibliographische Arbeiten series, vol. 14 (Tutzing: Hans Schneider, 1998), 44-47; Jon Gillock, *Performing Messiaen's Organ Music: 66 Masterclasses* (Bloomington: Indiana University Press, 2010), 49-98; Olivier Latry and Loïc Mallié, *L'œuvre d'orgue d'Olivier Messiaen. Œuvres d'avant-guerre* (Stuttgart: Carus, 2008), 120-86.

4. Peter Hill and Nigel Simeone, *Messiaen* (New Haven: Yale University Press, 2005), 60; Christopher Dingle, *The Life of Messiaen* (Cambridge and New York: Cambridge University Press, 2007), 55; Simeone, *Bibliographical Catalogue,* 46; quoted in Brigitte Massin and Olivier Messiaen, *Olivier Messiaen: une poétique du merveilleux* (Aix-en-Provence: Alinéa, 1989), 172.

1932–1943: Theological Order, Glorified Bodies, Apocalyptic Epoch

In terms of subject matter, the cycle derived from Messiaen's close reading of Marmion's *Christ in His Mysteries*.

Messiaen's curious embrace of the primacy of "grace" already seen in "The Lost Fiancée" (*Three Melodies* [1930]) preceded his encounter with Marmion. However, since Marmion's reflections on "divine adoption" (and, as a corollary, some version of "predestination") form a cornerstone of his theological vision, Messiaen would have found in him a sympathetic spirit.[5] The doctrinal centrality can immediately be seen in passages occurring early in Marmion's book:

> But the main reason for keeping alive such feelings within us is our status as children of God. The Divine Sonship of the Father's only-begotten is of the essence and eternal. But, in an infinitely free act of love, the Father has willed to add a sonship, a childship, of *grace*. He adopts us as His children, to the extent that one day we shall share in the beatitude of His own inner life. This is an inexplicable mystery; but faith tells us that when a soul receives sanctifying grace at baptism, that soul participates in the divine nature: "that you may become partakers of the divine nature" [2 Pet. 1:4]; the soul becomes truly a child of God: "You are gods, and all of you the sons of the Most High" [Ps. 81 (82):6; John 10:34]. . . . In a very real, a very true sense, we are divinely begotten by grace.[6]

> The marvels of divine adoption are so great that human language can never sound their depths. It is a wonderful thing for God to adopt us as His children; but the means He has chosen for effecting and establishing that adoption within us is something more wonderful still. And what is this means? It is His own Son: "in His beloved Son." I have already expounded this truth elsewhere [i.e., in *Christ, the Life of the Soul*, section 4], but so vital is it, that I cannot refrain from going back to it here.[7]

> That is why contemplation of the mysteries of Christ is so fruitful for the soul. The life, the death, the glory of Jesus are the example for our life, our

---

5. Marmion had already made this doctrine the cornerstone of the first book in his trilogy published in 1914. The first chapter is entitled "The Divine Plan of Our Adoptive Predestination in Jesus Christ." See Marmion, *Christ, the Life of the Soul*, trans. Alan Bancroft (Bethesda, Md.: Zaccheus Press, 2005), 3-36. For theology of the doctrine see Stephen Finlan and Vladimir Kharlamov, eds., *Theōsis: Deification in Christian Theology* (Eugene, Ore.: Pickwick, 2006).

6. Marmion, *Christ in His Mysteries*, 54.

7. Marmion, *Christ in His Mysteries*, 57.

1935-1939: Theological Turn, Young France, Baby Pascal

death, our glory. Never forget this truth: we are only acceptable to the Eternal Father *to the extent that we imitate His Son,* to the extent that He sees in us a resemblance to His Son. Why is that? Because this very resemblance is what, from all eternity, we have been destined [*prédestinés*] for. There is for us no other form of holiness than that which Christ has shown us; the measure of our perfection is fixed by *the degree of our imitation of Jesus.*[8]

The moral emphasis on the "imitation of Jesus" is thoroughly Catholic — and for Messiaen, for whom *The Imitation of Christ* was a key text (as it was for his mother), this emphasis would have great appeal.

However, the doctrines of "adoption" and "predestination" are unusual and idiosyncratic for a Roman Catholic thinker — so much so that a recent translator of *Christ in His Mysteries* felt the need to append a long note addressing the monk's use of the word *prédestiné* at the beginning of the book. (In fact, the translator deftly sidestepped the problem by translating *prédestiné* as "destined" instead of "predestined.")[9] Especially since its use by sixteenth-century Reformers to minimize (or deny) the cooperation of human will in personal salvation, Catholicism has tended to sideline this Augustinian doctrine and embrace instead a Thomistic emphasis on good works and a life of virtue.[10] And yet, Marmion boldly quotes the term as it occurs in Saint Paul's Letter to the Romans (in the Latin Vulgate) while commenting on the transfiguration:

> By the grace of Christ, this holiness has been like a light which has begun to shine within us, from the time of our baptism which inaugurated our

---

8. Marmion, chapter 1 ("The Mysteries of Christ Are Our Mysteries") in *Christ in His Mysteries*, 3-22, at 16, emphasis added.

9. See translator's note in Marmion, *Christ in His Mysteries*, 16 n. 65: "Marmion's word is *prédestinés*, 'predestined,' but it is important to keep in mind throughout the book that this word, and 'predestination' as Marmion uses it, does not in any way involve a denial of our wills being free to win heaven; not the slightest suggestion that God offers the eternal inheritance to some and not all." For "divinization" and the problem of grace and freedom in Western Christianity, see Karl Rahner, *Encyclopedia of Theology: The Concise Sacramentum Mundi* (New Delhi: Continuum, [1975] 2004), 596-98.

10. Although Marmion does not put this at the center of his work, he nevertheless does not neglect it: "Sanctifying grace is the first and fundamental element of our assimilation to God, of the divine likeness within us. But we must also be the image of our Father by our virtues. Christ Jesus told us this Himself: 'You, therefore, must be perfect, as your heavenly Father is perfect' [Matt. 5:48]. Imitate His goodness, His forbearance, His mercy: it is thus that you will reproduce His features in you. 'Be you,' repeats St. Paul after Jesus, 'imitators of God,' as is fitting for 'very dear children' [Eph. 5:1]." Marmion, *Christ in His Mysteries*, 56.

transformation into an image of Jesus. Here below, indeed, holiness is but an interior transfiguration modeled upon Christ: *Praedestinavit nos [Deus] conformes fieri imaginis Filii sui.* [God has predestined us to become conformed to the image of His Son.] By our fidelity to the action of the Spirit, this image grows little by little, develops, is perfected, until we attain the Light of eternity. Then, the transformation will become evident, in the sight of the angels and the elect. This will be the supreme ratification of "perfect adoption" [*l'adoption parfaite*] that will make spring forth within us an inexhaustible fount of joy.[11]

What would have been the appeal to Catholics of Marmion's somewhat idiosyncratic approach in the 1920s and 1930s? First, it is completely in sync with the more general wave of interest in "mysticism" (especially Eastern) of the 1920s that only increased in the 1930s. Like all forms of mysticism, Marmion's promised not merely union of the self with the divine — or perhaps better, dissolution of the boundaries between the two — but even more so, a radical transformation (not unlike the ancient promise of alchemy) of human substance into divine substance: "You are gods, and all of you the sons of the Most High."[12] Marmion manages to do all this while remaining thoroughly orthodox and echoing ancient Christian traditions of both Eastern *theosis* and Western divinization.

Second, by downplaying Catholicism's traditional emphasis on the human will and focusing instead on cosmic issues — that is, what a Creator might have done from the perspective of eternity — Marmion was once again thoroughly in sync with the postwar shift toward mysticism and metaphysics. The reach of human actions had been revealed in the catastrophe of the trenches; "civilization" had been unmasked. What was wanted in the postwar era was a return to asking the largest possible questions located against the widest possible horizon. By the end of the nineteenth century, liberal "religion" had

---

11. Marmion, chapter 12 ("On the Summit of Tabor [Second Sunday of Lent]"), in *Christ in His Mysteries*, 266-86, at 280-81; quoting Rom. 8:29 from the Vulgate; cf. Marmion, *Le Christ dans ses mystères. Conférences spirituelles* (Namur, Belgium: Abbaye de Maredsous; Paris and Bruges: Desclée de Brouwer et Cie, [1919] 1928), 270-71. Translation altered. *L'adoption parfaite* translates *adoptio perfecta,* a phrase adapted from the Collect for the feast of the transfiguration: see *Missel-Fr,* 1194; *Missal-En,* 1142; cf. Marmion, *Christ in His Mysteries,* 278; *Christ dans ses mystères,* 268. The importance of this passage for Messiaen may be glimpsed in the title of the "Amen of the Angels, of Saints, of Birdsong" (a variation on Marmion's "sight of the angels and the elect").

12. Marmion, *Christ in His Mysteries,* 54.

been transformed largely into rational moral or ethical systems. The appeal of "mysticism" in the early twentieth century, as opposed to "religion," lay precisely in its "primitive" attention to eternal (insoluble) mysteries.[13]

One particular aspect of this return to mysticism and metaphysics would have had special appeal for Messiaen: the emphasis on the *eternal*. In Marmion's scheme, God stands outside time and knows from all eternity not only his initial desires and designs for the universe but also the eventual outcomes. In other words (quoting Marmion's translator), "God, being outside time, knows which individuals will in the event achieve the eternal destiny planned for them."[14] Again, this raises the thorny problem of human will and predestination. But in his theology, as in his philosophy, astronomy, and other disciplines, Messiaen was a popularizer, not a hairsplitter. Ultimately insoluble theological paradoxes are not so important to him as are the big issues — and as we have repeatedly seen, perhaps the most consistently recurrent of those big issues is the often tragic temporal ephemerality saved by eternity.

Finally, on a more biographical level, Marmion's thought "saves" Cécile Sauvage. As opposed to a more conventional Catholicism insisting on confessional allegiance, sacramental practice, and observance of moral precepts, Marmion's emphasis on grace situates Cécile within the largest possible scheme of things — God's desires for her predestined from all eternity.

Summer 1935: The Structure of *The Nativity*

Armed with the doctrine of "divine adoption," we can make better sense of the structure of *The Nativity* (which can otherwise look somewhat hap-

---

13. Friedrich von Hügel, *The Mystical Element of Religion as Studied in Saint Catherine of Genova and Her Friends* (London: J. M. Dent, 1908); Evelyn Underhill, *Mysticism: A Study in the Nature and Development of Man's Spiritual Consciousness* (London: Methuen, 1911); Underhill, *Practical Mysticism: A Little Book for Normal People* (London: J. M. Dent and Sons; New York: Dutton, 1914); Underhill, *Mysticism and War* (London: J. M. Watkins, 1915). Michel de Certeau identified a distinctively late-nineteenth- and early-twentieth-century strain of talking about "mysticism": see Certeau, "Mysticism," trans. Marsanne Brammer, *Diacritics* 22, no. 2 (Summer 1992): 11-25; originally in *Encyclopaedia universalis* (1968); cf. Certeau, "History and Mysticism," in *Histories: French Constructions of the Past*, ed. Jacques Revel and Lynn Hunt, trans. Arthur Goldhammer et al. (New York: New Press, 1995), 437-47; originally "Histoire et mystique," *Revue d'histoire de la spiritualité* 89 (1972): 69-82. For the postwar "mystical" in France, see Stephen Schloesser, *Jazz Age Catholicism: Mystic Modernism in Postwar Paris, 1919-1933* (Toronto: University of Toronto Press, 2005), 116-19.

14. Translator's note, Marmion, *Christ in His Mysteries*, 16 n. 65.

1932–1943: Theological Order, Glorified Bodies, Apocalyptic Epoch

hazard).¹⁵ The work is divided into nine movements symbolizing the nine months of Mary's pregnancy: "Nine pieces in all to honor the maternity of the Blessed Virgin."¹⁶

The work is symmetrical in two ways. First, the center and fulcrum of the work is its meditation on the theological doctrine of divine adoption in the middle (fifth) movement: "The Children of God." As in *Ascension,* the titles are followed by their textual epigraphs upon which the music "comments":

1. The Virgin and Child¹⁷
Conceived by a Virgin a Child is born unto us, a Son has been given. Be transported by joy, daughter of Sion! Behold, your king comes to you, just and humble.

(Books of the Prophets Isaiah and Zechariah)

2. The Shepherds¹⁸
Having seen the Child lying in the crib, the shepherds returned home, glorifying and praising God.

(Gospel according to Saint Luke)

---

15. For alternative comparison of Marmion and Messiaen, see helpful schematic table in Massin and Messiaen, *Olivier Messiaen,* 72. For *Nativity* see Latry and Mallié, *L'œuvre d'orgue d'Olivier Messiaen,* 119-85; Gillock, *Performing Messiaen's Organ Music,* 49-98.

16. Messiaen, "Note de l'auteur," *La Nativité du Seigneur. Neuf méditations pour orgue,* 4 fascicles (Paris: Alphonse Leduc, 1936), fascicle 1, n.p.

17. "Let us also ask the Virgin Mary *to make us share the feelings that animated her* during the blessed days that preceded the birth of Jesus." "What shall we say of the Virgin when she gazed on Jesus? So pure, so humble and tender her gaze, so full of happiness — to what depths of the mystery it penetrated!" "Therefore let us abandon ourselves to joy and with the Church sing: 'For to us a Child is born, *to us* a Son is *given.*'" Marmion, chapters 6 ("The Divine Preparations [Advent]") and 7 ("O Wondrous Exchange! [Christmas]") in *Christ in His Mysteries,* 109-30 and 131-53, at 129, 151, 149. Compare chapter 9 ("The Virgin Mary, and the Mysteries of Christ's Childhood and Hidden Life [The Time after the Epiphany]"), 175-201, especially 178-83.

18. "These feasts are magnificent; they are also full of charm. The Church evokes the memory *of the angels singing songs* of 'Glory to the new-born Babe'; *of the shepherds,* simple souls who come to the manger to adore Him; *of the wise men* hastening from the East to render Him their adoration and offer Him rich gifts." "Then there are the shepherds, simple-hearted men, illumined by a light from on high . . . they have rendered Him their homage, and their souls have for a long time been filled with joy and peace." Marmion, *Christ in His Mysteries,* 132, 151, emphasis added.

1935–1939: Theological Turn, Young France, Baby Pascal

3. Eternal Designs[19]
God, in his love, predestined us [*nous a prédestinés*] to be his adoptive sons [*ses fils adoptifs*], through Jesus Christ, to the praise of the glory of his grace.
(Epistle of Saint Paul to the Ephesians)

4. The Word[20]
The Lord said to me: You are my Son. From his breast, before the dawn existed, he engendered me. I am the Image of the goodness of God, I am the Word of life, from the beginning.
(Psalms 2 and 109, Book of Wisdom, First Epistle of Saint John)

19. "All the blessings of God upon us have their source in the election He has made of our souls from all eternity, to make them 'holy and without blemish in His sight.' In this divine decree, so full of love, is included our destiny as adopted children of God, with the whole body of favors that attach to it." Marmion, *Christ in His Mysteries*, 109; see also translator's note, 109 n. 1.
   The theological doctrine of "eternal designs" (or "plans" — *Desseins*) is central in Marmion; it appears on the opening page of the first chapter of his book *Christ, the Life of the Soul*: "[The apostle Paul was] the one chosen by God to bring to light the 'dispensation of the mystery which has been hidden from eternity in God'; it is in those terms that Paul indicates *the Divine plan* concerning us. We see the great apostle labor without respite to make known *this eternal plan*. . . . Why do all the Apostle's efforts (as Paul takes care to say) aim at enlightening all men about the dispensation of *the Divine designs?*" See Marmion, *Christ, the Life of the Soul*, 3, emphasis added.
   20. "The Night Mass, all-enveloped in mystery, starts with these words that are full of solemnity: '*Dominus dixit ad me: Filius meus es tu, ego hodie genui te*' — 'The Lord has said to me: You are my Son, this day have I begotten you.' . . . 'This day' is first of all the 'today' of eternity — and eternity has no dawn, no waning." "Look at this Child lying in the manger. . . . In appearance, He is simply like every other child. And yet at this moment of your seeing Him, in that He is God, in that *He is the Word eternal*, . . . is He who is eternal and whose divine nature knows no change: 'He is always the same and His years are eternal!' He who was born in the sphere of time is also He who is before all time." Marmion, *Christ in His Mysteries*, 135, 137; cf. 114.

1932–1943: Theological Order, Glorified Bodies, Apocalyptic Epoch

> 5. The Children of God [i.e., divine adoption][21]
> To all those who received it, the Word gave the power to become children of God. And God sent into their hearts the Spirit of his Son which cried: Father! Father!
> *(Gospel according to Saint John and Epistle of Saint Paul to the Galatians)*

> 6. The Angels[22]
> The celestial army praised God and said: Glory to God in the highest heavens!
> *(Gospel according to Saint Luke)*

> 7. Jesus Accepts His Suffering[23]
> Christ says to his Father as he enters into the world: "You have accepted neither holocausts nor sacrifices for sin, but you have formed a body for me. Here I am!"
> *(Saint Paul, Epistle to the Hebrews)*

> 8. The Magi[24]
> The Magi left, and the star went before them.
> *(Gospel according to Saint Matthew)*

---

21. "What the Incarnate Word gives to humanity in return is an incomprehensible gift: it is a participation, a real and intimate participation in His divine nature: 'He ... has bestowed on us His divine nature': *Largitus est nobis suam deitatem.* In exchange for the humanity that He has taken to Himself, the Incarnate Word permits us to share in His divinity, He makes us participants in His divine nature: And thus is accomplished the most wonderful exchange we could ever celebrate. . . . By allowing us to share in His condition of Son, He will make us children of God." Marmion, *Christ in His Mysteries*, 138-39.

22. "Likewise the angels looked upon the New-born, the Word-made-flesh. They saw in Him their God, and so this knowledge threw those pure spirits into amazement and wonder at so incomprehensible an abasement. For He did not will to unite Himself to *their* nature, but to human nature: 'Nowhere does He take hold of angels: *but of the seed of Abraham He takes hold.*'" Marmion, *Christ in His Mysteries*, 151.

23. "The humanity of Christ makes God visible; but above all — and it is here that the Divine Wisdom is shown to be 'wondrous' — it makes God *capable of suffering.*" "'Therefore in coming into the world, He says, "Sacrifice and oblation you did not desire, but you have prepared *a body* for me. Then said I, Behold, I come . . . to do your will, O God."' It was by this oblation that Christ began to sanctify us." Marmion, *Christ in His Mysteries*, 145-46.

24. Marmion's entire chapter 8 ("The Epiphany") is devoted to the Magi. Marmion, *Christ in His Mysteries*, 154-174.

1935–1939: Theological Turn, Young France, Baby Pascal

9. God among Us[25]
Words of the communicant [receiving the Eucharist], of the Virgin, of the entire Church: He who created me has rested in my tent, the Word was made flesh and has dwelled within me. My soul glorifies the Lord, my spirit has shaken with joy [*a tressailli d'allégresse*] in God my Savior.
(Ecclesiastes, Gospels according to Saint John and Saint Luke)

The first four movements ascend to the climactic doctrine of divine adoption ("The Children of God") while the following four movements descend from it — not in the sense of decreased energy (for the most energetic movement is the final toccata), but in the sense of a dramatic denouement or unfolding. This theological centerpiece, "divine adoption" (or "divinization" or *theosis* as God's predestined "eternal design"), was a key doctrine in both Dom Guéranger and his successor Dom Marmion. It remained a central doctrine for Messiaen, and he eventually returned to it nearly thirty-five years later in *The Transfiguration* (1969) — a sign of its profound significance in his personal theology.[26]

The second symmetry is chiastic insofar as the acts leading up to and then down from the climax are also parallel with one another:

Virgin and Child   1 ↔ 9   God among Us
Shepherds   2 ↔ 8   Magi

25. "You see, it is a human-divine exchange. The child born on Christmas Day is at the same time God, and the human nature that God takes to Himself from us to serve as the instrument through which He communicates His divinity to us: 'As this man who has been born into our human nature has at the same time shone gloriously upon us as God, *so* — in the same way — this earthly substance may *communicate to us* what is *divine*.' Our offerings will be 'suitable to the mysteries' signified by the birth on Christmas Day if — by our contemplation of the divine work at Bethlehem and our reception of the Eucharistic Sacrament — we do share in the eternal life that Christ wishes to communicate to us through His humanity." "At the home of her cousin Elizabeth, she let the inner feelings of her soul overflow; she intoned that Magnificat which, in the course of the centuries, her spiritual children would repeat with her in praise of God for having chosen her from among all women: 'My soul glorifies the Lord, and my spirit rejoices in God my Savior....'" Marmion, *Christ in His Mysteries,* 133-34 and 180. Compare Hello, "Le moi-*Amen:* la Vierge" ("The Me-*Amen:* The Virgin"), in *Du néant à dieu,* ed. Jules-Philippe Heuzey, 2 vols. (Paris: Perrin et Cie, [1921] 1930), 1:171-72.

26. Messiaen returned to the doctrine of adoptive filiation in an explicit way in his oratorio *The Transfiguration* (1969). See Olivier Messiaen and Claude Samuel, *Music and Color: Conversations with Claude Samuel,* trans. E. Thomas Glasow (Portland, Ore.: Amadeus Press, 1994), 145.

1932–1943: Theological Order, Glorified Bodies, Apocalyptic Epoch

> Eternal Designs 3 ↔ 7 Jesus Suffering
> Word 4 ↔ 6 Angels
> 5
> Divine Adoption
> ("The Children of God")

The movements are in parallel:

- Movements 1 and 9 = commingling of humanity and divinity.
- Movements 2 and 8 = visiting onlookers, both lowly (shepherds) and lofty (Magi). (Compare the *Twenty Gazes at* [or *Looks at*] *the Infant Jesus* [1944].)
- Movements 3 and 7 = union of eternity with temporal suffering. God's "Eternal Designs" of predestination are accomplished necessarily through the incarnation and, as a corollary, temporal suffering.
- Movements 4 and 6 = atemporal beings (Word and angels) made manifest. The Word precedes all of creation and is paradoxically the "Son" (in the words of the Nicene Creed, "begotten, not made"). Like the Word, the angels also preceded temporal creation and exist outside of time; and yet they too, like the Word, manifest themselves in time at the birth of Christ.

Messiaen's text for the brilliant finale, "God among Us," is taken partly from Ecclesiastes and partly from the Gospels of Saint John and Saint Luke: the three figures of the *communicant* (Eucharist), *Virgin* (Maternity), and *entire church* represent continuity with earlier works: *Celestial Banquet* (1928), *Forgotten Offerings* (1930), *Resplendent Tomb* (1931), *Apparition of the Eternal Church* (1931-1932), and *Hymn to the Blessed Sacrament* (1932). This continuity is both reinforced and amplified in Marmion:

> There is the whole formula for sanctity: Adhere to the Word, to His doctrine, to His commands; and through Him, to the Father who sent Him and gives Him the words we ought to receive [cf. John 17:8].
> Finally, we remain united to the Word above all through the sacrament of union, the Eucharist. This is the Bread of Life, "the children's Bread" [sequence for feast of Corpus Christi, *Lauda Sion*]. Under the Eucharistic species is truly hidden the Word, He who is born eternally in the depths of the Godhead. What a mystery! He whom I receive in holy communion is

the Son, begotten of the Father from all eternity.... "He who eats my flesh ... abides in me and I in him" [John 6:57].[27]

Once again, the epigraph to *The Celestial Banquet*.

Messiaen's final words in *The Nativity*, a quotation of Mary's Magnificat — "my spirit has shaken (or trembled, quivered, or shuddered = *a tressailli*) with joy" — return to the central concern of both Guéranger and Marmion, indeed of Catholic Revivalism itself: *an increase in feeling*. And here, as in *Ascension*, the feeling being fostered is *joy:* "Therefore joy is one of the feelings that are most evident in the celebration of this mystery.... It is the joy of deliverance, of inheritance regained, of peace rediscovered, and, above all, of men being given the sight of God Himself: 'And he shall be called Emmanuel,' God-with-us."[28] God among us: *Dieu parmi nous*.

1935: La Spirale

The composition of *The Nativity* expressed Messiaen's desire in 1935 to situate himself more firmly within a tradition of theological doctrine and liturgical practice. Messiaen's personal aims were part of a broader 1930s shift to a "new humanism" going beyond the postwar contest between Stravinsky and Schoenberg: "Modernity as such, that of the evolution of artistic languages, of technological progress, and that dominating the formalist thought of Stravinsky's neo-classicism as well as Schoenberg's determinism, aroused visceral reactions among a good number of musicians."[29]

This generational reaction was also the context for the 1935 formation of the musical group La Spirale. Its members were all connected with the Schola Cantorum: Messiaen had been appointed to his post there teaching organ improvisation after the school's radical reorganization in December 1934.[30] La

---

27. Marmion, *Christ in His Mysteries*, 62.
28. Marmion, *Christ in His Mysteries*, 149.
29. Sylvain Caron and Michel Duchesneau, "La musique et la foi entre les deux guerres: vers un nouvel humanisme?" in *Musique, art et religion dans l'entre-deux guerres*, ed. Sylvain Caron and Michel Duchesneau (Lyon: Symétrie, 2009), 1-11, at 6.
30. Nigel Simeone, "La Spirale and La Jeune France: Group Identities," *Musical Times* 143, no. 1880 (Autumn 2002): 10-36; cf. Dingle, *The Life of Messiaen*, 45. Is it possible that the name came from Evelyn Underhill's book (published under her pseudonym, John Corderlier), *The Spiral Way: Being a Meditation on the Fifteen Mysteries of the Soul's Ascent* (London: John M. Watkins, 1912)?

1932–1943: Theological Order, Glorified Bodies, Apocalyptic Epoch

Spirale's committee members included its leader, Georges Migot, Messiaen and Claire, Daniel-Lesur (who had also just acquired his post teaching counterpoint at the Schola), and André Jolivet (who, along with his wife Hilda, lived close to the Messiaens). La Spirale's first concert took place in December 1935 with its manifesto printed on the program's front page: "to participate in the promotion of contemporary music, through concerts of French works, and through organizing exchange concerts with composers from other countries. It wishes to serve music and in order to do so, it will give fewer world premieres; instead, it will give repeat performances of significant works."[31]

At this first concert the Messiaens figured prominently: the program opened with Messiaen playing *Two Pieces for Organ* written by Claire (her name appeared as "Claire Delbos"). And it closed with Messiaen playing his own *Ascension* suite.[32] Daniel-Lesur was represented by three songs for tenor, string quartet, and piano (played by himself), and Jolivet by his recently written seminal work *Mana* (1935), about which Messiaen would soon write at length.[33] In January 1936, La Spirale offered a second concert dedicated to "contemporary French music." It opened with Jean Langlais playing his *Evangelical Poems* ("The Annunciation," "The Nativity," "The Palms" [1932]) on the organ. A third concert in March was dedicated to works of American composers: Messiaen accompanied a baritone's rendition of five songs by Charles Ives, including "Requiem," "The Innate," and "From 'Paracelsus.'" In April, a concert was devoted to "contemporary Hungarian music," including performances of Zoltán Kodály and Béla Bartók.[34] The manifesto's stated aim of cultural exchanges with com-

31. Quoted in Simeone, "Group Identities," 11.

32. See program (December 12, 1935) reprinted in Simeone, "Group Identities," 28. Delbos's composition is incorrectly identified as *Three Pieces (Trois pièces)*. Perhaps it is possible that Messiaen played the *Deux pièces* as well as some third composition.

33. Olivier Messiaen, "Billet parisien: Le *Mana* de Jolivet" ("Notes from Paris: *Mana* by Jolivet"), *La Sirène* (December 1937): 8-10; in *Olivier Messiaen: Journalism, 1935-1939*, ed. Stephen Broad (Surrey, UK, and Burlington, Vt.: Ashgate, 2012), Fr 34-36; Eng 95-97. Ten years later, Messiaen developed this article as an introduction to the published score: see Messiaen, "Introduction au *Mana* d'André Jolivet," in Jolivet, *Mana. 6 pièces pour piano* (Paris: Éditions Costallat, 1946), n.p. Both French and English versions are provided, the translation credited to "Pierre Messiaen and Rollo Myers." For Jolivet, see Deborah Mawer, "Jolivet's Search for a New French Voice: Spiritual 'Otherness' in *Mana* (1935)," in *French Music, Culture, and National Identity, 1870-1939*, ed. Barbara L. Kelly (Rochester, N.Y.: University of Rochester Press, 2008), 172-93; Jane F. Fulcher, *The Composer as Intellectual: Music and Ideology in France, 1914-1940* (New York: Oxford University Press, 2005), 275-323, especially 302-8; and entries for "Jolivet" in Vincent Perez Benitez, *Olivier Messiaen: A Research and Information Guide* (New York: Routledge, 2008).

34. All programs may be found in Simeone, "Group Identities."

240

posers from other countries served as a tool with which the 1930s interwar generation could pry open horizons over which the 1920s exerted a stranglehold.

1936: European Upheaval, Integral Humanism, Young France

In the ominous year of 1936, the search for a nonconformist third way between individualism and communalism became urgently concrete. In Spain, as the Great Depression dragged on, the left-wing Popular Front coalition won the February 1936 elections and established its government. The Popular Front in France followed suit and won the May elections. A general strike called during May-June resulted in the Matignon agreements (June 7), a pivotal moment in the establishment of twentieth-century workers' rights. On July 17, General Francisco Franco launched a coup d'état that inaugurated the Spanish Civil War (1936-1939). As outside fascist (Hitler, Mussolini) and communist (Stalin) powers took sides, the civil war would become a foreshadowing proxy war — a training ground and dress rehearsal for the great conflagration to come.[35]

The efforts of Messiaen and his age cohort — the self-styled "Young France" — embodied in miniature what one musicologist has called a "revolutionary spiritualism," a call for emotional composition freed from the spare vision of postwar neoclassicism, a less abstract and more "personal" style that was at once both "humanistic" and "mystical."[36] Both Messiaen and Jolivet "reflected the nonconformists' search for new ways to express man's existential

---

35. Martin Hurcombe, *France and the Spanish Civil War: Cultural Representations of the War Next Door, 1936-1945* (Burlington, Vt.: Ashgate, 2011).

36. For a recontextualization of La Jeune France as a musical "nonconformism" within a broader "revolutionary spiritualism" of French youth and musicians, see Fulcher, "Part 2: The Search for 'Oppositionality'; French Youth and 'Revolutionary Spiritualism,'" in *The Composer as Intellectual*, 285-301. Referring to Fulcher's work, Philip Nord writes that Jeune France "imagined a France gripped by a 'crisis of civilization.' What the nation needed was a new, spiritual art that, hovering above the earthbound musical partisanship of the day, would uplift and regenerate. From this angle, the Jeune France of 1936 looks much like a musical homologue to the neither-right-nor-left nonconformism espoused by the likes of Emmanuel Mounier, and so it has been argued by the best-informed scholar in the field." Nord, *France's New Deal: From the Thirties to the Postwar Era* (Princeton: Princeton University Press, 2010), 265; cf. Caron and Duchesneau, "La musique et la foi entre les deux guerres." For a detailed critique of Fulcher's position, see Stephen Broad, "Recontextualising Messiaen's Early Career," 2 vols. (Ph.D. diss., University of Oxford, 2005), 1:183-94; cf. Broad, "Messiaen: Poetics, Polemics and Politics," *Scottish Music Review* 1, no. 1 (2007): 83-98.

'essence,' and his endemic connection to a higher state of being."[37] In late 1935, the nonconformist Catholic Emmanuel Mounier published his essay "Our Humanism."[38] The next year saw the publication of Jacques Maritain's landmark *Integral Humanism: Temporal and Spiritual Problems of a New Christianity*.[39] Three years later, Messiaen would specify his own holistic humanism:

> There is much talk these days about a "return to the human" [*retour à l'humain*]. One should really speak of a "return to the divine" [*retour au divin*]. Man is neither angel nor beast, far less machine. He is man: flesh and conscience, body and soul [*chair et conscience, corps et âme*]. His heart is the abyss [*l'abîme*]: only the "divine" can fill it. Man is searching. Confusedly, doubtfully, he seeks God. Everywhere. In art, as elsewhere. One cannot separate the "return to the human" from the "return to the divine." When faith — which built our cathedrals — reigns over the arts, the "return to the human" — to the human in its entirety [*à l'humain tout entier*] — will be complete.[40]

Messiaen was fully immersed in the search for a new music, a new order, and a new "integral" humanism. More specifically, we see his turn away from the

---

37. Fulcher, *The Composer as Intellectual*, 302.

38. Emmanuel Mounier, "Notre humanisme," *Esprit* 37 (October 1935); cited in Pierre de Senarclens, *Le mouvement 'Esprit' 1932-1941: essai critique* (Lausanne: Éd. L'Âge d'homme, 1974), 327 n. 116.

39. Jacques Maritain, *Humanisme intégral: problèmes temporels et spirituels d'une nouvelle chrétienté* (Paris: F. Aubier, 1936). Somewhat ominously, it was also the year Erik Peterson published his book with an introduction by Maritain: *The Mystery of Jews and Gentiles in the Church, Followed by an Essay on the Apocalypse (Le mystère des Juifs et des gentils dans l'église, suivi d'un essai sur l'Apocalypse)* (Paris: Desclée de Brouwer, 1936)]. See Yvan Lamonde, "*La Relève* (1934-1939): Maritain et la crise spirituelle des années 1930," *Les Cahiers des dix* 62 (2008): 153-94.

40. Messiaen, "De la Musique sacrée" ("On Sacred Music") (June-July 1939); in *Olivier Messiaen: Journalism, 1935-1939*, 74-76, at 74; Eng 135-37, at 135-36, translation altered. Here again the influence of Pascal, both in the reference to the "abyss" and as the hybrid character of humanity: "Man is neither angel nor beast; and the misfortune is that he who would act the angel acts the beast." Pascal, *Pensées* (Pléiade), 572; (Lafuma) 678; (Sellier) 557; for Pléiade, see Pascal, *Œuvres complètes*, 2 vols. (Paris: Éditions Gallimard, 2000), vol. 2; for Lafuma, see Pascal, *Pensées*, trans. A. J. Krailsheimer, rev. ed. (New York: Penguin, 1995); for Sellier, see Pascal, *Pensées*, ed. and trans. Roger Ariew (Indianapolis: Hackett, 2005); cf. Stephen Schloesser, "1902-1920: The Hard Metier of Unmasking," in *Mystic Masque: Reality and Semblance in Georges Rouault, 1871-1958*, ed. Stephen Schloesser (Chestnut Hill, Mass.: McMullen Museum of Art, distributed by the University of Chicago Press, 2008), 79-104, at 91.

1935–1939: Theological Turn, Young France, Baby Pascal

disembodied Romantic "soul" toward a Thomistic (and Aristotelian) hylomorphic conception of the soul as a form of the body-soul composite.

The February 27, 1936, premiere of the *Nativity* suite and its subsequent publication (March 28) may be seen within this larger generational project. Messiaen did not premiere the work himself, instead dividing up the nine movements between three organists of his age cohort: Daniel-Lesur played movements 1-3, Langlais played 4-6, and Jean-Jacques Grunenwald (Dupré's student and assistant at Saint-Sulpice beginning in 1936) played 7-9. Meanwhile, Messiaen took the occasion to promulgate his evolving self-image as being at the service of Catholic theology. His short but dense personal manifesto, printed on small sheets of paper given to the audience, read in part:

> Emotion, the sincerity of the musical work.
> Which will be at the service of the dogmas of Catholic theology....
> Theological subject matter? The best, since it contains all subjects.
> And the abundance of technical means allows the heart to overflow freely.[41]

Messiaen's emphasis on "emotion" and the heart's overflow directly confronted postwar neoclassicism. Messiaen elaborated this generational intention in an article published about a month after this manifesto for the *Nativity*'s premiere:

> Yesterday, they spoke enthusiastically to us of the music of factories, of sports, of locomotives or aeroplanes, of dissonances capable of expressing, if not poeticizing, this aesthetic of noise. Then the wind changed: simplify! And, then, another question arose: "Who should I imitate to be original?"
> At the same time as these shocks, something germinated, one might say underground, something that could return to music the riches that it has lost. The young composers — the very young ones — think firstly of emotion, of emotion inspired by Love. Woman, Nature and Religion are sources of Love.
> The Christian faith gave us cathedrals, and it is this faith that will inspire musical masterpieces of love.[42]

Messiaen's desire to move to firmer "theological" footing was completely in sync with other nonconformist attempts to set down a new spiritual foun-

---

41. For facsimile see Simeone, *Bibliographical Catalogue*, 46; for another translation see Hill and Simeone, *Messiaen*, 60.

42. Olivier Messiaen, "La Transmutation des enthousiasmes" ("The Transmutation of Enthusiasms"), *La Page musicale* (April 16, 1936): 1; in *Olivier Messiaen: Journalism, 1935-1939*, Fr 61-62, at 61; Eng 123-24, at 123.

dation for Europe in 1936. However, the appellation "theological" lacked the needed expressive energy, and one of the most enthusiastic reviewers of the *Nativity*'s premiere instead fell back on familiar terms: "In this work, comprising nine *mystical* meditations for organ on the Nativity of Our Lord Jesus Christ, Olivier Messiaen has achieved a perfect and brilliant mastery of his art, at the same time as expressing a *mystical* sensibility of an incomparable nobility and quality."[43]

La Jeune France (Young France), a further expression of the drive toward a nonconformist new order, was the second and better-known group with which Messiaen would be associated. Although in later years Messiaen would minimize the importance that Jeune France had played in his earlier life, recently published translations of journalism he wrote during this time demonstrate that he was in fact deeply engaged in promoting the group's agenda: "One of the striking features of the journalism is Messiaen's unashamed promotion of those closest to him."[44] The group's first performance took place on June 3, 1936, exactly one month after the May 3 election of the Popular Front government — a revolutionary moment of socialist victory after a century and a half of failed dreams and attempts since the French Revolution. The atmosphere in France was giddy for some and foreboding for others. Into this atmosphere, La Jeune France — composed of Messiaen, Daniel-Lesur, Jolivet, and Yves Baudrier — launched its own nonconformist manifesto, setting a middle-way course between the "revolutionary" left and the "academic" (or formulaic) right. "As the conditions of life become more and more hard, mechanical and impersonal, music must always bring to those who love it, its spiritual violence and its courageous reactions. Young France [La Jeune France] ... a group of four young French composers who are friends ... proposes the dissemination of works [that are] youthful, free, [and] as far removed from revolutionary formulas [on the left] as from academic formulas [on the right]." This opening paragraph's first line seemed to come straight from the pen of Daniel-Rops, whose *World without Soul* (1932) was largely a critique of postwar "machinism." The paragraph's final line seemed to be a deliberate echo of Jacques Maritain's *Letter to Jean Cocteau* (1926), published exactly ten years earlier.[45] The manifesto continued:

43. Henri Sauget, in Hill and Simeone, *Messiaen*, 60, emphasis added.
44. Stephen Broad, introduction to *Olivier Messiaen: Journalism, 1935-1939*, 7.
45. See Daniel-Rops, *Le Monde sans âme* (1932), especially c. 3 ("L'Esprit et la Machine") and c. 4 ("L'Exigence de la Satisfaction"), an attack on *la civilisation machinique* and *la machinisme,* especially in America. Ten years earlier, Maritain had written that the "return to order" sought by Cocteau was "obviously, not the academic kind of order which

1935–1939: Theological Turn, Young France, Baby Pascal

The tendencies of this group will be diverse; their only unqualified agreement is in a common desire to be satisfied with nothing less than sincerity, generosity and artistic good faith. Their aim is to create and to promote a living music. ...

They also hope to encourage the performance of recent French scores which have been allowed to languish through the indifference or the penury of official powers, and to continue into this century the music of the great composers of the past who have made French music one of the pure jewels of civilization.[46]

The first concert included two of Messiaen's works — *Hymn to the Blessed Sacrament* and *The Forgotten Offerings* — and one of Jolivet's: the premiere of the *Incantatory Dance (Danse Incantatoire)* with "Monsieur et Mlle. Martenot" playing the new Ondes Martenot (invented in 1928).[47] Although the juxtaposition between Roman Catholic eucharistic devotion and the exotic quasi occultism of magical fetishism seems odd today, Messiaen's enthusiasm for Jolivet's work (especially *Mana*) makes sense within the broader context of the disintegrating 1930s: a distrust of the rational logic that had led to the current crisis; an embrace of the instinctive, intuitive, metaphysical, and surreal.

---

is a false one. ... What scandalizes our contemporaries the most is order: I mean order in spirit and in truth which is just as much the enemy of a stuffed-shirt order ... as it is of disorder." Maritain's sentiments grew logically out of what had first drawn him to Cocteau, a reading of his Collège de France address entitled "On Order Considered as Anarchy" (1923). Maritain wrote Cocteau: "It is a rare and enviable victory to have succeeded, as you have, in making 'order' seem as new and as disturbing as 'anarchy.'" See Schloesser, *Jazz Age Catholicism*, 188, 177. The parallels to Messiaen's own "anarchic dissonances" defended against while applying for the Trinité position are suggestive: "it is important not to disturb the piety of the faithful by using chords which are too anarchic." Letter of Messiaen to Curé Hemmer, August 8, 1931.

46. La Jeune France manifesto reproduced in Hill and Simeone, *Messiaen*, 63; cf. Stuart Waumsley, *The Organ Music of Olivier Messiaen* (Paris: Alphonse Leduc, 1968), 8.

47. Program for inaugural concert of La Jeune France (June 3, 1936) reproduced in Simeone, *Bibliographical Catalogue*, 16-17. For a near-contemporary French colonial representation of an African "incantation," see Georges Rouault's engraving for Ambroise Vollard's *Les Réincarnations du Père Ubu* (1932) entitled *Incantation;* in Schloesser, "1921-1929: Jazz Age Graphic Shock," in *Mystic Masque*, 133-55, at 146; 511-12 (plates 28a-b); cf. Félicien Rops' heliogravure *L'Incantation* (1888) reproduced at 237, fig. 5.

1932–1943: Theological Order, Glorified Bodies, Apocalyptic Epoch

Summer 1936: "Sacramental Warriors" in *Poems for Mi*

As the world erupted, Messiaen's musical imagination was more domestic than geopolitical during the hot days of summer 1936 at Petichet in Isère. Having successfully premiered the *Nativity* in February, he turned to composing *Poems for Mi* (his pet name for Claire)[48] for voice and piano. The decision to cast the piece in nine movements echoed that made for the *Nativity*, whose nine movements represented the Virgin Mary's nine months of maternity, and perhaps expressed a silent plea for Messiaen's own parental desires:

1. Thanksgiving *(Action de grâces)*
2. Landscape
3. The House
4. Terror
5. The Wife
6. Your Voice
7. The Two Warriors
8. The Necklace
9. Fulfilled Prayer

In the program for the work's premiere, Messiaen added the subtitle "Poems of O.M. on the Sacrament of Marriage."[49] (Marriage is one of seven sacraments in Catholic theology.) The marital theme is found in several of the movements, but nowhere so explicitly as in the seventh song, "The Two Warriors":

> Behold us two in one.
> Forward!
> Like warriors cased in iron! . . .

---

48. "Mi," the solfège syllable for E, is the highest note reached by a violin. "The top notes, however, are often produced by natural or artificial harmonics. Thus the E two octaves above the open E-string may be considered a practical limit for orchestral violin parts." Walter Piston, *Orchestration* (New York: Norton, 1955), 45. I am grateful to Peter Bannister for directing me to the significance of this name. Note also that the French word *mie* is an address of love. In his translation of *Romeo and Juliet*, Pierre Messiaen translated Romeo's address to Juliet — "And trust me, love" — as "Ma mie, crois-moi." See Shakespeare, *Œuvres*, 3:148; Shakespeare, *Romeo and Juliet*, act 3, scene 5, line 58, in *The Arden Shakespeare Complete Works*, ed. Richard Proudfoot, Ann Thompson, and David Scott Kastan, rev. ed. (London: Arden Shakespeare, 2011), 1029. See Messiaen letter to Claire below, p. 282.

49. Simeone, *Bibliographical Catalogue*, 52–55.

1935–1939: Theological Turn, Young France, Baby Pascal

Forward sacramental warriors!
Strain joyfully your shields,
shoot into the sky the arrows of devotion at dawn:
You will arrive at the gates of the City.[50]

The lyrics convey a sense of mission and battle — perhaps melodramatic in retrospect, but understandable within the overall atmosphere of 1935-1936: L'Ordre Nouveau, La Spirale, and La Jeune France.

But the text should also be seen within the proliferation of discourse about marriage within 1930s Catholic circles. As late as the Code of Canon Law promulgated in 1917 (just as the Great War was ending), drawing on the tradition of both Augustine and Aquinas, Canon 1013 defined two "ends" (or purposes) of marriage: a primary end of "procreation and nurture of children," and a secondary end of "mutual help and the remedying of concupiscence."[51] In short, Catholicism — at least in doctrine — lacked a sense of "companionate marriage" that had gradually evolved since the Reformation.

However, the Great War had changed society far more than anyone could have anticipated, especially in terms of gender relations.[52] By the end of the 1920s, such an archaic understanding of marriage had become inadequate. By 1924, Abbé Jean Viollet had begun his ministry of answering couples' inquiries about sexuality (and especially contraception), and he published frequently on the topics of marriage, family, contraception, sterilization, and eugenics: *Education about Purity and Feeling* (1925); *Education by the Family* (1926); *Familial Morality* (1927); *The Duties of Marriage* (several editions by 1928); *Eugenics, Sterilization, Their Moral Value* (1929).[53] In Germany, the lay

---

50. Olivier Messiaen, "The Two Warriors" ("Les Deux Guerriers"), in *Poems for Mi,* trans. Felix Aprahamian, in Olivier Messiaen, *Complete Edition,* 32 CDs (Germany: Deutsche Grammophon, 2008), 304-8, at 307.

51. *Codex Iuris Cononici* (1917), 1013; quoted in Robert E. Obach, *The Catholic Church on Marital Intercourse: From St. Paul to Pope John Paul II* (Lanham, Md.: Lexington Books, 2009), 121.

52. For introductions to this literature, see Whitney Chadwick, ed., *The Modern Woman Revisited: Paris between the Wars* (New Brunswick, N.J.: Rutgers University Press, 2003); Paul Smith, *Feminism and the Third Republic: Women's Political and Civil Rights in France, 1918-1945* (Oxford: Clarendon; New York: Oxford University Press, 1996); Mary Louise Roberts, *Civilization without Sexes: Reconstructing Gender in Postwar France, 1917-1927* (Chicago: University of Chicago Press, 1994).

53. Martine Sevegrand and Jean Viollet, *L'amour en toutes lettres: questions à l'abbé Viollet sur la sexualité, 1924-1943* (Paris: Albin Michel, 1996). See Abbé Jean Viollet: *Éducation de la pureté et du sentiment* (Paris: Association du mariage chrétien, 1925); *L'éducation par la*

theologian Dietrich von Hildebrand published his books *Purity and Virginity* (1928) and *Marriage* (1929).⁵⁴ These latter works immediately preceded the publication of the papal encyclical *Casti Connubii* (December 31, 1930), an unbending condemnation of contraception responding to the 1930 Anglican Lambeth Conference's reversal of its long-standing position on the matter.

In the encyclical's wake, the 1930s would be filled with Catholic publications attempting the reconciliation of tradition with modernity.⁵⁵ In France, Abbé Viollet published *Marriage* (1932), *The Psychology of Marriage* (1935), and *Christian Law and Marriage* (1936).⁵⁶ Also in 1936, the year Messiaen wrote *Poems for Mi,* Hildebrand's *Marriage* (German, 1929) appeared in French translation with the extended title *Love and the Mystery of Sacramental Marriage.* The following year (in which Messiaen's *Poems* was premiered), a French translation of Herbert Doms's groundbreaking (although somewhat unorthodox) *On the Meaning and End of Marriage* (1935) was published by Desclée de Brouwer.⁵⁷

It is difficult not to wonder whether Messiaen's "warrior" conception of marriage was not also, consciously or unconsciously, an overcompensation for his parents' marriage — not at all a tale of two "sacramental warriors." More acutely, one wonders whether it was not an attempt, on behalf of a childless couple, to reimagine Catholic marriage without procreation. In any event, "The Two Warriors" testifies to the kind of strict Catholicism that Messiaen

---

famille (Paris: Association du mariage chrétien, 1926); *Morale familiale* (Paris: Association du mariage chrétien, 1927); *Les Devoirs du mariage,* 4th ed. (Paris: Association du mariage chrétien, 1928). See also Viollet et al., *Pour restaurer la famille* (Paris: Éditions de la S.A.P.E., 1927); Viollet and André Lorulot, *L'Église et l'amour: controverse publique entre MM. l'abbé Viollet et André Lorulot* (Herblay, Seine et Oise: Aux Éditions de "l'idée libre," 1929); Viollet et al., *Eugénisme, stérilisation, leur valeur morale* (Paris: SPES, 1929).

54. Dietrich von Hildebrand, *Reinheit und Jungfräulichkeit* (Munich: Kösel & Pustet, 1927); Hildebrand, *Die Ehe* (Munich: J. Müller, 1929).

55. Shaji George Kochuthara, *The Concept of Sexual Pleasure in the Catholic Moral Tradition* (Rome: Editrice Pontificia Universita Gregoriana, 2007), 246-50.

56. See the following by Abbé Jean Viollet: *Le Mariage* (Tours: Mame, 1932); *La Psychologie du mariage* (Paris: Association du mariage chrétien, 1935); *La loi chrétienne du mariage: prescriptions et défenses* (Paris: Éd. Mariage et Famille, 1936). See also Viollet et al., *Où en sommes-nous? La doctrine familiale de l'Église catholique et le problème du mariage dans les deux mondes* (Paris: Éditions Mariage et Famille, 1932).

57. Dietrich von Hildebrand, *L'amour et le mystère du mariage sacramentel,* trans. Benoît Lavaud (Fribourg, Switzerland: Fragnière Frères, 1936); Hildebrand, *Le mariage* (Paris: Cerf, 1936); Herbert Doms, *Du sens et de la fin du mariage,* trans. Marie-Simone Thisse and Paul Thisse, 2nd ed. (Paris: Desclée de Brouwer, 1937); original *Vom Sinn und Zweck der Ehe* (1935).

1935–1939: Theological Turn, Young France, Baby Pascal

and Claire apparently embraced. So does the work's central movement, "The Wife."

> Go where the Spirit leads you,
> nothing can separate that which God has joined,
> go where the Spirit leads you,
> the wife is the extension [*le prolongement*] of the husband.
> Go where the Spirit leads you,
> as the Church is the extension [*le prolongement*] of Christ.[58]

Poems for Mi displays a number of influences on Messiaen at this time, especially those of Gregorian chant and Hindu rhythms. From the outset of the first movement, "Thanksgiving," the addition and subtraction of note values characterizing the *Nativity* are employed. In tandem with these syncopations, both the opening and closing movements are distinguished by elaborate melismatic lines, a seeming extension of Messiaen's "Vocalise-Study" published the previous year.[59] Evocative of plainchant, the soprano vocalizes the syllable "ah": on the word "Alleluia" in the first piece ("Thanksgiving") and on the word *âme* (soul) in the final piece ("Fulfilled Prayer"). The same technique is used in the horrifying fourth movement ("Terror") that concludes the first of the two "books" of poems: here the vocalization occurs on the fearful outburst — *Ha!*

"Terror" is intended to instill fear in the listener. As such, it displays Messiaen's propensity for opposite contrasts: the contentment of "Thanksgiving" is juxtaposed in "Terror" with an apocalyptic account of life's end:

> Ha, ha, ha, ha, ha, ha, ha, ho!
> Do not hide your memories in the earth, you might not find
> them again.
> Do not drag, nor crumple, nor tear.
> Bleeding tatters will follow you into the darkness
> like spasmodic vomiting,
> and the loud collision of the bolts of the door of no return

---

58. Messiaen, "The Wife" ("L'Épouse"), in *Poems for Mi,* in *Complete Edition,* 306.

59. Messiaen, *Vocalise-Étude pour voix élevées* (Paris: Alphonse Leduc, 1935). At the end of his life, Messiaen reworked this melody, one of his most beautiful, for oboe and orchestra. This "Vocalise" is the second movement in the *Concert à Quatre,* unfinished at the time of his death in 1992. It was premiered posthumously in 1994. See Simeone, *Bibliographical Catalogue,* 48-49, 184.

will energize your despair
to sate the fiery powers.⁶⁰

Just as in *Three Melodies* and *The Resplendent Tomb,* Messiaen imitates the surrealist rhetoric of Reverdy and Éluard.⁶¹ (Indeed, throughout the 1930s, surrealism had gained in strength, becoming increasingly apocalyptic as the Spanish Civil War approached and exploded in this same summer.) The grotesque language and mixed metaphors of "Terror" echo those found in "The Two Warriors" — "Your eye in my eye among the marching statues, / among the black howls, the downpours / of sulfurous geometries." Small wonder that one reviewer remarked: "The *Poems for Mi* of Olivier Messiaen, or nine melodies for voice and piano on the sacrament of marriage, are definitely not made for converting the unmarried [*célibataires*]. What harshness, and after the harshness, why so many false notes in our black landscape? The great masters knew how to render sadness more attractive. However, every now and then a charming sensibility breaks through."⁶² In *Poems,* terrestrial life is beautiful but ephemeral, eventually broken up by terrifying forces. The only lasting hope is to be found in the final movement ("Fulfilled Prayer"), celebrating the heart's "day of glory and Resurrection!" in a world beyond the boundaries of time.⁶³

There is a faint hint here that Messiaen had already begun reading Thomas Aquinas on the "glorified bodies" of resurrected human beings — a topic he would treat systematically three years later in *Glorified Bodies* (summer 1939). For example, in the third movement ("The House"), Messiaen again meditates on terrestrial ephemerality:

We shall be leaving this house:
I see it in your eye . . .
We shall *leave our bodies too.*

In the end, however, he concludes that all these "images of sorrow" will disappear

---

60. Messiaen, "Terror" ("Épouvante"), in *Poems for Mi,* 305-6.
61. Messiaen acknowledged his attempts to imitate Reverdy and Éluard; see Massin and Messiaen, *Olivier Messiaen,* 94.
62. "R.F.," review of the *Poems for Mi* performance (January 22, 1938), in *Le Ménestrel* 100, no. 4 (January 28, 1938): 21; excerpt in Simeone, *Bibliographical Catalogue,* 220-21.
63. Messiaen, "Fulfilled Prayer" ("Prière exaucée"), in *Poems for Mi,* 307-8, at 308.

1935–1939: Theological Turn, Young France, Baby Pascal

When we contemplate Truth,
in bodies that are pure, young and eternally luminous [*éternellement lum ineux*].[64]

Aquinas's term *clarté* (brilliance) does not yet appear here as one of the attributes of risen bodies, but *lumineux* suggests that Messiaen had begun focusing on their "lighted" aspect. It is worth reading Messiaen's extremely detailed analysis of the theme of "light" in Dukas's *Ariadne and Bluebeard,* which analysis appeared in the June 1936 issue of *La Revue musicale* just as Messiaen was leaving for summer vacation. (Dukas had died in April the previous year.) "The glow of 'Light' permeates the ensuing calm only to start up again as the act concludes with a kind of ethereal gigue," wrote Messiaen, "a frenzied dance in the clouds amidst the joys of *luminosity.* If I were asked what I like most in *Ariane et Barbe-bleue,* I would mention the scene with the precious stones. . . . But, above all else, I would put that inspired crescendo from dark to light that makes the second act not only Paul Dukas's masterpiece, but one of the masterpieces of all music."[65]

The "eternally luminous bodies" point to a broader shift: Messiaen now specifies "bodies" rather than the amorphous "souls" found in *The Lovable Host of Souls* (1928) and the *Simple Song of a Soul* (1930), the First and Second Souls in *The Death of Number* (1930), and the "souls" found in movements 2 and 3 of *Ascension* (organ version, 1933). While small in itself, the shift from "souls" to "bodies" suggests an enormous transition in imagining the "celestial life" of the beyond at the heart of Messiaen's music. It offers one more indication of the tonal shift from the "mystical" to the "theological" made between 1932 and 1935.

As in Dukas, precious stones (both luminous and colored) also figure here. In "Landscape," yet another imitation of the surrealists, the lake is "like a big blue jewel" — repeated three times — and so too is Mi: "There she is, green and blue like the landscape!"[66] "The Necklace," a lush impressionistic

---

64. Messiaen, "The House" ("La Maison"), in *Poems for Mi,* 305, translation altered, emphasis added.

65. Olivier Messiaen, "*Ariane et Barbe-bleue* de Paul Dukas" ("Paul Daukas's *Ariane et Barbe-bleue*"), *La Revue musicale* 166 (1936): 79-86; in *Olivier Messiaen: Journalism, 1935-1939,* Fr 15-21, at 20; Eng 79-84, at 83, emphasis added. One year earlier, on the death of Dukas, Messiaen had composed his *Pièce* for the collection *Le Tombeau de Paul Dukas: neuf pièces inédites composées pour piano, à la mémoire de Paul Dukas* (Paris: Revue Musicale, 1936), 23-24; cf. Simeone, *Bibliographical Catalogue,* 50-51.

66. Messiaen, "Landscape" ("Paysage"), in *Poems for Mi,* 305.

piece highly evocative of Debussy, begins with the colors of the "pale morning rainbow," which are then compared to the "Oriental necklace, chosen necklace multicolored with pearls both hard and comical!" The surrealism here is amplified by a slight synesthetic reference, as the necklace is a "tiny living cushion" of many colors bringing comfort to "my weary ears" rather than (as logically expected) worn-out eyes.[67]

A final thematic trope worth noting: as in earlier works, the Eucharist is the structural image that holds the work together. The first movement ("Thanksgiving") concludes with the divine "gifts" — one might almost say the "forgotten offerings" — for which the singer is grateful:

And Thou hast also given me Thyself,
in obedience and in the blood of Thy Cross,
and in a Bread sweeter than the freshness of the stars,
Lord God.
Alleluia.[68]

The final movement ("Fulfilled Prayer") similarly praises the Eucharist as healing balm for the "lone, old mountain of sorrow" and the "bitter waters of my heart":

O Jesus, Thou living Bread who givest life,
say but a single word and my soul will be healed.[69]

Around the middle of November in 1936, following Messiaen's premiere of *The Nativity* and the summertime composition of sacramental marriage poems, Claire once again conceived. During this pregnancy, Claire wrote a work for voice and piano entitled *The Budding Soul,* a musical setting of Cécile Sauvage's poems written three decades earlier during her pregnancy with Messiaen. Once again (as with her setting of poems from *Primrose,* pub-

---

67. Messiaen, "The Necklace" ("Le Collier"), in *Poems for Mi,* 307, translation altered.
68. Messiaen, "Thanksgiving *(Action de grâces),*" in *Poems for Mi,* 304-5, at 305.
69. Messiaen, "Fulfilled Prayer," 307. The line is a paraphrase from words spoken three times by the priest at Catholic Mass just before receiving the Eucharist: "Domine, non sum dignus, ut intres sub tectum meum: sed tantum dic verbo, et sanabitur anima mea" (Seigneur, je ne suis pas digne que vous entriez sous mon toit; mais dites seulement une parole, et mon âme sera guérie) (Lord, I am not worthy that Thou shouldst enter under my roof; but only say the word, and my soul shall be healed). The formula quotes words addressed to Jesus by the Roman centurion (Matt. 8:8). *Missal-En,* 790; *Missel-Fr,* 606.

lished in 1935), the score prominently featured the two women's names on the cover: "On Poems of CÉCILE SAUVAGE. Music by CLAIRE DELBOS."[70] The poems:

1. "Sleep"
2. "My heart's returning to its springtime . . ."
3. "I am here"
4. "And so you've left the nurturing cell"
5. "I knew it would be you . . ."
6. "And now he's born . . ."
7. "There you are, my little lover . . ."
8. "Could I have called you then from darkness . . ."[71]

In a typically audacious gesture, Messiaen reviewed his wife's work for the column "Notes from Paris" in the Belgian journal *La Sirène* in June 1937. He did not mention that the composer was his wife, the texts were by his mother, their subject matter was he himself, or that both he and Claire were cofounders of La Spirale: "Concerning the private concerts, I must point out first of all a song cycle for voice and piano by Claire Delbos: *L'Âme en bourgeon*, given by La Spirale. This cycle, of a passionate, tender and sad feminine sensibility, ornaments and delightfully embraces Cécile Sauvage's maternity poems." Messiaen then publicized La Jeune France, again without mentioning his own name as the group's fourth member: "I must also mention the sensational Jeune France symphonic concert that, under the magical direction of Roger Désormière, delighted the Parisian public with some sumptuous *premières* by Yves Baudrier, André Jolivet and Daniel-Lesur."[72]

---

70. *L'Âme en Bourgeon. Huit Mélodies avec accompagnement de piano*, Cécile Sauvage and Claire Delbos (Paris: Editions Fortin, 1937).

71. See poem numbers and pages from the Weller translation of *The Budding Soul* in *Olivier Messiaen: Music, Art, and Literature,* ed. Christopher Dingle and Nigel Simeone (Burlington, Vt.: Ashgate, 2007): "Sleep" (X, 225); "My heart's returning to its springtime . . ." (VIII, 215); "I am here" (VI, 210); "And so you've left the nurturing cell" (XI, 229); "I knew it would be you . . ." (XIV, 237); "And now he's born . . ." (XIII, 233); "There you are, my little lover . . ." (XVI, 241); "Could I have called you then from darkness . . ." (III, 201).

72. Olivier Messiaen, "Billet parisien" ("Notes from Paris"), *La Sirène* (June 1937): 14; in *Olivier Messiaen: Journalism, 1935-1939*, Fr 29; Eng 92.

1932–1943: Theological Order, Glorified Bodies, Apocalyptic Epoch

Charles Tournemire: Conflicted Connections?

A curious entry in Tournemire's memoirs written around the first week of October 1936 indicates that the master had grown both suspicious and jealous of his former apprentice. Tournemire wrote out by hand the melody to *Ascension*'s fourth movement ("Prayer of Christ Rising to His Father") so as to ridicule it. Then, attacking the "more or less distinguished amateurs" making a fuss in the press about the "genius" and the "renewal of organ music" by the "under 30" crowd, Tournemire complained about Messiaen's piece: "Here, among many others, is a sad example of the melodic destitution [*d'indigence mélodique*] that characterizes an organ music about which they speak today like some kind of revelation." Following the handwritten musical score, Tournemire added: "The rest is even more ugly. (*) The harmonies are implausible. It is a sauce in which the pepper and every kind of ingredient have been thrown together."[73] It is a mark of Tournemire's prickly personality that this October entry was written *after* the appearance of Messiaen's strongly enthusiastic review of his newly published text on organ technique in late June 1936.[74] Moreover, as already noted, it was Tournemire who had invited Messiaen to come to Sainte-Clotilde and play *Ascension;* when Messiaen did so on April 4, 1935, the audience numbered only seventy listeners.

The former mentor's jealousy of Messiaen's success is understandable: by the time of *Ascension*'s appearance in print (November 1934), the publication of Tournemire's mammoth *L'Orgue Mystique* had been going for six years (i.e., since 1928); the last volume would not appear until 1936. The contrast between its tepid reception and the enthusiasm stirred by the young Messiaen's work must have been a bitter pill for the old master.[75] But Messiaen's problematic

---

73. Charles Tournemire, journal entry for "From the end of September to October 1936," *Mémoires (1886-1939)*, 152-53. However, Tournemire's memoirs are not an entirely reliable source. They survive only in typewritten form, the handwritten originals having been destroyed after being transcribed (and edited) by Mme. Alice (*née* Espir) Tournemire. Thus, what remains is what Mme. Tournemire intended for posterity. (In the typescript, the [*] indicates excised material.) I am deeply grateful to the late Mme. Tournemire's niece, Mme. Odile Weber, for her kind permission to consult Tournemire's *Mémoires*.

74. Olivier Messiaen, review of "Charles Tournemire: *Précis d'exécution de registration et d'improvisation à l'orgue,*" *Le Monde musical* (June 30, 1936): 186; in *Olivier Messiaen: Journalism, 1935-1939*, Fr 53; Eng 115-16; cf. Broad, "Recontextualising Messiaen's Early Career," 1:53-54.

75. One example of Tournemire's chagrin over the *L'Orgue Mystique*'s reception can be found in the same journal entry containing the transcription from Messiaen's *L'Ascension:* "Priests in Frankfurt are organizing a Congress of Catholic Music. Naturally, *l'Orgue*

relationship with his former master was not unique. Following Tournemire's marriage to Alice Espir (his second wife) on July 18, 1934, Tournemire had a general falling-out with nearly everyone around him, including Daniel-Lesur, Langlais, and Messiaen. Langlais attributed this largely to what he perceived as Mme. Espir-Tournemire's "deceitful and manipulative" personality.[76]

Messiaen's relationship with Tournemire became the subject of a strange public exchange in early 1937 in the journal *La Page musicale*.[77] On February 5, Messiaen's article "Religious Music" appeared. Distinguishing between types of music that might be considered "religious," Messiaen wrote: *"Mystical music [La mystique] occupies a much higher rung [than conventional music]. But beware the false ecstasies of a vaguely religious sentiment! There are few truly mystical musicians [de vrais musiciens mystiques]*."[78] On February 19, Eugène Berteaux — who had written the libretto text for Tournemire's opera *The Gods Are Dead* almost twenty-five years earlier — accused Messiaen of asserting that Tournemire was dead.[79] Messiaen responded with an open letter to Berteaux published on February 26: "Placing Tournemire among the dead? Where the devil did you get that from? I wrote to him only yesterday . . . (do you perhaps suppose that I correspond with the other side? . . .)."[80] The episode closed with Berteaux's open letter to Messiaen pub-

---

Mystique is being excluded. It is in the order [of things], or rather, the disorder!! Oh the traitors!!" Tournemire, "From the end of September to October 1936," *Mémoires (1886-1939)*, 152.

76. James E. Frazier, *Maurice Duruflé: The Man and His Music* (Rochester, N.Y.: University of Rochester Press, 2007), 28; Ann Labounsky, *Jean Langlais: The Man and His Music* (Portland, Ore.: Amadeus Press, 2000), 106; cf. Andrew Thomson: ". . . by the 1930s, Tournemire — whose eight orchestral symphonies and three operas brought him little acclaim in the public arena — had become a depressed character, isolated from the wider musical world and, under the interfering Alice's not entirely helpful influence, estranged from some of his most devoted disciples, among them Messiaen and Daniel-Lesur." Thomson, "His Master's Voice," review of *"Dear Maître Tournemire": Charles Tournemire's Correspondence with Felix Aprahamian and His Visit to London in 1936*, ed. Nigel Simeone (Bangor, 2003), in *Musical Times* 144, no. 1884 (Autumn 2003): 66-67, at 66.

77. For this exchange see *Olivier Messiaen: Journalism, 1935-1939*, Fr 63-68; Eng 125-29.

78. Messiaen, "Musique religieuse" ("Religious Music"), *La Page musicale* (February 5, 1937): 1; in *Olivier Messiaen: Journalism, 1935-1939*, Fr 63-64; Eng 125.

79. For Berteaux and Tournemire collaboration, see Schloesser, *Jazz Age Catholicism*, 294-97.

80. Messiaen, "Derrière ou Devant la Porte? . . . (Lettre ouverte à M. Eugène Berteaux)" ("Behind or in Front of the Door? . . . [Open Letter to M. Eugène Berteaux]"), *La Page musicale* (February 26, 1937): 1; in *Olivier Messiaen: Journalism, 1935-1939*, Fr 65-67, at 66; Eng 127-28, at 127.

lished on March 5. Here it became clear that Berteaux had been expressing Tournemire's own anger in the episode — even as he was corresponding directly with Messiaen. "As for Charles Tournemire who, by a lack of precision, thought he had found himself sealed behind the heavy bronze door marked *in pace* — with rather too many flowers and wreaths heaped against it — you have certainly rescued him from this bad dream and taken pleasure today in paying deserved respect to 'his *language which is as new as it is inspired.*' It's perfect!"[81] Whatever his relationship with Tournemire after this exchange, Messiaen worked at promoting Tournemire's music. In May 1937 he published a review of Tournemire's *Postludes Libres,* and a year later he published an extremely enthusiastic review of *L'Orgue Mystique.*[82] Finally, Messiaen paid Tournemire the highest possible praise in his article "Sacred Music" that appeared in June-July 1939: "In *L'Orgue mystique,* Charles Tournemire shows how, on the contrary, one can modernize plainchant, adapt polytonality and Debussy's harmonies to the jubilant arabesques of the alleluias, in a rhythm at once supple and strikingly contemporary. Such a work is truly Catholic, liturgical and living. It is, perhaps, at this moment, the masterpiece of sacred art."[83] Weeks after this article appeared, the Second World War broke out and Messiaen was mobilized for the military. That November, after Sainte-Clotilde was shuttered because of its close proximity to the War Ministry, Tournemire died unexpectedly (and, to some, suspiciously).[84] In light of this tragic ending to a troubled relationship, perhaps Messiaen was grateful that he had concluded his review of Tournemire's *L'Orgue Mystique* in eschatological terms. Tournemire's final movement for Septuagesima Sunday, wrote Messiaen, "seems to comment on a phrase [*semble commenter une parole*] by Saint Paul in the day's epistle: 'Like a wrestler in the ring, I will run, I will fight, to win an incorruptible crown.'"[85]

---

81. Berteaux, "Devant ou Derrière la Porte? . . . (Réponse ouverte à M. Olivier Messiaen)" ("In Front of or Behind the Door? . . . [Open Response to M. Olivier Messiaen]"), *La Page musicale* (March 5, 1937): 1; Fr 67-68, at 68; Eng 128-29, at 129.

82. Messiaen, "*Post Ludes* [sic] *Libres* (Charles Tournemire)," *Le Monde musical* (May 31, 1937): 138; and "Billet Parisien: *L'Orgue mystique* de Tournemire" ("Notes from Paris: *L'Orgue Mystique* by Charles Tournemire"), *La Syrinx* (May 1938): 26-27; in *Olivier Messiaen: Journalism, 1935-1939,* Fr 54, 41-42; Eng 117, 101-3. Cf. Schloesser, *Jazz Age Catholicism,* 311.

83. Messiaen, "De la Musique sacrée" ("On Sacred Music"), *Carrefour* (June-July 1939 [double issue]): 75; in *Olivier Messiaen: Journalism, 1935-1939,* Fr 74-76; Eng 135-37, at 137.

84. Schloesser, *Jazz Age Catholicism,* 321.

85. Messiaen, "*L'Orgue mystique* de Tournemire," Fr 42; Eng 103.

1935–1939: Theological Turn, Young France, Baby Pascal

Summer 1937: Birth of Pascal and the International Exhibition

On April 28, 1937, when Claire's *Budding Soul* was premiered along with Messiaen's *Poems for Mi,* Claire was five and a half months pregnant with Pascal. The double premiere took place in a concert at the Schola Cantorum with Marcelle Bunlet singing and Messiaen accompanying. The same reviewer who disputed Messiaen's "harshness" and "false notes in a black landscape" had kinder words for Claire: *"The Budding Soul* of Mme. Claire Delbos, on eight poems about maternity, signals the possession of a very expressive talent. The great overall equality of the work makes a choice more difficult; however, we very much appreciated 'I am here' and 'And so you've left the nurturing cell.' "[86]

Messiaen quickly orchestrated the first movement of *Poems* — "Thanksgiving" — and premiered it on June 4. Like the *Nativity,* one wonders whether it wasn't intended as a votive offering for the health of both mother and child as Pascal's due date the following month drew near.[87] That same month also saw the publication of Messiaen's best-selling work, his choral arrangement of the ancient hymn "O Sacrum Convivium!" (subtitled a "Motet to the Blessed Sacrament").[88]

O sacrum convivium,	O sacred banquet [or: feast],
in quo Christus sumitur:	in which Christ is received:
recolitur memoria passionis eius;	the memory of His Passion is renewed;
mens impletur gratia	the mind is filled with grace
et futurae gloriae nobis pignus datur.	and a pledge of future glory given to us.

---

86. "R.F." (January 28, 1938), in Simeone, *Bibliographical Catalogue,* 220-21, at 221.

87. Although the phrase *action de grâce* may be translated simply as "thanksgiving," it connotes an action undertaken as an act of thanks or offering for some "grace" that has been received. Musically speaking, it was traditional to sing the Te Deum as such an act of thanksgiving. Note the title of Jean Langlais's *Hymne d'action de grâce "Te Deum"* from his *Three Gregorian Paraphrases (Trois paraphrases grégoriennes),* op. 5, 1933-1934; cf. Labounsky, *Jean Langlais,* 81-84.

88. "Since its first publication [in June 1937], *O sacrum convivium!* has been reprinted many times, and it is almost certainly Messiaen's best-selling work. According to Durand's printing records, it was reprinted 18 times between Jan 1954 (the first reprint, of 1000 copies) and Dec 1991 (the last printing before Messiaen's death, of 10,195 copies), amounting to a total of over 138,000 copies." Simeone, *Bibliographical Catalogue,* 60-61, at 61.

Undoubtedly, Messiaen was attracted to this particular text written by Thomas Aquinas in part because of its focus on time. Both past and future intersect as the mind is filled with grace in the present; the memory of Christ's passion *(memoria passionis)* in the past is renewed; and the Eucharist is given as a pledge of future glory *(futurae gloriae)* — as a "foretaste" *(praegustatum),* in the words of the later eucharistic hymn, "Ave Verum Corpus."

The following month, in what must have been an event brimming with anxious apprehension and profound relief, Pascal was born on Bastille Day (July 14) 1937. Why the name Pascal? It is tempting to think that Messiaen and Claire chose it for its evocation of Blaise Pascal, quintessential French philosopher, mathematician, literary artisan, and religious icon — perhaps in honor of Claire's father? Another connotation is suggested in "Rainbow of Innocence," one of the songs Messiaen would write for him the following summer:

You wriggle
like the clapper of a paschal bell [*de cloche pascal*].[89]

"Pascal" is the adjectival form of *Pâques* — that is, "Easter."

Two short weeks later, Messiaen's *Festival of Beautiful Waters,* an experimental work scored for a sextet of Ondes Martenot, was performed as part of the 1937 Paris world's fair. Officially entitled the International Exhibition of Arts and Technologies, the mammoth event ran from May 4 through November 27.[90] In terms of world politics, the fair was intended to present an image of "open" France in stark contrast to Germany's Nazi regime.[91] On the domestic scene, the socialist Popular Front government (which had come to power one year earlier) commissioned works like Messiaen's *Festival* in support of "popular" artistic endeavors, especially in this time of global economic depression.[92]

The "Festivals of Sound, Water, and Color" were an audiovisual spectacle

---

89. Messiaen, "Rainbow of Innocence (for My Little Pascal)" ("Arc-en-ciel d'innocence [pour mon petit Pascal]"), in *Songs of Earth and Sky (Chants de Terre et de Ciel),* trans. John Underwood, in *Complete Edition,* 308-14, at 312.

90. James D. Herbert, *Paris 1937: Worlds on Exhibition* (Ithaca, N.Y.: Cornell University Press, 1998); Shanny Peer, *France on Display: Peasants, Provincials, and Folklore in the 1937 Paris World's Fair* (Albany: State University of New York Press, 1998).

91. However, a recent book suggests that the event might have had the opposite effect as Germany's pavilion "seduced" the French. See Karen Fiss, *Grand Illusion: The Third Reich, the Paris Exposition, and the Cultural Seduction of France* (Chicago: University of Chicago Press, 2010).

92. Fulcher, *The Composer as Intellectual,* 199-241.

1935–1939: Theological Turn, Young France, Baby Pascal

that took place on and beside the Seine River between July 2 and August 29. At least fifteen musicians composed their sound and light shows, which began at 10 P.M. Since the summer sun in Paris sets so late, the effect of these concerts beginning as twilight set in must have been enchanting.[93] Titles included "1001 Nights," "Living Waters," "Dream," "Fire," and *"Fantastique."* Messiaen's own work was listed as *Great Waters* in the calendar of events.[94] Messiaen's piece must have had a remarkable effect: the melody includes the hauntingly melancholic section that was reworked three years later (in a German prisoner of war camp) as "Praise to the Eternity of Jesus," the fifth movement for cello and piano in *Quartet for the End of Time;* the sound of the six electronic instruments is unearthly, even heard today on a recording; and of course, it took place in the ambience of the warm summer's night show along the Seine. In the photograph showing the seven female performers (including the conductor), all are seated "wearing long white dresses in a flowing antique style."[95]

Messiaen's *Great Waters* was performed on Sunday, July 25 — eleven days after the birth of Pascal. Years later he explained his choice of instruments: "Since the music was, in any case, to be amplified by loudspeakers placed on all the buildings lining the Seine, the Onde Martenot seemed a marvellously apt choice for these outdoor performances. Specialized architects brought me enormous plans with detailed timing indications for the various parts of the display which had been allocated to me."[96] Although such a description might give a reader the impression of a twentieth-century version of Handel's *Music for Royal Fireworks,* the imagery Messiaen had in mind was something altogether different — with typically surrealistic juxtapositions:

> The music reflects the mystery of the night, the funereal aspect of the deep water, and the joyous, playful, carefree character of the fireworks. The jets of water, by contrast, seemed to be either fierce and terrible, or dream-like

---

93. For contemporaneous plans and accounts, see Nigel Simeone, "Music at the 1937 Paris Exposition: The Science of Enchantment," *Musical Times* 143, no. 1878 (Spring, 2002): 9-17.

94. For calendar see Simeone, *Bibliographical Catalogue,* 192-94. Messiaen listed the commissioned composers and gave descriptions of several of the works in his review of "Les Fêtes de la lumière" for *La Sirène* (July 1937). Messiaen, "Billet Parisien: *Les Fêtes de la lumière* ("Notes from Paris: The *Fêtes de la lumière*"), *La Sirène* (July 1937): 18-19; in *Olivier Messiaen: Journalism, 1935-1939,* Fr 30-31; Eng 92-94.

95. Photograph reproduced in *Beaux Arts,* Hors série no. 35, "Musée de la Musique" (Paris, 1996); described in Simeone, *Bibliographical Catalogue,* 192.

96. Messiaen commentary reprinted in the booklet for the 1996 recording; in Simeone, *Bibliographical Catalogue,* 194.

and contemplative. It is this last mood that predominates, and in the most worthwhile moments of *Fêtes des belles eaux* when, on two occasions, the jets of water shoot up to a great height, a long, slow phrase is heard — almost a prayer — which makes the water a symbol of Grace and Eternity, as in the words from the Gospel according to Saint John: "Anyone who drinks the water that I shall give will never be thirsty again: the water that I shall give will turn into a spring inside him, welling up to eternal life."[97]

Even here hovers the spirit of Dom Marmion: we need "to contemplate Him so as to conform our own lives . . . so that our thirst may be fully quenched," writes Marmion, for this knowledge is "a fountain of water, springing up into life everlasting."[98] Two years later, Messiaen echoed both John's Gospel and Marmion in his musical call to arms: "To express with its long-lasting power the struggle between darkness and the Holy Spirit, to throw open the doors of our flesh prison to the mountains, to give to our century of pistons, motors and killing machines *the living water that it needs,* would require a great artist, who must be as great a craftsman as he is a Christian."[99]

One particularly chilling image at the International Exhibition would soon become one of the century's most recognizable icons. On April 26, 1937, Guernica (in the Basque country of Spain) had been aerially bombarded by Hitler's and Mussolini's planes at the request of Francisco Franco's Spanish Nationalists.[100] In response, the leftist Spanish government commissioned Pablo Picasso to paint a commemorative work. He unveiled *Guernica,* one of the most iconic works of the twentieth century, at the Exhibition's Spanish Pavilion on May 23. Thus, although intended to be a festive event in the midst of the Great Depression, the gathering clouds of world war were fully evident at the 1937 fair, especially with the pavilions of Hitler's Germany and Stalin's Soviet Union competing for prominence and grandeur.[101]

---

97. Messiaen commentary quoting John 4:14; in Simeone, *Bibliographical Catalogue,* 194.

98. Marmion, *Christ in His Mysteries,* 9, 11.

99. Messiaen, "De la Musique sacrée" ("On Sacred Music") (June-July 1939), in *Olivier Messiaen: Journalism, 1935-1939,* Fr 74-76, at 76; Eng 135-37, at 137, emphasis added.

100. Russell Martin and Pablo Picasso, *Picasso's War: The Destruction of Guernica and the Masterpiece That Changed the World* (New York: Dutton, 2002); Gijs Van Hensbergen and Pablo Picasso, *Guernica: The Biography of a Twentieth-Century Icon* (New York: Bloomsbury, 2004).

101. Benjamin F. Martin, *France in 1938* (Baton Rouge: Louisiana State University Press, 2006); Talbot C. Imlay, *Facing the Second World War: Strategy, Politics, and Economics in Britain and France, 1938-1940* (New York: Oxford University Press, 2003).

1935–1939: Theological Turn, Young France, Baby Pascal

Ironically, the fair's leftist sponsor did not survive the event. Thanks to a worsening economy, a conservative parliament was voted into office, and the Popular Front effectively fell out of power on June 21, 1937, a little over a year after its victory, and about two months after the world's fair opened. Internal divisions about intervening in the Spanish Civil War caused the alliance to dissolve in late 1938.[102] This sharp political shift to the right would eventually provide a measure of continuity between the conservative French governments of 1938-1939 and the Vichy government after the German victory in 1940. The epoch had turned apocalyptic.

Summer 1938: From *Prisms* to *Songs of Earth and Sky*

In 1938, Messiaen once again spent the summer at Petichet, Isère, where he composed a work for voice and piano initially entitled *Prisms,* suggestive of the color spectrum produced by white light's passage through a prism.[103] This cycle of six songs continued the domestic focus that marked the previous year's *Poems for Mi* but with the new addition brought by baby Pascal's birth. The first four songs concerned Messiaen's wife and son:

1. "Union with Mi (for My Wife)"
2. "Antiphon of Silence (for the [Feast] Day of the Guardian Angels)"
3. "Dance of Baby-'Pill' (for My Little Pascal)"
4. "Rainbow of Innocence (for My Little Pascal)"

Although the topics suggest material easily sentimentalized (marriage, parenthood, childhood, domestic life), Messiaen used these pieces to experiment further in abstraction, a move effected by increased atonality and textual surrealism. The influence of Second Viennese atonalism may have come from the openness to "cultural exchange" already highlighted in the agenda of La Spirale and works by members of La Jeune France.

In particular, the "Antiphon of Silence" points ahead to the "Liturgy of Crystal" movement in *Quartet for the End of Time,* which would be composed and premiered during Messiaen's incarceration in a German prisoner of war

---

102. Julian T. Jackson, *Popular Front in France: Defending Democracy, 1934-1938* (New York: Cambridge University Press, 1988).

103. Simeone, *Bibliographical Catalogue,* 62-63. *Prisms* is later renamed *Songs of Earth and Sky* (or *Heaven*) *(Chants de Terre et de Ciel)* for voice and piano.

camp. Similarly, the text of the "Antiphon" of the "silent angel" prefigures *Quartet*'s "Vocalise for the Angel Who Announces the End of Time." Messiaen also extends his use of vocalization seen in "Vocalise" (1935) and *Poems for Mi*. However, the "Ha!" vocalized in the *Poems'* "Terror" now becomes the laughter of baby Pascal as he first attempts to say "Mama": "Malonlanlaine, ma. / Ma, ma, ma, io! Ha, ha, ha, ha, ha!"[104] The technique points ahead to *Harawi* (1945) and eventually *Five Refrains* (1948), in which the syllables will come from an invented language.

The final two movements form a diptych dedicated respectively to death and resurrection:

5. "Facing Up to Midnight Sharp *(for Death)*"
6. "Resurrection *(for Easter Day)*"

Messiaen's trademark juxtaposition of death and resurrection suggests a surrealist's eye. Indeed, by the late 1930s surrealism had become highly politicized as a mode of expressing apocalyptic despair over politics, especially in the Spaniards Picasso, Salvador Dali, and Joan Miró, who were horrified by their native land's civil war.[105] In particular, it seems likely that Messiaen would have been deeply influenced by the 1938 International Exhibition of Surrealism (Exposition Internationale du Surréalisme) preceding his summertime composition of *Prisms*. The epochal gathering in Paris, held between January 17 and February 24, occasioned a seminal publication: the *Summary Dictionary of Surrealism* by André Breton and Paul Éluard.[106]

In an article written to defend *Prisms* against critics, Messiaen himself

---

104. Messiaen, "Dance of Baby 'Pill' *(for My Little Pascal)*" ("Danse du bébé-Pilule *[pour mon petit Pascal]*"), *Songs of Earth and Sky*, 310-11, at 310.

105. See Steven Harris, *Surrealist Art and Thought in the 1930s: Art, Politics, and the Psyche* (New York: Cambridge University Press, 2004); Johanna Malt, *Obscure Objects of Desire: Surrealism, Fetishism, and Politics* (New York: Oxford University Press, 2004); Anne Umland, James Coddington, Joan Miró, et al., *Joan Miró: Painting and Anti-painting, 1927-1937* (New York: Museum of Modern Art, distributed in the United States and Canada by DAP/Distributed Art Publishers, 2008); Suzanne Pacé, *Années 30 en Europe: le temps menaçant 1929-1939: exposition du 20 février au 25 mai 1997, Musée d'art moderne de la ville de Paris* (Paris: Paris musées: Flammarion, 1997).

106. André Breton and Paul Éluard, *Dictionnaire abrégé du surréalisme. Photographies, illustrations, lettrines* (Paris: J. Corti, 1991; original, Paris: Galerie des beaux-arts, 1938). See Annabelle Görgen, *Exposition internationale du Surréalisme, Paris 1938. Bluff und Täuschung — Die Ausstellung als Werk. Einflüsse aus dem 19. Jahrhundert unter dem Aspekt der Kohärenz* (Munich: Schreiber, 2008); Elena Filipovic, "Surrealism in 1938: The Exhibition at War," in

called the fifth song — "Facing Up to Midnight Sharp" — the "central part of this work." His main intention, he wrote, was to express "remorse, the prayers, the anguish of agony amidst nocturnal bells, followed by the celestial release of death" — once more, a variation on the juxtaposed "terrestrial life" and "blessed eternity" of *Diptych* (1930). In this piece, the overall initial sound image is a clock striking exactly midnight — a "Clock-strike, my bones vibrate, / sudden number" — which reveals itself as the accumulation of sin and error — "debris of error and of the circles to the left, / nine, ten, eleven, twelve."[107] Messiaen knew Paris's nocturnal underbelly from his years of living in the Marais. He described midnight in the city streets in language both surrealist and Baudelairean, evocative of the urban pavement's spleen:

> City, stinking eye,
> devious midnights,
> rusty nails stuck in the corners of oblivion.
> Lamb, Lord!
>
> They dance,
> my sins dance!
>
> Deceitful carnival of the pavements of death.
> Great body of the streets all rotten
> beneath the hard street-lamps.
> Cross-road of fear!
> Cloak of madness and pride![108]

The terrifying scene is redeemed in the final movement, "Resurrection," which begins again with a vocalization on "Alleluia!" But even here, the lush romantic melismatic lines of *Poems for Mi* have given way to the influence of Viennese atonalism, giving the "resurrection" a cold, sharp, crystalline edge resisting sentimentalism:

> We have touched him, we have seen him.
> We touched him with our hands. [cf. 1 John 1:1]

Surrealism, Politics, and Culture, ed. Raymond Spiteri and Donald LaCoss (Burlington, Vt.: Ashgate, 2003), 179-203; and Herbert, *Paris 1937*.

107. Messiaen, "Midnight Obverse and Reverse *(to Death)*" ("Minuit Pile et Face [*pour la mort*]"), in *Songs of Earth and Sky*, 312-14, at 312.

108. Messiaen, "Midnight Obverse and Reverse *(to Death),*" 312.

Clipped surrealistic fragments preserve emotional distance even in the acts of "seeing" and "touching." Alliteration lends itself to vocalization, as in the explosive *p* linking angel, rock, embalming, sepulchral door, jewel, and Eucharist:

> An angel. || *Un ange.*
> Posed atop the rock. || *Sur la pierre il s'est posé.*
> Perfume, portal, pearl, || *Parfum, porte, perle,*
> unleavened [breads] of Truth. || *azymes de la Vérité.*[109]

The surrealist's textual gaps force the imagination to make explosive connections: the literal reading is "unleaveneds of Truth" instead of "unleavened breads" *(pains azymes de la Vérité);* thus, what is "unleavened" is not the absent "[bread]" but rather the perfume, the door, the pearl — an allusion to the doors made of pearls in the celestial city.[110]

Significant for Messiaen's abiding interest in visions is embedding the Eucharist here in the context of postresurrection apparition narratives (e.g., the road to Emmaus). The Eucharist is an act of vision, revelation, and recognition:

> Bread. || *Du pain.*
> He breaks it and their eyes are opened. || *Il le rompt et leurs yeux sont dessillés.*
> Perfume, portal, pearl, / || *Parfum, porte, perle,* /
> wash yourselves in Truth. || *lavez-vous dans la Vérité.*[111]

A phrase using the word *clarté* appears twice:

> put on your garment of brightness. || *revêtez votre habit de clarté.*

---

109. Messiaen, "Resurrection *(for Easter Day)*" ("Résurrection *[pour le jour de Pâques]*"), *Songs of Earth and Sky,* 314. The angel "Posed atop the rock" refers to the rock that had covered the opening or door (*porte* = portal) of Christ's tomb: "Et voici qu'il se fit un grand tremblement de terre; car un Ange du Seigneur descendit du Ciel, et s'approchant, il renversa la pierre *et s'assit dessus*" (Matt. 28:2 [Fillion]). The next two verses contain two of Messiaen's favorite motifs, brilliance and terror: "Son visage *était comme l'éclair*, et son vêtement blanc comme la neige. A cause de lui les gardes furent *atterrés d'effroi*, et devinrent comme morts" (Fillion, emphasis added). Compare these same elements in the transfiguration, Matt. 17:2, 6.

110. The juxtaposition of *porte* and *perle* comes from the hymn for the dedication of churches: "Les portes en sont de perles brillantes" ("The doors are made of brilliant pearls"). See discussion above of *Apparition of the Eternal Church,* p. 176.

111. Messiaen, "Resurrection *(for Easter Day),*" 314.

1935–1939: Theological Turn, Young France, Baby Pascal

The "garment" refers primarily to the white dress worn by a baby at the reception of baptism. Secondarily, it refers to the garments worn by the resurrected after death: "These are they who have come out of the great tribulation; they have washed their robes and made them white in the blood of the Lamb."[112] The word used here is not *lumière* or *lumineux,* as in the previous year's *Poems of Mi*. It is *clarté,* the technical term (Latin: *claritas* = clarity, lightness, brightness) denoted by Aquinas as one of the four attributes of glorified bodies.[113] *Prisms* leans forward into the next year's *Glorified Bodies.*

Prisms's sharp edges evoked its milieu. A month after Messiaen finished its composition and returned to Paris for another academic year, Germany, France, and Great Britain signed the Munich Agreement (September 29), allowing Hitler to take Czechoslovakia. Cheered by the masses at the time, the "Munich Appeasement" would go down in history as a moment of cynicism, betrayal, and capitulation.[114] The Popular Front, torn apart by internal dissension over the Spanish Civil War, dissolved itself soon after. In the United States, Orson Welles's Halloween broadcast of "The War of the Worlds" (October 30) terrified many who believed that aliens from outer space were actually invading earth. Seventy-five years later the event seems inexplicable; but interviews conducted immediately after the panic reveal that Americans, too, rattled by ten years of economic depression and gathering war clouds in both Europe and Asia, transferred their anxieties onto the possibility of Martian invasion.[115]

This was the ominous context in which *Prisms* was first performed on January 23, 1939. A February review in *Le Ménestrel* made clear the impression of novelty upon hearing it. "*Prisms* reveals in its author a singular sincerity and sensibility in our day; a mystical inspiration [*inspiration mystique*] as we know, but served by expressive means that are absolutely new, speaking both melodically and rhythmically, tending to the primitive simplicity of Gregorian chant. The accompaniment of these six poems for soprano and piano, elaborate and quite difficult, requires a distinctive piano technique which in any case seems to be new."[116] Four months later, in April, *Prisms* was published under a new title — *Songs of Earth and Sky* — again reminiscent of

---

112. Rev. 7:14.

113. For *clarté,* see above (p. 119 n. 105) on "clartés nouvelles" in *Three Melodies.*

114. Giles MacDonogh, *1938: Hitler's Gamble* (New York: Basic Books, 2009); David Faber, *Munich, 1938: Appeasement and World War II* (New York: Simon and Schuster, 2008).

115. Hadley Cantril, with the assistance of Hazel Gaudet and Herta Herzog, *The Invasion from Mars: A Study in the Psychology of Panic* (Princeton: Princeton University Press, [1940] 1982).

116. Michel-Léon Hirsch, review of first performance of Messiaen's *Prisms (Prismes),*

1932–1943: Theological Order, Glorified Bodies, Apocalyptic Epoch

Messiaen's abiding interest in the terrestrial and eschatological, summarized exactly one decade earlier in *Diptych for Organ: An Essay on Terrestrial Life and Blessed Eternity*. (Was the new twofold title intended to echo the one ten years earlier?) Despite the new name, complaints about the work's "dissonance" prompted Messiaen to defend the work: "It is not extravagant! I have studied harmony, fugue and composition long enough to have the pretension to know my *métier*. . . . Certain pages of Schoenberg and Jolivet, and certain French and Russian folksongs, have also influenced me. Add to that that I like Massenet, because he is tonal and well harmonized, and you will have some idea of my style. As to those who bellow about my so-called dissonances, I tell them quite simply that I am not dissonant: let them wash out their ears!"[117] *Songs of Earth and Sky* never achieved the popularity of *Poems for Mi*, and Messiaen never orchestrated them. They were published just months before the outbreak of world war. The year 1938 was the last full year of peace for Europe.

Summer 1939: *Apocalypse, Eschatology, Glorified Bodies*

Messiaen's plans for yet another "theological" organ work to succeed *The Nativity* seem to have been in the background of his article entitled "Around an Organ Work," appearing contemporaneously in April 1939 with the article "Around a Publication." Here Messiaen argued against the notion that his organ works, "because of their titles and because they can and should be played during services," were "more religious than the rest of my catalogue." This was not the case, he asserted, and he further complained "that the label of 'mystic' — which was so kindly pinned to my back at the first performance of my *Banquet céleste* — does not correspond to the truth." Rather, he simply sought to express his "Christian and Catholic faith," and this "act of faith" had been translated "most satisfactorily" in *The Nativity*.[118] The organ work that he was about to compose in the coming summer months — *Glorified Bodies* — would take the "theological" even further beyond the vague "mystical."

January 23, 1939, *Le Ménestrel* 101, no. 5 (February 3, 1939): 28; in Simeone, *Bibliographical Catalogue*, 221.

117. Messiaen, "Autour d'une Parution" (April 30, 1939), in *Olivier Messiaen: Journalism, 1935-1939*, Fr 57-59, at 59; Eng 119-21, at 121; in translation in Nigel Simeone, "Offrandes oubliées: Messiaen in the 1930s," 41, quoted in Broad, "Recontextualising Messiaen's Early Career," 1:82-83.

118. Messiaen, "Autour d'une Œuvre d'orgue" ("Around an Organ Work") (April 1939), in *Olivier Messiaen: Journalism, 1935-1939*, Fr 73-74, at 73; Eng 134-35.

1935–1939: Theological Turn, Young France, Baby Pascal

Messiaen's turn to eschatological and even apocalyptic themes in *Prisms* already suggested tranquility's numbered days.[119] However, when Messiaen left Paris on June 28, 1939, for his summer vacation at Petichet in the Alps, he could hardly have known that he would soon no longer be a civilian. As a sign of just how much he did not anticipate the outbreak of war on September 1, Messiaen wrote a letter on August 7 to one of the organizers of an international festival of music in Venice in September, at which he expected to appear and perform. The letter communicated (1) his curriculum vitae, (2) a list of his published works, (3) "several words about the religious character of my music and the technical particularities of my musical language" [*les particularités techniques de mon langage musical*], (4) the titles and subtitles of the work *(Songs of Earth and Sky)* to be performed at the Venetian festival, and (5) "Finally, an *analysis of this work. I must insist that this analysis be included in the program.*"[120] This letter makes clear that, as late as three weeks before the war's outbreak, Messiaen had no idea that traveling to Mussolini's Venice would be impossible in the month to follow.

Thus, Messiaen spent the final days of summer peacetime composing an

---

119. As Peter Manchester observes, "Christianity is a religion *about* time." See Manchester, "Time in Christianity," in *Religion and Time,* ed. Anindita Niyogi Balslev and J. N. Mohanty (New York: Brill, 1993), 109-37, at 109; cf. Jeremy S. Begbie, *Theology, Music, and Time* (New York: Cambridge University Press, 2000). For general overviews, see Eugen Weber, *Apocalypses: Prophecies, Cults, and Millennial Beliefs through the Ages* (Cambridge: Harvard University Press, 1999); Ulrich H. J. Körtner, *The End of the World: A Theological Interpretation* (Louisville: Westminster John Knox, 1995); Stephen D. O'Leary, *Arguing the Apocalypse: A Theory of Millennial Rhetoric* (New York: Oxford University Press, 1994). For Catholic apocalypticism in modern times, see Giovanni Filoramo, "Memory and the Metamorphosis of Apocalyptic Time in an Italian Millenarian Movement: The Case of Davide Lazzaretti and His Followers," in *Apocalyptic Time,* ed. Albert I. Baumgarten (Boston: Brill, 2000), 363-72. Messiaen's most direct statement about his firm beliefs in prophecies is found in his preface to Albert Roustit, *La Prophétie musicale dans l'histoire de l'humanité* (Roanne: Horvath, 1970); translated as Messiaen, preface to Roustit, *Prophecy in Music: Prophetic Parallels in Musical History,* trans. John A. Green (Paris: l'Imprimerie D.K. Paris Vème, 1975).

120. Olivier Messiaen (from Petichet) to unidentified recipient, August 7, 1939, Carlton Lake Collection of French Manuscripts, Harry Ransom Center, The University of Texas at Austin, 186.1. Emphasis (underlined) is Messiaen's. I am grateful to the Harry Ransom Center for kind permission to consult these documents. About the fifth point, Messiaen added: "This work, being long and complex, absolutely must have this commentary [*a absolument besoin de ce commentaire*], especially if you take into account the fact that it will be sung in French for an audience that is international and *Italian* in particular." The *Chants de Terre et de Ciel* was to be sung by Marcelle Bunlet with Messiaen accompanying at the piano. See also Hill and Simeone, *Messiaen,* 85.

eschatological masterwork, *Glorified Bodies: Seven Brief Visions of the Life of the Resurrected* for organ.[121]

Vision 1: "Subtlety of Glorified Bodies"
Vision 2: "The Waters of Grace"
Vision 3: "The Angel of Perfumes (or Incense = *parfums*)"
Vision 4: "Combat between Death and Life"
Vision 5: "Strength and Agility of Glorified Bodies"
Vision 6: "Joy and Clarity of Glorified Bodies"
Vision 7: "The Mystery of the Holy Trinity"

This is the first of Messiaen's works explicitly following Aquinas's text and argument.[122] Three movements represent qualities that Aquinas and other medieval thinkers attributed to glorified (i.e., resurrected) bodies: subtlety (Vision 1), agility (Vision 5), and clarity (Vision 6). Messiaen does not invoke the fourth attribute of "impassibility," but it is implicit in his use of "strength" (Vision 5).[123] Messiaen had definitely been preparing for the composition by a close reading of Aquinas's treatise at least a year and a half earlier, perhaps already in 1937. In his May 1938 review of Tournemire's *L'Orgue Mystique*, Messiaen used Aquinas's technical language to describe the work's rhythms, harmonies, modes, and melodies: they seemed "to penetrate matter with the subtlety of a glorified body" *(percer la matière avec la subtilité d'un corps glorieux).*[124]

Aquinas, both following and departing from his predecessor, Hugh of

---

121. Simeone, *Bibliographical Catalogue*, 64-67; Gillock, *Performing Messiaen's Organ Music*, 99-142; Latry and Mallié, *L'œuvre d'orgue d'Olivier Messiaen*, 187-230. In translating *glorieux* as "glorified" and not "glorious," I am following the common translation of Thomas Aquinas's discussions of "glorified bodies."

122. Massin and Messiaen, *Olivier Messiaen*, 31.

123. The discussion of "glorified bodies" in the *Summa Theologica*, found in questions 82-85 of the "Supplement to the Third Part" ("Supplementum Tertiae Partis"), was probably not written by Aquinas himself. The editor of the English translation notes: "The remainder of the Summa Theologica, known as the Supplement, was compiled probably by his companion and friend Fra Rainaldo da Piperno, and was gathered from St. Thomas's commentary on the Fourth Book of the Sentences of Peter Lombard." All quotations here are taken from *The "Summa Theologica" of St. Thomas Aquinas*, trans. Dominicans of the English Province, 22 vols., 2nd rev. ed. (London: Burns, Oates and Washbourne, 1920-1942); hereafter *ST*. For Aquinas's parallel writings on this topic, see Saint Thomas Aquinas and Sandra Edwards, *Quodlibetal Questions 1 and 2* (Toronto: Pontifical Institute of Mediaeval Studies, 1983).

124. Messiaen, review of Tournemire in *La Syrinx* (May 1938), 27, cited in n. 82 above.

St. Victor, recalls moments in Christ's life where he demonstrated these four gifts.[125] Christ demonstrated the gift of "agility" when he walked on water. His body demonstrated "subtlety" when he was born of the Virgin Mary and "came forth from the closed womb" — a reference to the traditional pious belief that Mary remained a virgin (i.e., her hymen was left intact) even after Christ's birth. He demonstrated "impassibility" when he escaped unhurt in situations where the crowd wanted to stone him or hurl him down a cliff. Finally, he demonstrated "clarity" (or "brilliance"), the only one of these gifts that "is a quality of the very person in himself," when he was transfigured.

The first trait Aquinas considers in his discussion of "glorified bodies" is the one that Messiaen does not include: impassibility.[126] This is the quality of being immune from suffering or undergoing any other change (i.e., "passion"). It might seem strange, in light of the overall thesis of this book, that Messiaen would not attempt to represent this attribute — if his aim is to represent a world that is beyond the vicissitudes, ephemerality, and whims of fortune in this one, "impassibility" would seem to be the trait he would most embrace.

On closer consideration, however, it seems Messiaen has indeed embraced this trait, although he has substituted the word "strength" *(force)* for it. His epigraph to Vision 5 ("Strength and Agility of Glorified Bodies") is taken from Saint Paul: "Their body, sown in weakness, shall rise in strength" (1 Cor. 15:43). This is the same passage Aquinas uses in his discussion of impassibility:

> *On the contrary,* Everything passible is corruptible, because "increase of passion results in loss of substance." Now the bodies of the saints will be incorruptible after the resurrection, according to 1 Cor. 15:42, "It is sown in corruption, it shall rise in incorruption." Therefore they will be impassible.
>
> Further, the stronger is not passive to the weaker. But no body will be stronger than the bodies of the saints, of which it is written (1 Cor.

---

125. "Of those four gifts, *clarity* alone is a quality of the very person in himself; whereas the other three are not perceptible, save in some action or movement, or in some passion. Christ, then, did show in Himself certain indications of those three gifts — of *agility,* for instance, when He walked on the waves of the sea; of *subtlety,* when He came forth from the closed womb of the Virgin; of *impassibility,* when He escaped unhurt from the hands of the Jews who wished to hurl Him down or to stone Him. And yet He is not said, on account of this, to be transfigured, but only on account of *clarity,* which pertains to the aspect of His Person." Aquinas, *ST,* IIIa, q. 45, a. 1, reply to the third objection. Emphasis added.

126. Aquinas, *ST,* Suppl., q. 82: "The impassibility of the bodies of the blessed after their resurrection."

15:43): "It is sown in weakness, it shall rise in power." Therefore they will be impassible.[127]

Messiaen may have preferred the concept of "strength" (or power = *la force*) because it is a positive statement of the attribute and not a negative definition (i.e., what does not undergo passion).

But there is another, more likely reason he chose "strength": "impassibility" carries with it a corollary problem to which Aquinas devotes a great deal of argumentation, namely, whether impassibility means that glorified bodies have no sensation. Eventually, Aquinas concludes that resurrected bodies will have those modes of sensation in which the sense organ receives the external "species" without themselves being changed — for example, receiving the color species of whiteness without the eye becoming white. However, glorified bodies will not possess those modes in which the sense organ receives the external "species" and is thereby changed — for example, the hand which itself becomes hot when touching (receiving the species of) a hot object.[128]

On the basis of these distinctions, Aquinas concludes that, although glorified bodies will experience neither touch nor taste, they will nevertheless possess the senses of smelling, hearing, and seeing (for all three the medium is the air). Messiaen had meditated on this question carefully. In Vision 3, "The Angel of Perfumes" — *parfum* translates as perfume, scent, fragrance, bouquet, or aroma — Messiaen quotes the book of the Apocalypse: "And with the prayers of the saints there went up before God from the angel's hand the smoke of the incense [*parfums*]."[129] Messiaen thus follows Aquinas's example for why the risen life must include the active sense of smell: "Smell also which is the object of the sense of smell will be there," writes Aquinas, "since the Church sings that the bodies of the saints will be a most sweet smell."[130]

However, most important for Messiaen is that glorified bodies will see light and hear music. "There will also be vocal praise in heaven," writes Aquinas; "hence a gloss says on Psalm 149:6, 'The high praises of God shall be in

---

127. Aquinas, *ST*, Suppl., q. 82, a. 1: "Whether the bodies of the saints will be impassible after the resurrection."

128. Aquinas, *ST*, Suppl., q. 82, a. 4: "Whether in the blessed, after the resurrection, all the senses will be in act." For background, see Robert Edward Brennan, *Thomistic Psychology: A Philosophic Analysis of the Nature of Man* (New York: Macmillan, 1941).

129. Apoc. 8:4 (Douay-CCD); cf. Fillion: "Et la fumée des parfums monta, avec les prières des saints, de la main de l'Ange devant Dieu."

130. Aquinas, *ST*, Suppl., q. 82, a. 4. Aquinas is presumably referring to 2 Cor. 2:14-16 and Eph. 5:2.

their mouth' that 'hearts and tongues shall not cease to praise God.' The same is had on the authority of a gloss on Nehemiah 12:27, 'With singing and with cymbals.'" As for sight, Aquinas argues: "The intensity of light does not hinder the spiritual reception of the image of color, so long as the pupil retains its diaphanous nature. . . . But the clarity of a glorified body does not destroy the diaphanous nature of the pupil, since glory does not destroy nature; and consequently the greatness of clarity in the pupil renders the sight keen rather than defective."[131]

"Subtlety" is the second trait Aquinas considers and Messiaen represents in his first vision. Here again, Messiaen's epigraph is identical to the one Aquinas quotes, signaling his close "theological" adherence to this section: "It is sown a corruptible body, it shall rise a spiritual body" (1 Cor. 15:44).[132] It would seem that Messiaen embraced "subtlety" and used it for the first of his seven visions partly because it links risen human bodies with the first created elements, the planets. (Compare the second vision of *Visions of Amen:* "Amen of the Stars, of the Planet with the Ring.") "Subtlety takes its name from the power to penetrate," writes Aquinas. This power may come either through "smallness of quantity" or else "through paucity of matter, wherefore rarity is synonymous with subtlety: and since in rare bodies the form is more predominant over the matter, the term 'subtlety' has been transferred to those bodies which are most perfectly subject to their form, and are most fully perfected thereby: thus we speak of subtlety in the sun and moon and like bodies."[133] Aquinas notes repeatedly that this kind of planetary "rarity" led certain ancients to postulate that glorified bodies were perfected by a "fifth, or heavenly, essence." Aquinas vehemently denies that the fifth essence can "enter into the composition of a body," insisting instead that the glorified body is in fact a material, corporeal one. This is amplified when he considers "Whether one glorified body can be in the same place together with another glorified body."[134] Predictably, his answer is negative: "if two bodies occupy the same place, one is penetrated by the other. But to be penetrated is a mark of imperfection which will be altogether absent from the glorified bodies. Therefore it will be impossible for two glorified bodies to be in the same place."

By making "subtlety" the first vision of *Glorified Bodies,* Messiaen followed Aquinas's own conclusion: "Consequently the first reason for spirituality in the

---

131. Aquinas, *ST,* Suppl., q. 82, a. 4.
132. Aquinas, *ST,* Suppl., q. 83, a. 1: "Whether subtlety is a property of the glorified body."
133. Aquinas, *ST,* Suppl., q. 83, a. 1.
134. Aquinas, *ST,* Suppl., q. 83. a. 4.

body is subtlety, and after that, agility and the other properties of a glorified body. Hence the Apostle, as the masters expound, in speaking of spirituality indicates subtlety: wherefore Gregory says (Moral. xiv, 56) that 'the glorified body is said to be subtle as a result of a spiritual power.'"[135]

Messiaen next turns to agility, again following Aquinas closely even in his epigraph's reproduction of Aquinas's own scriptural quotation: "It is sown in weakness, it shall rise in power." Here again Aquinas notes that some ancients attributed the gift of agility to the presence of "the fifth, i.e., the heavenly essence"; and once again he disapproves: "But of this we have frequently observed that it does not seem probable. Wherefore it is better to ascribe it to the soul, whence glory flows to the body."[136] For Aquinas, agility comes from the body's being "prompt and apt to obey the spirit in all the movements and actions of the soul." By means of this gift, "the glorified body will be rendered apt not only for local movement but also for sensation, and for the execution of all the other operations of the soul."

Asking "Whether saints will never use their agility for the purpose of movement," Aquinas must deal with an objection based on a fundamental principle of Aristotelian physics: "movement is the act of the imperfect" (*Physics* 3.2).[137] As his first countertexts, Aquinas appeals to two beautiful lines from Scripture:

> They shall run and not be weary, they shall walk and not faint. (Isa. 40:31)

> (The just) shall run to and fro like sparks among the reeds. (Wis. 3:7)

Aquinas concludes: "Therefore there will be some movement in glorified bodies." This can be seen in the seventh and final of Messiaen's *Visions of Amen*, the "Amen of Consummation"; it is a brilliant pianistic tour de force, a toccata boiling over with thrilling perpetual motion. Its rapid and lightly touched runs musically portray the velocity of these "sparks among the reeds."

For Messiaen, undoubtedly, it is Aquinas's linkage of movement and vision that is vitally important. Even after the saints have climbed the heavens, writes Aquinas, they will sometimes move as it pleases them to get a better view: "so that by actually putting into practice that which is in their power, they may show forth the excellence of Divine wisdom, and that furthermore

---

135. Aquinas, *ST*, Suppl., q. 83, a. 1.
136. Aquinas, *ST*, Suppl., q. 84, a. 1: "Whether the glorified bodies will be agile."
137. Aquinas, *ST*, Suppl., q. 84, a. 2.

their vision may be refreshed by the beauty of the variety of creatures, in which God's wisdom will shine forth with great evidence: for sense can only perceive that which is present, although glorified bodies can perceive from a greater distance than non-glorified bodies."[138] There is something wonderfully charming and fairy tale-like in this medieval outlook. The afterlife will be a spatial world filled with beautiful creatures. But to see them, the saints will have to change places by moving around to be able to perceive all these wonders through the eyes in their corporeal bodies.

But there is yet another problem embedded in the notion of movement: time. Aquinas asks "whether the movement of the saints will be instantaneous," and counters received opinion by reaffirming corporeal space and bodies: "*On the contrary,* In local movement space and time are equally divisible, as is demonstrated in [Aristotle's] Phys. vi, 4. Now the space traversed by a glorified body in motion is divisible. Therefore both the movement and the time are divisible. But an instant is indivisible. Therefore this movement will not be instantaneous."[139] Aquinas further notes that there cannot be any comparison here with the "movement" of an angel because "movement" for a body is not at all the same as "movement" for a pure spirit: again, the emphasis on the embodiedness of the saints is made by sharply distinguishing them from angels. He restates this even more firmly a while later: "Now it is impossible to take away from a body its being in some place or position, except one deprive it of its corporeity, by reason of which it requires a place or position: wherefore so long as it retains the nature of a body, it can nowise be moved instantaneously, however greater be the motive power. Now the glorified body will never lose its corporeity, and therefore it will never be possible for it to be moved instantaneously."[140] After much consideration, Aquinas finally agrees with those who "with greater probability hold that a glorified body moves in time, but that this time is so short as to be imperceptible." As for the problem of the "end of time," he simply concludes: "Although after the resurrection the time which is the measure of heaven's movement will be no more, there will nevertheless be time resulting from the before and after in any kind of movement."

"Clarity" (or "brilliance"), the fourth and final attribute — first appearing the previous year in *Songs of Earth and Sky* — is vitally important for Messiaen both here in 1939 and in the forthcoming *Visions of Amen* (1943) (as will

138. Aquinas, *ST,* Suppl., q. 84, a. 2.
139. Aquinas, *ST,* Suppl., q. 84, a. 3.
140. Aquinas, *ST,* Suppl., q. 84, a. 3.

be indicated in a cryptic quotation attributed to *Proverbs:* "from brilliance to brilliance" [*de clarté en clarté*].¹⁴¹ Once again Messiaen follows Aquinas closely as the sixth vision's epigraph quotes the same scriptural passage Aquinas does: "The just shall shine as the sun in the kingdom of their Father."¹⁴² Aquinas insists once more that, although "the cause of this clarity is ascribed by some to the fifth or heavenly essence," this explanation "is absurd, as we have often remarked." Rather, the glorified body, brilliant in its radiance, will still be a body: "clarity which in the soul is spiritual is received into the body as corporeal."

Finally, if we want to know just how brilliant the body will be, we can look at the sun and compare — for the glorified body will be brighter than the sun. However, even a nonglorified eye will not be destroyed by the effect of heating (as happens when looking at the sun) while looking at the glorified body. Rather, "though the clarity of a glorified body surpasses the clarity of the sun, it does not by its nature disturb the sight but soothes it: wherefore this clarity is compared to the jasper-stone (Apocalypse 21:11)."¹⁴³ In the book of Apocalypse, jasper, green although translucent, is the first of twelve listed precious stones upon which the celestial city is built.¹⁴⁴

By following Aquinas's argument so meticulously, Messiaen's *Glorified Bodies* takes his self-identity as a "theological" composer to new lengths. He has moved from the disembodied Neoplatonic "soul" to the hylomorphic Aristotelian-Thomistic "body-soul" composite. Nineteenth-century Romanticism and spiritualism — typical, for example, of his mother's affection for the poetry of Lamartine — has given way to more orthodox "theological" texts. As Dom Marmion himself explicitly observes: "God is so magnificently lavish in what He does for His Christ, that He wills that the mystery of the resurrection of His Son shall extend *not only to our souls but also to our bodies.* We shall rise again, we too. *That is a dogma of the Faith.* We shall rise again bodily, like Christ, with Christ. How could it be otherwise?"¹⁴⁵ Significantly, by becoming more theological, Messiaen had also become more eschatological — a fitting position as historical events turned apocalyptic.

---

141. See Messiaen's "Author's Note" for Vision 7 ("Amen of Consummation") of *Visions de l'Amen,* n.p. For discussion, see analysis below.

142. Aquinas, *ST,* Suppl., q. 85, a. 1: "Whether clarity is becoming to the glorified body."

143. Aquinas, *ST,* Suppl., q. 85, a. 2: "Whether the clarity of the glorified body is visible to the non-glorified eye."

144. Apoc. 21:18-19; cf. 4:3 and 21:11.

145. Marmion, chapter 15 (" 'If You Have Risen with Christ . . .' [Easter]"), in *Christ in His Mysteries,* 328-46, at 344, emphasis added. Cf. Messiaen, p. 242 above.

1935–1939: Theological Turn, Young France, Baby Pascal

September 1, 1939: The End of a Low Dishonest Decade

Messiaen finished composing *Glorified Bodies* on Tuesday, August 29, 1939.[146] Three days later, Hitler's army invaded Poland, putting an end to the "low dishonest decade" of the 1930s and inaugurating the Second World War. The date was immortalized in W. H. Auden's poem, "September 1, 1939":

> I sit in one of the dives
> On Fifty-second Street
> Uncertain and afraid
> As the clever hopes expire
> Of a low dishonest decade:
> Waves of anger and fear
> Circulate over the bright
> And darkened lands of the earth,
> Obsessing our private lives;
> The unmentionable odour of death
> Offends the September night.[147]

Just as it had been in *Songs of Earth and Sky* (or *Prisms*), Messiaen's eschatological vision of *Glorified Bodies* was entirely in tune with the menacing summer months during which it was composed. As such, it offers a vision of the end of time that is not the end of human life. "This time in which we live must come to an end one day," writes Messiaen. "At this moment both terrible and unexpected, the Elect — like the angels — will, to a certain extent, be able to participate in eternity."[148]

In response to the invasion of Poland, France and Great Britain declared war on Germany, and Messiaen was immediately called up for military service. He later recalled: "[*Glorified Bodies*] was in fact the last work I composed as a civilian." The manuscript was left in the countryside at Petichet.[149] It would have to wait another three years of clock time — an eternity in lived time — for Messiaen to return to it.

---

146. Simeone, *Bibliographical Catalogue*, 65. I am grateful to Nigel Simeone for verifying this date.

147. W. H. Auden, "September 1, 1939," in *Another Time* (New York: Random House, 1940), 98-101, at 98.

148. Messiaen, *Traité de rythme, de couleur, et d'ornithologie (1949-1992) en sept tomes*, 8 vols. (Paris: Alphonse Leduc, 1994-2002), 1:8.

149. Massin and Messiaen, *Olivier Messiaen*, 152; quoted in Simeone, *Bibliographical Catalogue*, 65.

CHAPTER 9

1940–1943

Music for the End Times

1939–1941: Apocalyptic Times

During August 1939, Claire and Pascal (now two years old) left Petichet to visit her mother and sister at the Delbos family château in Neussargues. When the Germans invaded, many other Parisians, fearing military advances on the capital, fled to the south for safety. But when the country was partitioned into a northern sector occupied by the Germans and a southern "neutral" sector with its government in Vichy — not far from Neussargues — they found themselves confronted with much bureaucratic red tape as they attempted to cross the border back into the north. These same obstacles delayed the return of Claire and Pascal. Twists of fate meant that they would remain in the south for the next two years, until the fall of 1941.

The period from September 3, 1939, to May 10, 1940, is known in France as the *drôle de guerre* — the "phony war." Although war had been declared, no shots were fired. It was a psychological terrorism, a period of terrifying anticipation. Messiaen had been called up into the army immediately after the declaration of war. He traveled from Petichet to Paris for his assignment, leaving behind the score for *Glorified Bodies*. Claire went into action on his behalf almost immediately, writing state officials in October 1939 about the possibility of his being assigned to national service at one of the several Parisian radio stations operating at that time. She signed her letter "Cl. Olivier Messiaen (Claire Victor-Delbos)."[1]

---

1. Claire Delbos-Messiaen (from Neussargues) to unidentified recipient, Saturday,

1940–1943: Music for the End Times

At the front, Messiaen delighted in receiving regular letters from Claire in Neussargues. One such letter, dated November 24-25, 1939, suggests Claire's fragile emotional state:

> I'd been thinking of Peace and I suddenly said to Pascal: "Just wait, my darling, when the war's over the bells in Jesus's House will ring really loudly," and thinking about that hour of deliverance made me sob even as I spoke (I'm still weeping as I write this). Pascal was distraught at my emotion and hurled himself on me: "Mummy, little Mummy. Come, come, Mummy, come here." And his little arms were held out to give a passionate embrace to his poor Mummy. I repeated what I'd said, with the same mixture of distress and hope, and my little boy embraced me in desperation. Five minutes earlier he had been behaving appallingly at table.[2]

On its face, Claire's letter reveals the tense emotions that would have afflicted many French men and women as they found themselves in frightening circumstances anticipating the worst. But read from the perspective of four years later, by which time Claire was exhibiting signs of the serious mental debilitation that would eventually require her commitment to an asylum, it foreshadows the effect wartime trauma was already having on her state of mind. It is hard to imagine that Messiaen did not intuit something of a parallel with his own traumatic 1914-1918 childhood: his father in the north at war; his distraught mother taking refuge with him at the family home in the south.

A January 1, 1940, letter written by Messiaen demonstrates just how "phony" the war was in his day-to-day experience. It was addressed to an unidentified editor about a forthcoming issue on the Venice Biennale; the return address read: "Soldier Messiaen (Olivier) — 620th R. I. Pionniers — 2nd Battalion, 5th Company, Postal sector 42." Messiaen wrote that he was "profiting from" the New Year's Day holiday, assembling brief autobiographical notes and a list of published works. Having laid out his past, Messiaen then detailed his daily life in the military, which was preventing almost any exercise of his musical skills, both as a performer and as a composer. Quickly changing topics, he made an appeal following up on the one made by Claire in her letter two months earlier: namely, whether he might not be reassigned as "mobilized in

---

October 23, 1939, Carlton Lake Collection of French Manuscripts, Harry Ransom Center, The University of Texas at Austin, 186.1. I am grateful to the Harry Ransom Center for kind permission to consult these documents.

2. Peter Hill and Nigel Simeone, *Messiaen* (New Haven: Yale University Press, 2005), 87-90, at 89.

place" *(mobilisé sur place)* in a capacity serving the French state's various radio stations in Paris. He underlined that he could serve *"in particular as a piano accompanist"* and could interpret any kind of music whatsoever *"with a great facility* and possessing an excellent technique as pianist." Messiaen concluded with a list of possible locations for assignment: "Radio Paris, Paris Mondial, Paris PTT, Radio-Cité, etc. etc. etc."[3]

On May 10, the Germans terminated the phony war by invading France and the Low Countries. Ten days later, Jehan Alain, the brilliant composer and organist three years Messiaen's junior, was killed in action. On June 14, the Germans took Paris. One day later, Verdun fell and Messiaen was taken prisoner. He was sent to the Görlitz prisoner of war camp in Silesia, Germany (now Poland). A week later, on June 22, an armistice was signed sealing France's astonishingly and suspiciously quick capitulation — what has come to be known as the Strange Defeat.[4] The armistice divided France into two zones: the Germans occupied the north as well as the entire Atlantic coast; in the south, an officially "neutral" government was set up with the vacation spa town of Vichy as its capital. Marshal Philippe Pétain, an eighty-four-year-old decorated veteran of the Great War, was appointed chief of the French state. The Vichy regime would inaugurate reactionary legislation with the motto Work, Family, Fatherland — a repudiation of the republican Liberty, Equality, Fraternity. It would become known for its high degree of willing collaboration with the Germans as well as anti-Jewish legislation that exceeded German requirements in the north.[5]

Three months after the German conquest of Paris, on September 21, 1940, a German ordinance was enacted that required Jews in the occupied zone to declare themselves at a police station or a subprefecture. Those who owned shops were required to display placards in the window identifying the establishment as Jewish-owned. On October 3, the first *Statut des juifs* (Jewish Statute) was enacted. It imposed quotas for Jews who worked in any societal sector that shaped public opinion, including entertainment (radio, cinema, op-

---

3. Olivier Messiaen (from military post) to unidentified recipient, January 1, 1940, Carlton Lake Collection, 186.1, emphasis in original.

4. Marc Léopold Benjamin Bloch, *L'étrange défaite; témoignage écrit en 1940* (Paris: Société des éd. Franc-tireur, 1940); Bloch, *Strange Defeat: A Statement of Evidence*, trans. Gerard Hopkins (London: Oxford University Press, 1949). A pioneering historian and member of the Resistance, Bloch (1886–June 16, 1944) was captured, tortured, and executed by the Gestapo during the Allied invasion of Normandy preceding the liberation.

5. Robert O. Paxton, *Vichy France: Old Guard and New Order, 1940-1944* (New York: Knopf, distributed by Random House, 1972).

era) and education. These quotas were also applied to the Paris Conservatory, where nearly all Jewish faculty were dismissed within a year.[6] One of these faculty members was André Bloch (1873-1960), professor of harmony since 1898. It was his seat that Messiaen would eventually occupy after his release from the Görlitz camp.[7]

During the fall and winter months of 1940-1941, Messiaen wrote what would become perhaps his most famous work: *Quartet for the End of Time*.[8] The awe-inspiring story of its composition and performance has become quasi-mythical, due largely to Messiaen's own publicity about it. It has been retold recently in a scholarly revisionist account, a riveting historical novel, and an illustrated children's book.[9] The work was first performed on January 15, 1941, in Stalag 8A at the Görlitz prisoner of war camp. In typical fashion, Messiaen preceded the performance with a commentary on the book of the Apocalypse of Saint John, focusing especially on its tenth chapter. "And the angel whom I saw standing on the sea and on the earth, lifted up his hand to heaven, and swore by him who lives forever and ever . . . that there shall be delay no longer; but that in the days of the voice of the seventh angel, when he begins to sound the trumpet, the mystery of God will be accomplished, as he declared by his servants the prophets."[10] The third movement of the work, "Abyss of the Birds" ("Abîme des oiseaux"), a clarinet solo that tests the met-

---

6. See Philippe Olivier, "The Fate of Professional French Jewish Musicians under the Vichy Regime," published on the Web site of the Orel Foundation: http://orelfoundation.org/index.php/journal/journalArticle/the_fate_of_professional_french_jewish_musicians_under_the_vichy_regime/. Olivier's referenced works include the following: Frederic Spotts, *The Shameful Peace: How French Artists and Intellectuals Survived the Nazi Occupation* (New Haven: Yale University Press, 2008), especially 192-220; Jean Gribenski, "L'exclusion des Juifs du Conservatoire (1940-1942)," in *La Vie Musicale sous Vichy*, ed. Myriam Chimènes (Brussels and Paris: Éditions Complexe, 2004); Amaury du Closel, *Les voix étouffées du Troisième Reich: entartete Musik: essai* (Arles: Actes sud, 2005); *Déracinements: musique, exil et transfert culturel pendant et après le Troisième Reich*, ed. du Closel and Philippe Olivier (Paris: Hermann, 2009).

7. Rebecca Rischin, *For the End of Time: The Story of the Messiaen Quartet* (Ithaca, N.Y.: Cornell University Press, 2003), 75.

8. For this and following, see Hill and Simeone, *Messiaen*, 97-103.

9. Rischin, *For the End of Time*; John William McMullen, *The Miracle of Stalag 8A: Beauty beyond the Horror; Olivier Messiaen and the Quartet for the End of Time* (Evansville, Ind.: Bird Brain Publishing, 2010); Jen Bryant, *Music for the End of Time*, illustrated by Beth Peck (Grand Rapids: Eerdmans Books for Young Readers, 2005). For an accessible analysis, see Anthony Pople, *Messiaen: Quatuor pour la fin du temps*, Cambridge Music Handbooks (New York: Cambridge University Press, 1998).

10. Apoc. 10:5-7 (CCD-Douay).

1932–1943: Theological Order, Glorified Bodies, Apocalyptic Epoch

tle of even the most skilled player, appears to have been written during the summer before Messiaen was captured. Its theme draws on one of Messiaen's favorite images, the "abyss" found in Pascal, Baudelaire, and Hello, as well as in the deep Alpine gorges in the Dauphiné region. But the word *abîme* is also found throughout the Apocalypse as the translation of the Latin *abyssus,* and it would seem that Messiaen was also drawing on this biblical apocalyptic imagery.[11]

In his notes for the work, Messiaen set up his fundamental opposition between time and eternity as a contrast between the "abyss" and "birds": "The abyss is Time, with its sorrows and its weariness. The birds are the opposite of Time; they are our desire for light, for stars, for rainbows and joyful songs!"[12] This new metaphysical and religious significance for birds — those beings who (not unlike angels) perch ambiguously on the margins between time and eternity, creation and the uncreated — undergirds *Quartet,* will be expanded in *Visions of Amen* (Vision 5: "Amen of the Angels, of Saints, of Birdsong"), and will inspire Messiaen's works throughout the rest of his career.

Biographically speaking, two other movements — both of them "Praises" ("Louanges") — are of poignant interest. Movement 5, "Praise to the Eternity of Jesus," is Messiaen's reworking (for cello and piano) of the "Prayer" ("Oraison") movement from *Festival of Beautiful Waters,* originally composed for six Ondes Martenot and premiered at the International Exhibition along the banks of the Seine River. Perhaps Messiaen simply loved the melody; it also seems likely that the 1937 "Prayer" was associated in his mind, especially during his incarceration in the prisoner of war camp, with his son Pascal, who had been born eleven days before the work's premiere.

The concluding movement 8 of *Quartet,* "Praise to the Immortality of Jesus," has a similar provenance: it is Messiaen's reworking (for violin and piano) of the slow second half of *Diptych* (1930), originally written for organ. It too

---

11. Apoc. 9:1, 2, 11; 11:7; 17:8; 20:3 (Fillion). For specific references to occurrences of the "abyss" in Messiaen, see Aloyse Michaely, "L'Abîme, Das Bild des Abgrunds bei Olivier Messiaen," *Musik-Konzepte 28: Olivier Messiaen* 28 (November 1982): 7-55, and Michaely, *Die Musik Olivier Messiaens: Untersuchungen zum Gesamtschaffen* (Hamburg: Verlag der Musikalienhandlung K. D. Wagner, 1987), 1 (658)–17 (674). Compare Ernest Hello's chapters entitled "Le vertige devant l'absolu" ("Vertigo before the Absolute"), "Communion spirituelle: les deux abîmes" ("Spiritual Communion: The Two Abysses"), "Prière à l'Abîme" ("Prayer to the Abyss"), and "Prière à l'Infini" ("Prayer to the Infinite"); all in Hello, *Du néant à dieu,* ed. Jules-Philippe Heuzey, 2 vols. (Paris: Perrin et Cie, [1921] 1930).

12. Messiaen, "Préface" to miniature score of *Quatour pour la fin du temps* (Paris: Durand, 1942), i-iv, at i; in Pople, *Messiaen,* 40.

would have had deep personal associations for Messiaen: *Diptych* had been composed immediately after the death of Cécile Sauvage; and its new scoring was for violin, an evocation of Claire Delbos. Messiaen can easily be imagined in his imprisonment recalling his son, mother, and wife in these new transcriptions. Recall that *Diptych* was subtitled *An Essay on Terrestrial Life and Blessed Eternity*. Here, the "blessed eternity" is contrasted to the sorrows of temporality, especially in the winter of 1940-1941; and Messiaen's vision is fixed on Jesus, in both his "eternity" and his "immortality." The two slow "Praises," then, punctuate, at the middle and at the end, *Quartet,* a work envisioned as yet another essay contrasting time ("abyss") with the promise of eternity ("birds").

Thanks largely to the intervention of Dupré with state officials — as all institutions (including schools) were now under the supervision of the German occupiers — Messiaen was liberated soon after this premiere.[13] A letter dated March 10 places him in Neussargues, where he had been reunited with Claire and Pascal. Two days later he was writing Claire from Vichy (not far from Neussargues), explaining to her the work and salary he might have working under Daniel-Lesur for the Association Jeune France (including Radio Jeunesse in Vichy).[14] But he also outlined possibilities for musical opportunities in Paris, including Trinité (which, he noted, was now unpaid along with other Parisian organ posts), the École Normale, and the Paris Conservatory, a position for which he would need to apply directly to the minister.[15] Soon after writing this letter, he did in fact make his formal application, on the letterhead of the Association Jeune France, for the harmony post at the Paris Conservatory, from which André Bloch had been removed. Messiaen would have been obliged by the Jewish Statutes of October 1940 to declare in writing: "I am not a Jew, my four grandparents are not Jewish, and there is absolutely no Jewish blood in my family."[16]

A letter written to Claire on March 28, 1941, confirms in plain language Messiaen's attitude toward terrestrial life, which is elsewhere expressed more subtly in musical code: "But it is likely that I will definitely leave for Paris in time for the third term of the academic year. In fact I have moved heaven and earth

---

13. Hill and Simeone, *Messiaen,* 103-4.
14. For this new Jeune France, Vichy's short-lived state-sponsored arts association (as distinct from the musical alliance formed in 1935), see Philip Nord, *France's New Deal: From the Thirties to the Postwar Era* (Princeton: Princeton University Press, 2010), 254, 262-72; Nord, "Pierre Schaeffer and Jeune France: Cultural Politics in the Vichy Years," *French Historical Studies* 30, no. 4 (Fall 2007): 685-709; cf. Hill and Simeone, *Messiaen,* 104-7.
15. Hill and Simeone, *Messiaen,* 105.
16. Hill and Simeone, *Messiaen,* 110.

1932–1943: Theological Order, Glorified Bodies, Apocalyptic Epoch

for the harmony job and I think it is going to happen. But I won't say any more about it, *because nothing is ever certain in this rotten world,* and it will be at least fifteen days before anything is definite."[17] If he had any qualms about so vigorously pursuing Bloch's forcibly vacated position, he did not express them here.

Messiaen used the term "neurasthenic" later in the letter, which calls to mind Pierre's observation a decade earlier that the adolescent Olivier, like Cécile, had been obsessed with "phobias." Messiaen seemed to be aware that both he and Claire were prone to anxiety attacks and probably depression:

> I will spend at least ten days at Neussargues before leaving for Paris. Another matter weighs heavily on my conscience as a result: will you come with me or not? How terrible it is swimming in all these worries! And I am dreadfully miserable on my own. If the harmony job comes to nothing and Lesur leaves for Marseille, nothing would give me the courage to stay, alone, without Mie, without Pascal and really without music, in order to be a paper-pusher. On the other hand, if they call me to Paris for the third term, I will need to ask for a passport in order to leave as quickly as possible. That will still leave us separated, perhaps for a long time? It's terrible and I no longer know what to think about it. It is obviously better that I go on my own, but — I repeat — it's terrible! *For your part, try not to be as neurasthenic about it as me:* you have Pascal and a lovely church very nearby to comfort you and keep you on an even keel. . . .
>
> My Mie, I love you, I love you. Write me a quick note to cheer me up and think about all these things. Forgive me if I am still an egoist. I want so much to make both you and Pascal happy! And above all not to leave you! It's my life to amuse Pascal and to talk endlessly to you . . . (forgive me!). You are my dear little children. Big kisses to both of you.[18]

The letter is especially intriguing in hindsight, in light of Claire's incipient mental deterioration, a condition that was surely catalyzed to some extent by the traumatic separation of the last year and a half and of the current chaos. According to Mme. Loriod, Claire lost her memory at just this time — April 1941 — and needed to be institutionalized in Neussargues in the Vichy Free Zone.[19]

These were the dismal circumstances in which Messiaen came to be ap-

---

17. Messiaen to Claire Delbos, March 28, 1941, in Hill and Simeone, 106-9, at 106, emphasis added.

18. Hill and Simeone, *Messiaen,* 108, emphasis added.

19. Rischin, *For the End of Time,* 76.

pointed as professor of harmony at the Paris Conservatory.[20] By the time the new term started on May 7, he had arrived in Paris, having successfully obtained his passport in order to leave the Free Zone and enter the Occupied Zone. Meanwhile, four days after the term's new start, his quickly composed work, *Choruses for a [Celebration of] Joan of Arc* (1941), was performed in Lyon and Marseille (both in the Free Zone) on May 11, a public holiday under the Vichy regime.[21] (From the 1920s to the present, Joan of Arc has been a patron saint of the political right.)[22] The date commemorated Joan of Arc's meeting with Charles (following the English retreat from Orléans on May 8, 1429) and convincing him to go to Rheims for his coronation. As Messiaen's primary biographers point out, "The score of Messiaen's choruses has not so far been discovered, but it is almost inconceivable that no copies survive given the large performing forces which were involved."[23]

It is understandable why Messiaen (and others) might have wanted this work to remain unrecovered. According to Messiaen's list of works compiled during the following year *(The Technique of My Musical Language)*, the choruses were the Te Deum and the Improperia. The latter, also known as the Reproaches, consists of contrasting oppositions between God's good actions and the Jews' alleged infidelities. Chanted at the Catholic liturgy for Good Friday, the verses include:

20. Stephen Broad's account contrasts with those offered by Jane Fulcher and Benjamin Ivry: "Messiaen was offered the post by the Conservatoire's then new director, Claude Delvincourt, who was, in fact, known for his intransigence in the face of the German occupying force. We might, in fact, suspect that Messiaen's pre-war popularity in the far-right press might have acted against him in Delvincourt's eyes. Yvonne Loriod later reported that she suspected Marcel Dupré's influence had helped secure Messiaen's nomination to the Conservatoire. Dupré had considerable influence at the wartime Conservatoire, having assumed administrative responsibility when the former director, Henri Rabaud, had fled in the face of the advancing German troops. When he ceded the post to Claude Delvincourt, he was doubtless in a strong position to promote Messiaen's career (as he had done previously with Messiaen's appointment to La Trinité)." Stephen Broad, "Recontextualising Messiaen's Early Career," 2 vols. (Ph.D. diss., University of Oxford, 2005), 1:187.

21. Hill and Simeone, *Messiaen,* 109; Simeone, *Bibliographical Catalogue,* 195. However, this was *not* the ecclesiastical feast day of Joan of Arc (canonized in 1920). Rather, that feast day was celebrated on May 30. See mass and vespers for "Sainte Jeanne d'Arc, Vierge," in the French supplement to the Roman Missal, *Missel-Fr,* 1332-38; cf. liturgical calendar for France, xv.

22. Martha Hanna, "Iconology and Ideology: Images of Joan of Arc in the Idiom of the Action Française, 1908-1931," *French Historical Studies* 14, no. 2 (Autumn 1985): 215-39. "La fête nationale de Jeanne d'Arc et du patriotisme" is celebrated annually on the second Sunday of May.

23. Hill and Simeone, *Messiaen,* 109.

1932–1943: Theological Order, Glorified Bodies, Apocalyptic Epoch

> O My people, what have I done unto thee? Or in what have I
>   offended thee?
>   Answer Me.
> Because I led thee out of the land of Egypt,
>   thou hast prepared a cross for thy Saviour.
> For thee did I scourge Egypt and its firstborn,
>   and thou hast given Me over to be scourged.
> I led thee out of Egypt, overwhelming Pharaoh in the Red Sea,
>   and thou hast delivered Me to the chief priests.[24]

Along with other elements of this liturgy (several of them revised or completely suppressed in post-1965 Catholic office books), the Reproaches had acquired distinctly anti-Semitic overtones during the centuries; sermons on them were "delivered in emotional and devastatingly anti-Jewish language."[25] Why did Messiaen choose these texts? Or were they chosen for him? And what did he do with them? Until the scores are rediscovered (if they still exist), these questions cannot be answered. In any event, Messiaen, who had already begun teaching in Paris, was not present for their premiere or their various other performances throughout the month of May 1941 in the Vichy Free Zone.[26]

What was the emotional climate of the occupied city to which Messiaen returned in May 1941? On May 10, three days after his first teaching day, the arrest of 4,000 foreign and stateless Jewish men was made possible by registrations decreed the previous September. The men were taken to Gare d'Austerlitz and then to camps at Pithieviers and Beaune-La-Rolande. Women and children would follow in July the next year. On May 26, Honoré d'Estienne d'Orves, a French navy officer from an aristocratic Catholic family, was condemned to death for espionage.[27] (The square in front of Trinité church and the Métro station would eventually be dedicated to him.) On June 2, the Second Jewish Statute tightened the controls imposed by the first. On August 29,

---

24. The "Reproaches" ("Improperia"), from Good Friday liturgy, *Missal-En*, 485-87; cf. "Impropères," *Missel-Fr*, 533-35.

25. See entry for "Improperia," in *Dictionary of Antisemitism from the Earliest Times to the Present*, ed. Robert Michael and Philip Rosen (Lanham, Md.: Scarecrow, 2006), 223-24.

26. Nord, *France's New Deal*, 271.

27. Pierre Guillain de Bénouville, *Vie exemplaire du commandant d'Estienne d'Orves: papiers, carnets et lettres* (Paris: Plon, 1950). Cf. Honoré d'Estienne d'Orves, *Honoré d'Estienne d'Orves: pionnier de la Résistance: papiers, carnets et lettres*, ed. Rose Honoré d'Estienne d'Orves and Philippe Honoré d'Estienne d'Orves (Paris: Éditions France-Empire, 2005); Étienne de Montety, *Honoré d'Estienne d'Orves: un héros français* (Paris: Perrin, 2001).

after having been ministered to by Fr. Franz Stock (the renowned German chaplain to prisoners in Paris), d'Estienne d'Orves was executed by firing squad without a blindfold, becoming the "first martyr of Free France." His execution was announced (along with that of two other prisoners) by placards in German and French posted throughout France: "Navy Lieutenant Henri Louis Honoré, COUNT [OF] D'ESTIENNES D'ORVES, French, born June 5, 1901 at Verrières, was condemned to death for espionage. [He] was shot to death today. Paris, 29 August 1941. [Signed:] *Der Militärbefehlshaber in Frankreich.*" The capital city was governed by a reign of terror.

On a more mundane level, navigating daily life under occupation had become challenging.[28] Fuel and transportation were rationed, curtailed, and unreliable. Curfews were imposed and food was rationed. As Sylvia Beach wrote a friend from her rural refuge on August 25 that year: "Food is missing completely in this countryside — not a chicken nor eggs nor butter nor cheese nor rabbits. . . . But I have been to all my relations here to prostrate myself to have a chicken, a duck, a goose with no result. . . . One may give me some eggs to be crushed on the trip to Paris with the mob I'll find on the trains at the end of the month."[29] Although Messiaen lived some distance from both Trinité and the Conservatory, he made a habit of walking — both because the Métro stopped running at 5:30 P.M. and because his financial straits forced him to choose between Métro fares and food. A midsummer letter of 1941 written to Claire in Neussargues (she was still unable to travel to the Occupied Zone) indicates Messiaen's financial concerns: "*Corps glorieux* [*Glorified Bodies*] sold to Leduc and my *Quatour* [*Quartet for the End of Time*] to Durand. All that and a month's salary from the Conservatoire, paid into the Crédit Lyonnais, will be for you: this money should help you . . . to buy music, to look after your health, and to get some treats and toys for Pascal."[30]

In addition to the overt terror and mundane miseries, a third aspect of

---

28. Ian Ousby, *Occupation: The Ordeal of France, 1940-1944* (New York: St. Martin's Press, 1998), especially 110-32; cf. Charles Glass, *Americans in Paris: Life and Death under Nazi Occupation* (New York: Penguin Press, 2010); Shannon Lee Fogg, *The Politics of Everyday Life in Vichy, France: Foreigners, Undesirables, and Strangers* (New York: Cambridge University Press, 2009); Richard Vinen, *The Unfree French: Life under the Occupation* (New Haven: Yale University Press, 2006); Rod Kedward, *France and the French: A Modern History* (Woodstock, N.Y.: Overlook Press, 2006); Robert Gildea, *Marianne in Chains: Daily Life in the Heart of France during the German Occupation* (New York: Metropolitan Books, 2003).

29. Sylvia Beach to Carlotta Welles Briggs, August 25, 1941, quoted in Glass, *Americans in Paris*, 195-96.

30. Messiaen to Claire Delbos, undated, in Hill and Simeone, *Messiaen*, 113.

the occupied city was a sense of isolation as the Germans attempted to control all sources of information. However, BBC radio broadcasts subverted that attempt.[31] In November 1939, immediately after Britain's declaration of war on Germany, the BBC began its Overseas Service. Broadcasting in all major European languages, the BBC provided an alternative news source for those who would secretly listen to it in occupied countries like France and Holland. By 1940, the "Radio London" broadcasts to France opened with: "This is London! The French speak to the French . . ." ("Ici Londres! Les Français parlent aux Français . . .").[32] One scholar describes the French situation in particular:

> With a controlled press and little or no postal or other contact with the outside world, including the Unoccupied Zone, the Occupied Zone was effectively sealed off. But there was an invisible hole — the airwaves. The Germans did their best to popularize their Radio-Paris, but it was hopelessly tarnished. In his travels around France Friedrich Grimm found that people thought of Radio-Paris as German, Radio-Vichy as collaborationist and the BBC as "*our* radio station." Throughout the country, tuning into the news from London — the volume kept low because of the harsh sanctions for listening — was a daily devotion. "It was listened to religiously at 8 in the evening with every family member sitting closely around the receiver as though around an altar."[33]

General Charles de Gaulle, self-appointed leader of the "Free French," first spoke to the French people from his London exile via the BBC on June 18, 1940. Jacques Maritain, self-exiled in New York City along with his (Jewish) wife Raïssa during the war, delivered messages to France in weekly broadcasts for the Voice of America as well as occasionally for the BBC.[34] Messiaen was

---

31. For the "war of the airwaves" during the occupation, see Nord, *France's New Deal*, 296-309.

32. Jacques Pessis, *La bataille de Radio Londres [1940-1944]. 70e anniversaire de l'appel du 18 juin* (Paris: Omnibus, 2010); Aurélie Luneau, *Radio Londres. Les voix de la liberté (1940-1944)* (Paris: Perrin, [2005] 2010); Martyn Cornick, "'Fraternity among Listeners': The BBC and French Resistance; Evidence from Refugees," in *Vichy, Resistance, Liberation: New Perspectives on Wartime France*, ed. Hanna Diamond and Simon Kitson (New York: Berg, 2005), 101-13.

33. "This is the scene as described by Henri Michel, but it can be found in account after account of the Occupation years." Spotts, *The Shameful Peace*, 55.

34. Gerd-Rainer Horn and E. Gerard, eds., *Left Catholicism, 1943-1955: Catholics and Society in Western Europe at the Point of Liberation* (Leuven: Leuven University Press, 2001), 25; Fourcade, "Jacques Maritain inspirateur de la Résistance," *Cahiers Jacques Maritain* 32

1940–1943: Music for the End Times

a committed Gaullist; his father, both Anglophone and Anglophile, undoubtedly listened to the BBC. The news service was always preceded by the Big Ben carillon chiming the Westminster theme. For many throughout the world, the theme became connected with hope and the promise of eventual liberation.

This was the occupied city to which the thirty-three-year-old Messiaen returned from imprisonment: German terror, everyday miseries, imposed isolation. Among the students in his first harmony class at the Conservatory was the extraordinarily talented seventeen-year-old pianist Yvonne Loriod. (Born in 1924, she was Messiaen's junior by sixteen years.) Loriod and the other pupils were "absolutely astonished" to see "a man who was quite young and whose fingers were swollen" because of his captivity. "Like other prisoners," Loriod recalled, Messiaen had "lost his hair and his teeth. When he returned, he had swollen fingers, chilblains, because he hadn't eaten." Since food was rationed in Paris as well and needed to be procured with tickets, Messiaen went for a stay at his maternal aunts' farm where there were eggs and milk and so on.[35] They nursed him back to health just as they had twelve years earlier during his bout with tuberculosis after his mother's death.

Claire did not accompany Messiaen to Paris; perhaps Pascal did not either, in which case Messiaen would have been living alone during this summer of 1941. Unfortunately, the picture is unclear since differing accounts offer differing timetables. In one version, both Claire and Pascal had to remain in Neussargues (in the southern Unoccupied Zone) that summer because they were unable to obtain permission to travel to the Occupied Zone. A November 30 letter in which Messiaen notes that "we" had dined with Pierre and Marguerite suggests that "at last Claire and Pascal had been allowed to travel from the free zone to Paris."[36] However, in another account given years later by Loriod, Messiaen had returned to Paris with Pascal (who would turn four on July 14, no longer celebrated as Bastille Day under the Occupation) but not with Claire. In this recollection, Claire

> had lost her memory and was put in an institution in the Free Zone. So it was Messiaen who raised this little boy (Pascal) all by himself in Paris. He didn't have anyone to help him. He heated the stove in the basement of

---

(1996): 14-57. The radio broadcasts on the Voice of America and other stations can be found under "Messages," in Jacques Maritain and Raïssa Maritain, *Œuvres complètes / Jacques et Raïssa Maritain,* ed. Jean-Marie Allion et al., 17 vols. (Fribourg, Switzerland: Éditions universitaires; Paris: Éditions Saint-Paul, 1982-2008), 8:381-508.

35. Loriod interview (1993); in Rischin, *For the End of Time,* 75, 76.
36. Hill and Simeone, *Messiaen,* 114-15.

1932–1943: Theological Order, Glorified Bodies, Apocalyptic Epoch

the house all alone and he went to restaurants to eat with his son. They ate very badly, obviously. He worked all the time, all the time. He had to earn a living, so he was professor at the Conservatory, organist at the Trinity; but he still didn't have a lot of money. He would always say: "I'm going to economize. I'm going to walk to work instead of taking the metro. Because, then, I'll be able to eat."[37]

Whether or not Pascal was in Paris at this time, Messiaen applied for permission to travel to Neussargues in the Unoccupied Zone for the 1941 summer holidays. However, authorization was delayed, and as late as July 22 he was in Paris at Trinité, playing *Glorified Bodies* (composed during the last week of peacetime in August 1939) for his students. He was eventually allowed to travel in August, but needed to return to Paris by September 29 for the new semester.[38]

In this fall semester the Conservatory enforced Jewish statutes against remaining students. Odette Gartenlaub (b. 1922), one of Messiaen's students and later a noted pianist, composer, and professor, received notification from the Conservatory director, Claude Delvincourt. "Delvincourt cited a decree by the French Ministry of National Education stating that it was forbidden to admit or instruct any Jewish student, and explained that Odette would be removed from the student lists in a week. The prominent musicologist Jacques Chailley, then secretary general of the Conservatory, went so far as to chase after Odette during one of her last days at school, saying, 'After September 30, you are no longer allowed to eat in the student cafeteria. Don't forget!' "[39]

---

37. Loriod interview (1993), 76. Loriod's account is perhaps bolstered by Messiaen's letter to Claire Delbos (March 28, 1941), in which he asks: "Did you not receive my first letter? In it I told you that the concert in Grenoble and the ones which follow it will take place at the end of April (between 25 and 30 April). There are so many things in my head!" Hill and Simeone, *Messiaen*, 106.

38. In this account, he returned without Claire. But if the first account above is correct, Claire had been allowed to enter the Occupied Zone and return to Paris (for the first time in two years) by November 30, dining at the home of Pierre and Marguerite Messiaen. Hill and Simeone, *Messiaen*, 114.

39. Benjamin Ivry, "Messiaen's Dark Past, II," *Commentary*, June 25, 2007; http://www.commentarymagazine.com/2007/06/25/messiaens-dark-past-ii/.

1940–1943: Music for the End Times

1942–1943: *Visions of Amen*

Messiaen spent the first months of 1942 readying genuinely "eschatological" works for publication.[40] *Quartet for the End of Time* was published in May. *Glorified Bodies,* completed during the last week prior to the war and left behind at Petichet, had been readied for publication and appeared on June 4. During the summer break in Neussargues, Messiaen worked on his treatise entitled *The Technique of My Musical Language* (published 1944) and completed it in Paris in October. At the same time, at least prior to October, Messiaen was forming an initial conception of a work "in five pieces" that would eventually become *Visions of Amen* — a work that, like *Glorified Bodies* and *Quartet,* was about the end (or final "consummation") of creation and time.[41]

We can sense the atmosphere by recalling the events of 1942. Although no one knew about it at the time, the year started out with the Wannsee Conference on January 20, the meeting in suburban Berlin at which "the Final Solution of the Jewish Question" — that is, the mass destruction of European Jewry (including the death camps) — was unveiled and discussed.[42] On March 30, the plan's implementation began with the first trainloads of Jews from Paris arriving at Auschwitz. Starting June 1, Jews in France, Holland, Belgium, Croatia, Slovakia, and Romania were ordered to wear yellow stars; as an extra measure, Jews in Paris were ordered to sit in segregated subway cars on the Métro.

July 16 and 17 remain days of infamy in French history; during the "Vel d'Hiv" roundup on those days, 12,887 Parisian Jews were rounded up, tem-

---

40. For Messiaen's diary during 1942, see Nigel Simeone, "Messiaen in 1942: A Working Musician in Occupied Paris," in Robert Sholl, *Messiaen Studies* (New York: Cambridge University Press, 2007), 1-33.

41. Utilizing an early version of *Visions of Amen* donated by Messiaen to the Bibliothèque Nationale de France, Yves Balmer provides a schematization of the work's initial outline containing five movements. Noting that Messiaen had completed his *Technique of My Musical Language* by October 1942, and that several of the musical examples in *Visions* provided in *Technique* differ from the published version, Balmer concludes that Messiaen had worked out this initial five-movement version before October — and that its composition had probably begun as early as summer 1942. See Balmer, "Édifier son œuvre: genèse, médiation, diffusion de l'œuvre d'Olivier Messiaen," 2 vols. (Ph.D. diss., l'Université Charles-de-Gaulle — Lille 3, 2008), 1:46, 95.

42. Mark Roseman, *The Wannsee Conference and the Final Solution: A Reconsideration* (New York: Metropolitan Books, 2002). For dramatization see *Conspiracy,* producer, Nick Gillott; writer, Loring Mandel; director, Frank Pierson (New York: HBO Home Video, [2001] 2002).

1932–1943: Theological Order, Glorified Bodies, Apocalyptic Epoch

porarily placed in the winter indoor cycling stadium (Vélodrome d'Hiver) without nourishment or sanitation, and sent to the Drancy internment camp just outside the city. There they soon boarded trains for Auschwitz. As one historian notes, "Few Parisians remained unaware of the day's events." In his journal for the evening of July 16, the twenty-eight-year-old novelist Claude Mauriac wrote: "In various spots in Paris and at different times of day, I came across buses where three French policemen guarded Jewish prisoners, going toward what fate? . . . The heart tightens, one is ashamed to be there, to be present at such ignominious sights and remain silent."[43] On August 26-28, another 7,000 Jews were arrested in the Unoccupied Zone where Messiaen was spending the summer. On November 10, faced with the growing threat of Allied incursions from North Africa into southern France, the Germans violated the 1940 armistice and invaded Vichy France. As of November 1942, all of France was an occupied zone. This is the atmosphere in which Messiaen returned to what would become *Visions of Amen*. He was able to begin composing in earnest after completing *The Technique of My Musical Language* in October.

Visions was conceived for two pianos. The more difficult first piano part was inspired by and intended for the virtuosity of Yvonne Loriod, now eighteen and having completed her first year as Messiaen's student. On December 26 the work received a "commission" from Denise Tual, the film producer who was the inspiration for the Concerts de la Pléiade series; this helped Messiaen pay copying costs. Messiaen later called this concert series — for which he wrote two of his most important works, *Visions of Amen* (1943) and *Three Small Liturgies* (1944) — "a kind of clandestine revenge against the Occupation."[44] Meanwhile, on the domestic front, Claire was exhibiting increasing signs of serious mental illness as the new year of 1943 arrived.

Visions of Amen was inspired by Ernest Hello's *Words of God*, which ends with a chapter-length panegyric to the word "Amen."[45] In Messiaen's original

---

43. Mauriac entry for evening of July 16, 1942; in Susan Zuccotti, *The Holocaust, the French, and the Jews* (New York: Basic Books, 1993), 109; cf. Renée Poznanski, *Jews in France during World War II* (Waltham, Mass.: Brandeis University Press in association with the United States Holocaust Memorial Museum; Hanover, N.H.: University Press of New England, 2001). For a historical fictional account of the Vel d'Hiv roundup, see Tatiana de Rosnay, *Sarah's Key* (New York: St. Martin's Press, 2007).

44. Nigel Simeone, "Messiaen and the Concerts de la Pléiade: 'A Kind of Clandestine Revenge against the Occupation,'" *Music & Letters* 8, no. 4 (November 2000): 532-50.

45. Hello, "Amen," in *Paroles de Dieu*, 247-51. Cf. Hello, "Méditation sur l'Amen" ("Meditation on Amen") and "Amen! Amen! Amen!" in *Du néant à Dieu*, 2:245-50, 251-52. Mes-

plan of five movements, the fulcrum balancing the whole was the "Amen of the Agony of Jesus," a title deriving from Pascal — "Jesus will be in agony until the end of the world" — that provides continuity with a quartet for "the end of time."[46] However, thanks to recent scholarship, we now know that, sometime between November 1942 and February 1943, Messiaen added an entirely new movement (Vision 4) devoted to the "Amen of Desire." In this new plan, the work's fulcrum shifted from agony to desire, suffering to yearning, both human and divine. This radical alteration of the work's structure and meaning can be seen schematically:

Pre-October 1942:
Vision 1: Amen of Creation
    Vision 2: Amen of Stars and Saturn
        Vision 3: Amen of the Agony of Jesus
    Vision 4: Amen of Angels, Saints, Birdsong
Vision 5: Amen of Consummation[47]

November 1942–February 1943:
Vision 1: Amen of Creation
    Vision 2: Amen of Stars and Saturn
        Vision 3: Amen of the Agony of Jesus
            Vision 4: Amen of Desire
        Vision 5: Amen of Judgment
    Vision 6: Amen of Angels, Saints, Birdsong
Vision 7: Amen of Consummation[48]

---

siaen lays out his "four different senses" of the word "Amen" in his author's note ("Note de l'Auteur") published in the score of *Visions de l'Amen* (1943), n.p.

46. Pascal, *Pensées* (Pléiade), 717; (Lafuma) 919; (Sellier) 749; for Pléiade, see Pascal, *Œuvres complètes*, 2 vols. (Paris: Éditions Gallimard, 2000), vol. 2; for Lafuma, see Pascal, *Pensées*, trans. A. J. Krailsheimer, rev. ed. (New York: Penguin, 1995); for Sellier, see Pascal, *Pensées*, ed. and trans. Roger Ariew (Indianapolis: Hackett, 2005); cf. Schloesser, "Notes on the *Miserere* Plates Exhibited in *Mystic Masque*," in *Mystic Masque: Reality and Semblance in Georges Rouault, 1871-1958*, ed. Stephen Schloesser (Chestnut Hill, Mass.: McMullen Museum of Art, distributed by the University of Chicago Press, 2008), 157-80, at 167.

47. Balmer, "Édifier son œuvre," 1:95.

48. The definitive version with seven movements was outlined by Messiaen on March 17, 1943, to Denise Tual, the film producer and patron who had "commissioned" the work in December (i.e., months after Messiaen had composed the first version). Hill and Simeone, *Messiaen*, 123.

1932–1943: Theological Order, Glorified Bodies, Apocalyptic Epoch

In addition, this change in plans significantly changed the character of what was originally envisioned as the "Amen of Creation." The "beautiful theme of Mozart" (Susanna's aria "Deh viene non tardar o gioia bella" from the *Marriage of Figaro*) had originally been intended for use in Vision 1 (creation). However, sometime during the winter of 1942-1943, Messiaen transferred it to his newly conceived "Amen of Desire" movement.[49] The first movement then acquired its present character as a stately carillon hymn. To maintain balance — a composition of six movements would not have had a central fulcrum — Messiaen added an extremely brief and brittle "Amen of Judgment" (Vision 5) and placed it immediately after the "Amen of Desire."[50] These two additions brought the number of visions and movements to seven — the biblical number of days of creation and of perfection.

On March 17, Messiaen announced the completion of composition and the turn to copying: "In 15 days I will have finished a first fair copy which I will give to Mlle Loriod so that we can start rehearsing together as soon as possible."[51] Two months later, on May 10, the piece received its premiere with Messiaen and Loriod performing it at the Galerie Charpentier. A second performance took place on June 22; this time the work was paired with *Poems for Mi*.

Embedded within this seemingly abstract account of archival material, plans, and alterations is a deeply poignant yet unspoken drama. Messiaen and his beloved "Mi" had been separated for over two years by the war; during that time, Claire's mental state had begun to deteriorate. She suffered memory loss, their home life had become erratic, and Messiaen was raising Pascal as best he could on the side of all his other commitments — all during a wartime of foreign occupation (during which he was employed by the state), shortages, and outages. In the midst of this bleakness, immediately upon his release from prison and repatriation to occupied Paris (without Claire), Messiaen seems to have fallen in love with the beautiful, brilliant, and much younger Loriod. *Visions of Amen* for two pianos, premiered by student (Piano 1) and composer (Piano 2), lays out the complexity of this drama on cosmic (creation and plan-

---

49. Balmer, "Édifier son œuvre," 1:120-23.

50. Messiaen's initial idea for the "Amen of Judgment" was textual, not musical: "*Amen of Judgment:* separation of light from darkness (Genesis), of the elect from the damned (parable of the King seated on the throne of majesty, Gosp. of St Mathew [sic]." Messiaen's handwriting uses only one *t* here for "Mathew." Balmer, "Édifier son œuvre," 1:152.

51. Messiaen to Tual, March 17, 1943, sent by pneumatic post, Hill and Simeone, *Messiaen*, 123.

ets), human (agony and desire), and eschatological (angels and saints) planes. In the work's centerpiece, desire had displaced agony.

At the second performance, the felt need to pair the work with the prewar *Poems for Mi* wordlessly suggests a story of divided hearts and tragic loss. It is around this time, not long after returning from imprisonment, that Messiaen asked his father where he might find his mother's missing manuscript of love writings, the book he called the *Book of Love* that he remembered her writing during the First World War. His father responded with rage, accusing German troops of having destroyed them during a pillage of the family's home in the country.[52] The tragedy was intergenerational but also mythically transcendent: Pelléas and Mélisande, Tristan and Iseult, the Lady of Shalott.

A poignant postscript: by 1945, Claire's behavior had become so erratic that Messiaen became increasingly anxious about his manuscripts, keeping drafts of works in progress with his bank. He also considered giving manuscripts away in order to keep them safe. It would seem that the autograph of *Visions of Amen* was donated to the Conservatory out of concern for its preservation.[53]

---

52. Béatrice Marchal, *Les Chants du silence. Olivier Messiaen, fils de Cécile Sauvage ou la musique face à l'impossible parole* (Sampzon: Éditions Delatour France, 2008), 107; cf. Hill and Simeone, *Messiaen*, 223.

53. Hill and Simeone, *Messiaen*, 179.

1943

Résumé: *Visions of Amen*

A Résumé of Three Decades: 1910s-1920s-1930s

Visions of Amen draws on an enormously wide variety of literature that Messiaen must have read by the time of its composition during the fall and winter of 1942-1943. Such works include popular works in science (especially astronomy), musicology, music history, history and theory of dance, literature (from Shakespeare to surrealism), and ornithology; he also immersed himself in the Bible, liturgical books, and contemplative writings of both Dom Marmion and Ernest Hello. Indeed, the seven distinct subject areas of *Visions of Amen* allowed Messiaen to use the composition as a résumé of many of his favorite themes, both those in the past and those he was about to embark on.

Moreover, given the precise details of his life immediately preceding the composition of *Visions* — his incarceration in a prisoner of war camp in 1940-1941; his assumption of a heavy teaching schedule immediately after release in 1941; and his intense preparations in 1941-1942 for the publication of *Glorified Bodies, Quartet for the End of Time,* and *The Technique of My Musical Language* — these readings must have been done during the 1920s and 1930s, that is, prior to his capture in June 1940. Some of the publication dates of works cited by Messiaen definitively place his encounter with them in the 1930s — for example, the works in astronomy that figure prominently in the "Amen of the Stars, of the Planet with the Ring." Other works more likely date from his years as a conservatory student during the 1920s, especially those where he studied music history under the tutelage of Maurice Emmanuel.

A Résumé of Three Decades: 1910s–1920s–1930s

Whatever the precise dates during which Messiaen encountered these writings, *Visions of Amen* offers a convenient end point for this first epoch in Messiaen's life. In *The Technique of My Musical Language*, it is, necessarily, the last work cited; he began it immediately after he prepared the *Technique* for publication. (Indeed, some examples attributed to *Visions* in the *Technique* did not actually appear in the finished composition.) *Visions* thus offers a snapshot of Messiaen's imaginary in 1943 at age thirty-four: as it had been assembled from his childhood years listening to Cécile and Pierre during the 1910s, his Conservatory training during the 1920s, and his young adult years during the 1930s.

Vision 1

Amen of Creation

Time & Eternity • Book of Genesis • Ernest Hello: Light & Life • Dostoyevsky: *Brothers Karamazov* • Alexis Carrel: *Man, the Unknown* • Rhythmic Characters in Stravinsky's *Rite of Spring* • Bergson: Duration and Clock Time • Augmentation & Diminution: Non-retrograde, Hindu & Greek Rhythms • Louis Vierne: Carillon of Westminster • Music of Peru and Bali • Dom Mocquereau: Greek *Arsis*

This first vision transports the listener back to the moment of creation when eternity was divided into time. Messiaen takes up the distinction between time and eternity at the very outset of his *Treatise,* introducing the section "Time and Eternity" with this epigraph from Saint Thomas Aquinas:

> Eternity is everything simultaneous,
> and in time there is a before and an after.[1]

---

1. Messiaen, "Time and Eternity" ("Temps et éternité"), in *Traité de rythme, de couleur, et d'ornithologie (1949-1992) en sept tomes,* 8 vols. (Paris: Alphonse Leduc, 1994-2002), 1:7-9, at 7; quoting *The "Summa Theologica" of St. Thomas Aquinas,* trans. Dominicans of the English Province, 22 vols., 2nd rev. ed. (London: Burns, Oates and Washbourne, 1920-1942), Ia, q. 10, a. 4: "Whether Eternity Differs from Time." For background, see Rory Fox, *Time and Eternity in Mid-Thirteenth-Century Thought* (Oxford and New York: Oxford University Press, 2006). For an important study in the 1930s, see Jean Guitton, *Le temps et l'éternité chez Plotin et Saint Augustin* (Paris: Boivin, 1933); cf. 3rd ed. (Paris: J. Vrin, 1959).

Vision 1: Amen of Creation

As the "Amen of Creation" opens, from the first nearly inaudible moment that the pianos are simultaneously struck by both pianists, the "simultaneity" of eternity has been broken. Time has been introduced, and even as we hear the resonance of the first chord beginning to fade, we are in a "present" that is always immediately passing into the past even as it turns into the future. This is the commencement of time; its fulfillment will come in Vision 7, the "Amen of Consummation."

In theological terms, Messiaen frames *Visions* with the creation and the eschaton, the study of which are protology and eschatology (the study of first and last things).[2] In Bergsonian terms, the amount of "clock time" that the universe will endure is unknown to us — current theory suggests that the universe is presently between 13.60 and 13.85 billion years old. By contrast, a "duration" is always a single indivisible entity — of a human being, a mountain, a star, a galaxy — regardless of the amount of external (spatialized) time used to measure the length of its existence. *Visions of Amen* can thus be thought of as the single indivisible duration of the created universe from its origin to its fulfillment, "creation" to "consummation" — a unique entity whose meaning and identity are determined from its outset in view of its ultimate end.

---

2. "Protology is a term formed on the analogy of eschatology to designate the dogmatic doctrine on the creation of the world and man, paradise, and the fall, hence the doctrine of the origins." Adolf Darlap, "Protology," in Karl Rahner, *Encyclopedia of Theology: The Concise Sacramentum Mundi* (New Delhi: Continuum, [1975] 2004), 319-20; cf. Darlap, "Beginning and End," 321-25. As Rahner notes, protology and eschatology are internally related: "Creation must also be seen . . . as constituting history; the creatural state must be seen as the basis of historicity and finally creation must be considered as constituting the possibility of the history of salvation. Viewed in this light, the doctrine of creation is a formal aspect of a doctrine of the history of salvation and therefore also the doctrine of condition governing the possibility of an eschatological completion." Karl Rahner, "Creature," in *Sacramentum Mundi*, 326. For a reading perhaps close to Messiaen's own view of predestination and divine adoption, see John Panteleimon Manoussakis: "If the truth of things lies *not* in their past, that is, in their origin, but in their future . . . then eschatology necessitates a re-examination of protology. If the kingdom holds the final word about who we are, about our identity, because it alone is the cause of every thing, then sin and evil should be redefined, not as a deviation from a supposedly perfect beginning — as in the traditional language of the 'fall' — but as a 'failing' to become who we are expected to be." Manoussakis, "The Anarchic Principle of Christian Eschatology in the Eucharistic Tradition of the Eastern Church," *Harvard Theological Review* 100, no. 1 (2007): 29-46, at 45.

1943: Résumé: Visions of Amen

Messiaen's "Author's Note"

Messiaen describes Vision 1 in his "Author's Note" to the published score:

> I. — Amen of Creation.
> Amen, let it be so! "God said: 'Let there be light! And there was light!'" (Genesis).
> The first piano plays a double rhythmic pedal like a carillon, on non-retrogradable rhythms, repeated in augmenting or diminishing the values with each repetition.
> The second piano expresses the theme of Creation, the principal theme of the entire work: large and solemn chords.
> The whole piece is a crescendo. It begins in absolute pianissimo, in the mystery of the primitive nebula which already in potency contains light, all the bells which tremble in this light — light and, as a consequence, Life.[3]

Commentary

1. Sound-Color: Light and Time

Along with time and eternity, light and vision are the key motifs in Messiaen's work. Happily, the Bible also begins with the association of those themes.

> In the beginning God created the heavens and the earth [*le ciel et la terre*].
> The earth was without form and empty:
> > darkness covered the face of the abyss [*les ténèbres couvraient la face de l'abîme*],
> and the Spirit of God moved over the waters.
> God said: Let there be light, and there was light
> > [*Que la lumière soit, et la lumière fut*].
> And God saw that light was good [*la lumière était bonne*];
> > and He separated light from darkness [*et Il sépara la lumière d'avec les ténèbres*].
> And God gave to light the name of Day [*donna à la lumière le nom de Jour*],
> > and to darkness the name of Night [*et aux ténèbres le nom de Nuit*];

---

3. Messiaen, "Note de l'Auteur," *Visions de l'Amen* (1943), n.p.

Vision 1: Amen of Creation

and of the evening and the morning was made the first day [*se fit le premier jour*].[4]

The creation of light marks the invention of "time" insofar as the division between light and darkness marks the division between day and night: the beginning of days, weeks, months, years, centuries, millennia, light-years (and, conversely, hours, minutes, seconds, nanoseconds). The earth's relationship to the sun and its light is the basis of time measurement.

There is something remarkable in realizing that we human beings, utterly insignificant in the great scheme of things, measure our lives by reference to the earth's revolutions on its own axis and around the sun. Messiaen explicitly refers to this phenomenon as he quotes from a best-selling popular scientific work of the 1930s by Alexis Carrel entitled *Man, the Unknown:* "The duration of a human being, the same as his size, varies according to the unit which serves as its measure. It is very large if we compare ourselves to smiles or to butterflies. It is very small with respect to the life of an oak tree. Insignificant when it is framed within the history of the earth. We measure it by the movement of the hands of a clock on the surface of its face. [The duration of a human life] is thus evaluated by units of solar time. It totals around five-hundred thousand days."[5]

The relationship between human beings and the sun is also one upon which the entire culture of the Bible is predicated — namely, the relationship between light and life. Dom Marmion makes the connection in his commentary on the Epiphany, the festival of light:

> And yet this Light is the Life of our soul. You will have noticed that in Holy Scripture the ideas of life and of light are frequently associated.... It is the same when Our Lord declares Himself "the light of the world." "He who follows me," He said (and there is more here than a mere juxtaposition of words) "does not walk in the darkness, but will have the *light of life.*" And this light of life proceeds from the light which in essence *is* life: "In Him was

---

4. Gen. 1:1-5, translating Fillion literally.

5. Alexis Carrel, *L'homme, cet inconnu* (Paris: Plon, 1935), 189; quoted in Messiaen, *Traité,* 1:20. Carrel had won the Nobel Prize in physiology or medicine in 1912. For an infamous negative reception see Roger Caillois, "Review of *L'Homme, cet inconnu,* by Dr. Alexis Carrel," *Nouvelle revue française* (March 1936): 438-39, reprinted in *The Edge of Surrealism: A Roger Caillois Reader,* ed. Claudine Frank, trans. Frank Naish and Camille Naish (Durham, N.C.: Duke University Press, 2003), 107-9.

life, and the life was the light of men." Our life in heaven will be to know the eternal light without veil, and to rejoice in its splendors.[6]

Messiaen again follows Marmion, and his final phrase in his "Author's Note" to the score (the dash and the capitalization are his own) makes it explicit: " — light and, as a consequence, Life."

The annual agricultural cycle (and, by extension, the liturgical year) is based on light; as I write, in the Northern Hemisphere, this year's spring equinox will be at 11:44 A.M. on March 20; the summer solstice at 5:45 A.M. on June 21; the fall equinox at 9:18 P.M. on September 22; and the winter solstice at 5:47 P.M. on December 21. Messiaen would have been intimately aware of the preconciliar Catholic liturgical year that observed these solar and lunar turns in minute detail (e.g., with the mandatory fasts on Rogation Days).

In turn, the agricultural activities of the four seasons on earth dependent on the sun — planting, growing, harvesting, and lying fallow — are what make life possible. Without adequate harvests human beings cannot survive, and such harvests depend on there being neither too much nor too little light, warmth, and water. Ernest Hello explicitly associates life and light:

> To listen to men, one would suppose that God had ordained no connection between the rays of the sun and the bread which they eat. They do not realize how the grain ripens. They forget the very light which nourishes them.
> ... Think of the close and mysterious relations between light and food. I spoke just now of sunshine and bread. Certainly the light and warmth that stream down upon our fields blessed with a golden harvest, in no way resemble a piece of bread. If men were as ignorant of the physical order of things as they sometimes are of the moral order, they would say with reference to bread: "What does light matter to us? What does warmth matter to us?" And yet, what is bread, except a ray of sunshine imprisoned in matter and kneaded into dough by the labor of man?
>
> The peasant who cannot read, but who, as he works in the fields, pauses a moment and lifts his cap when the *Angelus* [bell] rings, is nourished by Light and has need of God.
>
> No one can grasp in whole and in detail the action of Light on the world.[7]

---

6. Columba Marmion, chapter 8 ("The Epiphany"), in *Christ in His Mysteries*, trans. Alan Bancroft (Bethesda, Md.: Zaccheus Press, 2008), 154-74, at 155, emphasis in original.

7. Ernest Hello, "Light and the People," in *Life, Science, and Art: Being Leaves from*

Vision 1: Amen of Creation

And Messiaen was certainly aware of Dostoyevsky's poetic rendition connecting light and life in *The Brothers Karamazov:*

> Joy eternal pours its fires
> In the soul of God's creation,
> And its sparkle then inspires
> Life's mysterious fermentation.
>
> Joy fills with light the plants' green faces,
> Regulates the planets' runs,
> Fills immeasurable spaces
> With innumerable suns.[8]

Messiaen's allusion to the most ancient and anthropological is complemented by his reference to the most ultramodern: the "mystery of this primitive nebula." Messiaen cites works of popular astronomy from the 1930s containing photographs of nebulae. His description rings true: this primitive state in which light already exists "in potency [*en puissance*]" and in whose diffuse light primordial "bells" can be heard "trembling" or, perhaps better, twinkling.

All these images, however, are in service of LIFE. For Messiaen, the representation of life is the mark of genuinely "religious music." As he wrote in 1936, there were three types of "religious music" — conventional, mystical, and living — and the most important of these was the latter:

> *Living* music [*La vivante*]. Living through its subject, living through its language. The word "life" recurs constantly in the Gospels; our Catholic sacraments and liturgy are, above all, an organism of spiritual life, and all Christians aspire towards eternal life. The language of the musician-believer will thus try to express life [*exprimer la vie*]. This life — inexhaustible and ever fresh for those who seek it — calls for powerfully original and varied means of expression. For us, audacious harmonies, glittering rhythms, sumptuous modes and rainbow timbres![9]

Ernest Hello, trans. E. M. Walker (London: R. and T. Washbourne, 1912), 91-95, at 94-95. For extended reflections on the connection, see the popular science work by Albert Moitessier, *La lumière,* illustrated by G. Taylor et al., 2nd ed. (Paris: Hachette, 1880), especially c. 15, "La Lumière et la Vie" ("Light and Life"), 330-47.

8. Dostoyevsky, *The Brothers Karamazov,* trans. MacAndrew, 139.

9. Messiaen, "Musique religieuse" ("Religious Music") (November 29, 1936); in *Olivier*

1943: Résumé: Visions of Amen

2. *"Two Rhythmic Characters": First Piano (Duration)*

Messiaen's estimation of rhythm is summarized in his provocative challenge: "a musician is inevitably a rhythmician; if not, he does not merit the title musician."[10] Messiaen seems to have first developed the notion of "rhythmic characters" *(personnages rythmiques)* in a short two-page article written in 1939 entitled "Rhythm in Igor Stravinsky."[11] (Perhaps he had been inspired by Joan Miró's 1934 surrealist painting entitled *Personatges ritmics* [Fr.: *Personnages rythmiques*].)[12] In his analysis of Stravinsky's *Rite of Spring*, later expanded in his *Treatise,* Messiaen identifies two contrasting characters, one largely static (represented by the Elders) and the other dynamic (represented by the Elect whom the Elders have chosen for sacrifice).[13]

The "Amen of Creation" is also based on two "rhythmic characters,"

Messiaen: Journalism, 1935-1939, ed. Stephen Broad (Surrey, UK, and Burlington, Vt.: Ashgate, 2012), Fr 63-64; Eng 125. Emphasis in original.

10. Messiaen, *Traité,* 1:9; quoted in Andrew Shenton, "Observations on Time in Olivier Messiaen's *Traité,*" in *Olivier Messiaen: Music, Art, and Literature,* ed. Christopher Dingle and Nigel Simeone (Burlington, Vt.: Ashgate, 2007), 173-89, at 173. Messiaen saw himself as a composer, an ornithologist, and a rhythmician; see Olivier Messiaen and Claude Samuel, *Music and Color: Conversations with Claude Samuel,* trans. E. Thomas Glasow (Portland, Ore.: Amadeus Press, 1994), 67.

11. Gareth Healey, "Messiaen and the Concept of 'Personnages,'" *Tempo* 58, no. 230 (October 2004): 10-19.

12. See Anne Umland, James Coddington, Joan Miró, et al., *Joan Miró: Painting and Anti-painting, 1927-1937* (New York: Museum of Modern Art, distributed in the United States and Canada by DAP/Distributed Art Publishers, 2008).

13. Messiaen draws his theory of "rhythmic characters" from the theater, leading to speculation whether he had not been influenced by Henri Daniel-Rops's theorization of "abstract characters" *(personnages abstraits).* Messiaen writes: "In the language of theater, when a character, through feelings or actions, influences the feelings or actions of other characters, it is said that he is the 'lead' character in the scene. If this first character strikes a second character: the first is acting, the second is 'acted upon' or changed by the first. As the first takes on excessive importance the second declines. Let us imagine a third character, impassive, immobile, who watches, who is present at the conflict without intervening, functioning so to speak, as the scene's foundation: we would have the three main possibilities of scenic characters." Messiaen, *Traité,* 2:112. Messiaen devotes an entire chapter to the subject of "rhythmic characters" as found in Stravinsky's *Rite of Spring* as well as Messiaen's own *Turangalîla Symphony* (1946-1948), *Messe de la Pentecôte* (1950), and the *Livre d'Orgue* (1951). See *Traité,* 2:91-398; for Stravinsky, see 97-147, especially 112-19, 124-25. Cf. Daniel-Rops, "Les personnages abstraits dans le théâtre de H. R. Lenormand," *Revue hebdomadaire* 35, no. 10 (October 9, 1926): 162-77, reprinted in Daniel-Rops, *Sur le théâtre de H.-R. Lenormand* (Paris: Éditions des Cahiers libres, 1926).

Vision 1: Amen of Creation

assigned to the two pianists. The second piano plays the carillon's melody with metric regularity in accordance with "clock time"; the first plays with freedom, with seemingly improvised syncopations that lead the listener into unpredictable territories. These two distinctive characters seem to represent Bergson's theory of time. The first piano represents the "rhythmic character" of "duration"; the second the character of "clock time." As opposed to "clock time," a "duration" has free will to choose this end or that one, follow this path or go down another. The first piano, embodying duration, is characterized by indeterminacy.

Playing in the upper register, the first pianist, writes Messiaen, plays a double rhythmic pedal founded "on non-retrogradable rhythms, repeated by augmenting or diminishing the values in each repetition."[14] Later (in his *Treatise*) Messiaen specifies the three rhythmic cells that are repeated in various diminished and augmented forms, giving the appearance of indeterminacy:[15]

non-retrogradable || Hindu *dhenkî* by diminution || Greek amphimacer[16]

The "non-retrogradable rhythm" has already been encountered several times (beginning with *Apparition of the Eternal Church*) in references to Guillaume de Machaut: "My end is my beginning / And my beginning my end."[17] A non-retrogradable rhythm is a rhythmic palindrome: it reads the same forward and backward (retrograde). Since the "retrograde" version cannot be distinguished from the original version, it is "non-retrogradable." Messiaen later said he had first used it two years earlier in his *Quartet for the End of Time* (1941): since a palindrome reads the same both forward and backward, it is nonlinear. Messiaen uses it to represent an end to "time."[18]

---

14. Messiaen, "Note de l'Auteur."
15. The analysis of *Visions of Amen* is found in Messiaen, *Traité*, 3:229-75.
16. Messiaen, *Traité*, 3:231.
17. Messiaen, *Traité*, 1:45. In addition to Machaut, Messiaen also cites here J. S. Bach's *Musical Offering*, which includes, for example, the "Crab Canon." See Vision 7, note 56.
18. One scholar writes of the *Quartet for the End of Time*, which preceded the composition of *Visions of Amen* by two years: "This revolution in rhythm is best seen in the quartet's introductory movement, the 'Liturgy of Crystal.' ... Messiaen would later call this kind of thing a 'non-retrogradable rhythm.' Messiaen had rediscovered a medieval device called 'isorhythm,' in which unequal patterns of chords, pitches, and rhythms revolved around each other — except for medievalists, few musicians knew of the device until the 1950s. By avoiding metrically defined phrases and patterns of stressed and unstressed beats, these isorhythmic 'wheels within wheels' destroyed any sense of meter, and thus created a piece of music outside of 'time.'" Michael R. Linton, "Music for the End of Time," *First Things* 87

1943: Résumé: Visions of Amen

The second cell, the *dhenkî,* points to Messiaen's use of Hindu rhythms throughout his music, beginning most prominently with the *Nativity* (1935) suite for organ. The third cell, the Greek amphimacer (or Cretic foot), signals Messiaen's intimate acquaintance with rhythms in classical literature (a volume of his *Treatise* is devoted to Greek and Hindu meters).[19] First introduced by his parents' discussions of poetic meters, Messiaen later studied them under Maurice Emmanuel, a specialist in Greek antiquity.

The three rhythmic cells can be illustrated schematically:

non-retrogradable = ⌈1+2+3⌉⌈1+2⌉⌈1+2+3⌉
dhenkî = ⌈1+2⌉⌈1⌉⌈1+2⌉
amphimacer foot = ⌈1+2+3+4⌉⌈1+2⌉⌈1+2+3+4⌉

By juxtaposing these three and repeating the ensemble, Messiaen gives us this first rhythmic pattern:

⌈1+2+3⌉⌈1+2⌉⌈1+2+3⌉⌈1+2⌉⌈1⌉⌈1+2⌉⌈1+2+3+4⌉⌈1+2⌉⌈1+2+3+4⌉ etc.

Put another way:

3 + 2 + 3 + 2 + 1 + 2 + 4 + 2 + 4 etc.

Following this combination of these basic cells, Messiaen goes on to introduce even more variety and unpredictability by "augmenting" and "diminishing" values. (One of Hello's chapter titles comes to mind: "The Two Movements of Life: Expression and Contraction.")[20] This process parallels Bergson's image in which he compares the "duration" to an elastic band. When you stretch it out or relax its tension, you can see and trace its "movement in space" and over

---

(November 1998): 13-15. For historical perspective, see Margaret Bent, "What Is Isorhythm?" in *Quomodo Cantabimus Canticum? Studies in Honor of Edward H. Roesner,* ed. Cannata et al. (Middleton, Wis.: American Institute of Musicology, 2008), 121-43; Bent, "Isorhythm," in *Grove Music Online. Oxford Music Online.* http://www.oxfordmusiconline.com.proxy.bc.edu/subscriber/article/grove/music/13950.

19. Note the four topical chapters in the first volume of the *Traité:* 1. Time; 2. Rhythm; 3. Greek Meter; 4. Hindu Rhythms. As noted above, Messiaen is indebted to Dom Mocquereau, *Le Nombre musical grégorien, ou Rhythmique grégorienne, théorie et pratique,* 2 vols. (Rome, Tournay, and Paris: Société de Saint Jean l'Évangeliste, Desclée & Cie, 1908-1927).

20. Hello, "Les deux mouvements de la vie: expression et contraction," in *Du néant à dieu,* ed. Jules-Philippe Heuzey, 2 vols. (Paris: Perrin et Cie, [1921] 1930), 1:32-34.

Vision 1: Amen of Creation

"time"; yet it remains the same elastic band, the same "unit" of a single indivisible identity.[21] Messiaen's theory of augmentation and diminishment allows the identity of the rhythmic duration to remain the "same" unit even as it changes.

What can the average listener conclude from Messiaen's theories and uses of such rhythms? Simply put: in the "rhythmic character" of the first piano, Messiaen wants to subvert any predictable sense of "clock time" (as kept by the second piano). He is constructing a duration filled with indeterminacy and unpredictability — in short, the kind of freedom and seeming improvisation exhibited by the Creator in Genesis.

3. "Two Rhythmic Characters": Second Piano (Creation Theme)

Set in contrast against this indeterminacy is the second piano, in which "clock time" is sounded by the repetition of the "creation theme." This theme, the "principal theme" (notes Messiaen) of the entire *Visions*, is written in the form of a chorale or hymn.[22] There are four stanzas composed of the simplest possible rhythm: each note (or chord) receives a single beat, and the final notes of each stanza (or phrase) are elongated so that the singer can pause and breathe. A well-known analogy might be Isaac Watts's hymn "O God, Our Help in Ages Past" (based on Psalm 90):

> O God, our help in ages past,
> Our hope for years to come,
> Our shelter from the stormy blast,
> And our eternal home.

Much of the listening interest in this first movement comes from the interplay between these two "rhythmic characters," duration and metric time (i.e., the creation theme). While the first pianist (duration) keeps us guessing, the second pianist keeps metric time with the unvarying hymn-like steadiness of the "creation theme." This is time as measured from the exterior; yes, even here, the measurement of the musical beat is ultimately related to the earth's relationship to the sun. Marked in 4/4 time, there are four quarter notes to a

---

21. Henri Bergson, "Introduction à la métaphysique," published in 1903 in the *Revue de métaphysique et de morale;* reprinted in Bergson, *La pensée et le mouvant; essais et conférences* (Paris: F. Alcan, 1934); translated as *The Creative Mind,* trans. Mabelle L. Andison (New York: Citadel Press, [1946] 1992), 165.

22. Messiaen, "Note de l'Auteur"; repeated in *Traité,* 3:233.

1943: *Résumé:* Visions of Amen

measure with each quarter note receiving a beat; the metronome indication is fifty eighth notes (or twenty-five half notes) to the minute — a unit of measurement that ultimately refers to the revolution of the earth on its axis and the division of time into days and nights, darkness and light.

4. *The Carillon*

Messiaen observes that the first piano produces a double rhythmic pedal "like a carillon" *(en carillon).*[23] The image comes primarily from freestanding carillons in bell towers that ring out both melodic lines and chord clusters of bells. A secondary reference is the "Carillon" stop on a pipe organ, defined as an "organ stop composed of several pipes to each digital of the keyboard and giving a combination of several tones of different pitch when each key is depressed. The sound is high and tinkling in effect."[24] A carillon had been installed in the Salle des Fêtes of the old Palais du Trocadéro in 1878: a Cavaillé-Coll 1-3 rangs. Whether tinkling (oral) or twinkling (visual), this is the effect Messiaen intends in the "Amen of Creation." Thirdly, "carillon" refers to a popular genre for organ. (For more, see Vision 7, "Amen of Consumation.")

Perhaps the most well known of these pieces is Louis Vierne's "Carillon of Westminster," a thrilling organ work based on the theme of London's Big Ben clock chimes in the Palace of Westminster.[25]

When the world-famous bells sound the time ("Fourth Quarter"), they do so in two sections: first, the "Westminster" theme of four measures (as in a stan-

---

23. For Messiaen works with some reference to the bell and carillon, see Aloyse Michaely, *Die Musik Olivier Messiaens: Untersuchungen zum Gesamtschaffen* (Hamburg: Verlag der Musikalienhandlung K. D. Wagner, 1987), 207 (350)–210 (353).

24. "Carillon," in *The American History and Encyclopedia of Music: Musical Dictionary,* ed. W. L. Hubbard (New York: Irving Squire, 1908), 90.

25. Louis Vierne, "Carillon de Westminster," *Pièces de fantaisie. 3. Troisième suite* (op. 54) (Paris: Lemoine, 1927).

Vision 1: Amen of Creation

dard metric hymn like "O God, Our Help"); next, the single bell stroking once for each hour. The initial theme (lasting only about fifteen seconds), known throughout the world and imitated by many local bell towers, is constructed like the hymn tune "O God, Our Help"; it is also Messiaen's possible model for the creation theme: four stanzas of four equally spaced notes each.

Is it possible that the "creation theme" is in fact Messiaen's encoded version of the Westminster carillon's theme? In 1943, the chimes would have been immediately recognized as introducing the outlawed "Radio London" from the BBC's Overseas Service. Earlier, Messiaen characterized the Concerts de la Pléiade series — the series for which *Visions* was commissioned — as "a kind of clandestine revenge against the Occupation."[26] While this suggestion is purely speculative, it is not unreasonable. Indeed, one can only imagine what might have happened in an audience in occupied Paris in 1943 as they realized, but only gradually (i.e., by the creation theme's third entry), that they were listening to the chimes of Westminster, introducing, perhaps, a free broadcast escaping (and subverting) strictures imposed by occupying authorities.

Whether this association is true or not, it is enough to have noted that Big Ben is a close analogy for thinking of the carillon heard in the opening "Amen of Creation"; and to have mentioned it as a possible thematic source for this "creation theme."

5. Points for Close Listening[27]

In the primal moments of creation, the "tinkling" of the nebulous lights, waiting in potentiality to be actualized, is heard in the extreme upper register of the piano. It is rhythmic but not metric, arranged so as to give the listener an experience of unpredictability, openness, creativity, a truly free and undecided future. At the same time, in the extreme lower register, the creation theme is played through in its first statement (00:03–01:32). It is nearly inaudible, and its extreme slowness might at first prevent a listener from hearing the melody. The earth is unformed and empty; darkness hovers over the abyss; the spirit of God moves over the waters. Messiaen notes that the final three-note motif of the theme (E-F#-A) (01:19–01:32) "is Peruvian and Balinese." Peruvian

---

26. Nigel Simeone, "Messiaen and the Concerts de la Pléiade: 'A Kind of Clandestine Revenge against the Occupation,'" *Music and Letters* 8, no. 4 (November 2000): 532-50.

27. Timings here and after refer to the downloadable recording of *Visions* by Hyesook Kim and Stéphane Lemelin. A complete timing schedule is provided as an appendix to this book. See p. 533 below.

1943: *Résumé:* Visions of Amen

music is significant for Messiaen because it is the source of the *harawi* genre of tragic love. Balinese music is associated by Messiaen with dance — hence, the creation theme ends with the upward leap of a dancer, the accented *arsis* of the Greeks discussed in Dom Mocquereau. (For more on both Bali and dance see Vision 2, "Amen of the Stars.") Note that the dancer does not return to the ground: this incomplete rise-fall rhythm parallels the way in which the final period of this movement is clipped and incomplete.

The creation theme is played through a second time at increased volume and an octave higher (01:33–02:54). The listener can now hear the theme as a melody. The clarity increases as the theme is played through a third time with increased volume and at an octave higher (02:55–04:08). The melody has achieved solidity and form in the listener's ear. As Messiaen notes: "The whole piece is a crescendo" from primal darkness into light, and in this regard he probably had in mind his conservatory master. "But, above all else," Messiaen had written six years earlier, the "inspired crescendo from dark to light that makes the second act [of *Ariadne and Bluebeard*] not only Paul Dukas's masterpiece, but one of the masterpieces of all music."[28]

In what initially sounds like a fourth statement of the theme, the same steady metrical hymn-like stanza appears (04:09–05:58). However, the melody is actually an inverted phrase that opens by moving downward. There is an insistent vehemence to the theme as it is repeated four times by means of thrilling arpeggios imitating carillons: "Let there be light! And there was light!" Light is separated from darkness; daytime from nighttime. Time has been created. History has begun.

Finally, there is a coda in which the arpeggios increase in volume and flamboyance. This concluding phrase is repeated almost twice (05:10–06:00). I say "almost" because the final chord is not allowed to return to the home that has been established. Moreover, we have become accustomed to hearing eight-measure (thirty-two beats) phrases; this fifth and final statement ends one measure short, leaving the thirty-nine measures arranged as 8+8+8+8+7. The abrupt ending of this final and incomplete seventh measure leaves the listener expecting more. This expectation points to the movement that follows immediately; and, in the longer duration, it points ahead to the completion of all this material, which will be recapitulated and fulfilled only in the final "consummation."

---

28. Olivier Messiaen, "*Ariane et Barbe-bleue* de Paul Dukas" ("Paul Daukas's *Ariane et Barbe-bleue*"); in *Olivier Messiaen: Journalism, 1935-1939,* Fr 15-21, at 20; Eng 79-84, at 83.

Vision 2

Amen of the Stars, of the Planet with the Ring

Space & Fear • Pascal: *Pensées* • Fontenelle: Extraterrestrial Life • Life on Planet Mars • Marcel Boll: *Two Infinites* • Abbé Moreux: *Celestial Spheres* • Rudaux: *Astronomy* • Emmanuel: Greek *Orchestique* • Dom Mocquereau: Dance • Valéry: *Soul and Dance* • *Danse Sauvage* • Stravinsky: *Rite of Spring* • Cogniat: *Dances of Indochina* • Dance of Shiva • Aquinas: Aeviternity • Blackbird • Two Laws of Lived Duration

Whenever I think of this movement, I cannot help but remember comments I have overheard in two cathedrals. I heard the first while exiting a service at the Cathedral of Notre-Dame in Paris. Just behind me were two young men about twenty years old. Listening to the organ improvisation thundering from the loft above, one said to the other: "It's amazing, this capacity of modern music to express such powerful things."

I heard the second at the cathedral of Saint John the Evangelist in Milwaukee, Wisconsin. The preservice music was a quiet yet nonetheless disquieting work (for the uninitiated) by Messiaen. Two young men around twenty years old were sitting behind me. One whispered to the other: "What the hell's up with this outer space music?"

Certainly, the variance in reception in the two cathedrals stemmed partly from French and American cultural differences. However, I think Messiaen would have smiled at both. For Vision 2 is a superb example of modern music's

1943: *Résumé:* Visions of Amen

capacity to express powerful things, and it is meant to be "outer space music" — quite literally.

This movement transports the listener to outer space, to experience unfathomable distances and velocities (space and time). Here Messiaen is more modern than medieval. In the ancient cosmology proposed by Aristotle and Ptolemy, the heavenly bodies indeed "moved"; however, because they were composed of perfect substances and attached to their own individual crystalline spheres, their motion was constant, invariable, and circular (befitting timeless, flawless beings). Pythagoras's "music of the spheres" expressed the harmonious order of the universe.[1] Thomas Aquinas needed to distinguish Aristotle's godlike beings from the monotheistic God of Judaism, Christianity, and Islam. He was able to do this by accepting their unchangeable substantial being while at the same time emphasizing their changeability of place — local motion being a characteristic of temporality.

Messiaen, too, believed in a continuity between cosmic structures, musical consonances ("natural resonance"), and, ultimately, the divine.[2] But in this movement his imagination takes a giant leap as the planets do not merely "move" — they "dance" — and not only do they dance, but their dance is "brutal" and "savage" and their axial rotations are "violent."[3] The riotous Vision 2, following immediately on the slow and steady Vision 1 (with its abruptly in-

---

1. Joscelyn Godwin, *Harmony of the Spheres: The Pythagorean Tradition in Music* (Rochester, Vt.: Inner Traditions International, 1989); Godwin, *Harmonies of Heaven and Earth: Mysticism in Music from Antiquity to the Avant-garde* (Rochester, Vt.: Inner Traditions International, 1995); Jamie James, *The Music of the Spheres: Music, Science, and the Natural Order of the Universe* (New York: Copernicus, 1995).

2. Alex Ross suggests that the differing attitudes of Arnold Schoenberg and Olivier Messiaen over "natural resonance" were "ultimately theological. Schoenberg believed that God was unrepresentable, that His presence could be indicated only by placing a taboo on the familiar. Messiaen felt that God was present everywhere and in all sound. Therefore, there was no need for the new to supersede the old: God's creation gathered magnificence as it opened up in space and time." Ross, *The Rest Is Noise: Listening to the Twentieth Century* (New York: Farrar, Straus and Giroux, 2007), 448. For Messiaen's theory of "natural resonance," see James Mittelstadt, "Resonance: Unifying Factor in Messiaen's *Accords Spéciaux*," *Journal of Musicological Research* 28, no. 1 (January 2009): 30-60.

3. Had Messiaen read Nietzsche's *Thus Spake Zarathustra*? Nietzsche breathed the same late-nineteenth-century neoclassical air that led Maurice Emmanuel to study Greek dance; some of "the most startling images in *Zarathustra* use this topos of Weimar Classicism" — that is, the dance, combining "both Dionysian energy and Apollonian form." For example: "I would only believe in a god who knew how to dance"; "Only in dance do I know how to speak the symbol of the highest things." See Paul Bishop and Roger H. Stephenson, *Friedrich Nietzsche and Weimar Classicism* (Rochester, N.Y.: Camden House, 2005), 127-28. The

complete ending), is a surrealistic juxtaposition. If the first movement is almost unimaginably slow in its evocation of eternity's creation of time, this second movement aims at giving the listener an experience both thrilling and chilling — an interstellar roller-coaster ride.

Following the book of Job, Messiaen's evocation of the celestial spheres reminds human beings of their place in the universe. We humans have a tendency to become our own "suns" and the centers of our own self-referred universes (hence, the derivation of "solipsistic" from "solar"). Messiaen not only wants listeners to experience distance and velocity in numbers larger than they can imagine; he also indicates the emotional response he is trying to elicit: namely, *la crainte,* awe, dread, the fear of the Lord that is "the beginning of all wisdom."

Messiaen's "Author's Note"

Messiaen describes Vision 2 in his "Author's Note" to the published score:

> II. — Amen of the stars, of the planet with the ring
> Dance brutal and savage [*brutale et sauvage*]. Violent turning [*Tournent violemment*] of the stars, the suns, and Saturn, the planet with the multicolored ring. "God calls them and they say: Amen, here we are!" (Book of Baruch)[4]
> The second piano lays out the exposition of the theme of the dance of the planets.
> First development: beneath the polymodal whirling of the first piano, the second piano varies the rhythm and changes registers of the five notes beginning the theme with abrupt leaps [*en sauts brusques*].

---

first part of Nietzsche's *Zarathustra* was published in 1884; Emmanuel's dissertation was defended and published in 1895.

4. Messiaen has added the word "Amen" to the biblical line: "il les les appelle, et elles disent: '[Amen,] Nous voici!'" Baruch 3:35a (Crampon). Cf. Siglind Bruhn, *Messiaen's Contemplations of Covenant and Incarnation: Musical Symbols of Faith in the Two Great Piano Cycles of the 1940s* (Hillsdale, N.Y.: Pendragon Press, 2007), 108. Messiaen liked this line: he had quoted the second half in a prewar article published five years earlier: "Young composers: if you believe, step out in front and write us religious works that live and inspire, and which will bring us to say of them what the Scripture says of the stars: 'With cheerfulness they shewed light unto him that made them.'" Messiaen, "Musique religieuse" ("Religious Music"), *La Page musicale* (February 5, 1937): 1; in *Olivier Messiaen: Journalism, 1935-1939,* ed. Stephen Broad (Surrey, UK, and Burlington, Vt.: Ashgate, 2012), Fr 63-64, at 64; Eng 125.

1943: Résumé: Visions of Amen

Second development: notes from the theme's beginning [developed] by means of elimination, contrary motion, similar (or direct = *droit*) motion.

A third development is superposed: in the first piano: the beginning of the theme in rhythmic pedal; in the second piano: the beginning theme with changes in registrations.

Then an altered reprise of the dance of the planets.

All of these movements mixed together evoke the life of the planets and the astonishing rainbow that colors the rotating ring [*l'anneau tournant*] of Saturn.[5]

Commentary

1. Space and Fear: A Modernist Genealogy

Vast space has long been associated with fear in the modern era. In the seventeenth century, Pascal wrote in his *Pensées:*

> When I consider the brief duration of my life absorbed in the eternity that lies before and after — *The memory of a guest who stays only a day* — the small space I occupy and can even see, engulfed in the infinite immensity of spaces I do not know and that do not know me, I am frightened and astonished to see myself here rather than there [*je m'effraie et m'étonne de me voir ici plutôt que là*]; for there is no reason why I am here rather than there, why now rather than then [*ici plutôt que là, pourquoi à présent plutôt que lors*]. Who has put me here? By whose order and direction have this place and time been allotted to me?[6]

Three centuries later, during the postwar revival of "existentialist" philosophy, Martin Heidegger investigated the anxiety stemming from self-conscious awareness of being insignificant in time. As he wrote in *Being and Time* (1927):

---

5. Messiaen, "Note de l'Auteur," in *Visions de l'Amen* (1943), n.p.

6. Pascal, *Pensées* (Pléiade), 64; (Lafume) 68; (Sellier) 102; for Pléiade, see Pascal, *Œuvres complètes*, 2 vols. (Paris: Éditions Gallimard, 2000), vol. 2; for Lafuma, see Pascal, *Pensées,* trans. A. J. Krailsheimer, rev. ed. (New York: Penguin, 1995); for Sellier, see Pascal, *Pensées,* ed. and trans. Roger Ariew (Indianapolis: Hackett, 2005); cf. Stephen Schloesser, "1921-1929: Jazz Age Graphic Shock," in *Mystic Masque: Reality and Semblance in Georges Rouault, 1871-1958,* ed. Stephen Schloesser (Chestnut Hill, Mass.: McMullen Museum of Art, distributed by the University of Chicago Press, 2008), 133-55, at 150. Emphasis added.

Vision 2: Amen of the Stars, of the Planet with the Ring

In anticipating the indefinite certainty of death, Dasein opens itself to a constant *threat* arising out of its own "there" [*aus seinem Da selbst*]. In this very threat Being-towards-the-end must maintain itself. So little can it tone this down that it must rather cultivate the indefiniteness of the certainty [*die Unbestimmtheit der Gewißheit vielmehr ausbilden muß*]. How is it existentially possible for this constant threat to be genuinely disclosed? All understanding is accompanied by a state-of-mind. Dasein's mood brings it face to face with the thrownness of its "that it is there" [*vor die Geworfenheit seines "daß-es-da-ist"*]. . . . For this reason, anxiety as a basic state-of-mind belongs to such a self-understanding of Dasein on the basis of Dasein itself. Being-towards-death is essentially anxiety [*Das Sein zum Tode ist wesenhaft Angst*].[7]

Six decades later, John Updike's memoirs expressed this Pascalian and Heideggerian anxiety in American accents: "Yet isn't it a miracle, the oddity of consciousness being placed in one body rather than another, in one place and not somewhere else, in one handful of decades rather than in ancient Egypt, or ninth-century Wessex, or Samoa before the missionaries came, or Bulgaria under the Turkish yoke, or the Ob River Valley in the days of the woolly mammoths? Billions of consciousnesses silt history full, and every one of them the center of the universe. What can we do in the face of this unthinkable truth but scream or take refuge in God?"[8] For more than three centuries, moderns have been anxious over the fact of individuals being "thrown" into the flow of space-time.

And there is a corollary anxiety: the possibility that there is life on other planets. This was already true in a seventeenth-century "best seller," one of the first works of popular science to be so: Fontenelle's *Conversations on the Plurality of Inhabited Worlds,* first published in 1686, contemporaneous with Pascal's composition of the *Pensées*.[9] The book pretends to be the record of after-dinner conversations between the author and a fictional, anonymous

---

7. Martin Heidegger, *Sein und Zeit* (Tübingen: M. Niemeyer, 1972), 265, 266; *Being and Time,* trans. John Macquarrie and Edward Robinson (New York: Harper, 1962), 310; cf. Schloesser, "1921-1929," 151. For Heidegger, see Ethan Kleinberg, *Generation Existential: Heidegger's Philosophy in France, 1927-1961* (Ithaca, N.Y.: Cornell University Press, 2005).

8. John Updike, *Self-Consciousness: Memoirs* (New York: Knopf, 1989), 40.

9. Bernard le Bovier de Fontenelle, *Entretiens sur la pluralité des mondes habités* (Paris: C. Blageart, 1686). See Frédérique Aït-Touati, *Fictions of the Cosmos: Science and Literature in the Seventeenth Century,* trans. Susan Emmanuel (Chicago: University of Chicago Press, 2011).

"Marquise of ***" over the course of five evenings. On the fourth evening, the narrator talks about Saturn and its enormous distance from the sun. The inhabitants of Saturn are very bad off and have adapted to the lack of brightness and heat. "If we placed them in our coldest countries, in Greenland or Lapland," he says, "we'd see them sweat huge drops and die of the heat." "You give me an idea of Saturn which freezes me," responds the Marquise, "and a little while ago you were setting me on fire when you spoke of Mercury." "It's necessary," responds the narrator, speaking in rhetoric reminiscent of his contemporary, Pascal, "that the two worlds which are at the two extremities of this great vortex [*de ce grand Tourbillon*] should be opposite in all things."[10]

The narrator singles out Saturn's identifying characteristic as the planet with the multicolored ring: "As [Saturn's] year equals thirty of ours, and consequently it has countries where a single night lasts fifteen whole years, guess what Nature has invented to light such dreadful nights. She's not content to give five moons to Saturn, she's placed a great circle or ring about it which surrounds it completely and which, being placed high enough to be free of the shadow of the body of the planet, reflects the light of the Sun perpetually into places which can't see it."[11]

The marquise reacts to this information "like a person coming to, with astonishment [*avec étonnement*]": "all this is magnificently arranged; it really seems that Nature has had the needs of some living beings in view, and that the distribution of moons wasn't made haphazardly."[12]

On the fifth and final evening, the marquise confronts the possibility that the stars are also suns, each one the center of its own vortex with its own array of planets. She reasons: "The fixed stars are suns, too; our Sun is the center of a vortex [*le centre d'un Tourbillon*] which rotates around it; why shouldn't each fixed star also be the center of a vortex which moves about it?"[13] The

---

10. Bernard le Bovier de Fontenelle, *Conversations on the Plurality of Worlds*, trans. H. A. Hargreaves (Berkeley: University of California Press, 1990), 59-60; Fontenelle, *Entretiens sur la pluralité des mondes habités*, in *Œuvres complètes. Tome II*, ed. Alain Niderst, 9 vols. (Paris: Fayard, [1989-2001] 1991), 2:94. There are five "evenings" of conversations in the initial 1686 edition; in 1687, Fontenelle issued a second revised and corrected edition that included a sixth "evening." See editorial note of Alain Niderst in Fontenelle, *Œuvres complètes*, 2:6. The English edition used here concludes with the fifth evening; the French edition includes the sixth.

11. Fontenelle, *Conversations*, 58; *Entretiens*, 2:92.

12. Fontenelle, *Conversations*, 58; *Entretiens*, 2:92.

13. Fontenelle, *Conversations*, 63-64; *Entretiens*, 2:98. Note that this is the passage quoted in Abbé Théophile Moreux, *À travers les espaces célestes* (Paris: Flammarion, 1934), 74. See below.

Vision 2: Amen of the Stars, of the Planet with the Ring

marquise responds to her own reasoning with horror: "But here's a universe so large that I'm lost. I no longer know where I am, I'm nothing. . . . All this immense space which holds our Sun and our planets will be merely a small piece of the universe? As many spaces as there are fixed stars? This confounds me — troubles me — terrifies me [*me confond, me trouble, m'épouvante*]."[14]

The narrator, however, expresses an opposing reaction: "And as for me, this puts me at my ease. When the sky was only this blue vault, with the stars nailed to it, the universe seemed small and narrow to me; I felt oppressed by it. Now that they've given infinitely greater breadth and depth to this vault by dividing it into thousands and thousands of vortices, it seems to me that I breathe more freely, that I'm in a larger air, and certainly the universe has a completely different magnificence [*l'Univers a toute une autre magnificence*]."[15]

The marquise responds: "You offer me a kind of perspective so long that my eyes can't reach the end of it."[16]

The "plurality of worlds" was a hot topic once again in the early twentieth century. Abbé Théophile Moreux wrote about it in detail, specifically reacting to the American astronomer Percival Lowell's theory of intelligent life on Mars explicated in his books: *The Planet Mars* (1894), *Mars and Its Canals* (1906), and *Mars as the Abode of Life* (1908).[17] Abbé Moreux's *Are Other Worlds Inhabited?* first appeared in 1912 and was republished after the war with illustrations in 1923, and yet again in 1932.[18] Other contemporaneous publications add to a sense of the craze: Claude Farrère's *Stories from Foreign and Other Worlds* (1921); J.-H. Rosny's *Other Lives and Other Worlds* (1924); and *On Other Worlds . . .* (1937) by Lucien Rudaux.[19] Rudaux was read and quoted by Messiaen.

In 1938, the year following Rudaux's *On Other Worlds . . .* , Orson Welles's Mercury Theatre radio broadcast of *The War of the Worlds* — intended simply

---

14. Fontenelle, *Conversations*, 63; *Entretiens*, 2:98.
15. Fontenelle, *Conversations*, 63; *Entretiens*, 2:98.
16. Fontenelle, *Conversations*, 63; *Entretiens*, 2:99.
17. Mark Kidger, *Astronomical Enigmas: Life on Mars, the Star of Bethlehem, and Other Milky Way Mysteries* (Baltimore: Johns Hopkins University Press, 2005), 110. Cf. Percival Lowell: *The Planet Mars* (Flagstaff, Ariz.: Lowell Observatory, 1894); *Mars and Its Canals* (New York: Macmillan, 1906); *Mars as the Abode of Life: Illustrated* (New York: Macmillan, 1908).
18. Théophile Moreux, *Les autres mondes sont-ils habités?* (Paris: Éditions "Scientifica," 1912). Reprinted by G. Doin (Paris) in 1923 and 1932; and a new edition in 1950.
19. Claude Farrère, *Contes d'outre et d'autres mondes* (Paris: Dorbon-Ainé, 1921); J.-H. Rosny, *Les autres vies et les autres mondes* (Paris: G. Crès, 1924); Lucien Rudaux, *Sur les autres mondes . . .* (Paris: Librairie Larousse, 1937).

1943: Résumé: Visions of Amen

as a Halloween episode — terrified many American listeners who believed that a Martian invasion of Earth was actually in progress.[20] (Two years later, the reaction itself became the subject of scholarly study when Princeton University published *The Invasion from Mars: A Study in the Psychology of Panic.*)[21] The radio script was an adaptation of the novel *The War of the Worlds,* published by H. G. Wells in the fin-de-siècle and quickly translated into French as *La Guerre des mondes* (1900). It was published one year after Wells's *Time Machine* was published in translation — yet another work Messiaen knew intimately and quoted.[22] Given his father's love for English literature, it seems likely that Messiaen was introduced to Wells's works as a child.

In 1938, the year of the *War of the Worlds* panic, Marcel Boll published *The Two Infinites: Galaxies, Stars, Planets, Micelles, Fields, Nuclei, Neutrons, Photons.*[23] The work begins by laying out the "Two Infinites of Pascal" — that is, infinite being and infinite nothingness. (Sartre's work, *Being and Nothingness,* would be written five years later.) Boll then proceeded to the "Two Infinites of Einstein": a universe that was infinitely large — "galaxies, stars, planets" — and the atom, a world that was infinitely small — "nuclei, neutrons, photons." How do we know that Messiaen knew Boll's work when he wrote *Visions* in 1942-1943? Because in his *Twenty Gazes at the Infant Jesus* (1944), composed immediately after *Visions,* the commentary for the sixth movement, "By Him Everything Was Made," indirectly quotes Boll's *Two Infinites:* "Abundance of spaces and durations; galaxies, photons."[24] Boll's *Two Infinites* express both

20. Richard J. Hand, *Terror on the Air! Horror Radio in America, 1931-1952* (Jefferson, N.C.: Macfarlane and Co., 2006), 7.

21. Hadley Cantril, H. G. Wells, et al., *The Invasion from Mars: A Study in the Psychology of Panic* (Princeton: Princeton University Press, 1940).

22. H. G. Wells, *La guerre des mondes: roman,* trans. Henry-D. Davray (Paris: Société du Mercure de France, 1900); Wells, *La machine à explorer le temps: roman* (Paris: Société du Mercure de France, 1899). For citations of Wells's *Time Machine,* see Messiaen, *Traité de rythme, de couleur, et d'ornithologie (1949-1992) en sept tomes,* 8 vols. (Paris: Alphonse Leduc, 1994-2002), 1:20, 21, 33; 3:180. Messiaen's fondness for the works of Edgar Allan Poe has been noted above; so too has Poe's influence on Catholic Revivalist writers like Ernest Hello and Villiers de l'Isle Adam. For a study incorporating the works of Poe, Villiers de l'Isle Adam, and H. G. Wells (among others), see Martin Willis, *Mesmerists, Monsters, and Machines: Science Fiction and the Cultures of Science in the Nineteenth Century* (Kent, Ohio: Kent State University Press, 2006).

23. Marcel Boll, *Les deux infinis; galaxies, étoiles, planètes, micelles, réseaux, noyaux, neutrons, photons* (Paris: Larousse, 1938).

24. "Foisonnement des espaces et durées; galaxies, photons, spirales contraires, foudres inverses." Olivier Messiaen, "Note de l'Auteur," *Vingt Regards sur l'Enfant-Jésus* (Paris: Éditions Durand, 1944), II (VI. — "Par Lui tout a été fait."). The title comes from the Nicene

Vision 2: Amen of the Stars, of the Planet with the Ring

the unfathomably large (galaxies) and the unfathomably small (photons) in terms of space and time.[25]

Messiaen would later quote Boll's *Two Infinites* in his *Treatise*:

Man is a half-way being [*un être moyen*], situated half-way between the atom and the star. Look at a table of the scale of durations, going from the extremely long to the extremely short: it begins with the age of galaxies (immense duration, terrifying [*effroyable*], so extended that it requires a great effort on our part to think and express it), pass by the life of thorium, the solidification of the earth, the rotation of the Milky Way, human life, the threshold of perception of durations and sounds, the life of an excited atom, and finally reach the wave associated with the proton (a duration so infinitesimal [*infime*] that it is not even certain that the notion of time may be applied to it). (See Marcel Boll, *The Two Infinites*, p. 17).[26]

The transition from Vision 1 to Vision 2 is more than an imitation of the biblical account of creation or an association of light with suns and stars. It is also a situating of the human being in the universe — specifically, a position (like Job) of epistemological modesty, induced by awe *(la crainte)*, an awareness of one's true place in the great scheme of things. It is an imaginative move that has a specifically modern trajectory from the seventeenth century onward, especially in French literature.

Two final examples from twentieth-century literature make explicit this fear of what Walker Percy once called being "lost in the cosmos."[27] In the sprawling novel *Berlin Alexanderplatz* (1929), published just two years after Heidegger's *Being and Time,* Alfred Döblin's doomed character is pushed out of a car during a heist, a consequence of which will be the amputation of his right arm. Döblin inserts this philosophical-cosmological rumination:

Creed spoken by the priest or sung by the choir *(Credo)* at every Sunday Mass: "per quem omnia facta sunt" = "par qui toutes choses ont été faites." *Missel-Fr,* 591. The phrase comes from the New Testament: "Tout par lui a été fait" (John 1:3a); "tout a été créé par lui et pour lui" (Col. 1:16c) (Crampon).

25. See Siglind Bruhn, *Images and Ideas in Modern French Piano Music: The Extramusical Subtext in Piano Works by Ravel, Debussy, and Messiaen* (Stuyvesant, N.Y.: Pendragon Press, 1997), 317.

26. Messiaen, *Traité*, 1:20.

27. Walker Percy, *Lost in the Cosmos: The Last Self-Help Book* (New York: Farrar, Straus and Giroux, 1983).

1943: *Résumé:* Visions of Amen

The sun has risen. It is not certain what this sun is. Astronomers concern themselves a great deal with this body. According to them, it is the central body of our planetary system; for our earth is only a small planet, and what, indeed, are we? When the sun rises like that and we are glad, we should really be sad, for what are we, anyway; the sun is 300,000 times greater than the earth; and what a host of numbers and zeros there still are, and all they have to say is this: We are but a zero, nothing at all, just nothing....

... Surely that must be an error, a mistake, those terrible numbers with all the zeros![28]

A half century later, John Updike inflected this experience in particularly American cadences. One of his protagonist's earliest memories was "a fear of not getting home on time, of being stuck in a wrong place." Now, in his seventies, sitting in the movie theater with his grandchildren and realizing he was no longer young, he

> would be visited by terror: the walls of the theatre would fall away, the sticky floor become a chasm beneath his feet. His true situation in time and space would be revealed to him: a speck of consciousness now into its seventh decade, a mortal body poised to rejoin the minerals, a member of a lost civilization that once existed on a sliding continent. The curvature of the immense Earth beneath his chair and the solidity of the piece of earth that would cover Fulham's grave would become suffocatingly real to him, all in an instant; he would begin to sweat....
>
> Why? Why should he be afflicted here? The images and music emanating from the screen were somehow the means of conveying to his apprehension these leaden, unbearable truths.... All these films had in them episodes involving heights, great spaces, places one might never get back from. To be out there, among the stars![29]

---

28. Alfred Döblin, *Alexanderplatz, Berlin: The Story of Franz Biberkopf*, trans. Eugene Jolas (New York: Viking Press, 1931), 288-89; original Alfred Döblin, *Berlin Alexanderplatz* (Berlin: S. Fischer Verlag, A.G., 1929).

29. John Updike, "The Wallet" (1985), in Updike, *Trust Me: Short Stories* (New York: Knopf, distributed by Random House, 1987), 224, 225.

Vision 2: Amen of the Stars, of the Planet with the Ring

2. Sources in Popularized Science

Messiaen was an avid reader of popular science books — progenitors of present-day magazines like *American Scientist, Nature, Robot Magazine, Scientific American,* and so on.[30] As epigraphs to his analysis of Vision 2, Messiaen inserts three quotations from these kinds of publications. The first concerns the ring of Saturn: "An immense ring, formed of luminous dust particles [*poussières lumineuses*], veritable minuscule satellites reflecting the light of the sun like so many mirrors, circle around Saturn, around 12,000 kilometers around its equator. It thrusts out over the clouds like a gigantic rainbow with forms constantly changing, close to 68,000 kilometers large."[31] Messiaen's attraction is at least twofold: the light and the multicolored rainbow; and the "forms" of the ring in constant motion and change. In short: they "dance." As Moreux writes: "What a strange vision! [*Quelle étrange vision!*] With its ring and cortege of satellites, Saturn constitutes, without contest, the most astonishing marvel of the heavens [*la plus étonnante merveille du ciel*]."[32]

A second sentence is taken from the same book: "Arcturus, a star situated about 125 light-years away, is animated by a frightening velocity [*de la vitesse*

---

30. See especially the works quoted in Messiaen's *Traité,* 1:13-36, including the section "Bergsonian Time and Musical Rhythm." They include (in order of publication date): H. G. Wells, *La Machine à explorer le Temps* (1899); Pierre Termier, *À la gloire de la Terre. Souvenirs d'un géologue* (Paris: Desclée de Brouwer, 1922); Émile Borel, *L'Espace et le Temps* (Paris: Alcan, 1922); translation: *Space and Time* (London: Blackie, 1926); *Zeit und Raum: von Euklid bis Einstein* (Stuttgart: Frankh, 1931); Abbé Théophile Moreux, *À travers les espaces célestes* (1934); Téo Varlet, *Astronomie. Le Nouvel univers astronomique* (Paris: Société française d'éditions littéraires et techniques, 1934); Alexis Carrel, *L'Homme, cet inconnu* (1935); Lecomte du Noüy, *Le Temps et la vie* (Paris: Gallimard, 1936); translation: *Biological Time* (New York: Macmillan, 1937); Paul Couderc, *La Relativité* (Paris: Presses universitaires de France, 1941); Lucien Rudaux, *Manuel pratique d'astronomie,* rev. ed. (Paris: Larousse, [1925] 1941). Note that (excepting Wells's *Time Machine*) they were published between 1922 and 1941.

Perhaps one reason Messiaen's fascination with popular astronomy seems so fresh is that these topics are hot again today. "The most basic questions of astronomy are unanswered: Is there life elsewhere in the universe? How old is the universe? What is the ultimate fate of the universe? Those are the questions we are working to answer. It's an incredibly exciting moment in astrophysics." David Charbonneau, professor of astronomy and astrophysics, Harvard University; quoted in *Boston Globe* (April 5, 2009): http://www.boston.com/news/education/higher/articles/2009/04/05/heavy_requirements_not_in_harvards_stars/.

31. Moreux, *À travers les espaces célestes,* 40; quoted in Messiaen's analysis of Vision 2, in *Traité,* 3:234.

32. Moreux, *À travers les espaces célestes,* 39.

1943: *Résumé:* Visions of Amen

effrayante] of 413 kilometers per second."[33] Arcturus captures Messiaen's association of space-time with fear. It is also biblical, one of the celestial references God poses to Job:

> Where wast thou when I laid the foundations of the earth?
> Shalt thou be able to join together the shining stars the Pleiades,
> or canst thou stop the turning about of Arcturus?[34]

The religious significance is clear: human beings should have a certain amount of modesty about both their place in the universe and their understanding of it. Messiaen was attracted to Arcturus: it reappears the following year in *Three Small Liturgies of the Divine Presence* (1944).

A third passage is taken from another popular work: "The stars, launched across space like fantastical projectiles, in addition to their individual trajectories, form part of two great general currents. These currents pass diagonally, one across the other, like rivers of dust [*poussière*] whose particles (each one animated by its own proper movement) are suns!"[35] In his extremely dense analysis of this movement, Messiaen lays out two musical fragments (Fragments X and Y). Their many variations will play with, off, against, and across one another throughout the piece, just like the two great river currents of celestial "dust" — whose particles are suns — the marquise had been correct! — each one having its own particular trajectory along with playing its part in the more general ones. As with the two "rhythmic characters" in Vision 1, it is the

---

33. Moreux, "Les Mouvements propres des étoiles" ("Motion Belonging to Stars"), in *À travers les espaces célestes*, 71-78, at 73-74; cf. 78; quoted in Messiaen's analysis of Vision 2, in *Traité*, 3:234. Note Moreux's quotation here of the Fontenelle passage seen above in which the possibility is proposed that each star is actually, like our sun, its own vortex around which revolve numerous planets. See Fontenelle, *Conversations*, 63-64; *Entretiens*, 2:98; quoted in Moreux, 74.

34. Job 38:4a, 31-32. Moreux quotes this passage from the Crampon translation in *À travers les espaces célestes*, 72.

35. Messiaen's analysis of Vision 2, in *Traité*, 3:234; quoting Rudaux, *Manuel pratique d'astronomie* ([1924] 1941). Messiaen has cut and pasted fragments of three sentences: see Rudaux, 240-41 ("Mouvements propres des étoiles" ["Motion Belonging to Stars"]). It is somewhat surprising, given Messiaen's love for everything about fairy tales, that he did not quote a passage several pages earlier: "with a telescope, and even better photographically, one can contemplate the fairy-like spectacle [*féerique spectacle*] of actual clouds of sparkly dust [*de poussière étincelante*], each grain of which is a Sun!" (235-36). There is something poignant about his parents' use of dust *(poussière)*, usually connoting the Ash Wednesday command ("Remember, man, that thou art dust" ["Souviens-toi, ô homme, que tu es poussière"]), and this transformation of the morbid image into a sparkling sun.

Vision 2: Amen of the Stars, of the Planet with the Ring

interplay between order (two great general currents) and chaos (myriad suns each doing its own thing) that Messiaen represents in this movement's "dance."

What catalyzed Messiaen's introduction to these popular science publications? A careful look at Abbé Théophile Moreux's *Across the Celestial Spaces* (1934) with "18 individual helio-engraved illustrations" — the source of two of Messiaen's quotations — offers clues.

First, Moreux (as the title abbé denotes) was a Catholic priest. An astronomer and meteorologist, he founded the Bourges Observatory at the seminary of Saint Célestin (Bourges), where he was a professor of science and mathematics. He was famous as a "great popularizer" *(grand vulgarisateur)* of scientific works and produced a number of books with the Flammarion publishing house. His work continues today in the magazine *l'Astronomie,* a monthly popular science periodical founded by Camille Flammarion in 1882.[36] There is something subversive about this paradoxical figure. In a France where science was generally used as a weapon against Catholicism, a Catholic cleric was one of the greatest popularizers of science.

Second, Moreux's book was (not surprisingly) in service of a much larger project. It did not accept boundaries between "science" and "theology," let alone philosophical subdivisions like "physics" and "metaphysics." In this sense it was more like premodern "religion" — it was a cosmology, an attempt to see and understand the cosmos as a whole.

Across the Celestial Spaces was published in Flammarion's series entitled Good Readings. Other titles in this series indicate that its "scientific" subject matter stands apart from that of other issues: *A Papal Day; The Marriage of Love according to St. Francis de Sales; Images of Jesus Christ; Who Is Jesus Christ?; The Calvary of Louis XVI; The Curé d'Ars;* and *Saint Francis of Assisi.* In the copy I obtained and surveyed, an advertising brochure sewn into the middle of the book provided further evidence of the book's intended audience: it promoted six books by the popular and widely influential Dominican Fr. A.-D. Sertillanges, including *Saint Thomas Aquinas, God or Nothing?* and *The Catechism of Unbelievers;* two books by the popular war-wounded veteran from the Great War, Jesuit Fr. Paul Doncoeur, including *The Crisis of the Priesthood* and *Who Burned Joan of Arc?;* several works (including *Cardinal Mercier*) by Georges Goyau, the prolific Catholic apologist and intellectual (and member

---

36. Volume 118 (June 2004) of *l'Astronomie* dedicated a special dossier of articles to Abbé Moreux. See http://www2.saf-lastronomie.com/lastro/lasto406.htm; cf. http://encyclopedie.bourges.net/abbemoreux.htm and http://naturnet.free.fr/html/abbe.htm. I am very grateful to the editorial staff of *l'Astronomie* for graciously sending me a copy of the June 2004 issue.

1943: Résumé: Visions of Amen

of the Académie Française); and works by two key literary figures in Catholic Revivalism, Francis Jammes and René Johannet. Since all were figures central to the postwar Catholic Revivalist movement, we can situate Abbé Moreux's book here: it was published within the context of this Catholic milieu aimed at bringing religion back into the very center of intellectual and cultural discourse.[37] This is the same Catholic Revivalist world in which Messiaen's father Pierre and brother Alain were deeply embedded. Indeed, it seems very likely that one of them first passed the book on to him.

Knowing this milieu helps us understand the way in which Moreux lays out his book. The first chapter is entitled "Where Are We?" (Moreux had already published volumes posing questions echoing those made famous by Paul Gauguin's painting[38] a decade earlier: *Where Do We Come From?* [1909]; *Who Are We? Where Are We? Where Are We Going?* [1910].)[39] He begins by interrogating his reader:

> In those rare moments in which your hectic existence allows you some leisure for meditation, reader who has just purchased this work because you love Astronomy, have you posed for yourself this simple question: "Where am I?"
>
> — Where am I? But you will protest, I know my geographical place. I know very well that I live in a certain region of France, Switzerland, or

---

37. Yves Balmer makes this same point with regard to a book that is one of the cornerstones of Messiaen's theories on rhythm: "one discovers that *Les Rythmes et la vie* is hardly as secular as its title would suggest. Rather, it falls entirely within the vein of the Catholic Renaissance." Balmer, "Religious Literature in Messiaen's Personal Library," in *Messiaen the Theologian,* ed. Andrew Shenton (Burlington, Vt.: Ashgate, 2010), 23; Maxime Laignel-Lavastine, ed., *Les Rythmes et la vie* (Paris: Plon, 1947).

38. Paul Gauguin painted *D'où venons-nous? Que sommes-nous? Où allons-nous?* (Where do we come from? What are we? Where are we going?) in late 1897 and early 1898. Its title's questions "related it inevitably to the impending centenary transition" two years away. See Albert Boime: *Revelation of Modernism: Responses to Cultural Crises in Fin-de-siècle Painting* (Columbia: University of Missouri Press, 2008), 135.

39. Théophile Moreux, *D'où venons-nous?* (Paris: Maison de la Bonne presse, 1909); Moreux, *Qui sommes-nous?* (Paris: Maison de la Bonne presse, 1910); Moreux, *Qui sommes-nous?; Où sommes-nous?; Où allons-nous?* (Paris: Maison de la Bonne presse, 1910). The four questions were eventually collated into a single book entitled *Les Énigmes de la création* (1911); they were also available as individual volumes. Moreux immediately followed up these works with *Are Other Worlds Inhabited? (Les autres mondes sont-ils habités?)* (1912, cited above). Note that while Gauguin's title asked "WHAT [*Que*] are we?" Moreux's asked "WHO [*Qui*]?"

Vision 2: Amen of the Stars, of the Planet with the Ring

Spain, countries situated in Europe, and that Europe is itself part of the Earth.

— Perfect! But where is the Earth?
— In space, obviously.
— Very good! However, it is necessary for us to be yet more precise.[40]

From here, Moreux proceeds with prose like that quoted by Messiaen, namely, a statistical and descriptive summation of facts and figures designed precisely to make the reader *experience* just how small one is in the grand scheme.[41] Moreux opens with overwhelming numbers, velocities, and distances:

In order to respond to this new question, let's distance ourselves for a moment, leaving our modest stay [*séjour*]. Light, which goes faster than our airplanes and even more than our fastest bombshells, because it travels 300,000 kilometers a second, might, if you do not see it as inconvenient, serve as our vehicle.

— One, two, three, four . . . count the seconds.

At the end of an hour, you will have reached 3,600 seconds and we will have traveled a little more than a billion kilometers.

Let us voyage an entire day, 24 hours, at the rate of 300,000 kilometers per second, and we will have been transported in space approximately 26 billion kilometers. What a frightening distance! An airplane going 200 kilometers per hour would need just under 15,000 years in order to accomplish this fantastical trek.[42]

The abbé continues to lay out the universe as he moves toward the conclusion he wants to reach. If we are nothing but matter, briefly attached to the earth but soon enough dispersed to "the four winds of the heavens," then we should not be asking such questions. "Why, in this case, would man seek to understand the mystery of creation; why occupy oneself with the stars, the super-terrestrial Universe; why study Astronomy, why seek to calculate the distances of the stars, sound out the depths of the heavens? Why try hard to contribute to human progress if tomorrow we will no longer exist? Why strive to comprehend the constitution of the world, if we play no role, if we do not

---

40. Moreux, *À travers les espaces célestes*, 3.
41. For an American parallel, see Annie Dillard's rhetorical strategy in Dillard, *For the Time Being* (New York: Knopf, distributed by Random House, 1999).
42. Moreux, *À travers les espaces célestes*, 4.

1943: *Résumé:* Visions of Amen

contribute a single note in this sublime concert sung to the glory of the Creator?"[43] Having established the cosmological, ethical, and religious settings of the first chapter's question, "Where Are We?" Moreux proceeds systematically through the others: (2) "Our Place in the Solar System"; (3) "Simple Excursion into the Solar System"; (4) "Distance of the Stars"; (5) "The Stars of Space and Evolution of the Stars"; (6) "Movements Proper to Stars"; (7) "The Structure of the Universe." However, whereas scientific positivism of the nineteenth century had used such statistics to reduce the human being to an utterly insignificant material traveler, the abbé, not unexpectedly, comes to precisely the opposite conclusion: a song of praise.

> My mind may wander across the spaces, brush up against monstrous suns [*des soleils monstrueux*], lose itself within the nebulae springing out of chaos [*surgissant du chaos*], assist at the agony of aging systems, millions and millions of years not sufficing to visit these splendors. My ecstatic soul would not cease admiring, O divine Architect, this variety and this profusion of riches, because it is You that it would rediscover everywhere and always.
>
> *I am* is your name; this creation is your work; possibly it is not the only one, but all things, present, past, or future, are nothing in the face of your Being. Before You, everything is comparable to nothing; it is barely a light veil behind which shines the light of your infinite perfections.[44]

Moreux's influence on Messiaen was long lasting: compare this passage to the *Meditations on the Mystery of the Holy Trinity* (1969), *From Canyons to Stars* (1974), and *Book of the Blessed Sacrament* (1984).

For Messiaen, questions of astronomy and physics are as "religious" or "theological" as questions of religious doctrine. In this sense his mind is less modern than medieval. The modern mind draws strict boundaries between topics like Jesus Christ (religion) and the evolution of solar systems (science). Messiaen does not make these distinctions. Like the medievals, topics like time, space, and creation are essential to the meaning of topics like the incarnation, death, and resurrection of Jesus. These are all, in some respects, cosmological topics in the broadest sense — they have only one object in view: Being. Recall Messiaen's characterizations of "sacred music" published just prior to the war and *Visions:* "[religious art] expresses the search for a single thing, which is God, but a single thing that is everywhere, that may be found

---

43. Moreux, *À travers les espaces célestes*, 8.
44. Moreux, *À travers les espaces célestes*, 93-94.

in everything, above and below everything." And again: "The religious subject encompasses all subjects: it is God and all of his creation."[45]

3. The "Dance" of the Planets

We have already seen Maurice Emmanuel's enduring impact on Messiaen in music history and folk music. So too with dance: Emmanuel had first established himself academically with his dissertation exploring the Greek "orchestic" *(orchestique),* that is, the bodily combination of dance and gymnastics, accompanied by sung and instrumental music composed in Greek poetic meters, performed in Greek dramas.[46] Another strong influence on Messiaen's conception of dance came from a rather more unexpected source: the Benedictine Dom Mocquereau's scholarship on Gregorian chant, founding theories of plainchant on "natural" dance rhythms.

Messiaen devotes a section of his *Treatise* to dance, beginning with a remark illustrating his worldview more generally: "All natural periodicities are irregular. Walking does not escape this law. It is a series of falls which are always avoided, with more or less haste or nonchalance. Let us leave aside the [marching] 'without cadence' of soldiers, frighteningly anti-natural! Free walking — the true walking — is never composed of two groups of footsteps with absolutely identical durations."[47] Messiaen's contempt for the military march parallels his abhorrence of musical meter. ("No more rhythms made monotonous by their squareness. We want to breathe freely!" he cried before the war, pleading instead for "supple and sinuous rhythms and free-flowing

---

45. Messiaen, "Autour d'une Œuvre d'orgue" ("Around an Organ Work") (April 1939), and "De la Musique sacrée" ("On Sacred Music"), in *Olivier Messiaen: Journalism, 1935-1939,* Fr 73-74, 74-76; Eng 134-35, 135-37, at 134 and 136.

46. The term *mouvement orchestique* refers to the ancient Greek gymnastic combination of dance, athletic games, and "exercises with palm branches." It was the doctoral dissertation topic of Messiaen's teacher, Maurice Emmanuel: *Essai sur l'orchestique grecque: étude de ses mouvements d'après les monuments figurés . . . : thèse presentée de la Faculté des lettres de Paris* (Paris: Hachette, 1895). Its publication as a monograph altered the title so as not to confuse a broader audience: *orchestique* was simplified to *danse.* See Emmanuel, *La danse grecque antique d'après les monuments figurés* (Paris: Hachette, 1896); Emmanuel, *The Antique Greek Dance, After Sculptured and Painted Figures,* trans. Harriet Jean Beauley (London: John Lane, [1916] 1927). Emmanuel's work had a doubly profound influence on Messiaen, both directly as his Conservatory professor and indirectly through the musical theory of Dom Mocquereau.

47. Messiaen, "Danse," in *Traité,* 1:58-61, at 58.

1943: *Résumé:* Visions of Amen

imagination, unhindered by 'meter.' ")[48] For him both are "frighteningly antinatural"! Having declared that even everyday walking consists of unequal rhythms and durations, he distinguishes the art of dance:

> In other words, we walk in a space and a time which are imposed on us — the dancer, by contrast, tries to create a personal space and time [*un espace et un temps personnels*]. Philosophers establish a difference: between concrete or sense-accessible extension and conceptual or abstract Space; between the concrete or sense-accessible duration and conceptual or abstract Time. During the dance, the dancer, emerging out from himself, constructs an abstract space and time, objective, homogenous, a geometrical space, a quantitative time; his rhythm extends at once into the space and time designed by him: it becomes Number [*il devient le Nombre*].[49]

We have already encountered Messiaen's source for this argument in discussing *The Death of Number*. Messiaen follows Cuvillier's account of Bergson: "It is precisely because [space] is a principle of dividing up [*morcellement*], of division in the simultaneity, that space makes measurement possible: *space is the principle of number,* and not the inverse. . . . Thus, 'every clear idea of number [*toute idée claire du nombre*] implies a vision in space.' The very idea of the number two is already 'that of two different positions in space.'"[50]

From here, Messiaen evokes Paul Valéry and calls dance "the symbol of Life itself." ("Life," wrote Valéry in *The Soul and Dance,* "is a woman who dances.") "Life — like a dancer — soars and leaps outside of herself," writes Messiaen, "then falls back on herself, incessantly, such that the living being always finds itself again, from transformations into transformations, and this

---

48. Messiaen, "La Transmutation des enthousiasmes" ("The Transmutation of Enthusiasms"), April 16, 1936, in *Olivier Messiaen: Journalism, 1935-1939,* Fr 61-62, at 61; Eng 123-24, at 123.

49. Messiaen, "Danse," 1:58. This odd capitalization of "Number" recalls Messiaen's youthful composition, *The Death of Number (La mort du nombre).* Messiaen seems to have taken the word from Dom André Mocquereau's seminal work, *Le nombre musical grégorien, ou Rythmique grégorienne, théorie et pratique,* 2 vols. (Rome: Société de Saint Jean l'Evangeliste, Desclée, 1908-1927). Volume 1 had been published in 1908; Volume 2 was published in 1927, the year preceding the death of Messiaen's mother.

50. Armand Cuvillier, *Manuel de philosophie, Tome II: Logique, Morale, Philosophie générale* (Paris: Librairie Armand Colin, 1927), 558; quoting phrases from Bergson, *Essai sur les données immédiates de la conscience,* 36th ed. (Paris: Félix Alcan, 1938; original 1889), 59-68.

Vision 2: Amen of the Stars, of the Planet with the Ring

perpetual return assures its existence."[51] (Again, one of Hello's chapter titles comes to mind: "The Two Movements of Life: Expression and Contraction.")[52] This is the natural origin of rhythm; insofar as time and life are movement, they involve an endless rhythmic recurrence of what the ancient Greeks called the arsis and thesis, the rise (accented) and fall (unaccented) of metric lines. On this point, Messiaen quotes Dom Mocquereau at length:

> The frequently simultaneous employment of the three arts of movement — poetry, music, dance — has led them to make use of only a single rhythmic terminology. They borrow from a local rhythmic movement of dance two clear luminous expressions which they then apply to the rhythmic movement of sounds, either vocal or instrumental. In dance, they are called *arsis,* the ascending movement, the elevation of the body [*l'élan du corps*], and the *thesis,* the downward motion, the reposition of the body [*le repos du corps*] to its movement's terminus. As a result, in music (vocal or instrumental) and in poetry, the terms arsis, elevation, and *élan* denote those sounds and syllables corresponding to the body's ascent; and the terms thesis, deposition, and *repos* denote the sounds and syllables sung at the same moment as the dancers touch the floor — whether in order to get some simple support before rising up again, or in order to complete their motion with a definitive rest [*un repos définitif*]. Thus it is from the movement of dancers that the terms arsis and thesis come down to us. We call arsis the commencement and thesis the conclusion of an orchestic movement [*d'un mouvement orchestique*].[53]

For further analysis, Messiaen directs his reader to a chapter devoted to the arsis-thesis rhythm found in the fourth volume of his *Treatise*.[54]

To the reader unacquainted with Messiaen's extensive writings, his de-

---

51. Messiaen, "Danse," in *Traité,* 1:58; quoting Paul Valéry, *Eupalinos ou l'Architecte, précédé de l'Âme et la danse* (Paris: Éd. de la N.R.F., 1923); cf. Valéry, *Dance and the Soul: The Original French Text with a Translation,* trans. Dorothy Bussy (London: John Lehmann, 1951).

52. Hello, "Les deux mouvements de la vie: expression et contraction," in *Du néant à dieu,* ed. Jules-Philippe Heuzey, 2 vols. (Paris: Perrin et Cie, [1921] 1930), 1:32-34.

53. Messiaen quoting Dom Mocquereau, in "Danse," in *Traité,* 1:59, translation mine. For passage in English, see Mocquereau, *"Le Nombre Musical Grégorien": A Study of Gregorian Musical Rhythm,* trans. Aileen Tone (Rome, Tournay, and Paris: Société de Saint Jean l'Évangeliste, Desclée & Cie, 1932), 113.

54. Messiaen, "Dom Mocquereau et *le Nombre musical Grégorien,"* in *Traité,* 4:43-52; cf. Messiaen, "Théorie simplifiée de la rythmique grégorienne," in *Traité,* 4:52-65.

1943: Résumé: Visions of Amen

scription of "the life of the planets" as being necessarily represented as a "dance" can seem whimsical and merely picturesque. However, his cosmology has been carefully thought through and is the product of having read deeply in sources as different as Bergson, Cuvillier, Moreux, Emmanuel, and Mocquereau. The creation of "light" necessarily entails the creation of "time" insofar as daytime and nighttime are separated; this entails the spatialization of simultaneity, which results in number; number entails rhythm — the alternating rhythm of life, the sun's rising (arsis) and setting (thesis).

In the end, however, such abstractions are poetically gathered in the biblical account:

> God said: "Let there be bodies of light [*des corps de lumière*] made in the firmament of the sky, so that they might separate day from night; and let them serve as signs [*des signes*] to mark the seasons, days and years [*les temps, les jours et les années*]. Let them glimmer [*Qu'ils luisent*] in the firmament of the sky, and let them light up the earth [*qu'ils éclairent la terre*]." And thus it was done. God made two great luminous bodies [*deux grands corps lumineux*], the larger one to preside over day, the lesser one to preside over night: He also made the stars. And He put them in the firmament of the sky to glimmer over the earth [*luire sur la terre*], to preside over day and night, and to separate light from darkness [*la lumière d'avec les ténèbres*]. And God saw that this was good.
>
> And of the evening and morning was made the fourth day.[55]

The biblical account of light and time also explains a curiosity in Messiaen's commentary on his second vision as being about "stars, suns, and Saturn." To the modern reader, the distinction between "suns" and "stars" makes no sense. But in the Genesis account, there are two "suns" or "great lights" — the larger one (sun) presiding over day and the smaller one (moon) presiding over night. Their creation is followed by the stars. As in Vision 1: light and life are inextricably linked.

4. The Dance as "Savage (Wild)": A Sacrifice

The phrase *danse sauvage* has come down to the present perhaps most immediately meaning the floor show inaugurated in October 1925 by Josephine Baker

---

55. Gen. 1:14-19; literally translating Fillion.

Vision 2: Amen of the Stars, of the Planet with the Ring

and the *Revue nègre* at the Théâtre des Champs-Élysées.[56] But "savage dance" had precedents in the previous decade. It was the title of an experimental piano work (translated as *Wild Men's Dance*) composed around 1913 by Leo Ornstein, estimated to be "the single most important figure on the American modern-music scene in the 1910s."[57] When Ornstein shocked London audiences with *Danse Sauvage* on the eve of World War I, one critic enthused: "A year ago no one dreamt that, in a few short months a new star would arrive in the musical sky and effectually pale the fire of Schoenberg and Stravinsky. But the unexpected has happened, and the latest apostle of Futurism made his bow to a London audience at Steinway Hall. His name is Leo Ornstein."[58] At the other end of the Great War, Karol Szymanowski wrote the piano accompaniment for a violin piece by Paul Kochanski yet again entitled *Danse Sauvage* (1925).[59]

It would seem logical that Ornstein's *Wild Men's Dance* (ca. 1913) was inspired by Igor Stravinsky's *Rite of Spring*. The work's May 29, 1913, premiere provoked an audience uprising at the Théâtre de Champs-Élysées; it soon came to be associated with the sacrificial slaughter of youth in the atavistic Great War that followed.[60] It is also difficult not to suspect that Messiaen had

---

56. See Jody Blake, *Le Tumulte Noir: Modernist Art and Popular Entertainment in Jazz-Age Paris, 1900-1930* (University Park: Pennsylvania State University Press, 1999), 91-101; and numerous index entries for *danse sauvage* and *La Revue nègre* (both troupe and show) in Bennetta Jules-Rosette, *Josephine Baker in Art and Life: The Icon and the Image* (Urbana and Chicago: University of Illinois Press, 2007).

57. Carol J. Oja, "Leo Ornstein: 'Wild Man' of the 1910s," in Oja, *Making Music Modern: New York in the 1920s* (New York: Oxford University Press, 2000), 11-24, at 15; cf. Michael Broyles and Oja, "Ornstein, Leo," in *Grove Music Online. Oxford Music Online*, http://www.oxfordmusiconline.com.proxy.bc.edu/subscriber/article/grove/music/20486 (accessed March 3, 2011). For the work, see Leo Ornstein, *Danse Sauvage = Wild Men's Dance: op. 13, no. 2* (London: Schott, 1915). Several versions of Ornstein's *Danse Sauvage* are available on YouTube, including some visually accompanied by the score.

58. Review in the *London Globe* (1914); quoted in H. Thomas Hurley, "Leo Ornstein: The Man and His Music," *Wisconsin Academy Review* 34, no. 2 (March 1988): 16-19, at 17. The London concert (March 27, 1914) not only premiered *Danse Sauvage* and other works, it also marked Ornstein's solo debut as a modern virtuoso. See Oja, *Making Music Modern*, 14.

59. Pawel Kochański and Karol Szymanowski, *Danse Sauvage = Wild Dance* (New York: Carl Fischer, 1925). For Kochański's associations with Szymanowski and Stravinsky, see Mieczyslawa Hanuszewska, "Kochański, Pawel," in *Grove Music Online. Oxford Music Online*, http://www.oxfordmusiconline.com.proxy.bc.edu/subscriber/article/grove/music/15236 (accessed March 3, 2011).

60. Modris Eksteins, *Rites of Spring: The Great War and the Birth of the Modern Age* (Boston: Houghton Mifflin, 1989), 9-54; cf. Stephen Schloesser, *Jazz Age Catholicism: Mystic Modernism in Postwar Paris, 1919-1933* (Toronto: University of Toronto Press, 2005), 143.

1943: *Résumé:* Visions of Amen

Stravinsky's work in mind when he composed Vision 2, this "Dance brutal and savage [*brutale et sauvage*]. Violent turning [*tournent*] of the stars, the suns, and Saturn." As noted in Vision 1, Messiaen identifies two "rhythmic characters" in his analysis of Stravinsky's pivotal movement "Glorification of the Elect": the almost motionless Elders and the whirling Elect, violently turning up to her death. Messiaen writes:

> It is known that before writing the *Rite of Spring,* Igor Stravinsky had an initial vision of the work: a young girl, elected, chosen, to be sacrificed to the Earth, symbolizing the bud [*le bourgeon*] about to explode, *dances and turns all the way until death* [*dansait et tournait jusqu'à la mort*] in front of a lineup of dried up old men, silent and motionless, symbolizing the rough husk which the fragile bud is going to pierce.... We will soon see this young girl dance and die in a *rhythmic and geological orgy* [*une orgie rythmique et géologique*]: this will be the colossal "Sacred Dance."...
>
> The "Glorification of the Elect" is one of the most characteristic passages of the *Rite*. The savagery of the music, the brutality of the orchestration [*la sauvagerie de la musique, la brutalité de l'orchestration*], have made it justifiably famous.[61]

In Messiaen's imagination, the "brutal and savage dance" of the planets and the savage dance of the one elected to be sacrificed seem to be aspects of a more universal narrative ruling life. In Vision 3, the "Amen of the Agony of Jesus," this more general narrative of violence and sacrifice receives a new inflection.

As for the sacrificial girl symbolizing spring's "budding" life about to explode, recall the book of poems written by Cécile Sauvage about Messiaen when she was pregnant with him — *The Budding Soul*. Messiaen repeats some of this commentary several pages later as he analyzes Stravinsky's "Sacred Dance" section. Here the association of the "bud" with "pregnancy" is made more explicit:

> The Elected and her turning movement [*mouvement tournoyant*] symbolizes the tender and fragile bud [*le bourgeon*] which is going to pierce through the wooden shell in order to explode Life [*éclater la Vie*].... In the "Sacred Dance," the terrible and magnificent giving birth [*l'accouchement terrible et*

---

61. Messiaen, analysis of Stravinsky's *Rite of Spring*, in *Traité,* 2:97-147, at 111-12. The title of the "Glorification of the Elect (or: Chosen One)" movement was originally "Glorification-savage dance (Amazons)." See Pieter C. van den Toorn, *Stravinsky and "The Rite of Spring": The Beginnings of a Musical Language* (Berkeley and Los Angeles: University of California Press, 1987); http://ark.cdlib.org/ark:/13030/ft967nb647/, 24 (Table 1).

Vision 2: Amen of the Stars, of the Planet with the Ring

grandiose], the monstrous parturition [*l'effroyable parturition*] of the Earth in Spring, are carried to their climax. The "Sacred Dance" is the inducement for the entire *Rite:* it is both the initial cause and final accomplishment, the departure and the summit, the only possible conclusion. It is one in a million [*une chose inouïe*], this human sacrifice engenders the forces of Life, that this Greek orchestic death [*cette mort orchestique*],[62] by means of both dance and movement, in an orgy of numbers and values, in a Pythian delirium [*délire pythien*] expressed by oracles in gestures and in footsteps, resolving itself by Rhythm.[63]

This complex passage demonstrates Messiaen's remarkable capacity for synthesizing wide-ranging sources and metaphors, piling them on top of one another, layer upon layer: Stravinsky's original inspiration; Greek drama, gymnastic-dance *(orchestique),* and rhythm (thanks to Emmanuel and Mocquereau); the obvious though implicit evocations of his mother, merging her figure with that of Stravinsky's "Elected," her pregnancy with Messiaen "in bud," the "sacrifice" of a young woman as she dies giving birth to new life, an event both terrible and monstrous in its cosmic scale; equally obvious though unspoken, the "one in a million" figure of Christ's passion, sacrificial death, and resurrection; and the Christian extension of the Jewish Passover in spring. Sacrificial dance links Vision 2 (stars) to Vision 3 (agony of Jesus).

Messiaen's penchant for using "primitivist" elements to construct ultramodern music puts him squarely in the camp of Stravinsky, Picasso, and other high modernists.[64] This primitivism was intimately connected with the exposure to and importation of elements from the far reaches of European empires, including Africa, India, and the Far East. We have seen the effect made on Messiaen by his "sisters and brothers of Bali, who love rhythm as I do" at the International Exposition of 1931, as well as his enthusiastic endorsement of Jolivet's *Mana* in 1937.[65]

---

62. For the term *genre orchestique,* see n. 46 above.
63. Messiaen, analysis of Stravinsky's "Danse Sacrale" in the *Rite of Spring,* in *Traité,* 2:124. The "Pythian delirium" refers to the "delirious" visions of the oracle at Delphi, expressed in frequently violent dances and bodily trances.
64. As Michael North writes: "the modern itself is an unstable category when the new, in literature and in fashion, comes into being in such close association with the ancient." North, *Reading 1922: A Return to the Scene of the Modern* (New York: Oxford University Press, 1999), 29; quoted in Schloesser, *Jazz Age Catholicism,* 12; cf. 143, 332-33 n. 49.
65. Messiaen, "Danse," in *Traité,* 1:59; and Messiaen, "Billet Parisien: Le *Mana* de Jolivet" (December 1937), in *Olivier Messiaen: Journalism, 1935-1939,* Fr 34-36, 95-97.

1943: *Résumé:* Visions of Amen

The year after the International Exposition, Raymond Cogniat's coffee-table book entitled *Dances of Indochina* was published in the Discovery of the World series.[66] Inside its covers were sixty full-page photographs of dancers from contemporary Vietnam, Laos, and Cambodia. With remarkable variety, the book presents dancers engaged in highly stylized ritual dances within temple settings; posed dancers clothed in princely garments; long lines of dancers marching in streets; group and individual portraits; and seminude dancers, one engaged in the "Moi Dance of Seduction" and another with a shield engaged in a Moi combat dance.

These last two plates of the Moi particularly impressed Messiaen. He used this particular dyad — seduction and war — as yet another example of the rhythmic arsis-thesis pulsing throughout life:

> If we want to accurately account for how dances have two essential motors at their origin — combat and love — we bring dance back to two vital instincts, the instinct of preservation and the instinct of procreation: dances of war, dances of seduction. Departing from these origins, dance went on to satisfy other needs of human nature, emotional needs more often, which came to temper the brutality [*brutalité*] of instinctive needs. The intervening mystical necessity superposed rites on these gestures of passion and, the more advanced a race's evolution, the more this rite pushed farther into stylization, to the point of making it sometimes forget all of its original appearances.[67]

Rereading Messiaen's initial "author's note" on Vision 2 makes the "primitivist" aims of the movement clearer: "Dance brutal and savage [*brutale et sauvage*]. Violent turning [*Tournent violemment*]." In the Western cosmic tradition there might have been a "great chain of being" providing linkage from the most celestial forms to the most terrestrial, but it had a static character to it, a stationary ladder of "participation" in varying degrees of being and essence. Messiaen preserves this cosmic sense of unity. But his cosmos is radically different, in constant motion — or perhaps better, constant agitation — less like the calm, endless ebbing and flowing of the tides; more like the passionate instincts of the bedchamber and battlefield. This is true of Messiaen's suns, stars, and planets as well as of ancient dancers in Indonesia and Indochina.

---

66. Raymond Cogniat, *Danses d'Indochine* (Paris: Éd. des Chroniques du jour: G. di San Lazzaro, 1932).

67. Cogniat, *Danses,* quoted in Messiaen, "Danse," *Traité,* 1:59.

Vision 2: Amen of the Stars, of the Planet with the Ring

One final example of the oscillation underlying life deserves mention: Messiaen devotes the largest amount of text in his section on dance to Hinduism. The books he cites in his *Treatise* did not appear until 1951 and 1954 — *India, Divine Images: Nine Centuries of Unknown Hindu Art; (5th-13th Centuries)* (1954), and *Hindu Dance* (1951) — so they cannot have had a direct influence on his 1943 composition of *Visions*.[68] However, since they underscore Messiaen's frank confrontation with the linkage of destruction and creation, a brief look at his remarks on Hinduism is instructive.

Messiaen introduces Hinduism via the Balinese dancers: "We know that the dances and the music of Bali have their provenance from antique Hindu traditions." He then quotes from the 1951 work — "Hindu dance is the physical manifestation of cosmic rhythm" — and goes on to explain, specifying more rhythmic patterns:

> Shiva-Nataraja is the God Shiva under his aspect of eternal dancer. In dancing the dance Tandava, he perpetually destroys and reconstructs, annihilates and resuscitates illusions and disillusions. Numerous Hindu sculptures represent this dance of Shiva. [Quoting a 1954 work:] "The harmonious disposition of 6, 8, or 10 arms of the dancer, of his head and of his legs, expresses the unceasing perfect equilibrium between the creation and the destruction of the Universe, between birth and death. The contrast between the movement of his limbs and the immobility of his face expresses the paradox of time and of eternity, of mortal existence and of the indestructible Self." (Pierre Rambach and Vitold de Golish). . . . Shiva-Nataraja dances always [time] and everywhere [space]. Every activity of life is maintained by Shiva "in the numerous phenomena which he changes, creates, destroys turn by turn, these manifestations being always the expression of his cosmic dance." (Srimati Usha).[69]

Everywhere he turns, Messiaen locates rhythmic dyads that lend themselves to a surrealist's juxtaposition: creation and destruction; seduction and war; birth and death; movement and immobility; arsis and thesis; time and eternity. The dance of the planets — the dance of life — shot through with violence, yet from a certain standpoint, "unceasing perfect equilibirium."

68. Pierre Rambach and Vitold de Golish, *L'Inde, images divines: neuf siècles d'art hindou méconnu: Ve-XIIIe siècles* (Paris: Arthaud, 1954), and Usha Chatterji (Srimati Usha), *La danse hindoue,* trans. Manah Garreau-Dombasle (Paris: Éditions Véga, 1951).

69. Messiaen, "Danse," in *Traité,* 1:60; quoting Rambach and de Golish (1954) and Chatterji (Srimati Usha) (1951).

1943: Résumé: Visions of Amen

5. Birdsong

Although birdsong will be more explicit and more fully utilized in Vision 5 ("Amen of the Angels, of Saints, of Birdsong"), it makes its entrance here in Vision 2. This is another indication that the heavenly sphere of the planets (Vision 2) is explicitly meant to be linked with the "aeviternity" of the angels (Vision 5). Thomas Aquinas writes about those whose "being neither consists in change nor is the subject of change" and which nevertheless have "change annexed to them either actually or potentially": "This appears in the heavenly bodies, the substantial being of which is unchangeable; and yet with unchangeable being they have changeableness of place. The same applies to the angels, who have an unchangeable being as regards their nature with changeableness as regards choice; moreover they have changeableness of intelligence, of affections and of places in their own degree."[70] Birdsong shares this characteristic: inasmuch as any particular birdsong is unchangeable (the song of a blackbird, for example), it is also changeable insofar as particular motifs can be mixed and matched. Messiaen notes this as he describes the blackbird:

> *The Blackbird* — the most original and melodically the most complete of the bird singers. Plumage entirely black, yellow beak. Found in woods and groves. Sings at sunrise, afternoon, and at sunset. A strophic song with the melodic formulae frequently ending upwards on a high note. Made of melodic variations of an inexhaustible variety, linking together up to 7 different strophes. Its best song is towards 5 o'clock in the morning in April-May. Found throughout France. One must also cite the White-rumped Shama of Asia [*Copsychus malabaricus*], excellent singer, with a long black-and-white tail. Song brilliant, strong, and cheerful.[71]

In addition to Messiaen's capacity to form "seven different strophes" by linking fragments from the blackbird's song, Messiaen's notes also seem to bear on this movement in two other ways. First, this is a movement that is "early" — both in the day (5 A.M., just before sunrise) and in the annual cycle (springtime). Second, the white-rumped shama has a tail of tiered colors (black and white), perhaps evoking for Messiaen the "tiered" rings of Saturn.

---

70. St. Thomas Aquinas, *The "Summa Theologica" of St. Thomas Aquinas,* trans. Dominicans of the English Province, 22 vols., 2nd rev. ed. (London: Burns, Oates and Washbourne, 1920-1942), Ia, q. 10., a. 5, "The Difference of Aeviternity and Time."

71. Messiaen, analysis of Vision 5, in *Traité,* 3:256.

Vision 2: Amen of the Stars, of the Planet with the Ring

Like the Baroque rigaudon dance form used in this movement, birdsong is a highly stylized abstract motif that is, however, capable of widely various permutations and improvisations. It is appropriate that both should be introduced here in the planetary sphere, situated as it is between eternity and time. All four — angels, celestial bodies, dance forms, and birdsongs — would seem to occupy the hybrid metaphysical borderland mapped out by Aquinas: the substantial being of which is unchangeable; and yet with unchangeable being they also share changeableness.

6. Points for Close Listening

The "Theme of the Dance of the Planets" is first laid out (00:01-00:16) by the second piano (while the first piano remains silent) and then repeated without variation (00:17-00:30). It is "monophonic" — that is, only the one voice is heard (played by the two hands an octave apart) as if this were a plainchant. (Messiaen had used this monophonic technique in *Glorified Bodies,* especially in the first movement, "Subtlety of the Glorified Bodies," and again in *Quartet for the End of Time.*) Messiaen notes that this section has been composed in the form of a rigaudon, a Baroque dance genre originating in a folk dance "traditionally associated with southern France, especially the provinces of Vavarais, Languedoc, Dauphiné and Provence" — the region from which Messiaen's mother hailed, where he spent his childhood, and which he called home throughout his life.[72] Three more periods based on the theme (00:31-01:22) fix the dance firmly in the listener's ear.

This exposition is followed by three developments. Since Messiaen describes this movement (see above) as representing the "Violent rotation of the stars, the suns, and Saturn, the planet with the multicolored ring," it seems likely that the three developments are devoted one each to these celestial bodies: stars, suns, and Saturn.

Because the exposition is monophonic and chant-like, the first development (01:23-02:18) comes as an explosion of rhythm and tones as the first piano jumps into the fray, playing syncopated chords "rotating" (as the score indicates) in the upper register; meanwhile, fragments of the dance of the planets theme are played by the second piano with thunderous strikes — "brutal

---

72. Messiaen, analysis of Vision 2, in *Traité,* 3:235. Meredith Ellis Little, "Rigaudon," *Grove Music Online. Oxford Music Online,* http://www.oxfordmusiconline.com.proxy.bc.edu/subscriber/article/grove/music/23459 (accessed March 3, 2011).

and savage" — at both extreme ends of the spectrum. If these are the stars, we are perhaps meant to visualize them, as Messiaen writes, "launched across space like fantastical projectiles."

The second development (02:19–03:01) is marked "a little faster" with the indication that the notes are to be not only staccato but "hammered" *(martelé)*. Against steady forceful strikes in the first piano that set the pulse, the second piano plays a downward arpeggio rapidly and repeatedly (composed of the same five intervals as the dance theme, the quintuplets linked together in pairs so as to create recurring decuplets), creating a sense of "rotation" or swirling. It is easy to visualize Rudaux's "rivers of dust whose particles (each one animated by its own proper movement) are suns!" Perhaps, too, this is meant to represent Arcturus (cited in both the book of Job and Abbé Moreux), "animated by a frightening velocity [*de la vitesse effrayante*] of 413 kilometers per second."[73]

In the third development (03:02–04:17), marked "less fast" and "quasi legato," the effect is less "hammerlike" and more melodic. The increased emphasis here on "color" suggests that this is meant to represent the multicolored rotating ring of Saturn. The rapid arpeggios are taken over by the first piano and intermingled with various birdsongs, arranged so as to create a pattern based on the use of three Hindu rhythms: *râgavardhana, candrakalâ,* and *lakskmiça*. The entrance of the blackbird can be initially heard at 3:07, and immediately again a second time; it is then used repeatedly throughout the movement. Its song, as Messiaen notes, is "brilliant, strong, and cheerful," and since the blackbird sings "at sunrise, the afternoon, and sunset"[74] — that is, three different periods and effects of sunlight — it seems to represent Saturn's response to varieties of sunlight.

Finally, the fifth section (04:17–05:33) reprises the "Theme of the Dance of the Planets" that opened the movement. The listener might want to compare the five periods of this section with the parallel ones in the first exposition (00:01–01:22) to gain a sense of the piece's overall structure and equilibrium.

One last observation about "duration" and "clock time" seems worth noting. The total length of Vision 1 is 6:00; the total length of Vision 2 is 5:48. In "clock time" they are nearly identical. But it would seem that Messiaen has wanted to play here with his principles of time as it is internally experienced. It will be recalled (from the discussion above of *Diptyque*) that Messiaen summed up these two laws that "perfectly summarize lived duration":

---

73. Moreux, *À travers les espaces célestes,* 73-74; cf. 78; quoted in Messiaen's analysis of Vision 2, in *Traité,* 3:234.

74. Messiaen, analysis of Vision 5, *Traité,* 3:256.

Vision 2: Amen of the Stars, of the Planet with the Ring

a) *Feeling of the present duration.* Law: in the present, the more that time is filled with events, the more it will appear short — the more that it is empty of events, the more it will appear long.
b) *Retrospective appreciation of time passed.* Inverse law of the preceding: in the past, the more that time was filled with events, the more it will appear long now — the more it was empty of events, the more it will now appear short.[75]

Vision 1 is relatively "empty of events" while Vision 2 is "filled with events." They are almost exactly identical in length measured by the clock. The listener can decide whether they "appear" longer or shorter as they are happening; and then again, in retrospective appreciation.

---

75. Messiaen, *Traité*, 1:10, 23; summarizing Cuvillier, *Nouveau précis de philosophie. Tome I: La connaissance* (Paris: Armand Colin, 1963), 224-26; cf. discussion above of *Diptyque;* and Andrew Shenton, "Time in Olivier Messiaen's *Traité,*" in *Olivier Messiaen: Music, Art, and Literature,* ed. Christopher Dingle and Nigel Simeone (Burlington, Vt.: Ashgate, 2007), 179.

Vision 3

Amen of the Agony of Jesus

Hello: Word of Terror • Anne-Catherine Emmerich: *Dolorous Passion of Christ* • Prophet Isaiah • Éluard • Claudel • Gospels of Luke and Matthew • Greek Tragedy: Strophe-Antistrophe-Epode • Neoclassicism • Cocteau-Honneger: *Antigone* • Hello: "And Jesus Wept." • Star + Cross • Angels & Incarnation • Drops of Blood • Eliot: *Murder in the Cathedral*

The third vision transports the listener from the savage dance of limitless outer space into the suffocating confines of the Garden of Gethsemane. Agony is the necessary consequence of having become human — in this case, in the incarnation.[1] (In *Twenty Gazes at the Infant Jesus,* composed the following year, Messiaen will more explicitly develop his "star + cross" motive, inextricably linking the star at Bethlehem with the cross at Golgotha.) Years later, Messiaen summarized his vision of the incarnation in terms of eternity and time: "God, who's beyond Time . . . came in order to suffer with us. And

---

1. Compare Karl Rahner: "If we face squarely the fact of the incarnation, which our faith testifies to be the fundamental dogma of Christianity, we must simply say: God can become something, he who is unchangeable in himself can *himself* become subject to change *in something else.* . . . It follows — and this truth is now situated on a profounder level than before — that the creature is endowed, by virtue of its inmost essence and constitution, with the possibility of being assumed, of becoming the material of a possible history of God." Rahner, "On the Theology of the Incarnation," in *Theological Investigations,* trans. Cornelius Ernst, 23 vols. (Baltimore: Helicon Press, 1961-1992), 4:113, 115.

Vision 3: Amen of the Agony of Jesus

I express this in my music. . . . God is above us and still He comes to suffer with us."[2]

The paradox of an eternal and unchanging being undergoing temporal suffering lies at the very heart of Christianity. The problem was theologically solved in the first centuries by the doctrine of the Trinity; although there is a single "God" (Christianity being a monotheism), there are three distinct "persons" in that one God. Thus, one "person" (i.e., the Son) is capable of having become human and suffering; this allows "God" to truly suffer (and thus truly redeem) — but it also preserves another "person" (i.e., the Father) of this one "God" from any change whatsoever.[3] The reader of Messiaen's analysis will note how thoroughly Trinitarian this "Amen" is as the Son utters his "heart-rending moan" *(une plainte déchirante)* to the Father. His more elaborate Trinitarian analysis would appear nearly three decades later in *Meditations on the Mystery of the Holy Trinity* (1969).

When juxtaposed with the "Amen of the Stars," the "Amen of the Agony of Jesus" seems to be yet another example of the "two infinites." If the suns, stars, and planets represent the nearly infinite distance between the relative quantity of the life of a star or planet and the life of a human being — Pascal's "terror" of the "two infinites" — Jesus' hours in the Garden, confined within the finite space and time of a single human being, close to the moment of his life's end, represent the other end of that spectrum. Messiaen's title seemingly alludes to Pascal's meditation on Christ's agony in the Garden, sweating drops of blood while his followers fall asleep. Pascal writes: "Jesus will be in agony until the end of the world. We must not sleep during that time."[4]

---

2. Messiaen (June 11, 1972) in Almut Rößler, *Contributions to the Spiritual World of Olivier Messiaen,* trans. Barbara Dagg and Nancy Poland (Duisberg: Gilles & Francke, 1986), 48-56, at 52.

3. The opposite approach to this question is the third-century theory of Patripassionism (also known as Sabellianism). Coming from a conjunction of Latin words — *patri* = father; *passio* = suffer (or, more simply, to "undergo" change) — the name indicates the teaching that the "person" of the "Father" is also capable of suffering. Dom Marmion discusses this dilemma in his Christmas conference (7.4) entitled "The Incarnation Makes God Capable of Suffering, Capable of Expiating Our Sins by His Sufferings, and of Healing Us by His Humiliations." Columba Marmion, *Christ in His Mysteries,* trans. Alan Bancroft (Bethesda, Md.: Zaccheus Press, 2008), 144-48.

4. Pascal, *Pensées* (Pléiade), 717; (Lafuma) 919; (Sellier) 749; for Pléiade, see Pascal, *Œuvres complètes,* 2 vols. (Paris: Éditions Gallimard, 2000), vol. 2; for Lafuma, see Pascal, *Pensées,* trans. A. J. Krailsheimer, rev. ed. (New York: Penguin, 1995); for Sellier, see Pascal, *Pensées,* ed. and trans. Roger Ariew (Indianapolis: Hackett, 2005); cf. Stephen Schloesser, "Notes on the *Miserere* Plates Exhibited in *Mystic Masque,*" in *Mystic Masque: Reality and Semblance in*

1943: Résumé: Visions of Amen

Messiaen's "Author's Note"

Messiaen describes Vision 3 in his "Author's Note" to the published score:

> III. — Amen of the Agony of Jesus.
>
> Jesus suffers and weeps. "My Father, if this chalice cannot pass away without my drinking it, let thy will be done and not mine." (Gospel according to Saint Matthew). He accepts, let thy will be done, Amen.
>
> — Jesus is alone in the garden of Olives, face to face with his agony. Three musical motifs:
> 1) the curse of the Father on the sin of the world which Jesus represents in this moment;
> 2) a cry, rhythmic and expressive group: "anacrusis-accent-ending";
> 3) a heart-rending moan (or groan) [*une plainte déchirante*] based on 4 notes in contrary rhythms.
>
> — Then, recall of the Creation Theme. A great silence, divided into several pulsations, evokes the suffering of this hour; inexpressible suffering which the sweat of blood expresses a bit.[5]

Commentary

1. Agony: Psychophysiological Terror

Around 1933, Messiaen's brother Alain introduced him to Ernest Hello's *Words of God* (from which *Visions of Amen* took its inspiration).[6] Their mother had died about five years earlier, and Messiaen had recently taken over the organist position at La Trinité. It is impossible to say what exactly Alain had found so intriguing in this particular work, but one of its most curious aspects is that the fourth section is devoted to "tears in the Scriptures." Among the tears considered by Hello in his extended "commentaries" on scriptural texts are the following: tears in the desert; tears of the children of Israel; tears of Anna and Samuel; tears of Ezekiel, Esdras, Jeremiah, and Daniel; tears of the widows

---

Georges Rouault, 1871-1958, ed. Stephen Schloesser (Chestnut Hill, Mass.: McMullen Museum of Art, distributed by the University of Chicago Press, 2008), 157-80, at 167.

5. Messiaen, "Note de l'Auteur," *Visions de l'Amen* (1943), n.p.

6. Messiaen, in Brigitte Massin and Olivier Messiaen, *Olivier Messiaen: une poétique du merveilleux* (Aix-en-Provence: Alinéa, 1989), 155.

Vision 3: Amen of the Agony of Jesus

without tears; tears of God the Father; and the tears of Jesus at the tomb of Lazarus: "And Jesus wept."[7]

This attention to material bodily things like tears, sweat, and blood exemplified the work of Catholic Revivalist writers, whether highly sophisticated like Hello or more popular like Anne-Catherine Emmerich, who wrote *Dolorous Passion of Our Lord Jesus Christ* (1833).[8] (Mel Gibson's movie *The Passion of the Christ* [2004], famous for its prodigious use of blood, was based on Emmerich's classic work.) As Messiaen was well aware, Tournemire had based his composition *The Dolorous Passion of Christ* (1936-1937) on an extremely close reading of Emmerich's book.[9] Bodily secretions suffuse Emmerich's account of Jesus' passion and death.

> Simon [of Cyrene] was much annoyed, and expressed the greatest vexation at being obliged to carry Jesus's cross, because of the disgust provoked in him by all his bruises and his clothing soiled with blood [*toutes ses meurtrissures et ses vêtements souillés de sang*]; but Jesus wept, and cast such a pleading look upon him that he was touched, and instead of continuing to show reluctance, helped him to rise, while the executioners fastened one arm of the cross on his shoulders, and he walked behind our Lord, thus relieving him in a great measure from its weight; and when all was arranged, the procession moved forward.[10]

---

7. Hello, "Quatrième Partie: *Les larmes dans l'Ecriture*," in *Paroles de Dieu. Réflexions sur quelques textes sacrés,* ed. François Angelier (Grenoble: Jérôme Millon, [1877] 1992), 207-46.

8. See Hello, "Soupirs, larmes et sang" ("Sighs, Tears, and Blood"), in *Du néant à dieu,* ed. Jules-Philippe Heuzey, 2 vols. (Paris: Perrin et Cie, [1921] 1930), 2:72-74.

9. Parts of Tournemire's *Passion* were performed at the Pontifical Pavilion at the International Exhibition in Paris on October 30, 1937, several months after Messiaen's *Festival of Beautiful Waters.* See Joël-Marie Fauquet, *Catalogue de l'œuvre de Charles Tournemire* (Geneva: Éditions Minkoff, 1979), 95-96. *Passion* was also noted by Berteaux in his "open letter" to Messiaen: Berteaux, "'Ciment armé' . . . 'Derrière la Porte'!" ("'Reinforced Concrete' . . . 'Behind the Door'!"), *La Page musicale* (February 19, 1937): 1; in *Olivier Messiaen: Journalism, 1935-1939,* ed. Stephen Broad (Surrey, UK, and Burlington, Vt.: Ashgate, 2012), Fr 64-65, at 65; Eng 126-27, at 126. Tournemire's heavily underlined personal copy of Emmerich's book may be consulted at the Library of Congress in Washington, D.C. See Charles Tournemire Collection: Box-Folder 8/1: Anne-Catherine Emmerich, *La douloureuse passion de Notre-seigneur Jésus-Christ* (Tournai: Casterman, [18 —]); http://lccn.loc.gov/2006568223.

10. In this and subsequent quotations from Emmerich's text I have followed the published English translation but also altered it in places to conform better to the French translation (from the original German) by the Abbé Pasturel. For English, see Anna Katharina Emmerich, *The Dolorous Passion of Our Lord Jesus Christ* (Hawthorne, Calif.: Christian Book

1943: Résumé: Visions of Amen

Emmerich then follows this moment up with Jesus' encounter with Veronica, an episode not found in Scripture but enshrined within tradition.

> Among the people who gathered at the Temple from all directions were several who distanced themselves out of view of Jesus for fear of defiling themselves [*de peur de se souiller*]; others, less pharisaical, showed themselves to be accessible to compassion [*accessibles à la compassion*].[11] ... [A] woman of majestic appearance, holding a young girl by the hand, came out, and walked up to the very head of the procession. Seraphia was the name of the brave woman who thus dared to confront the enraged multitude; she was the wife of Sirach, one of the councillors belonging to the Temple, and was afterwards known by the name of Veronica, which name was given from the words *vera icon* (true portrait), to commemorate her brave conduct on this day.
>
> ... Those who were marching at the head of the procession tried to push her back; but she made her way through the mob, the soldiers, and the archers, reached Jesus, fell on her knees before him, and said, "Permit me to wipe the face of my Lord." At the same time, she took from her shoulders a beautiful shroud of fine linen [*un beau suaire de laine fine*] and presented it to Jesus, conforming to the usage established in Palestine to give a testimonial of sympathy to fatigued voyagers [*témoignage de sympathie aux voyageurs fatigués*], to the sick, and to afflicted persons. The Savior took the shroud in his left hand, wiped his bleeding face, and returned it with thanks. Seraphia kissed it, and put it under her cloak against her heart.... Both the Pharisees and the guards were greatly exasperated, not only by the sudden

---

Club of America, 1968); for French, see Emmerich, *La sainte chronique: ou, Nouvelle vie de Notre-Seigneur Jésus-Christ et de la très-sainte Vierge, d'après les visions d'Anne-Catherine Emmerich,* trans. M. l'Abbé Pasturel (Paris: V. Sarlit, 1861), Eng 257; Fr 514. The English translation (e.g., "so deplorable a condition of dirt and misery") sanitizes Emmerich's description, which follows the grotesque aesthetic embraced by nineteenth-century Catholic Revivalism. Cf. Stephen Schloesser, "1871-1901: Realism, Symbolism, Mystic Modernism," in *Mystic Masque,* 23-43, at 32-33; and Schloesser, *Jazz Age Catholicism: Mystic Modernism in Postwar Paris, 1919-1933* (Toronto: University of Toronto Press, 2005), 40-45.

11. The point of Emmerich's distinction here is an ironic one between legalism and compassion. Since the Pharisees become impure by coming into contact with Jesus' still-flowing blood and must then undergo ritual purification before entering the temple, they are reluctant to go near him. Ironically, those less concerned about religious purity laws are able to engage in compassionate acts. Since Simon of Cyrene is not Jewish ("a pagan"), although his sense of hygiene might be filled with "disgust" at so much blood, he does not have religious purity concerns about contact with it.

Vision 3: Amen of the Agony of Jesus

halt, but much more by the public testimony of veneration which was thus paid to Jesus, and they revenged themselves by striking and abusing him, while Seraphia returned in haste to her house.

... No sooner did she reach her room than she placed the woollen veil on a table, and fell almost senseless on her knees. A friend who entered the room a short time after, found her thus kneeling, with the child weeping by her side, and saw, to his astonishment, the bloody countenance of our Lord imprinted upon the veil, a perfect likeness, although heartrending and painful to look upon. He roused Seraphia, and pointed to the veil. She again knelt down before it, and exclaimed through her tears, "Now I shall indeed leave all with a happy heart, for my Lord has left me a testimony of love [*un gage de son amour*]."[12]

In the works of Hello, Emmerich, Léon Bloy, Joris-Karl Huysmans, and other Catholic Revivalists, blood, sweat, and tears figure prominently as symbolist transcendence penetrates bodily immanence. Messiaen emphasized the underpinnings of this incarnational paradox in his article "On Sacred Music" just before the war: "'Savior,' said Claudel, 'how wide and deep is the being you have created!' There is much talk these days about a 'return to the human.' One should really speak of a 'return to the divine.' Man is neither angel nor beast, far less machine. He is man: flesh and conscience, body and spirit. His heart is an abyss that only the 'divine' can fill."[13] Or, as Messiaen had written in his *Technique of My Musical Language* just prior to beginning *Visions:* "One point will attract our attention at the outset: the *charm of impossibilities*... simultaneously both voluptuous and contemplative."[14]

---

12. Emmerich, *Dolorous Passion,* 258-59; *La sainte chronique,* 514-16.

13. Messiaen, "De la Musique sacrée" ("On Sacred Music") (1939), in *Olivier Messiaen: Journalism, 1935-1939,* Fr 74-76, at 74; Eng 135-36, at 135. Messiaen quotes Paul Claudel, "Jésus est mis au tombeau," poem no. 14, from Claudel, *Le Chemin de la Croix* (Brussels: Durendal, 1911); and, indirectly, Pascal, *Pensées* (Pléiade), 572; (Lafuma) 678; (Sellier) 557; cf. Schloesser, "1902-1920: The Hard Metier of Unmasking," in *Mystic Masque,* 79-104, at 91.

14. Messiaen, *The Technique of My Musical Language,* trans. John Satterfield (Paris: Alphonse Leduc, 1956), 6; in Stephen Schloesser, "The Charm of Impossibilities: Mystic Surrealism as Contemplative Voluptuousness," in *Messiaen the Theologian,* ed. Andrew Shenton (Burlington, Vt.: Ashgate, 2010), 182. For the centrality of blood in medieval culture — and hence its appeal for nineteenth-century neo-medievalism — see Caroline Walker Bynum, *Wonderful Blood: Theology and Practice in Late Medieval Northern Germany and Beyond* (Philadelphia: University of Pennsylvania Press, 2007). For blood in Catholic Revivalism,

1943: Résumé: Visions of Amen

Vision 3 descends from this same genealogy and shares its emphasis on the body. Note two (of the four) quotations in Messiaen's *Treatise* analysis citing blood:[15]

Why is your robe red? The blood splashed back on my robe [*a rejailli sur ma robe*] and I stained all my clothes.

And the sweat became like drops of blood issuing forth [*découlant*] down to the earth.

The quotation from Isaiah demonstrates Messiaen's approach to texts and how he uses them. Here is the original passage from which it is taken:

Who is this that cometh from Edom,
    with dyed garments from Bosrah?
He is beautiful in his robe,
    and he walks in the greatness of his strength.
I, that speak justice, and am a defender to save.
Why then is thy robe red,
    and why thy garments like theirs that tread in the winepress?
I have trodden the wine press alone,
    and of the Gentiles there is not a man with me:
I have trampled on them in my indignation,
    and have crushed them in my wrath,
and their blood splashed up on my robe [*leur sang a rejailli sur Ma robe*],
    and I have stained all my apparel [*j'ai taché tous Mes vêtements*]. . . .
I have trodden down the people in my wrath,
    and have made them drunk in my indignation,
    and have brought down their strength to the earth.[16]

---

see Emmerich (noted above); Huysmans and Bloy in Schloesser, *Jazz Age Catholicism*, 40-45, 67-68; cf. Richard D. E. Burton, *Holy Tears, Holy Blood: Women, Catholicism, and the Culture of Suffering in France, 1840-1970* (Ithaca, N.Y.: Cornell University Press, 2004); Ellis Hanson, *Decadence and Catholicism* (Cambridge: Harvard University Press, 1997); Cristina Mazzoni, *Saint Hysteria: Neurosis, Mysticism, and Gender in European Culture* (Ithaca, N.Y.: Cornell University Press, 1996).

    15. Four quotations found in Messiaen, analysis of Vision 3, *Traité de rythme, de couleur, et d'ornithologie (1949-1992) en sept tomes*, 8 vols. (Paris: Alphonse Leduc, 1994-2002), 3:244.

    16. Isa. 63:1-3, 6 (Douay-CCD; altered following Fillion). Messiaen uses Fillion's translation.

Vision 3: Amen of the Agony of Jesus

There are many elements here: Bozrah was known for its iridescent dyes; Edom had always been associated with the color red; the trampled grapes and the sacrificed lifeblood are both associated with the stain on the garments that is the "glorious apparel" of a military victor.

However, Messiaen abstracts from these myriad associations and leaves us with the red robe, the blood, and the "splash back" that leaves an indelible stain. The speaker would seem to be Jesus, and, especially to a Catholic liturgical sensibility, the emotional atmosphere immediately conjures up the red vestments associated with feasts of sacrifice and martyrdom. Messiaen, always concerned with sound-colors, underscores the blood's red symbolism.[17]

Moreover, Messiaen seems to have chosen the one line from Isaiah because its verb *(rejaillir)* corresponds to that in a poem by the surrealist Éluard:

> Small tools,
> And those hands squeezing a balloon to burst it, so that the man's blood splashes his face [*le sang de l'homme lui jaillisse au visage*].
> And the wings held together like the earth and the sea.[18]

The shock of dream-like juxtaposition attracts Messiaen. Just as the balloon is filled with "empty" air one minute and splattering blood the next, so too do a diptych's opposites (earth and sea) "hold together" like wings.

Messiaen may also have been thinking of yet another wartime association made by Paul Claudel in one of his poems entitled "The Precious Blood" from *Other Poems during the War* (1916). As Claudel associates the sacrificial blood spilled by Great War soldiers with Christ's eucharistic blood, there is also the implication of eternity intersecting with spatiotemporal materiality — a sacramental predecessor to surrealism:

> The blood which is the Eternal Word,
> God who is in the mouth of his creature, in this
> heart in which he basks,
> This gulp of real wine![19]

---

17. In his reflections on the symbolism of various colors in *Traité*, 7:9-22, Messiaen quotes at length from René-Lucien Rousseau, *Les couleurs: contribution à une philosophie naturelle fondée sur l'analogie* (Paris: Flammarion, 1959).

18. Paul Éluard, "Ribbons" ("Rubans"), in *Capital of Pain,* trans. Mary Ann Caws, Patricia Terry, and Nancy Kline (Boston: Black Widow Press, 2006), 62-63.

19. Paul Claudel, "Le Précieux sang," in *Autres Poèmes durant la guerre* (1916); in *Œuvre poétique* (Paris: Gallimard, Édition N.R.F., [1957] 1962), 533.

1943: *Résumé:* Visions of Amen

Again the juxtaposition of opposites, surrealistic and yet thoroughly traditional: the abstract Eternal Word (Logos) is blood; the Creator becomes a creature drunk by another creature; the paradox of transubstantiation, the gulping of the real presence in "real wine" — the "celestial banquet."

In the second quotation, from the Gospel of Luke, physicality is doubly emphasized as the sweat becomes blood. In addition, Fillion's translation of the verb *(coulait)* is not *tombaient* (as in, for example, the Crampon and Segond translations), and Messiaen transforms it into the participial form of *découler,* connoting an issuance, emanation, or flow out of a source — normally a wound, but in this case, the sweat pores themselves function as the skin's orifices out of which blood flows.[20] At the same time, this most material of descriptions — sweating blood — is a mental one: it signifies the psychological terror Christ feels, made manifest in this extreme physicality.[21] In a literal sense, the sweating drops of blood are psychosomatic.

In Messiaen's third quoted epigraph, Hello emphasizes the mind-body connection: "Perhaps the crucifixion was felt in a more terrible manner in the Mount of Olives than on the cross. For on the cross it was felt in reality. In the Mount of Olives it was felt in the mind. The sweat of blood is the word of this terror." Messiaen musically represents this remarkable little passage in the most concrete musical way: the piano's low Cs at the end of the movement, he writes, are meant to "fall like drops of blood [*tombent comme les gouttes de sang*]."[22]

Hello designates this mental anguish as "terror" and "terrible." The word is a favorite of Messiaen's, associated in his mind with *la crainte:* awe, dread, wonder, fear of the Lord. In an interview given five years before his death, Messiaen said: "To speak of eternity, the unknowable, these are words evoking terror. All the traits of God evoke terror."[23] Messiaen's line improvises on

---

20. Messiaen's quotation of Luke 22:44 — "Et sa sueur devint comme des gouttes de sang découlant jusqu'à terre" — follows Fillion except for conjugating indicative *(qui coulait)* as participle *(découlant).* For the viscous and dynamic character of flowing blood in Catholic Revivalist works, see Frank Paul Bowman, "La circulation du sang religieux à l'époque romantique," *Romantisme* 31 (1981): 17-36.

21. This was a common trope in Huysmans: for his account of Grünewald's *Crucifixion,* see Schloesser, *Jazz Age Catholicism,* 40-41.

22. Messiaen, analysis of Vision 3, *Traité,* 3:244, 248; quoting Hello, "Coepit pavere et toedere" ("He Became Distressed and Troubled") (Mark 14:33), in *Paroles de Dieu,* 179-83, at 182. For bodily suffering in nineteenth-century symbolism, see Jeffrey Howe, "The Refuge of Art: Gustave Moreau and the Legacy of Symbolism," in *Mystic Masque,* 45-61.

23. Messiaen, interview with Patrick Szersnovicz, May 29, 1987, in "Olivier Messiaen: La Liturgie de l'arc-en-ciel," *Le Monde de la Musique* (July/August 1987): 34. I am grateful to Robert Sholl for providing this reference.

Vision 3: Amen of the Agony of Jesus

Hello's (in a work devoted to the "words" of God), which reads in reverse: "the word of this terror is the sweat of blood." (Is Hello the source for Claudel's "The blood which is the Eternal Word"?) The concept and the corporeal are one: the word is the sweat of blood irrupting from the body; it is the physical manifestation of the interior state. As Daniel-Rops had written in *Our Anxiety:* "In the Garden of Olives, Christ himself wept in distress [*a pleuré de détresse*]!"[24]

During this period of composition (December 1942–March 1943), mental anguish pervaded Messiaen's home as well as his father's. Alain, who had first given Messiaen Hello's book, was in a German prisoner of war camp. In the last pages of his diary for 1942, Messiaen speculated on possible avenues for securing Alain's release.[25] Meanwhile, as Claire's mental condition degenerated, the chaos at home would soon push Messiaen to try and find a studio where he could work without distraction.[26] The family's "bewilderment," notes Messiaen's biographers, "is reflected in a poignant document in [Olivier and Claire's son] Pascal's child's handwriting."

> To darling Mummy
>
> At a house-warming for our little place in Neussargues, we are planning a little party which will, I hope, be full of an atmosphere of "joy and friends" (the motto). I intend to make you laugh a little and you will be entertained. It is essential that we are happy. The revels will commence at 8.15, dinner at 8.45, the evening gathering at 9.15, and bedtime at 9.45. We are to respect the motto "joy and friendship," Mummy — I hope the spirit of our motto will last a long time. If I haven't mentioned "obedience," that's because, if you love your mother, you obey her.[27]

As Messiaen watched his son engage in creative efforts to cheer up his wife felled by depression, he cannot but have drawn the connection with his own childhood, similarly spent trying to ameliorate Cécile Sauvage's mental state.

It is hardly surprising that Messiaen would appreciate Hello's keenly psychological insights into the "terrible" ravages of mental anguish. One psychiatrist has noted that "The fact that we could disintegrate mentally by way of natural processes — as the schizophrenic does — is a monstrous uncanny

---

24. Henri Daniel-Rops, *Notre inquiétude, essais* (Paris: Perrin et Cie, 1927), 27.
25. Peter Hill and Nigel Simeone, *Messiaen* (New Haven: Yale University Press, 2005), 121.
26. Hill and Simeone, *Messiaen*, 157.
27. Pascal to Claire (1940s); quoted in Hill and Simeone, *Messiaen*, 158.

1943: Résumé: Visions of Amen

concept." A cultural historian expands that observation: "It is the fear of collapse, the sense of dissolution, which contaminates the Western image of all diseases, including elusive ones such as schizophrenia. . . . How we see the diseased, the mad, the polluting is a reflex of our own sense of control and the limits inherent in that sense of control."[28]

The last of Messiaen's epigraphic quotations to be considered comes from the Gospel according to Matthew's account of Jesus in the Garden: "Jesus said to them: My soul is sorrowful even unto death."[29] Given the importance of Bach's *Saint Matthew's Passion* in the history of music — in which appears Jesus' recitative "Meine Seele ist betrübt bis an den Tod, bleibet hier und wachet mit mir" — it seems appropriate that this serves as the first of Messiaen's four epigraphs. It seems worth remembering that this movement — one of Messiaen's "small passions" — was originally meant to be the centerpiece of a five-movement *Visions.*

2. Neoclassicism: Order Informing Chaos

On first glance, Messiaen's choice of neoclassical elements in this movement could simply be interpreted as using the neoclassical in the same way that it was popularly used during the Great War and the following "Jazz Age" decade of the 1920s. Already during the war, stoic and tragic forms of a classicist revival (endorsed by both the political right and left) seemed to offer "invaluable moral solace to a nation in mourning."[30] The United States' World War II Memorial on the Washington Mall serves as a recent example: the appeal to apparently timeless ancient genres (Roman arches, Grecian columns, laurel wreaths of victory) gives form to the random chaos of battle, if only by viewing

---

28. Sander L. Gilman, *Disease and Representation: The Construction of Images of Illness from Madness to AIDS* (Ithaca, N.Y.: Cornell University Press, 1988), 1, 3. Gilman is glossing a line from Manfred Bleuler, "What Is Schizophrenia?" *Schizophrenia Bulletin* 10 (1984): 8.

29. Matt. 26:38 (Fillion); quoted by Messiaen, analysis of Vision 3, *Traité,* 3:244. The line also has a poetic provenance in Lamartine; see "Pourquoi mon âme est-elle triste?" and *"Novissima verba,* ou Mon âme est triste jusqu'à la mort!" both in *Harmonies poétiques et religieuses* (Paris: C. Gosselin, 1830), in *Œuvres poétiques complètes de Lamartine,* ed. Marius-François Guyard (Paris: Éditions Gallimard, 1963), 424-30 and 472-88. For Lamartine's works transformed into Catholic expressions, see Mary Frances Dorschell, "Thérèse of Lisieux and Alphonse de Lamartine: The Spiritual Transformation of Romanticism," *Christianity and Literature* 58, no. 3 (Spring 2009): 403-27.

30. Martha Hanna, *The Mobilization of Intellect: French Scholars and Writers during the Great War* (Cambridge: Harvard University Press, 1996), 143.

Vision 3: Amen of the Agony of Jesus

tragedy from the perspective of eternity *(sub species aeternitatis)* and inculcating a sense of stoic endurance. "Classicism is Memory and Sorrow."[31]

However, in light of the remarks on disease above, Messiaen's use of the neoclassical might be read in a more textured way. Immanuel Kant's theory of the "sublime" is well known: we take material that would be, in actual existence, utterly chaotic and disintegrating for us, and we represent it within an orderly form. What would be utterly repellent in actual life becomes attractive in the sublime precisely because its orderly context means that it will not destroy us.

But it is not merely arctic shipwrecks, mass exoduses, vertiginous abysses, and other popular nineteenth-century subjects from which we desire safe distance. "Disease, with its seeming randomness," is yet another "aspect of the indeterminable universe that we wish to distance from ourselves."[32] Two decades after *Visions,* immediately following Claire's death, Messiaen would choose to frame *Chronochromie* (1960) using the same structural elements of Greek tragedy that he uses in this movement: strophe-antistrophe-epode. He uses those same elements here in 1943, as Claire's mental illness is beginning its long descent. They frame the vision of Jesus' own mental agony. They try to tame the terrible.

Messiaen notes that the movement is "Constructed like a chorus of Greek antiquity: Strophe-Antistrophe-Epode. The Antistrophe takes exactly the same elements but develops them . . . — the Epode is different and conclusive."[33] Messiaen identifies the strophe as consisting of three parts:[34]

1. The "curse of the Father on the sin of the world."
2. The "cry" of the Son in response.
3. The "tears of Jesus in his Agony." This four-note melody is inspired by Debussy's *Pelléas*.[35]

The second element, the "cry" of the Son, is itself tripartite in construction: anacrusis-accent-ending. The anacrusis, by beginning the "cry" with a nonaccent, gives it a sense of initial instability.[36] It then gathers speed, rushes

---

31. Vincent Scully, *Architecture: The Natural and the Manmade* (New York: St. Martin's Press, 1991), 297, quoted in Schloesser, *Jazz Age Catholicism,* 141.
32. Gilman, *Disease and Representation,* 4.
33. Messiaen, analysis of Vision 3, in *Traité,* 3:244.
34. Messiaen, "Note de l'Auteur."
35. Messiaen, analysis of Vision 3, in *Traité,* 3:246.
36. An anacrusis is essentially "an initiation on a non-accent, and as such it is rhyth-

toward an accent, and unfolds into its final inflection *(désinence)*. This particular rhythmic chain of accent and final inflection has neoclassicist overtones for Messiaen as he explicitly cites *Antigone* (1927), Arthur Honegger's operatic *tragédie musicale,* as a precedent.[37]

The timing of Messiaen's reference is intriguing. It suggests that he had attended the revival of *Antigone* in early February 1943 while still composing *Visions* (not completed until March). *Antigone* had been premiered sixteen years earlier; its libretto, originally Jean Cocteau's 1922 neoclassical adaptation of Sophocles' ancient drama, was set to music by Honegger (a member of Cocteau's musical "Group of Six" [*Les Six*]) five years later.[38] Since its first performances in 1927 had been failures with audiences, its wartime revival in occupied Paris was enormously (and unexpectedly) popular.[39] Antigone was likely embraced as a heroine of resistance. As one scholar notes, the success of the work is somewhat surprising in light of common perceptions about Vichy France in 1943:

> Unexpected as *Antigone*'s French triumph may have been, its occurrence in 1943, several months after the entry of German forces into previously unoccupied parts of France, is even more surprising. Just as perplexing, given this historical conjuncture, is that reviews in the collaborationist journals, *Je*

---

mically unstable: its most fundamental characteristic is the forward rhythmic impulse it generates towards the accent." Mine Doğantan, "Upbeat," in *Grove Music Online. Oxford Music Online,* http://www.oxfordmusiconline.com.proxy.bc.edu/subscriber/article/grove/music/28812 (accessed March 3, 2011).

37. Messiaen, analysis of Vision 3, in *Traité,* 3:245. On this same page, Messiaen notes that the first piano's melodic movement should make the listener think of Ravel's *Le tombeau de Couperin (Couperin's Tomb)* (composed 1914-1917). Ravel's six movements bear individual dedications to his friends killed in the Great War.

38. Jean Cocteau, *Antigone. Les Mariés de la Tour Eiffel* (Bruges: impr. Sainte-Catherine; Paris: libr. Gallimard; Éditions de la "Nouvelle Revue française," 1927); Arthur Honegger, Jean Cocteau, and Sophocles, *Antigone: Musikalische Tragödie in 3 Aufzügen* (Leipzig: Junne, 1927).

39. "When Arthur Honegger's *Antigone* was staged in Paris, sixteen years after its Brussels premiere, having first been rejected by the Paris Opéra as too 'advanced' for the public, its impact shattered all expectations. This time major critics proclaimed it a chef-d'oeuvre, lauding the director's courage in finally mounting this uncompromising work of bracing innovation in French operatic declamation and strident bi- and atonal music. Audiences, equally enthralled by Honegger and Jean Cocteau's still audacious, boldly modernist opera, pressed to its performances, irrepressibly, and inappropriately, interrupting it with applause." Jane F. Fulcher, "French Identity in Flux: The Triumph of Honegger's *Antigone,*" *Journal of Interdisciplinary History* 36, no. 4 (Spring 2006): 649-74, at 649.

Vision 3: Amen of the Agony of Jesus

suis partout and *Comoedia,* as well as in the Vichy-sanctioned *L'Information musicale,* had nothing but praise for both the opera's music and its text. The fact that both Vichy and Nazi authorities, as well as critics, approved the work, helps to crumble the notion that both regimes exercised strict ideological controls against modernism in music.[40]

For Messiaen, the appeal of *Antigone* (in addition to Honegger's setting) might have been the intersection of eternity and temporality in the tragic heroine. For Antigone, death is "the timeless eternity, the absolute principle to which she gives her undivided allegiance," and she "privileges it over mortal life."[41]

The classical figure of Antigone figured prominently in the open letters published in 1926 (the year before the original premiere of Honegger's *Antigone*) between Cocteau and Jacques Maritain. In a letter to Maritain, Cocteau wrote: "Now instinct always pushes me against the law. This is the secret reason why I translated *Antigone*. I would hate to have my love for order benefit from the meaning that is idly lent to that word. . . . I must salute, in its least high form, an unforeseen force opposed to Creon, to the foreseen mechanism of the law." Maritain responded:

> You have an admirably jealous longing for freedom. How well I understand your love for Antigone! Yet she herself tells us, and that is why she is dear to you, that in breaking human law she was following a better commandment — the unwritten and unchangeable laws.
>
> οὐ γάρ τι νῦν γε κἀφαχθες ἀφαλλ' ἀφαεί ποτε
> ζῇ ταῦτα, κοὐδεις ο ἴδεν, ἐξ ὅτου ἀ2φάνη[42]

---

40. Fulcher, "French Identity in Flux," 649.

41. See commentary in Sophocles, *Antigone,* trans. David Franklin and John Harrison (Cambridge: Cambridge University Press, 2003), 38; in Fulcher, "French Identity in Flux," 659.

42. Jean Cocteau and Jacques Maritain, *Lettre à Jacques Maritain. Réponse à Jean Cocteau* (Paris: Stock, 1926), 284, 325-26; Maritain and Cocteau, *Art and Faith: Letters between Jacques Maritain and J. Cocteau* (New York: Philosophical Library, 1948), 47, 100. See Schloesser, *Jazz Age Catholicism,* 185-90. The untranslated Greek is Antigone's response to Creon, an instruction about the precedence of eternal divine law over contingent human law. "For these [laws] have life, not simply today and yesterday, but forever, and no one knows how long ago they were revealed." Sophocles, "Antigone," in *Antigone, The Women of Trachis, Philoctetes, Oedipus at Colonus,* ed. and trans. Hugh Lloyd-Jones (Cambridge: Harvard University Press, 1994), Greek, 44, lines 456-57; English, 45. Greek phrase omitted in English translation. See Schloesser, *Jazz Age Catholicism,* 185-86.

1943: *Résumé:* Visions of Amen

Maritain likened Cocteau to Antigone, the *enfant terrible* from antiquity who broke contingent human customs in service of higher laws — invisible and eternal law, as primeval as the Greek script that preserved it in pristine purity. Although Messiaen had quite publicly repudiated Cocteau's neoclassicism in his formation of La Jeune France seven years earlier, he would nevertheless have had great sympathy with this heroine who represents "an unforeseen force opposed to . . . the foreseen mechanism of the law" — especially in occupied Paris.

Messiaen uses neoclassical formal elements to frame the subject matter of the "Agony of Jesus," that is, the terror of anguish, an experience both mental and physical. The classical tames the terror and produces the sublime; it serves as a vehicle for mourning; and it evokes invisible eternal forces opposed to (even as they intersect with) temporal tragedy.

3. The Price Paid for Taking on Spatiotemporality

As Messiaen notes, both the strophe and the antistrophe are composed of three elements: (1) the curse of the Father, (2) the cry of the Son, and (3) "a heart-rending moan (or groan) [*une plainte déchirante*]." This third element is, in turn, divided into two parts, which I have labeled 3a and 3b in my analysis:

```
00:49–01:42 = Part 3a:  Incarnation in Space-Time          mm. 17-28
01:43–02:29 = Part 3b:  Consequence: Tears of Jesus
                        in His Agony                       mm. 29-43
```

Although very simple, the melody in part 3a is among the most haunting and darkly romantic themes written by Messiaen.

Why do I call it the "Incarnation in Space-Time"? Because the melodic line (part 3a) is an almost exact quotation of the one opening Messiaen's *Nativity* (1935) suite for organ, written in the wake of Claire's multiple miscarriages. In the first movement to that, entitled "The Virgin and Child," the melody is played in the extremely slow tempo that Messiaen uses to represent eternity. It is played by the right hand in the highest possible register when using the stops Messiaen indicates (a 4' Flute and a 2⅔' Nazard). In the left hand, long, sustained chords in the upper middle register contribute to the experienced sense of timelessness. Messiaen's epigraph to this movement is taken from the prophet Zechariah:

Vision 3: Amen of the Agony of Jesus

> Conceived by a Virgin a Child is born unto us, a Son has been given us.
> Be transported by joy [*allégresse*], daughter of Sion!
> See how your king comes to you, just and humble.[43]

Now, seven years later, Messiaen transformed this same "Virgin and Child" melody (along with its opening chords lowered an octave) into the motive for Jesus' agony. However, in this new setting, Messiaen removed the original sense of timelessness. Partly this is due to the nature of the instruments: the organ sustains the chords uniformly as long as the fingers press the keys; on the piano, however, both chords and melody begin to fade as soon as the hammer strikes the strings. The organ version produces a chilly feeling from the sustained chords frozen in time. By contrast, the piano version is lushly romantic; the second piano's simple melody is accompanied by a pattern of ongoing movement played by the first piano above.

This quiet romantic motive (part 3a) is responded to by the motive Messiaen labels "The Tears of Jesus in His Agony" ("Les larmes de Jésus dans son Agonie") (part 3b), what my analysis labels the "Consequence," that is, the consequence of eternity taking on time.[44] In the score Messiaen gives this indication to the pianist at both entries of theme: "Sorrowful, weeping [*douloureux, en pleurant*]."[45]

Recall "Tears in the Scripture," the subject of the entire fourth section of Hello's *Words of God*. One chapter meditates on the father whose son is possessed: "And immediately the father of the child cried out in tears [*s'écria en pleurant*]: I believe, Lord, help my unbelief." The father of the child had asked if Jesus could do something. And Jesus replied with a strong "If!" Of this response, Hello says: "This 'if' is heart-rending [*déchirant*]!" — the same word Messiaen uses to describe Jesus' moan *(une plainte déchirante)*. Messiaen applies this heartrending "if" to Jesus, as his author's note begins with Christ's plea in the Garden: "My Father, *if* this chalice may not pass away without my drinking it, may your will be done and not mine."[46] The response reflects one of the four senses of "Amen" cited by Messiaen at the beginning of his work: "Amen, I submit, I accept. Let your will be done!"[47]

Hello's next chapter (following the father's tears) takes its title and textual

---

43. Messiaen has merged fragments: see Isa. 7:14; 9:6; and Zech. 9:9 (Fillion).
44. Messiaen, analysis of Vision 3, in *Traité*, 3:246.
45. Messiaen, *Visions de l'Amen*, 27, 30.
46. Messiaen, "Note de l'Auteur" for Vision 3; Messiaen has conflated verses 39 and 42 from Matt. 25. For Hello, see *Paroles de Dieu* (1992), 235-39, at 237.
47. Messiaen, opening of "Note de l'Auteur," *Visions de l'Amen,* n.p.

1943: *Résumé:* Visions of Amen

commentary from one of the shortest lines in Scripture: "And Jesus wept [*Et Jésus pleura*]."[48] Messiaen's immersion in Hello's thought is evident throughout. As Hello says in his commentary on Job, perhaps the title for the God of Job and Jesus should be "the God of Tears."[49]

> Tears play an immense role in the pages of the Holy Scriptures. What's more mysterious than tears? Is not the union of soul and body made clearly manifest by this physical phenomenon — a phenomenon which expresses outwardly all that is deepest and sincerest, most private and most touching, in the inward feelings of the heart? Tears are, perhaps, of all human things the most irresistible. At every instant — almost invariably — the Holy Scriptures, in telling us of a prayer that has been granted, point out that he who prayed wept while he was praying. It is as though this supreme weakness were productive of strength. Tears disarm the strong; they admit of no reply.[50]

Messiaen's "charm of impossibilities" — the inseparable (surrealist?) union of inward feelings and physical phenomena, the contemplative and the voluptuous — owes much to Hello.[51]

In this "Consequence" (part 3b), the first piano is silent as the second piano plays solo. In the right hand are four notes, repeated endlessly in syncopated rhythms, the falling downward second imitating weeping (in the style of Bach); in the left hand are harmonies whose use of major and minor seconds produces a feeling of space closing in tight, both constricting and suffocating. This harmony sequence, as noted, is from Debussy's *Pelléas*.[52] Does Messiaen intend more here than musical borrowing? Remember that the opera is about the intimate connection between love and suffering (even unto death) — a consequence that is unavoidable and seems to be destined. The "Amen of the Agony of Jesus" is followed immediately by the "Amen of Desire" — an association of cosmic suffering with human love. Remember too that in the original plan, the "Agony of Jesus" was the centerpiece of a five-movement work; in the final version, that structural role is displaced by the newly added "Desire" movement. The spirits of both Cécile Sauvage and Claire Delbos seem not

---

48. See Hello, *Paroles de Dieu*, 239-41.
49. Hello, *Paroles de Dieu*, 90; translation in Hello, *Life, Science, and Art: Being Leaves from Ernest Hello,* trans. E. M. Walker (London: R. and T. Washbourne, 1912), 168.
50. Hello, *Paroles de Dieu*, 238; translation in Hello, *Life, Science, and Art*, 173.
51. Schloesser, "The Charm of Impossibilities," 175.
52. For reference to Debussy's *Pelléas*, see Messiaen, analysis of Vision 3, *Traité*, 3:246.

Vision 3: Amen of the Agony of Jesus

far from this movement. For Messiaen, as in Debussy's *Pelléas* and Wagner's *Tristan,* love is intimately connected to tragic consequences.

Parts 3a and 3b function, then, as statement and response. By quoting the "Virgin and Child" motive from the *Nativity,* part 3a represents the paradoxical incarnation of the Eternal in space-time. In response, the heart-wrenching tears of mental anguish in part 3b represent the inevitable consequences of that divine love for humanity: the kind of psychological terror that irrupts on the body as sweating blood.

In *Visions of Amen,* Messiaen has not made the connection explicit for the audience: listeners would need to connect the "Virgin and Child" movement with the "Amen of the Agony of Jesus" on their own. However, one year later in *Twenty Gazes at the Infant Jesus,* Messiaen explicitly notes (in preface remarks for the "Gaze of the Star") that he has invented a single "star + cross" theme, a juxtaposition of the star of Bethlehem and the cross of Golgotha.[53] Already in *Visions of Amen,* then, it seems that part 3a, the "Incarnation in Space-Time," can be thought of as the star, while part 3b, the "Consequence," can be thought of as the cross. They refer back and forth to one another in an inescapable reciprocity: as a single "cross + star."

Yet another hint suggesting the spatiotemporal scandal of the incarnation for Messiaen can be found in *Twenty Gazes.* In his notes on the "Gaze of the Angels," Messiaen suggests "an astonishment bordering on jealousy on the part of the angels when they realize that the Word will be incarnated among humans rather than among them."[54] Like the "star + cross" association, this can be traced back to Dom Marmion: "Likewise the angels looked upon the Newborn, the Word-made-flesh. They saw in Him their God, and so this knowledge threw those pure spirits into amazement and wonder at so incomprehensible an abasement. For He did not will to unite Himself to *their* nature, but to human nature: 'Nowhere does He take hold of angels: *but of the seed of Abraham He takes hold.*'"[55] I have already noted the importance of "aeviternity" in Aquinas's work: God is eternal; human beings and other terrestrial beings are in time; but angels (and perhaps planets) live in "aeviternity." In this third boundary sphere, they have unchangeability as their nature; but as regards place, they are changeable (in that they can move). We can appreciate Mes-

---

53. See the discussion in Siglind Bruhn, *Messiaen's Contemplations of Covenant and Incarnation: Musical Symbols of Faith in the Two Great Piano Cycles of the 1940s* (Hillsdale, N.Y.: Pendragon Press, 2007), 138.

54. Bruhn, *Messiaen's Contemplations,* 139.

55. Marmion, chapter 7 ("O Wondrous Exchange! [Christmas]"), in *Christ in His Mysteries,* 131-53, at 151.

siaen's delight in reading Marmion, for here the Thomistic abstractions take on concrete thoughts and feelings. Why, indeed, must the angels have wondered, would God pass over "aeviternity" — in which, like God, there is no before and after — and instead take on the dimensions of spatiotemporality, in which there is before, after, change, and inescapable suffering *(passio)*?

The inevitably tragic character of the decision of timeless and immortal beings willingly taking on mortality for the sake of love has become the stuff of recent popular culture. Wim Wenders's *Wings of Desire* (1987) was popularized in the USA by Nicholas Cage and Meg Ryan in *City of Angels* (1998) — and followed up by *Faraway, So Close!* (1993). An angel must make a terrifying decision: whether or not to choose mortality after falling in love with a trapeze artist. In *Lord of the Rings*, after 3,000 years of immortality, Arwen Undómiel chooses mortality in order to marry Aragorn, the King Elessar, on Midsummer's day. In each case, it is the lure of love that appeals to the protagonists and lures them to sacrifice their own immortality in order to live with a human being until death. Notable trivia: Tolkien wrote the Ring trilogy between 1937 and 1949, contemporaneously with Messiaen's *Visions* and "Tristan Trilogy."

4. Drops of Blood / Creation Theme

In describing the epode, the third section of this movement that follows the strophe and antistrophe, Messiaen remarks that the creation theme (like a Wagnerian leitmotif) is quoted here in transposition: "The low C's fall like drops of blood. In the second measure, a recall of the Creation Theme, transposed into C major. . . . Why the Creation? Because the sufferings of Christ give grace and create the new man. It was like a second creation beginning with the sufferings of Christ, the New Adam. The first piano sounds an exhausted lament [*une plainte épuisé*], in changes of registration in the manner of Schoenberg. Two measures before the end: the final drops of blood."[56] This recall of the exuberant joy of Vision 1 (and foretaste of the consummation in Vision 7) can seem strange. However, the same general concept had been expressed shortly before the war in T. S. Eliot's play *Murder in the Cathedral* (1935). In his Christmas Day sermon, Thomas Becket, the soon-to-be-slain archbishop of Canterbury, joins the star and cross as he reflects on the nativity of Christ:

---

56. Messiaen, analysis of Vision 3, in *Traité*, 3:248.

Vision 3: Amen of the Agony of Jesus

For whenever Mass is said, we re-enact the Passion and Death of Our Lord; and on this Christmas Day we do this in celebration of His birth. So that at the same moment we rejoice in His coming for the salvation of men, and offer again to God His Body and Blood in sacrifice, oblation and satisfaction for the sins of the whole world. It was in this same night that has just passed, that a multitude of the heavenly host appeared before the shepherds at Bethlehem, saying "Glory to God in the highest, and on earth peace to men of good will"; at this same time of all the year that we celebrate at once the Birth of Our Lord and His Passion and Death upon the Cross. Beloved, as the World sees, this is to behave in a strange fashion. For who in the World will both mourn and rejoice at once and for the same reason? For either joy will be overborne by mourning, or mourning will be cast out by joy; so it is only in these our Christian mysteries that we can rejoice and mourn at once for the same reason.[57]

---

57. T. S. Eliot, *Murder in the Cathedral,* 2nd ed. (New York: Harcourt, Brace and Co., [1935] 1936), 47-48; cf. Eliot, "Murder in the Cathedral," in *The Complete Poems and Plays* (New York: Harcourt, Brace and Co., 1952), 173-221, at 198.

Vision 4

Amen of Desire

Temporality, Desire, Ends-in-View • Bergson: Duration
• Cuvillier: Degrees of Pasts & Futures • Terrible Love •
Mozart: Susanna's Aria *(Marriage of Figaro)* • Book of Song
of Songs • Massenet: *Manon Lescaut* • Breton: Surrealism

In this fourth vision, centerpiece of *Visions,* the listener experiences "the present moment" of becoming as both the arrival of the past and the longing for the future. If the last movement took place in the Garden of Gethsemane, this one takes place in what will soon become the "Garden of Sleeping Love" (movement 10, *Turangalîla Symphony* [1945-1948]), an allusion to the garden found in the biblical book Song of Songs.[1] Ever since Eden, gardens seem to be the price of being human, the desire that is also an agony. Put more abstractly, if Vision 3 was about the Eternal taking on temporality, Vision 4 is about temporality's fulfillment in eternity.

Considered from a Bergsonian perspective, this fulcrum movement is about the "present" that never really "is" but is always in a state of becoming: Heraclitus's famous "river" into which we can never step twice, always passing away, flowing forward toward the future. Emotionally speaking, the pres-

---

1. For a connection between sleep and desire, see Hello, "Le sommeil de Jacob: la vision et le désir" ("Jacob's Sleep: Vision and Desire"), and compare "L'homme de désir" ("The Man of Desire"), in *Du néant à dieu,* ed. Jules-Philippe Heuzey, 2 vols. (Paris: Perrin et Cie, [1921] 1930), 1:158-63, 2:63-66.

Vision 4: Amen of Desire

ent moment of becoming is experienced as desire. Vision 4 is the pivot point between first things and last things; between the firmly settled past and the future of limitless possibility. Desire is the fluidity of time, a period in which horizons have not been closed and in which freedom and creative novelty are open possibilities, its directionality shaped by ends-in-view.

However, recall that this movement (along with Vision 6 ["Amen of Judgment"]) was not in Messiaen's original plan. Initially, there were to be only five visions: two looking back protologically to prehistory ("Amen of Creation" and "Amen of the Stars"); two looking forward eschatologically to the end of history ("Amen of the Angels, of Saints, of Birdsong" and "Amen of Consummation"); with the "Agony of Jesus" serving as history's midpoint and fulcrum, the "new" or second creation. The decision to add the new movement of "Desire" and make it the center of the work was made in the course of composition during the winter of 1942-1943. It is a remarkable thing to displace the figure of Jesus as the work's center. And yet, the center of the work remains psychological and emotional, a different type of torment: a complex desire manifesting itself in the surrealistic alternating juxtaposition of "terrible love" with "harmonious silence."

Messiaen's "Author's Note"

Messiaen describes Vision 4 in his "Author's Note" to the published score:

> IV. — Amen of Desire.
> Two themes of desire.
> The first, slow, ecstatic, longing of a deep tenderness: already the calm perfume of Paradise.
> The second, extremely passionate: the soul is pulled by a terrible love [*amour terrible*] which expresses itself in a bodily [*charnelle*] manner (see the "Song of Songs"); but there is nothing here of the carnal [*charnel*], only a paroxysm of the thirst of Love.
> — A great calming down [*apaisement*] based on the first theme to conclude. The two principal voices seem to melt [or dissolve: *se fondre*] one into the other, and there is nothing other than the harmonious silence of Heaven. . . .

1943: Résumé: Visions of Amen

Commentary

1. Desire: The Marker of Time Being

Like the transition from the suns and Saturn to Jesus in the Garden, so too this passage from the agony of Jesus to a "desire" that may or may not be "carnal" can make *Visions of Amen* seem a thematic hodgepodge. Before turning to the specifics of the "terrible love" that Messiaen lays out, it might help to situate "desire" more broadly in a philosophical context — that is, as the emotional expression of a "duration."

Messiaen's notion of the "duration" owed a great debt, as we have seen, to Bergson. The "duration" of lived time is always singular. No matter how much clock time passes during an individual's existence, the "duration" of a June bug, a human being, and a star is uniquely one. Bergson's theorizing of internal duration, with its open-ended succession of internally indeterminate and qualitatively heterogenous states, served to combat the determinism that was seen to be an inherent corollary of nineteenth-century scientific positivism and materialism. Bergson's philosophy of duration provided a scientific framework for free will, the capacity to choose one future end-in-view over other possibilities.[2]

But "desire" aiming at an end-in-view was already implicit in Aristotle's notion of a final cause, a concept inherited and developed by Aquinas. Aquinas devotes several chapters in his *Summa contra Gentiles* to these theses:

> Every agent acts for an end.
> Every agent acts for a good.
> The end of everything is a good.
> All things are directed to one end, which is God.[3]

---

2. See Stephen Schloesser, *Jazz Age Catholicism: Mystic Modernism in Postwar Paris, 1919-1933* (Toronto: University of Toronto Press, 2005), 61-64; and Schloesser, "*Vivo ergo cogito:* Modernism as Temporalization and Its Discontents; A Propaedeutic to This Collection," in *The Reception of Pragmatism in France and the Rise of Roman Catholic Modernism, 1890-1914,* ed. David G. Schultenover (Washington, D.C.: Catholic University of America Press, 2009), 21-58, at 52-55.

3. Saint Thomas Aquinas, *Summa contra Gentiles,* bk. 3, vol. 1, cc. 2, 3, 16, 17, 18. For explanation see John F. Wippel, *The Metaphysical Thought of Thomas Aquinas: From Finite Being to Uncreated Being* (Washington, D.C.: Catholic University of America Press, 2000), 287, 412, 449, 480-82.

Vision 4: Amen of Desire

This is the source of philosophical "desire" in antiquity and the Middle Ages. At the end of the nineteenth and beginning of the twentieth century, a new attention to "temporality" (or "temporalization") — the fact (and implications) of our existing in time — arose in a transatlantic conversation about pragmatism.[4] In France, Bergson retrieved the ancient topic of "final causality" as the governing principle of free temporal agents moving forward.[5] On the other side of the Atlantic, Harvard University philosopher William James (who was in communication with Bergson) explored these same issues from an explicitly psychological perspective.[6] In 1890, James wrote in his *Principles of Psychology:*

> Every one knows what attention is. It is the taking possession by the mind, in clear and vivid form, of one out of what seem several simultaneously possible objects or trains of thought. Focalization, concentration, of consciousness are of its essence. It implies a withdrawal from some things in order to deal effectively with others, and is a condition which has a real opposite in the confused, dazed, scatter-brained state which in French is called *distraction,* and *Zerstreutheit* in German.

> But the whole feeling of reality, the whole sting and excitement of our voluntary life, depends on our sense that in it things are *really being decided* from one moment to another, and that it is not the dull rattling off of a chain that was forged innumerable ages ago.[7]

The American philosopher John Dewey, representing the generation inheriting James's pragmatism, published his naturalistic metaphysics, *Experience and Nature,* in 1925, and then again with revisions in 1929. In this work, Aristotle's "final cause" became Dewey's pragmatic "end-in-view." In 1929,

---

4. Schloesser, *"Vivo ergo cogito."*

5. Daniel J. Collins-Cavanaugh, "Aristotelian Theory of Duration and the History of Temporality" (Ph.D. diss., Duquesne University, 2005).

6. Frédéric Worms, "James and Bergson: Reciprocal Readings," trans. John J. Conley, and Donald Wayne Viney, "William James on Free Will: The French Connection with Charles Renouvier," both in *The Reception of Pragmatism in France,* 76-92, 93-121, respectively.

7. William James, "Attention" (c. 11), in *The Principles of Psychology,* 2 vols. (New York: Henry Holt, [1890] 1918), 1:403-4, 453; quoted with alteration in Winifred Gallagher, *Rapt: Attention and the Focused Life* (New York: Penguin Press, 2009), 6. Compare the chapter entitled "L'Attention" in Armand Cuvillier, *Manuel de philosophie. Tome I. Introduction générale: Psychologie* (Paris: Librairie Armand Colin, 1931), 358-80.

1943: *Résumé:* Visions of Amen

Alfred North Whitehead, the British mathematician and philosopher who emigrated in 1924 to teach at Harvard University, published *Process and Reality: An Essay in Cosmology,* another philosophical account putting temporal process, experience, feeling, and the "subjective aim" (his version of Aristotle's "final cause") at the heart of cosmology. Five years later, Dewey applied his basic theory to art and aesthetics, published as *Art as Experience.*[8] Pursuing an end-in-view with heightened attentive awareness was at the heart of a genuine "experience." In sum: envisioning reality as a temporal process governed by what is desired — final cause, end-in-view, or subjective aim — pervaded the intellectual-cultural air of the 1920s and 1930s.[9]

Dewey uses this notion of a desired end-in-view to distinguish between "events" and "experiences." Events are physical occurrences — without human beings ascribing meaning to them, they can be random, accidental, meaningless, and destructive.[10] Experiences, by contrast, are unified temporal durations, intentional events in which human beings act with an "end-in-view." That future end governs all the decisions that must be made in the present at various points in a process; this intended future end thus gives shape and meaning to the process (or duration) as a complete and continuous whole. In an "experience," the agent brings with it into the present the memories it has stored up from the past; and it interacts with each obstacle and invitation in terms of a desired end that keeps luring it into the future.

To illustrate his abstract theory, Dewey proposes a thought experiment in which he imagines a stone rolling down a hill that is capable of having an "experience," as opposed to a stone rolling down a hill that is a mere "event." We see that this imaginary stone "*looks forward with desire to the final outcome;* that it is interested in the things it meets on its way, conditions that accelerate and retard its movement with respect to their bearing on the end; that it acts and feels toward them according to the hindering or helping function it attributes to them; and that the final coming to rest is related to all that went before

---

8. John Dewey, *Experience and Nature* (New York: Norton, 1929); Alfred North Whitehead, *Process and Reality: An Essay in Cosmology; Oxford Lectures Delivered in the University of Edinburgh during the Session 1927-28* (Cambridge: Cambridge University Press, 1929); Dewey, *Art as Experience* (New York: Minton, 1934).

9. For Bergson, Dewey, and Whitehead, see Albert William Levi, *Philosophy and the Modern World* (Bloomington: Indiana University Press, 1959).

10. John Dewey, "Events and Meanings," *New Republic* 32 (1922): 9-10; republished in Dewey, *Characters and Events,* ed. Joseph Ratner, 2 vols. (New York: Henry Holt, 1929), 1:125-29; in Dewey, *The Middle Works, 1899-1924,* vol. 13, *1921-1922,* ed. Jo Ann Boydston (Carbondale and Edwardsville: Southern Illinois University Press, 1983), 276-80.

as the culmination of a continuous movement. Then the stone would have an experience, and one with esthetic quality."[11] Dewey and Bergson are agreed on this point: a duration's (or experience's) boundaries of "beginning" and "end" have nothing to do with the external spatialized measurements of a clock. Rather, the "end" will have arrived when the "end-in-view" — the overall aim or purpose guiding and governing the experience — has been achieved. Until then, every single moment, every decision to pursue path A and not path B, is interrelated with every other one in an organic and indivisible whole.

In his novel *The Long Goodbye,* Raymond Chandler nicely illustrates this outlook in his "methodical" description of brewing coffee:

> The coffee maker was almost ready to bubble. I turned the flame low and watched the water rise. It hung a little at the bottom of the glass tube. I turned the flame up just enough to get it over the hump and then turned it low again quickly. I stirred the coffee and covered it. I set my timer for three minutes. Very methodical guy, Marlowe....
>
> I cut the flame and set the coffee maker on a straw mat on the table. Why did I go into such detail? Because the charged atmosphere made every little thing stand out as a performance, a movement distinct and vastly important. It was one of those hypersensitive moments when all your automatic movements, however long established, however habitual, become separate acts of will. You are like a man learning to walk after polio. You take nothing for granted, absolutely nothing at all.[12]

Although the clock time plays a role here — it requires three minutes for the cooling — what defines the duration (or experience) is the conclusion. It is only when the required heterogenous actions have achieved their end or "function" (the perfect cup of coffee) that the duration comes to completion. This evokes another homey Bergsonian image: a duration, says Bergson, is like a melody.[13] A melody cannot be cut up into arbitrary pieces. Whether "long"

---

11. John Dewey, *Art as Experience,* in Dewey, *The Later Works, 1925-1953,* vol. 10, *1934,* ed. Jo Ann Boydston (Carbondale and Edwardsville: Southern Illinois University Press, 1987), 46, emphasis added.

12. Raymond Chandler, *The Long Goodbye* (New York: Vintage, [1954] 1992), 28.

13. Duration "prolongs the before into the after, keeping them from being mere snapshots appearing and disappearing in a present ceaselessly reborn. A melody to which we can listen with our eyes closed, heeding it alone ... we do away with the distinctive features of sound itself, retaining of it only the continuation of what precedes into what follows ... succession without separation, in order to finally rediscover basic time." Henri Bergson, *Du-*

1943: Résumé: Visions of Amen

or "short" in clock time, a melody is always a single unitary thing, whole and complete in itself. It is finished only when it is finished.

Aristotle, Aquinas, Bergson, Dewey, and Whitehead: these philosophers all share a *teleological* view of reality. Agents in the present are always aiming at some future goal or end *(telos)* — a final cause, a "lure for feeling" (Whitehead), an end-in-view to be accomplished, a formal outline to be realized, a dream to be materialized. After the positivistic materialism and determinism of the nineteenth century (worldviews excluding genuine creative novelty), pragmatism's new focus on teleology and investing the world with ends-in-view underscored two intertwined components: time and desire. We are "lured" by some future aim that we desire; this emotion then governs decisions about the future as well as about remembrances of the past.

As seen above in the discussion of *Preludes* and *Death of Number,* Messiaen explicitly embraced this Bergsonian view encountered in the textbook by Cuvillier.[14] Messiaen lays out these various aspects of the past-present-future continuum in emotional terms by distinguishing between three pasts and three futures: "the recent past and the immediate future; the distant past and the distant future. And the extremely distant past and future."[15] Having made these distinctions, Messiaen elaborates:

> The distant past is the true past; we can qualify it with Cuvillier as the "hardened past"; we reconstruct it with the aid of memory, but it is impossible to change anything about it: it was what it was. If we played a culpable role

---

ration and Simultaneity: With Reference to Einstein's Theory of Relativity, trans. Leon Jakobson (New York: Bobbs-Merrill, 1922), 44; original Bergson, *Durée et simultanéité, à propos de la théorie d'Einstein* (Paris: Félix Alcan, 1922). Cf. Bergson: "Pure duration ... forms both the past and the present states into an organic whole, as happens when we recall the notes of a tune, melting, so to speak, into one another." "We are thus compelled to admit that we have here to do with a synthesis which is, so to speak, qualitative, a gradual organization of our successive sensations, a unity resembling that of a phrase in a melody." When the hour strikes on a neighboring clock, "the sensations produced by each one of [several strokes], instead of being set side by side, had melted into one another in such a way as to give the whole a peculiar quality, to make a kind of musical phrase out of it." *Time and Free Will: An Essay on the Immediate Data of Consciousness,* trans. F. L. Pogson (New York: Humanities Press, [1910] 1971), 100, 111, 127; original *Essai sur les données immédiates de la conscience* (Paris: Félix Alcan, 1889).

14. See above, pp. 95-98; cf. pp. 118-19 n. 103.

15. Messiaen's discussion of "Philosophy of the Duration: Lived Duration, Structured Time," in *Traité de rythme, de couleur, et d'ornithologie (1949-1992) en sept tomes,* 8 vols. (Paris: Alphonse Leduc, 1994-2002), 1:9-12, at 11; quoting Cuvillier, *Nouveau précis de philosophie. Tome I: La connaissance* (Paris: Armand Colin, 1963), 227.

Vision 4: Amen of Desire

in it, it stays with us in the form of guilt; most often, it appears to us bathed in a soft light in which we develop transfigured, idealized, and gives rise to regret in us or nostalgic remembrance of that which is no more.

The extremely distant past is detached from us like a cadaver that falls: quite rightly we speak of extinct civilizations and dead languages. — The immediate future continues action already begun [in the past] or present desire [for a future end]. The distant future is the true future. The past gives rise to regret or guilt; the future engenders expectation. But since we often do not know what it will hold, the future allows all the fantasies of imagination. [As Bergson writes:] "What makes hope such an intense pleasure is that the future appears to us under a multitude of forms all at the same time, equally smiling on us, equally possible. Even if the most desired among these becomes realized, it will be necessary to sacrifice the others, and we will have lost a great deal. The idea of the future, large with an infinity of possibilities, is thus more fertile than the future itself, and this is why we find more appeal in hope than in possession, in dream than in reality." ... Of the three moments of time, the future is certainly the most elevated, because it is the one that clarifies and explains the two others: it is the future that directs the present, it is the future which excuses or approves the past. As for the extremely distant future, which we do not know at all, or which is a pure knowledge such as that given by science or Faith: the end of our planet, the life of glorified bodies, or quite simply the hour of our death.[16]

Drawing on Messiaen's tripartite division along with an image of the palindrome ("My end is my beginning/And my beginning my end"), the seven visions might be represented as a single indivisible duration:

$$\lfloor 3 + \lceil 1 \rfloor + 3 \rceil$$
$$\lfloor \text{Past (Visions 1-3)} + \lceil \text{Present (Vision 4)} \rfloor + \text{Future (Visions 5-7)} \rceil$$

The future — that is, the life of glorified bodies (Vision 5), the hour of our death (Vision 6), and the end of our planet and perhaps time itself (Vision 7) — "excuses or approves the past" — that is, the creation (Vision 1), the nearly inconceivable age in light-years of the celestial bodies (Vision 2), and

---

16. Messiaen, *Traite*, 1:11; summarizing Cuvillier, *Nouveau précis de philosophie. Tome I: La connaissance*, 226-29; and quoting Bergson, *Essai sur les données immédiates*, 7; Bergson, *Time and Free Will*, 9-10.

the terrestrial agony of Jesus in the Garden (Vision 3). At the same time, the future also acts as a final cause, subjective aim, or end-in-view: it "directs the present," which looks forward to the immediate future with desire.

Visions' palindrome is also a "non-retrogradable rhythm," a concept Messiaen had first employed (at least according to his own account) two years earlier in *Quartet for the End of Time:*

$$(3 + 1 + 3)$$

Thus, no matter how long the amount of "clock time," from the Bergsonian perspective of "duration" there is an indivisible timelessness about temporality: in the beginning, one already has the end-in-view: the creation (protology) already aims at the consummation (eschatology) just as, in Stravinsky's *Rite of Spring*, Messiaen sees the consummation of the sacrifice already implied in the "Sacred Dance." "The 'Sacred Dance,'" writes Messiaen, "has supported the whole structure of the *Rite:* it is both the cause and the accomplishment, the departure and the summit, the only possible conclusion."[17] Similarly, looking backward from the perspective of the end point, the past is "fulfilled." In a teleological view of existence, desire and time are inextricably bound together: desire governs the free pursuit of indeterminate ends.

Messiaen draws a Bergsonian conclusion: "The ephemeral being that lives several hours, the human being who lives several years, the mountain which endures several centuries, the star which lasts for thousands of centuries, have each brought their particular function complete up until death or disappearance: their duration is therefore the same. These times superimposed would only be different for a foreign observer; they are identical for those who live them, each one in the totality of its function, the power of duration."[18] A duration's boundary has nothing to do with its quantitative measure in "clock time." An experience is over when the originally envisioned and desired end-in-view has been realized.

Messiaen's preoccupation with Bergson's distinction between lived duration and structured (clock) time can seem abstract. However, the "Amen of Desire" flavors "lived time" with our emotional experiences of regret, remorse, and nostalgia for the past; of desire for multiple possibilities in the near and distant future, both realistic and wishful thinking; and of hope in the eternal

---

17. Messiaen, analysis of Stravinsky's *Rite of Spring*, in *Traité*, 2:93-147, at 124.
18. See Messiaen, "Bergsonian Theory Following Sivadjian," in *Traité*, 1:34-36, at 36.

Vision 4: Amen of Desire

beyond.[19] These emphases in twentieth-century pragmatism and process philosophy permeated Messiaen's intellectual formation. But "desire" was also deeply personal for Messiaen, especially in the winter of 1942-1943.

2. Terrible Love: 1940–1945

Messiaen's decision to make "desire" the midpoint fulcrum was made after an earlier five-movement work had been sketched out. The significance of this seeming afterthought is made even more tenuous by Messiaen's ambiguous use of the adjective *charnel* (fem. *charnelle*). Although translating most readily as "carnal" in the sexual sense, it can also mean something more general like "fleshly" or even "mortal." In this movement, writes Messiaen, "the soul" — that is, an incorporeal entity — "is pulled by a terrible love [*amour terrible*] which expresses itself in a bodily [*charnelle*] manner (see the 'Song of Songs'); but there is nothing here of the carnal [*charnel*], only a paroxysm of the thirst of Love." Messiaen negotiates this seeming contradiction by referring to the biblical book Song of Songs. The biblical text seems clearly to be about sexual or carnal love, but millennia of commentary on it (not to mention its original inclusion in the biblical canon) have interpreted it allegorically, symbolizing the relationship between God and his people.

But Messiaen's brief notes do not erase the ambiguity, the strangeness, and, perhaps, a sense of internal conflict. What does the addition of "desire" here mean — and what does it mean when the structure of the work as a whole is built on such a seemingly internally unstable foundation?

The movement opens with the first period of the "ecstatic and tender theme" (00:02–00:41). Messiaen notes that the melodic contour calls to mind "Mozart (Susanna's Aria, *Marriage of Figaro*)."[20] And indeed, listening to the

---

19. A distinction made by Whitehead between "abstract" and "real" possibility is implicit in Bergson's theory (as followed by Messiaen). Scholars explain: "There are abstract possibilities which are possible in principle to all human beings. That is, there is nothing in the definition of 'human being' which excludes the actualization of those possibilities. But not all of these things are really possible to every human being. There is an order among the abstract possibilities, so that certain ones cannot be actualized prior to the actualization of others. Hence, which of those things that are possible in principle to human beings are really possible for a particular person depends upon the tradition of actualization in which he or she stands." John B. Cobb Jr. and David Ray Griffin, *Process Theology: An Introductory Exposition* (Philadelphia: Westminster, 1976), 39.

20. Messiaen, analysis of Vision 4, in *Traité*, 3:249, referring to Susanna's recitative and aria: "No. 27. Giunse alfin il momento... Deh vieni, non tardar," in Wolfgang Amadeus

1943: Résumé: Visions of Amen

opening measures of Mozart's "Deh vienni non tardar" makes clear the source: Messiaen's melody is drawn from Mozart's setting of the text "Oh come, don't delay, my beautiful joy" *(Deh vienni non tardar, o gioja bella).*

The second period (00:42–01:43) begins with the fifth measure, about which Messiaen remarks: "Note the tenderness and the *pp* [pianissimo]." He also points out that in the second-to-last measure (1:21–1:29), the intervals recall those accompanying Susanna's words, "while the world is still, and calm is reigning" *(finchè l'aria è ancor bruna, e il mondo tace).* After offering several other analytical notes about the modes he has employed, Messiaen concludes: "For all of that, however, this entire analysis has little importance. What counts here is the indication '**with love.**'"[21]

Messiaen's employment of this aria in such an explicitly overt way intrigues. In the earlier, pre–October 1942 draft of *Visions* — the one with only five movements — this Mozartean melody was meant to appear in the first vision, the "Amen of Creation." When Messiaen decided to add these two other visions ("Amen of Desire" and "Amen of Judgment"), Susanna's melody was taken out of the creation movement and used here as the opening and primary theme. In light of the date, it would be tempting to interpret this late decision (and the "Amen of Desire" as a whole) as being inspired by Yvonne Loriod (for whose pianistic virtuosity the work was written) and Messiaen's growing relationship with her.

However, a less obvious reading is possible — for this is the aria that Susanna sings on the day of her marriage to Figaro. Knowing how important the sacrament of marriage was to Messiaen (cf. "Sacramental Warriors" [1936] just six years earlier), it is difficult to imagine him not referring this allusion to his own marriage. This seems especially likely since Messiaen seems to have intended the connection between Mozart's libretto and Song of Songs. Susanna's aria reads:

> Beloved, don't delay, the night is falling.
> Hasten where love's delight is sweetly calling.
> Until the stars grow pale, and night is waning,
> the brooklet rustles on, the breeze is blowing,
> and the timorous heart with hope is glowing.

Mozart and Lorenzo da Ponte, *Le Nozze di Figaro (The Marriage of Figaro): An Opera in Four Acts,* trans. Ruth and Thomas Martin (New York: G. Schirmer, [1947] 1951), 415-20.

21. "Ce qui compte ici, c'est l'indication '**avec amour.**'" Messiaen, analysis of Vision 4, in *Traité,* 3:250, emphasis in original.

Vision 4: Amen of Desire

> The flowers all with shining dew are gleaming,
> while the world is long asleep and dreaming.
> Come, my beloved, the starry sky above you.
> Come, beloved!
> Come, my beloved, with all my heart, I love you.
> Come, my beloved, with all my heart, with all my heart I love you.[22]

The biblical text reads:

> Arise, make haste, my love, my dove [*ma colombe*], my beautiful one, and come.
> For winter is now past, the rain is over and gone.
> The flowers have appeared in our land, the time of pruning is come.
>   The voice of the turtle is heard in our land;
>   the fig tree hath put forth her green figs.
>   The vines in flower yield their sweet smell [*leur parfum*].
> Arise, my love, my beautiful one, and come.
> My dove [*ma colombe*] in the clefts of the rock.[23]

Following this first, "ecstatic" theme (or "rhythmic character") comes a second, "passionate" theme described in terms evoking surrealism: "a terrible love [*un amour terrible*] which expresses itself in a bodily [*charnelle*] manner (see the 'Song of Songs'); but there is nothing here of the carnal [*charnel*], only a paroxysm of the thirst of Love."[24] In terms of analysis Messiaen writes with a seemingly wry smile: "A cry of passion doesn't analyze itself [*ne s'analyse pas*]."[25] This doesn't prevent him, however, from proceeding to lay out the alternations in transpositions of the theme's mode. Here, significantly, he uses the word "explosion" to mark certain moments: for example, "first explosion"; "new explosion"; "Then after the large harmonic line come the two explosions: F major/E flat major and the dominant of G major."[26] The word "explosion" fittingly describes the pianistic attacks representing the "paroxysm of the thirst of Love" — what Breton would call "convulsive beauty."[27]

---

22. Susanna's aria, "Deh vieni, non tardar," in Mozart and da Ponte, *Le Nozze di Figaro*, 417-19.
23. Song of Songs 2:10-14 (Douay-CCD; Fillion).
24. Messiaen, "Note de l'Auteur" for Vision 4, *Visions de l'Amen* (1943), n.p.
25. Messiaen, analysis of Vision 4, in *Traité*, 3:250.
26. Messiaen, analysis of Vision 4, in *Traité*, 3:251.
27. The phrase "convulsive beauty" appeared in André Breton's novel *Nadja* (1928)

1943: *Résumé:* Visions of Amen

In the analysis provided in the appendix below, I have presented the passionate theme as divided between a statement and a response (2a and 2b). In his analysis of the development of the passion theme, Messiaen notes that the chain of rapidly ascending chords (03:12–03:17) comes from Jules Massenet's opera *Manon Lescaut*.[28] Without context, a listener might simply associate this flight of passion with sensual rapture. But it seems worth remembering Massenet's conclusion: although the young Chevalier des Grieux has rescued Manon from her chains, he is — as in all cases of doomed love — too late. In their final exchange, des Grieux comforts Manon as she slips away from him in feverish visions.[29]

Both Susanna's aria and Manon's fevered farewell take place as night is falling. However, while Susanna's lyrics are an invitation to love throughout the night before morning's *alba* is announced, Manon's signal the approach of death. Messiaen's explicit citations of these works seem intended to recall more than melodic sources. The contrast between Susanna and Manon evokes the two poles of Messiaen's own lyrics for *The Death of Number:*

There was a sunbeam [*un rayon de soleil*] that slept in your hand.
You lifted your small fingers very high.
It began to shine with such brilliance [*d'un tel éclat*]
    that I could see nothing other than it.[30]

Time and space are dying!
So far off, joy! So far off, light! . . .
The end, the end, who can tell it? [*La fin, la fin, qui la dira?*]
I suffer! I suffer![31]

---

and in *Mad Love* (1937). See Sharla Hutchison, "Convulsive Beauty: Images of Hysteria and Transgressive Sexuality; Claude Cahun and Djuna Barnes," *symploke* 11, no. 1-2 (2003): 212-26.

28. "On trouve cet enchaînement dans *Manon* de Massenet." Messiaen describing the "passionate theme," analysis of Vision 4, in *Traité,* 3:250-51.

29. Note the parallel with delirium at the end of *Pelléas et Mélisande:* Mélisande: "However, it seems to me that I know something . . ." Arkel: "What are you saying? I don't understand you . . ." Mélisande: "I also don't understand what I am saying, You see . . . I don't know what I am saying . . . I don't know what I know . . . I no longer say what I want to . . ." Arkel: "You have had a bit of delirium lately, and you could no longer be understood. . . . But now, all that is long gone!" Maeterlinck and Debussy (act 5, scene 2), 372-73.

30. Olivier Messiaen, *La Mort du nombre* (Paris: Durand, 1931), 1.

31. Messiaen, *La Mort du nombre,* 9-11.

Vision 4: Amen of Desire

3. Carnal + Not Carnal: Beyond the Principle of Noncontradiction

Critics during this period accused Messiaen of writing music that was too sensual to be genuinely religious (or spiritual), "looking about anxiously like an angel wearing lipstick."[32] Responding to these charges in his *Treatise* analysis of *Visions,* Messiaen inserts these remarks about the obvious sensuality of the passion theme:

> The extreme mobility of tempo and the *very rubato* character of the second ["passionate"] theme oppose themselves in equal measure to the calm of the first ["ecstatic"] theme.
> Once again, what counts here is the cry of passion [*le cri de la passion*]. Its carnal character [*caractère charnel*] need not frighten. In the most unseemly [or "indecent": *inconvenants*] passages of the exquisite and audacious poem of oriental love [*d'amour oriental*] which is the *Song of Songs,* the Church Fathers saw symbols of the greatest spiritual union, and in this human love the inverted expression but also the reflection of divine love.[33]

This appeal to the Bible gives a traditional foundation for Messiaen's juxtaposition of the carnal and the spiritual. One might also recall the stage directions at the end of Cécile Sauvage's final work, *To Love after Death:* "the angels and the young human beings also lean towards one another in the same way, thus forming the figure of a mystical union between earth and heaven."[34]

However, another interpretation might be derived when the matter is viewed through the lens of surrealism. The overall form of the "Amen of Desire" is threefold: section A (00:02–04:23), in which the ecstasy theme and the passion theme are "equally opposed" to one another as thesis and antithesis; section A' (04:24–09:00), a reprise of both themes; and a coda (09:01–11:09), the "great calming down" *(apaisement).* In the coda, after an initial partial restatement of the first "ecstatic" theme in extremely slow tempo (09:01–09:37), time continues to approach a seeming point of zero movement. In this passage (9:37–10:18), says Messiaen, "The two principal voices (in the second

---

32. Claude Rostand; quoted by Nigel Simeone in liner notes for the *Trois petites Liturgies;* in Olivier Messiaen, *Complete Edition,* 32 CDs (Germany: Deutsche Grammophon, 2008), 250-51.

33. Messiaen, analysis of Vision 4, in *Traité,* 3:251, emphasis in original.

34. Sauvage, *Aimer après la mort,* in Cécile Sauvage and Béatrice Marchal-Vincent, *L'Œuvre poétique de Cécile Sauvage (1883-1927),* 2 vols. (Lille: Atelier National de Reproduction des Thèses, 1995), 2:216.

1943: *Résumé:* Visions of Amen

piano) seem to melt (or dissolve: *se fondre*) one into the other and all of the music seems to go back into itself as if absorbed by an interior abyss [*un abîme intérieur*]." Finally, in the nearly imperceptible three concluding measures (10:19–11:09), "An immaterial carillon [*un carillon immatériel*] superimposes itself on the foundation of a perfect G major chord, approaching closer and closer to silence [*de plus en plus proche du silence*]."[35] There is "nothing other than the harmonious silence of Heaven."[36]

Without the benefit of Messiaen's cryptic and seemingly self-contradictory remarks, this movement might be heard as a simple conflict opposing the spiritual and the carnal, concluded by a melodramatic victory of spirit over flesh. But the internal instability of his own notes — "carnal and not-carnal" — points instead to a surrealist listening. From such a viewpoint, as both Breton and Messiaen observe, oppositions between thesis and antithesis, spiritual and carnal, eternity and time are perceived as noncontradictions, grasped as they are by a synthesizing perspective. Once again quoting Messiaen from 1946, three years after the composition of the "Amen of Desire": "But if you define Surrealism as a mental vantage-point ('point de l'esprit') where visible natural realities and invisible supernatural realities are no longer in opposition to each other and where they cease to be perceived as contradictions, then I am a Surrealist composer.... In a present eternity, I glimpse infinite life unbounded by Time and Space."[37]

If we hear Susanna's aria as Claire's marriage call to Messiaen ten years earlier, and if we hear Manon's fevered final words as Claire's fading away — then perhaps the "Amen of Desire" is partly a lament for what has become of these "two sacramental warriors" during a tumultuous decade. However, as in *Harawi* two years later, although the farewell is fated to arrive before its time, from a perspective both surrealist and Christian, death is not the final word.

---

35. Messiaen, analysis of Vision 4, in *Traité*, 3:254, 255.
36. Messiaen, "Note de l'Auteur."
37. Olivier Messiaen, quoted in Ernest de Gengenbach, "Messiaen ou le surréel en musique," *Revue musicale de France* 1 (April 15, 1946): 1-3, 18, at 3; translation in Peter Hill and Nigel Simeone, *Messiaen* (New Haven: Yale University Press, 2005), 167.

Vision 5

Amen of the Angels, of Saints, of Birdsong

Avis, Aevum, Aeternitas • Aquinas: Planets & Angels • Rilke: Every Angel Is Terrible • Ezekiel: Eyes in the Wheels • William Blake • Ornithology • Prehistoric Birds: Tertiary Period, Oligocene and Miocene Epochs • History of Music • Blackbird • Nightingale • Shakespeare: *Romeo and Juliet* • Garden of Sleep • Blackcap • Finch • Chateaubriand: Nightingale • Nijni-Novgorod: "Lament of the Conscript" • Non-retrogradable Rhythm • European Serin • Cuckoo

This fifth vision transports the listener from the final stillness of the earthly garden — the last moments of temporality — to the realm of "aeviternity," the angelic sphere (in medieval cosmology) situated between time and eternity. The word derives from the Latin *aevum* (or *aevus*) designating "uninterrupted," "never-ending time," and "eternity": *in aevum* = "for all time." However, unlike *aeternitas* (eternity, endlessness, immortality), which is opposed to *tempus* (time), *aevum* can also be used in a more restricted sense of a definite time, period, age, epoch, or generation: a lifetime or "time of life."[1] Ambivalence about time and eternity is built into the word itself, appropriately so for the status of immortal angels and mortal saints who have been raised to eternal life.

In addition, Messiaen, the lover of language, would surely have delighted

---

1. *Oxford Latin Dictionary,* ed. P. G. W. Glare (Oxford: Clarendon; New York: Oxford University Press, 1982).

1943: Résumé: Visions of Amen

in *aevum*'s (and even more so *aevus*'s) near homonym of *avis* — "bird," as well as a bird of omen (or more generally, an omen). Significantly, however, the title of the movement names not birds but rather "birdsong." Although birds themselves do not have immortality, their songs are fixed according to species. Like forms and formal causes, birdsongs are identical and invariant in themselves; but when they take on material being, they assume variations as their interpreters improvise.

In the original plan for *Visions,* this vision of angels, saints, and birdsong would have been the fourth out of five movements. Visions 1 (creation) and 2 (planets, stars, and Saturn) would have been aspects of "protology": first things and the beginning of time. Vision 3 (agony of Jesus), the fulcrum and tipping point, would have provided the place of incarnation where eternity intersects with time. Visions 4 (angels, saints, and birdsong) and 5 (consummation) would have been aspects of "eschatology": last things and the end of time. This arrangement makes the parallelism of the original movements 2 and 4 more precise:

> Original Vision 2   "Amen of Stars and Saturn"
> Original Vision 3   "Amen of the Agony of Jesus"
> Original Vision 4   "Amen of Angels, Saints, Birdsong"

The later additions of the "Amen of Desire" (Vision 4 in final version) and "Amen of Judgment" (Vision 6 in final version) altered this simpler and more compact structure. As it stands in the final version, this movement of "aeviternity" now flows seamlessly out of the "harmonious silence of heaven" reached at the end of the "Amen of Desire," the "immaterial carillon" that approaches "closer and closer to silence." And since it precedes the "Amen of Judgment," that is, the eschatological judgment that marks the end of time, it reminds us that "aeviternity" stands above time.

In perhaps an unanticipated way, then, Messiaen's addition of "Desire" makes for a more complex understanding of time. The "present moment" in a Bergsonian sense is given temporal direction since it is marked by "desire" for some end-in-view (Dewey). This end-in-view, insofar as it is a "final cause" (Aristotle/Aquinas) or a "subjective aim" (Whitehead) toward which a duration moves as a consummation, serves to guide present choices. The "eschatological," then, is not merely about an imagined future. Rather, it makes its claim here and now. This intimate connection between the "Amen of Desire" and the eschatological "Amen of Angels, of Saints, of Birdsong" anticipates by two decades the theological understanding of Karl Rahner:

Vision 5: Amen of the Angels, of Saints, of Birdsong

Eschatology is not an advance report of events taking place "later." That is the basic intention of false apocalyptic as opposed to a genuine prophecy. Eschatology is a forward look which is necessary to man for his spiritual decision in freedom. . . . The gaze is directed towards the definitive fulfilment of precisely this human situation which is already an eschatological one. And it is intended to make possible a man's own enlightened decision in relation to what is obscure and open. . . . For that future presents itself as salvation now, precisely if it is accepted as God's action, incalculable in its when and how, because determined by God alone. . . . In other words, eschatology concerns redeemed man as he now is. With him as basis it knows what is to come as something blissfully incomprehensible which is to be accepted in freedom (and therefore in danger of being lost). What is to come (understood in this way) can be evoked in imagery but not described here and now in a report, and it is announced to man because he can only endure his present if he knows he is in movement towards his future, which is the incomprehensible God in his own very life.[2]

Messiaen's "Author's Note"

Messiaen describes Vision 5 in his "Author's Note" to the published score:

> V. — Amen of the Angels, of Saints, of Birdsong.
> Song of the purity of the Saints: Amen.
> Vehement vocalizing of the birds: Amen.
> "Angels prostrating themselves before the Throne: Amen." (Apocalypse of Saint John).
> First the song of Angels and Saints, spare, very pure. Then [second,] the "middle" based on birdsongs, offering a place for the most brilliant writing for piano. These are the actual songs of nightingales [*rossignols*], blackbirds [*merles*], finches [*pinsons*], warblers [*fauvettes*], and their smiling boisterous mixture. [Thirdly,] a reprise of the song of Saints, with a canon of non-retrogradable rhythms. . . . [Finally,] a short Coda on the birds.[3]

---

2. Karl Rahner, "Eschatology," in *Encyclopedia of Theology: The Concise Sacramentum Mundi* (New Delhi: Continuum, [1975] 2004), 436, 437.
3. Messiaen, "Note de l'Auteur," for Vision 5, *Visions de l'Amen* (1943), n.p.

1943: Résumé: Visions of Amen

Commentary

1. Aeviternity: Parallelism with Celestial Bodies

Messiaen underscores the movement's threefold character. Each of the three elements is first assigned its own "Amen": the *singing* of the "purity of the Saints"; the vehement *vocalizing (vocalise)* of the birds; and the *prostration (se prosternant)* of the angels. This dramatic cast is then mapped on to the movement's overall structure (A-B-A'-Coda). In the first section (A) we hear the song of the angels and saints. In the second (B) we hear the mixture of birdsongs. In the third (A') we hear a reprise (or recapitulation) of A, as the angels in worship prostrate themselves before the Uncreated beyond all time. A brief coda on birdsong serves as an ending. This threefold cast parallels that in Vision 2, described by Messiaen as the "violent rotation of [1] the stars, [2] the suns, and [3] Saturn." In the work's original five-movement framework, the parallelism between movements 1 and 5 (creation and consummation) and movements 2 and 4 (celestial bodies and angels/saints) provided balance and stability. Finally, the opening song — described by Messiaen as the "song of Angels and Saints, spare, very pure" — is monophonic (like a plainchant) and so parallels the opening "Theme of the Dance of the Planets" in Vision 2. Messiaen utilized this monophonic technique in *Glorified Bodies,* especially in the first movement, "Subtlety of the Glorified Bodies," and then again in *Quartet for the End of Time.*

However, the connection between the two categories (celestial bodies and celestial beings) is deeper and more significant in the medieval cosmological scheme — which in turn derives from and depends on ancient cosmology — and that connection points us, once again, to Messiaen's central preoccupation with varieties of temporality. Both planets and angels share this paradoxical situation in the medieval world: they *are* changeless in themselves; and yet, in some other respect, they *have* changeability. (Note the crucial distinction between *to be* and *to have*.) In his treatment of the question "What is the difference of aeviternity, as there is one time, and one eternity?" in *Summa Theologica,* Aquinas explicitly links planets and angels:

> Therefore the fact that an aeviternal thing is neither inveterate, nor subject to innovation, comes from its changelessness; and consequently its measure does not contain "before" and "after." We say then that since eternity is the measure of a permanent being, in so far as anything recedes from permanence of being, it recedes from eternity. Now some things recede from

Vision 5: Amen of the Angels, of Saints, of Birdsong

permanence of being, so that their being is subject to change, or consists in change; and these things are measured by time, as are all movements, and also the being of all things corruptible. But others recede less from permanence of being, forasmuch as their being neither consists in change, nor is the subject of change; nevertheless they have change annexed to them either actually or potentially. This appears in the heavenly bodies, the substantial being of which is unchangeable; *and yet with unchangeable being they have changeableness of place.* The same applies to the angels, who have *an unchangeable being as regards their nature with changeableness as regards choice;* moreover they have changeableness of intelligence, of affections and of places in their own degree.[4]

Heavenly bodies are composed of an unchangeable being — this comes from ancient cosmology. However, their location at any particular time in the sky is changeable. Likewise, angels are composed of unchangeable being. However, they must be capable of changing their minds and wills — they must have the free choice that makes some of them faithful courtiers in heaven and others of them infernal creatures, that is, "fallen angels" or devils. It might be objected that there is a profound difference between planets and angels. Aquinas himself notes this objection when he considers "Whether there is only one aeviternity": "Objection 2. Further, different genera have different measures. But some aeviternal things belong to the corporeal genus, as the heavenly bodies; and others are spiritual substances, as are the angels. Therefore there is not only one aeviternity."[5] After acknowledging that opinion is divided among authorities about whether there is more than one aeviternity, Aquinas restates his position that there is only one and answers the objection: "Although the heavenly bodies and spiritual things differ in the genus of their nature, still they agree in having a changeless being, and are thus measured by aeviternity."[6]

In summation, Aquinas delineates three modes of time (or its absence) — time, aeviternity, and eternity: "Therefore [planets and angels] are measured by aeviternity which is a mean between eternity and time. But the being that is measured by eternity is not changeable, nor is it annexed to change. In this way time has 'before' and 'after'; aeviternity in itself has no 'before' and 'after,'

---

4. *The "Summa Theologica" of St. Thomas Aquinas,* trans. Dominicans of the English Province, 2nd rev. ed., 22 vols. (London: Burns, Oates and Washbourne, 1920-1942), Ia, q. 10, a. 5, emphasis added. Hereafter cited as Aquinas, *ST.*

5. Aquinas, *ST,* Ia, q. 10, a. 6, second objection.

6. Aquinas, *ST,* Ia, q. 10, a. 6, reply to the second objection.

1943: *Résumé:* Visions of Amen

which can, however, be annexed to it; while eternity has neither 'before' nor 'after,' nor is it compatible with such at all."[7]

Messiaen chose to begin his multivolume *Treatise* with these considerations of Aquinas on the eternity of God. In the first two pages of the first volume, he considers the angels, reading Aquinas with a Bergsonian eye:

> It is known that the angels live in the *aevum* which is the intermediary between time and eternity. Time, *aevum,* eternity: Saint Thomas distinguishes and situates them very precisely: "Time implies succession before and after; the *aevum* has neither before nor after, but this condition of successive duration may be annexed [*s'y adjoindre*] to them; eternity has no succession and does not undergo it in any manner whatsoever (see article 5). Anteriority and posteriority are essential conditions of time; they may exist in the *aevum;* but they do not exist in what is stable, uniform, indivisible, in other words, in eternity: '*eternity is completely simultaneous.*' (see article 4)."[8]

Angels, saints, and the fixed patterns of birdsongs all share this liminal characteristic of straddling time and eternity; in their own being, that out of which they are created, they are unchangeable. At the same time, insofar as both angels and human beings have the choice to serve or not to serve, and insofar as birdsongs are fixed and yet capable of a creative multiplicity of riffs, variations, and improvisations, they all "have" changeability in a way that eternity does not.

2. "Every Angel Is Terrible!"

Our culture tends to picture angels sentimentally. There has been a recent wave of angel-related products: statues, pendants, greeting cards, lawn ornaments, and the television series *Touched by an Angel.* Like Clarence the guardian angel in the classic 1946 Christmas movie *It's a Wonderful Life* (directed by Frank Capra, a Catholic contemporary of Messiaen), these recent productions are homey and comforting: "Look, Daddy. Teacher says every time a bell rings an angel gets his wings."

---

7. Aquinas, *ST,* Ia, q. 10, a. 5.

8. Messiaen, "Time and Eternity," chapter 1, "Time," in *Traité de rythme, de couleur, et d'ornithologie (1949-1992) en sept tomes,* 8 vols. (Paris: Alphonse Leduc, 1994-2002), 1:7-8; material in quotation marks is a paraphrase of Aquinas, *ST,* Ia, q. 10, articles 4 and 5.

Vision 5: Amen of the Angels, of Saints, of Birdsong

For Messiaen, by contrast, angels are *"terrible."* In his remarks on "communicable language," Messiaen notes that the implications of aeviternity (and abstraction) are terrifying to human beings. Humans must communicate indirectly using conventions. For example, music "expresses nothing directly. It may suggest, evoke a feeling, a state of soul, touch the subconscious, enlarge the dreamlike faculties, and here lie its enormous powers: but it can absolutely not 'speak,' inform with precision."[9] Angels, by contrast, communicate directly and without the intermediate symbol-system of language:

> The angels alone have the privilege of communicating among themselves, without language, without convention, and still more wondrously, without needing to take any account of time and place. This is a power that completely outstrips us, a faculty of transmission that is almost dreadful [*presque effrayante*], and Rilke is correct to say: "Every angel is terrible!" [*Tout ange est terrible!*]

One can read this, in fact, in the *Summa Theologica* of Saint Thomas Aquinas (in the First Part on "Divine Government," question 107: "the language of angels"): "If an angel, by its will, orders its mental concept with a view to manifesting it to another, this other angel knows it immediately: in this manner the angel speaks to another angel." And later: "Angelic locution consists in an intellectual operation. Now, the intellectual operation of the angel makes an abstraction from time and place. This is why diversity in time or distance of place play no role here where it is made entirely by abstraction from time and place."[10]

Angelic capacities terrify us. Messiaen has more to say on this topic in his analysis of "The Eyes in the Wheels," the sixth movement of *The Organ Book*

---

9. Messiaen, discussion of "le langage communicable" in analysis of *Méditations sur le Mystère de la Sainte Trinité* (1969); in *Traité*, 3:366. Messiaen is partly paraphrasing the symbolist theory of Stéphane Mallarmé, who wrote that the ideal "is to *suggest* the object. It is the perfect use of this mystery which constitutes the symbol. An object must be gradually evoked in order to show a state of soul"; quoted in Stephen Schloesser, *Jazz Age Catholicism: Mystic Modernism in Postwar Paris, 1919-1933* (Toronto: University of Toronto Press, 2005), 215.

10. Messiaen, discussion of "le langage communicable," in *Traité*, 3:366, quoting Aquinas, *ST*, Ia, q. 107, a. 1, "Whether one angel speaks to another," and a. 4, "Whether local distance influences the angelic speech." Quotation of Rilke is from "Second Elegy," in *Duino Elegies*, trans. J. B. Leishman and Stephen Spender (New York: Norton, 1939), 28-33, at 28 (German), 29 (English).

(1951). Here he opens a discussion of angels by quoting from the opening lines of Rainer Maria Rilke's first of the *Duino Elegies:*

> For Beauty's nothing
> but beginning of Terror we're still just able to bear,
> and why we adore it so is because it serenely
> disdains to destroy us. Each single angel is terrible.[11]

Messiaen continues: "The divine visions of the Prophets have this terrifying beauty [*cette beauté terrifiante*]." Messiaen had very likely encountered this connection as a child while reading Dostoyevsky's *Brothers Karamazov* to his blind grandfather: "Beauty is a terrifying thing! [*La beauté, c'est une chose terrible et affreuse.*] It's so frightening [terrible] because it's indefinable and it's indefinable because God has surrounded us with nothing but riddles. Here the shores of a river meet, incompatibilities coexist.... The terrible thing is that beauty is not only frightening but a mystery as well. That's where God and the devil join battle, and their battlefield is the heart of man."[12] In this passage, Dostoyevsky implicitly follows both Pascal and Kierkegaard on the problem of being human: we are both angels and beasts (or insects), infinitely finite creatures capable of imagining infinity — and it is this suspension over the abyss that makes us capable of "dread" in the face of what is terrifying. The sublime twist is: beauty is terrible, both *tremendum* and *fascinans* (using Rudolf Otto's terms), repellent and fascinating at the same time.

Moreover, Messiaen is keenly aware that angels in the Bible are eschatological creatures associated with ultimate things: they can be prophetic, militaristic, and apocalyptic. Messiaen's "Eyes in the Wheels" refers to the prophet Ezekiel's chariot. The prophet identifies four creatures with "wings" as cherubim, angels from the celestial army who are God's throne-bearers. The chariot itself seems to be a throne, and it is terrifying: both its wheels and the cherubim are covered with eyes. After quoting Ezekiel's account almost in its entirety, Messiaen adds: "Everything struck me in this text: the wind of the tempest, the mass of fire, the noise of the great waters, the four living

---

11. Messiaen's analysis of "Les Yeux dans les roues," *Livre d'orgue* (1951), in *Traité*, 3:213-17, quoting Rilke at 213. See Rilke, "The First Elegy," in *Duino Elegies*, 20-27, at 20 (German), 21 (English).

12. Fyodor Dostoyevsky, *The Brothers Karamazov*, trans. Andrew R. MacAndrew (New York: Bantam Books, 1970), 126, 127 (bk. 3, chap. 3).

Vision 5: Amen of the Angels, of Saints, of Birdsong

creatures, flying in every sense like lightning, and finally *these extraordinary wheels, living, filled all around with eyes.*"[13]

Messiaen has dedicated Vision 5 to beings capable of flight and speed — angels, saints, and birds who sing. (The "agility" of saints' "glorified bodies" will be discussed in Vision 7.) His analytical commentary on "Eyes in the Wheels" reminds us, however, that these visions are not to be read sentimentally. "The divine visions of Prophets have this terrifying beauty. Terrifying, dazzling [*fulgurante*], and simultaneously bringing peacefulness [*pacifiante*]. They leave us crushed by communicating within us one part of their serene strength. 'Ezekiel,' says [Émile] Baumann, 'is the prophet of fire. His name means: God is strong. No one, except Saint John in his Apocalypse, will approach closer before the mystery where the invisible takes a form which the senses are able to apprehend.' "[14]

In the representation of the most monstrous fantastical [*du fantastique*], several painters, draftsmen, engravers, such as Goya and Picasso, have excelled. . . . Few have dared to tackle prophetic visions (except Dürer in his engravings of the Apocalypse, and Bosch in his representations of Hell and of Paradise). The vision of Ezekiel has been especially misrepresented. There is a "Vision of Ezekiel" by Raphael in the Pitt Palace of Florence: one clearly sees the four animals: man, lion, bull, eagle, but separated; no fire, no eyes, no wheels; it is very harmonious technically speaking, but . . . he did not dare. . . . In our own time, the surrealist painter [Félix] Labisse — more gifted for horror or black humor than for mysticity [*la mysticité*] — painted a "Cherubim" with a three-form head (eagle, man and lion), completely covered by his wings whose feathers imitate an armor of flames or gems: its subject is one of the four living creatures of Ezekiel. . . . Only William Blake (1757-1827) had the courage to represent the eyes in the wheels just as Ezekiel described them. (I won't speak about the celebrated "Eye of Silence" by Max Ernst which has nothing in common with our prophet.)[15]

---

13. Messiaen on "Les Yeux dans les roues," in *Traité*, 3:214, citing Ezek. 1:4-20.

14. One of the first associations evoked by the word *fulgurante* (dazzling) would be lightning bursts in an electrical storm. Messiaen is quoting the Catholic Revivalist author Émile Baumann, *Les nourritures célestes* (Paris: B. Grasset, 1943); see citation, *Traité*, 3:405. For Baumann, see Schloesser, *Jazz Age Catholicism*, especially 265-69.

15. Messiaen on "Les Yeux dans les roues," in *Traité*, 3:213. It is curious that William Blake alone has his birth and death dates cited. Note that Messiaen's father translated Blake: see Blake, *Chansons d'innocence (1789). Essai de traduction par Pierre Messiaen* (Le Puy-en-Velay: Impr. de la Haute-Loire; Saint-Étienne: Éditions des "Amitiés," 1934); Pierre Mes-

1943: Résumé: Visions of Amen

Whereas Messiaen's discussion of "aeviternity" is highly abstract, his description of the terrifying angels in Ezekiel's vision is extremely vivid. And yet, in search of suitable analogies, he must turn to visual artists. As noted above, Messiaen explicitly said that although music can represent terror, it cannot represent monsters: "in the art of sounds and rhythms there is an intellectual voluptuousness [*une volupté intellectuelle*] absolutely unsuitable for monstrosity and vileness — just as in laughter and the comical — indeed, [unsuitable for] all things excluded by an anthropomorphic criterion very distant from musical abstraction."[16]

3. Birdsong: Origin of Music

In 1943, Messiaen was only in the first stages of becoming known for his knowledge and use of birdsong. During the next decade, compositions drawing on birdsongs (including the monumental *Catalogue of Birds* [1956-1958]) would create a niche into which audiences and critics could place him. Messiaen worked to construct this identity himself by writing his seven-volume *Treatise on Rhythm, Color, and Ornithology*. The fifth volume is the largest, and its size required it to be published in two separate books (5-1 and 5-2). The 1,310 pages are divided precisely in half (as one might expect from a fastidious mathematical musician), with the first and second books spanning exactly 655 pages each.

Volume 5-1 is devoted to the "Songs of the Birds of France (and Also a Part of Europe)" and subdivided into sections: "Mountain Heights"; "Mountain Forests"; "Mountain Dwellers"; "Woods"; "Country Roads"; "Nocturnals"; "Vineyards"; "Prairies and Fields" (discovered spaces, great prairies, wheat fields); "Gardens and Parks"; "Cities"; "Deserts, Garrigues, Scrublands" (stony terrains, green oaks, cork oaks, bushes, Kermes oaks, low and prickly plants, thyme, lavender, boulders, and rocky hills); "Warblers, Reeds, Ponds, Riverbanks, Salt Earths"; "Oceans, Marine Coasts."

Volume 5-2 is devoted to "Birdsongs of Japan," "Birdsongs of the United States of America," "Birdsongs of New Caledonia," and "Birdsongs from Diverse Countries in the World" (along with an analysis of Messiaen's *Seven*

---

siaen, "William Blake, poète lyrique," *Revue bleue* (February 20, 1937). Messiaen quotes from and cites his father's translation of William Blake, *Poèmes et fragments — Oiseaux et Fleurs, de William Blake* (Paris: Desclée de Brouwer, n.d.); cf. Pierre Messiaen, *Les romantiques anglais: textes anglais et français* (Paris: Desclée de Brouwer, 1955), 95-233.

16. Messiaen, discussion of visual arts *(arts plastiques)* in the chapter on rhythm; in *Traité*, 1:65-68, at 68.

Haiku and other ornithological material). The arrangement of the American chapter gives the reader an idea of Messiaen's scope. The heading reads "Birdsongs of the United States of America, and Especially of Utah and the Western United States." There then follow forty individual entries, including "Mockingbird," "American Robin," "Sage Thrasher (NEVADA)," "Baltimore Oriole," "Pyrrhuloxia (ARIZONA)," "Cassin's Finch (UTAH)," "Prairie Chicken," "Canyon Wren (IDAHO, MONTANA)," "Great Horned Owl," "Redshafted Flicker," "Song Sparrow," "Cardinal," and twenty-eight others.

Both volumes 5-1 and 5-2 are prefaced with four epigraphs, each prominently displayed on its own page.[17] They immediately give the reader a sense that birds have profound symbolic meaning for Messiaen.

> O Cross, reconciliation of the Cosmos — height of the sky — depth of the earth — expanse of all that is visible — breadth of the universe. (Andrew of Crete)

> Ornithologist by passion, I am also one by reason. I have always thought that the Birds were great masters and that they had discovered everything: modes, neums, the rhythmical, melodies of tones, and even collective improvisation. (Olivier Messiaen, 1970)

> One discovers more in the woods than in books. The trees and rocks will teach you things that you otherwise know not how to hear. (Saint Bernard)

> All the creatures of the perceptible world lead us to God: they are the images of the Source, of Light, of eternal Plenitude, of the Sovereign Archetype. They are the signs which have been given to us by the Lord himself. (Saint Bonaventure)

The first epigraph, taken from Saint Andrew, archbishop of Crete in seventh- and eighth-century Byzantium, offers a cosmic interpretation of the mystery of the cross.[18] Christ's cross reconciles the cosmos with its two beams drawing to-

---

17. Messiaen, *Traité,* V-1 *(Chants d'oiseaux d'Europe):* 9-12; and V-2 *(Chants d'oiseaux extra-européens):* xiii-xvi.

18. Messiaen's source here is very likely Hugo Rahner, *Griechische Mythen in Christlicher Deutung: Gesammelte Aufsätze* (Zurich: Rhein-Verlag, 1945); translated as Rahner, *Mythes grecs et mystère chrétien,* trans. Henri Voirin (Paris: Payot, 1954), 67: "O Croix, réconciliation du cosmos, délimitation des étendues terrestres, hauteur du ciel, profondeur de la terre, lien de la création, étendue de tout ce qui est visible, largeur de l'Œcuméné." Cf. English:

gether the two (iconic) dimensions of space: width and height. Birds, implies Messiaen, are symbols of this cosmic reconciliation: they are cruciform when their wings are spread out; they traverse the totality of heights and depths; and their migrations take them to the four corners of the earth.

The third epigraph, an admonition from the Cistercian monk Saint Bernard of Clairvaux (1090-1153) to leave the monastic library for the fresh air of the woods, echoes Messiaen's own lament that twentieth-century city dwellers do not encounter birds: "I talk about birdsongs to urban dwellers who've never heard a bird in their lives. To hear birds, one has to live in the country, to get up at 4 o'clock in the morning, if need be, and at daybreak and in the evening twilight to listen to the birds greet the rising sun. In Paris, London or Berlin, that doesn't work."[19] The final epigraph fittingly comes from Saint Bonaventure (1221-1274), cardinal-bishop of Albano and one of the most famous friars of the order founded by Saint Francis of Assisi.[20] In this passage, Bonaventure takes the ancient sacramental theology of Saint Augustine and reformulates it for the medieval cult of light, most famously theorized by Abbot Suger.

Messiaen situates his self-quotation (the second epigraph) not in chronological order (in which case, it would follow the others) but rather before the two western medievals — perhaps because he felt it would be a mark of hubris to situate himself as the "terminus" of such an illustrious list.[21] Or perhaps he wanted to place himself in between eastern Byzantine and western Catholic Christianity, constructing himself as a bridge that precedes or reconciles or transcends the historical division between the two. At any rate, he succinctly

---

"It is particularly in Byzantine devotion that this cosmic interpretation of the mystery of the cross lives on. 'O Cross, thou atonement of the universe,' runs one of the panegyrics, 'thou boundary round the wide spaces of the earth, thou height of heaven and depth of the earth, thou binding bond of creation, thou that art the width of all that is visible and the breadth of the whole world.' Yet the same thing is also a very ancient theological heirloom of the Latin Christians of Rome and Africa." Rahner, quoting and citing Andrew of Crete, *In sanctam Crucem* (PG 97:1021C); in Rahner, *Greek Myths and Christian Mystery*, trans. Brian Battershaw (New York: Harper and Row, 1963), 52.

19. Messiaen (December 16, 1983); in Almut Rößler, *Contributions to the Spiritual World of Olivier Messiaen*, trans. Barbara Dagg and Nancy Poland (Duisberg: Gilles & Francke, 1986), 122. For Bernard source, see Robert Fallon, "The Record of Realism in Messiaen's Bird Style," in *Olivier Messiaen: Music, Art, and Literature*, ed. Christopher Dingle and Nigel Simeone (Burlington, Vt.: Ashgate, 2007), 115-36, at 131 n. 30.

20. It is possible that Messiaen's source for Bonaventure is Étienne Gilson, *L'esprit de la philosophie médiévale*, 2nd ed. (Paris: Librairie Philosophique, 1948), 245-46; see Fallon, "Record of Realism," 132 n. 32.

21. However, even with the generous assistance of other scholars (for which I am grateful), I have not been able to locate Messiaen's unspecified source in 1970.

Vision 5: Amen of the Angels, of Saints, of Birdsong

states what he wants to emphasize in his introduction ("Birdsong") to the first of the two volumes: "In the beginning was the Bird" — or more correctly, "Birdsong."

Messiaen's paragraph introducing the thirteen-hundred-page volume on ornithology is almost comical. It really *does* want to establish birdsong in the beginning, and in order to do that, it begins in a Jurassic park.

> We don't know anything about the voices of the Stegosaurus, the Tyrannosaurus, or the Diplodocus. And if the Brontosaurus made a noise like thunder (*brontē* in Greek [+*saurus* = "thunder lizard"]) it came from walking. What sounds came out of the Archaeopteryx, the flying reptile, the most ancient winged creature? Did the Pteranodon have a language of cries? At the beginning of the Tertiary Period (65 million years ago) Vultures and Flamingos already existed. In the Oligocene epoch [25-35 million years ago] appeared both Kites and Plovers. In the Miocene (26 million years ago), the majority of today's bird families were present. Around 500,000 years ago, at the arrival of Homo Sapiens, birds were there and they sang. And ever since then, they have always sung.[22]

Here again we see the logic of Messiaen's initial (i.e., pre–October 1942) outline for *Visions:* the "Amen of Stars and Saturn" paralleled the "Amen of Angels, Saints, Birdsong," pre- or posthistoric. Both planets and birdsongs put human being in its place (quite literally) — a relative latecomer in "history" (or prehistory). The parallelism also imitates the suspension of the human being between "the two infinites" — planets and photons, the infinitely large and infinitely small. Here, however, it is the planets and the birds — multicolored Saturn and colorful flamingos.

But it is not merely that birdsong preceded the evolution of human beings by 64 million years. They also were the progenitors of music itself.

> Music: in its double aspect of message, of communication — and of silence, of artistic joy — most certainly came out of the song of birds. (This was, moreover, the opinion of Wagner, succinctly expressed by Walther [von Stolzing, a character] in *Die Meistersinger von Nürnberg,* and by Siegfried in the *Ring* tetralogy.) This is why — abandoning to more knowledgeable ornithologists the study of other particularities of the bird, the wings, flight, colors of plumage, simple and triple vision [tetra-chromatic vision], noc-

---

22. Messiaen, "1re Introduction — Le chant des oiseaux," in *Traité,* 5-1:15.

1943: Résumé: Visions of Amen

turnal vision, the great mysteries of migration — I will here study only this last marvel: song, source of all music.[23]

The terms in which Messiaen then describes birdsong provide yet another parallel to remarks on planetary dancing in Vision 2. Like dance, birdsong is lifted out of the realm of the everyday. It is a highly stylized formula on which an individual bird can then improvise variations. "Certain birds possess innate song, which they bring about with them, as a birthright. Others learn to sing by listening to their elders (especially their father). All respect the style and esthetic proper to their species, and — except for several regional dialects — this style and esthetic have not varied over the course of centuries. On the contrary, human music has experienced anxiety, seeking, and numerous changes, above all during the last two hundred years."[24] In addition to the parallel with dance and the planets, Messiaen's attention to each species of birds having an individual language seems to link them as well with angels. For in medieval thought, each angel is its own species (since there is no matter by which they could be individuated).[25]

Messiaen then offers a quick overview of the history of human music. The topics fly by and dizzy the reader: ancient Egypt, Babylon, and Assyria; pentatonic music in China and the Andes; semichromatic music in India, Persia, and Greece; medieval plainchant; the Renaissance of Machaut, Monteverdi, and Le Jeune; the monopoly of the major mode and the metric bar in the seventeenth century (with traces of the past still present in Bach); the tonal music of Mozart and Beethoven. With Wagner comes a turning point, followed by Debussy's "rhythmic undulations" in *Pelléas and Mélisande* and *La Mer (The Sea)*, and Stravinsky's "return to rhythmic sources" in the *Rite of Spring*. Serial music arrives; after thirty years, Boulez and Stockhausen (both students of Messiaen) move beyond it. A "new somersault" comes with Xenakis (yet

---

23. Messiaen, "1re Introduction — Le chant des oiseaux," in *Traité,* 5-1:15-16. Compare the assessment of Abbé Marcel Hébert: "The gaiety of Siegfried, the joy of living and acting, filled up [Wagner's] own heart when, after having soldered back together the two sections of the sword: music and poetry, he embarked on combating the monster: false art, corrupted and corrupting, and conquered the divine virgin of all grace and every light, harmony and truth. [Like Siegfried, Wagner] also heard the bird singing in the forest, aerial being, 'living symbol of the soul [*vivant symbole de l'âme*],' which warbled great thoughts for him in a melodious rhythm [*sur un rythme mélodieux*]." Hébert, *Le Sentiment religieux dans l'œuvre de Richard Wagner* (Paris: Librairie Fischbacher, 1895), 97, quoting Alfred Ernst, *Richard Wagner et le drame contemporain* (Paris: Librairie moderne, 1887), 254.

24. Messiaen, "1re Introduction — Le chant des oiseaux," in *Traité,* 5-1:16.

25. Aquinas, *ST,* Ia, q. 50, a. 4: "Whether the angels differ in species."

Vision 5: Amen of the Angels, of Saints, of Birdsong

another Messiaen student) and his indeterminate "stochastic music" and the "mathematical study of chance." *Musique concrète,* electronic music, aleatoric music, and a number of other schools would last "only several months." In sharp contrast to all this, Messiaen brings us back to his topic:

> During this entire time birds continued to sing. . . .
>   This short resume of human music doesn't explain anything about my ornithological passion. One can't explain a passion. There is also no need to search for a secret preference in the names I have cited: no anathema is intended for the others! . . . silence is an oratorical effect necessary in a brief overview. . . . I simply wanted to display the frightening [*effrayant*] shrinkage of durations of the principal musical styles of human beings — and compare them to *the reassuring continuity of birdsong.*[26]

Again, ephemerality and eternity: while Messiaen finds the increasing shrinkage of musical trends "frightening," he turns to what is stable, continuous, and "reassuring": birdsong. Analogous to the aeviternal chants of the angels and the endlessly recurring rotations of the planets, birdsong has remained largely the same since prehistory.

4. Birdsongs, Hours, Seasons

At the beginning of his analysis of Vision 5, in the space where earlier movements were headed up by quotations from astronomers, Scripture, and devotional writers, Messiaen inserts "several words on the birds."[27] The webs of linked meanings that Messiaen discovers in birds are complex, and in the volume of his *Treatise* devoted to European birdsong, Messiaen draws a number of literary connections. For example, in his discussions of the lark, his debt to his parents' literary interests is apparent: he quotes long sections on the lark from his father's published translations of William Blake, Robert Burns, and Percy Bysshe Shelley.

Along with lines from Claudel, Messiaen also quotes from his mother's collection, *The Valley (Le Vallon),* dedicated to her secret love, Jean de Gourmont.

---

26. Messiaen, "1re Introduction — Le chant des oiseaux," in *Traité,* 5-1:17, emphasis added.

27. Messiaen, analysis of Vision 5, in *Traité,* 3:256-65, at 256.

1943: Résumé: Visions of Amen

Listen to the lark lost at the bottom of the sky. . . .

I saw the lark ascend,
Its voice constructing in the light air
A landscape of brilliance [*clarté*]. . . .

Soar upward, young lark!
Your eggs are laid in the wheat,
And the dew in droplets
Quivers on gilded blades of grass. . . .[28]

These lines were of more than passing interest for Messiaen, as he would explain later in life:

> Last of all, perhaps the most extraordinary of her prophecies was that she should have foreseen that one day, after her death, I would become an ornithologist [here he quotes lines from her poems that refer to birds]. . . . For indeed I was later to transcribe the songs of the turtle dove *(tourterelle),* the skylark *(alouette des champs),* the woodlark *(alouette lulu)* and the song-thrush *(grive musicienne),* as well as of the birds of Japan and New Caledonia. The skylark, rising effortlessly to its high point in the sky and spinning its great spirals of melody around a very high dominant, cost me literally hundreds of attempts at notation. And so it is that I always reread the following line with a very particular emotion: [*Listen to the lark lost at the bottom of the sky.*] . . .[29]

Messiaen's literary associations with birds and birdsongs go back to his earliest childhood and, more specifically, to his mother.

His remarks introducing the "Amen of the Angels, of Saints, of Birdsong" are divided (once again) into three: the thrush family (Fr. *Turdidés;* L. *Turdidae*); the Sylviidae songbird family (Fr. *Sylviidés;* L. *Silviidae*); and the Fringillidae family (Fr. *Fringillidés;* L. *Fringillidae*), also known as "New World seedeaters." His initial entry for the thrush family, already seen in the discus-

---

28. Messiaen, quoting poetry of Cécile Sauvage, in *Traité,* 5-1:254. For details, see the discussion in chapter 1, under the heading "1909-1912: *The Valley:* Companions in Poetry, Strangers in Worldview."

29. Messiaen, preface to Cécile Sauvage, *L'Âme en bourgeon. Préface d'Olivier Messiaen. Postface de Marie Dormoy* (Paris: Séguier Archimbaud, 1987), 10-11; in Weller, "Afterword" to Sauvage, *Budding Soul,* in *Olivier Messiaen: Music, Art, and Literature,* 254. Translation in brackets added.

Vision 5: Amen of the Angels, of Saints, of Birdsong

sion above of the "Amen of the Stars," is worth repeating since the blackbird figures so prominently in his works:

> *The Blackbird* — the most original and melodically the most complete of the bird singers. Plumage entirely black, yellow beak. Found in woods and groves. Sings at sunrise, afternoon, and at sunset. A strophic song with the melodic formulae frequently ending upwards on a high note. Made of melodic variations of an inexhaustible variety, linking together up to 7 different strophes. Its best song is towards 5 o'clock in the morning in April-May. Found throughout France. One must also cite the White-rumped Shama of Asia [*Copsychus malabaricus*], excellent singer, with a long black-and-white tail. Song brilliant, strong, and cheerful.[30]

The importance of the blackbird for Messiaen may also be seen in the short independent piece he wrote one decade after *Visions* as a competition test for students at the Paris Conservatory: *The Blackbird (Le Merle noir)* (1951) for flute and piano. He was attracted to the bird's capacity for an "inexhaustible" variety in melodies:

> The Blackbird sings in the morning, at afternoon's end and at sunset. Its most beautiful and most abundant songs are found early in the morning, at dawn and the first light [*à l'aube et à l'aurore*], towards 5:30 a.m. at the end of March and beginning of April, towards 4:00 a.m. in June and in the first days of July. Some bird species possess several typical themes which one finds in all the individuals of the same species: but this is not the case of the Blackbird. The style, the esthetic, are the same among all Blackbirds, but each individual has its personal collection of themes. At the end of winter, starting when it begins to become less cold, the Blackbird works: it seeks and perfects its motifs. Since it never abandons what it has found, each spring it takes up again the themes of the preceding springtime while adding its new productions. Thus it accumulates a large quantity of themes, and as it links them together, embroiders them, switches (or inverts) them, varies them into infinity, it can string together strophe after strophe, throughout a half hour or more, without ever repeating one.[31]

---

30. Messiaen, analysis of Vision 5, in *Traité,* 3:256.
31. Messiaen, "Le Merle noir *(Turdus merula)* — en anglais: Blackbird," in *Traité,* 5-1:483-90, at 483-84.

1943: Résumé: Visions of Amen

The thrush family also includes the nightingale *(Rossignol),* a bird with an impressive musical and literary pedigree. Stravinsky devoted his first opera to this bird: *The Nightingale (Le Rossignol)* (1908-1914; rev. 1962), based on the Hans Christian Andersen tale (with the same title); he later adapted it as a symphonic poem, *The Song of the Nightingale (Le Chant du Rossignol)* (1917); three years later he allowed Diaghilev to turn it into a ballet (premiered in 1920), later revived by Balanchine. About the nightingale Messiaen writes: "The Nightingale sings in springtime, season of loves. Whether it be to seduce the female or in order to 'joust' in the types of artistic tournaments with another male singer. It makes itself heard during the night, between midnight and 2:00 a.m., beginning in April. A song comprised above all of repeated notes (which [François] Couperin used for trills): a moving song with great tenderness."[32] Couperin's well-known *Nightingale in Love (Le rossignol-en-amour)* (1722) for harpsichord ends with an extraordinary fading-away, imitating the bird's trills.

Messiaen's aversion to mourning found company in Samuel Taylor Coleridge's poem "The Nightingale" (1798). Coleridge famously quoted John Milton's description of the nightingale as that "Most musical, most melancholy!" bird, and then proceeded to argue that nothing in nature is melancholic; rather it is filled with love and joy.[33] Using his father Pierre's translation, Messiaen quotes these lines from Coleridge:

> [*My Friend, and thou, our Sister! we have learnt*
> *A different lore: we may not thus profane*
> *Nature's sweet voices, always full of love*]
> And joyance! 'Tis the merry Nightingale
> That crowds and hurries, and precipitates
> With fast thick warble his delicious notes,
> As he were fearful that an April night
> Would be too short for him to utter forth
> His love-chant, and disburthen his full soul
> Of all its music![34]

---

32. Messiaen, analysis of Vision 5, in *Traité,* 3:256.

33. For Coleridge's ambivalent melancholy, see Eric G. Wilson, "Introduction: Speculative Gloom," in Wilson, *Coleridge's Melancholia: An Anatomy of Limbo* (Gainesville: University Press of Florida, 2004), 1-46.

34. Messiaen, "Le Rossignol *(Luscinia megarhynchos),*" in *Traité,* 5-1:422, quoting Samuel Taylor Coleridge, "The Nightingale: A Conversation Poem; April 1798" ("Le Rossignol. Poème familier, avril 1798"); in Pierre Messiaen, *Les Romantiques anglais. Textes anglais et*

Vision 5: Amen of the Angels, of Saints, of Birdsong

"It is Coleridge yet again," continues Messiaen, "who remarked on the difference between the slow and pianissimo sounds of the Nightingale and the victorious fortissimo of its trills, alluding at the same time to the competitions of song between several Nightingales":

[*But never elsewhere in one place I knew
So many nightingales;*] and far and near,
In wood and thicket, over the wide grove,
They answer and provoke each other's song,
With skirmish and capricious passagings,
And murmurs musical and swift jug jug,
And one low piping sound more sweet than all
[*Stirring the air with such a harmony,
That should you close your eyes, you might almost
Forget it was not day!*][35]

Yet again using his father Pierre's translation, Messiaen also quotes the final lines of John Keats's "Ode to a Nightingale." For the sake of space he has edited out lines. But reading them closely, one sees that Messiaen has excised Keats's trademark melancholy, homesickness, and forlornness:

Perhaps the self-same song that found a path
[*Through the sad heart of Ruth, when, sick for home,
   She stood in tears amid the alien corn;
   The same that oft-times hath*]
Charm'd magic casements, opening on the foam
   Of perilous seas, in faery lands forlorn.
      [*8
Forlorn! the very word is like a bell
To toll me back from thee to my sole self!
Adieu! the fancy cannot cheat so well
As she is fam'd to do, deceiving elf.
Adieu! adieu!*] thy plaintive anthem fades

---

français (Paris: Desclée de Brouwer, 1955), 334-39, at 336 (Eng), 337 (Fr). Italicized words in brackets not included by Messiaen. As Pierre notes, Coleridge quotes John Milton's "Il Penseroso" in line 13; see *Samuel Taylor Coleridge*, ed. H. J. Jackson (New York: Oxford University Press, 1985), 99-101, 701-2 n. 99.

35. Messiaen, "Le Rossignol," in *Traité*, 5-1:422; quoting Coleridge, "The Nightingale," in *Romantiques anglais,* 336 (Eng), 337 (Fr).

1943: Résumé: Visions of Amen

> Past the near meadows, over the still stream,
> Up the hill-side; and now 'tis buried deep
> In the next valley-glades:
> Was it a vision, or a waking dream?
> Fled is that music: — do I wake or sleep?[36]

Of additional interest here are the lines that Messiaen kept about visions, waking dreams, and the fine line that separates the two — an interest central to the surrealists.

Amplifying the nightingale's literary overtones, Messiaen quotes from his father Pierre's translation of Shakespeare's *Romeo and Juliet* after first prefacing the text:

> Shakespeare — in *Romeo and Juliet* — opposed the Lark and the Nightingale, assimilating the Nightingale to the forces of Night, of Love, and Ecstasy, and the Lark to the voice of Brangäne in Tristan and Iseult, in the voice of the night watchman in the Medieval "alba," the voice that announces the coming of day and the enemy forces:
> "Juliet. — Wilt thou be gone? it is not yet near day. It was the nightingale, and not the lark, That pierc'd the fearful hollow of thine ear; Nightly she sings on yond pomegranate tree: Believe me, love, it was the nightingale.
> "Romeo — It was the lark, the herald of the morn, No nightingale. Look, love, what envious streaks Do lace the severing clouds in yonder east. Night's candles are burnt out, and jocund day Stands tiptoe on the misty mountain tops."[37]

Messiaen might also have pointed to the ending of night visions in *A Midsummer Night's Dream,* one of his favorite Shakespearean plays as a child. As Queen Titania is wakened from the spell that has led to her "visions," and just before Bottom awakens from his own ("I have had a most rare vision"), Puck

---

36. Messiaen, "Le Rossignol," in *Traité,* 5-1:425; quoting John Keats, "Ode to a Nightingale" ("Ode à un rossignol"), in *Romantiques anglais,* 834-39, at 838 (Eng), 839 (Fr). Italicized words in brackets not included by Messiaen.

37. Messiaen, "Le Rossignol," in *Traité,* 5-1:422, quoting William Shakespeare, *Romeo and Juliet,* act 3, scene 5, lines 1-10; in *The Arden Shakespeare Complete Works,* ed. Richard Proudfoot, Ann Thompson, and David Scott Kastan, rev. ed. (London: Arden Shakespeare, 2011), 1028; Shakespeare, *Roméo et Juliette, Œuvres,* trans. Pierre Messiaen, 3:146-47. For the medieval *"alba,"* see discussion of *Five Refrains (Cinq Rechants)* (1948), pp. 483-84 below.

Vision 5: Amen of the Angels, of Saints, of Birdsong

notes the lark's announcement of dawn: "Fairy king, attend, and mark: / I do hear the morning lark."[38]

By its connections with the *alba,* ecstasy, star-crossed love, Romeo and Juliet, and Tristan and Iseult, the nightingale links this "Amen of Birdsong" back to the preceding "Amen of Desire" and a passion that is ominously foreboding. A few years later (in *Turangalîla Symphony* [1948]), Messiaen's notes would instruct the audience to "let sleep" rather than disturb the two lovers in the "Sleeping Garden."

Moving on to the Sylviidae songbird family, Messiaen singles out two varieties of warblers:

> *the Blackcap* [*la Fauvette à tête noire*], olive-greenish ash, with the male's top of the head black. One of the very best singers. In woods and gardens.
> *the Lesser Whitethroat* [*la Fauvette babillarde*], slate gray head, a black line on the eye — brownish upper face, white lower face washed with pink on the sides. In groves and hedges.[39]

In a more extended discussion in his *Treatise,* Messiaen once again links both time (seasons) and love in the blackcap:

> The Blackcap is a small bird, active, alert, and joyful. Its migration takes it into North Africa, and it spends the winter in Algeria or in Tunisia. It returns to France beginning in the month of April, and sings a lot during the morning and afternoon, until the end of June in Sologne and in Provence, until the end of July in the Dauphiné. . . . At the beginning of spring, the bird makes heard in each strophe the pianissimo chirping followed by the loud refrain. During the time of loves [*au moment des amours*], the Blackcap male executes long solos in which the chirping and the refrains are intimately intermingled, forming a truly melodic development. This takes place only

---

38. "Roi des fées, attention, écoute: / J'entends l'alouette matinale." William Shakespeare, *A Midsummer Night's Dream,* act 4, scene 1, lines 92-93, in *Arden Shakespeare,* 906; Shakespeare, *Le Songe d'une Nuit d'Été, Œuvres,* trans. Pierre Messiaen, 1:557. Messiaen recalled: "I was inclined toward fairy tales, and Shakespeare is sometimes a super-fairy tale; it was this aspect of Shakespeare that impressed me. . . . I loved *Macbeth* most of all because of the witches and Banquo's ghost, also Puck [in *Midsummer Night's Dream*] and Ariel [in *The Tempest*] for the same reasons." Olivier Messiaen and Claude Samuel, *Music and Color: Conversations with Claude Samuel,* trans. E. Thomas Glasow (Portland, Ore.: Amadeus Press, 1994), 26.

39. Messiaen, analysis of Vision 5, in *Traité,* 3:256.

for about 2 or 3 days. At the end of the season (June, July), one hears only the refrain alone at spaced intervals.[40]

Messiaen also associates this particular bird with Saint Francis of Assisi, perhaps not only because it is found in Italy, but also because its "black cap" reminded the composer of a "skullcap," that is, the zucchetto (*calotte* in French) originally used to keep the tonsured heads of clergy warm.

> The most striking thing about its livery is its black skullcap [*calotte,* from *zucchetto*] which won him his French name [*Fauvette à la tête noir* = warbler with black head], as in English (Blackcap) and in Italian (Capinera). This black skullcap descends all the way to the eyes. The Blackcap is common in Europe and is found just about everywhere in France. In Italy, it completely replaces the Garden Warbler [*la Fauvette des jardins*], and it is the bird type of the hermitage cave [*Carceri d'Assise* = the Carceri in Assisi] where Saint Francis and his companions lived. In my opera "Saint Francis of Assisi," [the Blackcap] is always there when Saint Francis is on stage, and it is the bird who interrupts from time to time in order to punctuate phrases of the "Sermon to the Birds."[41]

Concluding with the Fringillidae family, Messiaen makes this very short entry: "*the Finch* [*le Pinson*], cheerful and vivacious, whose song announces springtime."[42] He adds more in his considerations of European birdsong:

> [*The Finch*] Very common. Its song, vigorous, accelerated, with a small coda proper to each individual.
> A strophe that is victorious, optimistic, and triumphant.
> It sings all day, disturbing even the silence of the hot afternoon hours. It seeks out its short coda for weeks, and when it finds it, it will repeat its entire strophe throughout the summer.[43]

---

40. Messiaen, "La Fauvette à tête noire," under "Les jardins et les Parcs," in *Traité,* 5-1:314-69, at 314.

41. Messiaen, "La Fauvette à tête noire," in *Traité,* 5-1:314; for Messiaen's discussion of the garden warbler, see 5-1:370-418. It includes analysis of his piano work entitled *La Fauvette des Jardins* (composed 1970; published 1972); see 5-1:399-418; cf. Nigel Simeone, *Olivier Messiaen: A Bibliographical Catalogue of Messiaen's Works,* Musikbibliographische Arbeiten series, vol. 14 (Tutzing: Hans Schneider, 1998), 154-55.

42. Messiaen, analysis of Vision 5, in *Traité,* 3:256.

43. Messiaen, "Le Pinson — ou Pinson des arbres *(Fringilla cœlebs),*" in *Traité,* 5-1:471-72, at 471.

Vision 5: Amen of the Angels, of Saints, of Birdsong

Messiaen consistently connects birdsongs and time — with daily hours and yearly seasons. In doing so, since cycles of days and years depend on the earth's rotations with respect to the sun (and hence, light), birds also implicitly refer back to the "Amen of Creation" (Let there be light!) and the "Amen of the Stars."

But there is something more intriguing about the "mixture" of birdsongs in this movement; since they do not actually occur in the same time and place in terrestrial time, they can only sound like this in aeviternity — which shares eternity's characteristic of "simultaneity." The blackbird, for example, sings "in woods and groves." Although it sings at sunrise, in the afternoon, and at sunset, its "most beautiful and most abundant songs" are about 5:30 A.M. at the end of March and beginning of April, and about 4:00 A.M. in June and the first days of July. Hence, it could not possibly be singing at the same time and place as the nightingale, found "in gardens and parks," and mostly singing between midnight and 2:00 A.M. beginning in April. By contrast, the finch, found along with the nightingale in "gardens and parks," sings throughout the afternoon, even in the extreme heat. The blackcap tends to sing mostly during both the morning and the afternoon, in Sologne and in Provence until the end of June, in the Dauphiné until the end of July. However, the long solos are not heard during June and July; only the refrain is sung at spaced intervals. Moreover, it winters in Algeria or Tunisia. Clearly, aeviternity is oblivious to distinctions like early April and late July, springtime and winter. Finally, the blackcap (listed by Messiaen under birds to be found in "gardens and parks") would probably not be found singing along with the cuckoo (listed under birds dwelling on "country roads") unless one of the two had gotten lost.[44]

Messiaen's imagery of symphonic birdsong seems to be inspired by Chateaubriand's chapter (in *Genius of Christianity*) describing birdsong and how it was made for human ears. However, Messiaen's account almost seems designed to refute Chateaubriand's realism in which the nightingale does not partake in this joint effort with the other birds: "the nightingale disdains to waste her lays amid this symphony. She waits till night has imposed silence, and takes upon herself that portion of the festival which is celebrated in its shades." Nevertheless, Messiaen would undoubtedly have been inspired by Chateaubriand's imaginatively detailed description of the nightingale's "hymn to the Eternal":

44. Messiaen, *Traité*, 5-1:6.

1943: *Résumé:* Visions of Amen

She first strikes the echoes with lively bursts of pleasure. Disorder pervades her strains. She passes abruptly from flat to sharp, from soft to loud. She pauses; now she is slow and now quick. It is the expression of a heart intoxicated with joy — a heart palpitating under the pressure of love. But her voice suddenly fails. The bird is silent. She begins again; but how changed are her accents! What tender melody! Sometimes you hear a languid modulation, though varied in its form; sometimes a tune more monotonous, like the chorus of our ancient ballads — those master-pieces of simplicity and melancholy. *Singing is as often an expression of sadness as of joy.* The bird that has lost her young still sings. She still repeats the notes of her happy days, for she knows no other; but by a stroke of her art, the musician has merely changed her key, and *the song of pleasure is converted into the lamentation of grief.*[45]

Birdsongs, then, represent many things. They signal both love and war — the attempt to attract a mate sexually and the competitive jousting with a rival. They return from northern Africa to announce the coming of spring in France, and they punctuate the long hot hours of a summer's afternoon. They accompany sleep and lovemaking during nocturnal hours; and as daylight threatens to reveal secrets, birdsongs warn star-crossed lovers. However, their simultaneous performance in Vision 5 cannot actually take place in terrestrial time. It can only happen outside of time, in aeviternity — pointing once again to the eschatological character of this entire movement. And as represented in music, the juxtapositions are surrealistic.

5. Section A: Exposition of Angels and Saints

The first section (A), "Exposition of Angels and Saints," opens with the statement of the "Angels-Saints Theme" (00:01–00:30). The melody is monophonic — that is, both pianists play the same line (in different octaves) in pure simplicity, without harmony or counterpoint. This parallels the monophonic melody of the "Planets Theme" opening up Vision 2 (except there it is played

---

45. François-René de Chateaubriand, "Song of Birds — It Is Made for Man — Laws Relative to the Cry of Animals," in *Genius of Christianity; or, The Spirit and Beauty of the Christian Religion,* trans. Charles I. White, 13th rev. ed. (Baltimore: John Murphy and Co., [1856] 1880), 147-48; cf. Chateaubriand, "Chant des Oiseaux; Qu'il est fait pour l'Homme; Loi Relative aux Cris des Animaux," in *Génie du christianisme, ou beautés de la religion chrétienne* (1802), in *Essai sur les révolutions. Génie du christianisme,* ed. Maurice Regard (Paris: Éditions Gallimard, 1978), 566-67. Emphasis added.

Vision 5: Amen of the Angels, of Saints, of Birdsong

by the second piano alone). The same technique opens up *Glorified Bodies* for organ where the work's first movement, "The Subtlety of Glorified Bodies," consists entirely of a single line played like a chant without any harmonic or contrapuntal adornment. The form fits the image of the trait of the risen body's "subtlety," the power of being so thin and malleable as to be capable of penetrating matter. That movement is also related to the "Amen of the Angels, of Saints, of Birdsong" thematically since Messiaen has constructed its epigraph out of two scriptural passages referring to those raised from the dead: "Their body, sown as an animal body, will rise as a spiritual body. And they will be pure like the angels of God in heaven."[46] Messiaen makes clear the relationship between this *Glorified Bodies* movement and movement 5 of *Visions:* the "purity" of the unadorned opening monophonic line represents the "Song of the purity of the Saints: Amen."[47]

This opening motive is followed by a second, which I have labeled the "Creation Song" (00:31–00:58). This designation might be overly restrictive, however, because it is more complex than it initially appears. This second motive has two parts. The first is an evocation (marked "expressive and tender" by Messiaen) of the "creation theme" first encountered in Vision 1 and then briefly heard again at the very end of Vision 3 (the sacrificed blood of Jesus signaling "the Second Creation"). Its appearance here makes eminent sense: this eschatological movement of aeviternity already participates in — is a "foretaste" (*praegustatum* in the ancient hymn "Ave Verum Corpus") of — the "consummation" of creation (Vision 7).

This creation theme is then transformed imperceptibly into an extended variation. Without Messiaen's notes in his *Treatise*, it would be easy to assume that this is simply an improvisation on melodic material from the creation theme. However, Messiaen reveals that this melody (laid out in 00:37–00:39) comes from "a popular Russian song, lament [*complainte*] of Nijni-Novgorod."[48]

---

46. "Leur corps, semé corps animal, ressuscitera corps spirituel. Et ils seront purs comme les anges de Dieu dans le ciel." Messiaen, epigraph to the first movement of *Les Corps Glorieux* (Leduc, 1942), fasc. 1, pp. 1-2, at 1; citing 1 Cor. 15:44 and Matt. 22:30.

47. Messiaen, "Note de l'Auteur." Messiaen did not deviate from strongly held convictions about plainchant. First, he held that *all* liturgical music (as distinguished from "religious" music) ought to be plainchant. Second, he insisted that the chant should *not* be harmonized (in the nineteenth-century style) but rather sung freely and unaccompanied. This accounts in some part for his usage here in the "Angels-Saints Theme." This is a celestial "liturgy." For "liturgy" parallels both preceding and following *Visions,* see "The Liturgy of Crystal" movement in *Quartet for the End of Time* (1940), and *Three Small Liturgies of the Divine Presence* (composed 1943-1944).

48. Messiaen, analysis of Vision 5, in *Traité,* 3:258. Mily Alekseyevich Balakirev was

This obscure reference is to a collection of Russian folk songs entitled *Collection of Popular Russian Songs, Annotated and Harmonized by M. Balakirew*, which cites Saint Petersburg as the place of composition, Leipzig as the place of publication (1898), and its translation into French.[49] For each of the forty songs, Balakirev provides both melodies and lyrics along with a harmonized piano accompaniment. He also locates each song's geographical origin and assigns each one a genre: "Nuptial Song," "Nuptial Practical Joke," *"Branle"* (a sixteenth-century dance, a form of which is "rustic"), "Song of the Boatman" *(chant de haleur)*, "Song of the Streets," and "Lament" *(Complainte)*. Out of the eleven laments *(complaintes)* in the collection, only one gives the genre a specific name: the "Lament of the Conscript." It is #18 in Balakirev's collection, and he gives its place of origin: "Government of Nijni-Novgorod, District of Kniaguinine," situated at the confluence of the Oka and Volga Rivers.[50]

This "Lament of the Conscript" — more exactly, "Lament of Nijni-Novgorod" ("Complainte de Nijni-Novgorod") — is the song from which Messiaen borrowed the melodic fragment and seemingly connected it with the "creation theme." I say "seemingly" because Messiaen in his analysis reproduces a small fragment and indicates that this has been externally joined to the first two measures of the "creation theme."[51] However, on closer examination, we see that even the "creation theme" has been altered so that it is coextensive with the entire first line of the conscript's lament. Upon reflection, then, it seems that in fact Messiaen had most likely derived the first line of the "creation theme" itself from "Lament of Nijni-Novgorod," a melodic line bearing a remarkable resemblance to the Westminster carillon chimes. Whatever the chronological order of sources, the "creation theme" and the "conscript's lament" flow seamlessly together in this second motive, the "Creation Song."

There are several aspects of this little Russian folk song that must have appealed to Messiaen. He would have liked its "oriental" modalism, and it might have been intended as a small homage to Stravinsky, whom Messiaen credited with rediscovering rhythm for Western music and whose works (like the *Rite of Spring*) incorporated Russian folk songs from his native land. But

---

born in Nizhniy Novgorod in 1836/1837; he died in Saint Petersburg in 1910. See Stuart Campbell, "Balakirev, Mily Alekseyevich," *Grove Music Online. Oxford Music Online,* http://www.oxfordmusiconline.com/subscriber/article/grove/music/40685; cf. Messiaen's citation of Balakirev in his discussion of Russian folksong, in *Traité,* 7:83-84.

49. Balakirew, ed., *Recueil de chants populaires russes, notés et harmonisés par M. Balakirew,* trans. J. Sergennois (Leipzig: M. P. Bélaïeff, 1898); name follows French spelling.

50. Balakirew, *Recueil de chants populaires russes,* 30.

51. Messiaen, analysis of Vision 5, in *Traité,* 3:258.

further speculation about the significance of "conscription" is tempting, partly because it is a lament sung by conscripts being forcibly marched off to war, and partly because the action it recalls (the saying of "Farewell" and "Adieu") fits so aptly with so much leave-taking in Messiaen's life — bidding farewell to his father called off to war in 1914; to his mother as she died early from consumption; to his own wife and child as he had been conscripted just three years prior to this work's composition; the "Adieu! Adieu!" ("thy plaintive anthem") in Keats's "Ode to a Nightingale" (quoted by Messiaen);[52] and the "Farewell" that forms the midpoint and climax of the *Harawi* lament composed at the war's end. This last farewell, identified by Messiaen's biographers with Claire's decline, seems to have been linked with the traumatic effects of being left behind with young Pascal after Messiaen's conscription in September 1939.

In the Russian folk song of the conscript's lament, a young man is at a dance where his comrades are drowning their sorrows in wine. As he approaches the young women, he says:

> Adieu, young girls, adieu, ladies,
> For you can no longer be anything to us.
> They are leading us to the soldiers,
> To the soldiers, among the recruits,
> To a life of slavery,
> Beneath the weight of a rifle![53]

It is possible, of course, that Messiaen intended no allusion whatsoever to the content of this song from which he derived the "creation theme" and, more fully, this second motive of Vision 5. However, if he did intend it, it is intriguing to speculate why he inserted a lament at the very heart of this eschatological movement.

Here is one possible reading. We human beings were created for the earth and we are at home in it; when we are forced out of it into our "final" home — forced out of time into out-of-time — we cannot help but lament our leaving even as it is mixed in (perhaps) with joy. Then again, Messiaen might have had an extraordinarily personal reason for appealing to this folk song in these dark days of war, imprisonment, and now, occupation. His own conscription into the army and his farewell to Claire and Pascal had been only the beginning of an enormous unraveling of their lives together.

---

52. Messiaen, "Le Rossignol," in *Traité*, 5-1:425.
53. Balakirew, *Recueil de chants populaires russes*, 30.

1943: Résumé: Visions of Amen

This creation-lament material is followed by a bridge ("Motive 3" [00:59–01:16]) in a "non-retrogradable rhythm" — once again, a rhythmic palindrome, performed the same in reverse (retrograde) as it is performed forward, and hence a symbol of eternity. In this eschatological setting of the angels and saints, non-retrogradable rhythm provides an ideal bridge to section A's second part (01:17–01:41), almost exactly a reprise of the first part. Extending the image of a palindrome, the first and second parts provide a near-mirror image of one another:

Motive 1: Angels-Saints Theme
   Motive 2: Creation Song
     Motive 3: Bridge
   Motive 2: Creation Song
     Motive 3: Bridge
Motive 1: Angels-Saints Theme

6. Sections B and A′: Birdsong (Development) and Recapitulation

With its joyful and frenetic birdsong, the second section (B) forms a sharp surrealistic juxtaposition (a second "rhythmic character") with the meditative tranquility of section A. Messiaen divides the birdsong (again, not surprisingly) into three parts. Except for the song of the European serin (*Serinus serinus,* yet another finch) providing a full rhythmic stop in the last four seconds, part 1 is devoted almost entirely to the nightingale. Part 2 begins with the nightingale, but then the entrance of blackbirds introduces far more complicated rhythmic material: one sings its strophe while another provides counterpoint. After the European serin provides a rhythmic full stop, part 3 opens and the nightingale and blackbirds are joined by an increasingly "vehement cuckoo," whose song propels the energy into an ever more frenetic pace.[54]

Finally, the third section (A′) consists of a recapitulation of section A, that is, the initial "Exposition of Angels and Saints." However, this recapitulation is inflected with the difference that results from having passed through the development section of birdsong. For example, the opening "Angels-Saints Theme" (04:32–05:05) is still sung as a plainchant line, but it is now accompanied by rapid shimmering Debussyesque impressions in the upper register. The

---

54. As Messiaen notes, the cuckoo can repeat its simple two-note song "until it is satisfied, 3 times, 5 times, 9 times, and more." Messiaen, "Le Coucou *(Cuculus canorus),*" in *Traité,* 5-1:219.

Vision 5: Amen of the Angels, of Saints, of Birdsong

"Creation Song" (Motive 2) is also recapped here, but the placid timelessness of section A is replaced by unpredictable rhythmic attacks in both the lower and the upper registers that transfigure its lamentation into something much less melancholic. This is even truer in its restatement (05:55–06:24), when the attacks in the lower register are stronger and the atonal shimmering in the upper register carries it further still from any remaining association with melancholic lamentation. The restatement of the "Angels-Saints Theme" is here even more fully embedded within a Debussyesque setting.

The brief eleven-second coda ensures that the movement does not end ambivalently by drifting off into silence (as do Visions 3 and 4). The nightingale's rhythmic punctuation and a final brilliant glissando ensure that the conclusion is final and sealed. In other words, there is no chance that this vision of aeviternity, transcending terrestrial time, will blend into the next movement of judgment — a brief yet harsh vision of a human life's end.

Vision 6

Amen of Judgment

> Gospel of Matthew: Last Judgment • Excommunication •
> Book, Bell, Candle • *Pontificale Romanum* • *Fiat. Fiat. Fiat.* •
> Marlowe: *Doctor Faustus* • Baudelaire: *Hurlements* • *Victimae
> Paschali: Mors et Vita Duello* • Tam-tam • Poe: "The Pit and
> the Pendulum" • Pascal: The Abyss • Conversion by Terror

The sixth vision goes beyond aeviternity to the end of time. It is a "summing up" and hence "judgment" — either in the particular judgment of an individual (at the end of one's life) or at the general judgment at the end of time — the eschatological time of Revelation or, more fearfully, the Apocalypse. Like the "Amen of Desire," this movement was not in Messiaen's original plan. Did Messiaen merely feel theologically obligated to include a judgment before the final consummation of time and creation? Or did it perhaps have a more clandestine meaning in the context of the Concerts de la Pléiade in occupied Paris, a sense that present circumstances of oppression demanded the judgment of tyrants?

As opposed to the unpredictable carillon heard in the first vision, this movement pictures an ominously incessant tolling of the bell *(la cloche* as opposed to *le carillon)*. Messiaen's association of bells with death goes back at least as far as *Eight Preludes* (1928-1929) for piano, catalogued as his second opus. The sixth of eight movements is entitled "Bells of Anguish and Tears of Farewell" ("Cloches d'angoisse et larmes d'adieu"). He composed the work in the immediate aftermath of his mother's death the previous year, and "bells of anguish" were associated in his mind with funeral bells.

Vision 6: Amen of Judgment

Rhythmically speaking, the pace of Vision 6 is relentless in its uniformity and the bell tolling is predictably precise. It is the opposite of "rhythm" as Messiaen understood that word, instead exemplifying the metered "military march" he denounced. It is the one place in *Visions* where Bergson's "spatialized time" is represented: the unvarying, relentless swing of the pendulum. The metronome marking (132 sixteenth notes per minute) means that the "three frozen notes" actually do beat the seconds.

Messiaen's "Author's Note"

Messiaen describes Vision 6 in his "Author's Note" to the published score:

> VI. — Amen of Judgment.
> Three frozen notes [*notes glacées*] like the bell of evidence. In truth, I say to you, Amen. "Condemned, away from me!" (Gospel according to Saint Matthew). The damned are fixed in their state. Piece deliberately harsh and brief.

Commentary

1. Matthew 25: Judging Light and Darkness

As in his quotation of Baruch (in Vision 2), Messiaen's scriptural fragment adds the word "Amen" to the Gospel text. The source is Matthew:

> But when the Son of Man shall come in his majesty, and all the angels with him, then he will sit on the throne of his glory; and before him will be gathered all the nations, and he will separate them one from another, as the shepherd separates the sheep from the goats; and he will set the sheep on his right hand, but the goats on the left.
> Then the king will say to those on his right hand, "Come, blessed of my Father, take possession of the kingdom prepared for you from the foundation of the world." . . . Then he will say to those on his left hand, "Depart from me, accursed ones, into the everlasting fire [*Retirez-vous de Moi, maudits, allez au feu éternel*] which was prepared for the devil and his angels."
> . . . Then he will answer them, saying, "Amen I say to you [*En vérité, Je vous le dis*], as long as you did not do it for one of these least ones, you did not

1943: Résumé: Visions of Amen

do it for me." And these will go into everlasting punishment [*au supplice éternel*], but the just into everlasting life [*à la vie éternelle*].¹

This Gospel passage serves as the opening text for Hello's section (in *Words of God*) devoted to the New Testament.² It is from the eschatological discourse Jesus gives about the end times, and the parable immediately preceding this part ends with a clear reference to being cast out of light and into darkness: "But as for the unprofitable servant, cast him forth into the darkness outside [*jetez-le dans les ténèbres extérieures*], where there will be the weeping, and the gnashing of teeth."³ As such, it is the reversal of creation and of Vision 1: "Let there be light."

Beyond light and darkness, Messiaen would have found other eschatological tropes resonant in this account of the Last Judgment: eternity, angels, life versus death, and the end of time — which is to say, the end of possibility, desire, and free will. Choices are no longer possible. "The damned are fixed in their state." Messiaen's passage on past-present-future (seen in Vision 4) takes on much different significance in this new context: "The distant past is the true past; we can qualify it with Cuvillier as the 'hardened past'; we reconstruct it with the aid of memory, but it is impossible to change anything about it: it was what it was. If we played a culpable role in it, it stays with us in the form of guilt."⁴

2. "Bell of Evidence": Book, Bell, and Candle?

What is the "bell of evidence" to which Messiaen refers? Bells have played an unexpectedly important role in French history. Until the revolutionary legislation of 1793 (which outlawed bells and melted down many of them for other

---

1. Matt. 25:31-34, 41, 45-46 (Douay-CCD; comparing Fillion).

2. Ernest Hello, *Paroles de Dieu. Réflexions sur quelques textes sacrés*, ed. François Angelier (Grenoble: Jérôme Millon, [1877] 1992), 169-74. Hello's poignant meditation is on the vital necessity of hospitality for traveling foreigners in the ancient world.

3. Matt. 25:30 (Douay-CCD; comparing Fillion).

4. Olivier Messiaen, *Traité de rythme, de couleur, et d'ornithologie (1949-1992) en sept tomes*, 8 vols. (Paris: Alphonse Leduc, 1994-2002), 1:11, summarizing Armand Cuvillier, *Nouveau précis de philosophie. Tome I: La connaissance* (Paris: Armand Colin, 1963), 226-29, and quoting Henri Bergson, *Essai sur les données immédiates de la conscience* (Paris: Félix Alcan, 1889), 7; Bergson, *Time and Free Will: An Essay on the Immediate Data of Consciousness*, trans. F. L. Pogson (New York: Humanities Press, [1910] 1971), 9-10.

Vision 6: Amen of Judgment

purposes), the French countryside not only had a visual landscape but also an aural soundscape delimited and defined by bells.[5] (One wonders what kind of bells Messiaen heard in his Dauphiné childhood.) A village's boundary was delimited by whether or not a listener could hear the church bells ringing.

Every locality had a number of bells, depending on its wealth. Among these were the "elevation bell" *(cloche de l'élévation),* tolled during the elevation of the host and chalice during Mass; the "funeral bell" *(cloche funèbre)* was tolled to inform the village that someone was dying. (Recall Vierne's *Poem of the Funeral Bells* [1916] for piano.)[6] In the old soundscape, the "Angelus bell" rang at 6 A.M., noon, and 6 P.M., calling all within hearing distance to pause and pray the Angelus in honor of the Virgin Mary (a scene made famous in Jean-François Millet's *The Angelus,* painted in 1857-1859). The 1911 edition of the *Encyclopædia Britannica* listed a number of secular bells in the British soundscape, including not only smaller bells (the "Pancake Bell" rung on Shrove Tuesday, the Harvest Bell, Seeding Bell, Gleaning Bell, Oven Bell, and Market Bell) but also very large ones, like the tocsin, or alarm bell, used to signal fires, approaching storms and armies, and the shutting and opening of city gates.[7]

Among these many bells, there seems to be no exact match with Messiaen's

---

5. Alain Corbin, *Village Bells: Sound and Meaning in the Nineteenth-Century French Countryside,* trans. Martin Thom (New York: Columbia University Press, 1998); original Corbin, *Les cloches de la terre: paysage sonore et culture sensible dans les campagnes au XIXe siècle* (Paris: A. Michel, 1994); cf. Corbin, "Identity, Bells, and the Nineteenth-Century French Village," in *Hearing History: A Reader,* ed. Mark M. Smith (Athens: University of Georgia Press, 2004), 184-204. On July 23, 1793, the Revolutionary Committee on Public Safety (Comité du Salut Public) decreed that all bells should be taken down and used to make cannons. This caused unrest in the rural areas for which bells were "not only the mark of religion but also of time, of the hour." As late as June 1797, a young deputy from Lyon testified that while the law may have been obeyed in the cities, it was generally ignored in the countryside: "These bells are not only useful to the people, they are dear to them, they constitute one of the most sensual joys [*une des jouissances les plus sensibles*] that their religious practice [*son culte*] gives them." After Napoleon's signing of the papal concordat reestablished the church in France, the sounding of bells was once again allowed although regulated. The *Articles organiques* (April 1802) governing Catholic practice decreed that bishops would arrange the usage of bells in concert with the prefect, and they were not to be used except for the divine service. After having been silent for ten years, the great bell *(le bourdon)* of Notre-Dame was rung once again on April 18, 1802. See editorial note, François-René de Chateaubriand, *Essai sur les révolutions. Génie du christianisme,* ed. Maurice Regard (Paris: Éditions Gallimard, 1978), 1832-33 n. 1.

6. Vierne, *Poèmes des cloches funèbres,* op. 39; see discussion of Messiaen's *Eight Preludes* (1928-1929), pp. 88-89 above.

7. "Bell," *Encyclopædia Britannica* (1911). http://www.1911encyclopedia.org/Bell.

"bell of evidence" *(cloche de l'évidence)*. However, an 1894 British archaeological journal notes the existence of an "Excommunicating Bell": "When a person was excommunicated, the church bell was solemnly tolled, and the practice is still continued in Catholic countries."[8] The judicial nature of the "Amen of Judgment" as well as its compositional structure suggest that Messiaen may have had in mind the medieval ceremony of excommunication — the "bell, book, and candle." Its notoriously terrifying structure would have appealed to his attraction to both senses of "fear": fear *(la peur)* and awe *(la crainte)*.

The ceremony was a popular topic in nineteenth-century lore. In the 1867 translation of the fifteenth-century *Chronicles of Enguerrand de Monstrelet*, a detailed woodcut illustrated the ceremony. It conjured up the account in which a number of French noblemen, "by virtue of a bull of pope Urban V of happy memory ... were publicly excommunicated and anathematized in all the churches of the city of Paris, *by bell, book, and candle*."[9] Although Monstrelet offered no details of the ceremony, his fifteenth-century readers would presumably have known it. However, three centuries later, the Unitarian Joseph Priestley elaborated his account for anti-Anglican (i.e., anti-Trinitarian) purposes:

> In this [seventh century] period the sentence of excommunication became a much more dreadful thing than it had been before, and a proportionably greater solemnity was added to the forms of it. The most solemn part of the new ceremonial was the extinction of lamps or candles, by throwing them on the ground, with a solemn imprecation, that the person against whom the excommunication was pronounced, might in like manner be extinguished or destroyed by the judgment of God. And because the people were summoned to attend this ceremony by the sound of a bell, and the curses accompanying the excommunication were recited out of a book, while the person who pronounced them stood on some balcony or stage,

---

8. Elias Owen, F.S.A., "On the Use of Church Bells," *Archæologia Cambrensis*, 5th ser., 11, no. 43 (July 1894): 185-95, at 193. Owen also discusses other bells in belfries: the Passing Bell, Broth-Bell, Pudding-Bell, Joy-Bell, Fire-Bell, Ave Bell, Induction Bell.

9. Enguerrand de Monstrelet, *The Chronicles of Enguerrand de Monstrelet; Containing an Account of the Cruel Civil Wars Between the Houses of Orleans and Burgundy; of the Possession of Paris and Normandy by the English; their Expulsion Thence; and of Other Memorable Events that Happened in the Kingdom of France, as well as in Other Countries ... Beginning at the Year MCCCC, where that of Sir John Froissart Finishes, and Ending at the Year MCCCCLXVII, and Continued by Others to the Year MDXVI*, trans. Thomas Johnes, 2 vols. (London: William Smith, [1840] 1867), 1:196, emphasis added. The illustration is noted as being "From an original design."

Vision 6: Amen of Judgment

from which he would throw down his lights, we have the phrase of *cursing by bell, book and candle*. The first example of excommunication by throwing down lighted lamps was at Rheims, about the year 900, when the bishops excommunicated some murderers in this manner.[10]

At least this was how Priestley imagined things in 1782. Over a century later, the *Encyclopædia Britannica* (1911) explained the addition of the candle ceremony:

> To the spoken word was added the language of symbol. By means of lighted candles violently dashed to the ground and extinguished the faithful were graphically taught the meaning of the greater excommunication — though in a somewhat misleading way, for it is a fundamental principle of the canon law that *disciplina est excommunicatio, non eradicatio* [discipline is excommunication, not eradication]. The first instance, however, of excommunication by "bell, book and candle" is comparatively late (c. 1190).[11]

The contemporaneous *New International Encyclopædia* (1914), pushing the ceremony's origins back "as early as the eighth century," quoted the

---

10. Joseph Priestley, *A History of the Corruptions of Christianity to which are Appended Considerations in Evidence that the Apostolic and Primitive Church was Unitarian* (London: British and Foreign Unitarian Association, [1782] 1871), 206-7.

11. See entry for "Excommunication," *Encyclopædia Britannica* (1911) http://www.1911encyclopedia.org/Excommunication. This late dating would make the excommunication ceremony of Lord Gilbert in the movie *Becket* (1964) anachronistic since Thomas Becket had died in 1170. For this vivid cinematic portrayal of the excommunication's candle ceremony, see Richard Burton as Thomas Becket, archbishop of Canterbury, in *Becket* (1964), directed by Peter Glenville and produced by Hal B. Wallis; Joseph H. Hazen executive producer. The screenplay was adapted from the 1959 play *Becket or the Honour of God (Becket ou l'honneur de Dieu)* by Jean Anouilh. The excommunication scene largely follows the account described in the most recent *Encyclopaedia Britannica*: "When the assemblage had been convoked, a bishop appeared with 12 priests, and all 13 held lighted candles. The bishop, wearing violet vestments, then recited the formula, ending thus: 'We separate him, together with his accomplices and abettors, from the precious body and blood of the Lord and from the society of all Christians; we exclude him from our holy mother the church in heaven and on earth; we declare him excommunicate and anathema; we judge him damned, with the devil and his angels and all the reprobate, to eternal fire until he shall recover himself from the toils of the devil and return to amendment and to penitence.' Those present answered, 'So be it!' Then the bishop and the 12 priests extinguished their candles by dashing them to the ground, and (as a general rule) the ceremony then ended." See entry for "Bell, Book, and Candle": http://www.britannica.com/EBchecked/topic/59650/bell-book-and-candle.

pre-Reformation Scottish form of excommunication alluding to the candle: "Cursed be they from the crown of the head to the sole of the foot. Out be they taken of the book of life. And as this candle is cast from the sight of men, so be their souls cast from the sight of God into the deepest pit of hell. Amen." The rubric added: "And then the candle being dashed on the ground and quenched, let the bell be rung."[12]

Messiaen might have had access to a more complete overview of the ceremony by means of his father Pierre's associations within British-French Catholic Revivalist circles. In 1909, the English Jesuit Herbert Thurston published an article in the Jesuit periodical *The Month* aimed at refuting anti-Catholic propaganda using the "book, bell, and candle" ritual. After the Great War, he published a revised version of this article as a small popular tract for the Catholic Truth Society entitled *Excommunication by Book, Bell, and Candle*.[13] The text of the final lines of the excommunication rite — *"Et omnes respondent. Fiat. Fiat. Fiat.* (And all respond. *Let it be done. Let it be done. Let it be done)"* — and a woodcut illustration with a bishop surrounded by twelve priests (all holding candles) were reproduced in facsimile, both on the front cover and inside the pamphlet.[14]

The technical term for this ceremony, noted Thurston, is the "solemn anathema," which "does not generically differ from the greater excommunication, but it imports certain ceremonies which surround the promulgation of the sentence with *additional terror and solemnity.*" The ceremony had not been used "in any part of the Catholic Church within living memory," but it also had not been suppressed up to the most recent editions of the *Pontificale Romanum*. The rubrics provide for the bishop to be seated on his faldstool surrounded by twelve assisting priests in surplices, six on each side. They all hold lighted candles while the bishop reads the anathema. Thurston offers a translation of this reading's conclusion to which all respond with the threefold subjunctive *Fiat*: "So be it, so be it, so be it."[15]

The rubric then "directs that the Bishops and priests are to throw their lighted candles upon the pavement." While the *Pontificale* says nothing about

---

12. See entry for "Bell, Book, and Candle," in *The New International Encyclopædia*, 2nd ed. (New York: Dodd, Mead and Co., 1914), 3:105.

13. Herbert Thurston, S.J., *Excommunication by Book, Bell, and Candle* (London: Catholic Truth Society, 1926); revised from original publication in *The Month* (November 1909).

14. The reproduction was taken from the Giunta *Pontificale* (1520), one of the very earliest editions of the *Pontificale Romanum,* thus demonstrating that the Reformer Tyndale had grossly exaggerated his claims about the anathema in 1528. Thurston, *Excommunication*, 12-13.

15. Thurston, *Excommunication*, 10, emphasis added.

Vision 6: Amen of Judgment

the ringing of bells, Thurston notes that "earlier rituals prescribe that the bells are to be jangled both at the beginning and at the conclusion of the ceremony, seemingly as supplying *another element of horror and confusion.*" As for the throwing down of candles, "to which many of the older rubrics add stamping upon," Thurston observes that it "is intended clearly enough to symbolize the extinction of joy or of the light of grace in the soul of the offender. Indeed, many of the early mediæval formulæ, some as ancient as the ninth century, contain the express petition that 'his joy may be quenched in the face of all the Saints as these candles are extinguished before our eyes.'"[16]

Even if Messiaen had not been aware of the ceremony through any of these popular historical venues, he would have seen the ritual when he used the *Pontificale Romanum* as organist of Trinité during a bishop's visit. This book contains all the prayers and Gregorian chants (in plainchant notation) for rituals that are celebrated by a bishop, including the blessing of liturgical vessels, tabernacles, crucifixes, and images of the Virgin Mary; the baptism of adults and the celebration of marriage and the nuptial blessing; the solemn office following a funeral mass; and numerous other events. The most frequent ritual in a parish church would have been the visiting bishop's conferral of the sacrament of confirmation.[17]

The Latin title of the "bell, book, and candle" ritual is *Excommunicandi et absolvendi ordo* — The Order of Excommunication and of Absolution.[18] The ritual is twofold: the first half *(excommunicandi)* is for administering the solemn anathema; the second *(absolvendi)* for absolution of the repentant member and reception back into communion. The details of the rubrics read exactly as Thurston relates them: the bishop enters in procession with twelve attending priests, all carrying candles. The lengthy anathema is concluded with all answering: *Fiat. Fiat. Fiat.* Then the bishop and the priests "throw onto the ground the burning candles which they are holding in their hands [*projicere in terram candelas ardentes, quas in manibus tenebant*]."[19] This ceremony's central ritual action of extinguishing light fits well with both Matthew's eschatological Gospel scene and Messiaen's cryptic description: "Three frozen notes like the bell of evidence."[20]

---

16. Thurston, *Excommunication,* 11-12, emphasis added.

17. The version Messiaen would have known had been revised shortly after he took over the Trinité position in 1931. See *Pontificale Romanum: Summorum Pontificum* (Mechelen, Belgium: Dessain, 1934).

18. *Pontificale* (1934), 815-25.

19. *Pontificale* (1934), 822.

20. Messiaen, "Note de l'Auteur," *Visions de l'Amen* (1943), n.p.

1943: Résumé: Visions of Amen

This ceremony of light with its *Fiat* also provides a structural linkage between the "Amen of Judgment" and the "Amen of Creation." Messiaen's text for Vision 1: "Amen, let it be so! 'God said: "Let there be light! And there was light!"' "[21] is a vernacular translation of the Genesis verse that reads in the Latin Vulgate:

dixitque Deus fiat lux [God said let there be light]
et facta est lux [and there was light].[22]

The *"Fiat"* of the bishop and priests at the excommunication, along with extinguishing the light, reverses God's first act in creation: the original *fiat* that created (as Messiaen notes in Vision 1) "light and, as a consequence, Life." This is the second of Messiaen's "four different senses" of the word "Amen" (derived from Hello): "Amen, I submit, I accept. Let your will be done! [*Que votre volonté soit faite!*]."[23]

Vision 6's threefold structure outlined by Messiaen musically represents this ritual:

Form: First phrase: periods A / B / A / B extension concluding in E minor.
Second phrase: periods C / D / C / D extension concluding on B (dominant)
First phrase: periods A / B / A (new harmony) / B extension concluding in E minor — conclusion by four *ff* chords in E major
Each period is followed by "3 frozen notes like the bell of evidence." Three notes that say: **no**[24]

---

21. Messiaen, "Note de l'Auteur."
22. Gen. 1:3.
23. Messiaen, "Note de l'Auteur." For Hello's linkage between light and life, see above discussion of Vision 1; for his connections between "Amen" and "Fiat," see *Paroles de Dieu*, 247-51. For example: *"Fiat* translates in a certain measure the magnificent: *Amen."* "Yes! We may say *Amen* to the word who said: *Fiat lux* [Let there be light]."
24. Messiaen, analysis of Vision 6, in *Traité*, 3:266-69, at 266, bold in original. Messiaen identifies the three phrases as "first-second-first." To avoid confusion for the reader, in the appendix I have instead used "A-B-A'" to indicate that the third is a reprise of the first. Note that throughout this analysis of the *sixth* movement, Messiaen repeatedly plays on the number 6 as the product of 3 x 2. Phrase 1 = Periods A/B/A/B; Phrase 2 = Periods C/D/C/D; Phrase 3 = Periods A/B/A/B. Note too that in the series of numbers 1-7, only 4 and 6 (the two added movements) are not prime numbers.

Vision 6: Amen of Judgment

The rhythm of these three "frozen notes," says Messiaen, is anapestic and "contrasts throughout the piece by its fierce departure [*sa franchise énergique*] from the irregular rhythms of the rest." If "irregular rhythm" for Messiaen is in fact what "rhythm" is (as opposed to regular meter), then these three notes that say no are a refusal of rhythm itself — that is, of the dance of life. They prefer the death of the military march.[25]

The relentless "forward" motion of the pendulum in the first and third phrases swings in reverse in the middle phrase. The upward motion that marks the first and third phrases becomes a downward motion in the second; the three high notes become three low notes; and the thunderous crash in the lowest register (against the high notes) is inverted as a crash in the highest register (against the low notes). Messiaen seems to be drawing on an ancient practice of ringing bells backward as a tocsin or notice of danger. Ringing backward or "in a contrary direction" *(tout le contraire)* means ringing a muffled peal — that is, one of sorrow, not joy.[26] (I personally remember first hearing bells rung backward in the broadcasted 1997 funeral of Diana, Princess of Wales.) Sir Walter Scott uses the phrase in *The Betrothed:* "At first a single, long, and keen bugle-blast, announced the approach of the enemy; presently the signals of alarm were echoed from every castle and tower on the borders of Shropshire, where every place of habitation was then a fortress. Beacons were lighted upon crags and eminences, *the bells were rung backward in the churches and towns,* while the general and earnest summons to arms announced an extremity of danger which even the inhabitants of that unsettled country had not hitherto experienced."[27]

A more ancient ancestor of ringing backward comes from Christopher Marlowe's *Doctor Faustus:*

Bell, book, and candle; candle, book, and bell,
Forward and backward, to curse Faustus to hell.[28]

---

25. Messiaen, analysis of Vision 6, in *Traité,* 3:266.

26. See entry for "Bells" in Ebenezer Cobham Brewer, *Dictionary of Phrase and Fable, Giving the Derivation, Source, or Origin of Common Phrases, Allusions, and Words That Have a Tale to Tell,* rev. ed. (Philadelphia: Henry Altemus Co., 1898). Entry available online: http://www.bartleby.com/81/1642.html.

27. Sir Walter Scott, *The Betrothed* (Edinburgh: Constable, 1902), 29, emphasis added.

28. Christopher Marlowe, *Tamburlaine, Parts I and II; Doctor Faustus, A- and B-texts; The Jew of Malta; Edward II,* ed. David M. Bevington and Eric Rasmussen (New York: Oxford University Press, 1995), 165 (A-text: 3.1, lines 82-85), 217 (B-text: 3.2, lines 90-93).

1943: Résumé: Visions of Amen

The tripartite form of the stanzas imitates the threefold elements: forward, backward (retrograde), forward. Like Machaut's "My end is my beginning and my beginning my end," the phrase "bell-book-candle-book-bell" is analogous to a palindrome, the kind of non-retrogradable rhythm Messiaen uses when evoking eternity:

⌊bell → book → ⌈CANDLE⌋ ← book ← bell⌉

The tripartite structure — forward-backward-forward — is used to symbolize a curse that is "eternal" or "everlasting," both in Marlowe's *Doctor Faustus* and in Matthew's Gospel: "And these will go into everlasting punishment [*Et ceux-ci iront au supplice éternel*]."[29]

Having emphasized the "eternal" and "fixed state" aspects of Messiaen's movement, we note by contrast the anathema in the *Pontificale* — The Order of Excommunication and of Absolution: "For these reasons we, by the judgment of Almighty God, Father, Son, and Holy Ghost . . . pronounce him to be excommunicated and under anathema, and we declare him condemned with the devil and his angels and all the reprobate to eternal fire, *until he set himself free* from the devil's snares and *return to amendment and repentance*, making satisfaction to the Church which he has injured. Thus we deliver him to Satan for the destruction of the flesh *that his spirit may be saved in the day of judgment*."[30] The excommunication is not meant as the last word in a person's life. Rather, it is the first half of a twofold ritual (the second half being the absolution) intended to motivate the judged to "set himself free . . . and return to amendment and repentance." It ultimately aims not at damnation but rather at salvation. And here is where the analogy with Messiaen's "judgment" ends: the "hardened past" cannot be changed. Time is over. It was what it was.

2. "Hurlements": The "Wails" of Bells

Messiaen's peculiar language describing the sounds and emotional effects that should come from the piano in this movement is evocative but also provocative — peculiar enough to invite a closer look.

Messiaen describes the "frozen" three-note motive ("like the bell of evidence") concluding each period along with the crash that follows the motive:

---

29. Matt. 25:46a (Douay-CCD, Fillion).
30. Translation in Thurston, *Excommunication,* 11, emphasis added.

Vision 6: Amen of Judgment

After the 3 treble high-pitched notes, there is always a terrible "flam" [*un "fla" terrible*] on the bass drum [*de grosse caisse*] (extreme low register); after the 3 low-pitched notes, there is always a terrible "flam" on the sharp cymbal [*cymbale aiguë*] (extreme high register). These effects are repeated after the final periods of each phrase. The music belonging to the 2nd piano, the 1st piano accompanies it with shrill wails [*de hurlements stridents*] (or lower resonances) on a note and with counterpoints in range.[31]

In the immediately following analysis of the first phrase, Messiaen adds that in period A "the wail [*hurlement*] is on a g♮ surrounded by dissonances." At the end of the analysis, he notes that the first piano is to play "a G wailed more shrilly [*hurlé plus strident*] surrounded by supplementary dissonances."[32]

The description is metaphorical throughout: the "bass drum" is an orchestral instrument and the "sharp cymbal" is an organ stop — apparently, one of Messiaen's favorite stops since he added two of them to the Trinité organ during its renovations of 1934-1935 and 1962-1965.[33] The drum and cymbal are attempts to represent extremely low and high registers. The "flam" — a drum beat comprising a quick light stroke followed by a strong one — is a technical percussion term used most frequently with reference to a snare drum; it has little literal application to a bass drum, let alone an organ stop.[34] Calling it *"terrible"* is Messiaen's attempt to convey that, once again, the intended emotion is fear — not only everyday fear *(la peur)* but also awe, dread, or "fear of the Lord" *(la crainte)*. This metaphorical naming continues with the noun *hurlement,* from the verb *hurler;* although I have translated both the noun and verb as "wail" (because of the funereal connotations), other possibilities include "bawl," "bellow," "howl," "roar," "scream," "shout," "shriek," "yell," and "yowl."

Why does Messiaen use this word *(hurlé)* that refers so explicitly to the human voice in the very worst of times — those of loss, pain, bereavement, torture, agony — to describe a sound that is supposed to be the "bell of evidence"? The most immediate and obvious reference would seem to be Baudelaire, who makes explicit this connection between bells and wailing in one of several poems entitled "Spleen":

---

31. Messiaen, analysis of Vision 6, in *Traité,* 3:266.
32. Messiaen, analysis of Vision 6, in *Traité,* 3:266, 269.
33. The III Cymbale was added to the Trinité organ's Récit division in 1934; the IV Cymbale was added to the Grand-Orgue in 1962-1965. See Jon Gillock, *Performing Messiaen's Organ Music: 66 Masterclasses* (Bloomington: Indiana University Press, 2010), 363.
34. I am grateful to Yves Balmer for helping me negotiate these French references.

1943: Résumé: Visions of Amen

> then all at once the raging bells [*des cloches*] break loose
> hurling to heaven [*lance vers le ciel*] their awful caterwaul
>   [*un affreux hurlement*],
> like homeless ghosts with no one left to haunt
> whimpering their endless grievances.
>
> — And giant hearses, without dirge or drums,
> parade at half-step in my soul, where Hope,
> defeated, weeps, and the oppressor Dread [*l'Angoisse atroce*]
> plants his black flag on my assenting skull.[35]

As the image of the "giant hearses" passing by in the poet's soul indicates, these bells with the terrifying wail are funeral bells *(cloches funèbres).*

Baudelaire's use of the word *hurlement,* in turn, likely derived from Chateaubriand's small chapter on bells in his *Genius of Christianity* (1802).[36] In Chateaubriand, the angels "hurl" *(lancer)* the bells (presumably like lances or bolts of lightning), their consequent clanging sounds like screaming, shrieking, wailing, or whatever other image one might get from the word *hurlement:*

> Carillons of bells, in the midst of our festivals, seemed to heighten the public joy. In great calamities, on the contrary, the same clanging became *terrible* [*ces mêmes bruits devenaient terribles*]. The hair still stands erect at the remembrance of those days of murder and conflagration, all vibrating with the dismal noise of the tocsin [*des lugubres clameurs du tocsin*]. Who among us has forgotten the memory of those wails [*hurlements*] — those piercing shrieks succeeded by intervals of sudden silence, during which was now and then heard the discharge of a musket, some doleful and solitary voice, and, above all, the heavy tolling of the alarm bell [*le bourdonnement de la cloche*

---

35. Charles Baudelaire, "Spleen (IV)," in *Les Fleurs du mal: The Complete Text of the Flowers of Evil,* trans. Richard Howard (Boston: David R. Godine, 1982), 76-77 (Eng); 253-54 (Fr).

36. Baudelaire's initial 1857 version of this poem had not used the word *hurlement* but rather *gémissement,* derived from the verb *gémir,* meaning to groan, moan, whimper, or wail. In the 1861 version, *gémissement* was changed to *hurlement,* perhaps because he wanted an allusion to Chateaubriand; or perhaps because the syllables *(affreux hurlement)* are near homophones. See Aimée Boutin, "'Ring Out the Old, Ring In the New': The Symbolism of Bells in Nineteenth-Century French Poetry," *Nineteenth-Century French Studies* 30, no. 3-4 (Spring-Summer 2002): 267-81, at 272.

d'alarme], or the sound of the clock [*le son de l'horloge*] that calmly struck the hour which had just elapsed?

But, in a well-regulated society, the sound of the tocsin, suggesting the idea of succor, filled the soul with pity and terror [*de pitié et de terreur*], and thus touched the two great springs of tragical sensation [*les deux sources des sensations tragiques*]. . . . It was God himself who commanded the angel of victory to hurl up the *peals* [*l'ange des victoires de lancer des volées*] that proclaimed our triumphs, or the angel of death [*l'ange de la mort*] to sound forth the departure of a soul that had just returned to him.[37]

Messiaen's interest in the tocsin — the alarm sounded as an enemy approached — went back to childhood. He later recalled that one of the most attractive aspects of Shakespeare's plays (for which he built a toy theater and which he acted out) were the stage directions, especially "the famous instruction in the historical plays: 'alarums, skirmishes, the enemy enters the city.'"[38]

3. Beaumarchais: Tarare *(1787)*

Messiaen's descriptive use of drums and bells might also suggest another source of inspiration: the opera *Tarare* (1787). Its libretto was written by Pierre Beaumarchais, whose play *Marriage of Figaro* (1778) would later be the basis

---

37. François-René de Chateaubriand, *Genius of Christianity; or, The Spirit and Beauty of the Christian Religion,* trans. Charles I. White, 13th rev. ed. (Baltimore: John Murphy and Co., [1856] 1880), 480, 481; Chateaubriand, *Essai sur les révolutions. Génie du christianisme,* ed. Maurice Regard (Paris: Éditions Gallimard, 1978), 894-95, with variant *g,* 1832. Translation altered; emphasis added.

Baudelaire borrowed Chateaubriand's imagery for yet another poem entitled "Spleen (I)." Here, the bell is ambiguously called a *bourdon:* "A churchbell grieves . . . [*Le bourdon se lamente . . .*]." The word is rich in meaning: meaning a "bumblebee," it can also signify the "drone" *(faux-bourdon);* by extension, it signifies the great bell of a cathedral (which tolls for the dead); the phrase "to have the bourdon" *(avoir le bourdon)* means to feel blue. Messiaen would have enjoyed such a collection of overtones since "Bourdon" is the French word for the fundamental organ pipe, known in English as a "Diapason." See Baudelaire, "Spleen (I)," in *Les Fleurs du mal,* 74-75 (Eng); 251-52 (Fr). Note that the preceding poem is entitled "The Cracked Bell" ("La Cloche Felée"), 74 (Eng), 251 (Fr).

38. Olivier Messiaen and Claude Samuel, *Music and Color: Conversations with Claude Samuel,* trans. E. Thomas Glasow (Portland, Ore.: Amadeus Press, 1994), 26; Peter Hill and Nigel Simeone, *Messiaen* (New Haven: Yale University Press, 2005), 13 n. 23.

1943: *Résumé:* Visions of Amen

for Mozart's comic opera (premiered in 1784, three years before *Tarare*). Antonio Salieri wrote the score.

Although somewhat obscure, *Tarare* would have been known to Messiaen (who excelled in music history), especially given its idiosyncratic turns of fortune.[39] Just two years after its premiere came the Revolution of 1789. A new act was added: the "Crowning of Tarare" (with a "Scene of the Blacks" ["Scène des Nègres"]), which espoused the emancipation of slaves and gave the work a revolutionary denouement. However, in 1799, when the opera had its first revival toward the end of the Directory and on the eve of Napoleon's 18 Brumaire coup (November 9, 1799), political winds had reversed and the entire "Crowning of Tarare" (with its "Scene of the Blacks") was removed. (By 1802 Napoleon had reestablished slavery in France's colonies.) In 1819, with the post-Napoleonic "restoration" of European monarchies fully established, the opera's last remaining authorial intentions were erased in a thoroughgoing "revision" and yet another revival.[40]

The opera's final act contains a "judgment" scene. Atar, king of Ormus, addresses Astasie, the wife of the soldier Tarare, and issues this command:

> Leave me, wretched one [*Va, malheureuse*], I detest
> The unworthy love for you that burned me with desire.
> May you be delivered with [Tarare] to strictness of the laws!
> *(To the high priest.)*
> Pontiff, decide their lot.

The high priest Arthenée responds:

> They are judged [*Ils sont jugés*]: hoist the standard of death.
> The web of their criminal days is torn in shreds.[41]

Here, Beaumarchais offers stage directions specifying two banners

---

39. Beaumarchais's script would have been easily available to Messiaen: for example, Pierre-Augustin Caron de Beaumarchais, *Tarare. Opéra en Cinq Actes,* in *Œuvres de Beaumarchais. Nouvelle Édition* (Paris: Garnier Frères, 1876), 445-500.

40. Thomas Betzwieser and Arthur Groos, "Exoticism and Politics: Beaumarchais' and Salieri's 'Le Couronnement de Tarare' (1790)," *Cambridge Opera Journal* 6, no. 2 (July 1994): 91-112.

41. Pierre-Augustin Caron de Beaumarchais, *Tarare. Opéra en cinq actes,* in *Beaumarchais. Œuvres,* ed. Pierre Larthomas and Jacqueline Larthomas (Paris: Gallimard, 1988), 491-596, 1427-75; at 581 (act 5, scene 4); cf. *Œuvres de Beaumarchais* (1876), 493-94.

Vision 6: Amen of Judgment

(spelled out more fully in scene 5). One is white and on it letters have been written in gold: LIFE *(LA VIE)*; it is carried by a priest who leads a line of others clothed in white. A second is black and also carried in front of a line of priests, these covered in black crepe; on it is written in silver letters: DEATH *(LA MORT)*.[42] Now the high priest "tears into shreds the banner of Life" while the "priest in mourning dress [*en deuil*] raises up the banner of Death." The sound of funeral music *(un bruit funèbre)* is heard played by muffled instruments.[43]

Here follows the "Funeral Chorus of the Slaves" ("Choeur funèbre des esclaves"). Beaumarchais's directions indicate that he is adapting the excommunication ritual of bell, book, and candle and inflecting it through an Orientalist imagination.

(Astasie throws herself to her knees and prays throughout the chorus. The scrolls of judgment [*le livre des arrêts*], *covered in crêpe, are carried to the high priest. He signs the death sentence* [*l'arrêt de mort*]. *Two children in mourning dress each hand him a torch. Four priests in mourning dress present him with two large vases full of lustral water. He inserts the two torches in these vases and extinguishes them. During this time, the priests of life leave in silence. The shredded banner of Life falls to the ground.* <u>Three strikes of a funeral bell</u> [*d'une cloche funéraire*] <u>are heard.</u>)[44]

---

42. "Two lines of priests follow him; one in white, whose first priest carries a white banner on which is written, in gold lettering, these words: LIFE [LA VIE]. The other line of priests is in black, covered in crepe, whose first priest carries a black banner on which is written these words, in silver letters: DEATH [LA MORT]." Beaumarchais, *Tarare* (1988), 578 (act 5, scene 2); cf. *Œuvres de Beaumarchais* (1876), 491. Emphasis original.

43. Beaumarchais, *Tarare* (1988), 581 (act 5, scene 4); cf. *Œuvres de Beaumarchais* (1876), 494. The phrase *"instruments déguisés"* indicates instruments using various tactics to change their timbre. See editorial note (1988), 1472.

44. Beaumarchais, *Tarare* (1988), 581 (Act 5, Scene 4); cf. *Œuvres de Beaumarchais* (1876), 494. Note that the underlined words ("Three strikes of a funeral bell are heard") are not found in the main text but as variant: see (1988), 1472. As noted above, Beaumarchais rewrote parts of the libretto to accommodate the changing political circumstances following 1789.

The word *arrêt* can mean a judicial "judgment"; the *livre des arrêts* refers to the book in which decrees, laws, and arrest orders were recorded in ancien régime France. Beaumarchais would have had great familiarity with these since he was himself embroiled in a number of judicial cases against him. I am grateful to Ourida Mostefai for assistance with this passage.

Beaumarchais's text and ancien régime practice accord very well with biblical and medieval thought. In the *Summa Theologica,* Thomas Aquinas responds to the question "Whether after the resurrection every one will know what sins he has committed": "each

1943: Résumé: Visions of Amen

Are these three strikes Messiaen's source for the "three frozen notes like the bell of evidence"?[45]

Aspects of this episode at least suggest that Messiaen had it in mind as he composed the "Amen of Judgment." First, the association of the funeral bell's three strikes with the high priest's presentation of the "scroll of judgments" *(le livre des arrêts)* and the king's signing of the death warrant *(l'arrêt de mort)* offers a vivid portrayal of what Messiaen might intend with the image of "the bell of evidence." Second, the absolute opposition between LIFE and DEATH — strikingly displayed in the contrast between white garments and black (funereal) crepe and in the massive banners (or military standards) displaying the two words — is typical not only of late-eighteenth-century melodrama (the genre of *Tarare*) but also of apocalyptic or eschatological literature.[46]

Messiaen himself explicitly used the image in the seventh movement of his large work for organ, *Glorified Bodies,* completed in the last week of August 1939 but not published until 1942, just prior to taking up the composition of *Visions of Amen.*[47] Messiaen had first played two movements from *Glorified Bodies* on Christmas weekend in December 1941: Vision 4 ("Combat of Death and Life" ["Combat de la Mort et de la Vie"]) and Vision 6 ("Joy and Clarity of Glorified Bodies"). (Imagine hearing these pathbreaking works in occupied Paris three weeks after the Japanese attack on Pearl Harbor and America's entry into the war.) It was precisely Messiaen's surrealist affinity for opposing contrasts — the "combat" between black and white, life and death — that

---

man's conscience will be as a book containing his deeds on which judgment will be pronounced, even as in the human court of law we make use of records. Of these books it is written in the Apocalypse (20:12): 'The books were opened: and another book was opened, which is the book of life; and the dead were judged by those things which were written in the books according to their works.' ... But the book of life, of which the text goes on to speak, signifies each one's conscience, which is said to be one single book, because the one Divine power will cause all to recall their deeds, and this energy, in so far as it reminds a man of his deeds, is called the 'book of life.' Or else we may refer the first books to the conscience, and by the second book we may understand the Judge's sentence as expressed in His providence." *The "Summa Theologica" of St. Thomas Aquinas,* trans. Dominicans of the English Province, 2nd rev. ed., 22 vols. (London: Burns, Oates and Washbourne, 1920-1942), Suppl., q. 87 ("The knowledge which, after rising again, men will have at the judgment concerning merits and demerits"), a. 1.

45. Messiaen, "Note de l'Auteur."

46. Peter Brooks, *The Melodramatic Imagination* (New Haven and London: Yale University Press, [1976] 1995).

47. The galley proofs for *Glorified Bodies* were taken to the publisher on March 25, 1942 — around the time Messiaen would have been conceiving the original five-movement plan for *Visions of Amen.* Hill and Simeone, *Messiaen,* 115, 118.

Vision 6: Amen of Judgment

caught a reviewer's attention: "It is through his continual experiments into the opposition of ideas and of the clash of different moods that Olivier Messiaen attains the power to move us. In this respect, no musical instrument can serve him better than his own [i.e., the organ], which he plays with true virtuosity."[48]

Once again, the seven brief visions of *Glorified Bodies* (published 1942) and *Visions of Amen* (composed 1941-1942) are linked both chronologically and thematically. The imagery of the "combat of death and life" is explicitly eschatological; its epigraph comes from *Victimae Paschali,* the ancient Latin Sequence sung at Mass on Easter Sunday and each day of Easter Week.

Mors et vita duello / conflixére mirándo
dux vitae mórtuus, / regnat vivus.

Life and death battled / in stupefying conflict
the slain prince of life / reigns now living.[49]

Somewhat characteristically, Messiaen slightly altered the text to make his own perspective more explicit and emphatic. In his hand, the "Prince" *(dux)* of life becomes the "Author" of life, thus linking this combat explicitly back to the Creator and creation of life. The victory of life over death, as Messiaen states in the "Amen of the Agony of Jesus," is a "second creation." Thus, Messiaen's paraphrased epigraph to the "Combat":

"La mort et la vie ont engagé un stupéfiant combat;
l'Auteur de la vie, après être mort, vit et règne; et il dit:
'Mon Père, je suis ressuscité, je suis encore avec toi.'"

---

48. Norbert Dufourcq review of Messiaen's recital (Sunday, December 28, 1941), in *L'Information musicale,* January 23, 1942, 644; in Hill and Simeone, *Messiaen,* 115.

49. "Victimae Paschali laudes," sequence for Easter Sunday and its octave, in *Missal-En,* 540; *Missel-Fr,* 627. Translation mine. For other translations and commentaries, see Joseph Connelly, *Hymns of the Roman Liturgy* (New York: Longmans, Green and Co., 1957), 98-99; Matthew Britt, O.S.B., *The Hymns of the Breviary and Missal* (New York: Benziger Brothers, 1924), 141-44; Cornelius Canon Mulcahy, *The Hymns of the Roman Breviary and Missal* (Dublin: Browne and Nolan, 1938), 71.

Charles Tournemire's *Chorale-Improvisation on "Victimae Paschali"* was recorded on April 30, 1930, and appeared with other works on 78 rpm discs. Maurice Duruflé reconstituted five of Tournemire's recorded improvisations and published them in 1958. Tournemire's improvisation on "Victimae Paschali" (as reconstituted by Duruflé) is probably his most frequently performed work and has received numerous recordings.

1943: Résumé: Visions of Amen

"Death and life were locked in an astounding combat;
the Author of life, after being dead, lives and reigns; and he says:
'My Father, I am risen, I am still with you.' "[50]

This same cosmic battle between death and life, both eschatological and melodramatic, undergirds *Tarare*.

A third and final aspect of *Tarare* suggesting a linkage to the broader scheme of *Visions of Amen* is the "elaborate, allegorical prologue" preceding its five acts, a traditional *tragédie lyrique* structure going back to Jean-Baptiste Lully in the court of Louis XIV.[51] The prologue is a mythical account of creation, and, following the court practice of the "Dancing King," here too there is a mixture of music and dance. Beaumarchais's stage description for scene 1, "Nature and the Raging Winds," bears an uncanny resemblance to Messiaen's description of Vision 2, "Amen of the Stars, of the Planet with the Ring": "In the Overture is heard a violent noise in the air, a terrible shock [*choc terrible*] of all the Elements. As the curtain is raised, nothing is shown other than the clouds which roll, rage, and let us see the unchained winds. In their turbulence, they form *dances of the most violent agitation.*"[52] Into this cosmic chaos walks Nature, who addresses the winds "imperiously":

This is enough disruption in the universe:
Furious winds, stop agitating the air and the waves.

---

50. Olivier Messiaen, epigraph, *Les Corps glorieux: sept visions brèves de la vie des ressuscités: pour orgue* (Paris: Leduc, 1942); composed in summer 1939.

51. John A. Rice, "Tarare," in *The New Grove Dictionary of Opera,* ed. Stanley Sadie. See Grove Music Online. Oxford Music Online, http://www.oxfordmusiconline.com.

52. Beaumarchais, *Tarare* (1988), 513 (prologue, scene 1); cf. *Œuvres de Beaumarchais* (1876), 445. Note that the word I have translated "turbulence" *(tourbillonnant)* derives from the same word used by Fontenelle to describe celestial orbits (i.e., *tourbillon,* translated as "vortex" and "vortices"). See conversations for the fourth and fifth evenings in Bernard le Bovier de Fontenelle, *Entretiens sur la pluralité des mondes habités,* in *Œuvres complètes. Tome II,* ed. Alain Niderst, 9 vols. (Paris: Fayard, [1989-2001] 1991), 2:77-114; Fontenelle, *Conversations on the Plurality of Worlds,* trans. H. A. Hargreaves (Berkeley: University of California Press, 1990), 48-73. In his chapter on the philosophy of Fontenelle, Victor Delbos noted that in 1752, the ninety-five-year-old Fontenelle had written a defense of Descartes entitled *Theory of Vortices with Reflections on Attraction (Théorie des tourbillons avec des réflexions sur l'attraction).* See Delbos, "Fontenelle et Bayle," in Delbos, *La Philosophie française* (Paris: Plon-Nourrit et Cie, 1919), 133-52, at 136.

Vision 6: Amen of Judgment

That's enough: put your chains back on:
For Zephyr alone rules the world.[53]

Zephyr rises up out of the air. The overture and the noise calm down; the clouds dissipate; and "everything becomes harmonious and calm." The Demigod of Fire descends in a brilliant cloud over the eastern horizon, that is, over "the coast of the Orient." As in Messiaen's first two "Visions," the figure of Light, and especially the sun and the stars, dominates the stage.

Scene 2 consists of a dialogue between the Demigod of Fire and Nature. Fire praises the "bursting forth orb of the sun" while Nature praises the "Ardent demigod of the inflamed sphere [sun] / By which mine [Earth] is given life." Nature then describes the cosmos in terms of immensity similar to those in Pascal's *Pensées* and Fontanelle's *Conversations on the Plurality of Worlds*:

> Of all the races past,
> Dispersed in the immensity,
> I reassemble the elements
> In order to form a race
> Proximate to numerous humanity. . . .
> Humans not yet existing,
> Atoms lost in space
> Let each of your elements
> Come together and take its place
> Following the order, gravity,
> And all the immutable laws
> Which the dispensing Eternal
> Imposes upon your fellow beings.[54]

The prologue continues as Nature provides for climates and temperatures that will sustain human life. Nature also assigns Atar and Tarare their predestined roles in life: "I make a king of one and of the other a soldier." As they prepare themselves as spectators to watch history play itself out, Nature remarks to Fire that their "profound essence" — namely, Eternity — "devours space and time."

---

53. Beaumarchais, *Tarare* (1988), 514 (prologue, scene 1); cf. *Œuvres de Beaumarchais* (1876), 445.
54. Beaumarchais, *Tarare* (1988), 514, 515 (prologue, scene 2); cf. *Œuvres de Beaumarchais* (1876), 445, 446. For textual discrepancies see editorial notes (1988) 1464, 1465.

1943: Résumé: Visions of Amen

Tarare begins with a creation account, penultimately arrives at a climactic judgment in which Death appears to have bested Life, but finally works out its denouement in the ultimate melodramatic triumph of Life.

One final suggestive parallel with *Visions of Amen:* if Messiaen had consulted the score of the "Crowning of Tarare" (excised from the revival version following the revolution), he would have encountered several populist marches substituted by Salieri: an initial "march of the armed soldiers," a "second march of a group of peaceful citizens," and a "third march of a group of young farmers of both sexes." For each of these marches, Salieri directed that a bass drum be used in different ways. But since the bass drum was not notated, Salieri wrote out separate directions:

> "In this march the drum [*le tambour*] will beat very softly."
> "Here the drum [*le tambour*] will beat one bar softly [*piano*] and the other loudly [*forte*]."[55]

Salieri's description of a two-stroke drumbeat describes today's "flam" — a quick light stroke followed by a strong one. Compare it with Messiaen's oddly metaphorical analysis of the "Amen of Judgment": "After the 3 treble high-pitched notes, there is always a terrible 'flam' [*un 'fla' terrible*] on the bass drum [*de grosse caisse*]."[56] Finally, Beaumarchais's stage directions for a fourth march introduce an instrumental novelty: "Fourth march by a group of priests of Death [*prêtres de la Mort*], preceded by a TAM-TAM or suspended Indian bell [*d'un TAM-TAM ou cloche de l'Inde*] carried by two priests, forming a sort of tocsin."[57] Recall the tocsin: a warning bell of some impending danger, for example, a military invasion, an approaching storm, or a fire. The tam-tam (or gong) began to be used in European orchestras during the French Revolution and became associated with funeral marches. An encyclopedia of the time defines it as an "instrument of percussion in usage among the Orientals, and brought into our orchestras, from time to time, to produce terrible and mournful effects [*des effets terribles & lugubres*]. In its form, it is a type of tambourine [*tambour de basque*], completely made out of metal, which has an extraordinary vibration."[58] The "terrible and mournful effect" envisioned by Beaumarchais aims at dramatic effect:

55. Betzwieser and Groos, "Exoticism and Politics," 102.
56. Messiaen, analysis of Vision 6, in *Traité*, 3:266.
57. Betzwieser and Groos, "Exoticism and Politics," 102.
58. *Encyclopédie Méthodique: Musique* (Paris, 1818); quoted in Betzwieser and Groos, "Exoticism and Politics," 102 n. 39. For Messiaen works with some reference to the tam-

422

Vision 6: Amen of Judgment

"This imposing march makes the people step back [or recoil: *reculer*]" — presumably in terror.

New kinds of orchestration were on Messiaen's mind in 1942. During the following year he began work on *Three Small Liturgies of the Divine Presence* (composed 1943-1944). Note the instrumentation: piano solo, Ondes Martenot, celesta, vibraphone, maracas, Chinese cymbal, tam-tam, thirty-six women's voices, and strings. It makes its appearance in a small way in *Visions,* and it might have been inspired in part by revisiting *Tarare*.

4. The Pit and the Pendulum: The Abyss and Temporality

The Last Judgment sums up actions in time. The single duration of temporal creation and its openness to alternative future possibilities now come to a close. The judged are "fixed in their state" — whatever state that might be.[59] This is the terror of the "Amen of Judgment." The relentless pulses drive the feeling of clock time — seconds ticking by and our hearts beating with them — while rising chordal linkages *(enchaînements)* induce a dizzying feeling of vertigo.

As will be seen below in discussing *Turangalîla Symphony* (1946-1948), Messiaen associated the "Turangalîla 2" movement (no. 7), largely percussive and marked by atonalism, with Poe's story "The Pit and the Pendulum." He writes in his *Treatise:*

> The maximum effect of the passage resides in the striking of the tam-tam. The strike on the tam-tam must be very powerful, very violent: it is like an abyss repeatedly opening up without ceasing [*comme un gouffre sans cesse renouvelé*], more and more black, more and more deep, more and more terrible [*de plus en plus terrible*]....
>
> ... the tam-tam and the fourth chord are more and more gaping [*béants*], like a mouth opened infinitely wide, like a bottomless precipice [*un précipice sans fond*]. The opposition between diminution and augmentation, between the constriction and the enlargement of the 2 perpetually alternating rhythmic characters, recalls the double horror of [1] the reddened iron wall that tightens, and [2] the unspeakable, unutterable

---

tam, see Aloyse Michaely, *Die Musik Olivier Messiaens: Untersuchungen zum Gesamtschaffen* (Hamburg: Verlag der Musikalienhandlung K. D. Wagner, 1987), 206 (349).

59. Messiaen, "Note de l'Auteur," *Visions de l'Amen* (1943), n.p.

1943: Résumé: Visions of Amen

depths of the torture pit, in the famous story of Edgar Poe: "The Pit and the Pendulum."[60]

The "abyss" was much in Messiaen's imagination in this period.[61] In January 1941, in the prisoner of war camp, it appeared in *Quartet* as the second movement, "The Abyss of the Birds" ("Abîme des oiseaux"). Ten years later it would be represented in a most terrifying way in the third movement of the *Organ Book* (1951): "The Hands of the Abyss (for Penitential Seasons)" ("Les Mains de l'abîme [Pour les Temps de Pénitence]"), quoting Habakkuk 3:10: "The abyss uttered its cry; the depths lifted up their two hands."

The image of the "abyss" *(abîme* or *gouffre)* holds a prominent place in Francophone literature. Perhaps that is because its use in the French translation of the Latin Vulgate version of Genesis 1:2 was more literal than the King James Version.

Vulgate: *et tenebrae super* faciem abyssi
Crampon: *les ténèbres couvraient l'abîme*
Fillion: *et les ténèbres couvraient* la face de l'abîme
Douay-Rheims (CCD): *darkness covered* the abyss
King James: *and darkness was upon* the face of the deep.

Messiaen's attention to the "abyss" follows a venerable French tradition extending from Pascal to Hello and Baudelaire. Baudelaire's *Flowers of Evil* renders Pascal homage:

Pascal avait son gouffre, avec lui se mouvant.
— Hélas! tout est abîme —

---

60. Messiaen, analysis of "Turangalîla 2," in *Traité,* 2:289-331, 297. Compare Messiaen's liner notes for the 1991 recording: the movement has "a terrifying rhythm ... giving a double sensation of expansion and of retrenchment of height and of depth, each cycle ending in a great stroke on the tam-tam." Poe portrays a "double terror": on the one hand, the pendulum "slowly getting nearer the heart of the prisoner"; on the other hand, "the wall of red-hot iron closes in on him, and the unspeakable, indescribable depth of the torture pit." Messiaen notes on movement 7, "Turangalîla 2," *Turangalîla-Symphonie,* in *Complete Edition,* 32 CDs (Germany: Deutsche Grammophon, 2008), 281, trans. Paul Griffiths.

61. On the "abyss" in Messiaen, see again Aloyse Michaely, "L'Abîme, Das Bild des Abgrunds bei Olivier Messiaen," *Musik-Konzepte 28: Olivier Messiaen* 28 (November 1982); cf. Michaely, *Die Musik Olivier Messiaens,* 1 (658)–17 (674).

Vision 6: Amen of Judgment

Pascal had his abyss, it followed him.
But the abyss is All — action and dream,
language, desire! — and who could count the times
the wind of Fear has made my blood run cold![62]

For Pascal, the abyss represents either of the two infinites between which human beings live: infinity and nothingness (cf. Sartre, *Being and Nothingness*). He associates it with the fragility of our existential situation, but also deems it a corollary of our knowledge, and consequently, of our vain desire for certainty.

Whoever considers himself in this way will be afraid of himself, and seeing himself supported by the size nature has given him *between these two abysses* of the infinite and nothingness [*entre ces deux abîmes de l'infini et du néant*], he will tremble at these marvels [*il tremblera dans la vue de ces merveilles*]. . . . For, in the end, what is man in nature? A nothing compared to the infinite, an everything compared to the nothing, a midpoint between nothing and everything, infinitely removed from understanding the extremes: the end of things and their principle are hopelessly hidden from him in an impenetrable secret. . . . He is equally incapable of seeing the nothingness from which he is derived and the infinite in which he is engulfed. . . .

We burn with desire to find firm ground and an ultimate secure base on which to build a tower reaching up to the infinite. But our whole foundation cracks, and the earth *opens up into abysses* [*et la terre s'ouvre jusqu'aux abîmes*].[63]

It is easy to see the attraction Pascal's philosophy has for the surrealist imagination: the juxtaposition of opposites, or at least incongruent images

62. Baudelaire, "Le Gouffre" ("The Abyss"), in *Les Fleurs du mal*, 174 (Eng), 352-53 (Fr); Schloesser, "Notes on the *Miserere* Plates Exhibited in *Mystic Masque*," in *Mystic Masque: Reality and Semblance in Georges Rouault, 1871-1958*, ed. Stephen Schloesser (Chestnut Hill, Mass.: McMullen Museum of Art, distributed by the University of Chicago Press, 2008), 157-80, at 175.

63. Pascal, *Pensées* (Pléiade), 185; (Lafuma) 199; (Sellier) 230; for Pléiade, see Pascal, *Œuvres complètes*, 2 vols. (Paris: Éditions Gallimard, 2000), vol. 2; for Lafuma, see Pascal, *Pensées*, trans. A. J. Krailsheimer, rev. ed. (New York: Penguin, 1995); for Sellier, see Pascal, *Pensées*, ed. and trans. Roger Ariew (Indianapolis: Hackett, 2005); cf. Schloesser, "Notes on the *Miserere* Plates," 175-76. Emphasis added. Compare Hello, "Communion spirituelle: les deux abîmes" ("Spiritual Communion: The Two Abysses"), in *Du néant à dieu*, ed. Jules-Philippe Heuzey, 2 vols. (Paris: Perrin et Cie, [1921] 1930), 1:67-69.

1943: *Résumé:* Visions of Amen

(joy/blood; blood/stars), provokes the emotional explosion. So too in Pascal, where the emotional explosion is anxiety:

> This is our true state. It is what makes us incapable of certain knowledge or absolute ignorance. We float on a vast ocean, ever uncertain and adrift, blown this way or that. Whenever we think we have some point to which we can cling and fasten ourselves, it shakes free and leaves us behind. And if we follow it, it eludes our grasp, slides away, and escapes forever. *Nothing stays still for us.* This is our natural condition and yet the one farthest from our inclination. *We burn with desire to find firm ground* and an ultimate secure base on which to build a tower reaching up to the infinite. But our whole foundation cracks, and *the earth opens up into abysses.*
>
> Let us, therefore, not seek certainty and stability. Our reason is always deceived by inconstant appearances; nothing can affix the finite between the two infinites [of being and nothingness] that both enclose and escape it.[64]

Pascal sums up this juxtaposition of opposites:

> Man is neither angel nor brute, and the unfortunate thing
> is that he who would act the angel acts the brute.[65]

Two centuries later, Søren Kierkegaard would take Pascal's imagery and expand it. One scholar observes that Kierkegaard examines anxiety "not as a failure of the will or as a diseased weakness but as a sign of spiritual awareness of *the existential split between time and eternity*."[66] "If a human being were a beast or an angel, he could not be in anxiety. Because he is a synthesis, he can be in anxiety; and the more profoundly he is in anxiety, the greater is the man."[67] About four decades after Kierkegaard, Nietzsche also embraced the

---

64. Pascal, *Pensées* (Pléiade), 185; (Lafuma) 199; (Sellier) 230; cf. Schloesser, "Notes on the *Miserere* Plates," 176; Stephen Schloesser, "1871-1901: Realism, Symbolism, Mystic Modernism," in *Mystic Masque,* 23-43, at 37.

65. Pascal, *Pensées* (Pléiade), 572; (Lafuma) 678; (Sellier) 557; cf. Stephen Schloesser, "1902-1920: The Hard Metier of Unmasking," in *Mystic Masque,* 79-104, at 91.

66. Eric G. Wilson, *Coleridge's Melancholia: An Anatomy of Limbo* (Gainesville: University Press of Florida, 2004), 33, emphasis added.

67. Søren Kierkegaard, *The Concept of Anxiety: A Simple Psychologically Orienting Deliberation on the Dogmatic Issue of Hereditary Sin* [1844], ed. and trans. Reidar Thomte and Albert B. Anderson (Princeton: Princeton University Press, 1980), 155; quoted in Wilson,

Vision 6: Amen of Judgment

"abyss": humanity's anxiety-ridden suspension over the "abyss" is the source of its greatness:

> Man is a rope, tied between beast and overman — a rope over an abyss [*einem Abgrunde*]. A dangerous across, a dangerous on-the-way, a dangerous looking-back, a dangerous shuddering and stopping.
> What is great in man is that he is a bridge and not an end: what can be loved in man is that he is an *overture* and a *going under*.
> I love those who do not know how to live, except by going under, for they are those who cross over.[68]

In the literary sphere, the American Poe had a deep impact on the French: his stories were translated thanks largely to Baudelaire's assistance; they influenced the genre of the "fantastical tale" in writers like Hello. As seen in "Turangalîla 2," Messiaen loved Poe's story "The Pit and the Pendulum."

Poe's story recounts a "swoon," that is, a hallucinatory dream, which he endows with positive moral and aesthetic weight: "He who has never swooned, is not he who finds strange palaces and wildly familiar faces in coals that glow; is not he who beholds floating in mid-air the sad visions that the many may not view; is not he who ponders over the perfume of some novel flower — is not he whose brain grows bewildered with the meaning of some musical cadence which has never before arrested his attention."[69]

The story's events (at least as recounted by the hallucinating narrator) take place in Toledo during the time of Napoleon's "liberating" invasion of

---

Coleridge's Melancholia, 33. Compare Kierkegaard: "The spirit cannot do away with itself.... Neither can man sink down into the vegetative life.... He cannot flee from dread [anxiety]." Kierkegaard, *Concept of Dread,* trans. Walter Lowrie (Princeton: Princeton University Press, 1957), 139, 40. Both passages analyzed in Ernest Becker, *The Denial of Death* (New York: Free Press, 1973), 69.

68. "Der Mensch ist ein Seil, geknüpft zwischen Tier und Übermensch, — ein Seil über einem Abgrunde." Friedrich Nietzsche, *Also sprach Zarathustra. Ein Buch für Alle und Keinen* (1883-1885), in *Sämtliche Werke in Zwölf Bänden,* vol. 6 (Stuttgart: Alfred Kröner Verlag, 1964), 11; Nietzsche, *Thus Spoke Zarathustra: A Book for All and None,* trans. Walter Kaufmann (New York: Viking Press, [1954] 1966), 14-15 (part 1, Zarathustra's Prologue).

69. Edgar Allan Poe, "The Pit and the Pendulum" (1842), in Poe, *Poetry and Tales,* ed. Patrick F. Quinn, Library of America (New York: Literary Classics of the United States, distributed by the Viking Press, 1984), 491-505, at 492. Poe's opening line — "I was sick — sick unto death — " anticipates Søren Kierkegaard by seven years. See Kierkegaard, *The Sickness unto Death* (1849). Both writers are alluding to Jesus' words: "This sickness is not unto death" (John 11:4 Douay-CCD). Kierkegaard distinguishes between physical and spiritual death.

1943: *Résumé:* Visions of Amen

Spain. The protagonist received his judgment from the Spanish Inquisition: "The sentence — the dread sentence of death." Having heard "the inquisitorial voices" pronounce the verdict, the narrator fell into his swoon. The voices merged into "one dreamy indeterminate hum," and he formed an idea of "revolution" — not in our normal sense of a "revolt," but rather as associated with the ceaseless repetitive rotation of a mill wheel. The narrator saw "the lips of the black-robed judges" and "the decrees of what to me was Fate . . . still issuing from those lips."[70]

Then his "vision fell upon the seven tall candles upon the table." At first they seemed to him "white and slender angels" who would save him; but he was soon overcome with "a most deadly nausea" as "the angel forms became meaningless specters, with heads of flame" — a reference to the biblical angelic rank of seraphim ("burning ones"). Finally, light dissolved into darkness: "the figures of the judges vanished, as if magically, from before me; the tall candles sank into nothingness; their flames went out utterly; the blackness of darkness supervened; all sensations appeared swallowed up in a mad rushing descent as of the soul into Hades. Then silence, and stillness, and night were the universe."[71]

When he came back to consciousness, he was aware of both motion and sound: "the tumultuous motion of the heart, and, in my ears, the sound of its beating." As he tried to survey the extent of his dungeon cell in the darkness, he fell and was aware of something strange: "my chin rested upon the floor of the prison, but my lips and the upper portion of my head, although seemingly at a less elevation than the chin, touched nothing." Although he did not yet know it, his head was precariously poised over the pit. The "peculiar smell of decayed fungus" filled his nostrils. And then he realized his true circumstances:

> I put forward my arm, and shuddered to find that I had fallen at the very brink of a circular pit, whose extent, of course, I had no means of ascertaining at the moment. Groping about the masonry just below the margin, I succeeded in dislodging a small fragment, *and let it fall into the abyss.* For many seconds I hearkened to its reverberations as it dashed against the sides of the chasm in its descent; at length there was a sullen plunge into water, succeeded by loud echoes. . . .
>
> *I saw clearly the doom which had been prepared for me,* and congratu-

---

70. Poe, "Pit and the Pendulum," 491.
71. Poe, "Pit and the Pendulum," 491-92. For seraphim see Isa. 6:1-7.

Vision 6: Amen of Judgment

lated myself upon the timely accident by which I had escaped. Another step before my fall, and the world had seen me no more."[72]

The narrator then reflected on the Inquisition's legendary two kinds of death: a victim could be chosen for death by the "direst physical agonies" or death "with its most hideous moral horrors." The narrator presumed he had been "reserved for the latter," that is, "moral" (or mental) torture: "By long suffering my nerves had been unstrung, *until I trembled* at the sound of my own voice, and had become in every respect a fitting subject for the species of torture which awaited me."[73]

The narrator resolved "to perish rather than risk the terrors of the wells," which he imagined in the darkness as being placed in several locations in the dungeon. But he could not fulfill this resolution to kill himself: "In other conditions of mind," he reflected, "I might have had courage to end my misery at once *by a plunge into one of these abysses;* but now I was the veriest of cowards." After another deep sleep, he awakened and was able to see the exact dimensions of the dungeon. It was actually quite small and square. And in the center was only the circular pit.[74]

Gradually, however, the horror was amplified when he looked up at the ceiling. There, in one of the panels, was "the painted figure of Time as he is commonly represented, save that, in lieu of a scythe, he held what, at a casual glance, I supposed to be the pictured image of a huge pendulum such as we see on antique clocks." As he stared more intently at this "machine" — as in H. G. Wells's novel (which Messiaen also loved), this pendulum was a "time machine" (there being something mechanical and alienated about clock time) — he saw what he initially thought was an illusion but then realized was fact: the pendulum moved. He watched it for some minutes, "somewhat in fear, but more in wonder."[75]

---

72. Poe, "Pit and the Pendulum," 496, emphasis added.

73. Poe, "Pit and the Pendulum," 496, emphasis added. The next line begins: "Shaking in every limb . . ." Again, Poe's references to "trembling," "shaking," and the "abyss" predate Kierkegaard's work, in this case by just one year; cf. Kierkegaard, *Fear and Trembling* (1843). The title refers to Phil. 2:12: "work out your salvation with fear and trembling" (Douay-CCD).

74. Poe, "Pit and the Pendulum," 497, following the line beginning with "Shaking in every limb. . . ." Emphasis added.

75. Poe, "Pit and the Pendulum," 498-99. Note that Poe's word choice — "somewhat in fear, but more in wonder" — parallels Hello's contrast between fear *(peur)* and wonder or awe *(crainte)*.

1943: Résumé: Visions of Amen

Eventually he realized that the "machine" was in fact both a pendulum and the scythe of time. It had a razor's edge and was poised to cut across him directly at the heart. Just as he was about to be sliced, swarms of rats that had been gnawing at his bandages freed him. The pendulum receded into the ceiling. But then the walls of iron turned red hot and began to close in. He shrank away "from the glowing metal to the center of the cell. Amid the thought of the fiery destruction that impended, the idea of the coolness of the well came over [his] soul like balm." Poe ingeniously and vividly plays with the concept of existential vertigo, elucidated by Kierkegaard and popular among the Romantics: human beings are both terrified by infinity and, simultaneously, irrepressibly attracted to its unknownness.[76] The narrator now fully realized his predicament. On the one hand, he cried out: "any death but that of the pit!" On the other hand, he asked himself: "Could I resist its glow? Or, if even that, could I withstand its pressure?"[77]

The walls continued to close in, forcing him toward the pit. "At length for my seared and writhing body there was no longer an inch of foothold on the firm floor of the prison. I struggled no more, but the agony of my soul found vent in one loud, long, and final scream of despair. I felt that I tottered upon the brink — I averted my eyes."[78]

At just this moment the narrator was saved as Napoleon's army crashed

---

76. Kierkegaard: "One can compare anxiety with vertigo. One whose eye looks down into the swirling depths experiences vertigo — but why? The reason has as much to do with his eye as with the abyss. For what if he hadn't looked down? It is in this way that anxiety is the vertigo of freedom, occurring when the spirit wants to posit the synthesis and freedom looks down into its own possibility, and then grasps at finitude as something to hold on to. In this vertigo, freedom faints." Kierkegaard, *Concept of Anxiety*, 61, quoted in George Pattison, *The Philosophy of Kierkegaard* (Chesham, UK: Acumen, 2005), 55; cf. 83, 56.

Compare Karl Jaspers: "Vertigo *on the brink of a precipice* — when I feel the urge to hurl myself down, and draw back, shuddering"; "The frightened movements of dizziness and shuddering become a turning point in fear. I am aware that I can be extinguished. Anxiety is the vertigo and trepidation of freedom facing a choice"; and Jean-Paul Sartre: "Vertigo announces itself through fear." Jaspers, *Philosophy*, vol. 2, *Existential Elucidation* (Chicago: University of Chicago Press, 1970), 2:232; Sartre, *Being and Nothingness: An Essay on Phenomenological Ontology* (New York: Philosophical Library, 1956), 30; both quoted in Ulrich H. J. Körtner, *The End of the World: A Theological Interpretation* (Louisville: Westminster John Knox, 1995), 82, 83. For the quintessential Romantic visual representation of the abyss, see David Caspar Friedrich's *Wanderer above the Sea of Fog (Der Wanderer über dem Nebelmeer)* (1818), Kunsthalle Hamburg, Hamburg, Germany.

77. Poe, "Pit and the Pendulum," 504, 505.

78. Poe, "Pit and the Pendulum," 505.

Vision 6: Amen of Judgment

into Toledo and destroyed the Inquisition. "An outstretched arm caught my own as I fell, fainting, into the abyss."[79]

5. An Ultimately "Comic" Ending?

The three sources we have considered — the *Pontificale*'s solemn anathema ritual; *Tarare*'s melodramatic judgment; and Poe's Inquisitional torture — not only share elements of dread-inducing horror; they also share "comic" endings in the classical sense, that is, a reversal that brings about not tragic death but rather a final reconciliation. The anathema is only one half of the ritual; the other half is absolution. Excommunication is meant to catalyze repentance and return. *Tarare* is melodramatic and "comic" opera: a final reversal saves the players from death. Napoleon's army arrives to save the Inquisition's victim in the nick of time.

Messiaen's "Amen of Judgment" is horrific; yet it too, in the overall structure of *Visions,* is not final but rather penultimate, immediately followed by the "Amen of Consumption," the apocalyptic fulfillment and final restoration *(apokatastasis)* of creation. In this sense, the cryptic "bell of evidence" functions just as bells do in Chateaubriand's *Genius of Christianity* — a memento mori warning human beings that time is always passing and will eventually come to an end:

> This, however, is not the most remarkable character of the sound of bells. This sound has a thousand secret relations with man. How oft, amid the profound tranquillity of night, has the heavy tolling of the death-bell, like the slow pulsations of an expiring heart, startled the adultress in her guilty pleasures! How often has it caught the ear of the atheist who, in his impious vigils, had perhaps the presumption to write that there is no God! The pen drops from his fingers. He hears with consternation the funeral knell which seems to say to him, *And is there indeed no God?* Oh, how such sounds disturbed the slumbers of our tyrants! Extraordinary religion, which, by the mere percussion of the magic metal, can change pleasures into torments, appal the atheist, and cause the dagger to drop from the hand of the assassin! . . .
>
> Let bells, then, call the faithful together; for the voice of man is not

---

79. Poe, "Pit and the Pendulum," 505.

1943: Résumé: Visions of Amen

sufficiently pure to summon penitence, innocence, and misfortune to the foot of the altar.[80]

Thurston's 1926 "bell, book, and candle" pamphlet used other language to describe the same phenomenon:

> Similarly, the Church's object, when she has permitted the use of fierce and apparently inhuman anathemas, or of the ceremony of the clanging of bells and the stamping out of torches, must surely have been the well-intentioned one, which the rubrics or synodal decrees often clearly express, of striking terror into all who were present, *ut adjunctis horrificis solemnitatibus incutiat auditoribus terrorem* [so that by the accompanying horrific rites terror might strike into the hearts of listeners]. It is not easy to judge from the feeling of contemporaries in our own irreverent age, what "fearsome rites," if we may so translate *horrificæ solemnitates,* would have been most likely to inspire awe into populations a thousand years younger.[81]

Inspiring awe by striking terror into listeners: this seems to be a suitable epigraph for Messiaen's method of emotional experience, not only in this particular "Amen of Judgment" but throughout many other works as well. He will introduce a movement in *From Canyons to Stars* (1974) with an epigraph taken from Hello's *Words of God:* "The replacement of fear [*la peur*] by awe [*la crainte*] opens a window for adoration."[82]

---

80. Chateaubriand, *Genius of Christianity,* 480, 481; Chateaubriand, *Génie du christianisme,* 894, 895.

81. Thurston, *Excommunication,* 22-23.

82. Messiaen, epigraph to movement 5, "Cedar Breaks et le Don de crainte," in *Des canyons aux étoiles* (Paris: Leduc, 1974); in Messiaen, *Complete Edition,* 32-35, at 33; quoting Hello, *Paroles de Dieu,* 176.

Vision 7

Amen of Consummation

Proverbs: *De Clarté en Clarté* • Dom Marmion: *A Claritate in Claritate* • Divine Adoption • Transfiguration • Aquinas: Resurrected Bodies • *Apocalypse of Saint John* • Aaron's Breastplate: Twelve Precious Stones • Blanc-Gatti: *Chromophonie* • Rembrandt: "Philosopher in Meditation" • Organ Carillons • BBC Radio London: Westminster Carillon • Liberation

If Vision 6 is an experience of terror at the Last Judgment, Vision 7 transports the listener into a world of unbridled joy. The unrelenting monotony of the pendulum swing and the tocsin crash have given way to the carillon's exuberant peals. It is the consummation of creation, the day of liberation.

At the outbreak of the war, a distraught Claire wrote to Messiaen at the front: "I'd been thinking of Peace and I suddenly said to Pascal: 'Just wait, my darling, when the war's over the bells in Jesus's House will ring really loudly,' and thinking about that hour of deliverance made me sob even as I spoke (I'm still weeping as I write this)."[1] In this hour of deliverance that is the "consummation," bells ring "really loudly."

---

1. Peter Hill and Nigel Simeone, *Messiaen* (New Haven: Yale University Press, 2005), 87-90, at 89.

1943: Résumé: Visions of Amen

Messiaen's "Author's Note"

Messiaen describes Vision 7 in his "Author's Note" to the published score:

> VII. — Amen of Consummation.
>   Consummation, Paradise. Life of the glorious bodies in a carillon of light. "From brilliance into brilliance" [*De clarté en clarté*] (Book of Proverbs). Amen.
>   — The 2nd piano takes up again the theme of Creation in chords and turns it into a long chorale of glory. The first piano surrounds the 2nd (with both the lowest and highest registers played together) [with] an incessant carillon of chords and of brilliant sparkling rhythms, in *rhythmical canons* becoming *tighter and tighter:* precious stones of the *Apocalypse* which ring out, shock, dance, color and perfume the light of Life.

Commentary

1. *From Brilliance to Brilliance* (De Clarté en Clarté)

Messiaen immediately establishes the predominance of *light* in the consummation of creation — that is, the equivalence of "glory" with "light." The glorified bodies will possess the attribute of *clarté* — "clarity" or "brilliance" — which, thanks to translation peculiarities, becomes interchangeable with "glory."

To make the light-glory connection seem fresh again, think of an alternative metaphorical tradition: "glory" not as light but rather as water.[2] In the Hebrew Bible, the "glory" of God is associated with the storm cloud — and indeed, it has an aspect of light, that is, lightning bolts. But the "glory" comes predominantly from what the cloud brings, namely, rain. The Hebrew culture existed in a desert agricultural world; without crops to feed the people, the community dies. Moreover, as the Passover and exodus narratives (read during the annual rites of spring planting) make clear, death and life are closely inter-

---

2. On the biblical associations between the storm clouds, lightning, rain, and God's "glory," see F. M. Cross, *Canaanite Myth and Hebrew Epic* (Cambridge: Harvard University Press, 1973), 153 n. 30 and 165-67; Aloysius Fitzgerald, *The Lord of the East Wind* (Washington, D.C.: Catholic Biblical Association of America, 2002); A. R. W. Green, *The Storm-God in the Ancient Near East* (Winona Lake, Ind.: Eisenbrauns, 2003), 275-80. I am grateful to John Kselman for his assistance. Compare Ernest Hello's explicit connection between "light" and "life" noted above.

twined in water: in the great flood, when water (native home of Leviathan and other sea monsters) is unleashed to return to its primordial chaos, it destroys life. (Only through the ark is Noah saved.) The Israelites are delivered to life by drowning the Egyptians in the watery chaos. Thus, the "glory" of God, both cosmologically and historically, is watery — the capacity to send water in the right amount at the right time for the preservation of life in the human community.

In the Christian Scriptures and later tradition, as the linkage between the storm cloud's rainwater and lightning flash was decoupled, light acquired independence as an image. Its symbolism is most important in the writings of Saint Paul and Saint John: light comes into the world and darkness cannot extinguish it. In the French Middle Ages, light became associated most especially with the replacement of dark Romanesque churches by Gothic churches, the architectural embodiment of Abbot Suger's light theology in towering arched windows made possible by external buttresses.[3] As a boy, Messiaen's synesthesia was deeply affected by seeing the windows of Sainte-Chapelle for the first time. Messiaen's "carillon of light" is a "sound-color" owed to both Abbot Suger and Blanc-Gatti.

In his author's note, Messiaen's initial scriptural quotation has puzzled readers: "From brilliance into brilliance" *(De clarté en clarté),* attributed to Proverbs 4:18. In its Latin Vulgate, French, and most literal English translations (Douay-Rheims), the Proverbs passage does not read "from brightness to brightness" but rather "proceeds and increases":

> Latin: iustorum autem semita quasi lux splendens
> *procedit et crescit* usque ad perfectam diem.   *(Vulgate)*
>
> French: Le sentier des justes est comme la brillante lumière du matin,
> dont l'éclat *va croissant* jusqu'à ce que paraisse le jour.
> *(Crampon)*
> Mais le sentier des justes *s'avance* comme une lumière brillante
> *et qui croît* jusqu'au jour parfait.   *(Fillion)*

---

3. Lindy Grant, *Abbot Suger of St.-Denis: Church and State in Early Twelfth-Century France* (London and New York: Longman, 1998); Otto von Simpson, *The Gothic Cathedral: Origins of Gothic Architecture and the Medieval Concept of Order,* 2nd rev. ed., Bollingen Series 48 (Princeton: Princeton University Press, 1969).

1943: Résumé: Visions of Amen

English: But the path of the just, as a shining light,
   goeth forwards and increaseth even to perfect day.
(Douay-Rheims)
   But the path of the just is as the shining light,
   that *shineth more and more* unto the perfect day.
(King James Version)

It seemed that Messiaen's "from clarity into clarity" had been either a mistake or an invention.

However, a closely related phrase — "from glory to glory" — does occur in 2 Corinthians: "But to this day whenever Moses is read, a veil lies over their heart; but whenever a person turns to the Lord, the veil is taken away. Now the Lord is the Spirit, and where the Spirit of the Lord is, there is liberty. But we all, with unveiled face, beholding as in a mirror the *glory* of the Lord, are being transformed into the same image *from glory to glory,* just as from the Lord, the Spirit."[4]

Scholars have wondered: Was Messiaen thinking of this passage? And if so, how did he confuse 2 Corinthians with Proverbs? And even given his great devotion to the concept of *clarté,* how did "clarity" end up as his translation of "glory"?[5] Tracking this textual conundrum leads us (not surprisingly) once again to Marmion's *Christ in His Mysteries.* Messiaen's repetition of Marmion's alteration further demonstrates the great extent to which he relied on the monk's work for inspiration.

Messiaen has taken his cue from the penultimate paragraph in Marmion's conference on the Epiphany. Although his comments are situated within the Christmas cycle, Marmion uses eschatological "light" imagery from Saint John's Apocalypse:

> L'Écriture sainte compare la vie du juste à "une voie lumineuse qui va *de clarté en clarté*" jusqu'au jour où tous les voiles tombent, où toutes les ombres s'évanouissent, où apparaissent, dans *la lumière de la gloire,* les splendeurs éternelles de la divinité. Là, dit S. Jean, dans son livre si mystérieux de l'Apocalypse où il nous décrit les magnificences de la Jérusalem d'en haut, là

---

4. 2 Cor. 3:15-18, emphasis added.

5. For example, Bruhn speculates: "As he does so often, Messiaen may have paraphrased from memory, thinking of verse 4:18." Siglind Bruhn, *Messiaen's Contemplations of Covenant and Incarnation: Musical Symbols of Faith in the Two Great Piano Cycles of the 1940s* (Hillsdale, N.Y.: Pendragon Press, 2007), 88.

Vision 7: Amen of Consummation

il n'est pas besoin de lumière, parce que l'Agneau, c'est-à-dire le Christ, est lui-même la lumière qui éclaire et réjouit les âmes de tous les élus.

Ce sera l'Épiphanie céleste.[6]

Holy Scripture compares the life of the just man to "a luminous path which goes *from brilliance to brilliance*" — until that day when all veils fall away, when all shadows disperse, when in *the light of glory* the eternal splendors of the Godhead appear. There, says St. John in that rather mysterious book, the Apocalypse, in which he describes the magnificences of the heavenly Jerusalem, "the city has no need of the sun or the moon to shine upon it," for the Lamb — Christ — is Himself the Light that illumines and rejoices the souls of all the elect.

That will be the Epiphany of heaven.[7]

The confusion in attributing the source lies with Marmion; Messiaen was merely quoting him (and clearly did not look up the text in Proverbs for verification). However, one wonders how Marmion tripped over this confusion of texts in the first place. One explanation is that this particular quotation from the Scriptures is in French and not — as is the norm — in Latin quoted from the Vulgate. As Marmion was composing these conference meditations, he was very likely basing his improvisations on the *Imitation of Christ* by Thomas à Kempis. The phrase *de clarté à clarté* occurs in a popular French translation of the *Imitation* in a chapter arguing "That the body of Jesus Christ and Holy Scripture are very necessary for the faithful soul." Here on earth, writes à Kempis, both frequent reception of the Eucharist and reading of the Scriptures

---

6. Marmion, conference 8.4 (Epiphany), *Le Christ dans ses mystères. Conférences spirituelles* (Namur, Belgium: Abbaye de Maredsous; Paris and Bruges: Desclée de Brouwer et Cie, [1919] 1928), 166, emphasis added. For scriptural references in this passage, Marmion cites Prov. 4:18; Apoc. 21:23; 22:5. Here I follow Michaely's lead: he cites Marmion's quotation ("von Klarheit zu Klarheit"), citing Proverbs; he also points to Marmion's possible use of the *Imitation* ("von der Klarheit zur Klarheit" = "de claritate in claritatem"). Aloyse Michaely, *Die Musik Olivier Messiaens: Untersuchungen zum Gesamtschaffen* (Hamburg: Verlag der Musikalienhandlung K. D. Wagner, 1987), 131 (788). However, Michaely's use of German translations (of Scripture, à Kempis, Marmion, and Messiaen) is not as conducive as either French or English to seeing translation equivalences between "glory" *(die Herrlichkeit)* and "clarity" *(das Klarheit)* from the Latin *claritas*.

7. Marmion, chapter 8 ("The Epiphany"), in *Christ in His Mysteries,* trans. Alan Bancroft (Bethesda, Md.: Zaccheus Press, 2008), 154-74, at 174, emphasis added. Since the translator has substituted the text of Prov. 4:18 for Marmion's actual words, I have altered the translation to reflect the original French text.

are necessary for the luminous life.⁸ However, when this earthly life has come to its end and the faithful servant enters into the celestial life, such terrestrial remedies will no longer be necessary.

> I must content myself with the burning torch [*flambeau*] of true faith and walk in its light [*à sa lumière*] *up until the day* when eternal clarity [*de l'éternelle clarté*] *shall dawn, and when shadows* of figures *shall decline, but when what is perfect shall be renewed.* Then the use of sacraments will cease, because the blessed in celestial glory [*dans la gloire céleste*] have no more need of this remedy. For they rejoice without end in the presence of God, contemplating his glory face to face [*sa gloire face à face*]; and, transformed from clarity into clarity [*transformés de clarté en clarté*] in the abyss of his divinity [*dans l'abîme de sa divinité*], they taste the Word of God made flesh, just as it was from the beginning and will be in eternity.⁹

The source of the confusion over scriptural references seems solved: Marmion was reading the *Imitation of Christ* as inspiration for his Epiphany conference meditation. Although à Kempis is in fact quoting Saint Paul's two letters to the Corinthians (1 Cor. 13:12 and 2 Cor. 3:18), Marmion mistakenly thought the passage was from Proverbs. Messiaen, in turn, followed Marmion's lead.

However, this small textual stumble unexpectedly opens itself up to further examination of the "glory-light" linkage in Scriptures (especially in the works of Saints Paul and John), the medieval à Kempis, Marmion, and Messiaen himself. For if Marmion had read the *Imitation* in its original Latin, he would have encountered this:

> facie ad faciem gloriam eius speculantes;
> et *de claritate in claritatem* abyssalis Deitatis transformati.
>
> beholding His glory face to face,
> transformed *from clarity to clarity* of the ineffable Deity.¹⁰

---

8. Compare Hello, "La lumière du Verbe" ("The Light of the Word") and "L'union par le Verbe dans la vie lumineuse" ("Union by the Word in the Luminous Life"), in *Du néant à dieu,* ed. Jules-Philippe Heuzey, 2 vols. (Paris: Perrin et Cie, [1921] 1930), 2:80-86.

9. Thomas à Kempis, *L'Imitation de Jésus-Christ,* trans. R. P. de Gonnelieu, S.J., new ed. (Tournai: J. Casterman & Fils, [1712] 1855), 239-40, emphasis in original. The passage comes from book 4, chapter 11: "Que le corps de Jésus-Christ et l'Écriture sainte sont très-nécessaires à l'âme fidèle."

10. Thomas à Kempis, *De Imitatione Christi,* book 4, chapter 11, line 10, quoting 1 Cor.

Vision 7: Amen of Consummation

The possibilities for linking "glory" and "light" (that is, "clarity" or "brightness") come from the process of translating the Latin Vulgate of 2 Corinthians:

gloriam Domini speculantes
in eandem imaginem transformamur *a claritate in claritatem*. . . .[11]

When translating into French, these two words, distinct in Latin — *gloriam* and *claritate* — may be rendered by the single word *gloire* (glory):

contemplons comme dans un miroir la gloire *du Seigneur,*
nous sommes transformés en la même image, de gloire en gloire. . . .
(Segond)[12]

English translations (both Douay-Rheims and King James) may also use "glory" to translate both *gloriam* and *claritatem*:

beholding *the glory* of the Lord with open face,
are transformed into the same image *from glory to glory*. (Douay-Rheims)

with open face beholding as in a glass *the glory* of the Lord,
are changed into the same image *from glory to glory*. (KJV)

These somewhat slippery equivalences and intertextual references are more than serendipitous. As already seen (in the discussion of *Ascension* [1934]), what might have begun as translation confusions eventually evolve into Messiaen's core vision: "Glory, Grace, Light: it's all linked up together," he later says. "For that reason, my music is cheerful, it contains glory and light. Of course suffering exists for me, too, but I've written very few poignant pieces. I'm not made for that. I love Light, Joy, and Glory in the divine sense."[13]

13:12 and 2 Cor. 3:18; in Kenneth Michael Becker, *From the Treasure-House of Scripture: An Analysis of Scriptural Sources in "De Imitatione Christi"* (Turnhout, Belgium: Brepols, 2002), 692. Emphasis added. English translation altered.

11. "Nos vero omnes, revelata facie gloriam Domini speculantes, in eandem imaginem transformamur a claritate in claritatem, tamquam a Domini Spiritu" (2 Cor. 3:18), Vulgate, 1125, emphasis added.

12. However, contrast Fillion: "Et nous tous, qui contemplons la gloire du Seigneur à visage découvert, nous sommes transformés en la même image, de clarté en clarté, comme par l'Esprit du Seigneur."

13. Messiaen, interview with Rößler, April 23, 1979, in Almut Rößler, *Contributions to*

1943: *Résumé:* Visions of Amen

These equivalences provided the context for Messiaen's reading of the Apocalypse, life in the celestial city, and the "Amen of Consumation." The interchangeability of *gloire* and *clarté* — glory and brilliance, both expressions of the Latin *claritate* — is central to the medieval image of "glorified" bodies possessing the trait of *clarté*, that is, clarity, lightness, or brilliance. Here, too, we see the close connection, both chronologically and thematically, between *Glorified Bodies* (1939; published May 1942) and *Visions of Amen* (1943). Just prior to his initial sketch of the five-movement *Visions*, Messiaen had prepared the sixth movement of *Glorified Bodies* — "Joy and Clarity of the Glorified Bodies" ("Joie et Clarté des Corps Glorieux") — for publication. For that piece's epigraph, Messiaen followed Aquinas's own scriptural quotation used in his article on the topic: "The just shall shine as the sun in the kingdom of their Father."[14] Messiaen also followed Aquinas's eschatological linkage of clarity with the multicolored precious stones in the celestial city. For "though the clarity of a glorified body surpasses the clarity of the sun," writes Aquinas, "it does not by its nature disturb the sight but soothes it: wherefore this clarity is compared to the jasper-stone (Apocalypse 21:11)."[15]

Finally, other associations with "clarity" should not be forgotten: the "brilliance" *(clarté)* found in Debussy's *Pelléas and Mélisande* and in Dukas's *Ariadne and Bluebeard* (about which Messiaen had just published his lengthy article [1936] following his master's death); Victor Delbos's attention to conceptual clarity (evoking Descartes's "clear and distinct ideas") as the defining feature of French thought; and Delbos's daughter Louise Justine's adoption of the name Claire after meeting Messiaen.

2. Corps Glorieux: *Glorified Corporeality*

The "Amen of Consumation" is a thrilling toccata of motion, indeed, a perpetual motion machine. Certainly, this primary element of motion — movement — is a musical element. But more importantly for Messiaen, it is a musical representation of a theological understanding of the world of resurrected and

---

the Spiritual World of Olivier Messiaen, trans. Barbara Dagg and Nancy Poland (Duisberg: Gilles & Francke, 1986), 92.

14. *The "Summa Theologica" of St. Thomas Aquinas,* trans. Dominicans of the English Province, 22 vols., 2nd rev. ed. (London: Burns, Oates and Washbourne, 1920-1942), Suppl., q. 85, a. 1: "Whether clarity is becoming to the glorified body." The *Summa* is hereafter referred to as *ST.*

15. Aquinas, *ST,* Suppl., q. 85, a. 2: "Whether the clarity of the glorified body is visible to the non-glorified eye."

Vision 7: Amen of Consummation

glorified bodies: namely, that they will be constantly *on the move*. "Paradise" is not a static or sepulchral place for Messiaen; rather, it is bodies in perpetual motion. This "corporeal" (one might even say "carnal" [*charnel*]) aspect has been interpreted in the discussion above (of the turn from the disembodied "soul" to the body-soul composite) as a distinguishing marker of Messiaen's "new order" turn from the vague "mystical" to the more solid "theological" circa 1935. We saw Aquinas's discussion of these bodies in the treatment above of *Glorified Bodies*.

However, Aquinas has more to say on the subject. Some of the most important aspects of his thought for Messiaen might have been:

a. The bodies will be *corporeal*, not "spiritual." They are real bodies, albeit perfected.
b. They will be capable of *sensation*, most especially of sight and hearing.
c. They will preserve the *personal identity* of the person in this terrestrial historical life.
d. They will even preserve the *wounds* from this life.
e. As a corollary: the theological doctrine of glorified bodies takes the unique and unrepeatable history of the person in this world with ultimate seriousness — with all its trials and tragedies, wounds and griefs — and promises that these will be "redeemed," that is, healed and perfected.

Aquinas explicitly links glorified bodies and terrestrial suffering in his treatment of the transfiguration — a biblical passage Messiaen would treat in great detail twenty-five years later in the *Transfiguration* (1969). Messiaen said he began thinking about the transfiguration around 1945 (i.e., about when he was composing *Visions*) when he heard "an old priest deliver a sermon on light and filiation, the two principal ideas of my work."[16] The "old priest" was very likely expounding on a text in Aquinas that considers how "the clarity of the glory to come was foreshadowed in the Transfiguration." "The adoption of the sons of God [i.e., filiation] is through a certain conformity of image to the natural Son of God. Now this takes place in two ways: first, by the grace of the wayfarer, which is imperfect conformity; secondly, by glory, which is perfect conformity, according to 1 John 3:2: 'We are now the sons of God, and it hath not yet appeared what we shall be: we know

---

16. Olivier Messiaen and Claude Samuel, *Music and Color: Conversations with Claude Samuel*, trans. E. Thomas Glasow (Portland, Ore.: Amadeus Press, 1994), 145.

that, when He shall appear, we shall be like to Him, because we shall see Him as He is.'"[17]

It is very likely that the "old priest," like Messiaen himself, had read Aquinas through the interpretative lens of Marmion's treatment in *Christ in His Mysteries:*

> In the Transfiguration we see, indeed, a revelation of our future greatness. That glory which encircles Jesus is to become our portion. Why is that? Because He gives to us, as His members, the right to share in the inheritance He possesses as God's own Son. . . .
>
> The day will come when, lightning having lit up the earth and made it shake and tremble to its foundations, the just, in the words of Jesus Himself, "will shine forth like the sun in the kingdom of their Father." Their bodies will be glorious, like that of Christ upon Mount Tabor; the same glory as reflects on the humanity of the Word Incarnate will transfigure our bodies. St. Paul tells us expressly: Christ "will refashion the body of our lowliness, *configuratum corpori claritatis suae.*"[18]

As is customary, Marmion's text (in both French and English translations back then) quotes from the Vulgate without translation. It was up to the reader to look up the translation if necessary. In this passage, Messiaen would have read *configuratum corpori claritatis suae* and looked up the translation in Fillion: "conforming it to his glorified [*claritatis*] body" (Phil. 3:21). Messiaen's title, *Corps glorieux,* plays on the linguistic ambivalence discussed above: *claritas* in its various declensions is translated as both "glory" and "clarity." Thus, "glorified" *(glorieux)* bodies possess "clarity" *(clarté).*

When Aquinas asks, "What is the point of the Transfiguration?" — and answers, to "show His disciples the glory of His clarity" — he underscores its intimate linkage with suffering. It was Christ's "loving foresight" that allowed the disciples "to taste for a short time the contemplation of eternal joy, so that they might [later on] bear persecution bravely."[19] This linkage was built into the liturgical year itself as the transfiguration Gospel (Matt. 17:9) was appointed

---

17. Aquinas, *ST,* IIIa, q. 45, a. 4: "Whether the testimony of the Father's voice, saying, 'This is My beloved Son,' was fittingly added."

18. Marmion, chapter 12 ("On the Summit of Tabor [Second Sunday of Lent]"), in *Christ in His Mysteries,* 266-86, at 279-80, quoting Phil. 3:21.

19. Aquinas, *ST,* IIIa, q. 45, a. 1: "Whether it was fitting that Christ should be transfigured." Aquinas is quoting Saint Bede.

Vision 7: Amen of Consummation

to be read on the Second Sunday of Lent.[20] Its placement was intended to give the faithful a vision of the glorious end at which their forty Lenten days of fasting and penance were aiming. In Matthew's Gospel, Christ, having just foretold his passion to the disciples and exhorting them to follow him, knew that they could not move ahead in suffering with him without some vision of the ultimate end. Dom Marmion comments: "Thus Our Lord foresaw that His apostles would not be able to bear His being humiliated; that His cross would be for them an occasion of their falling-away.... He wished to forearm them against the scandal His state of humiliation would then cause to their faith. He wished to strengthen their faith through His transfiguration."[21]

Aquinas inherited and extended Aristotle's dicta "Every agent acts for an end" and "Every agent acts for a good."[22] In discussing the transfiguration, Aquinas applies these principles to Christ's transformation of the disciples' imaginations so that they would undergo persecution. "Now in order that anyone go straight along a road," writes Aquinas, "he must have some knowledge of the end. Above all this is necessary when hard and rough is the road, heavy the going, but delightful the end." (Compare the opening act of Messiaen's opera, *Saint Francis of Assisi:* "I am afraid . . . on the road [*J'ai peur . . . sur la route*].")[23] The passion, continues Aquinas, was the means by which "Christ achieved glory, *not only of His soul,* which He had from the first moment of His conception, *but also of His body.*" So the disciples might be braced for the sufferings they were about to endure, "it was fitting that He should show His disciples the glory of His clarity (which is to be transfigured), to which He will configure those who are His."[24] Compare Marmion: "St. Paul tells us expressly: Christ 'will refashion the body of our lowliness, conforming it to the body of His glory.'"[25]

When replying to the question "Whether the witnesses of the transfiguration were fittingly chosen," Aquinas reiterates the vision's purpose as arousing

---

20. "Le IIe Dimanche de Carême," *Missel-Fr,* 334-37, at 336; cf. *Missal-En,* 264-68, at 266-67.

21. Marmion, *Christ in His Mysteries,* 272.

22. Saint Thomas Aquinas, *Summa contra Gentiles,* bk. 3, vol. 1, cc. 2, 3, 16, 17, 18. See above discussion of "Amen of Desire."

23. The opera opens with Brother Leo singing: "I am afraid, I am afraid, I am afraid on the road. . . ." Messiaen, *Saint François d'Assise,* act 1, tableau 1 — The Cross; in Siglind Bruhn, *Messiaen's Interpretations of Holiness and Trinity: Echoes of Medieval Theology in the Oratorio, Organ Meditations, and Opera* (Hillsdale, N.Y.: Pendragon Press, 2008), 207.

24. Aquinas, *ST,* IIIa, q. 45, a. 1.

25. Marmion, *Christ in His Mysteries,* 280, quoting Phil. 3:21.

desire for the end-in-view: "Christ wished to be transfigured in order to show men His glory, and *to arouse men to a desire of it* [*ut gloriam suam hominibus ostenderet, et* ad eam desiderandam homines provocaret], as stated above." Moreover, when replying to whether it might not have been more fitting to make angels the primary witnesses, Aquinas insists on the corporeality of this glorified body: "By His transfiguration Christ manifested to His disciples the glory of His body, which belongs only to human beings. It was therefore fitting that He should choose human beings and not angels as witnesses [*ideo convenienter non Angeli, sed homines pro testibus*]."[26] As Messiaen (following Marmion) will soon remark in notes for *Twenty Gazes at the Infant Jesus* (1944), the angels were scandalized that God chose not to become an angel (pure spirit) but rather a human being.[27]

Human beings are not angels. We are essentially embodied creatures and our identities are indistinguishable from those material bodies that distinguish our personal identities from one another. Aquinas's insistence on the corporeality and individual identities of those raised from the dead at the end of time is unequivocal, and the length to which he goes to refute any possible objections is instructive. When considering the "Conditions of those who Rise Again, and first of their Identity," Aquinas first asks "Whether the body will rise again identically the same." He notes that philosophers both ancient and modern have held different viewpoints. For those who believed in the transmigration of souls, the union of soul and body at the resurrection "was not with the selfsame body that was laid aside in death, but with another, sometimes of the same, sometimes of a different species."[28]

Some believed that the soul could pass "into the body of some other animal to whose manner of living it had conformed in this life, for instance into the body of a dog on account of lust, into the body of a lion on account of robbery and violence, and so forth." Others went to the opposite extreme. Believing that earthly bodies were not suitable or noble or perhaps "spiritual" enough, they held that souls migrated, not into their former bodies, but instead into "heavenly bodies, or again to bodies subtle as the wind." Both errors, says

---

26. Aquinas, *ST*, IIIa, q. 45, a. 3, reply to the first objection. Translation altered. Underline emphasis added.

27. "And the stupefaction of the angels grows greater — because it is not to them but to the human race with which God has been united." Messiaen, "Note de l'Auteur," *Vingt Regards sur l'Enfant-Jésus* (Paris: Éditions Durand, 1947), i-iv, at iii; following Marmion, chapter 7 ("O Wondrous Exchange! [Christmas]"), *Christ in His Mysteries,* 131-53, at 151.

28. Aquinas, *ST,* Suppl., q. 79, a. 1: "Whether in the resurrection the soul will be reunited to the same identical body."

Aquinas, conceive of the soul as being related to the body not substantially but in only an accidental way, "as a man to his clothes." Today I put on a blue suit but perhaps tomorrow I will wear green.[29] This is what allows them to maintain that "the soul pre-existed before being infused into the body begotten of natural generation."

In contrast to both sides, Aquinas insists: "For we cannot call it resurrection unless the soul returns to the same body, since resurrection is a second rising, and the same things rise that fall: wherefore resurrection regards the body which after death falls rather than the soul which after death lives. And consequently if it be not the same body which the soul resumes, it will not be a resurrection, but rather the assuming of a new body. . . . Thus the matter that will be brought back to restore the human body will be the same as that body's previous matter."[30] In the next article under the same question, Aquinas considers "Whether it will be identically the same man that shall rise again." Here Aquinas considers what is at stake for him in the idea of the resurrection: human beings cannot fulfill or accomplish the final end-in-view for which they are created in a soul separated from its body. If we are to avoid saying that we are made without purpose or without being able to accomplish our end, "it is necessary for the selfsame man to rise again; and this is effected by the selfsame soul being united to the selfsame body."[31]

In medieval fashion, Aquinas then explores minuscule details of this question, the kinds of minutiae that either charm or appall modern readers depending on their temperament. Considering "The integrity of the bodies in the resurrection,"[32] Aquinas asks "Whether all the members of the human body will rise again." He notes various objections: it seems that "genital members" will not rise again because Christ had said that after the resurrection people "shall neither marry, nor be married" (Matt. 22:30). Furthermore, it seems that the intestines (entrails) will not rise again: "For they can neither rise full, since thus they contain impurities, nor empty, since nothing is empty in nature." Aquinas replies that if the risen body must "correspond entirely to the soul" and its powers, then "all the members that are now in man's body

---

29. Aquinas, *ST,* Suppl., q. 79, a. 1. Caroline Bynum discusses these medieval anxieties about change and identity (for example, in werewolves); see Bynum, *Metamorphosis and Identity* (New York: Zone Books; Cambridge, Mass., distributed by the MIT Press, 2001); cf. Bynum, *The Resurrection of the Body in Western Christianity, 200-1336* (New York: Columbia University Press, 1995).

30. Aquinas, *ST,* Suppl., q. 79, a. 1, reply to the third objection.

31. Aquinas, *ST,* Suppl., q. 79, a. 2.

32. Aquinas, *ST,* Suppl., q. 80.

must needs be restored at the resurrection." This includes both the genitalia and intestines, although these latter "will be filled not with vile superfluities but with goodly humors."[33]

Pressing the matter further, Aquinas considers "Whether the hair and nails will rise again in the human body."[34] Here again, Aquinas argues in the affirmative: "hair and nails were given to man as an ornament," and risen bodies "ought to rise again with all their adornment." Moreover, "hair and nails are in man for the protection of other parts" of the body, so they "belong to the secondary perfection." Pressing even further, Aquinas considers "Whether the humors will rise again in the body," and most especially the "chief humor" (i.e., the fluid), which is blood. Distinguishing between three kinds of "humidity" (or "fluidity") the medievals found in the body — *ros, cambium,* and *gluten* — Aquinas notes that this third type "has already reached its ultimate perfection that nature intends in the body of the individual, and has already undergone transformation and become incorporate with the members."[35] Hence, it will arise with them. As liturgical evidence, Aquinas cites the Eucharist: "Now in Christ's resurrection His blood rose again, else the wine would not now be changed into His blood in the Sacrament of the altar. Therefore the blood will rise again in us also, and in like manner the other humors."[36]

Two other specifications are both intricate and instructive. First, Aquinas asks whether all will rise again in the youthful age. In typical Aristotelian fashion, Aquinas focuses on the mean by distinguishing the extremes. At one end of the spectrum, children are defective because they have not yet attained the ultimate perfection of human nature; at the other end are the aged, who have regressed from the ultimate perfection. Since human beings "will rise again without any defect of human nature," Aquinas concludes that bodies will be raised to the state of their ultimate perfection, "which is in the youthful age, at which the movement of growth terminates, and from which the movement of decrease begins."[37] A second question is "Whether all will rise again of the male sex." The question comes from the Aristotelian theory that held that females were produced by "a fault in the formative power of the seed, which is unable to bring the matter of the fetus to the male form: wherefore [Aristotle]

---

33. Aquinas, *ST,* Suppl., q. 80, a. 1, replies to the first and second objections.
34. Aquinas, *ST,* Suppl., q. 80, a. 2.
35. Aquinas, *ST,* Suppl., q. 80, a. 3.
36. Aquinas, *ST,* Suppl., q. 80, a. 3, *sed contra.* For context see Caroline Walker Bynum, *Wonderful Blood: Theology and Practice in Late Medieval Northern Germany and Beyond* (Philadelphia: University of Pennsylvania Press, 2007).
37. Aquinas, *ST,* Suppl., q. 81, a. 1: "Whether all will rise again of the same age."

says that 'the female is a misbegotten male.'" Aquinas argues that the begetting of females "is in the intention of universal nature, which requires both sexes for the perfection of the human species."[38] Thus human bodies will rise again as they were sexually differentiated in life, male and female. Replying to an objection raised by citing Saint Paul (Eph. 4:13), Aquinas further specifies that "When it is said: We shall all meet 'Christ unto a perfect man,' this refers not to the male sex but to the strength of soul which will be in all, both men and women."[39]

Messiaen's concerns about a stable celestial life following on the unstable ephemerality of terrestrial existence accord with Aquinas's arguments about the necessity of the resurrection. Aquinas follows Aristotle in claiming that the "last end which all men desire naturally is happiness."[40] However, he disagrees sharply with those ancients who believed "that man is able to attain this end in this life: wherefore they had no need to admit another life after this, wherein man would be able to attain to this perfection." This opinion, says Aquinas, "is confuted with sufficient probability by *the changeableness of fortune,* the weakness of the human body, the imperfection and instability of knowledge and virtue, all of which are hindrances to the perfection of happiness, as Augustine argues at the end of *The City of God* (xxii,22)."[41] Messiaen was no stranger to fortune's changeability, especially in 1941-1942.

At the other end of the spectrum, Aquinas also disagrees with those who say that life after death is a life of the soul only. The saying of Porphyry captures this opinion: "The soul, to be happy, must avoid all bodies."[42] These dualists too, then, did not believe in the resurrection of the body. It is *this* body, *my* body, here and now, that carries the past and present into the future. The insistence on the substantial embodiedness of the human being and the "self-same" identity in this life and the next marks individual history as a unique and unrepeatable identity — and this is the identity that survives into eternity.

Since the scars of wounds in Christ and the saints are not defects but rather "signs of the most steadfast virtue," seeing them increases the joy of both the saints and those who see them. Appealing to ancient authority, Aquinas quotes Augustine: "We feel an undescribable love for the blessed martyrs so

---

38. Aquinas, *ST,* Suppl., q. 81, a. 3; see third objection and reply. For this traditional "one-sex theory," see Thomas Walter Laqueur, *Making Sex: Body and Gender from the Greeks to Freud* (Cambridge: Harvard University Press, 1990).
39. Aquinas, *ST,* Suppl., q. 81, a. 3, reply to the first objection.
40. Aquinas, *ST,* Suppl., q. 75, a. 1: "Whether there is to be a resurrection of the body."
41. Aquinas, *ST,* Suppl., q. 75, a. 1, emphasis added.
42. Aquinas, *ST,* Suppl., q. 75, a. 1.

1943: Résumé: Visions of Amen

as to desire to see in that kingdom the scars of the wounds in their bodies, which they bore for Christ's name. Perchance indeed we shall see them for this will not make them less comely but more glorious. A certain beauty will shine in them, a beauty though in the body, yet not of the body but of virtue."[43] Messiaen's "Amen of Consummation" represents this Augustinian-Thomistic tradition. He is keenly aware of the often painful vicissitudes of *fortune,* of the wounds that accrue with time, and of the ephemerality of human life, and his insistence on the risen glorified body is an impassioned act of faith: that terrestrial life is not meaningless, and that celestial life is not a fiction. After Christ's resurrection, the doubting Thomas said to his companions: "Unless I see in his hands the print of the nails, and put my finger into the place of the nails, and put my hand into his side, I will not believe."[44] Messiaen seems to say with Christ: Behold the wounds in this glorified body. Believe.

3. Dazzlement: Precious Stones

Messiaen describes Vision 7 as the "Life of glorified bodies in a carillon of light," an "incessant carillon of chords and of brilliant sparkling rhythms . . . : precious stones of the *Apocalypse* that ring out, shock, dance, color and perfume the light of Life."[45] The "carillon of light" simultaneously evokes aural sounds and visual images — "sound-colors" — suggesting the influence of surrealism, of synesthetic research and experience, and very specifically, of Blanc-Gatti's painting *Carillon de Malesco.*[46] Scripturally speaking, the image derives from the passage

---

43. Augustine, *City of God* 23.19; quoted by Aquinas, *ST,* Suppl., q. 82, a. 1 ("Whether the bodies of the saints will be impassible after the resurrection"), reply to the fifth objection.

44. John 20:25 (Douay-CCD).

45. Messiaen, "Note de l'Auteur," in *Visions de l'Amen* (Paris: Durand, 1943), n.p.; cf. Olivier Messiaen, *Traité de rythme, de couleur, et d'ornithologie (1949-1992) en sept tomes,* 8 vols. (Paris: Alphonse Leduc, 1994-2002), 2:55-61. Messiaen's observation that the ceaseless carillon is structured "in *rhythmic canons* that become tighter and tighter" again suggests the influence of Lyapunov's "Carillon" (see below, p. 453). There too the theme (an Orthodox hymn) is heard in canon.

46. Messiaen specifically cites this piece in his commentary on "Rhythmic Orders": "I had a friend afflicted with this gratifying illness, of which he was very proud: Charles Blanc-Gatti, the painter of sounds. At this very moment, I am looking at his paintings: 'Modulation,' 'Sound Waves of Organs,' 'Carillon of Malesco,' whose titles sufficiently express that he painted what he heard." Messiaen, *Traité,* 1:67, emphasis in original. For reproductions of Blanc-Gatti's works, see table of illustrations in Charles Blanc-Gatti, *Sons et couleurs,* 2nd ed. (Paris and Neuchâtel: Attinger, [1934] 1958), 180.

Vision 7: Amen of Consummation

in the Apocalypse that lists the twelve stones undergirding the walls of the celestial city. Messiaen quotes this passage as the epigraph to his *Treatise* analysis:

"The Throne was encircled by a rainbow.

"Then he showed me a river of the water of life, clear as crystal; flowing from the Throne of God and of the Lamb, down the middle of the street of the city.

"And the foundations of the wall of the city were garnished with all manner of precious stones. The first foundation was jasper; the second, sapphire; the third, a chalcedony; the fourth, an emerald; the fifth, sardonyx; the sixth, sardius; the seventh, chrysolyte; the eighth, beryl; the ninth, a topaz; the tenth, a chrysoprasus; the eleventh, a jacinth; the twelfth, an amethyst." (Apocalypse of Saint John)[47]

The stones have multiple layers of symbolism associated with them, because some were part of Aaron's "breastplate of judgment" *(pectoral du jugement)*.[48] The twelve stones represent the twelve tribes of Israel; they later come to represent the twelve apostles, that is, the human foundations of the heavenly Jerusalem. One of the earliest sets of linkages between the stones and various "apostles" (including Paul) was made by Andreas, tenth-century bishop of Caesarea:

Jasper	Peter	greenish
Sapphire	Paul	blue
Chalcedony (Carbuncle)	Andrew	milky
Emerald	John (Evangelist)	green
Sardonyx	James (Great)	semiprecious, two layers
Sardius	Philip	orangish red
Chrysolite	Bartholomew	gold gleaming
Beryl	Thomas	aquamarine / emerald
Topaz	Matthew	yellow / brown

47. Rev. 4:3; 22:1-2; 21:19-20; in Messiaen, analysis of Vision 7, in *Traité*, 3:270. Messiaen also quotes this passage in his consideration of color symbolism; see *Traité*, 7:21.

48. A chapter is entitled "The High-Priest's Breastplate" in George Frederick Kunz, *The Curious Lore of Precious Stones: Being a Description of Their Sentiments and Folk Lore, Superstitions, Symbolism, Mysticism, Use in Medicine, Protection, Prevention, Religion, and Divination, Crystal Gazing, Birthstones, Lucky Stones and Talismans, Astral, Zodiacal and Planetary* (London: Lippincott, 1913; reprint, New York: Dover, 1971), 275-306. For the "breastplate (or breastpiece) of judgment," see Exod. 28:15; cf. Kunz, 276-77.

1943: Résumé: Visions of Amen

Chrysoprase	Thaddaeus	gold
Jacinth	Simon (Zealot)	orange-yellow-red
Amethyst	Matthias	fiery: purple-violet[49]

The association of precious stones with the apostles — especially the martyred ones — also recalls Messiaen's longtime affection for "Caelestis urbs Jerusalem" and "Urbs Jerusalem beata," hymns to the celestial city sung on the feast of the dedication of a church.[50]

The "Amen of Consumption" represents the "perpetual dazzlement" of the celestial city, "an eternal music of colors, an eternal color of musics."[51] (This theme would be explored in more detail in his *Colors of the Celestial City* [1963] for piano, wind, and percussion.) Messiaen's finale evokes a prediction made at the turn of the century in a book entitled *Light Waves and Their Uses:*

> I venture to predict that in the not very distant future there may be a color art analogous to the art of sound — a *color music,* in which the performer, seated before a literally chromatic scale, can play the colors of the spectrum in any succession or combination, flashing on a screen all possible gradations of color, simultaneously or in any desired succession, producing at will the most delicate and subtle modulations of light and color, or the most gorgeous and startling contrasts and chords! It seems to me that we have here at least as great a possibility of rendering all the fancies, moods, and emotions of the human mind as in the older arts.[52]

Messiaen had surely seen Blanc-Gatti's *Chromophonie,* either on its completion in 1939 or on his return from captivity after 1941. Vision 7 is his response.

---

49. Kunz, *Curious Lore of Precious Stones,* 311-14. To accommodate Saint Paul as one of the twelve apostles, Andreas of Caesarea seems to have forgotten James, son of Alphaeus (James the Less). For more references to gems in literature, including biblical references, Shakespearean references, and writings by Marbodius, bishop of Rennes (ca. 1035-1123), see Bruce G. Knuth, *Gems in Myth, Legend, and Lore* (Thornton, Colo.: Jewelers Press, 1999).

50. See discussion of *Apparition of the Eternal Church,* pp. 171-77 above.

51. Messiaen, in Rößler, *Contributions,* 66; quoted in Jeremy S. Begbie, *Resounding Truth: Christian Wisdom in the World of Music* (Grand Rapids: Baker Academic, 2007), 169.

52. Albert A. Michelson, *Light Waves and Their Uses* (Chicago: University of Chicago Press, 1903); quoted in Clark Farmer, "'Every Beautiful Sound Also Creates an Equally Beautiful Picture': Color Music and Walt Disney's *Fantasia,*" in *Lowering the Boom: Critical Studies in Film Sound,* ed. Jay Beck and Tony Grajeda (Urbana: University of Illinois Press, 2008), 183-200, at 185; quoted in Faber Birren, *Color Psychology and Color Therapy: A Factual Study of the Influence of Color on Human Life* (New Hyde Park, N.Y.: University Books, 1961), 165.

Vision 7: Amen of Consummation

Why does Messiaen emphasize in his "Author's Note" that these "carillons of brilliant sparkling rhythms" are woven "in *rhythmical canons* becoming *tighter and tighter*"? Again, linkage between the "Amen of Consummation" and *Colors of the Celestial City* appears. This mathematical use of canons, an extension of the non-retrogradable rhythms already seen, will later be developed as "symmetrical permutations" and used in that work. Messiaen's description of *Celestial City* also applies to the "Consummation": "The work does not end, having never really begun: it turns on itself, interlacing its temporal blocks, like the rose window of a cathedral with its vivid invisible colors."[53] One scholar elaborates: increasingly tighter rhythmical canons return the listener more and more quickly to the beginning of the canon, creating the effect of a kaleidoscope or a rose window in endless circular motion.[54] Another scholar offers an electrical analogy: all these devices (rhythmical canons, non-retrogradable rhythms, and other forms of symmetrical permutations) create a "closed circuit"; "embodied in the closed circuitry of each innovation, Messiaen found expressions of eternal life."[55]

In other words, these various symmetries are all attempts to square the circle, paradoxically representing eternity by the temporal medium of music. This is a Baroque vision, demonstrated in Rembrandt's 1632 painting *Philosopher in Meditation* (with the seemingly endless staircase in the background, easily viewed by Messiaen at the Louvre), and in the "riddle canons" of Bach's *Musical Offering* (1747), examples of the *canon perpetuus* or, more generally, *perpetuum mobile* — canons repeated indefinitely.[56] (Compare "this staircase that doesn't end" in *Death of Number* [1930] and "The Stairs Repeat" in *Harawi* [1945].) More specifically, Messiaen associated chromatic counterpoint with the works of Bach.[57] Modern painters were also inspired by Bach's mathe-

---

53. Messiaen, quoted in Paul Griffiths, *Olivier Messiaen and the Music of Time* (Ithaca, N.Y.: Cornell University Press, 1985), 201; in Begbie, *Resounding Truth,* 170.

54. For this parallel see Begbie, *Resounding Truth,* 170.

55. Jean Marie Wu, "Mystical Symbols of Faith: Olivier Messiaen's Charm of Impossibilities," in *Messiaen's Language of Mystical Love,* ed. Siglind Bruhn (New York and London: Garland, 1998), 113.

56. See Douglas R. Hofstadter, *Gödel, Escher, Bach: An Eternal Golden Braid* (New York: Basic Books, 1979), 2-15, 199-203, 665-68, 681-83, 715-42. One scholar writes of Rembrandt's *Philosopher in Meditation:* "Rembrandt has the meditation of a scholar paralleled visually by the unending movement of a winding staircase." Rudolf Arnheim, "The Virtue of Endlessness," *British Journal of Aesthetics* 40, no. 2 (April 2000): 225-27, at 225.

57. In an interview (December 16, 1983), Messiaen said of Bach: "The beauty lies in the counterpoint, in the meetings of these counterpoints which yield nearly modern harmonies. . . . chromatic counterpoints move up and down. Their meeting-points produce an

matical forms. For both composers and painters, the attraction was "the tight yet flexible structure of the Bach fugue; comparison with the fugue became a fashionable way of characterizing preoccupation with structure." Franz Marc, for example, described the work of Robert Delaunay (Messiaen's favorite artist) as "pure sounding fugues."[58] Recall that even Disney's *Fantasia* (1940), a masterpiece of the sound-color movement, opened with Stokowski's arrangement of Bach's *Toccata and Fugue in D Minor*. Messiaen's canons represent color and eternity.

Messiaen's concluding words — "the light of Life" — intentionally bring us back full circle to Vision 1: " — light and, as a consequence, Life." (Note Messiaen's capitalization of "Life" [*la Vie*] in his notes for both Visions 1 and 7.) Light and Life are intrinsically connected for Messiaen, as they are for the Scriptures, Hello, and Marmion. " 'He who follows me,' He said (and there is more here than a mere juxtaposition of words), 'does not walk in the darkness, but will have the *light of life*.' And this light of life proceeds from the light which in essence *is* life: 'In Him was life, and the life was the light of men.' Our life in heaven will be to know the eternal light without veil, and to rejoice in its splendors."[59] Blanc-Gatti reminds us that we perceive light *as color*. And yet the precious gems are only stepping-stones to a greater synesthetic unity; they "ring out, shock, dance, color and perfume the light of Life." Thoroughly in keeping with the theme of the "consummation" of creation, the movement ends up as an organic synesthetic whole: all of creation is unified. As such, the stones are the "living stones" polished in the sufferings of terrestrial life, now become "glorified bodies" gifted by strength, subtlety, agility, and above all, clarity (or brilliance); the stones "ring out" (they are *heard* as sound); they "shock, dance, and color" (they are *seen* as light and motion); and they "perfume" (they are *smelled* as odorous). Multisensory "dazzlement."[60]

---

almost Debussy-like harmonic language, most unusual for that time. The contrapuntal and harmonic aspects of Bach are really brilliant, not only in his organ works, but above all, in the glorious B Minor Mass." Rößler, *Contributions*, 139.

58. John Gage, *Color and Culture: Practice and Meaning from Antiquity to Abstraction* (Boston: Little, Brown, 1993), 241; quoted in Farmer, "Every Beautiful Sound," 192.

59. Marmion, *Christ in His Mysteries*, 154-74, at 155, emphasis in original.

60. Sander van Maas, *The Reinvention of Religious Music: Olivier Messiaen's Breakthrough toward the Beyond* (New York: Fordham University Press, 2009), 33-35.

Vision 7: Amen of Consummation

4. Westminster Carillon: A Clandestine Revenge?

A precedent for composing a pianistic "carillon" can be found in Sergey Lyapunov's *Twelve Studies of Transcendent Execution (Douze études d'exécution transcendante)*, published around 1900. The third of these "transcendental studies" featured a Russian Orthodox Church theme heard in canon in the upper register of the piano.[61]

However, the French carillon genre more generally descends from the organ tradition, itself emerging from a fascination with imitating the newly invented carillons of the sixteenth and seventeenth centuries.[62] For example, *The Carillons of Paris*, by the seventeenth-century composer Louis Couperin, was always played on the organ of Saint-Gervais between the vespers of All Saints' Day and that of All Souls' Day (i.e., November 1-2). In the early eighteenth century, the only organ book published by Pierre Dandrieu contained the *Carillon or Bells* (1714).[63] Although bells had been outlawed in 1793 during the French Revolution, the bells of Notre-Dame cathedral in Paris rang out again after Napoleon signed the Concordat in 1802. This was the same year that Chateaubriand's chapter celebrating bells (seen above in the "Amen of Judgment") appeared in his *Genius of Christianity*.

More particularly, the genre of large fantasies based on the musical themes of carillons was mostly owed to the orchestral organs of Aristide Cavaillé-Coll (1811-1899) built between circa 1840 and 1900.[64] One of the most significant changes was enlarging the pedal division and filling it with massive high-pressure reeds. (For example, the pedal division in the organ installed in the new Basilica of Sainte-Clotilde [completed 1859] included a Bassoon 16, Bombarde 16, Trompette 8, and Clarion 4.) Brilliant toccatas could now be created in which the manuals played feverishly in the upper registers while melodies

---

61. Sergey Lyapunov, *Douze études d'exécution transcendante (Twelve Studies of Transcendent Execution)* (Leipzig, 1900-1905). The third étude is entitled "Carillon." See Edward Garden, "Lyapunov, Sergey Mikhaylovich," in *Grove Music Online. Oxford Music Online*, http://www.oxfordmusiconline.com.proxy.bc.edu/subscriber/article/grove/music/17241.

62. The carillon developed from clock chimes, and the "technique of grinding the bells to bring overtones into tuneful and harmonic relationships was developed in the Low Countries in the mid-17th century." Jeremy Montagu, "Carillon," in *The Oxford Companion to Music*, ed. Alison Latham, *Oxford Music Online*, http://www.oxfordmusiconline.com.proxy.bc.edu/subscriber/article/opr/t114/e1174.

63. Corliss Richard Arnold, *Organ Literature: A Comprehensive Survey*, 3rd ed., 2 vols. (Metuchen, N.J.: Scarecrow, 1995), 1:127, 136. The "day of the dead" refers to All Souls' Day, November 2.

64. Arnold, *Organ Literature*, 1:199-201.

1943: Résumé: Visions of Amen

(imitating carillon themes) bellowed forth bombastically in the pedals. The "Amen of Consummation" imitates this manuals-pedal division as the first piano plays feverishly in the upper register while the carillon melody thunders below in the second piano.

Examples of the "carillon" genre (by date of publication) illustrate the lineage:

> 1886: Adolphe Marty: *Carillon des cloches de Saint-Paul d'Orléans*
> 1890: Boëllmann: *Carillon* from *Douze Pièces*, op. 16
> 1911: Henri Mulet: *Carillon-sortie* (Schola Cantorum, n.d.; ded. Joseph Bonnet)
> 1914: Louis Vierne: *Carillon: sur la sonnerie du Carillon de la chapelle du Château de Longpont (Aisne)*, in *Pièces en style libre*, op. 31, no. 21 (earliest bell piece)
> 1920: Leo Sowerby: *Carillon* (composed 1917)
> 1921: Émile Bourdon: Carillons from *Dix Pièces*, op. 7
> 1924: Marcel Dupré: *Les Cloches de Perros-Guirec, Suite Bretonne*, op. 21
> 1926-1927: Louis Vierne: *Carillon de Westminster* (3e suite, op. 54) and *Les cloches de Hinckley* (4e suite, op. 55); in *Pièces de Fantaisie*, 4 vols.
> 1928: Charles Tournemire: "Paraphrase-Carillon," *L'Orgue Mystique* (35: Assumption)
> 1931: Marcel Dupré: *Carillon*, from *Sept Pièces*, op. 27
> 1941: Henri Nibelle: *Le Carillon orléannais*
> 1949: Herbert Murrill: *Carillon*
> 1962: Maurice Duruflé: *Fugue sur le thème du Carillon des heures de la cathédrale de Soissons*, op. 12 (on twenty-fifth anniversary of death of Louis Vierne)

Among the most famous in this genre is Vierne's *Carillon of Westminster*, composed and published as one of *Twenty-four Fantasy Pieces* in 1926-1927. Extremely familiar today, it was brand-new during the Conservatory's autumn 1927 semester in which Messiaen took up the organ. Vierne played it for the first time in public on that November 29 — about three months after the death of Cécile Sauvage — when it served as the recessional piece for the closing of the Forty Hours (a eucharistic devotion) at Notre-Dame. Eight days later, it received its formal premiere in Vierne's recital inaugurating the restored organ at Saint-Nicolas-du-Chardonnet, Paris.[65] Messiaen had just begun taking organ

---

65. See Rollin Smith, *Louis Vierne: Organist of Notre-Dame Cathedral* (Hillsdale, N.Y.:

Vision 7: Amen of Consummation

lessons with Dupré that September; it is difficult to imagine that he did not attend this inaugural recital. In 1941-1942, as Messiaen composed *Visions*, the memory of Vierne would have been quite vivid; he had died a very dramatic and public death less than five years earlier.[66]

Structural similarities are apparent between Vierne's *Carillon of Westminster* and Messiaen's visions of "Creation" and "Consummation." In the upper register, both of Messiaen's movements have free variations suggesting brilliant toccata-like organ improvisations. (Vierne, like Tournemire and Messiaen himself, was a great improviser.) In the lower register, Messiaen uses the "creation" theme as a repeating ostinato in the same way Vierne uses the theme from Westminster. In each, the slow, stable melody booms forth against the upper register, unifying and stabilizing the feverish high-pitched activity.

In 1927, Vierne's use of the Westminster clock's theme would have been just another example of such borrowings from carillons. However, in 1943, when Messiaen premiered *Visions* in German-occupied Paris, the Westminster theme had taken on an entirely different significance: preceding a broadcast of Radio London, the clandestine BBC news service transmitted from London to occupied France, the chimes symbolized resistance and hoped-for liberation.[67]

Is it too much of a stretch to postulate that Messiaen's "creation theme" intentionally refers to the Westminster carillon theme? Recall that *Visions* had been commissioned by Denise Tual as the fourth concert in the Concerts de la Pléiade series — the series Messiaen referred to as "a kind of clandestine revenge against the Occupation."[68] *Visions* was his first composition after re-

---

Pendragon Press, 1999), 555-59, and Iain Simcock, "Louis Vierne and the '24 Pièces de Fantaisie,'" *Musical Times* 130, no. 1758 (August 1989): 495, 497, 499.

66. On June 2, 1937, Vierne was playing his 1,750th recital before an audience of 3,000 at Notre-Dame cathedral in Paris. At about the midpoint of his concert, having just concluded his *Stele for a Deceased Child (Stèle pour un enfant défunt)*, Vierne inhaled his bottle of smelling salts, said, "I'm going to be ill," and died as his foot pushed down a long low E on the pedal. A representative emerged and explained to the audience what had happened, asking them "to stay a few minutes to pray for the repose of Vierne's soul." Smith, *Louis Vierne*, 419-25.

67. Martyn Cornick, "'Fraternity among Listeners': The BBC and French Resistance; Evidence from Refugees," in *Vichy, Resistance, Liberation: New Perspectives on Wartime France*, ed. Hanna Diamond and Simon Kitson (New York: Berg, 2005); Jacques Pessis, *La bataille de Radio Londres (1940-1944). 70e anniversaire de l'appel du 18 juin* (Paris: Omnibus, 2010); Aurélie Luneau, *Radio Londres. Les voix de la liberté (1940-1944)* (Paris: Perrin, [2005] 2010).

68. Nigel Simeone, "Messiaen and the Concerts de la Pléiade: 'A Kind of Clandestine Revenge against the Occupation,'" *Music and Letters* 8, no. 4 (November 2000): 532-50.

1943: *Résumé:* Visions of Amen

turning to occupied Paris from his incarceration in the German POW camp. Is the creation theme in itself a clandestine revenge against the occupation? An encoded version of the carillon is first heard faintly in the "Amen of Creation," emerging from the nebulae in the primal moments of time; it approaches closer in the "Agony of Jesus"; and closer still in the "Amen of the Angels, of Saints, of Birdsong." Finally, on the day of creation's "Consummation," it exuberantly thunders forth with thrilling rhythmic power as the "Carillon of the Seventh Day" (Léon Bloy).[69]

*   *   *

Whatever historical and personal meanings Messiaen might have invested in the "Amen of Consummation," a concluding theological point is worth underscoring. In the Hebrew Scriptures, creation and liberation — Genesis and Exodus — go hand in hand. Isaiah prophesied to a people conquered and exiled by a foreign power:

> Behold I do new things,
> and now they shall spring forth, verily you shall know them.
> I will make a way in the wilderness, and rivers in the desert.

The Christian book of the Apocalypse continues this ancient tradition even as it depicts creation's final epic battle and the overthrow of tyranny:

> And he who was sitting on the throne said,
> "Behold, I make all things new!"[70]

---

69. In his journal entry for October 18, 1892, Bloy noted "all the dungheaps in the East or West, crying out in anguish, since the eternities, waiting for the Carillon of the Seventh Day" [tous les fumiers de l'Orient ou de l'Occident, et qui crie d'angoisse, depuis les éternités, en attendant le Carillon du Septième Jour]. *Journal de Léon Bloy,* ed. Joseph Bollery, 2 vols. (Paris: Mercure de France, [1956] 1963), 1:55.

70. Isa. 43:19; Apoc. 21:5 (Douay-CCD).

PART IV

1943–1992

Legacy

CHAPTER 10

1943–1949

Postwar *Liebestod*

Visions of Amen marks the end of a certain period in Messiaen's life. In October 1942, just prior to beginning its composition, he had concluded *The Technique of My Musical Language*. It was published in February 1944, six months before the liberation of Paris. In this work Messiaen assembled a catalogue of his works published up until that date: the last work included is *Visions*, and, since it would not be published until 1950, it did not include the name of a publisher.[1] Thus, *Visions* closes out the first period of Messiaen's life as he summarized it upon returning to Paris from the prisoner of war camp.

On a domestic level, *Visions* signaled the entrance of Yvonne Loriod into Messiaen's life. Although neither Messiaen nor Loriod knew it at the time, this too was the beginning of a closure to the first period of Messiaen's life. The "Amen of Desire," introduced sometime after October 1942, would already seem to represent this transition.

Of course, Messiaen had by this time lived slightly less than half his life, and during the next four decades he would write the massive works that established him as one of the twentieth century's most important musicians. What follows in this final section is a brief and necessarily superficial survey of those works in their chronological contexts. It is meant to offer the listener new to Messiaen's works an introductory framework. The section is divided into three brief chapters. Chapter 10 surveys the immediate postwar period, from the premiere

1. Olivier Messiaen, *Technique de mon langage musical*, 2 vols. (Paris: Alphonse Leduc, 1944), 1:64-67, at 64.

of *Visions* through the "Tristan Trilogy," concluding in December 1949. This "trilogy" of three works was inspired by the Tristan and Isolde myth. Chapter 11 considers the Cold War decade of birdsong — *Catalogue of Birds* — as a body of work whose abstraction was in sync with the postwar avant-gardism but might also be considered a form of coded language. It ends with the death of Claire Delbos in 1959. Chapter 12 offers brief indications for listening to the music of 1960 and beyond, that composed during Messiaen's marriage to Yvonne Loriod and marked by an explicit return to theological themes.

1944-1945: *Liturgies, Twenty Gazes,* Liberation, and "Controversy"

Between the time Messiaen's *Visions of Amen* was composed in the autumn-winter of 1942-1943 and the time it was first performed in May and June 1943, the psychology surrounding the war changed significantly. On February 2, 1943, the Germans had surrendered to the Soviets at Stalingrad. British observers described the event as the salvation of European civilization.[2] To be sure, the Holocaust's horrors escalated as the Germans, having lost their hope of conquering the Soviets and Africa, focused energy on exterminating Jews within Europe's boundaries. On March 14 came the liquidation of the Jewish ghetto in Krakow. Between March and June, four new gas chambers and crematories were built at Auschwitz; by June 25, they had reached a daily capacity of incinerating 4,756 bodies. By November, the ghettos of Vilna, Minsk, and Riga had been liquidated. From the perspective of the Holocaust, no end was in sight. But from the military perspective and that of occupied Paris, the Stalingrad victory in February, German and Italian surrenders in May, and the Allied invasion of Sicily in early July marked a turning of the tide.

During this period of nascent, growing hopefulness about the possibility of liberation, Messiaen composed, between November 15, 1943, and March 15, 1944, his *Three Small Liturgies of the Divine Presence,* a work for orchestra, chorus, and a virtuoso pianist.[3] Having finished it, he immediately began composing a massive work for solo piano that would put Loriod's formidable technique on display all alone. The monumental *Twenty Gazes at the Infant Jesus* was composed in 1944, between March 23 and September 8, a period en-

---

2. Geoffrey Roberts, *Stalin's Wars: From World War to Cold War, 1939-1953* (New Haven: Yale University Press, 2006), 154.

3. For Messiaen's *Trois petites Liturgies de la Présence Divine,* see Nigel Simeone, *Olivier Messiaen: A Bibliographical Catalogue of Messiaen's Works,* Musikbibliographische Arbeiten series, vol. 14 (Tutzing: Hans Schneider, 1998), 84-87.

veloping D-Day and the Allied invasion of Normandy from June 6 to June 30.[4] (The invasion catalyzed the German terror: the Jewish French historian Marc Bloch, author of *Strange Defeat,* was executed on June 16.) Pierre Messiaen's memoirs, so deeply marked by his experience of the First World War, were published on June 30, just as the invasion reached a successful conclusion.

The liberation of Paris then came quickly, albeit with much bloodshed. On August 15, the gendarmerie, the police, and the employees of the Paris Métro went on strike; postal workers followed suit the following day. A more general strike broke out on August 18, completely paralyzing transportation of goods and city services. The following day, French Resistance forces took the battle to the streets of Paris, fighting until the German surrender on August 25. Numerous plaques throughout the city, easily missed by tourists who do not understand French, mark the exact places at which Resistance fighters were felled in the guerilla warfare. On August 26, 1944, Charles de Gaulle triumphantly marched down the Champs-Élysées in a victory parade.

However, the surface show of unity was short-lived. A "wild" or "savage cleansing" *(épuration sauvage)* immediately followed in which collaborators, and most especially women who had formed romantic relationships with German occupiers, were hunted down, publicly humiliated (the collaborating women had their heads shaved [the *femmes tondues*]), tortured, and even killed. Along with this popular uprising came the "legal cleansing" *(épuration légale),* during which the government detained, tried, and convicted — some (like Marshal Pétain himself) condemned to death — those judged to have collaborated with the Germans.[5]

The March and April 1945 premieres of Messiaen's two works composed during the previous year were indeed held in a liberated Paris — but also in a traumatized nation, embroiled in bitter battles over treason and collaboration. On March 26, 1945, Yvonne Loriod premiered *Twenty Gazes at the Infant Jesus;* about a month later, on April 21, *Three Small Liturgies of the Divine Presence* received its first performance in a Concert de la Pléiade at the Paris Conservatory. (The previous week, on April 15, Messiaen had given a second

---

4. For Messiaen's *Vingt Regards sur l'Enfant-Jésus,* see Simeone, *Bibliographical Catalogue,* 88-91. The title page of the first edition gives the date of composition as "Paris, 23 March–8 Sept 1944." Note that September 8 is not only an important feast day in the Catholic calendar, that is, the Nativity of the Blessed Virgin Mary; it is intimately related to the subject matter of *Vingt Regards.*

5. Antony Beevor and Artemis Cooper, *Paris after the Liberation, 1944-1949* (New York: Doubleday, 1994); Jean-Paul Cointet, *Expier Vichy: L'épuration en France (1943-1958)* (Paris: Perrin, 2008).

performance of his organ work *Glorious Bodies* at the Palais de Chaillot.) On May 8 Germany surrendered unconditionally.

It was in response to the March 26, 1945, premiere of *Twenty Gazes* that Messiaen received the first highly critical review in what would come to be known as "the Messiaen Controversy" *(Le Cas Messiaen)*.[6] Another venomous review, this one devoted to Messiaen's performance of *Glorified Bodies,* would appear on April 21, the same date as the premiere of *Three Small Liturgies,* which was about to cause a small uproar. Messiaen's text, which he composed, drawing on both Buddhist and Christian sources (including Aquinas), was nearly pantheistic in its claims for divine immanence in the historical world of space and time.

> The Son is the presence,
> The Spirit is the presence!
> Present in the blood of the soul,
> Soul-breathing star,
> Everywhere present, winged mirror of days,
> Through Love,
> The God of Love! . . .
> Whole in all places,
> Whole in each place, . . .
> The successive you is omnipresent,
> In these spaces and times that you created, . . .
> Present in the movement of Arcturus,
> In the rainbow, with one wing after the other, . . .
> Present in the hidden race of my cells,
> In the blood that repairs its banks,
> Present, through Grace, in your Saints.[7]

The sources that influenced *Visions of Amen* are easily seen here: the reference to Arcturus; and Boll's "Two Infinites," the infinite largeness of outer space and the infinite smallness of the "hidden race of my cells."

---

6. For an exhaustive study see Lilise Boswell-Kurc, "Olivier Messiaen's Religious Wartime Works and Their Controversial Reception in France (1941-46)" (Ph.D. diss., New York University, 2001). See also Peter Hill and Nigel Simeone, *Messiaen* (New Haven: Yale University Press, 2005), 142-67.

7. Olivier Messiaen, "Three Short Liturgies of the Divine Presence" ("Trois petites Liturgies de la Présence Divine"), trans. Stewart Spencer, in Olivier Messiaen, *Complete Edition,* 32 CDs (Germany: Deutsche Grammophon, 2008), 315-19.

1943–1949: Postwar Liebestod

A half century later, Claude Samuel looked back at the scandal: "today's listeners must feel only astonishment and be at a loss to explain the violent and often offensive remarks provoked by the first performance of the *Trois petites Liturgies*."[8] Perhaps — but then again, it is worth imagining what it might have been like to listen to Messiaen's immanentist effusions about divine presence in a blood-soaked city and traumatized culture. Even in the best of times, such claims might be expected to have a difficult reception. These were not the best of times.

Perhaps a preparatory contributing factor to the "controversy" had been *The Technique of My Musical Language,* published one year earlier. In addition to its self-evident presumption — what other composer who had only achieved fame two years earlier, with *Quartet for the End of Time*, would devote an extended analytical work to himself? — Messiaen's call for (and perhaps self-appointment as) the long-awaited "liberator" likely evoked a bad taste in an occupied city impatiently awaiting its liberation:

"To express with a lasting power our darkness struggling with the Holy Spirit, to raise upon the mountain the doors of our prison of flesh, to give to our century the spring water for which it thirsts, there shall have to be a great artist who will be both a great artisan and a great Christian." Let us hasten by our prayers the coming of the liberator. And, beforehand, let us offer him two thoughts. First, that of [Pierre] Reverdy: "May he draw in the whole sky in one breath!" And then that of [Ernest] Hello: "There is no one great except him to whom God speaks, and in the moment in which God speaks to him."[9]

---

8. Claude Samuel, liner notes for Messiaen, *Réveil des oiseaux. Trois petites Liturgies de la Présence Divine,* with Kent Nagano, Yvonne Loriod, et al., trans. Stewart Spencer, [1992] 1996, by Erato Disques S.A., Erato 0630-12702-2, compact disc.

9. Olivier Messiaen, *The Technique of My Musical Language,* trans. John Satterfield (Paris: Alphonse Leduc, 1956), 1:8; Messiaen, *Technique de mon langage musical,* 1:4. Messiaen's quotations are from his own essay that had been published just before the war: "De la Musique sacrée" ("On Sacred Music") (June-July 1939), in *Olivier Messiaen: Journalism, 1935-1939,* ed. Stephen Broad (Surrey, U.K., and Burlington, Vt.: Ashgate, 2012), Fr 74-76, at 76; Eng 135-37, at 137. Note his paraphrase of Marmion: "to contemplate Him so as to conform our own lives . . . so that our thirst may be fully quenched"; for this knowledge is "a fountain of water, springing up into life everlasting." Columba Marmion, chapter 1 ("The Mysteries of Christ Are Our Mysteries"), in *Christ in His Mysteries,* trans. Alan Bancroft (Bethesda, Md.: Zaccheus Press, 2008), 3-22, at 9, 11. For the references to Hello and Reverdy, see Ernest Hello, *Paroles de Dieu. Réflexions sur quelques textes sacrés,* ed. François Angelier (Grenoble: Jérôme Millon, [1877] 1992), 197; and Reverdy, "La jetée" ("The Toss"),

As Stephen Broad's recently published collection of Messiaen's journalistic writings from 1935 to 1939 shows, however, his penchant for audacity and stirring up passions had already been well established prior to the war.

In the "controversy," critics attacked Messiaen's practice — rooted in largely nineteenth-century understandings of the symbolist project and the "mystical" project of "commenting on" texts — of providing extensive commentaries on his works at performances, in program notes and occasionally in long oral discourses. However, the more significant charge lodged against his music was that it was not appropriate to the "religious" nature of his titles and texts. There was too much "sensuality" in music that should have been "religious" — and by this, apparently, his opponents meant "spirituality" and "austerity." One critic wrote in *Mondes:* "to judge by the title and the words, the spirit of this work ought to be religious, but the music does not lead us to a mood of contemplation owing to its multifariousness: meditation is followed by jazzy uproar, and that in turn by easy-on-the-ear passages, often reminding us of a charming operetta finale. To sum up, far from ascending in a fine continuous line towards the ethereal spheres, the work follows a downward curve and heads unerringly towards a prosaic world which it ought to eschew."[10] This review is significant because it unwittingly highlights Messiaen's surrealistic technique of juxtaposing opposites. Messiaen's own manifesto in *Technique* had opened himself to this charge of "multifariousness": "One point will attract our attention at the outset: the *charm of impossibilities* [*le charme des impossibilités*]."[11]

A corollary charge was that Messiaen, although posing as an orthodox Catholic "mystic," was nothing of the sort. His "sensual dynamism" and the "whiff of sulphur" (i.e., of the devil or at least of heresy) in his music were incompatible with his "mysticism." Although he shifted in 1935 from the "mystical" label to the "theological" one, critics continued to evaluate his work using

---

in *Les Ardoises du toit* (Paris: Paul Birault, 1918), n.p. Reverdy's text reads: "La voix vient de plus haut / L'homme vient de plus loin / Tu voudrais respirer à peine / Et l'autre aspirerait le ciel tout d'une haleine" (no final punctuation). Messiaen's alteration reads: "S'il veut bien chanter, qu'il aspire le ciel tout d'une haleine."

10. Roger Blanchard, quoted in Matthew Schellhorn, "*Les Noces* and *Trois petites Liturgies:* An Assessment of Stravinsky's Influence on Messiaen," in *Olivier Messiaen: Music, Art, and Literature,* ed. Christopher Dingle and Nigel Simeone (Burlington, Vt.: Ashgate, 2007), 39-61, at 40. For the accusation that Messiaen's music was too "sensual" to be "spiritual," see Boswell-Kurc, "Olivier Messiaen's Religious War-time Works," 313-83.

11. Messiaen, *Technique* (1956), 1:13; Messiaen, *Technique* (1944), 1:5. Emphasis in original.

1943–1949: Postwar Liebestod

their customary categories and attacking his "mystico-poetic" commentaries.[12] One famously described *Liturgies* as "a work of tinsel, false magnificence and pseudo-mysticism ... looking about anxiously like an angel wearing lipstick."[13] Throughout the episode, Messiaen had supporters as well as detractors, and he defended himself in print with stinging rebuttals.

In April 1946, aiming to put the episode to rest, *Le Figaro littéraire* asked: "Is there a 'Messiaen Controversy'?" After presenting the replies of various critics, *Figaro* answered no — but also counseled an end to textual commentaries: "We believe that this enquiry has exploded the myth of a 'Cas Messiaen.' Almost all the replies describe Messiaen as a very great musician of our time. The majority are also in agreement about rejecting all the literature and commentaries which the composer or certain bumbling exegetes place around his works, and concur that these do the music a disservice."[14]

Asking whether or not there had in fact "been" a "Messiaen controversy" was perhaps understandable at that time. But posing the question this way today blurs the precise timing of its historical context: it began with the end of the occupation and only calmed down as a new republic (the Fourth Republic) was being worked out, bringing to closure (however imperfectly) the question of France's identity. The furious postwar "cleansing" — whether the popular "wild" type *(l'épuration sauvage)* or the state-sponsored "legal" process *(l'épuration légale)* — was a judgment not only on what "France" had been during the 1940-1944 occupation, but also on what it would become. What would be continuous and what would need to be excised or forgotten? This would be the question during France's "long liberation" from 1944 to 1947.[15]

Messiaen was an ambivalent figure in this culture; while from a logical point of view, his music ought to have been the ideal expression of Vichy, as a matter of historical fact, he was unacceptable to the regime. One scholar sums up the situation: "Messiaen should have suited Vichy well — an ex–war prisoner, a devout Catholic, the organist at Trinité in Paris and the pre-eminent composer of religious works. . . . [However,] his name was notoriously absent from the list of those who received commissions from the state. So while never

---

12. Hill and Simeone, *Messiaen*, 165.

13. Claude Rostand, quoted by Nigel Simeone in liner notes for the *Trois petites Liturgies*, in Messiaen, *Complete Edition*, 250-51.

14. "Y-a-t-il un 'Cas Messiaen'?" *Le Figaro littéraire*, April 13/20, 1946; in Hill and Simeone, *Messiaen*, 166-67.

15. Andrew Knapp, ed., *The Uncertain Foundation: France at the Liberation, 1944-47* (New York: Palgrave Macmillan, 2007); cf. Rosemary Wakeman, *The Heroic City: Paris, 1945-1958* (Chicago: University of Chicago Press, 2009).

banned, he was marginalized. . . . [The] only possible conclusion is that his type of Modernism was unacceptable to the authorities."[16] Perhaps Messiaen's music was seen as the kind of "degenerate music" *(entartete Musik)* reviled by the Nazis.[17] But there are other suggestive possibilities. For example: as seen above, Messiaen described the Concerts de la Pléiade series — for which he wrote both *Visions* and *Three Small Liturgies* — as "a kind of clandestine revenge against the Occupation." Another example: Messiaen's enthusiasm for the poetical works of Éluard since the 1920s has already been seen. During the 1930s, Éluard distanced himself from the surrealists as he became increasingly involved with the communists. During the occupation, as his writing became identified with the Resistance, Messiaen's attraction only increased. In his *Technique,* Messiaen explicitly identified Éluard as one of a handful of major influences on his thought and music. The composer and poet would exchange correspondence soon after the war's end. Messiaen had also been an exceptionally strong supporter of Darius Milhaud, the Jewish composer who had to flee France with his wife and take refuge in the United States during the war. Finally, Messiaen deeply admired Charles de Gaulle, stemming from his time in the POW camp. These scattered fragments of evidence suggest that Messiaen's "type of Modernism" may indeed have been unacceptable to the authorities — and perhaps intentionally so.[18]

16. Frederic Spotts, *The Shameful Peace: How French Artists and Intellectuals Survived the Nazi Occupation* (New Haven: Yale University Press, 2008), 219. Compare Nigel Simeone: "Leslie Sprout has observed that Messiaen was 'one of the very few composers liberated from prisoner of war camps in Germany not to receive a commission from Vichy,' and that 'while Messiaen's music was never banned, his compositions were none the less relegated to the periphery of Parisian musical life.' Sprout argues convincingly that this marginalisation was primarily on aesthetic grounds. Was Messiaen irritated by the marginalisation?" Nigel Simeone, "Making Music in Occupied Paris," *Musical Times* 147, no. 1894 (Spring 2006): 23-50, at 50; citing Leslie Sprout, "Les Commandes de Vichy," in *La Vie musicale sous Vichy,* ed. Myriam Chimènes (Brussels: Complexe, 2001), 157-78, at 164-65.

17. Richard A. Etlin, *Art, Culture, and Media under the Third Reich* (Chicago: University of Chicago Press, 2002), 56-64.

18. For the Concerts de la Pléiade, see Nigel Simeone, "Messiaen and the Concerts de la Pléiade: 'A Kind of Clandestine Revenge against the Occupation,'" *Music and Letters* 8, no. 4 (November 2000): 532-50. For Milhaud, see Stephen Broad, "Interpreting Messiaen's Reception of Milhaud," in *Wiener Jahrbuch für Jüdische Geschichte Kultur & Museumswesen: Musik & Widerstand,* ed. Michael Haas (Vienna: Jüdisches Museum der Stadt Wien, 2008), 58-67; cf. Broad, "Messiaen: Poetics, Polemics and Politics," *Scottish Music Review* 1, no. 1 (2007): 83-98. For de Gaulle see Nigel Simeone, "Messiaen in 1942: A Working Musician in Occupied Paris," in *Messiaen Studies,* ed. Robert Sholl, Cambridge Composer Studies (New York: Cambridge University Press, 2007), 19; and Messiaen, "Des paroles d'esprit: Entre-

1943–1949: Postwar Liebestod

The question of what constituted authentic "religious" music in 1944-1946 can also be situated within the Catholic crisis left behind by Vichy. The Catholic hierarchy in France had been profoundly compromised in its relationship with the Germans; the cardinal archbishop of Paris, Emmanuel Suhard, was so tainted by his activities during the occupation that General de Gaulle forbade him from attending the Te Deum service of thanksgiving at his own cathedral of Notre-Dame.[19] One historian notes: "Because he had welcomed Marshal Pétain to Notre-Dame in April 1944 and in June 1944 had celebrated the funeral of Philippe Henriot, the collaborationist information minister assassinated by Resistance fighters, [Suhard] was considered as a traitor by the liberators of France. For some Christian-democrats, he also betrayed true Catholic values."[20]

De Gaulle's extraordinary assertion of a layman's military authority over the cardinal archbishop not only demonstrates how conflicted French Catholicism was in the summer of 1944; it also points to the bloody retribution against collaborators — the *épuration*. Moreover, the *épuration* would be in large measure revenge exacted on the right by the left (especially communists), who had been tortured and killed for the Resistance. To some extent it was yet another act in the 1930s drama between right and left, one that extended back to the Dreyfus affair.

Whatever the causes and content of the "Messiaen Controversy," and no matter how much Messiaen might have minimized it in later years, it certainly had a powerful effect. Messiaen did not provide spoken commentaries on his works after this. He also turned away from explicitly religious subjects — and

---

tien avec Olivier Messiaen," in *Charles de Gaulle,* ed. Michel Cazenave and Olivier Germain Thomas (Paris: L'Herne, 1973), 44-46. For Éluard, see Philip Nord, *France's New Deal: From the Thirties to the Postwar Era* (Princeton: Princeton University Press, 2010), 307; Stephen Schloesser, "The Charm of Impossibilities: Mystic Surrealism as Contemplative Voluptuousness," in *Messiaen the Theologian,* ed. Andrew Shenton (Burlington, Vt.: Ashgate, 2010), 166, 177-78, 181; and letters of Olivier Messiaen to Paul Éluard, March 13, 1945, and undated, Carlton Lake Collection of French Manuscripts, Harry Ransom Center, The University of Texas at Austin, 66.1. I am grateful to the Harry Ransom Center for kind permission to consult these documents.

19. German snipers fired shots from the galleries up near the roof of Notre-Dame cathedral as the congregation assembled for the Te Deum thanksgiving service on August 26, 1944. Although congregants took cover under their seats, Charles de Gaulle "calmly stood through the service, joining fervently in the 'Magnificat.'" Charles Williams, *The Last Great Frenchman: A Life of General de Gaulle* (New York: Wiley, 1993), 275.

20. Emmanuel Godin, "French Catholic Intellectuals and the Nation in Post-war France," *South Central Review* 17, no. 4 (Winter 2000): 45-60, at 47.

turned toward the myth of Tristan and Isolde — for reasons already implicit in the "Amen of Desire."

Before leaving these last explicitly "religious" works appearing in the turbulent days following the liberation, one small element found in *Twenty Gazes at the Infant Jesus* deserves mention: Messiaen's invention of the "star + cross" motif.[21] The motif is first found implicitly in the "Amen of the Agony of Jesus."[22] But in his commentary on the "Gaze of the Star" movement, Messiaen's reflection on the intrinsic relationship between sites of birth and

---

21. The title *Twenty Gazes* is admittedly strange in English; the French word *regard* can be translated a number of ways, including as "look," "glance," "gaze." I have chosen "gaze" because it includes the act of "looking" while suggesting the longer duration of "contemplation" implied in Marmion's text, the inspirational source of Messiaen's composition. Marmion recalls a variety of "gazes" at the infant Jesus: the ox and the ass saw "that which an animal can *see:* the form, the size, the color, the movement — a wholly rudimentary knowledge, not going beyond the realm of the senses." The "passers-by, the curious" have also "*seen* the child." Then there are the shepherds, who were illumined by a light from on high and hence saw more: "they have *recognized* in this child the Messiah, promised and awaited." Likewise, in the passage quoted here, "the angels *looked* upon the new born." And then: "What shall we say of the Virgin when she *gazed* on Jesus? So pure, so humble and tender her *gaze,* so full of happiness — to what depths of the mystery it penetrated!" Finally comes "(but it is something untellable) the *gaze* of the Father contemplating His Son, made flesh for mankind." These are the various "gazes" *(regards)* that inspired Messiaen's cycle. See Marmion, *Christ in His Mysteries,* 150, 151, emphasis added. For a detailed analysis, see David Butler Cannata, "Messiaen Reads the Infancy Gospels: The *Vingt Regards sur l'Enfant-Jésus* as Christology," in *"Quomodo cantabimus canticum"? Studies in Honor of Edward H. Roesner,* ed. Cannata et al. (Middleton, Wis.: American Institute of Musicology, 2008), 235-77.

22. Messiaen writes in his "Author's Note" introducing the score of *Twenty Gazes at the Infant Jesus:* "The *Star* and the *Cross* [movements] have the same theme because one opens and the other closes the terrestrial period of Jesus." Olivier Messiaen, *Vingt Regards sur l'Enfant-Jésus* (Paris: Durand, 1944), ii. See movements 2 ("Gaze of the Star") and 7 ("Gaze of the Cross"). As Siglind Bruhn notes, the deeper source of this association comes from Dom Marmion's meditations on Christmas; see Marmion, chapter 7 ("O Wondrous Exchange! [Christmas]"), in *Christ in His Mysteries,* 131-53, at 145-46. See Siglind Bruhn, *Messiaen's Contemplations of Covenant and Incarnation: Musical Symbols of Faith in the Two Great Piano Cycles of the 1940s* (Hillsdale, N.Y.: Pendragon Press, 2007), 138. Bruhn also notes the study of Aloyse Michaely pointing to late-medieval and early-modern paintings representing a cross above the manger, including Albrecht Dürer's *Birth of Christ* (1503) and Roger van der Weyden's *Adoration of the Magi* (1460). Bruhn, 153, citing Michaely, "*Verbum Caro:* Die Darstellung des Mysteriums der Inkarnation in Olivier Messiaens Vingt Regards sur l'Enfant-Jésus," *Hamburger Jahrbuch für Musikwissenschaft* 6 (1983): 225-345, at 252. Pierre Messiaen would almost certainly have made his son aware of the same connection between Christmas and sacrifice laid out in T. S. Eliot's *Murder in the Cathedral* (1935), first performed and published a decade earlier.

death derives from Marmion's *Christ in His Mysteries,* the devotional model for *Twenty Gazes.* Marmion writes:

> As you will not be unaware, we had to wait until the immolation of Calvary before the expiation would be complete: but, as St. Paul has told us, it was at the first moment of His incarnation that Christ expressed acceptance of the accomplishment of the will of His Father, acceptance of His offering Himself as a Victim for the whole human race . . . ; and it was as far back as the manger that He inaugurated the life of suffering that He willed to live for our salvation, an earthly life of which Golgotha was the appointed end, and which, by its destruction of sin, restored friendship with His Father to us. The manger was undoubtedly only the first stage, but it contained at root all the others.[23]

The manger is but the first stage in a multiple-staged acceptance by Christ of human suffering.

The star + cross motif provides the key to interpreting the text of a short (about four minutes) work entitled *Song of the Deported* (1945).[24] Messiaen had received a commission from Radio France to write it for a "Concert of French Music in Memory of the Deported who died in Germany." It was premiered at that concert at the Palais de Chaillot on November 2, 1945 (All Souls' Day in the Catholic calendar), with Pierre Boulez, Messiaen's student, playing the piano part. The work called for not only orchestra but also huge forces in the chorus. Messiaen himself wrote the poetic text, and in the juxtaposition of "the form of a cross / The kiss of the star," we see the "star + cross" motif that runs through *Twenty Gazes,* premiered the previous year: the intersection of the manger in Bethlehem and the cross at Golgotha. Being born into the human condition entails suffering and death.

> Progressing towards death,
> Higher, groaning sun,
> I shall find my sky and my night.
>
> My pain takes *the form of a cross*
> *The kiss of the star* and of the night

---

23. Marmion, *Christ in His Mysteries,* 145, 146.
24. Hill and Simeone, *Messiaen,* 163.

A cipher on the register of pain,
My portion of sky, my portion of night.

My fairest love, my sister, my France,
I am going, groaning sun.
Truth, accomplish my release
That I may drink my sky, my night from you.

All eyes disappear at night
And peace returns at night.[25]

1945–1948: Terrible Love and the Turn to Myth — the "Tristan Trilogy"

Between 1945 and 1948 Messiaen composed three pieces that became known retrospectively as his "Tristan Trilogy": *Harawi* (1945), *Turangalîla Symphony* (1945-1948), and *Five Refrains* (1948-1949).[26] This "trilogy" did not result from Messiaen's premeditated decision to write a unified triptych; the works do not share that much in common. What they do share is the theme of love that is fatalistically doomed, tragic, and perhaps only realizable after death. These themes amplified Messiaen's decisive boyhood encounter with Debussy's *Pelléas et Mélisande,* an encounter he had within the context of his parents'

---

25. Olivier Messien, *Song of the Deported (Chant des déportés),* trans. Sister Christophora, in *Complete Edition,* 320, emphasis added. Note that the alphabetical index to these liner notes lists the work as *Chants* (plural); presumably this is a typographical error.

When Messiaen writes that "My pain takes the form of a cross," implying that the deportations (including those of Jews) were in some sense a sharing in the suffering and death of Christ, one wonders whether he had been influenced by Jacques Maritain's writings as the Holocaust became public knowledge. Maritain, searching for a theological explanation of the horror, theorized that the Jewish people were undergoing the passion of Christ — in March 1944 he read the Holocaust as "the mass crucifixion of the Jewish people, and that new passion which Christ is now undergoing in His people and race." See Richard Francis Crane, *Passion of Israel: Jacques Maritain, Catholic Conscience, and the Holocaust* (Scranton, Pa.: University of Scranton Press, 2010), 97; and Schloesser review of Crane in *Shofar: An Interdisciplinary Jewish Review* (Spring 2011); http://www.case.edu/artsci/jdst/reviews/Passion.htm.

26. Audrey Ekdahl Davidson, *Olivier Messiaen and the Tristan Myth* (Westport, Conn.: Praeger, 2001); Siglind Bruhn, *Messiaen's Explorations of Love and Death: Musico-poetic Signification in the Tristan Trilogy and Three Related Song Cycles* (Hillsdale, N.Y.: Pendragon Press, 2008).

1943–1949: Postwar Liebestod

somewhat tragic marriage. One also wonders whether, from oral readings of Dostoyevsky's *Brothers Karamazov* to his blind maternal grandfather, Messiaen would have had boyhood memories of these poignant lines: "Because sensual lust is a tempest — worse than a tempest! Beauty is a terrible and awful thing! It is terrible because it has not been fathomed and never can be fathomed, for God sets us nothing but riddles. Here the boundaries meet and all contradictions exist side by side. I am not a cultivated man, brother, but I've thought a lot about this. It's terrible what mysteries there are!"[27] Whether Messiaen remembered this passage or not, it expresses succinctly his own vision of the *terrible,* both aesthetic and religious: "All the traits of God evoke terror."[28]

An invitation to compose incidental music for Lucien Fabre's *Tristan and Isolde* must have come as a timely inspiration, a new opportunity (following the "Controversy") to leave behind explicitly "religious" works. It seems likely that the tandem of public "controversy" and Claire's increasing deterioration at home had become too heavy a burden. Perhaps he also appreciated the possibility of writing in coded language, one provided by a timeless symbolic myth. And yet there is continuity: Messiaen always connected human love with the cosmic. In this he followed his mother's final work, *To Love after Death,* which concludes with the dramatic instructions: "the angels and the young humans lean forward toward one another, making the figure of the mystical union of earth and of heaven."[29]

---

27. Fyodor Dostoyevsky, *The Brothers Karamazov: A Novel in Four Parts and an Epilogue,* trans. Constance Garnett (New York: Macmillan, 1922), 109-10 (book 3, chap. 3). Note the use of the word *terrible* in the 1923 French edition: "Car la sensualité est une tempête, et même quelque chose de plus. La beauté, c'est une chose terrible et affreuse. Terrible, parce qu'indéfinissable, et on ne peut la définir, car Dieu n'a créé que des énigmes. Les extrêmes se rejoignent, les contradictions vivent accouplées." Dostoevsky, *Les Frères Karamazov, roman en quatre parties et un épilogue,* trans. Henri Mongault and Marc Laval, 3 vols. (Paris: Éditions Bossard, 1923). The French translation suggests a "surrealistic" approach: "Extremes rejoin, contradictions live united (literally: 'coupled together' [*accouplées*])."

28. Olivier Messiaen, interview with Patrick Szersnovicz, May 29, 1987, in "Olivier Messiaen: La Liturgie de l'arc-en-ciel," *Le Monde de la Musique* (July/August 1987): 34. See also Messiaen's explanation of "the gift of fear" *(le don de crainte)* in the sense of "awe" or dread; in Olivier Messiaen and Claude Samuel, *Music and Color: Conversations with Claude Samuel,* trans. E. Thomas Glasow (Portland, Ore.: Amadeus Press, 1994), 164-65; hereafter "Messiaen and Samuel (1994)"; and Hello, *Paroles de Dieu,* 225-29.

29. Cécile Sauvage, *Aimer après la mort;* in Cécile Sauvage and Béatrice Marchal-Vincent, *L'Œuvre poétique de Cécile Sauvage (1883-1927),* 2 vols. (Lille: Atelier National de Reproduction des Thèses, 1995), 2:216.

1943–1992: Legacy

1945: *Harawi* — Postwar Surrealism

On May 8, 1945, the Germans surrendered unconditionally and the war in Europe ended. About two months later, on July 17, Messiaen, Claire, and Pascal left Paris for vacation in Grenoble.[30] Messiaen composed *Harawi* — the "incidental music" for Tristan — within two months, finishing the work by September 17. The Grenoble vacation must have been somewhat grim. Claire's illness had become so erratic that Messiaen feared for his scores; Loriod, who, like Mélisande, had emerged in the middle of an obscure forest, was back in Paris. And the "Messiaen Controversy" refused to die. A month after Messiaen returned to Paris from summer vacation, the Jesuit monthly *Études* published "Music and Mystic: The Messiaen 'Controversy'" in October; it was soon followed by another article entitled "Olivier Messiaen: Mystical Composer?" in December.[31] The opaque hybridization of Norse and Peruvian themes in *Harawi*, woven together in surrealist fragments, must have seemed attractive.

Hawari is subtitled *Song of Love and Death*. The French title *(Chant d'Amour et de Mort)* is a play on words that doesn't translate into English: the words *d'Amour* and *de Mort* are near homophones — that is, the words "love" and "death" sound nearly the same in French. This would seem to be Messiaen's evocation of Wagner's *"Liebestod"* (love-death), the final dramatic aria in *Tristan and Isolde* in which erotic love can be consummated only after death. Messiaen said that he borrowed from Wagner's love-death "only the idea of a love that is fatal, irreversible, that in theory leads on to death and, in a certain way, calls upon death, for it is a love that goes beyond the soul, a cosmic love."[32] Note too: the pronunciation of Messiaen's *Chant d'Amour et de Mort* is a near echo of his mother's *Aimer après la mort (To Love after Death)*.

One scholar who had numerous conversations with the composer has interpreted *Harawi* as a lament for Messiaen's passionate love for Loriod, which cannot be consummated in this life.

---

30. Hill and Simeone, *Messiaen*, 154-55; Simeone, *Bibliographical Catalogue*, 92-94. Simeone's note that Claire had entered a sanatorium by this time was written before his access to the Messiaen archives. I am grateful to Nigel Simeone for verifying the correct date of 1953.

31. Bernard Gavoty, "Musique et mystique: Le 'Cas' Messiaen," *Études* (October 1945): 21-37; Henry Barraud, "Olivier Messiaen: Compositeur mystique?" *Contrepoints* 1 (December 1945): 101-2.

32. Messiaen, quoted by Renaud Machart in liner notes for *Harawi*, trans. Daphné Anglès, in *Complete Edition*, 253-54, at 253.

1943–1949: Postwar Liebestod

In reality separated from his wife who had to live for many years in a nursing home, Messiaen remained joined to her until her death by the sacrament of marriage. He was overwhelmed, however, by a love of unique force and depth, which precisely mirrored the legendary love of Tristan and [Isolde], or, much closer to our own times, the passion which Wagner and Mathilde Wesendonk felt for each other, a passion which finds its artistic transfiguration in Wagner's *Tristan*. Messiaen . . . lived throughout these years, blazing and pure, joined only in spirit and communing through music alone with the object of his passion.[33]

However, a more recent, second interpretation of *Harawi* has been offered by Messiaen's biographers. Here, the focus is not Loriod but Delbos: "Seeing Claire as the subject of *Harawi* explains the work's mood of almost unbearably passionate lament."[34] This interpretation is based on the specific genre of the *harawi* — namely, a Peruvian love song that is also a lament in which the lovers are destined to be united only in death. (Again Cécile: "to love after death.") As noted in the discussion of Messiaen's *Preludes,* Messiaen had most likely encountered the *harawi* in *The Music of the Incas* soon after its 1925 publication.[35] The dove in *Preludes* evokes his mother's death.

In *Harawi,* the dove returns, but now as a surreal green dove. Messiaen explained: "At the time I wrote [*Harawi*] I was a great reader of Pierre Reverdy and Paul Eluard, and also a very good book by André Breton on Surrealism and painting. It is thus an almost entirely Surrealist work, apart from some images borrowed from the mountains of the Dauphiné (because I have never seen the Andes *cordillera*), and certain Peruvian Surrealist phrases such as the 'green dove.' The dove is a symbol for a girl in Peru, and the color green represents spring."[36] Interpreting *Harawi* as a lamentation for Claire rests on the work's structure of twelve songs and noting that the "Farewell" comes

---

33. Antoine Goléa, in Hill and Simeone, *Messiaen,* 157.

34. Hill and Simeone, *Messiaen,* 158.

35. Hill and Simeone, *Messiaen,* 156. See Raoul d'Harcourt and M. d'Harcourt, *La Musique des Incas et ses survivances,* 2 vols. (Paris: Librairie Orientaliste Paul Geuthner, 1925).

36. Interview with Antoine Goléa, in Hill and Simeone, *Messiaen,* 157. The painting is Roland Pemrose's *Seeing Is Believing (L'Île invisible)* (1937). The publication reference is to André Breton, *Le surréalisme et la peinture; suivi de Genèse et perspective artistiques du surréalisme et de fragments inédits* (New York: Brentano's, 1945); a new edition of an earlier publication, André Breton and Max Ernst, *Le Surréalisme et la peinture: avec 77 photogravures d'après Max Ernst* (Paris: Gallimard, 1928). As Hill and Simeone note (393 n. 24), Messiaen also knew Breton's *Second Manifesto of Surrealism* (1930) well. Cf. Messiaen to Éluard, March 13, 1945, and undated.

not at the end of the work but at the "midpoint."³⁷ The lovers part in song #7, "Farewell" ("Adieu"), where the love theme of the "green dove" (song #2) appears a second time:

> Farewell, green dove,
> Farewell, limpid pearl.

But this is not the story's end: in song #9 the lovers are reunited after death:

> Let us invent the love of the world
> To seek each other, to weep for us,
> To dream of us,
> To find us....³⁸

In #10, "Love Bird of a Star," serenity is regained. The imagery of eyes, birds, and stars in these final lines echoes the love song to Claire in *Songs of Earth and Sky*.

Songs of Earth and Sky (1938) "Union with Mi"	*Harawi* (1945) "Love Bird of a Star"
Your mortal eye, / my mortal eye, our mortal hands, / to weave the atmosphere, the mountain of the atmosphere.	Star bird, / your eye, singing towards the stars,
Star of silence / for my mortal heart, to my mortal lips, / little ball of sun complementary to my earth.	Your head uplifted under the sky. Your starry sky, / falling chains, towards the stars, The shortest path from shadow to heaven.
	All the birds of the stars, ...
The union, My sweet companion to my bitter shoulder.	Star, increased silence of heaven. your eye, your neck, the sky.³⁹

---

37. Interpretation here following is in Hill and Simeone, *Messiaen*, 159.

38. Olivier Messiaen, *Harawi: A Song of Love and Death (Harawi. Chant d'Amour et de Mort)*, trans. Universal Music Classics France, in *Complete Edition*, 320-27, at 322, 325, translation altered.

39. Messiaen, "Union with Mi *(for my wife)* ("Bail avec Mi [*pour ma femme*]"), in *Songs*

1943–1949: Postwar Liebestod

In this view, Messiaen has written a lament for Claire, mourning that their love can only be consummated after death.

However, a third interpretation occurs, traceable to both Dostoyevsky and Breton: a surrealist interpretation in which time and timelessness, life and death, are not simple contradictions but rather two conjoined (or coupled) aspects of a single reality. Imagine the piece as yet another *Diptych,* not unlike the one Messiaen wrote for organ immediately after Cécile's death, subtitled *An Essay on Terrestrial Life and Blessed Eternity* (1930). *Harawi*'s structure would have two wings or panels:

1. The sleeping city, you
  2. Good morning, green dove
    3. Mountains
      4. Doundou tchil
        5. The love of Piroutcha
          6. *Planetary repetition*   [*eternity*]
          7. *Farewell*   [*temporality*]
        8. Syllables
      9. The stair repeats, gestures of the sun
    10. Love bird of a star
  11. Katchikatchi the stars
12. In the dark

Because of the even number of movements, there is no "midpoint," strictly speaking; there is, instead, the side-by-side juxtaposition of "planetary repetition" — which in the thought of Aristotle and Aquinas is the nearest approximation to "eternity" that can be found in temporality — and "farewell," the very essence of time passing and the dissolution of things. In other words, the two central movements constitute the juxtaposition of diametrical opposites. Situating this construction in the context of Messiaen's postwar immersion in surrealism, the words of Breton's *Second Manifesto of Surrealism* take on added significance: "Everything tends to make us believe that there exists a certain point of the mind at which life and death ... cease to be perceived as contradictions."[40]

---

of Earth and Sky, trans. John Underwood, in *Complete Edition,* 308-9; "Love Bird of a Star" ("Amour oiseau d'étoile"), in *Harawi,* 325-26.

40. André Breton, *Manifestoes of Surrealism,* trans. Richard Seaver and Helen R. Lane (Ann Arbor: University of Michigan Press, [1969] 1972), 123-24.

Although the first half of *Harawi* seems to be temporal with "Farewell" signaling the end of existence, the preceding "Planetary repetition" suggests otherwise (as does the following repeating staircase evoking Claire's first appearance in *The Death of Number* [1930]). From a perspective both Christian and surrealist, life and death are somehow inextricably linked.

However we interpret *Harawi*, note that almost one decade earlier Messiaen had written "The Two Warriors" (1936) with the supreme confidence (one might say arrogance) of a recently-wed twenty-seven-year-old:

Behold us two in one.
Forward! . . .
Forward sacramental warriors! . . .
You will arrive at the gates of the City.[41]

In the summer of 1945 — after a decade marked by war, imprisonment, exile, separation, reunion, and increasing dementia — the song was still about a city.

Farewell to thee, green dove,
saddened angel. . . .

My love, my breath!
Dove, green dove,
the figure five for thee,
the double violet will double,
far away, so quietly.
The sleeping city.[42]

But the ravages of time had tempered the vision. Modesty replaced militancy; the Bible's white dove acquired a green Incan surrealist coat; and the "city" was quietly left to rest in lower case.

Harawi was first performed at a concert in a private home on June 26, 1946. Marcelle Bunlet sang, Messiaen accompanied on piano, Loriod turned pages, and Claire sat in the audience. The following evening was the work's first public performance in Brussels; a second followed the next day in Ant-

---

41. Messiaen, "The Two Warriors," in *Poems for Mi,* trans. Felix Aprahamian, in Messiaen, *Complete Edition,* 307.

42. Messiaen, "Farewell" ("Adieu") and "In the Dark" ("Dans le noir"), in *Harawi,* 322-23, 326-27.

werp. Reversing years of practice, Messiaen provided no commentary for the work — "surely a most eloquent silence."[43]

1946–1949: *Turangalîla* and Tanglewood: Cold War Holidays

By October 10, 1945, Messiaen had been commissioned by Serge Koussevitzky, longtime music director of the Boston Symphony Orchestra from 1924 to 1949, to write a symphonic work.[44] Already in the 1920s, Koussevitzky had been a great champion of contemporary music and commissioned a number of such works, including Prokofiev's *Fourth Symphony* (1929), Stravinsky's *Symphony of Psalms* (1930), and Ravel's *Piano Concerto in G* (1929-1931). After his second wife died in 1942, he founded the Koussevitzky Music Foundations in her honor, to support the composition of new music, including Messiaen's commission. Beginning in late October 1945, Messiaen's project evolved gradually, achieving its completion in 1948 as the mammoth *Turangalîla Symphony*.[45]

Turangalîla's composition takes Messiaen's story out of France and into the infinitely expanded, new postwar world. Perhaps his awareness of this broad new horizon accounted for its overwhelming scale. The world war was over and the Cold War was under way as European nations were aligned (even divided within themselves like Germany) with either the USA or the USSR. Czechoslovakia serves as a particularly poignant example of this ongoing shift. On March 5, 1946, Winston Churchill delivered his "Iron Curtain" speech at Westminster College in Fulton, Missouri. "From Stettin in the Baltic to Trieste in the Adriatic," he warned, "an 'iron curtain' has descended across the Continent. Behind that line lie all the capitals of the ancient states of Central and Eastern Europe." That same March, Messiaen and Loriod traveled to Prague for several concerts.

However, just two years later, a series of intervening events made such a visit impossible (or at least not a simple task). In 1947, the United States announced the European Recovery Program, better known as the "Marshall Plan," a massive American investment in European infrastructure intended to rebuild economies and bolster confidence in democracy. The Soviets retaliated with a Czechoslovakian coup d'état in February 1948. That June, the Soviets blockaded the city of West Berlin. The Berlin airlift would last until the following May, 1949.

43. Hill and Simeone, *Messiaen*, 164.
44. Hill and Simeone, *Messiaen*, 160.
45. Simeone, *Bibliographical Catalogue*, 95-99.

1943–1992: Legacy

One effort to firm up transatlantic relations entailed cultural exchanges between the USA and other nations, including France. The Fulbright student exchange program was founded in 1946. It was to the benefit of the postwar boom in air travel that government and industry strategized to make France an attractive American tourist destination. The American film industry, one small player in a much broader "cultural Cold War" (heavily funded by the CIA), created nostalgic and alluring images of France at a time when the country itself was still in postwar turmoil.[46] Vincente Minnelli's *An American in Paris* (1951), employing the music of a 1928 George Gershwin composition, garnered numerous Academy Awards; so too would Minnelli's extravagant MGM musical *Gigi* (1958), starring Maurice Chevalier. (Chevalier, who had been accused of collaboration in the postwar "cleansing," was personally rescued by the testimony of General Dwight D. Eisenhower, soon to become president.) The *Turangalîla* played a role in this transatlantic context and, as a result, a key role in catapulting Messiaen to international prominence.

Messiaen finished the symphony in December 1948. In one of its later stages, it seems to have consisted of nine movements — an odd number would have provided a distinctive midpoint. However, the final version consisted of ten movements, an even number placing the structure's center weight on the juxtaposition of two contrasting elements, most conducive to a surrealist perspective:

1. "Introduction" (Moderate, somewhat fast)
2. "Love Song 1" (Moderate, heavy)
3. "Turangalîla 1" (Almost slow, dreamy)
4. "Love Song 2" (Moderate)
5. *"Joy of the Blood of the Stars" (Fast, passionate, with joy)*
6. *"Garden of Love's Sleep" (Very moderate, very tender)*
7. "Turangalîla 2" (Somewhat fast — moderate)
8. "Development of Love" (Moderate)
9. "Turangalîla 3" (Moderate)
10. "Finale" (Moderate, almost fast, with a great joy)

46. Richard T. Arndt and David Lee Rubin, *The Fulbright Difference, 1948-1992* (New Brunswick, N.J.: Transaction, 1993); Christopher Endy, *Cold War Holidays: American Tourism in France* (Chapel Hill: University of North Carolina Press, 2004); Tony Shaw, *Hollywood's Cold War* (Edinburgh: Edinburgh University Press, 2007). For bibliography on CIA see p. 489 n. 1, in chapter 11, below, introducing the 1950s.

Recall that the "Amen of Desire" had juxtaposed two motives within a single movement: first, a "slow, ecstatic, longing of a deep tenderness: already the calm perfume of Paradise"; and second, "extremely passionate: the soul is pulled by a terrible love [*amour terrible*] which expresses itself in a carnal [*charnelle*] manner."[47] Now, five years later, these two motives find individual expression in two self-enclosed pieces: movements 5 and 6.

The "extremely passionate" motive is expressed in "Joy of the Blood of the Stars," the title itself a surrealist image juxtaposing oppositions: the violence of "blood" is juxtaposed with joy while its thick liquid viscosity is juxtaposed with the fire and light of stars. Messiaen called this piece "a long, frenetic dance of joy." (Recall the *danse sauvage* of the stars and Saturn in Vision 2 of *Visions of Amen*.) He continued: "In order to understand the qualities of excess in the movement, one must remember that the union of true lovers is for them a transformation, and a transformation on a cosmic scale."[48] For support and illustration he then cites Breton, Shakespeare's *Romeo and Juliet*, and the myth of Tristan and Isolde.

A contrasting slow ecstatic longing is represented in "Garden of Love's Sleep." Messiaen calls this movement a "single expansive phrase on the 'love theme,'" and sees it as being "in total contrast with its predecessor. The two lovers are enclosed in love's sleep, landscape comes out of them. The garden around them is called Tristan; the garden around them is called [Isolde]. It is a garden full of shadow and light, of new plants and flowers, of bright and melodious birds. 'All the birds of the stars . . .' to quote *Harawi*. Time flows forgotten. The lovers are outside time: let us not wake them."[49]

One of the most interesting aspects of *Turangalîla Symphony* is the way it is an extended meditation on time and timelessness. These themes emerged in Messiaen's very earliest writings, but in 1945-1948 they are more overtly connected with the complicated inner world of human desire. Movement 5 is a surrealistic juxtaposition of passionate violence; movement 6 is its opposing contrast, an experience of lovers suspended in time, outside time, time forgotten.

Messiaen's penchant for juxtaposition returns in movement 8, "Develop-

---

47. See above, pp. 359, 367-72.

48. Olivier Messiaen, notes on *Turangalîla-Symphonie* (1948), trans. Paul Griffiths, in *Complete Edition*, 275-82; here, notes on movement 5, "Joy of the Blood of the Stars," 280.

49. Messiaen, notes on movement 6, "Garden of Love's Sleep," *Turangalîla-Symphonie*, in *Complete Edition*, 281. The metaphor of the garden comes from Song of Songs 4:12: "Ma sœur, mon épouse est un jardin fermé; elle est un jardin fermé, une fontaine scellée" (Fillion).

ment of Love." "This terrible title," writes Messiaen — again, *terrible* — "can be understood in two ways." First, it means love as a "constantly growing passion, multiplying itself to the infinite" — mortal beings who are finite in space suddenly find themselves expanded into infinity. Second, it means infinity in time as well — forever and ever: "Lovers who can never detach themselves, like Tristan and [Isolde], whom the 'love potion' has united for ever."[50]

Messiaen seems to have read a well-known text attributed to Pascal and circulated by late-nineteenth-century symbolists like the painter Gustave Moreau:

> human knowledge [*la connaissance humaine*]
> is like a sphere which
> will grow without ceasing as
> it increases its volume, increasing
> the number of contact points
> with the unknown [*avec l'inconnu*].[51]

Whether or not Pascal actually wrote these words, they do sum up his fundamental view about what causes human beings to experience "anxiety" or "dread" — that is, the *terrible*. For Pascal, humans are finite beings "suspended" between two "abysses." One is the abyss of infinity or "being"; thanks to human knowledge, humanity can approach this unknown asymptotically. The other is the abyss of "nothingness," that is, where finitude diminishes to the point of zero; due to human animality, humanity also approaches this abyss in death.[52]

"Development of Love" is yet another expression of this quintessentially modern picture of the human being as a finite-infinite hybrid — and hence, "anxious." Love's "development" is "terrifying" because the *infinite* is at stake. Infinity makes things "terrible" for finite mortals, in both space (desire's "con-

---

50. Messiaen, notes on movement 8, "Development of Love," *Turangalîla-Symphonie*, in *Complete Edition*, 281.

51. Attributed to Blaise Pascal; quoted in Stephen Schloesser, "1871-1901: Realism, Symbolism, Mystic Modernism," in *Mystic Masque: Reality and Semblance in Georges Rouault, 1871-1958*, ed. Stephen Schloesser (Chestnut Hill, Mass.: McMullen Museum of Art, distributed by the University of Chicago Press, 2008), 23-43, at 37.

52. On the "abyss" in Messiaen, see Aloyse Michaely, "L'Abîme, Das Bild des Abgrunds bei Olivier Messiaen," *Musik-Konzepte 28: Olivier Messiaen* 28 (November 1982): 7-55; and Michaely, *Die Musik Olivier Messiaens: Untersuchungen zum Gesamtschaffen* (Hamburg: Verlag der Musikalienhandlung K. D. Wagner, 1987), 1 (658)-17 (674).

stantly growing passion, multiplying itself to the infinite") and time ("united for ever").[53]

Interpreting "Development of Love" (movement 8) this way explains in turn "Turangalîla 2" (movement 7). Messiaen's excursus on "Turangalîla 2" recalls a line from *The Death of Number* (1930) originating in Edgar Allan Poe: "wall that crushes me!" Almost two decades later, he returned to this same terror that comes with time and space "closing in" on a person: "a terrifying rhythm, using the 'chords theme' and the metal percussion, giving a double sensation of expansion and of retrenchment of height and of depth, each cycle ending in a great stroke on the tam-tam. This recalls the double terror of the pendulum blade slowly getting nearer the heart of the prisoner while the wall of red-hot iron closes in on him, and the unspeakable, indescribable depth of the torture pit, in Edgar Allan Poe's celebrated story *The Pit and the Pendulum*."[54] The "double terror" is that of time and space: spatialized time represented by the pendulum and its blade coming ever closer; the shrinking of space represented by the red-hot walls closing in; and finally, Pascal's abyss over which human beings are suspended, represented by the "indescribable depth of the torture pit."

In light of these considerations of being and nothingness, infinity and finitude, timelessness and time, and human beings suspended over the abyss, Messiaen's construction of movements is clear:

Movement 5 ("Joy of the Blood of the Stars"): the finitude of true lovers is nearly infinite — "transformation on a cosmic scale."
Movement 6 ("Garden of Love's Sleep"): the lovers are "outside time," in a sense rescued from the dilemma of human anxiety.
Movement 7 ("Turangalîla 2"): the "double terror" of both time (pendulum) and space (abyss).
Movement 8 ("Development of Love"): the "terrible title" evokes those "Lovers who can never detach themselves, like Tristan and [Isolde], whom the 'love potion' united for ever," that is, for eternity.

While movements 5 and 6 may be the midpoint, Messiaen calls movement 8 the "peak of the whole" ten-movement symphony. The two individual figures

---

53. Messiaen, notes on movement 8, "Development of Love," *Turangalîla-Symphonie,* in *Complete Edition,* 281.

54. Messiaen, notes on movement 7, "Turangalîla 2," *Turangalîla-Symphonie,* in *Complete Edition,* 281. For Poe, see analysis of *The Death of Number;* for tam-tam and "Pit and the Pendulum," see analysis of the "Amen of Judgment," pp. 117, 423-24, 427-31 above.

of Tristan and Isolde are now "transcended by Tristan-Isolde" — that is, the alchemical union of the two as one. Here, Messiaen concludes, as the tam-tam is struck one last time, "one hears resonances from the *languages of the beyond,* and the 'statue theme' *bends over the abyss.*"[55] In the "Finale" (movement 10), the "love theme" melody "rests in suspense, in a state of luminous expectation, and this great gesture towards an end that does not exist (Glory and Joy are without end) attracts and inspires the coda, a brilliant, vehement peroration on the first theme," a fanfare for trumpets and horns.[56]

Having finished the symphony in December 1948, Messiaen traveled to the USA in July 1949 to lecture on composition at Tanglewood, the Boston Symphony's summertime home and educational outreach center. On August 14, Koussevitsky concluded the Berkshire Festival with a performance of Messiaen's *Ascension* suite. Messiaen left for France in late August, but returned to America in late November for the December 2 premiere of the *Turangalîla* at Symphony Hall in Boston. Leonard Bernstein conducted and Yvonne Loriod played the piano.[57] Soon afterward, the New Year inaugurated the 1950s. The Boston premiere offered a preview of the international stature that Messiaen would acquire throughout the coming decade.

1948: *Five Refrains (Cinq Rechants)*

However, as public acclaim grew, Messiaen's domestic life declined. Perhaps nothing encapsulates this inverse relationship more than the composition of *Five Refrains,* the third and final work of the "Tristan Trilogy." After Messiaen had finished composition of the *Turangalîla* on November 29, he immediately began composing *Five Refrains;* it was likely finished within two months, since he received payment for it in early February 1949.[58] During its

---

55. Messiaen, notes on movement 8, "Development of Love," *Turangalîla-Symphonie,* in *Complete Edition,* 281, 282, emphasis added. For the "abyss" see Pascal, Baudelaire, the "Hands of the Abyss" in *Livre d'orgue* (1951), and Michaely, "L'Abîme, Das Bild des Abgrunds bei Olivier Messiaen." For "languages of the beyond" *(les langages de l'au-delà),* compare "Illuminations from the Beyond . . ." ("Éclairs sur l'Au-Delà . . .") (1991), Messiaen's final completed work (premiered posthumously).

56. Messiaen, notes on movement 10, "Finale," *Turangalîla-Symphonie,* in *Complete Edition,* 282.

57. Hill and Simeone, *Messiaen,* 187-93. Note photo from Tanglewood, 1949: Messiaen with Koussevitzky, Aaron Copland, and Leonard Bernstein, 188, fig. 95.

58. Simeone, *Bibliographical Catalogue,* 102-3; Hill and Simeone, *Messiaen,* 179-80.

composition, Claire underwent a hysterectomy in January. Perhaps because of the effects of a general anesthetic, the operation was performed with an epidural; this would later be blamed for "a drastic further deterioration in her memory."[59] Claire's erratic behavior made life in their Paris home chaotic and increasingly difficult for Messiaen; he could not find the peaceful space in which to compose, and when he did write, he feared for the safety of his manuscripts. As Claire spent more and more time alone at Neussargues, the two lived increasingly separate lives. This is the domestic context in which *Five Refrains* was written.

The title of the work came from the poem "Le Printemps" ("Spring") by Claude Le Jeune (ca. 1528-1600), the most famous composer of French secular music in the sixteenth century. Messiaen writes that there are three traditional elements in *Five Refrains*:

> In [Le Jeune's] *Spring,* the couplets are called *chants* and the refrains *rechants.* . . . The melodic sources [of *Five Refrains*] are twofold: the *harawi* or *yaravi,* a folkloristic love-song from Peru and Ecuador; and the *alba,* a medieval morning-song, in which a supernatural voice warns the lovers that the night of love is about to end (listen to the love-songs by the troubadour Jaufré Rudel, to the *alba* by the troubadour Folquet de Marseille, and also, in the same spirit, to Brangäne's voice in the second Act of Wagner's *Tristan,* and to certain words of Shakespeare's Juliet or Debussy's Mélisande . . .).[60]

The *harawi* genre is familiar from both *Preludes* and *Harawi*: it is a love song–lamentation in which lovers are destined to be united only in death. The medieval literary genre of the alba (from the Latin for "dawn") also intimates doomed (or at least dangerously clandestine) love. The alba, "or dawn song, is sung by a lover whose secret tryst with a beloved is interrupted by the rising of the sun, which signals the end of their meeting." In Old Provençal (of which Messiaen would have been deeply aware, given his mother's connections to Avignon and Mistral), the word *alba* means "white" and evokes the brightness of dawn. An alba is characterized by "its theme of separation, its use of dia-

---

59. Hill and Simeone, *Messiaen,* 179.
60. Olivier Messiaen, liner notes for *Five Refrains (Cinq Rechants),* in Messiaen, *Complete Edition,* 126-27 (Fr), 255-56 (Eng); reprint from Messiaen, *Quatour pour la Fin du Temps. Cinq Rechants,* performed by Solistes des Choeurs de l'O.R.T.F. et al., under the direction of Marcel Couraud, trans. Universal Music Classics France (Paris: Erato Disques S.A., [1963, 1968] 1993), 9-10 (Fr), 17-18 (Eng). Translation altered.

logue," and "the use of a watchman figure."[61] Among the most familiar albas might be the predawn argument between Romeo and Juliet. Romeo argues:

> It was the lark, the herald of the morn,
> No nightingale. Look, love, what envious streaks
> Do lace the severing clouds in yonder east.
> Night's candles are burnt out, and jocund day
> Stands tiptoe on the misty mountain tops.
> I must be gone and live, or stay and die.[62]

Messiaen explicitly referred to Shakespeare's passage in his writings, but the alba in *Five Refrains* most immediately refers to Brangäne's "dawn song" in *Tristan*, which Messiaen once described as the "most beautiful page in Wagner."[63] Ultimately, the alba is a poem of grief — "grief for what one has and now must lose"; the "unwilling departure of the lover is normally surrounded by a note of somber heroism in the face of a climactic and really formidable separation."[64]

A polyphonic work written for twelve voices (three sopranos, three altos, three tenors, three basses), *Five Refrains* was "absolutely new" in every respect, including its difficulty, making "everything written up until then seem like child's play."[65] Even the text was challenging. Lines in medieval French following Le Jeune's "chant" and "rechant" pattern are interwoven with a second text written "in an imaginary language, with Sanskrit consonances, and syllables 'chosen for their aptitude in stressing the music.'"[66] In his prefatory

---

61. Sigrid Kind, "Lyric," in *Encyclopedia of Medieval Literature*, ed. Robert T. Lambdin and Laura C. Lambdin (Westport, Conn.: Greenwood Press, 2000), 362-76, at 370; cf. Gale Sigal, *Erotic Dawn-Songs of the Middle Ages: Voicing the Lyric Lady* (Gainesville: University Press of Florida, 1996).

62. William Shakespeare, *Romeo and Juliet*, act 3, scene 5, lines 6-11; in *The Arden Shakespeare Complete Works*, ed. Richard Proudfoot, Ann Thompson, and David Scott Kastan, rev. ed. (London: Arden Shakespeare, 2011), 1028.

63. Messiaen, interview with Antoine Goléa; in Hill and Simeone, *Messiaen*, 180.

64. Sara Thorne-Thomsen, "'Adam's Aubade' and the Medieval Alba," *South Atlantic Review* 54, no. 1 (January 1989): 13-26, at 14-15; quoting R. E. Kaske, "The Aube in Chaucer's *Troilus*," in *Chaucer Criticism: Troilus and Criseyde and the Minor Poems*, ed. Richard J. Schoeck and Jerome Taylor, 2 vols. (Notre Dame, Ind.: University of Notre Dame Press, 1961), 2:167-79; and Jonathan Saville, *The Medieval Erotic Alba: Structure as Meaning* (New York: Columbia University Press, 1972).

65. Marcel Couraud in 1953 recalling his first encounter with *Five Refrains*; in Hill and Simeone, *Messiaen*, 183.

66. Hill and Simeone, *Messiaen*, 181.

note to the text, Messiaen simply instructed that the "words in imaginary or pseudo-Hindu language should be pronounced as written."[67]

What is the point of Messiaen's increased turn to abstraction and surrealist juxtapositions — now not merely the explosive juxtapositions of incongruent imagery, but the invention of an imaginary language intertwined with late-medieval French? His biographers interpret it "as an expression — albeit sublimated, and in heavily disguised Surrealist code — of Messiaen's agonizing predicament."[68] This provides a key to understanding the "Tristan Trilogy": if *Harawi* (1945) can be seen as a final "passionate elegy to Claire," *Five Refrains* (1948), half written in secret code, suggests that a fateful eternal step has been taken with Loriod. In between the two stands *Turangalîla Symphony* (composed 1946-1948), an extended meditation on love as something both placid and frenzied, contemplative and *terrible*. In the notes for "Garden of Love's Sleep," Messiaen had written of the lovers' eternity: "The lovers are out of time: let us not wake them."[69] But *Five Refrains* is built around the alba: it is dawn now and the time for dreaming is over — time to wake up.

By December 19, 1949, *Five Refrains* had been performed and published; it was performed a second time in May 1950. As the work closes Messiaen's "Tristan Trilogy" of the late 1940s, it also *seems* to mark a chasm of sorts, because the compositions of the 1950s, primarily using birdsong, seem to have no connection to what preceded. However, if we focus on the "coded" aspect of *Harawi*, but even more so *Five Refrains*, there is more continuity than is first apparent. Messiaen's work in the next decade, primarily using the songs of birds as his "texts," might be viewed as a continuation of his desire at the end of the 1940s to express himself in coded language — a nonhuman extension beyond the "imaginary or pseudo-Hindu language" of *Five Refrains*. Messiaen's experimentalism was certainly at one with the dominant currents of 1950s musical avant-gardism. But it is also worth considering whether the circumstances of his personal life impelled him toward the composition of works based on linguistic codes that were thoroughly expressive and yet remained largely known only to him (and perhaps Loriod, their main interpreter).

Moreover, birdsong is a remarkable thing in that it is both fixed and eternal while at the same time capable of endless improvised variations in time.[70] Birdsong possesses the same double-edged (or surrealistic) mixture of time

---

67. Simeone, *Bibliographical Catalogue*, 103.
68. Hill and Simeone, *Messiaen*, 182.
69. Messiaen, notes for "Garden of Love's Sleep," in *Complete Edition*, 281.
70. I am grateful to Paul Breines for this suggestion.

and eternity — a hope in the transcendence of death — that Messiaen imagined in *Five Refrains:* "the Beloved One is standing above Time, beyond any musical, rhythmical or literary technique, even beyond death, like Edgar Poe's Ligeia, while, very mysteriously, 'her eyes keep wandering, into the past, into the future....'"[71]

* * *

Before leaving the 1940s, we must note the germ of an idea that would not be realized for another thirty years. Messiaen would later say, commenting on his massive opera, *Saint Francis of Assisi* (composed 1975-1983), that he had been thinking about his subject "for thirty years without imagining what it might lead to."[72] Certainly, his immersion in birdsong during the 1950s would provide a fitting context in which to situate the saint who legend says famously preached a sermon to the birds.

However, Messiaen's dating of three decades prior to 1975 indicates 1945 — and here, a more specific source for thinking about Saint Francis would have been the publication of his father Pierre's scholarly edition of *The Little Flowers: Life and Miracles of Saint Francis of Assisi, of His Companions, and of Saint Claire* (1947).[73] Also, in 1950 Roberto Rossellini released his postwar neorealist film, *The Flowers of St. Francis* (in Italian, *Francesco, giullare di Dio*,

71. Messiaen, notes for *Five Refrains*, in *Complete Edition*, 255-56, at 256. The reference is to the character whose name becomes the title of Edgar Allan Poe's short story "Ligeia" (1838). The story might be based on one of Poe's opium hallucinations.

72. Messiaen and Samuel (1994), 216; in Simeone, *Bibliographical Catalogue*, 165.

73. Godefroy de Paris, *Les Fioretti: vie et miracles de saint François d'Assise, de ses compagnons et de sainte Claire*, trans. and ed. Pierre Messiaen (Paris: La Renaissance du livre: Marcel Daubin, 1947). This book was published in the Histoire, Philosophie, Religion series, of which Pierre was the general editor. The copy I consulted (from the library at Tulane University) has an inscription: "À Madame et à Garrett Mattingly. Cordial hommage. P. Messiaen — ." Mattingly (1900-1962), professor of European history at Columbia University, had spent the academic year 1937-1938 on a Guggenheim Fellowship researching in European archives. Three years later, just before the United States entered the war, he published *Catherine of Aragon* (Boston: Little, Brown, 1941).

Messiaen might have been introduced to the topic even earlier by G. K. Chesterton's *Saint François d'Assise*, trans. Isabelle Rivière, Le Roseau d'or Oeuvres et Chroniques series, no. 4 (Paris: Plon-Nourrit et Cie, 1925); original Chesterton, *St. Francis of Assisi* (London and Toronto: Hodder and Stoughton, 1923). The French translation of the newly converted Chesterton's work would have piqued Pierre Messiaen's interest. Chesterton, who had converted in 1922, famously said that he had turned to Catholicism because it was the only religion that could have produced a Saint Francis. The Roseau d'or series was a publishing

1943-1949: Postwar Liebestod

or "Francis, Jester of God"), cowritten by Rossellini and Federico Fellini. Although Messiaen's *Saint Francis* opera would not premiere for another thirty years (in late 1983) — following the upheavals of the 1960s and 1970s — Messiaen traced its inspiration back to this immediate postwar period.[74]

---

venture of Jacques Maritain. See Stephen Schloesser, *Jazz Age Catholicism: Mystic Modernism in Postwar Paris, 1919-1933* (Toronto: University of Toronto Press, 2005), 181-85.

74. However, 1983 was the same year that Julien Green, long associated with Catholic Revivalism, published his own approach to Saint Francis, one that would attain immediate successive and multiple translations. See Green, *Frère François* (Paris: Éditions du Seuil, 1983); cf. Green, *God's Fool: The Life and Times of Francis of Assisi,* trans. Peter Heinegg (San Francisco: Harper and Row, 1985). For Green's close association with Maritain, including his anxieties over homosexuality, see Schloesser, *Jazz Age Catholicism,* 184, 202-3.

In addition to Chesterton's *Saint François,* other interwar works devoted to the saint included the following: Saint Francis of Assisi, *Les petites fleurs de saint François d'Assise,* trans. André Pératé, illustrated by Maurice Denis (Paris: Impr. et Libr. de l'Art catholique, 1926); Saint Francis, *Les Petites Fleurs,* trans. Frédéric Ozanam (Paris: Payot, 1927); Francis Jammes, *Le Rêve franciscain. Suivi des Petites fleurs de saint François d'Assise,* trans. Frédéric Ozanam, illustrated by Angelina Beloff (Paris: l'Adolescence catholique, 1927); *Les Petites Fleurs de saint François,* original watercolors by Émile Bernard, wood engravings printed by Marthe Féguet (Paris: Ambroise Vollard, 1928); Saint Francis of Assisi, *Les petites fleurs* (Paris: Librairie de l'Art catholique, 1946); Saint Francis, *Les petites fleurs de saint François d'Assise: (fioretti) suivies des considérations des très saints stimates,* trans. T. de Wyzewa (Paris: Librairie académique Perrin, 1947). For an overview of Saint Francis in French literary culture, see Damien Vorreux, *François d'Assise dans les lettres françaises* (Paris: Desclée de Brouwer, 1988). Finally, note that Charles Tournemire had composed and published *Sei fioretti. Pages d'orgue,* op. 60, 2 vols. (Paris: Hérelle, 1933).

CHAPTER 11

1949–1959

Cold War Ornithology

The 1950s are primarily marked by Messiaen's monumental *Catalogue of Birds* and the research that preceded the composition. On the domestic scene, *Five Refrains* had first been performed by the date of their publication, December 19, 1949. Almost four years later to the day, Claire was diagnosed with "incurable cerebral atrophy," on December 18, 1953. She was brought to a nursing home from which she would never leave, dying five and a half years later on April 22, 1959. The 1950s were thus a period of inexpressible tragedy for Messiaen. Perhaps this is why the "texts" upon which he commented during this period were songs without words provided by birds.

1949–1953: Rhythmic Études and Organ Works

Messiaen's initial work during the 1950s is inextricably linked with the new Cold War situation, especially the newly created nation of West Germany after the postwar division between the Soviets and the Western Allies. The year 1949 signaled a turning point in the transition from the extremely brief postwar honeymoon period (during which the USA and USSR had been allies) to a new "cold" wartime era: in May the Berlin airlift ended, signaling the permanent division of the city and Germany itself; in August the USSR tested its first nuclear device, setting off the arms race; and in October, Mao Zedong proclaimed the formation of the People's Republic of China. The Cold War would be conducted on a cultural plane as well as on the level of nations and armies.

1949–1959: Cold War Ornithology

An aggressive campaign, partially orchestrated and funded by the USA's Central Intelligence Agency, promoted certain artistic practices (like the New York School of abstract expressionism) in opposition to the Soviet Union's officially sanctioned socialist realism.[1] In the world of music, along with jazz, the dominant, officially promoted practice was serialism, a repudiation of the tonalism mandated by official Soviet ideology and a musical representation of Western "freedom" from traditional strictures.[2]

From the decade's onset, Messiaen's composition and teaching became involved in — if only because it provided him income — this overall cultural Cold War. The first productions were four piano works experimenting with time and rhythm that were later grouped as *Four Studies in Rhythm* (1949-1950).[3] The first study, "Mode of Values and Intensities," was composed in Darmstadt in 1949. Messiaen returned to Darmstadt in 1950 to give a lecture on rhythmic analysis.

Darmstadt, a city in the southwest corner of the newly formed Federal Republic of Germany (West Germany), became famous for its Internationale Ferienkurse für Neue Musik (International Summer Courses for New Music).

---

1. For the CIA and the "cultural Cold War," see Serge Guilbaut, *How New York Stole the Idea of Modern Art: Abstract Expressionism, Freedom, and the Cold War*, trans. Arthur Goldhammer (Chicago: University of Chicago Press, 1983); Naima Prevots, *Dance for Export: Cultural Diplomacy and the Cold War* (Middletown, Conn.: Wesleyan University Press; Hanover, N.H.: University Press of New England, 1998); Frances Stonor Saunders, *The Cultural Cold War: The CIA and the World of Arts and Letters* (New York: New Press, distributed by Norton, 2000); David Caute, *The Dancer Defects: The Struggle for Cultural Supremacy during the Cold War* (New York: Oxford University Press, 2003); Hugh Wilford, *The Mighty Wurlitzer: How the CIA Played America* (Cambridge: Harvard University Press, 2008).

2. For an issue dedicated to Cold War music, see the *Journal of Musicology* 26, no. 1 (Winter 2009). Articles include: Peter J. Schmelz, "Introduction: Music in the Cold War": 3-16; Laura Silverberg, "Between Dissonance and Dissidence: Socialist Modernism in the German Democratic Republic": 44-84; Leslie A. Sprout, "The 1945 Stravinsky Debates: Nigg, Messiaen, and the Early Cold War in France": 85-131. For France in particular, see Mark Carroll, *Music and Ideology in Cold War Europe* (New York: Cambridge University Press, 2003). For jazz, see Uta G. Poiger, *Jazz, Rock, and Rebels: Cold War Politics and American Culture in a Divided Germany* (Berkeley: University of California Press, 2000); Penny M. Von Eschen, *Satchmo Blows Up the World: Jazz Ambassadors Play the Cold War* (Cambridge: Harvard University Press, 2004); Stephen A. Crist, "Jazz as Democracy? Dave Brubeck and Cold War Politics," *Journal of Musicology* 26, no. 2 (April 2009): 133-74.

3. Nigel Simeone, *Olivier Messiaen: A Bibliographical Catalogue of Messiaen's Works*, Musikbibliographische Arbeiten series, vol. 14 (Tutzing: Hans Schneider, 1998), 104-11. The order in which the four pieces were composed is not the order in which Messiaen collated them as a group and designated them to be played.

1943–1992: Legacy

The project was launched in 1946, a year after the Third Reich's defeat in May 1945 freed German musicians from Nazi ideological strictures. The Darmstadt program aimed at promoting new musical repertoire by commissioning and recording new works, and collaborating with radio stations to broadcast and disseminate them.[4] Along with Messiaen, its many lecturers would eventually include an international cast of the epoch's towering figures: Theodor W. Adorno, Milton Babbitt, Luciano Berio, Pierre Boulez, John Cage, Morton Feldman, Hans Werner Henze, Ernst Krenek, György Ligeti, Luigi Nono, Karlheinz Stockhausen, Edgard Varèse, Iannis Xenakis, and many others. Because of its unique position on the USA's "frontier" with the USSR, West Germany soon assumed the role of a "Cold War musical hothouse, a nation whose cultural mission was to cultivate modernist and avant-garde repertoire that was too fragile or too thorny to flourish in any other soil." Such "support was also extended to composers from abroad, some of whose works were ignored or maligned in their own countries."[5] This latter category included Messiaen, whose work was being neglected by French musicians in postwar Paris, a nostalgic and "morose" musical scene not open to the avant-garde.[6]

The second of the four rhythmic studies, "Rhythmic Neums," was composed at Tanglewood, Massachusetts — again, a Cold War setting significant for its Franco-American exchange — during Messiaen's summer residency prior to the December premiere in Boston of *Turangalîla Symphony*. The last two études, "Island of Fire 1" and "Island of Fire 2," were composed in Paris in 1950. The four pieces were first performed on November 6, 1950, by Messiaen himself, in the somewhat unexpected venue of Tunis. They were published individually that same month. Messiaen later instructed that they "should always be played" in this order: (1) "Island of Fire 1"; (2) "Mode of Values and Intensities"; (3) "Rhythmic Neums"; (4) "Island of Fire 2."

Messiaen composed his *Mass of Pentecost* (for solo organ) contemporane-

---

4. Christopher Fox, "Darmstadt School, The," in *Grove Music Online. Oxford Music Online;* http://www.oxfordmusiconline.com. See also Amy C. Beal, *New Music, New Allies: American Experimental Music in West Germany from the Zero Hour to Reunification* (Berkeley: University of California Press, 2006); David Monod, *Settling Scores: German Music, Denazification, and the Americans, 1945-1953* (Chapel Hill: University of North Carolina Press, 2005); and Elizabeth Janik, *Recomposing Music: Politics and Tradition in Cold War Berlin* (Boston: Brill, 2005).

5. Joy H. Calico, "Schoenberg's Symbolic Remigration: *A Survivor from Warsaw* in Postwar West Germany," *Journal of Musicology* 26, no. 1 (Winter 2009): 17-43, at 18.

6. Peter Hill and Nigel Simeone, *Olivier Messiaen, Oiseaux exotiques* (Aldershot, England, and Burlington, Vt.: Ashgate, 2007), 5, 12. For the conservative music scene in postwar France, see Carroll, *Music and Ideology in Cold War Europe*.

ously with the four rhythmic études, beginning at Tanglewood in the summer of 1949 and finishing up in Paris in 1950.[7] The work reflects an organist's duty of improvising at key points at a "low mass," and Messiaen later said that the work was to some extent a résumé "based on — or . . . a summation of — his improvisations at the Trinité."[8] The work has the same five-movement structure as the fifty-one masses in Tournemire's *L'Orgue Mystique:* Entrance, Offertory, Consecration (or Elevation), Communion, and Sortie (Exit). However, unlike Tournemire's masses, Messiaen's assigns each movement a colorful descriptive title and states the text upon which the improvisation "comments":

I-ENTRANCE (Tongues of Fire)
"Tongues of fire rested upon each of them" (Acts of the Apostles [2:3])

II-OFFERTORY (Things visible and invisible)
"Things visible and invisible" (Nicene Creed)

III-CONSECRATION (Gift of Wisdom)
"The Holy Spirit will remind you of all that I have told you" (Gospel of Saint John [14:26])

IV-COMMUNION (Birds and springs)
"Springs of water, bless the Lord; birds of the sky, bless the Lord" (Canticle of the Three Youths [Book of Daniel 3:77, 80])

V-SORTIE (Wind of the Spirit)
"A violent wind filled the entire house" (Acts of the Apostles [2:2])

However, this "résumé" of rhythmic experiments in *Mass of Pentecost* does not call to mind Tournemire so much as Messiaen's own contemporaneous *Four Studies in Rhythm.* Here is just a sampling of Messiaen's notations denoting rhythmic types in this Mass:

"Greek rhythms treated in irrational values"
"3 Hindu rhythms: tritîya, caturthaka, hinçankalîla — transformed into

---

7. Simeone, *Bibliographical Catalogue,* 112-13; Jon Gillock, *Performing Messiaen's Organ Music: 66 Masterclasses* (Bloomington: Indiana University Press, 2010), 143-61.
8. Simeone, *Bibliographical Catalogue,* 113. Following quotations are from the score: Messiaen, *Messe de la Pentecôte* (Paris: Alphonse Leduc, 1951).

rhythmic characters: the 1st does not change, the 2nd augments, the 3rd diminishes"
"Hindu rhythm simhavikrama"
"Neums in the plainchant style"
"Inversions based on 5 chromatic durations"

Mass of Pentecost was composed almost exactly ten years after Messiaen's last large masterwork for organ, *Glorified Bodies: Seven Brief Visions of the Life of the Resurrected,* completed just before the September 1, 1939, outbreak of war. Listening to the two works side by side demonstrates the enormous intellectual, emotional, and musical distance Messiaen had traveled between August 1939 (at Petichet, Isère) and August 1949 (at Tanglewood). And of course, the context was radically new. One scholar — recalling that the USSR exploded its first nuclear device in August 1949 while Messiaen was at Tanglewood and began composing the mass — has interpreted the work as a response to the seemingly imminent atomic apocalypse.[9] *Mass of Pentecost* was premiered at La Trinité during the Mass for Pentecost Sunday, 1951. It was the last completely religious work that Messiaen would compose during the next ten years — until December 1960, following Claire's death.

In 1951, Messiaen composed a second work for organ — *The Organ Book: Seven Pieces for Organ.* This would be his last composition for organ until December 1960 as well, until after Claire's death.[10] It was commissioned for the inauguration of the new organ installed in the Villa Berg Studio in Stuttgart. Villa Berg had been restored after being leveled by Allied bombing raids (along with the rest of Stuttgart), and the studio served the West German radio and television station Süddeutscher Rundfunk (SDR) (South German Broadcasting), founded in 1949. Akin to London's Abbey Road, Villa Berg would become a premier recording destination for classical, jazz, and rock musicians during the coming decades.

Although the *Organ Book*'s opening and closing movements are named for compositional techniques, Messiaen associated the other five movements with a liturgical feast or season by means of both title and text being "commented" on:

---

9. Robert Fallon, "Birds, Beasts, and Bombs in Messiaen's Cold War Mass," *Journal of Musicology* 26, no. 2 (Spring 2009): 175-204.

10. Simeone, *Bibliographical Catalogue,* 116-17; Gillock, *Performing Messiaen's Organ Music,* 162-92.

1. Repetition by interversion
2. Trio (for Trinity Sunday):
    "For now we see through a glass, darkly" (1 Cor. 13:12)
3. The Hands of the Abyss (for Times of Penitence):
    "The abyss uttered its cry, and lifted up its hands"
    (Hab. 3:10)

4. Birdsong (for Eastertide):
    Afternoon of the Birds: blackbird, robin,
    song thrush — and nightingale
    when night falls . . .

5. Trio (for Trinity Sunday):
    "For of him, by him, and for him are all things"
    (Rom. 11:36)
6. The Eyes in the Wheels (for Pentecost Sunday):
    "And the rims of the four wheels were full of eyes round about.
    For the spirit of living being was in the wheels" (Ezek. 1:18, 20)
7. Sixty-four Durations[11]

The *Organ Book* marks an even greater step forward in Messiaen's rhythmic complexities and mathematical abstractions in the heyday of postwar surrealism. His comments on the seventh piece, "Sixty-four Durations," suggest the influence of Bergsonian "duration" and the experiment with fast and slow tempi in *Diptych* (1930); as well as that of Boll's *Two Infinites* (1938):

> [In "Sixty-four Durations"], I've tried to make the listener grasp some extremely long note-values whose differences are exceedingly minute. This is very difficult for a human being to appreciate. We are average-sized creatures of medium height and, alas! of average thinking capacity, and our time is apportioned in an average manner; we're halfway between the microcosm and the macrocosm. So we perceive very long durations with difficulty, and the very tiny durations, which can contrast the long durations, with still greater difficulty.[12]

---

11. For table of contents see *Livre d'orgue, pour orgue* (1950), in Olivier Messiaen, *Complete Edition*, 32 CDs (Germany: Deutsche Grammophon, 2008), 21-22.

12. Olivier Messiaen and Claude Samuel, *Music and Color: Conversations with Claude Samuel*, trans. E. Thomas Glasow (Portland, Ore.: Amadeus Press, 1994), 118; hereafter "Messiaen and Samuel (1994)."

And yet, movements 3, 4, and 6 are remarkably and concretely picturesque: the despair of the "abyss" seems truly bottomless; the birds sing, both in the afternoon and at night; and perhaps most spectacularly, the terrifying apparition of the "eyes in the wheels" recorded in Ezekiel's prophecy demand a new level of virtuosity. Somewhat paradoxically, as both the "abyss" and the "eyes in the wheels" demonstrate, Messiaen is capable of deploying the most extreme limits of mathematical abstraction in service of conveying a profoundly concrete experience of fear: "All the traits of God evoke terror."[13] His awareness of this paradox is evident in his answer to a question asking whether his *Organ Book* had "primarily theoretical significance" in the same way as Bach's *Art of Fugue*. Messiaen responded with imagery derived from both Hello and Pascal:

> Yes, in a certain sense, but in it are also violent colors and new effects. For instance, "Les mains de l'abîme" ["Hands of the Abyss"] was written while contemplating the meandering of the Romance River through the terrifying mountain pass of the gorges of the Infernet. It's a truly impressive chasm; I wanted at the same time to pay homage to the sensation of vertigo it imparts and, symbolically, to the two gulfs of human misery and divine pity. A verse by the prophet Habakkuk served as a motto: "The abyss uttered its cry! The deep lifted up both hands." . . . According to [Ernest] Hello's admirable commentary, "It is necessary that the very lowest abyss show, below man, death, so the abyss above may exhibit, higher than him, life." To translate this vertiginous feeling into music, I juxtaposed the extremes of the organ, taking advantage of the wide range of this instrument's registers. I wrote, therefore, a very low voice that represents the bottom of the abyss of human misery, with a deep and terrifying sonority, a bit like the cavernous trumpetings and chants of Tibetan priests, and at the same time, above, the voice of God in reply — but it isn't a terrifying voice of thunder and lightning; it's a mysterious, distant, high-pitched, almost tender voice, barely audible. One voice is so low and the other so high, one has absolutely no idea what one is hearing, and the timbres are so strange that it's impossible to make out the notes. To me, this seems to convey marvelously the ideas of penitence, reverence, and vertigo before holiness.[14]

---

13. Messiaen, interview with Patrick Szersnovicz, May 29, 1987, in "Olivier Messiaen: La Liturgie de l'arc-en-ciel," *Le Monde de la Musique* (July/August 1987).

14. Messiaen and Samuel (1994), 119.

Undoubtedly Messiaen was thinking here of Hello's chapter fragment entitled "Vertigo before the Absolute."[15]

On April 23, 1952, Messiaen inaugurated Villa Berg's new organ by premiering the *Organ Book* as part of the Day of Contemporary Music (Tage zeitgenössischer Musik). He also gave a lecture on rhythmic analysis in Saarbrücken. However, as his connections to the new postwar West German scene multiplied, things worsened at home. Perhaps at his father's suggestion (given Pierre's own fond memories of having acquired English in England and Scotland), Messiaen had sent fifteen-year-old Pascal to London for the ostensible reason of improving the boy's facility in English. Presumably Claire was no longer capable of helping Messiaen raise their son; but Pascal's absence must also have been a great loss for her.

Claire wrote and published the last work of her life in 1952 — that is, contemporaneous with Messiaen's "Hands of the Abyss" — a piece for organ solo entitled *Parce, Domine ["Lord, Spare Your People"] for the Season of Lent*.[16] "Parce Domine," a Gregorian chant refrain derived from Joel 2:17, is used during the forty-day penitential season of Lent that precedes Easter. More specifically, it is one of the responsories designated to be sung by the choir during the imposition of ashes on Ash Wednesday (at which the priest says: "Remember man, that thou art dust, and unto dust thou shalt return").[17] The brief, harsh text suggests Claire's desperate state of mind:

Parce Dómine, párce pópulo túo: Spare, Lord, spare your people:
ne in aetérnum irascáris nóbis.[18]   do not be angry with us into eternity.

The organ was an appropriate instrument for expressing these sentiments; but one wonders whether Claire was not also making some kind of appeal to Messiaen.

---

15. Ernest Hello, "Le vertige devant l'absolu," in *Du néant à dieu,* ed. Jules-Philippe Heuzey, 2 vols. (Paris: Perrin et Cie, [1921] 1930), 1:38-41.

16. Claire Delbos, *Parce, Domine: (pour le temps du carême); pour orgue = Pardonnez, Seigneur, à votre peuple . . .* (Paris: Rouart, Lerolle et Cie, 1952); cf. Nigel Simeone, "Delbos, Claire," in Grove Music Online. Oxford Music Online.

17. *The Liber Usualis with Introduction and Rubrics in English,* ed. Benedictines of Solesmes (Tournai, Belgium: Desclée & Co., [1939] 1949), 523-25, at 524 ("Ash Wednesday"); cf. *Missal En,* 218: "Between the porch and the altar, the priests, the Lord's ministers, shall weep and shall say: Spare, O Lord, spare Thy people; and shut not the mouths of them that sing to thee, O Lord" (Joel 2:17).

18. *Liber Usualis,* 1868 ("At a Time of Penance").

1943–1992: Legacy

The year 1953 brought a more explicit "awakening of birds" in Messiaen's life. Of course, he had been flirting with birdsong for some time: it had appeared a decade earlier in *Quartet for the End of Time* and *Visions of Amen*. More recently, the Communion piece for *Mass of Pentecost* was entitled "Birds and Springs"; an examination piece composed in 1951 for a Conservatory competition was entitled *The Blackbird* for flute and piano.[19] And, as seen, the midpoint of the *Organ Book* associated Easter with birdsong.

However, study of birdsong took a significant step forward in *Awakening of Birds* (1953), a twenty-minute piece for piano and orchestra dedicated in homage to Yvonne Loriod.[20] Once again West Germany played an important role when *Awakening* was premiered on October 11, 1953, at the city hall of Donaueschingen. Hans Rosbaud conducted the Orchestra of Südwestfunk (SWR) (Southwest Broadcasting) and Yvonne Loriod played the piano. Unfortunately, *Awakening* was not received with much interest, and Messiaen became anxious that Durand would lose interest in publishing his music. Perhaps due to a loss in confidence, he would not compose anything for the next two years.

Awakening of Birds evokes a moment of joy and new life, birds waking up at 4 A.M. and a great chorus singing out as light appears on a spring morning. However, the domestic circumstances in which it was composed and premiered could not have been more autumnal. Early that summer of 1953, Claire left their home in Paris for a final time and traveled alone to Neussargues. Without other options, Messiaen brought Pascal along with him to West Germany in July for the summer institute at Darmstadt. On October 25, two weeks after the premiere of *Awakening of Birds* in Donaueschingen, Claire's neighbors in Neussargues alerted Messiaen to her worsening condition. He made an emergency journey there and brought Claire back to a temporary nursing home in Paris. On November 19, she was admitted to Paris's Salpetrière hospital, noted since the nineteenth century for its research in mental illnesses. On December 2, a diagnosis was rendered: "cerebral atrophy, incurable." On December 18, Yvonne Loriod's mother Simone assisted in taking Claire to the nursing home at La Varenne. Messiaen began his custom of visiting Claire every week on Sundays, after the Mass at Trinité and before returning to play vespers. As Claire declined and became incontinent during 1955, "it fell to Messiaen to purchase the necessities to cope with this."[21]

---

19. Simeone, *Bibliographical Catalogue*, 114-15.

20. Simeone, *Bibliographical Catalogue*, 122-23.

21. Peter Hill and Nigel Simeone, *Messiaen* (New Haven: Yale University Press, 2005), 209, 213.

1949–1959: Cold War Ornithology

Messiaen's turn to birdsong — a language offering great possibilities for the encoding of meaning — should be seen within this profoundly desperate personal context. A Conservatory student later recalled Messiaen's demoralization during the year 1955-1956: "We are all in a profound night," Messiaen would say to his class, "and I don't know where I am going; I'm as lost as you."[22] This is a remarkable statement from a personality so thoroughly marked by metaphors of light and seeing: visions, apparitions, gazes, lightning flashes, dazzlement, *clarté*. It provides a lens through which we might read "Trio (for Trinity Sunday)" from the *Organ Book* (1951): "For now we see through a glass, darkly." Small wonder that the movement is immediately followed by one of Messiaen's other favorite metaphors: "The abyss uttered its cry, and lifted up its hands."[23]

1953–1959: *Catalogue of Birds*

Messiaen's first note referring to birdsong sketches was recorded on the evening of October 6, 1953 — one week before the West German premiere of *Awakening* and three weeks before Claire's collapse. His notebook for 1954 and throughout the spring and summer of 1955 brims over with notations, detailing expeditions to the coast of Britanny, the southern Alps, and Germany's Black Forest, as well as notes made from 78 rpm recordings of Mexican and North American birdsong.[24] For example: "14 July, 8 p.m., on the right the Téléferique and Fort Rabot, at the end, by the town hall and the belfry of St-André, in the garden, scarlet cannas, pink hortensias ... geraniums, pansies, thousands of blue, purple and pink violets, some zinnias adding a striking note of orange. Coming out of the belfry of the old church, a ballet of swallows, criss-crossing the sky in curves, crosses, stars, flowers — all kinds of shapes."[25] For those acquainted with the book *The Plant That Makes Eyes Open with Wonder* (1927), it is difficult not to note the remarkable similarity between Messiaen's meticulous notations of place, date, and time of day, along with detailed descriptions of surroundings and bird activities and songs, and the similarly detailed recordings of

---

22. Hill and Simeone, *Messiaen*, 214.
23. Epigraphs to movements 2 and 3 from *Organ Book* (1951): 1 Cor. 13:12 and Hab. 3:10.
24. Hill and Simeone, *Messiaen*, 210-15.
25. Messiaen notebook for July 14, 1955; in Hill and Simeone, *Messiaen*, 214.

mescaline-induced hallucinations in *Peyote*.²⁶ Also notable is the way in which Messiaen's picturesque impressions and metaphors strongly resemble his mother's nature poetry.

After a two-year hiatus, when Messiaen returned to composition on October 5, 1955, the result was *Exotic Birds* (1956), a piece for piano and instrumental ensemble lasting around fifteen minutes. The instrumentation represents experimental percussive resources upon which Messiaen was drawing in order to effect his rhythmic aims: glockenspiel, xylophone, temple blocks, three gongs, and tam-tam.²⁷ Completed on January 23, 1956, *Exotic Birds* was premiered on March 10 with Yvonne Loriod at the piano — this time not in West Germany but back home in Paris, under the auspices of the Concerts du Domaine musical series.

Meanwhile, Messiaen's students began to make their mark. On June 18, 1955, Pierre Boulez premiered *The Hammer without a Master*, a setting of René Char's surrealist poetry for alto voice and six instrumentalists. The notoriety that eventually marked the event helped promote Boulez's avant-garde image. The French committee members of the International Society for Contemporary Music declined to sanction the work as France's official entry at its festival in Baden-Baden. Heinrich Strobel, director of music at the Südwestfunk and an advocate of Boulez, had already arranged fifty rehearsals with Hans Rosbaud. He went ahead with the premiere at Baden-Baden; it was "an instant and sensational success," even as the "French contingent made a dignified exit from the hall, although certain of its members were later to rally around." During the following months, *Le Marteau sans maître* was performed and celebrated in Vienna, Zurich, Munich, London, New York, and Los Angeles; Stravinsky judged it a "masterpiece of new music."²⁸

A year later, Karlheinz Stockhausen premiered his groundbreaking *Canticle of the Youths* on May 30, 1956, in the broadcast auditorium of the Westdeutscher Rundfunk (WDR) (West German Broadcasting) in Cologne. Stockhausen had first encountered Messiaen's work in the summer of 1951 at Darmstadt, where he listened to Messiaen's "Island of Fire 2" "over and over again, both fascinated and overwhelmed by what he called 'fantastic music of

---

26. Alexandre Rouhier, *La plante qui fait les yeux émerveillés: le peyotl* (Paris: Gaston Doin et Cie, 1927).

27. Simeone, *Bibliographical Catalogue*, 126-27.

28. Dominique Jameux, *Pierre Boulez*, trans. Susan Bradshaw (Cambridge: Harvard University Press, 1991), 73-81, at 73-74, 80. See also Pierre Grondines, "Le Marteau sans maître: Serialism Becomes Respectable," trans. Jane Brierley, *La Scena Musicale* 6, no. 4 (December 1, 2000); http://www.scena.org/lsm/sm6-4/serialisme-en.html.

the stars.'"[29] In 1952, Stockhausen came to Paris to study with Messiaen, whose Conservatory course in analysis and aesthetics that year concentrated on the subject of rhythm.[30] Returning to Cologne to work in the WDR's electronic music studio, Stockhausen sought to bridge the German world of electronically generated music and the French world of electronically altered recorded acoustical sounds *(musique concrète)*.[31] *Canticle of the Youths* began with the recording of a twelve-year-old boy singing the divine praises told of in the biblical story of three young men cast into the fiery furnace by Nebuchadnezzar (Dan. 3): the phrase "Praise the Lord" *(Preiset/Lobet/Jubelt den [de] Herrn)* recurs as the textual refrain.[32] Stockhausen then extracted fragments of this recorded speech, resynthesized them to alter the acoustical sounds, and "set out to create an electronic work in which the sounds of a human voice mysteriously condense out of a plasma of electronically-realized phonemic particles."[33] Conceived as both a sacred cantata and a sacred ritual, Stockhausen's landmark piece referred back to Messiaen's explorations in multiple ways.

In a discussion of the "magic names" found in Stockhausen's later work *Stimmung* (1968), one scholar suggests that a foreshadowing might be found in "the 'magic syllables' of Messiaen's *Harawi*."[34] It seems worth recalling his *Five Refrains* as well; it too integrates encoded "phonemic particles," both medieval French and pseudo-Hindu Sanskrit. Moreover, in light of Stockhausen's experiments in voices, cannot bird strophes also be considered "phonemic particles" woven into Messiaen's larger musical narratives?

In October 1956, after the premiere of *Exotic Birds,* Messiaen began com-

---

29. Karl H. Wörner, *Stockhausen: Life and Work,* trans. and ed. Bill Hopkins (Berkeley and Los Angeles: University of California Press, 1973), 80-81.

30. Robin Maconie, "Paris, 1952," in *The Works of Karlheinz Stockhausen* (Boston: Marion Boyars, [1976] 1981), 30-40, at 36; cf. 95-99.

31. For the work's eventual labeling (rightly or wrongly) as *musique concrète,* see Maconie, in *Works of Karlheinz Stockhausen,* 98-99.

32. Maconie, in *Works of Karlheinz Stockhausen,* 97. For the vocalized speech sounds see Robin Maconie, *Other Planets: The Music of Karlheinz Stockhausen* (Lanham, Md.: Scarecrow, 2005), 166-71, at 169. Stockhausen had originally intended the work, written out of religious conviction, to be performed in the Cologne cathedral. The request was refused, and he was bitterly disappointed. Michael Kurtz, *Stockhausen: A Biography,* trans. Richard Toop (Boston: Faber and Faber, 1992), 82. The text from the book of Daniel is commented on by Messiaen in the "Communion" movement of *Mass of Pentecost.*

33. Description is Maconie, *Other Planets,* 167.

34. For this and other parallels see Maconie, *Works of Karlheinz Stockhausen,* 36-37; for *Stimmung* see 239-43. The German noun *die Stimmung* can mean "tuning," "tune," or "temper" (as in Bach's "Well-Tempered Clavier"); it derives from *die Stimme,* one of whose meanings is "voice."

posing the monumental *Catalogue of Birds,* an effort that would require nearly two full years.[35] This massive cycle of thirteen movements for solo piano — symbolically divided, once again, into *seven* books — takes about two and a half hours to perform.

Book I
1. The Alpine Chough *(Coracia graculus)*
2. The Golden Oriole *(Oriolus oriolus)*[36]
3. The Blue Rock Thrush *(Monticola solitarius)*

Book II
4. The Black-eared Wheateer *(Oenanthe hispanica)*

Book III
5. The Tawny Owl *(Strix aluco)*
6. The Woodlark *(Lullula arborea)*

Book IV
7. The Reed Warbler *(Acrocephalus scirpaceus)*

Book V
8. The Short-toed Lark *(Calandrella brachydactyla)*
9. Cetti's Warbler *(Cettia cetti)*

Book VI
10. The Rock Thrush *(Monticola saxatilis)*

Book VII
11. The Buzzard *(Buteo buteo)*
12. Black Wheatear *(Oenanthe leucura)*
13. The Curlew *(Numenius arquata)*

As there are seven books and thirteen movements, the cycle has a definitive midpoint at movement 7 in Book IV: "The Reed Warbler." Messiaen intends this movement as a form of "non-retrogradable rhythm," the kind of

---

35. Simeone, *Bibliographical Catalogue,* 128-31.
36. "Le Loriot" is pronounced the same as Yvonne Loriod's maiden name — a coincidence that delighted Messiaen.

isorhythmic or palindromic plan that, capable of being read the same both forward and backward, suggests eternity: "The whole piece is a great curved movement, stretching from midnight / 3 a.m. through to the next midnight / 3 a.m. The events from afternoon to night repeat in reverse order, the events from night to morning."[37]

Each movement bears the title of a bird species and utilizes its song, while extensive notes accompanying each piece describe the melody of each title bird's song, its habitat, season of year and time of day it sings, and other physical conditions of that particular species. However, Messiaen's imagination transcends the limitations imposed by actual terrestrial life: by introducing various other species as well, each movement consists of a number of species singing together that could not, in reality, sing together. Their actual lives are separated by barriers as large as continents and seasons, and as small as hours of the day. They sing here, however, in utopian — or perhaps eschatological — choirs.

Given the highly-abstract nature of this work, both musically and in its lack of linguistic texts, it might initially seem an ill fit for Messiaen's customary work, which is both highly programmatic and descriptive. However, Messiaen's notes are surprising as he uses them to describe the entire spectrum of human emotions. For example, Messiaen's affinity for the frightful finds apt expression in his idiosyncratic description of the Tawny Owl (Book III, no. 5):

> Plumage spotted with brown and rust, enormous facial discs, a solemn expression, stamped with mystery, wisdom and the supernatural. Even more than its aspect, the voice of this night bird provokes terror.... Shadows, fear, a heart beating too fast, mewing and yelping of the Little Owl, cries of the Long-eared Owl; and here is the call of the Tawny; sometimes lugubrious and distressing, sometimes vague and disturbing (with a strange trembling), sometimes screamed in horror like the cry of a murdered child! ... Silence. More distant hooting, seeming like a bell from another world.[38]

Clearly, the "Messiaen Controversy" circa 1944-1946 had not put a permanent lid on Messiaen's colorful exegeses!

Relations of fathers and sons intersected with the composition of the

---

37. Messiaen notes for "The Reed Warbler *(Acrocephalus scirpaceus)*" ("La Rousserolle effarvatte"), *Catalogue of Birds (Catalogue d'oiseaux)* (1958), in *Complete Edition*, 204-11, at 207, translation altered.

38. Messiaen notes for "The Tawny Owl *(Strix aluco)*" ("La Chouette hulotte"), in *Complete Edition*, 206-7.

catalogue at two junctures. First, on May 26, 1957, Pierre Messiaen died unexpectedly at the age of seventy-four.[39] Once again, while going through his father's papers, Messiaen had hoped to find his mother's missing manuscript of love writings, the mysterious *Book of Love*. Once again he was disappointed and discovered nothing. Second, on August 2, during the final month of composition, twenty-one-year-old Pascal married. Messiaen was invited to the wedding but chose not to attend. (Eventually, however, whatever had caused the hurt feelings, Messiaen bought the newlywed couple an apartment.) About a month later, on September 1, the catalogue was finally finished, after two long years of work. Three months later, on December 10, 1958, Messiaen turned fifty.

Catalogue of Birds made its triumphal premiere on April 15, 1959.[40] Yvonne Loriod played the piano at the Salle Gaveau in Paris, under the auspices (as with *Exotic Birds*) of the Concerts du Domaine musical series. One critic's review praised Loriod's "amazingly accurate fingers," which were able to tease the piano "from its twittering heights down to its booming depths 'of terror.'"[41]

39. Pierre Messiaen (b. March 13, 1883) died suddenly on May 26, 1957; Hill and Simeone, *Messiaen*, 7, 223. As seen above in his translation of *Les Fioretti* (1947), published in the Histoire, Philosophie, Religion series, of which he was the general editor, Pierre had continued his involvement with Catholic Revivalist circles after the war. Compare another book he published in that series that same year — a Catholic genealogy of the "doctrinal Baudelaire": Pierre Messiaen, *Sentiment chrétien et poésie française: Baudelaire, Verlaine, Rimbaud* (Paris: La Renaissance du livre, 1947). For background, see Lawrence B. Leighton, "Review: A Doctrinal Baudelaire," *Kenyon Review* 7, no. 2 (Spring 1945): 321-24; and Stanislas Fumet, *Notre Baudelaire*, Le Roseau d'or Œuvres et Chroniques series, no. 8 (Paris: Plon-Nourrit et Cie, 1926). Fumet was the secretary of Maritain's "Roseau d'or" venture. See Stephen Schloesser, *Jazz Age Catholicism: Mystic Modernism in Postwar Paris, 1919-1933* (Toronto: University of Toronto Press, 2005), 181.

At the end of his life, Pierre held the position of *professeur* at the Institut Catholique in Paris (as indicated on the title page of his *Romantiques anglais* [1955]) and continued to publish with the Desclée Catholic publishing house. His last published work seems to have been a French translation of meditations written by Fr. Paul de Jaegher, S.J., a Belgian Jesuit who had specialized in the study of "mysticism." See de Jaegher, *La Vertu d'amour*, trans. Pierre Messiaen (Paris: Desclée de Brouwer; Bruges: les Presses Saint-Augustin, 1956); English translation from Dutch original, de Jaegher, *The Virtue of Love: Meditations* (New York: Kennedy, 1955). Cf. Pierre Messiaen, *Les Romantiques anglais. Textes anglais et français* (Paris: Desclée de Brouwer, 1955). After his death, Desclée published a new edition of Pierre's translation of the complete works of Shakespeare (1961-1964) with newly added introductions and essays by other authors.

40. Simeone, *Bibliographical Catalogue*, 129; Hill and Simeone, *Messiaen*, 226.

41. Suzanne Demarquez, "Le *Catalogue d'oiseaux* d'Olivier Messiaen," *Guide du concert* 233 (May 1, 1959): 42; in Hill and Simeone, *Messiaen*, 228.

Life imitated art as this climactic moment of triumph coincided with tragedy. Exactly one week after the premiere, Claire Delbos died, on April 22, 1959.

Might not Messiaen's *Chronochromie* (1960) be thought of as a funereal work for Claire? Sometime during 1959, Messiaen began composing *Chronochromie* in response to a commission by the Südwestfunk, where *Awakening of Birds* had premiered in 1953.[42] A work for large orchestra suffused with birdsong, its title is a neologism combining two Greek words — *chronos* (time) and *chroma* (color) — signifying "time-color." Like the hybridized title, the work's structure is Greek in origin, and Messiaen's use of it suggests a debt owed to *The Antique Greek Dance* (1896) of Maurice Emmanuel, his music history teacher at the Conservatory.

1. Introduction
   [SYSTEM A]
2. Strophe I   [RIGHT TURN]
3. Antistrophe I   [LEFT TURN]
   [SYSTEM B]
4. Strophe II   [RIGHT TURN]
5. Antistrophe II   [LEFT TURN]
   [FREESTANDING]
6. Epode   [CENTER: CLIMACTIC]
7. Coda[43]

Messiaen's employment of the strophe-antistrophe structure imitates the fundamental structure of Greek tragedy. (He had already used it in miniature in the "Amen of the Agony of Jesus.") The literal meaning of the word *strophē*

---

42. Simeone, *Bibliographical Catalogue*, 132-33.
43. These choreographic indications are not Messiaen's. They are mine, drawing on the approach of Leo Aylen, *The Greek Theater* (Cranbury, N.J.: Associated University Presses, 1985). One of the advantages of consulting Aylen's approach is his insistence on ancient Greek tragedy's having been both sung and danced throughout; as a corollary, the varieties of Greek meter, so important to Messiaen, are inseparable from danced movement. Thus, Aylen's work complements Maurice Emmanuel's pioneering studies. Using the analogy of Balinese music (again, so important to Messiaen), Aylen makes the point strongly at the beginning of his chapter devoted especially to "dance drama": "Dance, then, is not just an element in the staging of the fifth-century plays like costumes or music. It is a central flavor of the culture, as perhaps it is still in Bali. Until we appreciate this, we cannot approach the work of Aeschylus and Sophocles. To make the chorus of a fifth-century play stand and recite free verse is much more ludicrous even than making the chorus of a modern musical do so." Aylen, 114-40, at 114-15. For notes on some Greek meters, see 357-59.

is "turning"; *antistrophē* is a "turning back."⁴⁴ When taken together, the pair constitutes a "system." Messiaen has structured the work so that it has two systems (each system in turn composed of two interrelated stanzas) and a third freestanding element, the chorus's climactic "Epode."⁴⁵ As Messiaen notes in his analysis of the work: "The Epode, as in Greek choirs, is completely different from all the rest."⁴⁶ Messiaen uses the full resources of the orchestra only in the introduction and coda, which would serve, if this were a stage production, as music accompanying entrance and exit.

Finally, here again Messiaen has organized the work so that it will embody the symbolic number seven (cf. *Glorified Bodies; Visions of Amen; Catalogue of Birds*). Seven is the Jewish and Christian number for perfection and, perhaps more importantly, completion or consummation (seven days of creation, seven sacraments, seven gifts of the Holy Spirit, the seventh "Amen," the "Amen of Consummation"). *Chronochromie* thus evokes Messiaen's recurrent image of the end of time *(chronos)* and the celestial city marked by dazzling color *(chroma)*. But it might also symbolize a more personal "consummation."

Chronochromie was premiered by conductor Hans Rosbaud in the Donaueschingen Stadthalle on October 16. Messiaen's 1950s had begun in West Germany; they also ended there. One suspects that the event, structured along the lines of a Greek tragedy, served an encoded funereal function memorializing the end of Claire's life. And yet, following Machaut's lead, "My beginning is in my end." Thus began a third epoch in Messiaen's life: the first had been

44. Graham Ley, *A Short Introduction to the Ancient Greek Theater* (Chicago: University of Chicago Press, 1991), 48-56, at 49; cf. Aylen, *The Greek Theater*, 121. Simon Goldhill, "The Language of Tragedy: Rhetoric and Communication," in *The Cambridge Companion to Greek Tragedy*, ed. P. E. Easterling (New York: Cambridge University Press, 1997), 127-50, at 128.

45. "A system consists of a *strophē* and *antistrophē*, two metrically identical stanzas sung to the same tune. In the *antistrophē* identical dance movement is performed to that in the *strophē*, though in the opposite direction." The "epode" tends to be "climactic and require more excited movement," suggesting that during it the chorus might have moved closer to the front. Aylen, *The Greek Theater*, 355-56, 121; cf. 106-7. Another scholar's work (preceding Aylen's) also underscores the necessarily deliberate and perhaps exaggerated nature of bodily movement in the Greek theater, given its vast size and the audience's distance from the stage: "So actions must have been large and distinct. There is no place in this theater for fidgeting, for the idiosyncratic twitch and reflex: stance, large use of the arms, and the whole style of movement must convey both the ethos of the characters and the significant action of the play." Oliver Taplin, *Greek Tragedy in Action* (Berkeley and Los Angeles: University of California Press, 1978), 15.

46. Messiaen, analysis of *Chronochromie* (1960), in Messiaen, *Traité de rythme, de couleur, et d'ornithologie (1949-1992) en sept tomes,* 8 vols. (Paris: Alphonse Leduc, 1994-2002), 3:79-120, at 81 and 97.

marked by Cécile Sauvage; the second by Claire Delbos. The third — by far the longest — would be lived with Yvonne Loriod.

*   *   *

Before leaving the 1950s, we might ask: Why birds and birdsong? Several possible answers come to mind.

First, birdsong offered the possibility of extending the kind of coded language employed by imaginary or pseudo-Hindu words in *Five Refrains* (1948). Coded language allows for self-expression while, at the same time, concealing significance from those who do not know the code — a useful device in the circumstances in which Messiaen was writing about love and loss.

Second, birdsong is, in a sense, an entire language that is coded; while it allows birds to communicate among themselves, it is largely incomprehensible to us as human beings. In this it approaches the problem (in Messiaen's view) of representing eternal beings and concepts; hence the impulsion, in the 1960s, for Messiaen's invention of a *langage communicable* (communicable language), a musical alphabet for encoding.

Third, during the vogue of serialism, birdsong allowed Messiaen to straddle two competing views of music. Even more than its twelve-tone predecessors, serialism was imagined as liberating musicians from anything fixed, natural, given, or even communal.[47] (In retrospect, its embrace by Western composers during the Cold War in opposition to Soviet strictures makes much sense.) But for Messiaen, committed to "natural resonance" (based on the overtone series) and "simultaneous contrast" (based on the light spectrum) — not to mention the metaphysics of Thomas Aquinas — this kind of "freedom" from natural structures would have made little sense. However, birdsong could bridge this divide: on the one hand, it is comprised of instinctively given and fixed fragments within its own natural environment; on the other, when appropriated by a human being as a set, group, or pattern on which to develop, it can sound as free, independent, arbitrary, and even chance-like as anything else. Birdsong could allow Messiaen to participate in the highly-

---

47. In the words of Karlheinz Stockhausen, one of Messiaen's students: "So serial thinking is something that's come into our consciousness and will be there forever: it's relativity and nothing else. It just says: Use all the components of any given number of elements, don't leave out individual elements, use them all with equal importance and try to find an equidistant scale so that certain steps are no larger than others. It's a spiritual and democratic attitude toward the world." Stockhausen, in Jonathan Cott, *Stockhausen: Conversations with the Composer* (New York: Simon and Schuster, 1973), 101.

abstract antirepresentational world of 1950s serialism while, at the same time, remaining connected to and grounded in natural structures.

Finally, birdsong is not quite eternal — but, as seen in Messiaen's historical overview of birds back to the era of dinosaurs, it is primordial. Like the angels, created yet eternal, birdsong occupies a liminal space. On the one hand, it is eternally fixed and particular to a species; on the other hand, it is temporal, capable of numerous permutations as individual birds improvise on the given series. In the philosopher's categories, birdsongs are both fixed and mutable, necessary and free. As such, they are yet one more variation on Messiaen's recurrent theme: time and eternity.

CHAPTER 12

1960–1992

Et Exspecto Resurrectionem Mortuorum

1960–1969: Return to the "Theological" in a Revolutionary Decade

In December 1960, following the October 16 premiere of *Chronochromie*, Messiaen composed what might be considered the first work of the next phase of his life: *Verset for the Feast of the Dedication*. In itself, the work seems relatively insignificant, a small piece for organ intended for use in the Conservatory's competition.[1] However, the work's larger meaning might be gathered by re-

---

1. Nigel Simeone, *Olivier Messiaen: A Bibliographical Catalogue of Messiaen's Works*, Musikbibliographische Arbeiten series, vol. 14 (Tutzing: Hans Schneider, 1998), 134-35; Jon Gillock, *Performing Messiaen's Organ Music: 66 Masterclasses* (Bloomington: Indiana University Press, 2010), 193-98. While I have suggested that the reason for Messiaen's abstention from writing explicitly "sacred" music from *Mass of Pentecost* (1950) and *Organ Book* (1951) until *Verset* (December 1960) was for largely personal reasons, this reading would not be incompatible with an argument made by Stephen Broad. He speculates that the lack of religious works could be correlated with the Vatican's denunciation of the "mania of novelty" and the "so-called modern movement in art" in 1950-1951. See Broad, "Messiaen and Modern *Art sacré*" (paper presented at the Fourth Biennial International Conference on Twentieth-Century Music, University of Sussex, UK, 2005); cited in Andrew Shenton, ed., *Messiaen the Theologian* (Burlington, Vt.: Ashgate, 2010), 34 n. 16. For the controversy embroiling *L'Art sacré*, see Françoise Caussé, *La revue "L'Art sacré." Le débat en France sur l'art et la religion (1945-1954)* (Paris: Les Éditions du Cerf, 2010); Aidan Nichols, O.P., "The Dominicans and the Journal *L'Art sacré*," *New Blackfriars* 88, no. 1013 (January 2007): 25-45; for parallels with the painter Georges Rouault, see Sheila Nowinski, "Creating Rouault's Legacy, 1945-1965: Commander in the Légion d'honneur, Artist of Catholic Modernity," in *Mystic Masque: Reality and Semblance in Georges Rouault, 1871-1958*, ed. Stephen Schloesser

turning to the autumn of 1931, when Messiaen assumed his new position at Trinité. The annual feast of the dedication of Saint John Lateran was celebrated on November 9; it would seem most likely that Messiaen's composition of *Apparition of the Eternal Church*, a "commentary" on the vespers hymn for the feast of the dedication of a church, had been inspired by that liturgical event. It had preceded Messiaen's marriage to Claire the following June.

This is the text — that is, the office for the Dedication of a Church — to which Messiaen now returns. On the surface, he is to write a somewhat perfunctory work for a Conservatory competition. However, it is the first work for organ he has composed since *The Organ Book* (1951), inaugurating the Stuttgart Villa Berg organ; and it is the first fully religious-themed organ work since *Mass of Pentecost*, finished in Paris in 1950.

The overall significance of the dedication of a church is eschatological: terrestrial life shapes and polishes the human beings who will become the precious stones of the celestial city. In *Apparition of the Eternal Church,* this process, latent with suffering, was expressed in an overwhelming and terrifying way. By contrast, *Verset,* written three decades later, is meant to evoke joy and consolation. The work begins with Messiaen's idiosyncratic quotation of the plainchant "Alleluia of the Dedication." A section marked "Slow, rocking" (as in a cradle) follows, again identified as the "Alleluia of the Dedication." An extremely quiet section *(ppp* in the left hand) follows, marked "Very moderate *(like a consolation [comme une consolation])*." Next comes a quicker section, identified as the birdsong of a song thrush *(Grive musicienne),* to be "rhythmic, with a strange joy" *(rythmé, avec une joie étrange).* This structure is then repeated: "Alleluia of the Dedication"; "Slow, rocking"; "like a consolation." A new element appears in stark contrast: a very loud passage *(fff)* marked "Moderate *(supplication)*" — prayer in supplication, presumably, for the departed. The song thrush returns, "rhythmic, with strange joy"; the plainchant "Alleluia of the Dedication" is restated; the entire piece ends in quiet *(ppp)* "ecstasy": "Very slow *(ecstatic [extatique])*."[2]

Within the context of Messiaen's personal life, the work seems to be a *re*dedication of sorts: a rededication to life after "consolation," "strange joy," and even "ecstasy." In 1961, *Verset* was published on March 27. On July 1, Messiaen and Yvonne Loriod married one another in a civil ceremony; two days

---

(Chestnut Hill, Mass.: McMullen Museum of Art, distributed by the University of Chicago Press, 2008), 401-11, at 403-6, 409 n. 26.

2. Messiaen, *Verset pour la fête de la dédicace, pour orgue* (Paris: Alphonse Leduc, 1961); cf. Simeone, *Bibliographical Catalogue,* 134-35.

later came the religious one, a small gathering without music or ceremony, not at Trinité, but at the church of Sainte-Geneviève-des-Grandes-Carrières. They kept their marriage secret for three years in order to quell gossip, and it was not until 1964 that Messiaen moved to join Loriod permanently in her expanded apartment on the rue Marcadet in the Eighteenth Arrondissement.[3] They would live there for nearly three decades, until Messiaen's death. They would also travel all over the world, beginning with a trip to Japan in the summer of 1962. Their visit to Hiroshima — the city's atomic destruction had been just seventeen years earlier — hosted by a Belgian priest, Fr. Ernest Goossens, made an unforgettable impression.[4] The voyage resulted in Messiaen's *Seven Haiku: Japanese Sketches for Solo Piano and Small Orchestra* (1962).[5]

Launched by the brief yet symbol-laden *Verset for the Feast of the Dedication,* the 1960s would be marked by Messiaen's production of four important works. Each was not only explicitly religious and even "theological" in subject matter; it was also eschatological — a consideration of celestial life. He had written earlier apocalyptic works when in his thirties during a grim historical epoch: *Glorified Bodies* (1939), *Quartet for the End of Time* (1940), and *Visions of Amen* (1943). The works in the 1960s were those of a middle-aged man: his mother and father were deceased; so too was his first wife; his son had just married; and he himself had just remarried. Messiaen now viewed life after a half century's experience, a good deal of it tragic, through an eschatological prism. In the words of the creed sung every Sunday, *Et exspecto resurrectionem mortuorum:* "I await the resurrection of the dead."

His first work, *Colors of the Celestial City* (1963), a piece lasting about twenty minutes, was written for piano solo (again, Loriod), wind orchestra, and percussion.[6] Like the hymn for the feast of dedication, it is about the precious gems — the human stones — chiseled and fashioned during their earthly and purgatorial journeys in order to become the foundation of the heavenly Jerusalem. But in this work, Messiaen draws on another key eschatological aspect of the celestial city: the stones are multicolored (as in the book of Revelation). Messiaen's synesthesia (color-sounds) had first played an important role in *Apparition of the Eternal Church,* composed soon after meeting Blanc-Gatti. Although it had receded in importance with the pursuit of birdsong during the 1950s, synesthesia made an explicit return in the 1960s and 1970s,

---

3. Peter Hill and Nigel Simeone, *Messiaen* (New Haven: Yale University Press, 2005), 239-41.
4. Hill and Simeone, *Messiaen,* 245-51.
5. Simeone, *Bibliographical Catalogue,* 136-37.
6. Simeone, *Bibliographical Catalogue,* 140-41.

especially in interviews Messiaen used during these years to shape his legacy. The color-sound fusion symbolized Messiaen's vision of the afterlife, a dazzling city built of brilliant multicolored gems.

During that same year of 1963, Messiaen received a state commission to write a work honoring "the dead of two World Wars," to be premiered in 1965, twenty-five years after the German invasion of 1940.[7] (The commissioner was André Malraux, the first minister of cultural affairs serving under President Charles de Gaulle.) The resulting piece was *Et Exspecto Resurrectionem Mortuorum* (1964) — "And I look forward to (or: await, expect) the resurrection of the dead" — one of the Latin affirmations in the Nicene Creed sung every Sunday and solemn feast day at Mass.[8]

This work played a significant role in shaping the self-image that Messiaen projected in his mature years — quite successfully, as it turned out. As noted in the introduction, in the year of Messiaen's death, one critic summed up his countercultural stance: "Messiaen's music is different from its age not so much for the techniques it discovers but *for its refusal to mourn*. Not since Haydn perhaps, has a composer had the effrontery to be so happy, so serene: to suffuse his music with such confidence and composure."[9] In interviews conducted during the 1970s, Messiaen observed: "it isn't my nature to bury myself in suffering"; "Glory, Grace, Light: it's all linked up together. For that reason, my music is cheerful, it contains glory and light. Of course, suffering exists for me, too, but I've written very few poignant pieces. I'm not made for that. I love Light, Joy, and Glory in the divine sense."[10] Yvonne Loriod later noted that, rather than a Requiem Mass (like Benjamin Britten's *War Requiem*), Messiaen had chosen to commemorate the war dead by writing *Et Exspecto Resurrectionem Mortuorum*, saying: "Death? That exists, but I myself emphasize the Resurrection." Loriod added, "He always said, 'I have no wish to waste my time on harrowing subjects. *I am a musician of joy.*'"[11]

---

7. Hill and Simeone, *Messiaen*, 261.

8. Simeone, *Bibliographical Catalogue*, 142-45.

9. Bernard Holland, "Remembering Messiaen with Works of His Own," *New York Times*, November 10, 1992, emphasis added.

10. Messiaen, June 1972 and April 23, 1979, both in Almut Rößler, *Contributions to the Spiritual World of Olivier Messiaen*, trans. Barbara Dagg and Nancy Poland (Duisberg: Gilles & Francke, 1986), 52, 92; cf. Robert Sholl, "The Shock of the Positive: Olivier Messiaen, St. Francis, and Redemption through Modernity," in *Resonant Witness: Conversations between Music and Theology*, ed. Jeremy S. Begbie and Steven R. Guthrie (Grand Rapids: Eerdmans, 2011), 162-89.

11. Yvonne Loriod, in an interview with Peter Hill, in *The Messiaen Companion*, ed. Peter Hill (Portland, Ore.: Amadeus Press, 1995), 294-95, emphasis added.

1960-1992: Et Exspecto Resurrectionem Mortuorum

Messiaen was aware that in these revolutionary years of the 1960s and 1970s — years during which political theology and liberation theology were in ascendance — some critics reproached him for pursuing "a kind of *theologia gloriae* [theology of glory] which scarcely has anything to do with the actual situation of today's human being and his need for redemption." Messiaen's response is notable for the way that he too appealed to human suffering in history — but emphasized instead the incarnation: "God, who's beyond Time . . . came in order to suffer with us. And I express this in my music. . . . God is above us and still He comes to suffer with us. This is expressed by means of bird- and color-themes."[12] The decision not to write a requiem but rather *Et Exspecto* seemed to summarize the twentieth-century musician "set apart," "a man out of his time and place," the one "who refused to mourn."[13]

Two brief comparisons illustrate Messiaen's difference by contrast. The first is Benjamin Britten's *War Requiem*, premiered on May 30, 1962, and written for the reconsecration of Coventry Cathedral, which had been destroyed by German air raids during the Battle of Britain. It is a bitter piece, ironically intermingling fragments from the Latin Requiem Mass with the antiwar poetry of the British war poets. The second is Leonard Bernstein's *Kaddish* (third) symphony, first performed in Tel Aviv the following year, on December 10, 1963 (three weeks after the assassination of President Kennedy), with Bernstein conducting the Israel Philharmonic Orchestra. The work's title refers to the Jewish prayer chanted during the service for the dead. However, in this work, Bernstein's narrator recounts for God all the faults of creation; then, in his dream, he proposes an alternative vision of how the world might be. In the end, the narrator and God conclude a

---

12. See remarks by Dutch theologian Johan Vos in a roundtable discussion (June 11, 1972) and Messiaen's response; in Rößler, *Contributions*, 48-56, at 51, 52; cf. Andrew Shenton, *Olivier Messiaen's System of Signs: Notes towards Understanding His Music* (Aldershot, UK, and Burlington, Vt.: Ashgate, 2008), 28. For further discussion of this question, see Jeremy S. Begbie, *Resounding Truth: Christian Wisdom in the World of Music* (Grand Rapids: Baker Academic, 2007), 174-76. Both aspects of Messiaen's response can be found in Marmion. For the "infinite distance separating the creature from the Creator," see Columba Marmion, chapter 8 ("The Epiphany"), in *Christ in His Mysteries*, trans. Alan Bancroft (Bethesda, Md.: Zaccheus Press, 2008), 154-74, at 154; and for the incarnation's making "God *capable of suffering,*" see chapter 7 ("O Wondrous Exchange! [Christmas]"), 131-53, at 144.

13. Paul Griffiths, "Messiaen," in *The New Grove Dictionary of Music and Musicians* (London, 2001), 16, 491; unsigned obituary, "Olivier Messiaen," *Times* (London), April 29, 1992, in *Olivier Messiaen: Journalism, 1935-1939*, ed. Stephen Broad (Surrey, UK, and Burlington, Vt.: Ashgate, 2012), 1; and Holland, "Remembering Messiaen with Works of His Own."

new covenant in which they will cocreate a new world.[14] Generally speaking, Messiaen's use of traditional religious material in a nonironic way departed from trends of the transatlantic 1960s. To find a close counterpart, one would need to turn eastward toward Krzysztof Penderecki, the Polish composer writing religious works in a serialist vein behind the Iron Curtain, explicitly defiant repudiations of Soviet ideology and policy: *Stabat Mater* (1962), *Saint Luke Passion* (1965), *Dies Irae* (from the Requiem Mass, 1967), and *Utrenja* (Morning Prayer, 1969-1971).

The first performance of *Et Exspecto* took place on May 7, 1965, one day before the twentieth anniversary of V-E Day. The setting, Sainte-Chapelle, had been deeply meaningful to Messiaen since boyhood when he saw it after first moving to Paris; the brilliance of its stained glass windows dazzled him. The second performance took place on June 20 after High Mass in Chartres Cathedral, with President Charles de Gaulle in attendance.

Eight days later, Messiaen began composing yet another enormous work for chorus and orchestra commissioned for a festival in Lisbon: an oratorio entitled *The Transfiguration*.[15] Messiaen regarded this work highly:

> *The Transfiguration* is one of my most important works. I even consider it one of my most successful.... I'd been considering the subject of *The Transfiguration* for years, perhaps twenty years, ever since the day when I heard, in a little country church in the Dauphiné region, in Motte-d'Aveillans, an old priest deliver a sermon on the light and the filiation, the two principal ideas of my work. This was on 6 August, the Feast of the Transfiguration, so I devoted the first septenary to the idea of light, because Christ transfigured became radiant: "His countenance was like lightning, and his raiment white as snow." The second septenary is based on the idea of the filiation: a voice emerges from the cloud saying, "This is my Son, whom I love." There are two kinds of filiation: eternal filiation of the Word-become-Man in Jesus Christ, and the adoptive filiation of all the poor human beings that we are.[16]

---

14. Bernstein's *Mass* (1971) is composed in much the same vein. By contrast, however, Bernstein's hopeful and even peaceful *Chichester Psalms* was premiered on July 15, 1965, two months after the first performance of Messiaen's *Et Exspecto*.

15. Simeone, *Bibliographical Catalogue*, 146-49. See also Howard E. Smither, *A History of the Oratorio*, 4 vols. (Chapel Hill: University of North Carolina Press, 1977-2000), 4:670-76; Siglind Bruhn, *Messiaen's Interpretations of Holiness and Trinity: Echoes of Medieval Theology in the Oratorio, Organ Meditations, and Opera* (Hillsdale, N.Y.: Pendragon Press, 2008), 57-147.

16. Olivier Messiaen and Claude Samuel, *Music and Color: Conversations with Claude*

1960-1992: Et Exspecto Resurrectionem Mortuorum

Two points seem worth underscoring: first, Messiaen had first embraced the centrality of the doctrine of filiation in the early 1930s when he encountered it in Dom Marmion's *Christ in His Mysteries*.[17] We have already seen its key theological and compositional position in *The Nativity* (1935). Thirty years later, it appears in *The Transfiguration,* most explicitly in movement 10 — "Adoptionem filiorum perfectam" — following Marmion:

> In declaring [in the transfiguration] that Jesus is His Son, the Father declares that those who share, through grace, in His, the Father's, divinity are likewise His children, albeit by a different title to be so. It is through Jesus, the Word Incarnate, that this adoption is given to us: "He has begotten us through the Word of Truth," *Genuit nos veritatis* [James 1:18]. And by adopting us as His children, the Father gives us the right of one day sharing in His divine and glorious life. That is the "completed adoption," *adoptio perfecta*.[18]

Marmion's *adoptio perfecta* (in Latin) is adapted from the Collect for the Mass celebrated on the August feast of the transfiguration: *et adoptiónem filiórum perféctam* = "the perfect adoption of sons." Messiaen uses this phrase for the title of his tenth movement: "Adoptionem filiorum perfectam." Like Messiaen himself, the "old priest" on transfiguration day — if indeed he existed — would undoubtedly have been inspired by Marmion.

A second point about chronology: Messiaen's recollection of the sermon on the feast of the transfiguration dates it "perhaps twenty years" prior to 1965 — that is, sometime around August 6, 1945, the day of the bombing of Hiroshima. Indeed, one of the chilling aspects of celebrating this ancient major feast of the church year in the wake of that horrific twentieth-century event is the appointed Gospel reading: the apostles see everything transformed by the blinding light turning garments "as white as snow." Note that in 1962, three years prior to beginning *The Transfiguration,* Messiaen had been deeply moved

---

Samuel, trans. E. Thomas Glasow (Portland, Ore.: Amadeus Press, 1994), 143-51, at 145; hereafter "Messiaen and Samuel (1994)."

17. See the discussion above of the concept of filiation as the central fulcrum — that is, movement 5, "The Children of God" — on which the structure of *The Nativity* (1935) is balanced.

18. Marmion, chapter 12 ("On the Summit of Tabor [Second Sunday of Lent]"), in *Christ in His Mysteries*, 266-86, at 278. Note that Marmion's emphasis on divine adoption ultimately follows Dom Guéranger's. See, for example, Guéranger's treatment of the feast of the transfiguration in Dom Prosper Guéranger, O.S.B., *The Liturgical Year,* trans. Benedictines of Stanbrook, 15 vols. (Westminster, Md.: Newman Press, 1949), 13:271-84.

by his visit to Hiroshima. (This visit to Japan had resulted in the composition of *Seven Haiku* [1962].) And he was surprisingly frank in voicing his idiosyncratic association of the atomic bombing with the effects of Christ's resurrected body. He explained that he believed in the Shroud of Turin "because it seems to me not like a miracle but like a natural phenomenon. At Hiroshima bodies of the victims were found etched on the walls. In the same way the Resurrection was like an atomic explosion: Christ rose at a stroke and his image was imprinted on the Shroud."[19]

Messiaen would also have been intimately aware of Penderecki's utterly terrifying *Threnody to the Victims of Hiroshima* (1960), a competition prize-winner that brought the young composer from behind the Iron Curtain to international prominence. The piece had originally been entitled *8'37"*, "referring to its duration in minutes and seconds" (and perhaps imitative of John Cage's *4'33"*, premiered in 1952).[20] The work's premiere in 1961 by the Polish Radio Symphony Orchestra was taped; this recording was then played that May in Paris, winning Penderecki the UNESCO Prize of the International Composers' Jury. After an influential musicologist and critic interpreted it as a "profoundly disturbing piece of apparently hopeless cataclysmic atmosphere," Penderecki changed the name and dedicated it to "the victims of Hiroshima." On December 1, 1964, Penderecki traveled to Japan to give a performance of *Threnody* in Hiroshima, describing the 1945 atomic bombing of the city as a "tragedy of mankind" in a letter to the city's mayor.[21]

Is it a coincidence that Messiaen had traveled to Hiroshima in the summer of 1962; Penderecki performed *Threnody* there in December 1964; and five months later Messiaen began composing *The Transfiguration*? If not, then Penderecki's and Messiaen's works offer two contrasting memorials of the date August 6: one, a horrifically cacophonous evocation of air raid sirens

---

19. Jean-Christophe Marti, "Entretien avec Olivier Messiaen," in *Saint François d'Assise: Messiaen* (Paris: l'Avant-Scène Opéra, 1992), 11; quoted in Robert Fallon, "Birds, Beasts, and Bombs in Messiaen's Cold War Mass," *Journal of Musicology* 26, no. 2 (Spring 2009): 180; cf. Alex Ross, *The Rest Is Noise: Listening to the Twentieth Century* (New York: Farrar, Straus and Giroux, 2007), 446.

20. Wolfram Schwinger, *Krzysztof Penderecki: His Life and Work; Encounters, Biography, and Musical Commentary*, trans. William Mann (New York: Schott, 1989), 124; original Schwinger, *Penderecki: Begegnungen, Lebensdaten, Werkkommentare* (Stuttgart: Deutsche Verlags-Anstalt, 1979), 116. For *"4'33"* see Kyle Gann, *No Such Thing as Silence: John Cage's "4'33"* (New Haven: Yale University Press, 2010).

21. Schwinger, *Krzysztof Penderecki*, 28, 35; Schwinger, *Penderecki*, 32, 41.

1960–1992: Et Exspecto Resurrectionem Mortuorum

and dropping bombs, "a naturalistic representation of Chaos";[22] the other, an eschatological representation of Christ's blinding transformation.

If Messiaen intended *The Transfiguration* to be linked (inexplicitly) with August 6, 1945, it would be tied historically to *Et Exspecto Resurrectionem,* and both would be memorializations of the Second World War. They are also, in any event, linked with one another scripturally, liturgically, and doctrinally, Christ's transfiguration being seen as a prefiguration of the resurrection.[23] As Thomas Aquinas writes, both are experiences of sense dazzlement and hence of fear or awe (in the face of the *terrible*):

> It was fitting [at the transfiguration] that the disciples should be afraid and fall down on hearing the voice of the Father, to show that the glory which was then being revealed surpasses in excellence the sense and faculty of all mortal beings; according to Exodus 33:20: "Man shall not see Me and live." This is what Jerome says on Matthew 17:6: "Such is human frailty that it cannot bear to gaze on such great glory." But men are healed of this frailty by Christ when He brings them into glory. And this is signified by what He says to them: "Arise, and fear not."[24]

Hence the significance of movement 12: *"Terribilis est locus iste."* This is a terrifying place.[25]

Messiaen worked on *The Transfiguration* from June 28, 1965, until Feb-

---

22. Schwinger, *Krzysztof Penderecki,* 124; Schwinger, *Penderecki,* 117.

23. Although (as noted above) the Gospel account of the transfiguration was read in early spring on the Second Sunday of Lent, Marmion noted that it was also appointed to be read again in summer: "The Church provides for the Gospel account of the Transfiguration to be read to us twice: on the Second Sunday of Lent, to strengthen our resolve to bear the Lenten mortifications through a distant view of the glory Christ promises us by His Transfiguration; and a second time on August 6th, the Solemnity devoted solely to honoring the manifestation of the divine splendor in Jesus on Mount Tabor." Marmion, *Christ in His Mysteries,* 267 n. 2.

24. *The "Summa Theologica" of St. Thomas Aquinas,* trans. Dominicans of the English Province, 22 vols., 2nd rev. ed. (London: Burns, Oates and Washbourne, 1920-1942), Suppl., q. 45 ("Christ's Transfiguration"), a. 4, reply to the fourth objection.

25. This line from Gen. 28:17 (Vulgate) is used for the first line of the Mass (i.e., the Introit) for the feast of the dedication of a church. See *The Liber Usualis with Introduction and Rubrics in English,* ed. Benedictines of Solesmes (Tournai, Belgium: Desclée & Co., [1939] 1949), 1250; *Missel-Fr,* 930; *Missal-En,* 1388-89: "Terrible is this place: it is the house of God, and the gate of heaven; and shall be called the court of God." Since masses were named after the first word of the Introit, the Mass for a dedication anniversary is simply *Terribilis* — yet another reason for Messiaen's use of it beginning with *Apparition.*

ruary 20, 1969. Its wide variety of source materials exemplifies Messiaen's self-image as a "theological" musician: the Gospel of Saint Matthew, Genesis, Psalms, the Book of Wisdom, Paul's Letter to the Hebrews, Thomas Aquinas's *Summa Theologica,* and the liturgical offices (Mass and Hours) for the feast of the transfiguration. The subject matter and timing of *The Transfiguration* — that is, the transformation of what is lowly and even despised into what is glorious — also suggest that Messiaen encountered the work of Hans Urs von Balthasar in the process of writing this work. The first volume (entitled *Apparition*) of von Balthasar's monumental multivolume work appeared in French translation in 1965 under the title *La gloire et la croix (The Glory and the Cross).*[26] Among the numerous aspects of von Balthasar's "theological aesthetics" are the notions of *sur-figure* and *dé-figure* — both the glorification and the debasement of the figure of Christ. The crucifixion would be a *dé-figure* of Christ's form; the transfiguration would be a *sur-figure* of the same form.

That Messiaen worked for nearly four years on this is remarkable in itself. But 1965-1969 were years of extraordinary social, political, intellectual, and cultural upheaval on both sides of the Atlantic. This was the period during which a new generation that had not known the Second World War — but had been born and raised within the post-1945 arrangements — came of age and rejected those arrangements.

In the USA, the 1965 escalation of America's war in Vietnam triggered what would later be thought of as the turbulent 1960s. In retrospect, it can be seen as a post-1945 Cold War arrangement coming to an end: riots against both the Vietnam War and racial discrimination proliferated in 1965-1968. In West Germany, some youth rejected their country's twenty-year-old position as an American quasi satellite. A riot in Berlin on June 2, 1967, occasioned by an official visit of the Shah of Iran, produced the martyr's death that catalyzed radical leftism in what would eventually be a decade of domestic terrorism, dominated by the image of the Baader-Meinhof complex. Three days later, the Six Day War (June 5-10, 1967) between Israel and Egypt inaugurated a period of destabilization in the Middle East that endures to this day. During the following year, revolutions broke out across the globe.[27]

26. Hans Urs von Balthasar, *La gloire et la croix: les aspects esthétique de la révélation. 1: Apparition,* trans. Robert Givord (Paris: Aubier, 1965); original von Balthasar, *Herrlichkeit, eine theologische Ästhetik. 1: Schau der Gestalt* (Einsiedeln: Johannes Verlag, 1961). The work has been published in English as *The Glory of the Lord,* a title that translates the German original more literally than does the French.

27. Jeremi Suri, *Power and Protest: Global Revolution and the Rise of Detente* (Cam-

1960–1992: Et Exspecto Resurrectionem Mortuorum

May 1968 has acquired quasi-mythical status for the student riots throughout Europe that shook the continent to its foundations. In Paris, streets filled with students and workers imagining a new world was opening up for them, and their protests challenged conservative structures in French society (especially its elitist educational structures). Although government forces prevailed and workers felt abandoned by students and intellectuals (as they had in the past), the events catalyzed the following year's collapse of Charles de Gaulle's government (January 8, 1959–April 28, 1969), a decade-long reign originating in the Algerian War crisis. The events of May 1968 would become the stuff of legends and divisions within the "Generation of 1968" (the *soixante-huitards*) that would dominate politics for the coming decades.[28] In the United States, 1968 was also a landmark year — "the year that rocked the world."[29] The assassinations of Martin Luther King Jr. (April 4) and Robert F. Kennedy (June 5) preceded the Chicago Riots at the Democratic National Convention in August; Richard M. Nixon was elected in November. Finally, in Czechoslovakia, the Soviet invasion in September brutally suppressed and finished off the Prague Spring. On December 8, at the far end of this cataclysmic year, Messiaen turned sixty years old.

Within this genuinely world-historical context, *The Transfiguration* received its Lisbon premiere on June 7, 1969. Its Paris premiere followed soon afterward on October 20. When Messiaen began its composition in June 1965, France was commemorating the Second World War beneath the firm hand of President de Gaulle. Just before its premiere, de Gaulle's seemingly eternal government had been swept out of power.

In the midst of such terrestrial upheaval, perhaps it is not surprising that Messiaen's final composition of the 1960s was a daunting organ cycle, *Meditations on the Mystery of the Holy Trinity* (1969).[30] These meditations considered the Trinitarian Godhead *in itself* (the "immanent Trinity") — in its eternal and

---

bridge: Harvard University Press, 2003); Suri, *The Global Revolutions of 1968: A Norton Casebook in History* (New York: Norton, 2007).

28. Andrew Feenberg and Jim Freedman, *When Poetry Ruled the Streets: The French May Events of 1968* (Albany: State University of New York Press, 2001); Kristin Ross, *May '68 and Its Afterlives* (Chicago: University of Chicago Press, 2002); Julian Bourg, *From Revolution to Ethics: May 1968 and Contemporary French Thought* (Montreal and Ithaca, N.Y.: McGill-Queen's University Press, 2007).

29. Mark Kurlansky, *1968: The Year That Rocked the World* (New York: Ballantine, 2004).

30. Simeone, *Bibliographical Catalogue,* 150-53; Gillock, *Performing Messiaen's Organ Music,* 199-239.

unchanging inward self — and not as it works *for us* in history (the "economic Trinity"). In this work, Messiaen leaves behind the world of time completely, preferring instead the contemplation of timeless realities. In the first edition, the meditations were numbered but untitled, each preceded by a commentary. Messiaen's later notes identified the nine movements:[31]

I The Unbegotten Father	↔	VI The Son, Word and Light
II The Holiness of Jesus Christ	↔	VII By the Holy Spirit, the Father and Son love themselves and us
III The real relation in God: being identical with its essence	↔	VIII God is simple
IV I am, I am!	↔	IX I am He who is

V God is immense, eternal, immovable
— the Breath of the Spirit — God is Love

Throughout the work, Messiaen emphasizes timeless existence: the "Unbegotten" character without origin; God as the only being whose existence is identical with his essence (a fundamental Thomistic distinction); the appeal to the translation of God's self-revelation in Exodus as "I am who I Am" (both movements IV and IX). Musically speaking, *Meditations* is the work in which Messiaen most fully deployed both serialism and his own invention of "communicable language."[32]

1971–1974: *From Canyons to Stars*

Almost immediately after completing *Meditations,* Messiaen was commissioned by Alice Tully to compose a work to commemorate the American bicentennial year of 1976. The result was *From Canyons to Stars* (1974), yet another gigantic work for a large chamber ensemble that outstripped Messiaen's previous compositions in terms of duration.[33] In the spring of 1972, to prepare himself, Messiaen traveled to the canyons of Utah and noted what

---

31. Simeone, *Bibliographical Catalogue,* 151.
32. For Messiaen's *langage communicable,* see Shenton, *Olivier Messiaen's System of Signs,* 83-136.
33. Simeone, *Bibliographical Catalogue,* 156-59.

he found: "Red-violet, a red orange, rose, dark red carmine, scarlet red, all possible varieties of red, and extraordinary beauty."[34] In the most literal sense, these rock colors were *chronochromie* — time-colors — hues delineating enormous layers of primeval time. One music historian notes, "this color was the color of time, for the layered rock of Utah slices into the history of the earth, brings the deep past into the present — as the stars do, shining from far away and long ago. Messiaen's combination of themes — the red rock strata and the constellations in the still-blue desert sky — provided him with favorite imagery, and at the same time enabled him to answer the commission, with music of stars and stripes."[35]

In addition to writing a "geological" work, Messiaen also wanted to write an "astronomical" work — and in this respect, the clearest precedent for *From Canyons* is the "Amen of the Stars" in *Visions of Amen,* composed three decades earlier.

> But I also wanted to write an astronomical work and to raise myself up from the depth of the canyons to the beauty of the stars. I was interested in astronomy in my childhood and, here, I focused on Aldebaran, one of the brightest stars in the firmament. Having left the canyons to climb to the stars, I had only to keep going in the same direction to raise myself up to God. So my work is at once geological, ornithological, astronomical, and theological. Despite the importance of color and birds, it's above all a religious work of praise and contemplation.[36]

In addition to discovering Utah, 1972 brought a very different kind of discovery for Messiaen. After his maternal aunt, Germaine Tatin, died that September, Messiaen received the copies of his mother's clandestine works written during World War I while she and young Olivier lived in André Sauvage's apartment.[37] She had confided them to her sister. Messiaen had been shy of his sixth birthday when the war broke out; he was now just short of celebrating his sixty-fourth. We have no written record of his reaction to

---

34. Messiaen, in Harriet Watts, "Canyons, Colours and Birds: An Interview with Olivier Messiaen," *Tempo* 128 (1979): 2-8; quoted in Paul Griffiths, liner notes for *From Canyons to Stars (Des canyons aux étoiles)* (1974), in Olivier Messiaen, *Complete Edition,* 32 CDs (Germany: Deutsche Grammophon, 2008), 286-90, at 286.

35. Griffiths, liner notes for *From Canyons to Stars,* 286-87.

36. Messiaen and Samuel (1994), 163.

37. Cécile Sauvage, *Écrits d'amour,* edited, introduced, and annotated by Béatrice Marchal (Paris: Les Éditions du Cerf, 2009), 24.

discovering the precise nature of his mother's awful grief and depression of those early years.

We do, however, have Yvonne Loriod's 1973 recording of Messiaen's youthful *The Lady of Shalott* (1917). As Cécile Sauvage's biographer observes, Messiaen's discovery of his mother's hidden writings in September 1972 perhaps explains the recording of this work fifty-six years after its composition: "in having Yvonne Loriod play it a year after the full revelation of the passion lived by his mother, he seems to have testified that it had acquired a new importance in his eyes. He finally understood why she had loved this poem so much which, by means of its symbolism, offered a discreet identification with the Lady of Shalott."[38] However, Messiaen did not tell Loriod of the discovery of his mother's writings for another fifteen years.

Messiaen was sixty-three years old when he visited Utah and sixty-five when he completed the vast tableau of *From Canyons*. It summarizes numerous themes spanning various decades of his life, quoting the Catholic Revivalist Ernest Hello, indulging his penchant for outer space, illustrating many varieties of birds, and ending up in Utah's Zion National Park, a stand-in for the heavenly Zion or "celestial city." The work's twelve movements symbolically recall the twelve tribes of Israel, the twelve apostles, and the twelve varieties of precious stones out of which the celestial city will be built. The twelve movements are themselves divided into two parts: 5 + 7. The two parts thus function as a somewhat asymmetrical diptych, recalling the *Diptych* (1930) subtitled *An Essay on Terrestrial Life and Blessed Eternity*. Here too, part 1 is devoted to terrestrial history while part 2 is devoted to celestial life, represented by birds.

Part 1[39] [Terrestrial Life]
1. "The Desert." Messiaen quotes Ernest Hello: "He who is to be found is vast: one must discard everything in order to take the first steps towards him. . . . Go deep into the Desert of deserts."[40]

---

38. Béatrice Marchal, *Les Chants du silence. Olivier Messiaen, fils de Cécile Sauvage ou la musique face à l'impossible parole* (Sampzon: Éditions Delatour France, 2008), 112. Yvonne Loriod's 1973 recording of *La Dame de Shalott* was included in her eight-LP set of Messiaen's piano music for the Erato label.

39. For the following, see Griffiths, liner notes for *From Canyons to Stars*, in Messiaen, *Complete Edition*, 286-90.

40. Ernest Hello, *Paroles de Dieu. Réflexions sur quelques textes sacrés*, ed. François Angelier (Grenoble: Jérôme Millon, [1877] 1992), 77, 78; quoted in Messiaen, titles and inscriptions to movements of *From Canyons to Stars*, in *Complete Edition*, 32-35, at 32. Cf. Hello,

2. "The Orioles." A song of North America's "most jubilant birds," dominated by the orchard oriole.
3. "What is written in the stars . . ." Messiaen uses the musical alphabet of his "communicable language" (fully developed in *Meditations on the Mystery of the Holy Trinity*) to inscribe the cryptic message written on the wall at Belshazzar's feast: *Mene Tekel Upharsin.*

Was Messiaen making a statement about the ephemerality of even the American empire? The scriptural interpretation of this prophecy is given by Daniel: "And this is the interpretation of the word. MANE: God hath numbered thy kingdom, and hath finished it. THECEL: thou art weighed in the balance, and art found wanting. PHARES: thy kingdom is divided, and is given to the Medes and Persians."[41] Surely this would have been a disturbing reference at the work's premiere at Alice Tully Hall at Lincoln Center in 1974, just after Watergate and as American troops were drawing down in Vietnam. Whatever Messiaen's meaning, the effect is chaotic, a sharp contrast between the eternal stars and empires that rise and fall.

4. "The White-Browed Robin." The bird is from Africa: Did Messiaen intend it as a reference to the African American slave trade? The form is roughly palindromic, that is, largely the same whether read from beginning to end or from end to beginning.
5. "Cedar Breaks and the Gift of Awe [*le Don de Crainte*]." As this movement is the climax of the first part of the work, it is not surprising that it is the most dense in philosophical and theological meaning. It reprises the long-standing influence on Messiaen of both Pascal and Ernest Hello. As in the first movement, Messiaen inserts words of Hello as an epigraph: "The replacement of fear [*la peur*] by awe [*la crainte*] opens a window for adoration."[42] The abyss of Cedar Breaks embodies two infinites, one of depths (nothingness) and the other of heights (being): "a vast amphitheater, dropping to a deep gorge, whose rocks — orange, yellow, brown, red — rise in curtain walls, columns, towers, turrets, and keeps."[43] The "gift of awe" leads to "adoration": awareness of one's nearly infinite smallness

---

"Trois puissances: le néant, le vide, le désert" ("Three Powers: Nothingness, Emptiness, the Desert"), in *Du néant à dieu,* ed. Jules-Philippe Heuzey, 2 vols. (Paris: Perrin et Cie, [1921] 1930), 1:93-96.

41. Dan. 5:25-28 (Douay-CCD).
42. Hello, *Paroles de Dieu,* 176; quoted in Messiaen, *Complete Edition,* 33.
43. Messiaen, in Griffiths, liner notes, *Complete Edition,* 288.

in the face of infinity — "holy and venerable is his name. The fear of the Lord is the beginning of all wisdom."[44]

As Messiaen's commentary on this passage is perhaps the most detailed of all his remarks about "fear" and "awe," it is worth considering at length:

> As I've said, Cedar Breaks was a frightening place, and to evoke it, I thought of the different stages of fear: first the fear of the policeman or, if you prefer, the fear of punishment, then the fear that the Bible calls awe, which is the beginning of wisdom. Awe here signifies the sense of the sacred. When Moses approaches the burning bush and a voice says to him, "I am the One who is," he is afraid. It's not the fear felt before death, but a feeling caused by an extraordinary event that is beyond you. It's a reverence for the sacred, and if we pursue this line of thinking, we arrive at theology and the knowledge of God. The fifth piece was the most difficult one in the whole work for me to compose.
>
> . . . because I wanted to translate this feeling of awe, which is not fear but a feeling of reverence before something higher. I'll give you a simple example: suppose that an extraterrestrial comes into this room. He would be stunned to see us, and we, too, would be stunned to see him. We wouldn't be able to understand each other — Well, then, the gift of awe is a little like that: the impossibility of understanding, and it isn't easy to translate into music.[45]

Part 2 [Celestial Life]

6. "Interstellar Call." A lonely horn sounds between stars. This movement also has an elaborate meaning for Messiaen: it "sums up all the questioning about misfortune and suffering" in this world; and it then answers that questioning "by showing, alongside the atrocities surrounding us, the miraculous beauties of our planet and the hope of still greater beauties after death."[46]

7. "Bryce Canyon and the Red-Orange Rocks." The movement mirrors movement 5 (about Cedar Breaks) insofar as the two infinites appear

---

44. Ps. 110 (111):9b-10; cf. Prov. 9:10 Douay-CCD. See Fillion translation parallel with Vulgate: "Son nom est saint et terrible. La crainte du Seigneur est le commencement de la sagesse" ("Sanctum et terribile nomen ejus. Initium sapientiae timor Domini"); "La crainte du Seigneur est le principe de la sagesse" ("Timor Domini principium sapientiae").

45. Messiaen and Samuel (1994), 164-65.

46. Messiaen and Samuel (1994), 165.

1960–1992: Et Exspecto Resurrectionem Mortuorum

again: the infinite being of the Celestial City (chorales, bell sounds, alleluias) and the infinite nothingness of the abyss (the tam-tam and low trombone). Messiaen considered it "the central piece of the entire work" as it "evolves through all shades of red, violet, and orange, with the most varied nuances: red-orange, purple-red, hyacinth-violet, etc."[47]

8. "The Resurrected and the Song of the Star Aldebaran." This peaceful song recalls "Garden of the Sleep of Love" from *Turangalîla Symphony,* though now the "lovers" have been raised from the dead, spending eternity singing as birds.
9. "The Mockingbird." A second piano solo for Yvonne Loriod — and Australian birds also sing here.
10. "The Wood Thrush." An image of the "new name" promised for each individual (Rev. 2:17).
11. "Omao, Leiothrix, Elepaio, Shama." These birds all live in Hawaii — the United States' fiftieth state. The work revisits *Exotic Birds* (1956).
12. "Zion Park and the Celestial City." As did America's nineteenth-century pioneers, so too Messiaen finds in Zion Park a terrestrial representation of the Celestial City marked by choruses of birdsong.

From Canyons to Stars was premiered on November 20, 1974, in Alice Tully Hall at Lincoln Center — which had just opened in 1969 — with Yvonne Loriod playing the piano. President Richard Nixon had resigned his office three months earlier, and Vice President Gerald Ford had stepped into the presidency. When commissioning the bicentennial work in 1971, Alice Tully could hardly have imagined what shape the United States would be in three years later: its government having just survived a constitutional crisis; its war winding down; a peace treaty negotiated following years of frustrating peace talks in Paris, the origin of French Indochina's colonial power. The historical situation was filled with ironies. Perhaps best for all in a bicentennial mode, *From Canyons* focused on the enduring rather than the transient.

Throughout the 1950s-1960s epoch dominated by serialism, Messiaen's music remained something of an outsider. However, the 1974 premiere of *From Canyons* reminds us that classical music was radically changing during the 1970s. The shift toward a "postmodern" eclecticism that retrieved Western traditional elements along with "ethnic" ones (i.e., from recently decolonized

---

47. Messiaen and Samuel (1994), 167. In this discussion of sound-color correspondence, Messiaen here also cites Paul Dukas's *Ariadne and Bluebeard* and the Swiss painter Blanc-Gatti.

parts of the world) had already begun in the 1960s: Terry Riley's *In C* (1964, often cited as the first minimalist composition); George Rochberg's *Music for the Magic Theater* (1965); Steve Reich's *Violin Phase* (1967); Luciano Berio's *Sinfonia* (1968). Even more so in the 1970s: Leonard Bernstein's *Mass* (1971); Henryk Górecki's *Symphony No. 3* (1976); and Philip Glass's *Einstein on the Beach* (1976). In 1981, Reich composed *Tehillim*, a setting of several psalms in the original Hebrew text; it was premiered at Westdeutscher Rundfunk (West German Radio) in Cologne. If music was on the move, it was moving toward, not away from, Messiaen. By the time *Saint Francis* premiered in 1983, the postmodern shift was already well under way.

1975–1986: *Saint Francis of Assisi* and *Book of the Blessed Sacrament*

With the premier of *From Canyons* in November 1974 now behind him, and just a few years remaining before his seventieth birthday, Messiaen turned to the lifework he had considered for thirty years.[48] He would eventually compose an opera, *Saint Francis of Assisi (Franciscan Scenes)*, based on the beloved medieval Italian saint closely identified with animals, especially birds.[49] (Francis was famously reputed to have preached a sermon to the birds; this event is recalled in act 2, tableau 6: "Sermon to the Birds.") The work's composition, orchestration, and copying required eight long years of Messiaen's life (1975–1983), some of them quite difficult.[50] Failing health and accumulating anxiety culminated in an emotional crisis around his seventy-third birthday in December 1981. Loriod later recalled that Messiaen "was subdued and exhausted, unable to decide what to do; he was prone to fits of weeping, and was convinced the opera would never be finished." The crisis was solved after Messiaen agreed to let Loriod assist in the process of copying. He also began to get physical exercise, and resumed a practice begun in 1980 during the renovation of the organ at Trinité: climbing the hill to Montmartre to attend evening Mass at the Sacré-Coeur Basilica.[51]

The opera was premiered in late 1983 with a performance on both sides of Messiaen's seventy-fifth birthday: first, on November 28, Seiji Ozawa conduct-

---

48. Messiaen and Samuel (1994), 216; in Simeone, *Bibliographical Catalogue*, 165. See discussion above following *Five Refrains* at the end of the 1940s.

49. Simeone, *Bibliographical Catalogue*, 160–65; Bruhn, *Messiaen's Interpretations*, 149–202; English translation of libretto at 207-18.

50. For the story see Hill and Simeone, *Messiaen*, 304–41.

51. Hill and Simeone, *Messiaen*, 334.

ing; and second, on December 14, Kent Nagano conducting. It was the summit and consummation of Messiaen's vision. Fortunately for today's reader, there are multiple recordings, both aural and visual.

I began this book with observations about Messiaen's self-image as a "musician of joy." The meaning of "joy" was called into question with the surrealistic title of one of Messiaen's most famous movements, "Joy of the Blood of the Stars" from *Turangalîla Symphony*. When we arrive at the end of Messiaen's life and work, the meaning of "joy" for Messiaen is both questioned and resolved in *Saint Francis of Assisi*. One of the opera's main leitmotifs is "perfect joy" *(la joie parfaite)*. Messiaen explained this leitmotif in an interview:

> So the keyboards announce the first scene, which should have been called "Perfect Joy." I rejected this title because it might have been misinterpreted. According to Saint Francis, *to feel perfect joy is to suffer like Christ,* in penance for all the sins of mankind. *This is a strange joy,* and I thought it simpler to entitle the scene "The Cross." In fact, at the end of the scene, a large cross produced by a laser beam appears. During the course of the scene, Saint Francis explains to Brother Leo that, having reached the door of the monastery, exhausted by a walk of forty kilometers, starving, thirsty, soaked by rain, driven off by a doorkeeper who not only pretended not to recognize him but beat him with a stick, he finally knows what he calls "perfect joy." Brother Leo is dumbfounded. The curtain falls as the chorus repeats the words of Christ: "He would walk in my steps, let him renounce himself, take up his cross and follow me."[52]

And yet even the saint must learn this lesson in a way uniquely his own. The forward motion of the opera is driven by Saint Francis's fear — his "fear on the road" of life's journey. One of his deepest fears is of lepers. A moment of climax in the opera comes when Saint Francis overcomes this fear and kisses the leper. At this moment he too understands "perfect joy," not only theologically but also experientially. And his fear is turned into fear of the Lord, opening up a window on adoration.

After 1983 ended with the premiere of *Saint Francis,* Messiaen turned to his last work for organ, the sprawling *Book of the Blessed Sacrament.* The source

---

52. Messiaen and Samuel (1994), 223. For an overview of this leitmotif, see Robert Fallon, "Two Paths to Paradise: Reform in Messiaen's *Saint François d'Assise,*" in *Messiaen Studies,* ed. Robert Sholl, Cambridge Composer Studies (New York: Cambridge University Press, 2007), 206-31.

of its inspiration seems certain in light of Messiaen's December 1981 crisis: he had recommenced an earlier practice of walking up Montmartre's slope for evening Mass at the Basilica of the Sacré-Coeur, a perennially popular tourist destination. Since 1885, even before the basilica's construction had been completed, the Blessed Sacrament has been exposed for perpetual adoration without interruption: twenty-four hours a day, seven days a week.[53] Although the meditations in the massive *Book of the Blessed Sacrament* are undoubtedly the result of decades of theological study and meditative contemplation, their more immediate source of inspiration would seem to have been Messiaen's daily experience of seeing the exposed monstrance at Sacré-Coeur throughout 1982-1983. Perhaps, once again, the composition can be seen as a kind of votive offering, in this case a work of gratitude for having lived long enough to see the opera premiered the previous year.

Book of the Blessed Sacrament had been commissioned by the city of Detroit and the American Guild of Organists for its annual meeting.[54] The work was premiered by Almut Rössler on July 1, 1986, at the Metropolitan Methodist Church in Detroit. It is touching that Messiaen would return at the end of his life to material he had begun with: his first work had been *The Celestial Banquet* (1928) for organ in the summer following his mother's death. Sixty years later, he returned to this theme in a massive endeavor that helped establish for posterity his self-understanding as a "theological" musician. He later said of the piece's premiere: "On 27 June [1986], I undertook another trip to the United States for the registrations of my last organ work, *Livre du Saint Sacrement*. . . . This was a private concert for the American Guild of Organists, which has two thousand members. So my work was first performed before an audience of two thousand, all professional organists. It was a very great success for Almut Rössler and for the work and, on my part, a great act of faith in the Real Presence of Jesus Christ in the Blessed Sacrament."[55] However, it is also possible that Messiaen intended, at least in part, to intervene in postconciliar Catholicism, that is, within the context of liturgical and theological upheaval following the Second Vatican Council (1962-1965) — changes that Messiaen, along with numerous other French Catholic organists (including Maurice Duruflé and Jean Langlais),

---

53. Raymond Anthony Jonas, *France and the Cult of the Sacred Heart: An Epic Tale for Modern Times* (Berkeley: University of California Press, 2000).

54. Simeone, *Bibliographical Catalogue*, 166-69; Gillock, *Performing Messiaen's Organ Music*, 240-344.

55. Messiaen and Samuel (1994), 258; in Simeone, *Bibliographical Catalogue*, 168. Translation altered.

opposed.[56] During and following that upheaval, the medieval scholastic doctrine of transubstantiation as an explanation of the "Real Presence" of Christ in the Eucharist underwent serious theological scrutiny. The doctrine and its medieval metaphysical underpinnings had been affirmed at the Council of Trent four centuries earlier. However, in the 1960s, theologians asked whether this formulation made sense to moderns for whom the substance-accident metaphysical system, both in its original medieval scholastic form and in its nineteenth-century neoscholastic retrieval, was no longer meaningful.[57] The debates reached such a pitch that Pope Paul VI, even before the closure of the council in December 1965, felt compelled to publish an encyclical naming the crisis and underscoring his insistence on retaining the language of transubstantiation — as opposed to competing paradigms like "transignification" or "transfinalization."[58]

For Messiaen, the doctrine of transubstantiation is simply beyond question. He inserts it in *Book of the Blessed Sacrament* at the center of his eighteen-movement composition, just following the Easter Sunday events:

    VII. The Resurrected and the Light of Life
        VIII. Institution of the Eucharist [i.e., Last Supper on Holy
        (Maundy) Thursday]
        IX. The Darkness [i.e., Good Friday]
        X. The Resurrection of Christ [i.e., Easter morning]

---

56. Karin Heller, "Olivier Messiaen and Cardinal Jean-Marie Lustiger: Two Views of the Liturgical Reform according to the Second Vatican Council," in *Messiaen the Theologian*, 63-82.

57. For example, Edward Schillebeeckx, "Transubstantiation, Transfinalization, Transignification," *Worship* 40 (June-July 1966): 324-38; reprinted in Schillebeeckx, *The Eucharist* (New York: Sheed and Ward, 1968); Karl Rahner, "The Presence of Christ in the Sacrament of the Lord's Supper," *Theological Investigations,* vol. 4, *More Recent Writings,* trans. Kevin Smyth (Baltimore: Helicon Press, 1966), 187-311; Piet Schoonenberg, "Presence and the Eucharist Presence," *Cross Currents* 17 (1967): 39-54; reprinted in "The Real Presence in Contemporary Discussion," *Theology Digest* 15 (1967): 3-11; Joseph M. Powers, *Eucharistic Theology* (New York: Herder and Herder, 1967). For a present-day overview, including postmodern critiques, see John H. McKenna, C.M., "Eucharistic Presence: An Invitation to Dialogue," *Theological Studies* 60 (1999): 294-317.

58. "Nor is it allowable to discuss the mystery of transubstantiation without mentioning what the Council of Trent stated about the marvelous conversion of the whole substance of the bread into the Body and of the whole substance of the wine into the Blood of Christ, speaking rather only of what is called 'transignification' and 'transfinalization.'" Pope Paul VI, *Mysterium Fidei* (September 3, 1965), ¶ 11; http://www.vatican.va/holy_father/paul_vi/encyclicals/documents/hf_p-vi_enc_03091965_mysterium_en.html.

XI. The Appearance of the Risen Christ to Mary Magdalene
[i.e., Easter morning]
XII. Transubstantiation

It is easy to understand why, for Messiaen, the doctrine of transubstantiation is nonnegotiable. It embodies the dialectical interpenetration — of Creator and creature, divinity and humanity, eternity and temporality — that underpins Messiaen's cosmic vision.

Moreover, given Messiaen's single-minded attention to *vision,* the doctrine is perhaps most distinguished by its contrast between appearance and reality: that is, the deepest reality of the Eucharist, its "substance" — divinity — is hidden from sense perception, which reaches only appearances, that is, "accidents." Messiaen specifically foregrounds this visual doctrinal aspect in movements 3 and 4: "Hidden God" and "Act of Faith." It also stands at the very beginning of the work, which opens with a movement entitled *Adoro te,* Messiaen's "commentary" on the hymn text written by Thomas Aquinas. The first stanza of *Adoro te* explicitly refers to the quality of hiddenness, concealment, and appearances:

> Devoutly I adore You, hidden Deity,
> Under these appearances concealed.
> To You my heart surrenders self
> For, seeing You, all else must yield.

The final stanza asserts belief that Christ's concealment beneath the "veils" of external accidents will be uncovered at the end of one's life.

> Jesus, Whom now I see enveiled,
> What I desire, when will it be?
> Beholding Your fair face revealed,
> Your glory shall I be blessed to see.[59]

---

59. "Adoro te devote, latens Deitas," Latin original and translation in *Devoutly I Adore Thee: The Prayers and Hymns of St. Thomas Aquinas,* trans. and ed. Robert Anderson and Johann Moser (Manchester, N.H.: Sophia Institute Press, 1993), 68-71. For other translations and commentaries see Joseph Connelly, *Hymns of the Roman Liturgy* (New York: Longmans, Green, 1957), 128-31; Matthew Britt, O.S.B., *The Hymns of the Breviary and Missal* (New York: Benziger Brothers, 1924), 190-92; Cornelius Canon Mulcahy, *The Hymns of the Roman Breviary and Missal* (Dublin: Browne and Nolan, 1938), 92-93.

1960–1992: Et Exspecto Resurrectionem Mortuorum

The epigraph for "Trio (for Trinity Sunday)" of the *Organ Book* comes to mind: "For now we see through a glass, darkly" (1 Cor. 13:12).

The same focus on the *visual* explains Messiaen's insertion of the *apparition* of Christ to Mary Magdalene in between "The Resurrection of Christ" and "Transubstantiation." Like the later revelation of Christ to the disciples on the road to Emmaus, the appearance to Mary on the morning of Easter is an apparition narrative: the true identity formerly hidden from recognition is suddenly capable of being seen. Nearly five decades earlier, Messiaen had already linked the Eucharist and recognition in "Resurrection (for Easter Day)" in *Songs of Earth and Sky* (1938):

> Bread. ǁ *Du pain.*
> He breaks it and their eyes are opened. ǁ *Il le rompt et leurs yeux sont dessillés.*

For Mary Magdalene — who initially mistakes Christ for the gardener — the recognition is triggered only when she *hears Christ's voice* speak her name. Surely, Messiaen would have delighted in this privileged position of the auditory as the only sure pointer toward recognition of the divine presence. Indeed, Aquinas himself inscribed this very observation in the second verse of *Adoro te,* associating hearing with what Christ had spoken:

> Sight and touch and taste here fail;
> Hearing only can be believed. [*Sed auditu solo tuto creditur.*]
> I trust what God's own Son has said.
> Truth from truth is best received.[60]

The theological sophistication and contemplative complexity found in *Book of the Blessed Sacrament* reward close reading.

Undoubtedly, Messiaen would have been absolutely delighted with the turn of events at the Grammy Awards in 2011. Organist and Juilliard professor Paul Jacobs became the first organist ever to win a Grammy, receiving the award for Best Instrumental Soloist Performance (without Orchestra) for his recording of Messiaen's *Book of the Blessed Sacrament.* For Jacobs, Messiaen's work is "a music of terrifying joy."[61]

---

60. Aquinas, "Adoro te," 69.

61. Paul Jacobs, *Livre du Saint-Sacrement* ([Hong Kong]: Naxos, 2010) (Naxos 8.572436–8.572437). In a 2005 interview accompanying his monumental performance of Messiaen's complete organ works, Jacobs said: "We're living in a cynical and jaded age, and Messiaen is the antithesis of our cynicism. He is first and foremost a composer of

1943–1992: Legacy

1987–1992: *Lightning Flashes of the Beyond...*

In August 1987, one year shy of his eightieth birthday, Messiaen accepted a commission from Zubin Mehta and the New York Philharmonic Orchestra for its 150th anniversary. Two months later, Messiaen shared with Loriod the clandestine writings of his mother, Cécile Sauvage, which he had obtained in 1972 following the death of his aunt, Germaine Tatin.[62] For fifteen years Messiaen had not disclosed these to Loriod; now he felt compelled to do so. As age eighty approached, he seems to have wanted to make sure that death did not doom these writings to oblivion.

This small fact about sharing his mother's works adds poignancy to the title he chose for the New York commission: *Éclairs sur l'au-delà*... Although frequently translated as "Illuminations of the Beyond," the title is not quite accurate; instead of the French *illumination,* Messiaen chose the more specific word *éclair,* which has no simple English equivalent. The word most immediately refers to the flashes of light — the "lightning flashes" sometimes called "heat lightning" (as opposed to lightning bolts) — that light up the sky in electrical storms. They are not the obvious and frequently terrifying brilliant flashes of lightning but rather the generally diffused light that seems to appear on some far-off distant horizon. Not the loud clap of thunder but rather the muffled rumor of angels.

So, while it is not entirely incorrect to translate Messiaen's final finished work as "illuminations," it slightly misrepresents his last statement. For these are not the "illuminations" of a seer (as in Rimbaud's *Illuminations*), the self-confident (and perhaps smug) revelation of something once shrouded in darkness and now seen clearly face-to-face. Rather, the opposite is intended: these are brief, diffuse, distant, momentary glimpses, fleeting intuitions, perhaps, of what lies beyond. The tentativeness of the seeing is emphasized by the insertion of the ellipsis at the end of the title, as if to say: "To be continued..."

The eleven movements have detailed programmatic titles taken largely from the final biblical book of Revelation.

---

faith. His music is one of brightness and joy. It dazzles the listener in the most profound and beautiful way. I believe our time needs to hear a message of joy, a music of terrifying joy." Jacobs in Chris Pasles, "Faith in the Magic of Messiaen," *Los Angeles Times,* October 28, 2005.

62. Cécile Sauvage, *Écrits d'amour,* 24.

Appendix

Timing Indications for the Downloadable Recording of *Visions* by Hyesook Kim and Stéphane Lemelin

Timing numbers in the following analyses (left-hand column) correspond to the recording of *Visions of Amen* by Professors Hyesook Kim and Stéphane Lemelin available in downloadable format at the web address below.

www.eerdmans.com/schloesser_audio

Appendix

I. AMEN OF CREATION[1]
Performance time = 6:00

00:03–01:32   Period A: creation theme ostinato with four phrases   mm. 1-8

    00:03–00:25 = Phrase 1   mm. 1-2
    00:26–00:48 = Phrase 2   mm. 3-4
    00:49–01:10 = Phrase 3   mm. 5-6
    01:11–01:32 = Phrase 4   mm. 7-8

01:33–02:54   Period A': creation theme ostinato with four phrases   mm. 9-16

    01:33–01:54 = Phrase 1   mm. 9-10
    01:55–02:14 = Phrase 2   mm. 11-12
    02:15–02:34 = Phrase 3   mm. 13-14
    02:35–02:54 = Phrase 4   mm. 15-16

02:55–04:08   Period A'': creation theme ostinato with four phrases   mm. 17-24

    02:55–03:13 = Phrase 1   mm. 17-18
    03:14–03:33 = Phrase 2   mm. 19-20
    03:34–03:51 = Phrase 3   mm. 21-22
    03:52–04:08 = Phrase 4   mm. 23-24

04:09–05:09   Period B: creation theme ostinato developed / inverted   mm. 25-32

    04:09–04:23 = Phrase 1   mm. 25-26
    04:24–04:38 = Phrase 2   mm. 27-28
    04:39–04:54 = Phrase 3   mm. 29-30
    04:55–05:09 = Phrase 4   mm. 31-32

05:10–06:00   CODA   mm. 33-39

    05:10–05:22 = Phrase 1   mm. 33-34a
    05:23–06:00 = Phrase 2   mm. 34b-39

---

1. Overall plan of Vision 1: four periods of four-phrase ostinato (creation theme) + coda. For analyses see Messiaen, *Traité de rythme, de couleur, et d'ornithologie (1949-1992) en sept tomes,* 8 vols. (Paris: Alphonse Leduc, 1994-2002), 3:231-33; Aloyse Michaely, *Die Musik Olivier Messiaens: Untersuchungen zum Gesamtschaffen* (Hamburg: Verlag der Musikalienhandlung K. D. Wagner, 1987), 128 (785)–129 (786); Joachim Claucig, "Die musikalische und philosophische Botschaft Olivier Messiaens anhand der Analyse von 'Visions de l'Amen'" (Diplomarbeit, Universität für Musik und Darstellende Kunst Wien [Institut für Analyse, Geschichte und Theorie der Musik], 2003), 76-83; Gareth Healey, "Form: Messiaen's 'Downfall'?" *Twentieth-Century Music* 4, no. 2 (September 2007): 163-87, at 167.

Appendix

II. AMEN OF THE STARS, OF THE PLANET WITH THE RING[2]
Performance time = 5:48

00:01–01:22 SECTION A: EXPOSITION of
    "Theme of the Dance of the Planets" mm. 1-48

    00:01–00:16 = Period 1 mm. 1-10
    00:17–00:30 = Period 2 mm. 11-19a
    00:31–00:48 = Period 3 mm. 19b-28
    00:49–01:02 = Period 4 mm. 29-37
    01:03–01:22 = Period 5 mm. 38-48

01:23–02:18 SECTION B: Development 1 mm. 49-79

02:19–03:01 SECTION C: Development 2 mm. 80-106

03:02–04:17 SECTION D: Development 3 mm. 107-147

04:18–05:33 SECTION E: REPRISE of "Theme of the
    Dance of the Planets" mm. 148-195

    04:18–04:32 = Period 1 mm. 148-157
    04:33–04:45 = Period 2 mm. 158-166a
    04:46–05:02 = Period 3 mm. 166b-175
    05:03–05:15 = Period 4 mm. 176-184
    05:16–05:33 = Period 5 mm. 185-195

05:33–05:48 CODA mm. 196-199

2. For analyses of Vision 2 see Messiaen, *Traité*, 3:234-43; Michaely, *Die Musik Olivier Messiaens*, 250 (393); Claucig, "Die musikalische und philosophische Botschaft," 84-92; Healey, "Form," 167. Note that Michaely counts 199 total measures; Claucig counts 198.

Appendix

III. AMEN OF THE AGONY OF JESUS[3]
Performance time = 7:02

00:01–02:29 SECTION A: STROPHE		mm. 1-43
00:01–00:31 = Part 1: Curse of the Father on the sin of the world	mm. 1-12	
00:32–00:48 = Part 2: Outcry of the Son	mm. 13-16	
00:49–01:42 = Part 3a: Incarnation in Space-Time ("Nativité" motive)	mm. 17-28	
01:43–02:29 = Part 3b: Consequence: Tears of Jesus in His Agony	mm. 29-43	
02:30–05:17 SECTION B: ANTISTROPHE		mm. 44-94
02:30-03:07 = Part 1: Curse of the Father on the sin of the world	mm. 44-56	
03:08–03:29 = Part 2: Outcry of the Son	mm. 57-62	
03:30–04:18 = Part 3a: Incarnation in Space-Time ("Nativité" motive)	mm. 63-74	
04:19–05:17 = Part 3b: Consequence: Tears of Jesus in His Agony	mm. 75-94	
05:18–07:02 SECTION C: EPODE		mm. 95-102
05:18–05:33 = Part 1: Three drops of sweat-blood	mm. 95-95	
05:34–05:45 = Part 2: Creation theme quotation	mm. 96-97a	
05:46–06:02 = Part 3: *Plainte épuisée* [in style of Schoenberg]	mm. 97b-98a	
06:03–06:14 = Part 2': Creation theme quotation	mm. 98b-99a	
06:15–06:35 = Part 3': *Plainte épuisée* [in style of Schoenberg]	mm. 99b-100a	
06:36–06:46 = Part 1': Three drops of sweat-blood	mm. 100b-101a	
06:47–07:02 = Concluding Chord and final drop of sweat-blood	mm. 101b-102	

3. For analyses of Vision 3 see Messiaen, *Traité*, 3:244-48; Michaely, *Die Musik Olivier Messiaens*, 81 (492)-85 (496); Claucig, "Die musikalische und philosophische Botschaft," 93-101; Healey, "Form," 167. For strophe, antistrophe, and epode, see above discussion of *Chronochromie* (1960).

Appendix

IV. AMEN OF DESIRE[4]
Performance time = 11:09

00:02–04:23 SECTION A	mm. 1-86
00:02–00:41 = Period 1: Ecstasy theme 1a	mm. 1-4
00:42–01:43 = Period 2: Ecstasy theme 1b	mm. 5-10
01:44–01:58 = Period 3: Passion theme 2a	mm. 11-18
01:59–02:12 = Period 4: Passion theme 2b	mm. 19-25
02:13–02:26 = Period 5: Passion theme 2a'	mm. 26-33
02:27–02:40 = Period 6: Passion theme 2b'	mm. 34-40
02:41–02:56 = Period 7: Passion theme 2a/b	mm. 41-48
02:57–04:23 = Period 8: Development of Passion theme 2b	mm. 49-86
04:24–09:00 SECTION A'	mm. 87-175
04:24–05:07 = Period 1: Ecstasy theme 1a	mm. 87-90
05:08–06:19 = Period 2: Ecstasy theme 1b	mm. 91-96
06:20–06:24 = Introduction of ostinato rhythm	mm. 97-99
06:25–06:38 = Period 3: Passion theme 2a	mm. 100-107
06:39–06:52 = Period 4: Passion theme 2b	mm. 108-114
06:53–07:05 = Period 5: Passion theme 2a'	mm. 115-122
07:06–07:19 = Period 6: Passion theme 2b'	mm. 123-129
07:20–07:34 = Period 7: Passion theme 2a/b	mm. 130-137
07:35–09:00 = Period 8: Development of Passion theme 2b	mm. 138-175
09:01–11:09 CODA	mm. 176-184
09:01–10:18 = Period 1	mm. 176-182
10:19–11:09 = Period 2	mm. 183-184

---

4. For analyses of Vision 4 see Messiaen, *Traité*, 3:249-55; Michaely, *Die Musik Olivier Messiaens*, 100 (511); Claucig, "Die musikalische und philosophische Botschaft," 102-11; Healey, "Form," 167. Healey: Theme 1, Theme 2, Reprise of theme 1, Reprise of theme 2, Coda.

Appendix

V. AMEN OF THE ANGELS, OF SAINTS, OF BIRDSONG[5]
Performance time = 7:12

00:01–02:10   SECTION A: EXPOSITION OF ANGELS AND SAINTS   mm. 1-44

PART 1

00:01–00:30 = Motive 1: Angels-Saints Theme   mm. 1-11
00:31–00:58 = Motive 2: Creation Song
   00:31–00:36   Creation theme quotation   mm. 12-13a
   00:37–00:58   *Complainte de Nijni-Novgorod*   mm. 13b-18
00:59–01:16 = Motive 3: Bridge
   (non-retrogradable rhythm: eternity)   mm. 19-23

PART 2

01:17–01:41 = Motive 2': Creation Song
   01:17–01:21   Creation theme quotation   mm. 24-25a
   01:22–01:41   *Complainte de Nijni-Novgorod*   mm. 25b-30
01:42–01:51 = Motive 3': Bridge
   (non-retrogradable rhythm: eternity)   mm. 31-33
01:52–02:10 = Motive 1': Statement of
   Angels-Saints Theme   mm. 34-44

02:11–04:31   SECTION B: BIRDSONG   mm. 45-148

PART 1

02:11–02:18 = Motive 1: Nightingale [4 + 3]   mm. 45-51
02:19–02:29 = Motive 1: Nightingale [4 + 3]   mm. 52-62
02:30–02:32 = Bridge 1   mm. 63-64
02:33–02:41 = Motive 1': Nightingale [3 + 3]   mm. 65-69
02:42–02:45 = Bridge 2: European serin   mm. 70-71

PART 2

02:46–02:51 = Motive 1: Nightingale [4 + 3]   mm. 72-76
02:52–03:04 = Motive 2: Blackbirds
   (strophe + counterpoint)   mm. 77-89
03:05–03:08 = Bridge 3: Blackbird variation   mm. 90-91
03:09–03:17 = Motive 1': Nightingale [3 + 3]   mm. 92-96
03:18–03:21 = Bridge 3: European serin   mm. 97-98

---

5. For analyses of Vision 5 see Messiaen, *Traité*, 3:256-65; Michaely, *Die Musik Olivier Messiaens*, 109 (766)–110 (767); Claucig, "Die musikalische und philosophische Botschaft," 112-17; Healey, "Form," 167. Healey: Part 1, Birdsong, Reprise of part 1, Coda.

Appendix

PART 3

03:22–03:35 = Motive 1: Nightingale [4 + 3]	mm. 99-112
03:36–03:56 = Motive 2: Blackbirds (strophe + counterpoint)	mm. 113-130
03:57–03:59 = Bridge 1	mm. 131-132
04:00–04:25 = Motive 1': Nightingale [3 + 3]	mm. 133-146
04:26–04:31 = Bridge 4	mm. 147-148

04:32–07:00 SECTION A': RECAPITULATION OF
ANGELS AND SAINTS   mm. 149-192

PART 1

04:32–05:05 = Motive 1: Angels-Saints Theme	mm. 149-159
05:06–05:33 = Motive 2: Creation Song	
05:06–05:11 Creation theme quotation	mm. 160-161a
05:12–05:33 *Complainte de Nijni-Novgorod*	mm. 161b-166
05:34–05:54 = Motive 3: Bridge (non-retrogradable rhythm)	mm. 167-171

PART 2

05:55–06:24 = Motive 2': Creation Song	
05:55–06:00 Creation theme quotation	mm. 172-173a
06:01–06:24 *Complainte de Nijni-Novgorod*	mm. 173b-178
06:25–06:35 = Motive 3': Bridge (non-retrogradable rhythm)	mm. 179-181
06:36–07:00 = Motive 1': Statement of Angels-Saints Theme	mm. 182-192

07:01–07:12 CODA   mm. 193-198

07:01–07:06 = Motive 1: Nightingale [4 + 3]	mm. 193-196
07:07–07:12 = Bridge 4	mm. 197-198

Appendix

VI. AMEN OF JUDGMENT[6]
Performance time = 2:45

00:02–00:52 PHRASE 1 (A)   mm. 1-19

    00:02–00:12 = Period A   mm. 1-4
    00:13–00:23 = Period B   mm. 5-8
    00:24–00:34 = Period A   mm. 9-12
    00:35–00:52 = Period B   mm. 13-19

00:53–01:43 PHRASE 2 (B)   mm. 20-38

    00:53–01:03 = Period C   mm. 20-23
    01:04–01:14 = Period D   mm. 24-27
    01:15–01:25 = Period C   mm. 28-31
    01:26–01:43 = Period D   mm. 32-38

01:44–02:35 PHRASE 3 (A′)   mm. 39-57

    01:44–01:54 = Period A   mm. 39-42
    01:55–02:05 = Period B   mm. 43-46
    02:06–02:16 = Period A   mm. 47-50
    02:17–02:35 = Period B   mm. 51-57

02:36–02:45 CODA   mm. 58-59

---

6. For analyses of Vision 6 see Messiaen, *Traité,* 3:266-69; Michaely, *Die Musik Olivier Messiaens,* 134 (791); Claucig, "Die musikalische und philosophische Botschaft," 118-21; Healey, "Form," 167.

Appendix

VII. AMEN OF CONSUMMATION[7]
Performance Time = 7:31

STONE 1: JASPER

0:02–00:31	Period A: creation theme ostinato with four phrases (A major) [identical to "Amen of Creation" period 1]	mm. 1-8
	00:02–00:08 = Phrase 1	mm. 1-2
	00:09–00:16 = Phrase 2	mm. 3-4
	00:17–00:23 = Phrase 3	mm. 5-6
	00:24–00:31 = Phrase 4	mm. 7-8

STONE 2: SAPPHIRE

00:32–01:05	Period B: creation theme ostinato with three phrases	mm. 9-17
	00:32–00:38 = Phrase 1	mm. 9-10
	00:39–00:46 = Phrase 2	mm. 11-12
	00:47–01:05 = Phrase 3 [elongated]	mm. 13-17

STONE 3: CHALCEDONY

01:06–01:34	Period A transposed into C# major	mm. 18-25
	01:06–01:12 = Phrase 1	mm. 18-19
	01:13–01:19 = Phrase 2	mm. 20-21

---

7. For analyses of Vision 7 see Messiaen, *Traité*, 3:270-75; Michaely, *Die Musik Olivier Messiaens*, 131 (788)–132 (789); Claucig, "Die musikalische und philosophische Botschaft," 122-28; Healey, "Form," 167. Michaely and Claucig divide the movement into nine sections. Healey divides into ten sections: Period 1, Period 2, Period 1 transition, Period 3, Period 1, Period 2 transition, Transitional, Period 1 reprise, Period 3, New period. My division into twelve sections follows Messiaen's indications:

1. Première période en la majeur
2. Deuxième période, page 79, 2ᵉ mesure
3. Première période transposée en ut # majeur — page 80, 3ᵉ mesure
4. Troisième période, page 81, 2ᵉ système
5. Page 82, mesures 2 et 3: 1/2 période concluant en mode de Ré de plain-chant
6. Page 82, 1ʳᵉ mesure — Page 82, 2ᵉ mesure, 2ᵉ systéme, 1/2 période
7. Première période en fa majeur
8. Page 84, deuxième période, transposée en fa majeur
9. Page 85, 2e système: période transitoire, modulante
10. *Page 88, reprise de la 1ʳᵉ période en la majeur* (italics in original)
11. Troisième période en la majeur
12. Page 93, 2e système, nouvelle période

The labeling of these sections with the names of the twelve stones listed in the book of Revelation should not be attributed to Messiaen. The labels are my own association; they are simply intended to suggest symbolic reasons for Messiaen's twelve-section division.

Appendix

01:20–01:27 = Phrase 3   mm. 22-23
01:28–01:34 = Phrase 4   mm. 24-25

STONE 4: EMERALD

01:35–01:56   Period C: reproduces "Amen of Creation" periods 2 and 3   mm. 26-31

01:35–01:42 = Phrase 1   mm. 26-27
01:43–01:49 = Phrase 2   mm. 28-29
01:50–01:56 = Phrase 3   mm. 30-31

STONE 5: SARDONYX

01:57–02:04   Half-period concluding in plainchant mode Re, transposed   mm. 32-33

01:57–02:04 = Phrase 1   mm. 32-33

STONE 6: SARDIUS

02:05–02:18   Half-period concluding in plainchant mode Sol, transposed   mm. 34-37

02:05–02:18 = Phrase 1   mm. 34-37

STONE 7: CHRYSOLITE

02:19–02:48   Period A in F major   mm. 38-45

02:19–02:26 = Phrase 1   mm. 38-39
02:27–02:33 = Phrase 2   mm. 40-41
02:34–02:40 = Phrase 3   mm. 42-43
02:41–02:48 = Phrase 4   mm. 44-45

STONE 8: BERYL

02:49–03:21   Period B transposed into F major   mm. 46-54

02:49–02:55 = Phrase 1   mm. 46-47
02:56–03:04 = Phrase 2   mm. 48-49
03:05–03:21 = Phrase 3 [elongated]   mm. 50-54

STONE 9: TOPAZ

03:22–04:20   Transitional period modulating   mm. 55-70

03:22–03:28 = Phrase 1   mm. 55-56
03:29–03:36 = Phrase 2 [repeats theme modulated]   mm. 57-58
03:37–03:47 = Phrase 3   mm. 59-61
03:48–04:05 = Phrase 4   mm. 62-63a
04:06–04:20 = Phrase 5 [four thematic statements = coda]   mm. 63b-70

Appendix

STONE 10: CHRYSOPRASE

04:21-04:46   Period A reprise in A major   mm. 71-78

    04:21–04:27 = Phrase 1   mm. 71-72
    04:28–04:33 = Phrase 2   mm. 73-74
    04:34–04:40 = Phrase 3   mm. 75-76
    04:41–04:46 = Phrase 4   mm. 77-78

STONE 11: JACINTH

04:47–05:41   Period C in A major   mm. 79-94

    04:47–04:53 = Phrase 1   mm. 79-80
    04:54–04:59 = Phrase 2   mm. 81-82
    05:00–05:12 = Phrase 3 [elongated]   mm. 83-86
    05:13–05:27 = Phrase 4 [elongated]   mm. 87-90
    05:28–05:34 = Phrase 5 [creation statement]   mm. 91-92
    05:35–05:41 = Phrase 6 [creation statement]   mm. 93-94

STONE 12: AMETHYST

05:42–07:31   Period D: recalls periods A, B, C   mm. 95-124

    05:42–05:48 = Phrase 1a   mm. 95-96
    05:49–05:54 = Phrase 1b   mm. 97-98
    05:55–06:00 = Phrase 2a   mm. 99-100
    06:01–06:06 = Phrase 2b   mm. 101-102
    06:07–06:26 = Phrase 3   mm. 103-108
    06:27–06:47 = Phrase 4   mm. 109-114a
    06:48–07:05 = Phrase 5   mm. 114b-119
    07:06–07:31 = Coda   mm. 120-124

Abbreviations

Crampon	*La Sainte Bible,* trans. Augustin Crampon (1904), new ed. (Paris and Tournai: Desclée et Cie, 1939).
Douay-CCD	*New Catholic Edition of the Holy Bible,* trans. Confraternity of Christian Doctrine, new ed. (New York: Catholic Book Publishing Co., [1949] 1954).
Fillion	Abbé Louis-Claude Fillion (1843-1927), *La Sainte Bible: (texte latin et traduction française; commentée d'après la Vulgate et les textes originaux; à l'usage des séminaires et du clergé,* 9th ed., 8 vols. (Paris: Librairie Letouzey et Ané, 1927-1931). Dates of individual volumes published: vol. 1 (1888); vol. 2 (1889); vol. 3 (1891); vol. 4 (1892); vol. 5 (1894); vol. 6 (1896); vol. 7 (1901); vol. 8 (1904).
Missal-En	*The New Roman Missal in Latin and English,* ed. F. X. Lasance and Francis Augustine Walsh (New York: Benziger Brothers, [1937] 1950).
Missel-Fr	*Missel-Vespéral liturgique très complet. Messes de chaque jour — vêpres — dévotions — prières* (Tours: Maison Mame, [1947] 1951).
Segond	*La Sainte Bible, qui comprend l'Ancien et le Nouveau Testament,* trans. Louis Segond (Paris: [58, rue de Clichy], 1928).
Vulgate	*Biblia Sacra vulgatæ editionis: Sixti V Pont. Max. iussu recognita et Clementis VIII auctoritate edita,* ed. Michael Hetzenauer, 3rd ed. (Ratisbon, Germany: F. Pustet, 1929).

Index of Names and Subjects

Abbreviation "OM" refers to Olivier Messiaen. Page numbers in **bold** indicate complete chapters.

abyss/vertigo: anxiety compared with vertigo by Jaspers, 430n76; and the Apocalypse of Saint John, 280; Baudelaire, Charles, 280, 424-25; and the Dauphiné Alps, 39, 280; and Genesis 1:2, 424; and Habakkuk 3:10, 424, 493, 494, 497; and Pascal's *Pensées,* 424-25. *See also* fear *(la peur)* and awe *(la crainte);* Hello, Ernest; Pascal, Blaise; Poe, Edgar Allan; staircases; sublime; vertigo; Messiaen, Olivier, WORKS: *From Canyons to Stars; The Organ Book,* "The Hands of the Abyss (for Times of Penitence)"; *Quartet for the End of Time,* "The Abyss of the Birds"; *Turangalîla Symphony,* "Development of Love"

Action Française, 8, 9, 58; Cécile Sauvage's association with, 74; cofounding by Charles Maurras and Léon Daudet, 66n65; and Jean Tenant, 66n65; Pope Pius XI's condemnation of, 74n97. *See also* Barrès, Maurice; Bernanos, Georges; Maurras, Charles

Act of Separation (1905), xiii, 13, 27-28

adoptio perfecta, 230-31, 232n11, 236-39, 513. *See also* divine adoption

Alain, Jehan, 278

alarm (tocsin). *See* bells

alba ("dawn song"): and Brangäne's song in Wagner's *Tristan,* 392, 483, 484; and OM's *Five Refrains,* 484-85; in *Romeo and Juliet,* 392-93, 483-85; and Susanna's aria, 370

Andreas of Caesarea, 450

angels: the Angel of Death, 59, 415; birds linked with, 373-74, 375, 386, 387; and eternity, 373; and Eucharist vision of OM's *Diptych,* 264; and God's choice to become human, 444; "movement" of, 273; and planets, 377, 386; sentimental views of, 378; terrifying qualities of, 379-80. *See also* terrible; Messiaen, Olivier, WORKS: *The Organ Book,* "The Eyes in the Wheels (for Pentecost Sunday)"; *Vi-*

sions of Amen, "Amen of the Angels, of Saints, of Birdsong"

Antigone: Honegger's operatic *tragédie musicale*, 350-51; and Maritain, 351-52. See also Greek culture; neoclassicism

anxiety: and Cécile Sauvage, postpartum depression, 16-17; Cécile Sauvage, wartime longing, 34-36; and ephemerality, xviii-xix, 99-101; and Heidegger's *Being and Time*, 312-13; wartime trauma/apocalyptic times, 276-78, 284-87. See also Claudel, Paul; Cuvillier, Armand; Daniel-Rops, Henri; Heidegger, Martin; Kierkegaard, Søren; melancholy; Pascal, Blaise; Poe, Edgar Allan; Updike, John

Apocalypse of Saint John: and abyss, 280; "light" imagery from, 436-37; and OM's *Lightning Flashes of the Beyond...*, 530-31; stones of, 171, 274, 440, 448-49, 509. See also Messiaen, Olivier, WORKS: *Apparition of the Eternal Church*; *Visions of Amen*, "Amen of Consummation"

apocalypticism: Great Depression background of OM's *Resplendent Tomb*, 127; heat death of the universe theories, 189; music for end times, **276-93**. See also eschatology; Messiaen, Olivier, WORKS: *Apparition of the Eternal Church*; *Glorified Bodies*; *Quartet for the End of Time*; *Songs of Earth and Sky*; *Visions of Amen*

apparition, xix, 36, 40, 152, **153-93**, 212, 238, 264, 494, 497, 508-9, 515n25, 516, 529, 531. See also Blanc-Gatti, Charles; drugs; Messiaen, Olivier, WORKS: *Apparition of the Eternal Church*; Shakespeare, William; synesthesia; visions

Aquinas, Thomas: *Adoro te*, 528, 529; "Ave Verum Corpus," 84; on Christ's transfiguration as prefiguration of the resurrection, 515; clarity of, 120,

269, 269n125, 271, 440; on "glorified bodies," 268-72, 441-48; impossibility of, 269, 269n125; as inspiration to OM, 8, 81, 120, 251-52, 528, 529; and late-nineteenth-century Catholic education, 8n7; subtlety of, 269; on time and eternity, 296, 378. See also body; desire; end-in-view

Aristotle: end-in-view/final cause perspective of, 360, 361-62, 364, 474. See also body: and body-soul (hylomorphic) composite; desire

Arnold, Matthew, "Dover Beach," 183-84. See also eternity; waves

arsis and thesis. See dance; Greek culture; Mocquereau, (Dom) André, O.S.B.; rhythm: rhythmic dyads; waves

astronomy, 319-25, 531; Boll's *Two Infinites*, 316-17, 462; Fontenelle's *Conversations on the Plurality of Inhabited Worlds*, 313-15, 320n33, 420n52. See also Messiaen, Olivier, WORKS: *Visions of Amen*, "Amen of the Stars, of the Planet with the Ring"; Moreux, Abbé Théophile; Rudaux, Lucien; stars; terrestrial/celestial contrast; Wells, H. G.

Augustine, 7, 209-10n41, 247; and Bonaventure's sacramentalist theology of light, 384; *The City of God*, 447-48

Aulnoy, Madame (Countess) Marie-Catherine d', "The Bluebird," 37, 125. See also bird families; Maeterlinck, Maurice: *The Bluebird*

awe *(la crainte)*: and "the beginning of all wisdom," 310-11. See also fear *(la peur) and awe (la crainte)*; sublime

Bach, J. S.: *canon perpetuus* in *Musical Offering* of, 451; chromatic counterpoint of, 451-52, 451-52n57, 494; *Saint Matthew's Passion*, 348

Balakirew, Mily Alexeïewitch (or Mily Alekseyevich Balakirev): *Collection of*

Index of Names and Subjects

Russian Folk Songs, 113, 398. *See also* "Lament of Nijni-Novgorod"
Bali/Balinese: Balinese/Indonesian dance, 308, 331-34; and creation theme from OM's *Visions of Amen,* "Amen of Creation," 307-8; and "dance drama," 503n43; and Hinduism, 333-34; and OM's self conception as a rhythmician, xiv, 24, 216n62, 331. *See also* International Colonial Exposition (1931); Jolivet, André
Balthasar, Hans Urs von, 516. *See also* glory
Balzac, Honoré de, and OM's parents' literary interests, 23, 40, 192
Barbey d'Aurevilly, Jules-Amédée, 8, 66n65
Barrès, Maurice, 8-9, 11-12n21, 19, 28, 66n65, 67, 70, 74. *See also* Action Française
Barzun, Jacques, on the fin-de-siècle's paradoxical "logic of progress," 24n65
Baudelaire, Charles, 63, 88n33, 154, 263; and the "abyss," 280, 424; and Chateaubriand, 414-15, 415n37; "funeral bell" imagery, 63, 89, 413-15, 414n36, 415n37; on modernity, 186, 186n99; *Poem of Hashish,* 158; "Spleen," 413-15, 415n37; and synesthesia, 154, 155, 158-59, 169; translations of Poe, 117n100, 427. *See also* Catholic Revivalism; fear *(la peur)* and awe *(la crainte);* symbolist movement
Baumann, Émile, 67, 381. *See also* Catholic Revivalism
BBC Overseas Service, 286-87, 307, 455. *See also* Westminster carillon
Beach, Sylvia, 285
Beaumarchais, Pierre: instrumental effects of *Tarare,* 422-23; judgment scene of *Tarare,* 415-18, 420-23; *Tarare* as melodramatic triumph of life, 420-22
bells: "bell, book, and candle" ritual, 404-12; in Chateaubriand's *Genius of Christianity,* 226, 414-15, 415n37, 431-32, 453; Couperin's *Carillons of Paris,* 453; and death, 402; funeral bells, 412-15; in Gibon's *Breton Cemetery,* 44; of Notre-Dame cathedral, 405n5, 453; ringing backward of, 411-12; Thurston's "Bell, Book, and Candle," 408, 409, 412n30, 432; tocsin (alarm/alarum), 41, 44, 162, 405, 411, 414-15, 422, 433. *See also* Baudelaire, Charles; carillon; Shakespeare, William
Benjamin, René, 74
Bergson, Henri, 95-98, 328; *The Creative Mind,* 89-90n37; on duration/number, xv, xvii, 89-90n37, 95-96, 118-19n103, 120, 138, 360, 363-64n13, 366-67; and Whitehead's distinction between "abstract" and "real" possibility, 367n19. *See also* Cuvillier, Armand; desire; end-in-view; eternity; rhythm; Messiaen, Olivier, WORKS: *The Death of Number; Eight Preludes,* "Deceased Instants"
Berio, Luciano, *Sinfonia* (1968), 524. *See also* postmodern
Bernanos, Georges, 58, 67-68, 69n79, 71n88, 74-75, 121. *See also* Action Française; Catholic Revivalism; Sauvage, Cécile
Bernard of Clairvaux, 384
Bernstein, Leonard: OM's *Turangalîla Symphony* premiered in Boston by, 482; WORKS: *Kaddish* (third) symphony, 511-12; *Mass,* 512n14, 524. *See also* postmodern
bird families:
    blackbirds, 336, 388-89, 395
    blackcap warblers, 393-94, 395
    bluebirds: and d'Aulnoy, 37, 125; and Maeterlinck, 125
    doves: and Cécile Sauvage, 91, 473; green doves, 473, 474, 476; and the *harawi* genre of love songs, 93-95, 473; OM's *Eight Preludes,*

547

Index of Names and Subjects

"The Dove," 89, 91, 95, 473. *See also* Messiaen, Olivier, WORKS: *Harawi*

finches, 394-95

larks: Cécile Sauvage's poem about, 20-21, 21n55, 388; and Shakespeare, 392

nightingales, 395-96; and Coleridge, 390-91; and Couperin, 390; and de Gourmont, 26; and Keats, 391-92, 399; and Shakespeare, 392; and Stravinsky, 390

thrushes: song thrush, 388-89, 508

birds: and angels, 373-74, 375, 386, 387; and Chateaubriand, 395-96; and cosmic reconciliation, 383-84; and dinosaurs, 385, 506; and eternity, xviii, 280, 281, 373-74, 378, 385-87, 395, 506, 511; and OM's *Three Melodies*, "Why?," 104; and planetary dancing, 386; and serialism, 387, 505-6; in Shakespeare, 484. *See also* bird families; Messiaen, Olivier, WORKS: *The Blackbird*; *Catalogue of Birds*; *Exotic Birds*; *From Canyons to Stars*; *The Organ Book*, "Birdsong (for Eastertide)"; *Quartet for the End of Time*, "The Abyss of the Birds"; *Visions of Amen*, "Amen of the Angels, of Saints, of Birdsong"

Bismarck, Otto von, 5

Blake, William, 381-82n15, 387

Blanc-Gatti, Charles: *Carillon de Malesco*, 448; *Chromophonie*, 161, 450; influence on OM, 159-61, 160n25, 162, 163-65, 435, 452, 509, 523n47; and the living stones in the Apocalypse, 171, 448-49, 452; sound and light as waves, 163-64; *Sounds and Colors*, 160, 161-65, 193. *See also* sound-color

Bloch, André, 279, 281-82

Bloch, Marc, 278n4, 461

Blondel, Maurice, 198, 200, 201, 203

blood: as the "chief humor," 446; "Joy of the Blood of the Stars" movement of OM's *Turangalîla Symphony*, 180n84, 182, 479, 481, 525; red symbolism of, 344-46; sacrificial/ eucharistic blood, 179-80, 345; sweating blood, 343, 346, 347; which is the Eternal Word, 346-47. *See also* Catholic Revivalism; Claudel, Paul; Emmerich, Anne-Catherine; star + cross motif; symbolist movement

Bloy, Léon, 66n65, 74, 343; "Carillon of the Seventh Day," 456n69; and joy (*l'allégresse*), 224n87, 226n93. *See also* Catholic Revivalism; Tenant, Jean

body: and body-soul (hylomorphic) composite, 243, 250-51, 274; glorified bodies, 266-74, 441. *See also* resurrection; sensual mysticism; soul; Messiaen, Olivier, WORKS: *Et Exspecto Resurrectionem Mortuorum*; *Glorified Bodies*; *The Transfiguration*; *Turangalîla Symphony*, "Garden of Love's Sleep"; *Visions of Amen*, "Amen of Desire"

Boll, Marcel, *The Two Infinites*, 316-17, 462

Bonaventure, 383, 384

Bonnet, Joseph, 60

Bordes, Charles, 44n53, 110-11. *See also* Schola Cantorum

Boulez, Pierre: *The Hammer without a Master*, 498; and OM's legacy, 490; and serial music, 386; studies with OM, 102-3, 469

Breton, André: "certain point of the mind" (*point de l'esprit*), 102, 103, 163, 372, 475; on dreaming, 89-90n37, 90; *Manifestoes of Surrealism*, 102, 128-29n136; on the marvelous, 128-29n136. *See also* juxtaposition of contrasts; surrealism

Britten, Benjamin, *War Requiem*, 510, 511

Bruyr, José: OM's interview with, 121, 144-45, 175; Tournemire's interview with, 142-43

Büllow, Hans von, 165

Burke, Edmund, xvii

Index of Names and Subjects

Burns, Robert, 387

Cage, John, on OM's organ improvisation, 147. *See also* improvisation
Calderón del la Barca, Pedro, *Life Is a Dream*, 58, 59
carillon: Bloy's "Carillon of the Seventh Day," 456
carillon of light: and phrase "from brilliance into brilliance," 434-40, 448; and stained glass windows of Sainte-Chapelle, 435, 512
Carillon or Bells (Dandrieu), 453; French carillon genre, 453-54; and Lyapunov's "Carillon" in *Twelve Studies of Transcendent Execution*, 448n45, 453. *See also* bells
Carrel, Alexis, *Man, the Unknown*, 299
Carter, Jimmy, 227
"Cas Messiaen, Le." *See* "Messiaen Controversy"
Cathedral of Notre-Dame de Paris, 47, 52, 60, 62, 89, 132, 148, 209, 309, 454-55; bells of, 405n5, 453; Te Deum thanksgiving service in 1944 at, 467, 467n19. *See also* de Gaulle, Charles; Vierne, Louis
Catholic Revivalism: increase in feeling, 239; and juxtaposition of "Catholic" and "modern," xii-xiii; and mysticism, 138-39; and OM's work, 138, 138n31; and Poe, 316n22; and symbolist movement, 138-39. *See also* Baumann, Émile; Bloy, Léon; Claudel, Paul; de Noailles, Comtesse Anna; Hello, Ernest; Jammes, Francis; Maritain, Jacques; Péguy, Charles
Cavaillé-Coll, Aristide, 189, 306, 453
Chandler, Raymond, *The Long Goodbye*, 363
Chartres: and Cécile Sauvage, 61-63; Chartres Cathedral, premiere of OM's *Et Exspecto* at, 512; windows of, 62n53
Chateaubriand, François René de:

Genius of Christianity, 226, 395-96, 414-15, 415n37, 431-32, 453; and "joy" (*l'allégresse*), 224n87, 226; *mal du siècle* (malady of the century), 208n38; and Pierre Messiaen's literary education, 8
Chénier, André, 23
clarity (*clarté*): and Aquinas, 119-20n105, 120, 128, 265, 442-43; as both "light" and "glory," 222; and *claire*/Claire Delbos, 119, 129; and Dukas's *Ariadne and Bluebeard*, 116n99, 125, 251, 308, 440; and the illuminating "inner voice," 127-28; Maritain's reading of, 83, 119-20n105, 120; OM on glory, grace, and light as equivalent, 222, 439, 510; in OM's *Death of Number*, 128; in poetry of Cécile Sauvage, 388. *See also* Delbos, Victor; *éblouissement* (dazzlement); stones/gems
Claudel, Paul, 8-9, 22, 52; *Ars poétique*, 22n59; *The City*, 13-14; "The Precious Blood," 345. *See also* Catholic Revivalism
Cocteau, Jean: and *Antigone*, 350-52; and OM, 81n9, 352
Cogniat, Raymond, *Dances of Indochina*, 332
Cold War, **488-506**; and OM's *Catalogue of Birds*, 460; and OM's *Turangalîla Symphony*, 477, 478; and serialism, 505; Vietnam War, 516; West Germany as "Cold War musical hothouse," 488-90. *See also* Darmstadt
Coleridge, Taylor: "The Nightingale," 390-91; on the sound-like power in light, 155. *See also* melancholy
Copland, Aaron, on OM's organ improvisation, 147. *See also* improvisation
Couperin, François, *Nightingale in Love*, 390. *See also* bird families: nightingales
Couperin, Louis, *The Carillons of Paris*, 453

549

Crampon, Augustin, iin2, 224n87, 346, 435
creation, ix, xviii, 22n59, 82, 85n24, 238, 280, 289, 291-92, **296-308**, 310n2, 311, 317, 322-25, 328, 333, 340, 356-57, 359, 365-66, 368, 374, 376, 383-84n18, 395, 397-401, 402, 404, 410, 419-20, 422-23, 431, 433-34, 452, 455-56, 504, 511
creation theme, 305, 307-8, 340, 356, 397-99, 455-56, 533-34, 536, 538-39, 541
Crémieux, Benjamin, 208n38
Cuvillier, Armand: and Bergsonian thought summarized by OM, 100, 364-65, 404; *Manuel de philosophie*, 95-98, 95-96n45, 100n60, 328; philosophy of duration of, 96-99, 100-101; *Précis de philosophie*, 100n60. See also desire; end-in-view

dance: arsis and thesis, 308, 327-28, 332-33; Balinese/Indonesian, 308, 331-34; birdsong related to, 386; of the planets, 311-12, 330, 334, 335-37, 376; and Emmanuel, 310-11n3; Nietzsche on, 310-11n3; and Valéry, 326. See also Emmanuel, Maurice; Greek culture; Mocquereau, (Dom) André, O.S.B.; Stravinsky, Igor
Dandrieu, Pierre, 453
Daniel-Lesur, Jean-Yves: and La Spirale, 240; and the Schola, 240; and Tournemire's *L'Orgue Mystique*, 205
Daniel-Rops, Henri: "abstract characters" *(personnages abstraits)*, 302n13; and L'Ordre Nouveau, 210-11; *Our Anxiety*, 144, 181n89, 206, 208-9, 211, 347; *World without Soul*, 211-12, 244
Darmstadt, 489-90, 496, 498. See also Cold War
Daudet, Léon, 66n65, 74
Dauphiné Alps: OM's childhood in, 30, 39, 61, 280, 335, 393, 395, 405, 473, 512; OM's funeral in, 531. See also abyss/vertigo
dazzlement. See *éblouissement*

Debussy, Claude: influence heard in OM's *Visions of Amen*, "Amen of the Angels, of Saints, of Birdsong," 400-401; and modernist-primitivism, 44n53, 81n9, 147n62; WORKS: *Apparition*, 173n65; *La Mer* (The Sea), 386; *Pelléas and Mélisande*, 40, 44-46, 46n57, 138, 186, 186n100, 293, 349, 370n29, 386, 440, 470-71; *Preludes*, 88; *Three Ballads of François Villon*, 51. See also Gibon, Jean (Jehan) de; symbolist movement
Dedication of a Church (liturgical office): and OM's *Transfiguration*, "Terribilis est locus iste," 515, 515n25; and plainchants "Caelestis urbs Jerusalem" and "Urbs Jerusalem beata," 172, 173-74, 174-75n67, 176-77, 180, 450; two feasts of, 172-76. See also Dedication of Saint John Lateran; Messiaen, Olivier, WORKS: *Apparition of the Eternal Church; Verset for the Feast of the Dedication*
Dedication of Saint John Lateran, 153, 172, 508. See also Dedication of a Church (liturgical office)
de Gaulle, Charles, 512; on BBC radio, 286; and OM's *Et Exspecto*, 510, 512; and liberation of Paris, 461, 467; 1969 collapse of government of, 517; OM's admiration of, 286-87, 466. See also BBC Overseas Service; Messiaen, Olivier, WORKS: *Et Exspecto Resurrectionem Mortuorum*
de Gourmont, Jean, and Cécile Sauvage, 18-19, 26, 27, 28-29, 34, 49, 65-66, 73, 387
de Gourmont, Remy, 19
Delarue-Mardrus, Lucie, 19, 66-67n68, 68
Delaunay, Robert, 452. See also juxtaposition of contrasts; simultaneous contrast
Delbos, Claire (OM's first wife): birth of, 113, 197; as "Cl. Olivier Messiaen" (Claire Victor-Delbos), 276; death

Index of Names and Subjects

of, 55, 349, 503; declining mental state of, xvi, xx, 202, 276-77, 282, 290, 292-93, 347-48, 349, 399, 482-83; and Manon Lescaut's farewell, 370; marriage to OM, 111-12, 121, 153, 197-98, 205; "Mi" as OM's pet name for, 205; miscarriages, xvi, 216-18, 229, 352; name of Claire adopted by, 197, 440; and OM's acceptance of truths of Catholic faith, 128-29; and OM's *Harawi*, 472-75; and OM's *Songs of Earth and Sky*, 474; Schola Cantorum musical studies of, 111, 113, 204; and Susanna's aria, 372; and Victor Delbos (father), 197-98; WORKS: *The Budding Soul*, 252-53; *Primrose*, 218, 252; *Two Pieces for Organ*, 215, 229, 240; *The Virgin Rocks the Child*, 216, 229

Delbos, Louise Justine. *See* Delbos, Claire

Delbos, Victor (OM's father-in-law): and clarity *(clarté)*, 201-2, 440; and the "clear and distinct ideas" of Descartes, 201, 213, 420n52, 440; death of, 292; on Fontenelle, 420n52; legacy of, 95-96n45, 198n4, 203-4; and Maurice Blondel, 198, 200, 201, 203; and prewar Catholic Revivalism, 198-201. *See also* Delbos, Claire

de Noailles, Comtesse Anna, 8, 19, 66-67n68, 67, 70. *See also* Catholic Revivalism

De Quincey, Thomas, *Confessions of an English Opium Eater*, 158. *See also* drugs; visions

Descartes, René: "clear and distinct ideas" of, 201, 213, 420n52, 440; and Fontenelle, 420n52; and synesthetic research as reaction against, 156

desire, 360-70. *See also* Bergson, Henri; body; Cuvillier, Armand; end-in-view; sensual mysticism; time

Dewey, John: *Art as Experience*, 362-63; end-in-view/teleological view of reality, 361-63, 364, 374; "events" and "experiences" distinguished, 362-63. *See also* Bergson, Henri; desire; end-in-view

Dickens, Charles, 23, 40

Dillard, Annie, 323n41

dinosaurs, 385, 506

Disney, Walt: and Blanc-Gatti, 161; *Fantasia*, 112, 157, 161, 452. *See also* sound-color

divine adoption, 229-33, 234, 236-38, 297n2, 513n18. *See also* filiation (adoptive); Guéranger, (Dom) Prosper, O.S.B.; Marmion, (Dom) Columba, O.S.B.; predestination; Messiaen, Olivier, WORKS: *The Nativity of the Lord*; *The Transfiguration*

Döblin, Alfred, *Berlin Alexanderplatz*, 317-18

Dostoyevsky, Fyodor: *Brothers Karamazov*, 180, 301, 380, 471; and OM's childhood, 23. *See also* terrible

dove. *See* bird families; *harawi*; Harcourt, Marguerite and Raoul d'; Peru/Peruvian; Sauvage, Cécile; surrealism

Dreyfus affair: and French Catholicism, 4-6, 13, 467; and Pierre Messiaen, 4-6, 13; politicization and polarization of French music, 110. *See also* Act of Separation

drugs: altered states of consciousness, xix, 157-59; cannabis/hashish, 157-58, 157-58n18, 170; mescaline-induced hallucinations, xv, 165, 165n43, 167, 169, 170, 182, 191, 497-98; opium, exotic aura of, 157-58; *Peyote: The Plant That Makes Eyes Open with Wonder* (Rouhier), 165-70, 165n43, 182, 497-98; and Poe, 427-28, 486n71; "Squeaky Blonde" in Festa's *Apparition of the Eternal Church*, 190-92; "visions" of the celestial city likened to drug-induced hallucinations, 173n65. *See also* synesthesia

Dukas, Paul: *Ariadne and Bluebeard*, 116, 116n99, 125, 251, 308, 440,

523n47; OM's composition studies with, 214-15n57; *The Peri*, 214-15n57; *Sorcerer's Apprentice*, 112, 157. *See also* clarity *(clarté)*; stones/gems

Dupré, Marcel: OM's conservatory studies with, 43, 55n25, 133-34; OM's 1935 organ concert with, 218-19; OM's Paris Conservatory position, 281; rivalry with Tournemire, 43n50, 135; *Treatise on Organ Improvisation*, 55; and Widor, 99; WORKS: *Three Preludes and Fugues*, 99. *See also* improvisation; Messiaen, Olivier, WORKS: *Diptych (Diptyque) for Organ*; Paris Conservatory

duration: and abiding *(demeurer)*/ eternity in OM's *Celestial Banquet*, 84, 87, 99; and achievement of "end-in-view," 363-64; and Boll's *Two Infinites*, 317; and Plotinus's concept of "number," 118; as "rhythmic character" in OM's *Visions of Amen*, 302-5; "Sixty-four Durations" from OM's *Organ Book*, 493; time as duration's "death," 97-98. *See also* Boll, Marcel; Cuvillier, Armand; end-in-view; Messiaen, Olivier, WORKS: *Diptych (Diptyque) for Organ*; nonretrogradability; "rhythmic characters"; time

Easter. *See* resurrection

éblouissement (dazzlement), xv, 51, 114, 128-29, 448, 450, 452, 497, 515; of the celestial city, 114-15n97, 450; and "living stones," 452; and OM's synesthesia, 51, 159-60n24, 162, 171-72n59; in OM's work, 114-15, 114-15n97, 450; and Saint John of the Cross, 114-15n97; and terrifying beauty *(fulgurante)*, 381. *See also* clarity *(clarté)*; fear *(la peur)* and awe *(la crainte)*; synesthesia

electronic music, 387, 499. *See also* Stockhausen, Karlheinz

Élie, Marguerite, marriage to Pierre Messiaen, 75

Eliot, T. S., *Murder in the Cathedral*, 180n84, 356-57, 468n22. *See also* Breton, André: "certain point of the mind" *(point de l'esprit)*; juxtaposition of contrasts

Éluard, Paul, 64, 65, 88, 122, 126-28, 154, 163, 208n36, 250, 262, 345, 466-67, 473. *See also* surrealism

émerveiller ("enmarvellement"), 165-66n44. *See also* drugs; marvelous; *Peyote: The Plant That Makes Eyes Open with Wonder*

Emmanuel, Maurice: *The Antique Greek Dance*, 503; and Greek antiquity, 54, 304, 310n3, 325, 503n43; and OM's self-conception as a "rhythmician," 54-55, 55n27, 304, 325, 325n46, 328; *Sonatina IV: On Hindu Modes*, 139. *See also* Greek culture; Hindu; Harcourt, Marguerite and Raoul d'; Peru/Peruvian; "Lament of Nijni-Novgorod"; Schola Cantorum

Emmerich, Anne-Catherine, *Dolorous Passion of Our Lord Jesus Christ*, 341-43, 341-42nn10-11

emotions. *See* abyss/vertigo; awe *(la crainte)*; desire; ephemerality; fear *(la peur)* and awe *(la crainte)*; grief; joy; lament; melancholy; terrible

end-in-view: and Aquinas on the transfiguration, 443-47; Aristotle's final cause perspective of, 360, 361-62, 364, 474; and Bergson's concept of duration, 360, 363-64, 366; and desire/subjective aim, 360, 364, 366-67; Dewey's teleological view of reality, 361-63, 364, 374. *See also* duration; Whitehead, Alfred North

ephemerality: and Claudel, 20-21, 22n59; and impassibility of "glorified bodies," 250, 269; and Job 14:1-2 *(Homo natus de muliere)*, 215-16n60; and melancholy, xvi, xviii-xix; of mosquitoes, 3, 13-14; and OM's Bergsonian notion of "duration," 366; and terrestriality, 250. *See also*

Index of Names and Subjects

desire; duration; rhythm; terrestrial/celestial contrast; time

Escaich, Thierry, 148. *See also* improvisation

eschatology: and angels, 380-82; fin-de-siècle concern with end times, 189; Rahner on, 297n2, 374-75. *See also* apocalypticism; Messiaen, Olivier, WORKS: *Celestial Banquet; Et Exspecto Resurrectionem Mortuorum; Glorified Bodies; Lightning Flashes of the Beyond . . . ; Visions of Amen*

eternity: and Bach's *canon perpetuus*, 451-52; and Cuvillier's philosophy of duration, 96-99; and endless staircases, 116, 191, 476; and ephemerality, xvi, xviii-xix, 99-101; Eucharist as foretaste of, 84-85; and God's capacity for suffering, 511; and human divinization *(potentia oboedientia)*, 85, 85n24; OM's explanation of his single-minded attention to, 181; OM's summary of incarnation in terms of, 338-39; organ as ideal instrument for expression of, 138, 189; palindrome as symbol of, xvii, 124, 187-88, 303, 365-66; and perpetual motion machines, 188-89; primordial Aegean Sea, 184, 189; and threefold church, 173n63. *See also* Messiaen, Olivier, WORKS: *Apparition of the Eternal Church*; nonretrogradability; palindrome; staircases; terrestrial/celestial contrast; time

Eucharist, xvii, 41, 84-87, 107, 112, 137n28, 142, 166-67, 182, 185, 214, 219, 237-38, 245, 252, 258, 264, 297n2, 345, 437, 446, 454, 527-29; and Emmaus, 264, 529; as erotic exchange in Cécile Sauvage, 35; as foretaste *(praegustatum)* of eternity, 84-85; and hymn *Adoro te*, 528-29; and hymn "Ave verum corpus," 84, 258, 397; and John 6:37-40, 86n25; and John 6:51-55, 86; and John 6:57, 86, 239; and Requiem Mass for the dead, 86, 105-6, 510-11, 512; sacrificial/eucharistic blood, 179-80, 345; as sign of love, 107; transubstantiation, 85, 145, 346, 526-29. *See also* Messiaen, Olivier, WORKS: *Book of the Blessed Sacrament; Celestial Banquet; The Eucharistic Banquet; The Forgotten Offerings; Hymn to the Blessed Sacrament*

Exodus, book of: creation and liberation in, 456; God's self-revelation in, 518

Fabre, Lucien, *Tristan and Isolde*, 471. *See also* Messiaen, Olivier, WORKS: "Tristan Trilogy"

Fauré, Gabriel, *Requiem*, 105

"F.D.": Fernand Drogoul possibly identified with, 208n36; OM's *Hymn to the Blessed Sacrament* reviewed by, 213-15; OM's *Resplendent Tomb* reviewed by, 208, 212-13

fear *(la peur)* and awe *(la crainte)*, xvi-xvii; and Aquinas on transfiguration, 515; distinguished by Hello, xvii, 39n38, 177-78, 429n75, 432; genealogy of, xvi-xvii; and humanity's place in universe, 317-18; and OM's *Apparition*, 189-93; and OM's childhood fascination with fearful things, 39-41, 192, 193; OM's commentary on, 522; and OM's *Transfiguration*, "Terribilis est locus iste," 515, 515n25; and Psalm 110:9b-10, 521-22; and recent work on "history of emotions," 192-93; and the sublime, xvii. *See also* abyss/vertigo; Baudelaire, Charles; *éblouissement* (dazzlement); Dostoyevsky, Fyodor; Hello, Ernest; Otto, Rudolf; Pascal, Blaise; Poe, Edgar Allan; Shakespeare, William; sublime; terrible

Festa, Paul, *Apparition of the Eternal Church*, 189-92. *See also* postmodern

filiation (adoptive), 237n26, 441, 512-13. *See also* divine adoption

Fillion, Abbé Louis-Claude: French

553

translation of Latin Vulgate by, 264n109, 270n129, 280n11, 299n4, 328n55, 344n16, 346n20, 404, 424, 435, 439n12, 442; and OM's self-conception as a theological musician, 223-24

Fischinger, Oskar, 157, 161

Flaubert, Gustave, *Madame Bovary*, 11

Fontenelle, Bernard Le Bovier de, *Conversations on the Plurality of Inhabited Worlds*, 313-15, 320n33, 420n52. *See also* astronomy; fear *(la peur)* and awe *(la crainte)*; Pascal, Blaise

Francis of Assisi: blackcap warbler associated with by OM, 394; Fellini and Rossellini, 486-87; and Flammarion series, 321; Franciscan order founded by Saint Bonaventure, 384; and "perfect joy," 182; Pierre Messiaen's scholarly edition of *The Little Flowers*, 486; Tournemire's *Trilogy Faust — Don Quixote — Saint Francis of Assisi*, 177n73. *See also* Messiaen, Olivier, WORKS: *Saint Francis of Assisi*

Frank, César: OM's "Franckist" past, 227; and Tournemire, 142-43

Fuligny, 79-80, 84-85, 106, 121, 129, 136-37, 142, 146n56, 287

Gajard, (Dom) Joseph, O.S.B., 140

Gallon, Jean, 49, 131, 133; OM's studies with, 49

Gauguin, Paul, 322, 322n38

Gautier, Théophile, 157-58

gaze, ii, 181, 225, 234n17, 238, 355, 375, 460-70, 497, 515. *See also* Messiaen, Olivier, WORKS: *Twenty Gazes at the Infant Jesus*; visions

gems. *See* stones/gems

Genesis, book of: creation and liberation in, 298-99, 456; improvisation of Creator in, 305; and tree of knowledge of good and evil, 166. *See also* abyss/vertigo; astronomy; creation; light and life; Messiaen, Olivier,

WORKS: *Visions of Amen*, "Amen of Creation"

Gibon, Jean (Jehan) de, 43-44, 134

Gibon, Joseph de. *See* Gibon, Jean (Jehan) de

Gide, André, 19, 52n16

Glass, Philip, *Einstein on the Beach*, 524. *See also* postmodern

glory, i, ii, xv, 144, 151, 173-74, 178-79, 181-82, 221-25, 230-31, 234-36, 250, 257-58, 271-72, 324, 357, 403, 434-44, 482, 510-11, 515-16, 528, 531-32

Gontier, Canon Augustin-Mathurin, *Rational Method of Plainchant*, 109

Górecki, Henryk, *Symphony No. 3*, 524. *See also* postmodern

Great War. *See* World War I

Greek culture: arsis and thesis (rising and falling metric lines), 308, 327; and Cécile Sauvage, 61; and dance, 503n43; Plotinus, 118, 118n102; primordial Aegean Sea, 184, 189; rhythm in drama and poetry of, xiv, 325, 327, 331; strophe-antistrophe-epode structure of Greek tragedy, 349-50, 503-4, 504n45. *See also* Antigone; Emmanuel, Maurice; Mocquereau, (Dom) André, O.S.B.; neoclassicism

Green, Julien: and Catholic Revivalism, 487n74; on OM's organ improvisation, 146-47, 177-78. *See also* improvisation

grief, xviii, xix, xxi, 31-34, 36, 64, 79-129, 215-16, 277, 281, 293, 347, 349, 352, 354-55, 372, 396, 399, 415, 441, 460, 472-77, 484, 485, 488, 495, 496, 503-6, 519

Grunenwald, Jean-Jacques, 243

Guéranger, (Dom) Prosper, O.S.B., 237; and "divine adoption," 237, 513n18; *The Liturgical Year (L'Année liturgique)*, 149-50, 175, 176

Guillou, Jean, 148. *See also* improvisation

hallucination, xv, 158, 165n43, 166,

Index of Names and Subjects

173n65, 192n110, 193, 427, 486n71, 497. *See also* drugs; visions
harawi (Peruvian genre of love song), 92-95, 166, 307-8, 473, 483; and Rouhier's *Peyote*, 166. *See also* bird families: doves; Harcourt, Marguerite and Raoul d'; Peru/Peruvian; Messiaen, Olivier, WORKS: *Five Refrains; Harawi*
Harcourt, Marguerite and Raoul d', *The Music of the Incas*, 56, 92-93, 117, 473. *See also* Emmanuel, Maurice; *harawi*; Peru/Peruvian
Hébert, Abbé Marcel, 386n23
Hebrews, book of, quoted by Dostoyevsky, 180
Heidegger, Martin, 97n51, 208n37; *Being and Time*, 312-13, 317. *See also* anxiety
Hello, Ernest, 343; *Du néant à dieu*, 82; fear *(la peur)* and awe *(la crainte)* distinguished by, xvii, 39n38, 177-78, 346-47, 429n75, 432; Hello's "Vertigo before the Absolute" chapter, 280n11, 494-95; on light and life, 300; on tears in the Scriptures, 340-41; *Words of God*, 177, 340, 353-54, 404, 432. *See also* abyss/vertigo; Catholic Revivalism
Henze, Hans Werner, 490
Hindu: dance, 333; and Hinduism, 139-40; OM's use of, 54-55, 229, 249, 303-4, 333, 336, 491-92; pseudo-Hindu language in OM's *Five Refrains*, 262, 485, 499, 505; rhythms and language, xiv-xv, xvii. *See also* Emmanuel, Maurice
Hiroshima. *See* Japan
Hitler, Adolf, 207, 241, 265
Honegger, Arthur, *Antigone*, 350-51. *See also* neoclassicism; Vichy regime; Young France
Huysmans, Joris-Karl, 343. *See also* symbolist movement

Imitation of Christ (De Imitatione Christi, Thomas à Kempis), i, 62, 214, 231, 437-38; and Cécile Sauvage, 61
improvisation, 131-33, 136-37, 145-47, 148, 153, 177, 239, 254n74, 305, 309, 335, 378, 383, 397, 419n49, 455, 491; as "commentary" or "paraphrase" of a "mystical" composer on a sacred text, 111, 137, 145, 147, 148, 151-52, 178, 257n87, 454, 491. *See also* Debussy, Claude; Dupré, Marcel; Green, Julien; *lectio divina*; Mallarmé, Stéphane; Marmion, (Dom) Columba, O.S.B.; "rhythmic characters"; symbolist movement; Tournemire, Charles
Indy, Vincent d', 55n25, 92n43, 110-11, 204, 208. *See also* Schola Cantorum
International Colonial Exposition (1931), 123-24. *See also* Bali/Balinese; Jolivet, André
International Exhibition of Arts and Technologies (1937), 258-61, 280, 341n9
International Exhibition of Surrealism (1938), 262. *See also* surrealism
Isaiah, book of, and the Virgin and Child, 234

Jacobs, Paul, 529, 529-30n61
James, William, *Principles of Psychology*, 361
Jammes, Francis, 8-9, 11-12n21, 19. *See also* Catholic Revivalism
Jansenism, 106
Japan: birdsongs of, transcribed by OM, 382, 388; OM's *Seven Haiku*, 382-83, 509, 514; OM's travels to, 509, 514; Penderecki's *Threnody to the Victims of Hiroshima*, 514. *See also* Messiaen, Olivier, WORKS: *The Transfiguration*
Jaspers, Karl, 430n76. *See also* abyss/vertigo
Jeune France, La. *See* Young France
Jews and Judaism: execution of Marc Bloch, 461; Good Friday liturgy

"Reproaches" *(Improperia)*, 283-84; Jewish Statutes of October 1940, 281; and liquidation of the Jewish ghettos, 460; and the Occupation, 289-90; and OM's *Song of the Deported*, 469-70, 470n25; and Paris Conservatory, 279, 281-83, 285, 287; and Vichy regime, 278-79, 281, 284, 466. *See also* World War II

John, Gospel of, and adoptive filiation, 236, 237, 238-39. *See also* Messiaen, Olivier, WORKS: *Ascension; Celestial Banquet*

John of the Cross, 114-15n97

Jolivet, André: and La Spirale, 240; *Mana*, 240, 331. *See also* Bali/Balinese

Jolivet, Hilda, 216

joy, i, xv-xvi, xviii, 117-18, 125, 176, 179-82, 201, 221-26, 232, 234, 237, 239, 247, 251, 259, 268, 280, 301, 347, 353, 356-57, 368, 370, 385, 386, 390, 393, 396, 399, 400, 405, 406, 409, 411, 414, 418, 426, 433, 439, 440, 442, 447, 478, 479, 481-82, 496, 508, 510, 525, 529, 529-30n61, 532; and Bloy, 224n87, 226n93; and Chateaubriand, 224n87, 226; in epigraphs to movements of OM's *Nativity*, 224n87, 352-53; and Guéranger, *The Liturgical Year*, 176; "Joy of the Blood of the Stars" movement of OM's *Turangalîla Symphony*, 180n84, 182, 479, 481, 525; OM's self-definition as a "musician of joy," xv-xvi, xviii, 182, 182n91, 225, 510, 525; and OM's "Virgin and Child" melody, 353; "perfect joy" explained in OM's *Saint Francis of Assisi*, 182; and Psalm 46:6, 222

juxtaposition of contrasts: between "terrible love" and "harmonious silence" in OM's *Turangalîla Symphony*, 478-82; between "terrible love" and "harmonious silence" in OM's *Visions of Amen*, 359, 360, 371, 374, 479; as feature of OM's musical thought, 102-3, 159-60n24, 171-72n59, 185n98, 475; of large (galaxies) and small (photons) in Boll's *Two Infinites*, 316-17, 462; in OM's *Diptych*, 98-103; in OM's *Five Refrains*, 485; modernist-primitivism, 44n53, 331-32; and paradox of transubstantiation ("celestial banquet"), 346; and rhythmic dyads, 333-34; and sound-color, 181, 185, 185n98. *See also* Breton, André: "certain point of the mind" *(point de l'esprit);* Delaunay, Robert; Éluard, Paul; Eucharist; simultaneous contrast; stones/gems; surrealism; synesthesia; terrestrial/celestial contrast

Kant, Immanuel: philosophical opponents of, 8; and the sublime, xvii, 349, 352

Keats, John: "Ode to a Nightingale," 391-92, 399; and Pierre Messiaen, 20, 38, 64

Kierkegaard, Søren, anxiety compared with vertigo by, 426-27, 429n73, 430, 430n76. *See also* abyss/vertigo

Koussevitsky, Serge, and OM's *Ascension*, 226-27n95, 482

Krenek, Ernst, 490

The Lady of Shalott, symbolism of, 38, 45, 293, 520

La Fontaine, Jean de, 23

Lamartine, Alphonse de: and Cécile Sauvage's poetry, 16-17nn33,35, 118n102; and literary imagination OM inherited from his parents, 8; and Pierre Messiaen, 8; "The Valley," 24. *See also* soul

lament, 51, 56, 89, 92-95, 113-15, 117, 215-16, 356, 372, 396, 397-401, 415, 472-73, 475, 483. *See also* bird families: doves; ephemerality; grief; "Lament of Nijni-Novgorod"; melancholy; Peru/Peruvian

"Lament of Nijni-Novgorod," 397-400.

Index of Names and Subjects

See also creation theme; Messiaen, Olivier, WORKS: *Visions of Amen*, "Amen of Consummation"
"Lament of the Conscript," 397-400
Langlais, Jean: on Dupré, 133n10; and La Spirale, 240; OM's friendship with, 205; performance of OM's *Nativity* suite, 243; and postconciliar Catholicism, 526-27; *Three Gregorian Paraphrases*, 257n87; and Tournemire, 255. *See also* improvisation
lark. *See* bird families
La Spirale, 227, 253
Latry, Olivier, 148. *See also* improvisation
lectio divina, 148-52, 178-80. *See also* improvisation
Leguay, Jean-Pierre, 148. *See also* improvisation
Le Jeune, Claude, 386, 483, 484
Liber Usualis, 223n84, 495nn17-18, 515n25
life. *See* creation; light and life
Ligeti, György, 490
light. *See* Bonaventure; clarity *(clarté)*; *éblouissement* (dazzlement); glory; light and life; Sainte-Chapelle; sound-color; stones/gems; Suger, Abbot; visions
light and life, 299, 301, 328, 452
lightning flash, 36, 59, 154, 210, 435, 497, 530-31. *See also* visions
Loriod (Loriod-Messiaen), Yvonne (OM's second wife), 227; and clandestine writings of Cécile Sauvage, 530; marriage to OM, 460, 508-9; and OM's *Lady of Shalott*, 520; OM's meeting of, 287, 290; and OM's *Twenty Gazes*, 461; piano performances of, 292-93, 460-61, 477, 482, 496, 498, 502, 520, 523; and *Visions of Amen*, 292-93
Lowell, Percival, 315
Luke, Gospel of, and adoptive filiation, 236-38
Lyapunov, Sergey, "Carillon" in *Twelve*

Studies of Transcendent Execution, 448n45, 453

Mabille, Pierre, *Mirror of the Marvelous*, 128-29n137, 165-66n44. *See also* Breton, André; drugs; surrealism; visions
Machaut, Guillaume de, "My end is my beginning" *(Ma fin)*, 187-88, 187-88nn101-3, 303, 412, 504; and nonretrogradability/eternity, 365. *See also* palindrome
Maeterlinck, Maurice: *The Bluebird*, 125; and Debussy's *Pelléas and Mélisande*, 40, 44-45, 46n57, 370n29; and Dukas's *Ariadne and Bluebeard*, 116, 116n99, 125, 251, 440, 523n47. *See also* Aulnoy, Madame (Countess) Marie-Catherine d', "The Bluebird"
Mallarmé, Stéphane, xv, 8, 154n1, 379n9. *See also* symbolist movement
Marc, Franz, 452
Maredsous Abbey, 148-49. *See also* Marmion, (Dom) Columba, O.S.B.
Maritain, Jacques, 74-75; and *Antigone*, 351-52; *Antimoderne*, 58, 83; *Art and Scholasticism*, 81-83, 120; Bernanos's attacks on, 75; broadcasts for BBC Overseas Service and Voice of America, 286; and clarity *(clarté)*, 83, 119-20n105, 120; on the Holocaust, 470n25; *Integral Humanism*, 242; *Letter to Jean Cocteau*, 244, 244-45n45; self-exile in New York of, 286; suicide pact of, with Raïssa Maritain (*née* Oumançoff), 24n65. *See also* Catholic Revivalism
Marmion, (Dom) Columba, O.S.B.: and *adoptio perfecta*, 230-31, 236-39, 513; confusion over scriptural references by, 437-38; on divine grace (Rom. 8:18 and 2 Cor. 4:17), 182; on the glorified body, 442-43; on God's suffering, 339n3; and Guéranger, 149-50, 152, 237; on human suffering, 180; and *lectio divina*, 148-52, 178-81; and

Index of Names and Subjects

OM's turn away from the "mystical" toward the "theological," 228-29; and postwar mysticism and metaphysics, 232-33; on predestination, 106, 231-33; and star + cross motif, 180-81, 229-30, 468nn21-22, 469; WRITINGS: *Christ in His Mysteries*, 148-52, 178-82, 228-29, 231-33, 234nn17-18, 235nn19-20, 236nn21-23, 237n25, 238-39, 260, 274, 299-300, 339n3, 355, 436-37, 442, 443, 444, 459, 463n9, 468nn22-23, 469, 511n12, 513, 513n18, 515n23; *Christ, the Life of the Soul*, 235n19. *See also* divine adoption; filiation (adoptive); Maredsous Abbey; predestination; Messiaen, Olivier, WORKS: *Apparition of the Eternal Church; Glorified Bodies; The Nativity of the Lord; The Transfiguration; Twenty Gazes at the Infant Jesus*

marvelous, 128, 128-29n136, 165-66n44, 214n56, 527n58. *See also* Breton, André; drugs; Mabille, Pierre; surrealism; visions

Mary Magdalene, 105-6, 529. *See also* apparition

Matthew, Gospel of, and adoptive filiation, 236

Maurras, Charles, 8-9, 11-12n21, 28, 66n65, 74, 75. *See also* Action Française

melancholy, **30-46**; and Cécile Sauvage, xvi, 14, 16, 24-25, 34-37, 42, 49-51, 61, 519; Coleridge's "The Nightingale," 390-91; and ephemerality, xvi, xviii-xix; "Melancholy" by Cécile Sauvage, 26, 27n78, 69, 91; and OM's *Forgotten Offerings*, 112; OM's joyously melancholic *The Resplendent Tomb*, 124-25; and OM's "Praise to the Eternity of Jesus," 259, 280; and OM's self-definition as "musician of joy," xv-xvi, xviii, 182, 182n91, 225, 510, 525; OM's setting of poetry of, 103-4; poem about a lark by Cécile Sauvage, 20-21, 21n55, 388; as recurrent theme in OM's life, xv-xvi, 3, 191. *See also* anxiety; bird families: doves; bird families: nightingales; ephemerality; grief; *harawi*; lament; star + cross motif

Messiaen, Alain (OM's brother), 121; birth of, 69, 70; and Catholic Revivalism, 322; and Hello, 340, 346; *The Valley* by Cécile Sauvage dedicated to, 73

Messiaen, Charles-Marie (OM's half brother), 75; birth of, 75, 121

Messiaen, Jacques (OM's half brother), death of, 215

Messiaen, Léon (OM's uncle), 33

Messiaen, Olivier:

CHILDHOOD INFLUENCES: *The Budding Soul* by Cécile Sauvage dedicated to, 73; Catholic faith and parents' religiosity, xiii, 22-23, 58-60, 148; fascination with visions and apparitions, 166-67, 170-71; in Fuligny, 79, 80, 84-85, 106, 121, 129, 136, 137, 142; parents' literary interests, 8, 20, 23, 40, 192, 387; Sainte-Chapelle and synesthesia, 47, 51, 435, 512; self-discovery as a musician, 38; and Shakespeare, 40-41, 90n38, 128, 170, 392-93, 415

THOUGHT: on city dwellers and birds, 384; crib and tomb/star + cross linkage in music of, 16, 120; *éblouissement* (dazzlement), 51, 114-15, 114-15n97, 128; and history of human music, 386-87; and juxtaposition of contrasts, 102-3, 475; and organ commentary, 136-37; and organ improvisation, 131, 133, 146-47, 177-78; "phonemic particles" and "magic syllables," 499; and popular science, 319-25; self-conception as a rhythmician, xiv, xvii, 54-55, 304, 325, 325n46, 328; self-definition as a "musician of joy," xv-xvi, xviii, 182, 182n91, 225, 510, 525; self-image as a "mystical"

558

composer, and Cécile Sauvage, 36, 59-60, 76, 118n102, 121; self-image and the "Messiaen Controversy," 138, 462-65, 467-68; self-image and the organ, 130, 142; self-image and plainchant, 111-12, 144; self-image and rejection/transition away from, 206, 228; self-image and *Technique of My Musical Language*, 226-27; self-image and *The Celestial Banquet*, 84, 88; self-image and *The Forgotten Offerings*, 142, 144; self-image as a "theological" musician/biblical composer, 147, 206, 224, 228-29, 511, 516; self-image and "The Transmutation of Enthusiasms," 326; self-image and Tournemire, 111, 136-38, 142-45

TRAVELS: to Japan, 509, 514; to Utah, 518-20; to Washington, D.C., 227. *See also* Tanglewood

WORKS:
  Apparition of the Eternal Church (1931-1932), xix, **153-93**, 238, 264n110, 508; continuity with *The Nativity*, 238; and eternity/perpetual motion, 183-85, 188-89; fear, 189-93; introductory poem for, 171, 531; and juxtaposition of *porte* and *perle*, 176, 264n110; and *lectio divina*, 152, 178-81; office for the Dedication of a Church, 175, 508; paraphrasing of, 531; synesthesia in, 509; and visionary aspects of mysticism, 36. *See also* Dedication of a Church (liturgical office)
  Ascension: Four Symphonic Meditations for Orchestra (1932-1934): composition of, xix; OM's rating of, 226-27; orchestration of, 205-6. *See also* Carter, Jimmy; Tanglewood
  Ascension: Four Symphonic Meditations for Organ (1934), 205, 218-23, 251

Awakening of Birds (1953), 496, 497, 503
The Blackbird (1951), 389, 496
Book of the Blessed Sacrament (1984), 324, 525-29; and human divinization *(potentia oboedientia)*, 85; Paul Jacobs Grammy Award–winning performance of, 529; and transubstantiation, 527-29
Catalogue of Birds (1956-1958), 460, 499-501, 502-3; epigraphs to, 383-85
Celestial Banquet (1928), 99, 238; composition of, 80, 83-87, 95; and Tournemire's *L'Orgue Mystique*, 136-38; and "What celestial life" *(Quelle céleste vie)* by Cécile Sauvage, 87-88
Choruses for a Joan of Arc (1941), 283
Chronochromie (1960), 349, 503
Colors of the Celestial City (1963), 172, 450, 451, 509-10
The Death of Number (1930): and Claire Delbos, 119-20, 197; composition of, 112, 113-20, 197; and "far-off"/"endless" staircase, 125, 186n100, 451, 476; and Poe's "Pit and the Pendulum," 481
Diptych (Diptyque) for Organ: An Essay on Terrestrial Life and Blessed Eternity (1930), 98-103, 154, 263, 266, 281
Éclairs sur l'au-delà . . . See Lightning Flashes of the Beyond . . . (1991)
Eight Preludes (1928-1929), 55-56, 88-98; 1. "The Dove," 89, 91, 95, 474; 2. "Song of Ecstasy in a Sad Landscape," 89, 90; 3. "The Light Number," 89, 95, 96, 98; 4. "Deceased Instants," 89, 95, 98, 118; 5. "The Impalpable Sounds of Dreaming," 89, 90; 6. "Bells of Anguish and Tears of

Farewell," 116-17, 402; 7. "Quiet Lament," 89, 92; 8. "Reflection in the Wind," 89, 90-91, 155

Et Exspecto Resurrectionem Mortuorum (1964), 510-12, 515

The Eucharistic Banquet (1928), 85

Exotic Birds (1956), 498, 499-502; revisited in *From Canyons to Stars*, 523

Festival of Beautiful Waters (1937) (or *Great Waters*), 258-60, 341n9; and *Quartet for the End of Time*, 280

Five Refrains (Cinq Rechants) (1948): *alba*, 483-84, 499; pseudo-Hindu language of, 262, 485, 499

The Forgotten Offerings (1930), 134, 238; binary and ternary groupings inspired by plainchant in, 108-9, 112, 123-24, 188; composition of, 80, 106-7, 111-12; "eternity" represented in, 124, 127; and OM's self-image as "mystical" composer, 111, 142, 144

Four Studies in Rhythm (1949-1950), 489-90, 491-92. *See also* Cold War; Darmstadt

From Canyons to Stars (1974), 39, 177, 432, 518-24

Glorified Bodies: Seven Brief Visions of the Life of the Resurrected (1939): and Aquinas, 120, 265, 268-73, 274, 441; eschatological vision of, 289; and *Visions of Amen*, 418, 422, 440-41

Harawi (1945), 55-56, 93, 116, 262, 372, 399, 451, 470, 472-77, 483, 485, 499; and Claire Delbos, 472-75

Hymn to the Blessed Sacrament (1932), 238, 245; reviews of, 145, 213-15

The Lady of Shalott (1917), 38, 45, 520

Lightning Flashes of the Beyond . . . (1991), 482n55, 530-32; and visionary aspects of mysticism, 36, 59, 154, 210, 530-31

Mass of Pentecost (1950), 172, 490-92, 496, 499n32, 507-8n1, 508

Meditations on the Mystery of the Holy Trinity (1969), 517-18

The Nativity of the Lord: Nine Meditations for Organ (1935): composition of, 227, 228; epigraphs to movements of, 224n87; and Fillion, 224; and OM's post-Franckist aesthetic, 227, 229; premiere of, 243-44; structure of, 233-39

The Organ Book: Seven Pieces for Organ (1951), 379-80, 492-95, 497; epigraph for, 529; 1. "Repetition by Interversion," 493, 497; 2. "Trio (for Trinity Sunday)," 493; 3. "The Hands of the Abyss (for Times of Penitence)," 424, 493, 494, 497; 4. "Birdsong (for Eastertide)," 493, 494; 5. "Trio (for Trinity Sunday)," 493; 6. "The Eyes in the Wheels (for Pentecost Sunday)," 379-80, 493, 494-95; 7. "Sixty-four Durations," 493

Poems of Mi (1936), 250-52, 257, 261, 262, 263-64, 265, 266

Prisms. See Songs of Earth and Sky

Quartet for the End of Time (1940): eschatological vision of, 289; German POW camp premiere of, xi, 4-5n2, 261-62, 279; and "non-retrogradable rhythm," 303, 303-4n18; as palindrome, 366; 1. "Liturgy of Crystal," 261-62, 397n47; 2. "Vocalise, for the Angel Who Announces the End of Time," 262; 3. "The Abyss of the Birds," 279-80, 424; 5. "Praise to the Eternity of Jesus," 259, 280; 6. "Dance of Fury

for the Seven Trumpets," 531;
8. "Praise to the Immortality of
Jesus," 280-81
The Resplendent Tomb (1931), 210,
238; composition of, 120-22, 128-
29; irregular rhythmic patterns
in, 123-25, 188; reviewed by
"F.D.," 208, 212-13; surrealist
imagery of, 125-28
The Sadness of a Great White Sky
(1925), 55-56, 92, 95
Saint Francis of Assisi (1983),
114n97, 182, 443, 524-25; libretto
for, xiv, 138, 182n91
*Seven Haiku: Japanese Sketches for
Solo Piano and Small Orchestra*
(1962), 382-83, 509, 514
A Smile (Un Sourire) (1989),
104n69
Song of the Deported (1945), 469-
70, 470n25
Songs of Earth and Sky (1938),
originally entitled *Prisms*): and
"clarity," 273; eschatological and
apocalyptic themes in, 267, 275;
writing of, 261-66; 1. "Union
with Mi *(for My Wife),*" 261;
2. "Antiphon of Silence *(for
the [Feast] Day of the Guardian
Angels),*" 261; 3. "Dance of Baby
'Pill' *(for My Little Pascal),*"
262; 4. "Resurrection *(for
Easter Day),*" 262, 264n109, 529;
5. "Facing Up to Midnight Sharp
(for Death)," 262-63; 6. "Rainbow of Innocence *(for My Little
Pascal),*" 258, 261
Theme and Variations (1932), 205.
See also Delbos, Claire: marriage
to OM
Three Melodies (1930): and OM's
piety and theology, 105-6; poetry by OM and his mother in,
103-4, 106, 113, 114
*Three Small Liturgies of the Divine
Presence* (1944): and Arcturus,

320, 462; and Beaumarchais's
Tarare, 423; composition of,
423, 460; and the Concerts de la
Pléiade, 290, 461-62, 466
The Transfiguration (1969): and
adoptive filiation, 237, 512-13;
and glorified bodies, 441; world-
historical context of composition of, 513-17
"Tristan Trilogy," xx, 470, 482,
485. *See also Five Refrains;
Harawi; Turangalîla Symphony*
Turangalîla Symphony (1945-1948),
182, 477-82, 525; "Development
of Love," 479-81; "Garden of
Love's Sleep," 479, 479n49, 481;
"Joy of the Blood of the Stars,"
180n84, 182, 479, 481, 525; and
Poe's "Pit and the Pendulum,"
423-24
Twenty Gazes at the Infant Jesus
(1944): and Boll's *Two Infinites,*
316; comparison with "gazes"
in OM's *Nativity,* 238; composition of, 154, 238, 460-61;
critical review of, 462; and
nonretrogradability, 187n101,
188; premiered by Loriod, 461;
quotation from 2 Corinthians
4:17-18, ii; star + cross motif in,
44, 180n84, 182n91, 338, 355,
468-69, 468nn21-22; title from
Nicene Creed, 316-17n24
Two Ballads of Villon (1921), 51,
53-54
Verset for the Feast of the Dedication
(1961), 172, 507-9
Vingt Regards (1944). *See Twenty
Gazes at the Infant Jesus*
Visions of Amen (1943), 441, 519;
and Beaumarchais's *Tarare,*
422-23; composition of, 289n41,
290-92, 460; eschatological
vision of, 289; as palindrome,
365-66; and popular science,
294, 319-25; premiere in

Index of Names and Subjects

German-occupied Paris of, 455-56; as résumé of OM's reading and thinking, xx; as snapshot of OM's imaginary in 1943, 294-95; and *tragédie lyrique*, 420; and visionary aspects of mysticism, 36, 60, 154

Vision 1: "Amen of Creation," **296-308**; and "rhythmic characters," 302-6; and Westminster carillon theme/creation theme, 306-8, 398, 455-56

Vision 2: "Amen of the Stars, of the Planet with the Ring," **309-37**; and birdsong, 385-86; OM's analysis of, 320n35, 332, 420

Vision 3: "Amen of the Agony of Jesus," **338-57**; and Beaumarchais's *Tarare*, 419-20

Vision 4: "Amen of Desire," **358-72**; and emotional and experiential aspects of time, xviii

Vision 5: "Amen of the Angels, of Saints, of Birdsong," **373-401**; as palindrome, 400-401

Vision 6: "Amen of Judgment," **402-32**; and Beaumarchais's *Tarare*, 418, 422

Vision 7: "Amen of Consummation," **433-56**; and clarity *(clarté, claritas)*, 222n82; creation theme of, 397-98, 455; and "perpetual dazzlement" of the celestial city, 450

WRITINGS:

"De la Musique sacrée" ("On Sacred Music"), 242n40

"Musique religieuse" ("Religious Music"), 301

Technique of My Musical Language, composition of, xx, 4-5n2

Treatise on Rhythm, Color, and Ornithology (1949-1992) in Seven Volumes, 397, 423-24; "Bergsonian Theory Following Sivadjian," 366; "Bergsonian Time and Musical Rhythm," 319n20; on birds and birdsong, 385-87, 392n37, 393-95; Boll's *Two Infinites* quoted, 317; and "Creation Song" in *Visions of Amen*, "Amen of Consummation," 397-98; Cuvillier's Bergsonian thought summarized in, 100-101, 364-65, 404; on dance, 325, 326-27, 333; epigraph to, 449; on Greek and Latin meters, 20n52, 54, 139, 304; Machaut's *Ma fin* quoted in, 187n101, 303n17; Plotinus on colors in, 118n102; on "rhythmic characters," xiv, 302-3, 302n13; on "sound-color," 160, 165n43, 345n17, 449n47; "Time and Eternity," 296-97, 378; *The Valley* by Cécile Sauvage, quoted in, 21n55

Messiaen, Pascal (OM's son), 257-58, 276-77, 280-82, 285, 287-88, 292, 347, 399, 433, 472, 495-96, 502. *See also* Messiaen, Olivier, WORKS: *Songs of Earth and Sky*

Messiaen, Paul (OM's uncle), 33

Messiaen, Pierre (OM's father): Blake translated by, 381-82n15, 387; *The Budding Soul* by Cécile Sauvage commented on, 16; and Catholic Revivalism, 322; and Coleridge, 390-91; crib and tomb symbolism in memoirs, 16; death of, 502; and the Great War, xvi; and Keats, 20, 38, 64; and Maritain, 58; marriage to Marguerite Élie, 75, 121; military service, 14, 17; position of *professeur* at Institut Catholique, 502n39; publication of *Images*, 461; scholarly edition of *The Little Flowers*, 486; Shakespeare translated by, 4-5n2, 20, 28-29, 49, 392, 502n39; and Villon, 53. *See also* Sauvage, Cécile

"Messiaen Controversy" ("Le Cas Messiaen"), iii, 148, 462-65, 467-68, 472. *See also* Catholic Revivalism; improvisation; symbolist movement

Index of Names and Subjects

meter: arsis and thesis (rising and falling metric lines), 308, 327; Greek meter, 503n43; OM on Greek and Latin meters, 20n52, 54, 139, 304; OM's disdain for, 325-26, 411; OM's *Forgotten Offerings* and resistance to, 112; OM's "three frozen notes," 403, 410-11, 418. *See also* Mocquereau, (Dom) André, O.S.B., rhythm; time

Michelson, Albert A., *Light Waves and Their Uses,* 450. *See also* waves

Migot, Georges, and La Spirale, 240

Milhaud, Darius, 466

Mistral, Frédéric, 15, 15n30, 19, 27, 34, 67, 483

Mocquereau, (Dom) André, O.S.B., 108, 108-9n76, 325, 328; on arsis and thesis, 308, 327; *The Gregorian Musical Number,* 108-9n76, 326n49. *See also* rhythm; Solesmes Abbey

Moreux, Abbé Théophile: *Across the Celestial Spaces,* 314n13, 319, 320-22, 320n33, 336; *Are Other Worlds Inhabited?* 315, 322, 328. *See also* astronomy

Mounier, Emmanuel, "Our Humanism," 241n36, 242

Mounier, Joseph, 12, 66

Mozart, Wolfgang Amadeus: and OM's *A Smile (Un Sourire),* 104n69; Susanna's aria from *Marriage of Figaro,* 292, 367-70, 372

musique concrète, 387, 499

Mussolini, Benito, 207, 241

"My end is my beginning" *(Ma fin). See* Machaut, Guillaume de

mysticism: and mescaline intoxication, 170; of OM's *Visions of Amen,* "Amen of Desire," 354; postwar "mystical" vogue, 118n102, 139-40, 232-33; visionary aspects of, 36, 59, 154, 165-66, 210. *See also* improvisation; sensual mysticism; star + cross motif

Napoleon: Concordat signed by, 405n5, 453; and Poe's "Pit and the Pendulum," 427-28, 430-31

neoclassicism, 348-52; and OM's *Visions of Amen,* "Amen of the Agony of Jesus," 352; and OM's *Chronochromie,* 349-50. *See also* Antigone; Greek culture; Young France

Nicene Creed: "begotten, not made," 238; "by him everything was made" of OM's *Twenty Gazes,* 316-17n24; OM's *Et Exspecto,* 509; "Things visible and invisible," 491

Nietzsche, Friedrich, 19; on anxiety/the abyss, 426-27; on dancing, 310-11n3; philosophical opponents of, 8

nightingale. *See* bird families

Nono, Luigi, 490

nonretrogradability: and Bergson's elastic band image of duration, 304-5; and OM's *Apparition,* 188; and OM's *Quartet for the End of Time,* 303, 366; and OM's *Twenty Gazes,* 187n101, 188; and OM's *Visions of Amen,* "Amen of Creation," 298, 303-5; and OM's *Visions of Amen,* "Amen of the Angels, of Saints, of Birdsong," 375; representing stasis/simultaneity (eternity), 124, 303-5, 412; and structure of OM's *Visions of Amen,* 365-66. *See also* eternity; Machaut, Guillaume de; palindrome

Notre-Dame cathedral. *See* Cathedral of Notre-Dame de Paris

Office for the Dedication of a Church. *See* Dedication of a Church (liturgical office)

organs: and carillon genre, 453-54; and eternity/perpetual motion, 87, 138, 183-85, 188-89; and sound-color, 156, 160. *See also* Cathedral of Notre-Dame de Paris; Cavaillé-Coll, Aristide; improvisation

Otto, Rudolf, *Idea of the Holy,* xvii, 380. *See also* sublime; terrible

palindrome: Machaut's "My end is my beginning" *(Ma fin),* 187-88,

187-88nn101-3, 303, 412, 504; OM's *Apparition* as, 188; and OM's binary and ternary groupings inspired by plainchant, 124; and phrase "bell-book-candle-book-bell," 411-12; as symbol of eternity, xvii, 124, 187-88, 303, 365-66, 399-400, 412. *See also* eternity; nonretrogradability; rhythm; time

Paris: International Colonial Exposition (1931), 123-24; liberation of, xiii, 461; occupation of, 278-79, 285-86, 290, 455-56, 465-67; and OM's "Midnight Obverse and Reverse *(to Death),*" in *Songs of Earth and Sky,* 263n107; and OM's *Visions of Amen* creation theme as musical code for liberation of, 456; Stavisky Riots, 215, 228

Paris Conservatory, xix, xx, 43, **47-76**, 98, 105n70, 110, 111n87, 113, 116n99, 131-36, 141, 142, 186n100, 187-88n103, 189, 218, 279, 281-83, 285, 287-88, 293, 294-95, 308, 325n46, 389, 454, 461, 496, 497, 499, 503, 507, 508. *See also* Dukas, Paul; Dupré, Marcel; Emmanuel, Maurice; Schola Cantorum; Tournemire, Charles

Pascal, Blaise, xvi, xviii, 13, 20, 22, 39, 118n102, 209, 242n40, 258, 280, 291, 312, 313, 314, 316, 339, 343n13, 380, 421, 424-26, 480, 481, 482n55, 494, 521. *See also* abyss/vertigo; anxiety; astronomy; Boll, Marcel; ephemerality; Fontenelle, Bernard Le Bovier de; Hello, Ernest; Kierkegaard, Søren; Nietzsche, Friedrich; Poe, Edgar Allan; Rouault, Georges; terrible

Paul VI, Pope, *Mysterium Fidei* on transubstantiation, 527. *See also* Eucharist

Péguy, Charles, 212n47. *See also* Catholic Revivalism

Penderecki, Krzysztof, 512; *Threnody to the Victims of Hiroshima,* 514-15

Percy, Walker, 317

Peru/Peruvian: and creation theme, 307-8; *harawi* (love song genre), 92-93, 166, 307-8, 473, 483; d'Harcourt, Marguerite and Raoul, on Peruvian love potions, 117; *The Music of the Incas* (d'Harcourt and d'Harcourt), 56, 92-93. *See also* bird families: doves; Emmanuel, Maurice; Messiaen, Olivier, WORKS: *Eight Preludes,* "The Dove"; *Five Refrains; Harawi*

Peyote: The Plant That Makes Eyes Open with Wonder (Rouhier), 165-70, 165n43, 182, 497-98. *See also* apparition; drugs; *émerveiller* ("enmarvellement"); hallucination; marvelous; sound-color; visions

Picasso, Pablo, modernist-primitivism, 44n53, 331

Pius X, Pope: *motu proprio* mandating plainchant restoration, 43n51; *Pascendi Dominici Gregis* and Roman Catholic Modernism, 15; and timing of OM's first communion (Eucharist), 41n47

Pius XI, Pope: Action Française condemned by, 74n97; contraception condemned by, 217-18

plainchant: "Celestial City of Jerusalem" ("Caelestis urbs Jerusalem"), 172, 173-74, 174-75n67, 176-77, 180, 450; and OM's convictions about liturgical music, 397n47; revival/restoration of, 43n51, 109-10; and Tournemire's *L'Orgue Mystique,* 144, 256

Plotinus, 118, 118n102

Poe, Edgar Allan: and Catholic Revivalist writers, 316n22; impact on French literature, 427; "Ligeia," 486; and OM's *Turangalîla Symphony,* 423-24, 424n60; opium hallucinations of, 486n71; "The Pit and the Pendulum," 63, 117, 117n100, 423-24, 427-31, 427n69, 481; translated by Baudelaire, 117n100, 427. *See also* Baudelaire, Charles; fear *(la peur)*

Index of Names and Subjects

and awe *(la crainte)*; juxtaposition of contrasts; terrible
postmodern, 523-24; and Festa's *Apparition of the Eternal Church,* 189-93. *See also* Bernstein, Leonard
Pourrat, Henri, 73, 73-74n95. *See also* Action Française; Vichy regime
predestination: and Cécile Sauvage, 106, 233. *See also* divine adoption; eternity; filiation (adoptive); Messiaen, Olivier, WORKS: *The Nativity of the Lord; The Transfiguration*

Racine, Jean, and Cécile Sauvage, 20, 23, 61
Rahner, Karl, 231n9, 297n2, 338n1, 374-75, 383-84n18; on human divinization *(potentia oboedientia),* 85n24
Ravel, Maurice, *Pavane pour une infante défunte* and OM's *Eight Preludes,* "Deceased Instants" ("Instants défunts"), 98
Reich, Steve: *Tehillim,* 524; *Violin Phase,* 524. *See also* postmodern
Rembrandt van Rijn, *Philosopher in Meditation,* 116n99, 451, 451n56
resurrection, 176n69, 250, 262-65, 269-70, 273-74, 324, 331, 417-18n44, 444-48, 509-10, 514, 515, 527, 529. *See also* Messiaen, Olivier, WORKS: *Book of the Blessed Sacrament; Et Exspecto Resurrectionem Mortuorum; Glorified Bodies; Poems of Mi; Songs of Earth and Sky,* "Resurrection *(for Easter Day)*"
Reverdy, Pierre, 89, 250, 463, 463-64n9, 473. *See also* surrealism
rhythm: influence of "nonmusical rhythms" on musical rhythm, 193; isorhythm, xvii, 187n101, 303-4n18, 500-501; military march as nonrhythmic, 111, 325, 403, 411, 422; OM's self-conception as rhythmician, xiv, xvii, 54-55, 304, 325, 325n46, 328; rhythmic dyads, 333-34. *See also* arsis and thesis; Bergson, Henri; Bali/Balinese; dance; duration; Emmanuel, Maurice; Greek culture; Hindu; juxtaposition of contrasts; meter; Mocquereau, (Dom) André, O.S.B.; nonretrogradability; palindrome; plainchant; "rhythmic characters"; time; Messiaen, Olivier, WORKS: *The Death of Number; Diptych (Diptyque) for Organ; The Forgotten Offerings; Four Studies in Rhythm; The Nativity of the Lord;* Messiaen, Olivier, WRITINGS: *Technique of My Musical Language; Treatise on Rhythm, Color, and Ornithology (1949-1992) in Seven Volumes*
"rhythmic characters" *(personnages rythmiques):* and "clock time," 303; and Daniel-Rops's "abstract characters" *(personnages abstraits)* theories, 302n13; and duration, 303; and improvisation of Creator in Genesis, 305; and OM's *Visions of Amen,* "Amen of Creation," 302-6; and Stravinsky's *Rite of Spring,* 302, 330-31. *See also* duration; juxtaposition of contrasts; Messiaen, Olivier, WORKS: *Diptych (Diptyque) for Organ;* nonretrogradability; surrealism
Riley, Terry, *In C,* 524. *See also* postmodern
Rilke, Rainer Maria, *Duino Elegies,* 379-80
Robin, Jean-Baptiste, 148. *See also* improvisation
Rochberg, George, *Music for the Magic Theater,* 524. *See also* postmodern
Roosevelt, Franklin Delano, 207
Rosicrucians, xiv. *See also* symbolist movement
Rossellini, Roberto, 486-87
Rossetti, Christina, 91
Rossier, Henri, 224
Roth, Daniel, 148. *See also* improvisation
Rouault, Georges, xii, 162n31, 245n47, 507n1

Index of Names and Subjects

Rouhier, Alexandre. *See Peyote: The Plant That Makes Eyes Open with Wonder*
Rudaux, Lucien, 315-16, 320n35, 336. *See also* astronomy

Saint-Eustache (church), 60. *See also* Paris
Saint-Sulpice (church), 60-61. *See also* Paris
Sainte-Chapelle, 47, 51, 435, 512. *See also éblouissement* (dazzlement); Paris; sound-color; synesthesia
Sainte-Clotilde (church), 61; Cavaillé-Coll organ in, 453; and Tournemire's *L'Orgue Mystique*, 205
Sainte-Geneviève-des-Grandes-Carrières (church), OM and Loriod marriage at, 509
Salieri, Antonio, and Beaumarchais's *Tarare*, 416, 422
Sauvage, André (OM's uncle), 10, 36, 48, 55, 519
Sauvage, Cécile (OM's mother): and Action Française, 74; and Ariadne, 116n99; clandestine writings of, to Jean de Gourmont, 26, 35-36, 293, 519-20, 530; death of, xvi, 63, 65-66, 80, 175-76, 197, 349; influence of poetry on OM, 59-60, 87-88, 214; isolation and loneliness of, xvi, 14, 16, 24-25, 34-37, 42, 49-51, 61, 519-20; and Jean de Gourmont, 18-19, 28-29, 34, 49, 65-66, 73, 387; modernity detested by, 52; and OM's *Three Melodies*, 103-4, 106; phobias of, 49-50; and poem about a lark, 20-21, 21n55, 388; postpartum depression following OM's birth, xvi, 17; predestination for eternity of, 106, 233; star + cross imagery in writing of, xvi, 16, 21-23; writings quoted by OM, 21n55, 387-88
  WRITINGS: *The Budding Soul*, 16, 73, 252-53, 257; and Claire Delbos's settings of, 218, 252; "The Cow," 18; "Melancholy," 26, 27n78, 69, 91; *Mystic Embrace*, 35-36, 65, 72, 73; "On Re-reading Villon," 51-52, 53; *Primrose*, 62n53, 72-73; "The Smile," 103-4; *Souvenirs of Digne*, 54; *To Love after Death*, 58-59, 61, 471; *The Valley (Le Vallon)*, 70, 73, 387; "What celestial life" from *Saint Mary the Egyptian*, 87-88; *Wisps of Smoke*, 26n74, 27n78, 73
Sauvage, Prosper (OM's grandfather), 13, 37, 39, 40-41
Schleiermacher, Friedrich, xvii
Schoenberg, Arnold, 239, 266, 310n2, 329, 356
Schola Cantorum: anti-Dreyfusard character of, 110; Claire Delbos's musical studies at, 111, 113, 204; and Daniel-Lesur, 240; and d'Harcourt, Marguerite, 92n43; and La Spirale, 239; plainchant revival at, 110-11; Tournemire's dislike of, 111n87. *See also* Bordes, Charles; Emmanuel, Maurice; Indy, Vincent d'
Segond, Louis, *La Sainte Bible*, 224n7, 439
sensual mysticism: and Christ's passion and death, 341-43; Debussy's *Pelléas and Mélisande*, 45-46; and *Liebestod* (love-death), 459-87; of love poetry of Cécile Sauvage, 35-36, 104-5; and OM's composition of *Visions of Amen*, 290-93; and "terrible love," xviii, 359, 367-69, 479; of Wagner's *Tristan*, 472, 484. *See also* Debussy, Claude; juxtaposition of contrasts; mysticism; star + cross motif; surrealism; Messiaen, Olivier, WORKS: *Turangalîla Symphony*; *Visions of Amen*, "Amen of Desire"
serialism: and Cold War, 505; and OM's interest in birdsong, 386-87, 505-6; and OM's *Meditations on the Mystery of the Holy Trinity*, 518; Penderec-

Index of Names and Subjects

ki's religious works in, 512. *See also* Darmstadt

Shakespeare, William, xvi; and Cécile Sauvage, 37-38, 41, 61; *Midsummer Night's Dream,* 90n38, 170, 392-93; OM's childhood interest in, 40-41, 90n38, 128, 170, 392-93, 415; Pierre Messiaen's French translation of, 4-5n2, 20, 28-29, 49, 502n39; *Romeo and Juliet,* 246n48, 392-93, 479, 483-85. *See also* fear *(la peur)* and awe *(la crainte)*

Shelley, Percy Bysshe, 20, 155, 387

simultaneous contrast, 159, 159-60n24, 162, 163, 171-72n59, 185, 185n98, 505. *See also* Breton, André: "certain point of the mind" *(point de l'esprit);* Delaunay, Robert; Eucharist; juxtaposition of contrasts; surrealism

Solesmes Abbey, 140; *Liber Usualis,* 223n84, 495nn17-18, 515n25; and *ressourcement* ("return to the sources"), 44n53, 111, 147; and theorization of Gregorian chant as "free," 108-10. *See also* Guéranger, (Dom) Prosper, O.S.B.; Mocquereau, (Dom) André, O.S.B.; plainchant

soul, 15-16, 17, 19, 20, 21, 33, 53, 56, 57, 59, 61, 69, 71, 73, 87, 104, 105, 113-20, 118n102, 128, 145, 149n66, 150, 151, 155, 171-75, 179-81, 185, 197, 209, 211-13, 214, 220-25, 230, 235n19, 237, 239n30, 242-43, 244, 249, 251, 252, 253n71, 272, 274, 299, 301, 326-27, 348, 354, 359, 367, 379, 386n23, 390, 408-9, 414-15, 428, 430, 437, 441, 443-45, 447, 453, 462, 469, 472, 479

sound-color: and blood's red symbolism, 345; and carillons of light, 434-40, 448, 512; and Disney's *Fantasia,* 452; and juxtaposition of contrasts by OM, 181, 185, 185n98; and light and time, 298-301; and OM's *From Canyons to Stars,* 39, 522-23; in OM's *Treatise,* 160, 160n26, 165n43, 345n17, 449n47. *See also* Blanc-Gatti, Charles; synesthesia

staircases: enchanted staircase in OM's *Resplendent Tomb,* 124; and eternity, 116, 191, 476; "far-off"/"endless" staircase in OM's *Death of Number,* 125, 186n100, 451, 476; in Festa's *Apparition of the Eternal Church,* 190; "The Stairs Repeat" in OM's *Harawi,* 116, 451. *See also* abyss/vertigo; eternity

Stalin, Joseph, 241

star + cross motif, 16n34, 180n84, 182n91, 338, 355, 468, 469; and Eliot's *Murder in the Cathedral,* 180n84, 356-57, 468n22; and Marmion, 180-81, 468nn21-22, 469; and OM's *Song of the Deported,* 469-70, 470n25. *See also* blood; melancholy; mysticism; stars; terrestrial/celestial contrast

stars: Arcturus, 319-20, 336, 462; and book of Job, 320, 336; "Joy of the Blood of the Stars" movement of OM's *Turangalîla Symphony,* 180n84, 182, 479, 481, 525; Orson Welles's broadcast of "War of the Worlds," 265, 315-16. *See also* astronomy; Moreux, Abbé Théophile; Rudaux, Lucien; star + cross motif; terrestrial/celestial contrast; Messiaen, Olivier, WORKS: *From Canyons to Stars; Visions of Amen,* "Amen of the Stars, of the Planet with the Ring"

Stockhausen, Karlheinz, 386, 490, 498-99; *Canticle of the Youths,* 498-99; "phonemic particles" and "magic syllables," 499; *Stimmung,* 499

stones, living: in Apocalypse of Saint John, 171, 440, 448-49, 509; of celestial city, 171-76, 264n110; as light of life, 452; and OM's *Apparition,* 171; and OM's *Colors of the Celestial City,* 172, 450-51, 509. *See also* Dedication of a Church (liturgical office); *éblouissement* (dazzlement); eschatology; light and life; Messiaen, Olivier,

567

Index of Names and Subjects

WORKS: *Glorified Bodies;* sound-color; visions

stones/gems: apostles linked with, 449-50

Stravinsky, Igor: and modernist-primitivism, 44n53, 331; on organ as monster, 87n29; *The Nightingale,* 390; *Rite of Spring,* 112, 302, 330-31, 366, 386. *See also* dance; "rhythmic characters"

sublime: Kantian theory of, 349, 352; and "new order" of divine reality, 228-29; and Romanticism, xvii, 154-55; and terrifying beauty, 380. *See also* awe *(la crainte);* fear *(la peur)* and awe *(la crainte);* terrible

Suger, Abbot, light theology of, 435. *See also* Bonaventure; visions

surrealism: and *Diptych,* 102-3; and "endless" staircase, 125; and rhythmic dyads, 333-34. *See also* Breton, André: "certain point of the mind" *(point de l'esprit);* Éluard, Paul; juxtaposition of contrasts; Reverdy, Pierre

Susanna's aria from Mozart's *Marriage of Figaro:* and *alba* ("dawn songs"), 370; as Claire Delbos, 372; and *Visions of Amen,* "Amen of Desire," 292

symbolist movement: and Catholic Revivalism, xiv; and synesthetic visionary, 154-55; and Tournemire's "paraphrasing" of liturgical texts, 137n27, 151-52. *See also* Baudelaire, Charles; Bloy, Léon; Debussy, Claude; Hello, Ernest; Huysmans, Joris-Karl; Mallarmé, Stéphane; Rosicrucians; Tournemire, Charles; Wagner, Richard

synesthesia: and Baudelaire, 154, 155, 158-59, 169; Blanc-Gatti's "synopsia," 159, 159-60n24, 161-62; and blood's red symbolism, 345-46; cultural historical overview of, 153-59; and dazzlement of celestial city, 173n65, 450; and OM's "carillon of light," 434-40, 448; OM's form of "synopsia," xi, 51, 159-60n24, 162, 171-72n59; and peyote, 169; and surrealist unity of opposites, 154. *See also* Blanc-Gatti, Charles; drugs; juxtaposition of contrasts; sound-color; visions

Tanglewood: OM's *Ascension* suite conducted at, 226-27n95, 482; and OM's *Four Studies in Rhythm,* 490; OM's lectures on composition, 482; and OM's *Mass of Pentecost,* 492; and OM's *Turangalîla Symphony,* 477, 490. *See also* Cold War

Tatin-Sauvage, Germaine (OM's aunt), 61, 62; death of, 519, 530

Tenant, Jean, 12, 66-72, 74-75, 79, 121. *See also* Action Française; Bernanos, Georges; Delarue-Mardrus, Lucie; de Noailles, Comtesse Anna; Maurras, Charles; Sauvage, Cécile

Tennyson, Alfred Lord, 38

terrestrial/celestial contrast: and Aquinas's views of "glorified bodies," 271-72, 441-42, 447-48; and Daniel-Rops, 181n89; geological and astronomical contrasts in OM's *Visions of Amen,* 330, 519; and "living stones," 171-73, 452; and OM's *Apparition,* 153; OM's attitude toward, 181, 210, 281-82, 448; and OM's *Celestial Banquet,* 84, 87, 99-100; and OM's *Diptych,* 99-103, 116, 281; and OM's *Songs of Earth and Sky,* 265-66. *See also* ephemerality; eternity; juxtaposition of contrasts; star + cross motif; stones/gems; Messiaen, Olivier, WORKS: *Diptych (Diptyque) for Organ; From Canyons to Stars; Harawi*

terrible, 259, 275, 282, 318, 331, 346-47, 349, 378-80, 413, 414, 420, 422, 423, 471, 480, 485, 515, 522n44; and "harmonious silence" in OM's *Visions of Amen,* 359, 360, 371, 374, 479; and OM's sensual mysticism, xviii, 359, 367-69; and Song of Songs, 359, 367-69; and OM's *Turangalîla Symphony,*

Index of Names and Subjects

479-82. *See also* fear *(la peur)* and awe *(la crainte)*
terror. *See* terrible
Thomas à Kempis. *See Imitation of Christ*
Thurston, Herbert, S.J., "Bell, Book, and Candle," 408, 409, 412n30, 432
time: "clock time," and creation theme, 305-6; "clock time," distinguished from "duration" by Bergson, 96-97; "clock time," as "rhythmic character," 303; eternity, and ambivalence, 373; eternity, Aquinas on, 296, 378; eternity, as contrast between "abyss" and "birds," 280; eternity, and OM's *Apparition*, 185; eternity, OM's emotional response to, xvii-xviii, 99-100, 108-9, 112, 298-99; eternity, and OM's *Visions of Amen*, "Amen of the Angels, of Saints, of Birdsong," 373; eternity, and the organ, xix, 185; eternity, and rhythmic dyads, 333; and Kierkegaard, 426; and mescaline intoxication, 170; meter, and death of number, 108; meter, OM's binary and ternary groupings of notes inspired by plainchant, 108-9, 112, 123-24, 188. *See also* Bergson, Henri; Cuvillier, Armand; desire; ephemerality; eternity; meter; palindrome; rhythm; Messiaen, Olivier, WORKS: *The Death of Number; Eight Preludes,* "Deceased Instants"
Tolstoy, Leo, 23, 40
Tournemire, Charles, 61, 111n87; *César Frank,* 143; improvisation based on plainchant by, 111; La Trinité, OM's position as organist at, 129, 144-47, 154, 340; and liturgical commentary/paraphrases, 136-37, 137n27; and OM's *Mass of Pentecost,* 491; OM's relationship with, 106, 108, 143-44, 205, 254-56; WORKS: *Chorale-Improvisation on "Victimae Paschali,"* 419n49; *The Dolorous Passion of Christ,* 341, 341n9; *L'Orgue Mystique,*

144, 147, 185, 205, 254, 256; *Trilogy Faust — Don Quixote — Saint Francis of Assisi,* 177n73. *See also* improvisation; symbolist movement
transfiguration, 231-32, 237, 264n109, 441-44, 512-17. *See also* Messiaen, Olivier, WORKS: *The Transfiguration*
transubstantiation, 526-29. *See also* Aquinas, Thomas: *Adoro te;* Eucharist; Messiaen, Olivier, WORKS: *Book of the Blessed Sacrament*
Tual, Denise: commissioning of OM's *Visions of Amen* for Concerts de la Pléiade series, 290, 291n48, 455; *Olivier Messiaen et les oiseaux* directed with Michel Fano, 160n25

Updike, John, 313, 318
Urban V, Pope, 406

Valéry, Paul, on dance as the symbol of life, 326
Varèse, Edgard, 490
vertigo: Hello's "Vertigo before the Absolute" chapter, 280n11, 494-95; in Kierkegaard, 426-27, 429n73, 430, 430n76; and terror/abyss of Last Judgment, 423. *See also* abyss/vertigo; fear *(la peur)* and awe *(la crainte);* Messiaen, Olivier, WORKS: *From Canyons to Stars;* Poe, Edgar Allan; staircases; sublime
Vichy regime, 261, 276-79; and French Catholicism, 467; and Honegger's *Antigone,* 350-51; and Joan of Arc, 283; and the Occupation, 290; OM's marginalization during, 465-66, 466n16; and Pierre Messiaen's political views, 4-5n2, 66n65; and Pourrat, 73-74n95. *See also* World War II
Vierne, Louis, 60; "carillon" genre works of, 454; "Carillon of Westminster," 306, 454-55; death of, 455n66; and Dupré, 133n10; *Poems of Funeral Bells,* 89, 405; on Widor, 132. *See also* Cathedral of Notre-Dame de Paris

Villon, François, 23, 51; and Cécile Sauvage, 51-52, 53; and Pierre Messiaen, 53
visions: OM's fascination with, 166-67, 170-71. *See also* apparition; drugs; *éblouissement* (dazzlement); gaze; hallucination; light and life; lightning flash; Shakespeare, William; sound-color; synesthesia
Vulgate, 16, 424, 435

Wagner, Richard: *Art and Revolution*, 155; on birds, 385-86, 386n23; mystical experience evoked by, 112; *Tristan*, 355, 392, 472, 483, 484. *See also* symbolist movement
waves, 59, 125-26, 162-63, 164, 169, 171, 183, 286, 317, 420, 448n46, 450. *See also* arsis and thesis; astronomy; Blanc-Gatti, Charles; rhythm; sound-color; synesthesia
Welles, Orson, broadcast of "War of the Worlds," 265, 315-16
Wells, H. G.: *Time Machine*, 316, 319n30, 429; *War of the Worlds*, 316
Westminster carillon: and creation, 306-7, 397-98, 455-56; Vierne's "Carillon of Westminster," 306, 454-55. *See also* BBC Overseas Service; bells; creation theme
Whitehead, Alfred North, teleological view of reality of, 362, 364, 367n19. *See also* Aristotle; Bergson, Henri; Cuvillier, Armand; desire; Dewey, John; end-in-view
Whitman, Walt, 4-5n2
Widor, Charles-Marie, 60-61; and Dupré, 99, 131-33; and OM, 131, 189; Organ Symphony No. 5, 188-89
Woolf, Virginia, 42
Wordsworth, William, 20, 155
World War I (Great War): and Cécile Sauvage's melancholic isolation, xvi, 24-25, 34-37, 42, 61; end of, 89, 472; and Pierre Messiaen, 31-34, 461
World War II: end of, 460-62, 472; OM's *Et Exspecto*, 510. *See also* Hitler, Adolf; Jews and Judaism; Paris; Vichy regime

Xenakis, Iannis, 386-87, 490

Young France (La Jeune France), 244-45; first concert of, 244-45, 253; and La Spirale, 227; and musical "nonconformism," 241n36; and OM, 228, 253, 281, 352. *See also* neoclassicism

Zechariah, book of, and the Virgin and Child, 234
Zola, Émile, 50

Index of Scripture References

OLD TESTAMENT

Genesis
1:1-15	298-99
1:2	424
1:3	410
1:14-19	328
3:19	60
28:17	515n25

Exodus
28:15	449
33:20	515

Nehemiah
12:27	271

Job
14:1-2	16n33, 215
14:18-22	216
38:4a	320

Psalms
2	235
45(46):4	180
46:6	222-23
81(82):6	230
109	235
110:9b-10	521-22
149:6	270-71

Proverbs
4:18	434-36

Ecclesiastes
	237, 238

Song of Songs
2:10-14	368-69
4:12	479

Isaiah
7:14	353n43
43:19	456
63:1-3	344-45
63:6	344-45

Ezekiel
1:4-20	380-82
1:18	493-94
1:20	493-94

Daniel
3:77	80, 491, 499

Joel
2:17	495

Habakkuk
3:10	424, 493, 494, 497

Zechariah
9:9	223-24, 224n87, 353

NEW TESTAMENT

Matthew
5:48	231-32n10
17:2	264n109
17:6	264n109, 515
17:9	442-43
22:30	445
25	57
25:30-31	403-4
25:46a	412
26:38	348
28:2	264n109

Index of Scripture References

Luke
1:46-47	224n87
22:44	346, 346n20

John
1:3a	316-17n24
6:37-40	86n25
6:51-55	86
6:57	86, 239
10:34	230
11:4	427n69
11:21-27	86n25
14:26	491
17:1	221-22
17:18	238

Acts of the Apostles
2:2	491

Romans
8:18	182n90
8:29	231-32
11:36	493

1 Corinthians
13:12	438, 438-39n10, 493, 497, 529

15:42-43	269-70
15:42-44	269, 271, 397n46

2 Corinthians
3:15-18	436, 438-39, 438-39nn10-11
4:17-18	ii, 182n90
4:18	xviii-xix

Ephesians
	235
1:5	235
4:13	447

Philippians
3:21	442

Colossians
1:12	221
1:16	316-17n24

Hebrews 236

James
1:18	513

2 Peter
1:4	230

1 John
1:1	263
3:2	441-42

Apocalypse of Saint John
2:17	523
2:19-20	171, 449
4:3	449
5:9	179
5:13	179
7:3	531
7:9	179
7:14	265
8:4	270
10:5-7	279
21:1	449
21:5	456
21:11	440
21:15	456

www.ingramcontent.com/pod-product-compliance
Lightning Source LLC
Chambersburg PA
CBHW031538300426
44111CB00006BA/99